ANTHONY TROLLOPE. See Biographical Note on p. ix and Chronology pp. x–xv.

DAVID SKILTON was educated at King's College, Cambridge and the University of Copenhagen. After holding posts at the Universities of Stockholm and Glasgow and at Lampeter, he is now Professor of English at Cardiff, and Head of the School of English Studies, Communication and Philosophy there. His books include *Anthony Trollope and His Contemporaries* (Longman, 1972), *Defoe to the Victorians* (Penguin, 1985), *The Early and Mid-Victorian Novel* (Routledge, 1993) and editions of numerous Victorian novels, including the Everyman editions of George Eliot's *The Mill on the Floss* and Trollope's *He Knew He Was Right*.

ANTHONY TROLLOPE

The Last Chronicle of Barset

Edited by
David Skilton
University of Wales, Cardiff

J.M. Dent
London
Charles E. Tuttle Co.
Rutland, Vermont
EVERYMAN'S LIBRARY

First published in Everyman in 1993

Introduction and other critical apparatus
© J.M. Dent 1993

Made in Great Britain by
The Guernsey Press Co. Ltd, Guernsey, C.I.
J.M. Dent
Orion Publishing Group
Orion House
5 Upper St Martin's Lane
London WC2H 9EA
and
Charles E. Tuttle Co., Inc.
28 South Main Street
Rutland, Vermont
05071, USA

ISBN 0 460 87234 6

Everyman's Library
Reg. US Patent Office

CONTENTS

A BIOGRAPHICAL NOTE ON ANTHONY TROLLOPE

Born in London in 1812, the fourth surviving child of a failing barrister with a difficult personality and grandiose expectations, Anthony Trollope spent a miserable childhood and youth. Because of his poverty he felt himself an outcast at Harrow and Winchester, where he was a scholastic failure. He felt further rejected when his mother abandoned him for four years at the age of twelve to go to America in a vain attempt to save the family's fortunes. After his father went bankrupt, she supported the family by her writing. Through a family contact, Anthony was found a clerkship in the Post Office, and after a period in London he was posted to Ireland, where he became a reliable and energetic public servant. He married Rose Heseltine in 1844. Until retiring in 1867 he managed to combine full-time Post Office work, reorganizing large parts of the postal service of Great Britain, Ireland and the West Indies, with a huge literary output, and with life in society and on the hunting field. He published his first novel in 1847, but had only just become well-known on his return to London in 1859. He was immensely popular in the 1860s, and made new efforts after 1870 to retain his market position. When he died in 1882 he had written nine volumes of stories and sketches, nine works of non-fiction and forty-seven novels, including two six-volume cycles, the *Chronicles of Barsetshire* and the Palliser novels. He journeyed extensively in Europe, North America, Australia, New Zealand and South Africa, writing fiction and factual books about his travels. He recounted his upbringing and his working life in a fascinating and moving autobiography, published posthumously in 1883. He is also celebrated for introducing the pillar box into Britain.

CHRONOLOGY OF TROLLOPE'S LIFE

Year	Age	Life
1815		Born at Keppel St, Russell Square, London, on Monday 24 April
1817	2	
1818	3	
1819	4	
1820	5	
1821	6	
1823	8	Attends Harrow as a day boy until 1825
1825	10	Attends private school at Sunbury, Middlesex, until 1827
1827	12	Attends Winchester until 1830
1829	14	
1830	15	Returns to Harrow until 1834
1832	17	
1833	18	
1834	19	Family flees creditors to Belgium
		Enters General Post Office as a clerk
1837	22	
1838	23	
1840	25	Suffers a serious illness
1841	26	Appointed surveyor's clerk in the Central District of Ireland
1842	27	
1843	28	Starts to write *The Macdermots of Ballycloran* (pub. 1847)

CHRONOLOGY OF HIS TIMES

Year	Literary Context	Historical Events
1815	*Emma* [Austen]	Battle of Waterloo
1817	*Biographia Literaria* [Coleridge]	
1818	*The Heart of Midlothian* [Scott] *Frankenstein* [M. Shelley]	
1819		Peterloo massacre
1820	*Prometheus Unbound* [P. Shelley]	Death of George III
1821	*Defence of Poetry* [P. Shelley]	
1823		
1825		
1827		
1829		Catholic Emancipation Act passed
1830	*Poems, Chiefly Lyrical* [Tennyson] *Rural Rides* [Cobbett]	
1832		Reform Act passed
1833		Establishment of Oxford Movement
1834		
1837	*Pickwick Papers* [Dickens]	Accession to throne of Victoria
1838	*Sartor Resartus* [Carlyle] *Nicholas Nickleby* [Dickens]	Emergence of Chartism
1840	*The Old Curiosity Shop* [Dickens]	Introduction of the Penny Post
1841		Peel becomes Prime Minister
1842	*Poems in Two Volumes* [Tennyson]	Collapse of Chartist movement
1843	*Martin Chuzzlewit* [Dickens]	Peel sends troops to Ireland

Year	Age	Life
1844	29	Marries Rose Heseltine (1821–1917)
1846	31	
1847	32	
1848	33	*The Kellys and the O'Kellys*
1850	35	*La Vendée*
1851	36	Tours of duty reorganizing the posts in southwest England and Wales until 1852
1852	37	
1855	40	*The Warden*; writes *The New Zealander* (pub. 1872)
1857	42	*Barchester Towers*; *The Three Clerks*
1858	43	Postal mission to Suez; *Doctor Thorne* Reorganizes postal routes in the West Indies
1859	44	*The Bertrams*; becomes Surveyor of the Eastern District of England
1860	45	*Framley Parsonage* April 1860–April 1861; *Castle Richmond*
1861	46	*Orley Farm* March 1861–October 1862; *Brown, Jones and Robinson* August 1861–March 1862; travels to USA
1862	47	*The Small House at Allington* September 1862–April 1864; *North America*
1863	48	*Rachel Ray*
1864	49	*Can You Forgive Her?* January 1864–August 1865
1865	50	*Miss Mackenzie*; *The Belton Estate* May 1865–January 1866
1866	51	*The Claverings* February 1866–May 1867 *Nina Balatka* July 1866–January 1867 *The Last Chronicle of Barset* December 1866–July 1867
1867	52	*Phineas Finn* October 1867–May 1869 *Linda Tressel* October 1867–May 1868 Edits *St Paul's Magazine* until 1870; resigns from Post Office
1868	53	*He Knew He Was Right* October 1868–May 1869 Postal mission to USA
1869	54	*The Vicar of Bullhampton* July 1869–May 1870
1870	55	*Ralph the Heir* January 1870–July 1871 *Sir Harry Hotspur of Humblethwaite* May–Dec 1870

Year	Literary Context	Historical Events
1844	*Poems* [Barrett]	O'Connell tried for conspiracy
1846		Ireland devastated by famine
		Peel resigns after corn-law repeal
1847	*Vanity Fair* [Thackeray]	
1848	*Wuthering Heights* [E. Bronte]	Revolution sweeps Europe
	History of England [Macaulay]	
	Communist Manifesto [Marx/ Engels]	
1850	*In Memoriam* [Tennyson]	
1851		Opening of Great Exhibition
1852	*The History of Henry Esmond* [Thackeray]	
1855	*Little Dorrit* [Dickens]	Civil Service exams introduced
1857	*Scenes of Clerical Life* [Eliot]	
1858		
1859	*Adam Bede* [Eliot]	
	The Origin of Species [Darwin]	
1860	*Great Expectations* [Dickens]	
	The Mill on the Floss [Eliot]	
1861	*Silas Marner* [Eliot]	American Civil War begins
1862	*Utilitarianism* [Mill]	Unification of Italy
1863	Thackeray dies	
1864	*Dramatis Personae* [Browning]	
1865		American Civil War ends
1866	*Poems and Ballads* [Swinburne]	Hyde Park riot
	Felix Holt, The Radical [Eliot]	
1867	*The English Constitution* [Bagehot]	Second Reform Act passed
	Das Kapital [Marx]	
1868	*The Moonstone* [Collins]	
	The Ring and the Book [Browning]	
1869	*Culture and Anarchy* [Arnold]	
	The Subjection of Women [Mill]	
1870	Dickens dies	Franco-Prussian War
	Poems [D. G. Rossetti]	Start of Irish Home Rule movement
		Married Women's Property Act

Year	Age	Life
1871	56	*The Eustace Diamonds* July 1871–February 1873
		Travels to Australia and New Zealand, May 1871–December 1872
1872	57	*The Golden Lion of Granpere* January–August
1873	58	*Lady Anna* April 1873–April 1874; *Phineas Redux* July 1873–January 1874; *Australia and New Zealand*; *Harry Heathcote*
1874	59	*The Way We Live Now* February 1874–September 1875
1875	60	*The Prime Minister* November 1875–June 1876
		Travels to Australia and USA, March–October
		Starts *An Autobiography* (compl. 1876, pub. 1883)
1876	61	*The American Senator* May 1876–July 1877
1877	62	*Is He Popenjoy?* October 1877–July 1878
		Travels to South Africa
1878	63	*John Caldigate* April 1878–June 1879
		An Eye for an Eye August 1878–June 1879; *South Africa*
1879	64	*Cousin Henry* March–May
		The Duke's Children October 1879–July 1880
		Thackeray
1880	65	*Dr Wortle's School* May–December
1881	66	*Ayala's Angel*; *The Fixed Period* October 1881–March 1882
		Marion Fay December 1881–June 1882
1882	67	*Kept in the Dark* May–December
		Mr Scarborough's Family May 1882–June 1883
		The Landleaguers November 1882–October 1883
		Dies 6 December, at Welbeck Street, Cavendish Square, London
1883		*An Autobiography*
1884		*An Old Man's Love*

Year	Literary Context	Historical Events
1871	*The Descent of Man* [Darwin]	
1872	*Middlemarch* [Eliot]	
1873		
1874	*Far From the Madding Crowd* [Hardy]	Irish Home Rule movement grows
1875		
1876	*Daniel Deronda* [Eliot]	Victoria made Empress of India
1877		
1878	*Poems and Ballads: second series* [Swinburne]	Congress of Berlin
1879	*Daisy Miller* [James]	Irish National Land League formed
1880	Eliot dies	Charles Parnell tried for conspiracy
1881	*Portrait of a Lady* [James] *Washington Square* [James]	Land League outlawed
1882		
1883		
1884		Third Reform Act passed

INTRODUCTION

The Last Chronicle of Barset has always been one of Trollope's
most popular works, and appeared at a time when his star was
in the ascendant over the literary marketplace. During the
novel's run – it came out in weekly parts over the seven months
from December 1866 to July 1867 – it attracted enormous
attention in the press, and confirmed him as 'a writer . . . born
to make the fortune of circulating libraries'.[1] His reputation
depended in part on the series of novels now known as the
Chronicles of Barsetshire, consisting of *The Warden* (1855),
Barchester Towers (1857), *Doctor Thorne* (1858), *Framley
Parsonage* (1860–61), *The Small House at Allington* (1862–4)
and the ominously titled *Last Chronicle of Barset*. One critic
'found the loneliness very oppressive since he was told that he
was never again to meet almost the best known and most typical
of his countrymen again', while another pointed out that 'the
fortunes of these inhabitants of Mr Trollope's county of Barsetshire obtain such a thorough hold on the interests of readers
that they are anxious to hear more about them, more even than
Mr Trollope is willing to tell'.[2]

All this represented enormous success for a writer who had
not come before the public until he was thirty-two. He was
never a brilliant and fêted young genius like Dickens or Disraeli,
and when he achieved his first great popular success in 1860, at
the age of forty-four, he was not only in the toga of manhood
(as he himself might have expressed it), but had entered his
increasingly solid middle age. Indeed, prosperity and authorship
were intimately linked in his life. After a miserable childhood
and youth, when he felt deprived of the social status and
comforts which should have been his by birth, he had finally

achieved celebrity and economic security by his literary efforts. As he explains in his *Autobiography* (1883):

> I have ever wished to be liked by those around me, – a wish that during the first half of my life was never gratified ... It was not till we had settled ourselves at Waltham that I really began to live much with others. The Garrick Club was the first assemblage of men at which I felt myself to be popular.[3]

He was forty-six at this time. A sense of belonging seems to have been all-important, and this not just in Trollope's own life but in the awareness and ideology of large segments of Victorian society.

By origin Trollope's family belonged to the gentry, but his father, a difficult and mentally troubled man, and a notably unsuccessful barrister, brought ruin to the family, from which it was only saved by the literary exertions of Anthony's mother, the prolific novelist, Fanny Trollope. During his childhood and youth, which he movingly describes in his *Autobiography*, Trollope felt himself to be unloved at home, and an outcast at Harrow and Winchester, where he was despised and shunned as a clumsy, ill-clad dunce. When he was twelve his mother left him for four years to travel to America with others of her children, abandoning him to the care of his father, who was at best moody, and at worst insane, and who was probably damaged by the overuse of a mercury-based medicine prescribed for his recurrent migraines. After the family's inevitable bankruptcy and their flight to Belgium, a Civil Service clerkship was found for the twenty-year-old Anthony in the Post Office, and following some years of minor dissipation in London, chance saved him in the form of a posting in Ireland. This happy move seems to have given him what he needed in order to mature, and, relieved to be away from the pressures and temptations of London, he turned himself into a confident and respected public servant. He also married Rose, about whom we know regrettably little, except that she was a very capable domestic manager, and that he had exceptional trust in her literary judgment all his life. In Ireland, too, he began to write novels, and by the time he returned permanently to live near London in 1859, he was known as the author of *The Warden*, *Barchester Towers* and *Doctor Thorne*, and of *The Three Clerks* and four other novels.

The outcast schoolboy had become a successful man of the world and popular author, dubbed by *The Times* 'the mighty monarch of books that are good enough to be read ... the Apollo of the circulating library'.[4] His first serial fiction, *Framley Parsonage* (1860–61), which was the fourth of the *Chronicles of Barsetshire*, was outstandingly successful, and from then on, throughout the 1860s, his were the most widely read novels, and his too were the fictional standards which for the time dominated the literary marketplace.

The transformation from failure to success was as striking in his Civil Service career: the progress of Johnny Eames from hobbledehoy to confident adult in the last two of the *Chronicles* (*The Small House at Allington* and *The Last Chronicle of Barset*) is based on the author's own life. Trollope's early life left him with a profound understanding of the value of social belonging and the horror of social exclusion, and taught him that personality and public persona are to an important degree the product of experience, and the cumulative result of myriad decisions of the individual in the small as well as the large occasions of life. His prosperity and social position were achieved by an exertion which was extraordinary even in Victorian terms. The fictional worlds which he wrote in novel after novel in order to maintain them, show all the concern with material well-being and social status that we infer from his life. His biographers detect a nightmarish underside to his success, as though all that he had could be negated at any time by failure and insanity like his father's. The same shadow fell across his fiction, with Mr Crawley in *The Last Chronicle of Barset* as the most striking and wilfully self-destructive of his characters.

To understand the impact of Victorian serial fiction we have to remember that a novel would be read over a period as long as nineteen months, that a series of novels (and Trollope wrote two consisting of six novels each) might be spread over a decade or more, and that the consumer might be engaged in reading several very different novels at a time. As a reviewer in *The Times* put it in 1862, 'A novel-reader will go on reading novels to all eternity, and sometimes even will have several in hand at once – a serial of Mr Trollope's here, a serial of Mr Dickens's there, and the last three-volume tale into the bargain.'[5] Just as novelists in a later century make a good living only if they sell the film and television rights of a novel as well as the book rights, so with few exceptions mid-Victorian novelists would be prosperous in proportion to their success as serial writers.

Competition for public attention was intense, and the fiction which flourished best was customarily classified into two types: that which appealed to the public by resembling the stream of events making up the narratives which readers made for themselves to explain their own 'real lives'; and that which made modern life resemble a nightmare in which events overwhelmed the individual, with the hero alone able to follow a clue through the labyrinth of plot. Trollope discusses this classification in his *Autobiography*:

> Among English novels of the present day, and among English novelists, a great division is made. There are sensational novels and anti-sensational, sensational novelists and anti-sensational; sensational readers and anti-sensational. The novelists who are considered to be anti-sensational are generally called realistic. I am realistic. My friend Wilkie Collins is generally supposed to be sensational. The readers who prefer the one are supposed to take delight in the elucidation of character. They who hold by the other are charmed by the construction and gradual development of a plot.[6]

For most of the 1860s Trollope was the foremost proponent of what he here calls 'realism'.[7]

The Last Chronicle of Barset is a perfect example of his refusal to promote sensational effect above character-study, since it would be a simple matter to rearrange the story of a clergyman suspected of having stolen a cheque, to generate suspense, shock and scandalous revelations. As it is we have a serial fiction which contains a mystery, an amateur detective, a race across Europe and a last-minute solution, but all without playing upon the reader by means of the regular 'cliffhangers' which characterize sensation novels. For some critics the climax of *The Last Chronicle* is not even the revelation of how the cheque came into Mr Crawley's hands, but the moment in Chapter 83 when the wealthy archdeacon recognizes the impoverished perpetual curate as his equal as a gentleman – a far cry indeed from the climax of a sensation novel. As quite often in Trollope, the drama of social acceptance is more important than the creation of surprise, and one morally enlightening moment greater than any amount of suspense.

It was perhaps inevitable that Trollope should be a 'non-sensational writer, who does not rest his interest on playing bopeep with a secret',[8] because of an avowed inability to work out an intricate plot: 'to construct a plot so as to know, before the story is begun, how it is to end, has always been to me a labour of Hercules beyond my reach.'[9] The purpose – or at least the effect – of all literature, every Victorian writer agreed, was to teach moral conduct, and this could only be done, Trollope said, by adhering to 'truth-to-life':

> [he] who tells tales in prose can hardly hope to be effective as a teacher unless he binds himself by the circumstances of the world which he finds around him. Humour and truth there should be, and pathos and humour, but he should so constrain them that they shall not seem to mount into nature beyond the ordinary habitations of men and women.[10]

The realist might refuse to mount to 'higher' regions, but there were novelists and critics for whom the purpose of fiction was:

> to take man from the low passions, and to beguile weary and selfish pain, to excite a generous sorrow at vicissitudes not his own, to raise the passions into sympathy with heroic struggles – and to admit the soul into that serener atmosphere from which it rarely returns to ordinary existence, without some memory or association which ought to enlarge the domain of thought and exalt the motives of action . . .[11]

At the time this kind of fiction was usually called 'idealist', and the American novelist Nathaniel Hawthorne – himself an idealist – showed a friendly sympathy for the quite different aims and methods of his English contemporary:

> Have you read the novels of Anthony Trollope? They precisely suit my taste, – solid and substantial, written on the strength of beef and through the inspiration of ale, and just as real as if some giant had hewn a great lump out of the earth and put it under a glass case, with all its inhabitants going about their daily business, and not suspecting that they were being made a show of.[12]

A hundred years later few people would think that realism was as unproblematic as Hawthorne seemed to believe, and the idea that a novelist could present the world without imposing ideological values on the resultant fiction would be untenable.

Since Trollope's heyday, many critics have found the ideas presented in 'realistic' fiction more interesting than those in idealistic or sensational fiction, and such critics find it very much to Trollope's credit that he was greatly admired by one great moralist, Tolstoy, and that another, George Eliot, asserted that the example of novels like the *Chronicles of Barsetshire* encouraged her to attempt the large social picture of *Middlemarch*, which some have held to be the greatest single novel in the English language.

The techniques of large-scale social fiction had to be learned, and Trollope and his contemporaries owed a huge debt to Sir Walter Scott, whose *Waverley* novels taught them how to analyse the experience of ordinary individuals in relation to the great movements of history. Scott's Scottish novels seek to explain the current state of the country by describing the life of private individuals in the historical conflicts out of which early nineteenth-century Scotland was made. For their part the mid-Victorians experienced their own time as history, being more conscious than any previous people in peacetime of living in an age of rapid change. Industrialization and capital accumulation aggravated wealth differences and class conflicts, producing unprecedented improvements in the standard of living for the well-to-do, counterbalanced by a fearful increase in poverty in town and country alike. Railways and industrial development transformed the country beyond recognition in a matter of decades, not only in the big centres of population but also in the remote countryside. Rapid change breeds alarm and insecurity even among those whom it does not reduce to misery, and consequently a frequent syndrome in the period was a simultaneous excitement at and approval of 'progress', and a yearning after a more secure state of things. This in turn led to the construction of a myth of a secure society, which supposedly existed in the recent past or in some remote part of the land. Such a place was Trollope's fictional county of Barsetshire to readers during the Second World War, and such might it have been to many of his contemporaries too, were it not that even in Barsetshire the nineteenth-century world intruded powerfully, disallowing facile nostalgia. One of Trollope's best contemporary critics, Richard Holt Hutton, the literary editor of the *Spectator*, summed up the condition of the high-Victorian individual by a comparison between Trollope and Jane Austen. The inner portions of Trollope's characters, Hutton says, are invaded by the outside world, while Austen's people are themselves alone:

> Everybody in Miss Austen . . . is leisurely, giving one a great sense of perfect seclusion, ample opportunity, plenty of scope, and plenty of

time. Everybody in Mr Trollope is more or less under pressure, swayed hither and thither by opposite attractions, assailed on this side and on that by the strategy of rivals; everywhere someone's room is more wanted than his company; everywhere time is short ... The atmosphere of affairs is permanent. The Church or the world, or the flesh or the devil, seem always at work to keep men going, and prevent them from being themselves alone. Mr Trollope's people are themselves so far as the circumstances of the day will allow them to be themselves, but very often are much distorted from their most natural selves.[13]

The world was certainly very much with Trollope's characters, including the clergy.

Because this was an age of Church reform, the internal political stresses in the institution were daily manifest, and the struggle between the High Church Archdeacon Grantly and the Low Church Proudies, who had been appointed by a Whig administration as part of an attempt to change the social, doctrinal and financial face of the Church of England, was echoed in every diocese in the country. Many anomalies remained, such as the appalling position of perpetual curates, who were beneficed clergymen appointed to perform the entire duties of a parish on an income appropriate to an ordinary curate or assistant cleric. Such an unfortunate is Mr Crawley, who is a gentleman by birth, education and temperament, and who must keep up appearances as a clergyman of the Church of England – and hence as a 'gentleman' – on an income altogether insufficient for the purpose.

Despite his threadbare coat, Crawley was a gentleman. He was one who 'belonged' by right, but was excluded in practice. The concept of 'the gentleman' is one of the most important for understanding the fiction of the period, and involves a complex combination of financial, social and moral criteria, and a novel like *The Last Chronicle* acted out the anxieties of a large number of its readers – as well as the genteel aspirations of many others. Crawley is a social *memento mori* for the vulnerable among the 'respectable' middle class. He has, we cannot help noticing, a very conservative intellectual position. Nobody at that time doubted that a knowledge of Greek was important to a man's intellectual development, but a thorough schooling in this dead language was not to prove a motive force for later Victorian developments. We remember that in Chapter 80 of *The Last Chronicle* Johnny Eames, who is a practical administrator of the nineteenth-century world, thinks he might 'go deep into Greek', but gives it up when he finds it too difficult to revive the learning of his schooldays. It is also by implication not necessary. Crawley can be compared with Trollope's father, who devoted himself to impossible scholarly tasks in the almost complete absence of resources, and of whom the novelist said, 'The touch of his hand seemed to create failure . . . We were all estranged from him, and yet I believe that he would have given his heart's blood for any of us. His life as I knew it was one long tragedy.'[14] *The Last Chronicle of Barset* is of enormous significance for Trollope personally and for the age in which he lived. That is why there is such a charge for the Victorian reader in the moment when Grantly recognizes Crawley as his equal.[15]

One of the recognizable signs of a genteel upbringing was the ability to deploy literary quotations, and examples of the common currency of literary references can be found in the explanatory notes of the present edition. Latin quotations are particularly significant, since they were familiar to Trollope's middle- and upper-class male readers, who had learned them at school in literature 'set texts', or as grammatical examples to be learned off by heart from Latin textbooks. They thus acted as a kind of shibboleth of social belonging. Quite a number of women learned the Latin language up to a certain level, but they were often teachers and presented as stereotyped spinsters, like the Misses Prettyman in *The Last Chronicle*. Trollope is giving contradictory signals to his original readers in having Grace Crawley both skilled in the Classics and a highly attractive woman. Crawley, a true scholar and a lover of literature, educates his daughters in the things he holds dear and believes to be of supreme importance. To the original readers this might have been a sign of his eccentricity and impracticability; to the modern reader the fact that the beautiful, young Grace is better educated than her well-to-do lover is a source of gratification. And Trollope's creative imagination is large enough to encompass this case, though one doubts whether Dickens's would have been.

The Last Chronicle of Barset is unusual in its stress on Greek, which is at once a sign of Crawley's greater learning and a signal of the tragic dimension of his story. Crawley reads Aeschylus and Sophocles with his daughters, and among English works, Milton's *Samson Agonistes*. The narrator also hints at tragedy in referring to one of the plays, when Archdeacon Grantly suffers a severe hurt to his paternal feelings in Chapter 83 at a place where three roads meet – the very description of the spot in Sophocles' *Oedipus* at which Oedipus kills his father. But in the case of the archdeacon and the major, we have long ago recognized that comic conventions are at work, and that all will turn out well. Crawley's case is considerably more alarming.

The Last Chronicle is the most complex of the Barsetshire novels, and the only one approaching the force of tragedy. The series began with small-scale drama in *The Warden*, which, without the power of *The Last Chronicle*, mirrors tragic form in the irreconcilable clash of opposing principles, in which the upright protagonist is defeated. But the tone of *The Warden* is merely one of melancholy for the passing of more picturesque days. Thereafter the tone of the Barsetshire books is light, as they expand the fictional world beyond the confines of the city of Barchester, charting the whole county and some adjoining parts, and thoroughly supplying them with gentry, aristocracy and clergy. In *The Last Chronicle* Trollope sets himself the task of telling the anguished story of Mr Crawley and his doubts about his own sanity, while at the same time gathering up all the strands which have been running through the previous books. The result is a fine example of the Victorian multiplot novel – a flexible form which offers the author the chances enjoyed by English Renaissance playwrights to interlink plots, or to compare situations in parallel plots, and to produce the effects of closure in some plot lines, while leaving others open. For a number of generations the multiplot novel was thought to result from a lack of aesthetic thinking, and many critics echoed Henry James's sentiments about it as 'a loose, baggy monster'. Critical opinion has, however, largely swung away from James's position in the second half of the twentieth century.[16]

For Trollope's control in *The Last Chronicle* is considerable. As an example, the plot involving Major Grantly and Grace Crawley is interdependent with the plot of the stolen cheque, while Johnny Eames's adventures in London, and the affairs of Lily Dale are parallel plots, offering social and moral comparisons with the world of Barset and the 'healthier' love of the Crawley–Grantly alliance. These comparisons are available, but the narrator – that familiar mid-Victorian construct – is a tolerant guide, apparently not coercing us into judgments, but seeming to let common sense hold sway – that sense which appears to be held in common in the reader's community as well as the fictional one. This impression is, of course, an illusion. The narrative is strongly informed with the moral assumptions of the Victorian middle class, and the author's trickery is in convincing so many readers that there is something 'natural', timeless and universal about these. Although they do not parade complexity, Trollope's novels are not simplistic.

The multiplot structure of *The Last Chronicle* is complicated by the fact that there are five earlier novels which must be rounded off as well. Readers who find the multiplicity of characters a little confusing towards the end of *The Last Chronicle of Barset* will find that they are drawn back to read its precursors. When they do so they will admire the skill and economy with which Trollope has arranged closure for certain strands of plot, while others which seemed closed before have been going on ever since. Although the *Last Chronicle* is exactly what it says, and although all the storylines are neatly tied up at the end, the impression of life continuing in an alternative world is maintained simply because that fictional life has been sustained through thousands of pages, published over a dozen years. The reason Barsetshire has seemed idyllic to those readers who have completely suspended their disbelief, may be this illusion of characters existing without plots to worry them.

The Last Chronicle of Barset has been thought by many, including Trollope himself, to be his best novel, and it certainly is one of the great novels of the period. It shows that his kind of 'realism', which some critics have found too bland, is capable of disturbing insights into a distressed mind and aberrant behaviour, and provides a sombre alternative to that mid-Victorian confidence which later ages have found rather indigestible. In particular it provides a fine introduction to the darker side of our greatest Victorian novelist.

> *David Skilton*
> University of Wales, Cardiff
> 1993

Notes
1. *Saturday Review*, 11 (4 May 1861), 451–2.
2. *Spectator* 51 (13 July 1867), 778–80, and Geraldine Jewsbury (anon.), *Athenaeum* no. 2075 (3 August 1867), 141.

3. *An Autobiography* (World's Classics, 1980), p.159.

4. E. S. Dallas (anon.), 'Anthony Trollope', *The Times*, 23 May 1859, 12.

5. E. S. Dallas (anon.), *The Times*, 18 November 1862, 8.

6. *An Autobiography*, pp.226–7.

7. For a fuller discussion of the use of the term in the period see D. Skilton, *Critical Contexts: The Early and Mid-Victorian Novel* (Routledge, 1993), chapters 4 and 5.

8. *Saturday Review* 24 (21 September 1867), 381–2.

9. 'A Walk in a Wood', *Good Words*, September 1879, 595.

10. *Ibid.*, 600.

11. Preface to the 1845 edition of Edward Bulwer Lytton's *Night and Morning*.

12. See *An Autobiography*, pp. 144–5.

13. 'From Miss Austen to Mr Trollope', *Spectator* 55 (16 December 1882), 1609–11.

14. *An Autobiography*, p.32.

15. For more about the Victorian concept of the 'gentleman', see R. Gilmour, *The Idea of the Gentleman in the Victorian Novel* (George Allen and Unwin, 1981), and Chapter 2 of B. Dennis and D. Skilton (eds.), *Reform and Intellectual Debate in Victorian England* (Croom Helm, 1987).

16. See P. Garrett, *The Victorian Multiplot Novel* (New Haven: Yale University Press, 1980), and for a theoretical approach to some of the issues involved see M. Bakhtin, *The Dialogic Imagination*, translated C. Emerson and M. Holquist (Austin: University of Texas Press, 1981).

NOTE ON THE TEXT

The Last Chronicle of Barset was written between 21 January and 15 September 1866, and came out in weekly parts from 1 December 1866 to 6 July 1867. The two volumes of the first book edition were published in March and July 1867.

The present edition follows the first edition, with a few minor errors corrected, and a few spellings modernized which might impede the modern reader.

THE LAST CHRONICLE
OF BARSET
Volume One

CHAPTER 1

How did he get it ?

'I can never bring myself to believe it, John,' said Mary Walker, the pretty daughter of Mr George Walker, attorney of Silverbridge. Walker and Winthrop was the name of the firm, and they were respectable people, who did all the solicitors' business that had to be done in that part of Barsetshire on behalf of the Crown, were employed on the local business of the Duke of Omnium who is great in those parts, and altogether held their heads up high, as provincial lawyers often do. They, – the Walkers, – lived in a great brick house in the middle of the town, gave dinners, to which the county gentlemen not unfrequently condescended to come, and in a mild way led the fashion in Silverbridge. 'I can never bring myself to believe it, John,' said Miss Walker.

'You'll have to bring yourself to believe it,' said John, without taking his eyes from his book.

'A clergyman, – and such a clergyman too !'

'I don't see that that has anything to do with it.' And as he now spoke, John did take his eyes off his book. 'Why should not a clergyman turn thief as well as anybody else ? You girls always seem to forget that clergymen are only men after all.'

'Their conduct is likely to be better than that of other men, I think.'

'I deny it utterly,' said John Walker. 'I'll undertake to say that at this moment there are more clergymen in debt in Barsetshire than there are either lawyers or doctors. This man has always been in debt. Since he has been in the county I don't think he has ever been able to show his face in the High Street of Silverbridge.'

'John, that is saying more than you have a right to say,' said Mrs Walker.

'Why, mother, this very cheque was given to a butcher who had threatened a few days before to post bills all about the county, giving an account of the debt that was due to him, if the money was not paid at once.'

'More shame for Mr Fletcher,' said Mary. 'He has made a fortune as butcher in Silverbridge.'

'What has that to do with it? Of course a man likes to have his money. He had written three times to the bishop, and he had sent a man over to Hogglestock to get his little bill settled six days running. You see he got it at last. Of course, a tradesman must look for his money.'

'Mamma, do you think that Mr Crawley stole the cheque?' Mary, as she asked the question, came and stood over her mother, looking at her with anxious eyes.

'I would rather give no opinion, my dear.'

'But you must think something when everybody is talking about it, mamma.'

'Of course my mother thinks he did,' said John, going back to his book. 'It is impossible that she should think otherwise.'

'That is not fair, John,' said Mrs Walker; 'and I won't have you fabricate thoughts for me, or put the expression of them into my mouth. The whole affair is very painful, and as your father is engaged in the inquiry, I think that the less said about the matter in this house the better. I am sure that that would be your father's feeling.'

'Of course I should say nothing about it before him,' said Mary. 'I know that papa does not wish to have it talked about. But how is one to help thinking about such a thing? It would be so terrible for all of us who belong to the Church.'

'I do not see that at all,' said John. 'Mr Crawley is not more than any other man just because he's a clergyman. I hate all that kind of clap-trap. There are a lot of people here in Silverbridge who think the matter shouldn't be followed up, just because the man is in a position which makes the crime more criminal in him than it would be in another.'

'But I feel sure that Mr Crawley has committed no crime at all,' said Mary.

'My dear,' said Mrs Walker, 'I have just said that I would rather you would not talk about it. Papa will be in directly.'

'I won't, mamma; – only—'

'Only! yes; just only!' said John. 'She'd go on till dinner if any one would stay to hear her.'

'You've said twice as much as I have, John.' But John had left the room before his sister's last words could reach him.

'You know, mamma, it is quite impossible not to help thinkng of it,' said Mary.

'I dare say it is, my dear.'

'And when one knows the people it does make it so dreadful.'

'But do you know them? I never spoke to Mr Crawley in my life, and I do not think I ever saw her.'

'I knew Grace very well, – when she used to come first to Miss Prettyman's school.'

'Poor girl. I pity her.'

'Pity her! Pity is no word for it, mamma. My heart bleeds for them. And yet I do not believe for a moment that he stole the cheque. How can it be possible? For though he may have been in debt because they have been so very, very poor; yet we all know that he has been an excellent clergyman. When the Robartses were dining here last, I heard Mrs Robarts say that for piety and devotion to his duties she had hardly ever seen any one equal to him. And the Robartses know more of them than anybody.'

'They say that the dean is his great friend.'

'What a pity it is that the Arabins should be away just now when he is in such trouble.' And in this way the mother and daughter went on discussing the question of the clergyman's guilt in spite of Mrs Walker's previously expressed desire that nothing more might be said about it. But Mrs Walker, like many other mothers, was apt to be more free in converse with her daughter than she was with her son. While they were thus talking the father came in from his office, and then the subject was dropped. He was a man between fifty and sixty years of age, with grey hair, rather short, and somewhat corpulent, but still gifted with that amount of personal comeliness which comfortable position and the respect of others will generally seem to give. A man rarely carries himself meanly, whom the world holds high in esteem.

'I am very tired, my dear,' said Mr Walker.

'You look tired. Come and sit down for a few minutes before you dress. Mary, get your father's slippers.' Mary instantly ran to the door.

'Thanks, my darling,' said the father. And then he whispered to his wife, as soon as Mary was out of hearing, 'I fear that unfortunate man is guilty. I fear he is! I fear he is!'

'Oh, heavens! what will become of them?'

'What indeed? She has been with me to-day.'

'Has she? And what could you say to her?'

'I told her at first that I could not see her, and begged her not to speak to me about it. I tried to make her understand that she should go to some one else. But it was of no use.'

'And how did it end?'

'I asked her to go in to you, but she declined. She said you could do nothing for her.'

'And does she think her husband guilty?'

'No, indeed. She think him guilty ! Nothing on earth, – or from heaven either, as I take it, would make her suppose it to be possible. She came to me simply to tell me how good he was.'

'I love her for that,' said Mrs Walker.

'So did I. But what is the good of loving her ? Thank you, dearest. I'll get your slippers for you some day, perhaps.'

The whole county was astir in this matter of this alleged guilt of the Reverend Josiah Crawley, – the whole county, almost as keenly as the family of Mr Walker, of Silverbridge. The crime laid to his charge was the theft of a cheque for twenty pounds, which he was said to have stolen out of a pocket-book left or dropped in his house, and to have passed as money into the hands of one Fletcher, a butcher of Silverbridge, to whom he was indebted. Mr Crawley was in those days the perpetual curate of Hogglestock, a parish in the northern extremity of East Barsetshire ; a man known by all who knew anything of him to be very poor, – an unhappy, moody, disappointed man, upon whom the troubles of the world always seemed to come with a double weight. But he had ever been respected as a clergyman, since his old friend Mr Arabin, the dean of Barchester, had given him the small incumbency which he now held. Though moody, unhappy, and disappointd, he was a hard-working, conscientious pastor among the poor people with whom his lot was cast ; for in the parish of Hogglestock there resided only a few farmers higher in degree than field labourers, brickmakers, and such like. Mr Crawley had now passed some ten years of his life at Hogglestock ; and during those years he had worked very hard to do his duty, struggling to teach the people around him perhaps too much of the mystery, but something also of the comfort, of religion. That he had become popular in his parish cannot be said of him. He was not a man to make himself popular in any position. I have said that he was moody and disappointed. He was even worse than this ; he was morose, sometimes almost to insanity. There had been days in which even his wife had found it impossible to deal with him otherwise than as with an acknowl-edged lunatic. And this was known among the farmers, who talked about their clergyman among themselves as though he were a madman. But among the very poor, among the brickmakers of Hoggle End, – a lawless, drunken, terribly rough lot of humanity, – he was held in high respect ; for they knew that he lived hardly, as they lived ; that he worked hard, as they worked ; and that the outside world was hard tc him, as it was to them ; and there had been an apparent sincerity of godliness about the man, and a manifest struggle to do his duty in spite of the world's ill-usage, which had won its way even with the rough ; so that Mr Crawley's name had stood high with many in his parish, in spite of the unfortunate peculiarity of his disposition. This was the man who was now accused of stealing a cheque for twenty pounds.

But before the circumstances of the alleged theft are stated, a word or two must be said as to Mr Crawley's family. It is declared that a good wife is a crown to her husband,* but Mrs Crawley had been much more than a crown to him. As had regarded all the inner life of the man, – all that portion of his life which had not been passed in the pulpit or in pastoral teaching, – she had been crown, throne, and sceptre all in one. That she had endured with him and on his behalf the miseries of poverty, and the troubles of a life which had known no smiles, is perhaps not to be alleged as much to her honour. She had joined herself to him for better or worse, and it was her manifest duty to bear such things ; wives always have to bear them, knowing when they marry that they must take their chance. Mr Crawley might have been a bishop, and Mrs Crawley, when she married him, perhaps thought it probable that such would be his fortune. Instead of that he was now, just as he was approaching his fiftieth year, a perpetual curate, with an income of one hundred and thirty pounds per annum, – and a family. That had been Mrs Crawley's luck in life, and of course she bore it. But she had also done much more than this. She had striven hard to be contented, or, rather, to appear to be contented, when he had been most wretched and most moody. She had struggled to conceal from him her own conviction as to his half-insanity, treating him at the same time with the respect due to an honoured father of a family, and with the careful measured indulgence fit for a sick and wayward child. In all the terrible troubles of their life her courage had been higher than his. The metal of which she was made had been tempered to a steel which was very rare and fine, but the rareness and fineness of which he had failed to appreciate. He had often told her that she was without pride, because she had stooped to receive from others, on his behalf and on behalf of her children, things which were very needful, but which she could not buy. He had told her that she was a beggar, and that it was better to starve than to beg. She had borne the rebuke without a word in reply, and had then begged again for him, and had endured the starvation herself. Nothing in their poverty had, for years past, been a shame to her ; but every accident of their poverty was still, and ever had been, a living disgrace to him.

They had had many children, and three were still alive. Of the eldest, Grace Crawley, we shall hear much in the coming story. She was at this time nineteen years old, and there were those who said that, in spite of her poverty, her shabby outward apparel, and a certain thin, unfledged, unrounded form of person, a want of fulness in the lines of her figure, she was the prettiest girl in that part of the world. She was living now at a school in Silverbridge, where for the last year she had been a teacher; and there were many in Silverbridge who declared that very bright prospects were opening to her, – that young Major Grantly of Cosby Lodge, who, though a widower with a young child, was the cynosure of all female eyes in and round Silverbridge, had found beauty in her thin face, and that Grace Crawley's fortune was made in the teeth, as it were, of the prevailing ill-fortune of her family. Bob Crawley, who was two years younger, was now at Marlbro' School, from whence it was intended that he should proceed to Cambridge, and be educated there at the expense of his godfather, Dean Arabin. In this also the world saw a stroke of good luck. But then nothing was lucky to Mr Crawley. Bob, indeed, who had done very well at school, might do well at Cambridge, – might do great things there. But Mr Crawley would almost have preferred that the boy should work in the fields, than that he should be educated in a manner so manifestly eleemosynary. And then his clothes! How was he to be provided with clothes fit either for school or for college? But the dean and Mrs Crawley between them managed this, leaving Mr Crawley very much in the dark, as Mrs Crawley was in the habit of leaving him. Then there was a younger daughter, Jane, still at home, who passed her life between her mother's work-table and her father's Greek, mending linen and learning to scan iambics, – for Mr Crawley in his early days had been a ripe scholar.

And now there had come upon them all this terribly-crushing disaster. That poor Mr Crawley had gradually got himself into a mess of debt at Silverbridge, from which he was quite unable to extricate himself, was generally known by all the world both of Silverbridge and Hogglestock. To a great many it was known that Dean Arabin had paid money for him, very much contrary to his own consent, and that he had quarrelled, or attempted to quarrel, with the dean in consequence, – had so attempted, although the money had in part passed through his own hands. There had been one creditor, Fletcher, the butcher of Silverbridge, who had of late been specially hard upon poor Crawley. This man, who had not been without good nature in his dealings, had heard stories of the dean's good-will and such like, and had loudly expressed his opinion that the perpetual curate of Hogglestock would show a higher pride in allowing himself to be indebted to a rich brother clergyman, than in remaining under thrall to a butcher. And thus a rumour had grown up. And then the butcher had written repeated letters to the bishop, – to Bishop Proudie of Barchester, who had at first caused his chaplain to answer them, and had told Mr Crawley somewhat roundly what was his opinion of a clergyman who ate meat and did not pay for it. But nothing that the bishop could say or do enabled Mr Crawley to pay the butcher. It was very grievous to such a man as Mr Crawley to receive these letters from such a man as Bishop Proudie; but the letters came, and made festering wounds, but then there was an end of them. And at last there had come forth from the butcher's shop a threat that if the money were not paid by a certain date, printed bills should be posted about the county. All who heard of this in Silverbridge were very angry with Mr Fletcher, for no one there had ever known a tradesman to take such a step before; but Fletcher swore that he would persevere, and defended himself by showing that six or seven months since, in the spring of the year, Mr Crawley had been paying money in Silverbridge, but had paid none to him, – to him who had been not only his earliest, but his most enduring creditor. 'He got money from the dean in March,' said Mr Fetcher to Mr Walker, 'and he paid twelve pounds ten to Green, and seventeen pounds to Grobury, the baker.' It was that seventeen pounds to Grobury, the baker, for flour, which made the butcher so fixedly determined to smite the poor clergyman hip and thigh. 'And he paid money to Hall, and to Mrs Holt, and to a deal more; but he never came near my shop. If he had even shown himself, I would not have said so much about it.' And then a day before the date named, Mrs Crawley had come to Silverbridge, and had paid the butcher twenty pounds in four five-pound notes. So far Fletcher the butcher had been successful.

Some six weeks after this, inquiry began to be made as to a certain cheque for twenty pounds drawn by Lord Lufton on his bankers in London, which cheque had been lost early in the spring by Mr Soames, Lord Lufton's man of business in Barsetshire, together with a pocket-book in which it had been folded. This pocket-book Soames had believed himself to have left at Mr Crawley's house, and had gone so far, even at the time of the loss, as to express his absolute conviction that he had so left it. He was in the habit of paying a rentcharge* to Mr Crawley on behalf of Lord Lufton, amounting to twenty pounds four shillings, every half-year. Lord Lufton held the large tithes* of Hogglestock, and paid annually a sum of forty pounds eight shillings to the incumbent. This amount was, as a rule, remitted punctually by Mr Soames through the post. On the occasion now spoken of, he had had some reason for visiting Hogglestock, and had paid the money personally to Mr Crawley. Of so much there was no doubt. But he had paid it by a cheque drawn by himself on his own bankers at Barchester, and that cheque had been cashed in the ordinary way on the next morning. On returning to his own house in Barchester he had missed his pocket-book, and had written to Mr Crawley to make inquiry. There had been no money in it, beyond the cheque drawn by Lord Lufton for twenty pounds. Mr Crawley had answered this letter by another, saying that no pocket-book had been found in his house. All this had happened in March.

In October, Mrs Crawley paid the twenty pounds to Fletcher, the butcher, and in November Lord Lufton's cheque was traced back through the Barchester bank to Mr Crawley's hands. A brickmaker of Hoggle End, much favoured by Mr Crawley, had asked for change over the counter of this Barchester bank, – not, as will be understood, the bank on which the cheque was drawn – and had received it. The accommodation had been refused to the man at first, but when he presented the cheque the second day, bearing Mr Crawley's name on the back of it, together with a note from Mr Crawley himself, the money had been given for it; and the identical notes so paid had been given to Fletcher, the butcher, on the next day by Mrs Crawley. When inquiry was made, Mr Crawley stated that the cheque had been paid to him by Mr Soames, on behalf of the rentcharge due to him by Lord Lufton. But the error of this statement was at once made manifest. There was the cheque, signed by Mr Soames himself, for the exact amount, – twenty pounds four shillings. As he himself declared, he had never in his life paid money on behalf of Lord Lufton by a cheque drawn by his lordship. The cheque given by Lord Lufton, and which had been lost, had been a private matter between them. His lordship had simply wanted change in his pocket, and his agent had given it to him. Mr Crawley was speedily shown to be altogether wrong in the state-ment made to account for possession of the cheque.

Then he became very moody and would say nothing further. But his wife, who had known nothing of his first statement when made, came forward and declared that she believed the cheque for twenty pounds to be a part of a present given by Dean Arabin to her husband in April last. There had been, she said, great heartburnings about this gift, and she had hardly dared to speak to her husband on the subject. An execution had been threatened in the house by Grobury, the baker, of which the dean had heard. Then there had been some scenes at the deanery between her husband and the dean and Mrs Arabin, as to which she had subsequently heard much from Mrs Arabin. Mrs Arabin had told her that money had been given, – and at last taken. Indeed, so much had been very apparent, as bills had been paid to the amount of at least fifty pounds. When the threat made by the butcher had reached her husband's ears, the

effect upon him had been very grievous. All this was the story told
by Mrs Crawley to Mr Walker, the lawyer, when he was pushing
his inquiries. She, poor woman, at any rate told all that she knew.
Her husband had told her one morning, when the butcher's threat
was weighing heavily on his mind, speaking to her in such a humour
that she found it impossible to cross-question him, that he had still
money left, though it was money which he had hoped that he would
not be driven to use; and he had given her the four five-pound
notes, and had told her to go to Silverbridge and satisfy the man
who was so eager for his money. She had done so, and had felt no
doubt that the money so forthcoming had been given by the dean.
That was the story as told by Mrs Crawley.

But how could she explain her husband's statement as to the
cheque, which had been shown to be altogether false? All this
passed between Mr Walker and Mrs Crawley, and the lawyer was
very gentle with her. In the first stages of the inquiry he had simply
desired to learn the truth, and place the clergyman above suspicion.
Latterly, being bound as he was to follow the matter up officially,
he would not have seen Mrs Crawley, had he been able to escape
that lady's importunity. 'Mr Walker,' she had said, at last, 'you do
not know my husband. No one knows him but I. It is hard to have
to tell you of all our troubles.' 'If I can lessen them, trust me that I
will do so,' said the lawyer. 'No one, I think, can lessen them in this
world,' said the lady. 'The truth is, sir, that my husband often
knows not what he says. When he declared that the money had
been paid to him by Mr Soames, most certainly he thought so.
There are times when in his misery he knows not what he says, –
when he forgets everything.'

Up to this period Mr Walker had not suspected Mr Crawley of
anything dishonest, nor did he suspect him as yet. The poor man
had probably received the money from the dean, and had told the
lie about it, not choosing to own that he had taken money from his
rich friend, and thinking that there would be no further inquiry. He
had been very foolish, and that would be the end of it. Mr Soames
was by no means so good-natured in his belief. 'How should my
pocket-book have got into Dean Arabin's hands?' said Mr Soames,
almost triumphantly. 'And then I felt sure at the time that I had left
it at Crawley's house!'

Mr Walker wrote a letter to the dean, who at that moment was
in Florence, on his way to Rome, from whence he was going on to
the Holy Land. There came back a letter from Mr Arabin, saying
that on the 17th of March he had given to Mr Crawley a sum of
fifty pounds, and that the payment had been made with five Bank
of England notes of ten pounds each, which had been handed by

him to his friend in the library at the deanery. The letter was very short, and may, perhaps, be described as having been almost curt. Mr Walker, in his anxiety to do the best he could for Mr Crawley, had simply asked a question as to the nature of the transaction between the two gentlemen, saying that no doubt the dean's answer would clear up a little mystery which existed at present respecting a cheque for twenty pounds. The dean in answer simply stated the fact as it has been given above; but he wrote to Mr Crawley begging to know what was in truth this new difficulty, and offering any assistance in his power. He explained all the circumstances of the money, as he remembered them. The sum advanced had certainly consisted of fifty pounds, and there had certainly been five Bank of England notes. He had put the notes into an envelope, which he had not closed, but had addressed to Mr Crawley, and had placed this envelope in his friend's hands. He went on to say that Mrs Arabin would have written, but that she was in Paris with her son. Mrs Arabin was to remain in Paris during his absence in the Holy Land, and meet him in Italy on his return. As she was so much nearer at hand, the dean expressed a hope that Mrs Crawley would apply to her if there was any trouble.

The letter to Mr Walker was conclusive as to the dean's money. Mr Crawley had not received Lord Lufton's cheque from the dean. Then whence had he received it? The poor wife was left by the lawyer to obtain further information from her husband. Ah, who can tell how terrible were the scenes between that poor pair of wretches, as the wife endeavoured to learn the truth from her miserable, half-maddened husband! That her husband had been honest throughout, she had not any shadow of doubt. She did not doubt that to her at least he endeavoured to tell the truth, as far as his poor racked imperfect memory would allow him to remember what was true and what was not true. The upshot of it all was that the husband declared that he still believed that the money had come to him from the dean. He had kept it by him, not wishing to use it if he could help it. He had forgotten it, – so he said at times, – having understood from Arabin that he was to have fifty pounds, and having received more. If it had not come to him from the dean, then it had been sent to him by the Prince of Evil for his utter undoing; and there were times in which he seemed to think that such had been the manner in which the fatal cheque had reached him. In all that he said he was terribly confused, contradictory, unintelligible, – speaking almost as a madman might speak, – ending always by declaring that the cruelty of the world had been too much for him, that the waters were meeting over his head,* and praying for God's mercy to remove him from the world. It need hardly be said that his poor wife in these days had a burden on her shoulders that was more than enough to crush any woman.

She at last acknowledged to Mr Walker that she could not account for the twenty pounds. She herself would write again to the dean about it, but she hardly hoped for any further assistance there. 'The dean's answer is very plain,' said Mr Walker. 'He says that he gave Mr Crawley five ten-pound notes, and those five notes we have traced to Mr Crawley's hands.' Then Mrs Crawley could say nothing further beyond making protestations of her husband's innocence.

CHAPTER 2

By Heavens he had better not!

I must ask the reader to make the acquaintance of Major Grantly of Cosby Lodge, before he is introduced to the family of Mr Crawley, at their parsonage in Hogglestock. It has been said that Major Grantly had thrown a favourable eye on Grace Crawley, – by which report occasion was given to all men and women in those parts to hint that the Crawleys, with all their piety and humility, were very cunning, and that one of the Grantlys was, – to say the least of it, – very soft, admitted as it was throughout the county of Barsetshire, that there was no family therein more widely awake to the affairs generally of this world and the next combined, than the family of which Archdeacon Grantly was the respected head and patriarch. Mrs Walker, the most good-natured woman in Silverbridge, had acknowledged to her daughter that she could not understand it, – that she could not see anything at all in Grace Crawley. Mr Walker had shrugged his shoulders and expressed a confident belief that Major Grantly had not a shilling of his own beyond his half-pay and his late wife's fortune, which was only six thousand pounds. Others, who were ill-natured, had declared that Grace Crawley was little better than a beggar, and that she could not possibly have acquired the manners of a gentlewoman. Fletcher the butcher had wondered whether the major would pay his future father-in-law's debts; and Dr Tempest, the old rector of Silverbridge, whose four daughters were all as yet unmarried, had turned up his old nose, and had hinted that half-pay majors did not get caught in marriage so easily as that.

Such and such like had been the expressions of the opinion of men and women in Silverbridge. But the matter had been discussed further afield than at Silverbridge, and had been allowed to intrude itself as a most unwelcome subject into the family conclave of the archdeacon's rectory. To those who have not as yet learned the fact from the public character and well-appreciated reputation of the

man, let it be known that Archdeacon Grantly was at this time, as
he had been for many years previously, Archdeacon of Barchester
and Rector of Plumstead Episcopi. A rich and prosperous man he
had ever been, – though he also had had his sore troubles, as we all
have, – his having arisen chiefly from want of that higher ecclesiastical promotion which his soul had coveted, and for which the whole
tenour of his life had especially fitted him. Now, in his green old
age, he had ceased to covet, but had not ceased to repine. He had
ceased to covet aught for himself, but still coveted much for his
children; and for him such a marriage as this which was now
suggested for his son was encompassed almost with the bitterness
of death. 'I think it would kill me,' he had said to his wife; 'by
heavens, I think it would be my death!'

A daughter of the archdeacon had made a splendid matrimonial
alliance, – so splendid that its history was at the time known to all
the aristocracy of the county, and had not been altogether forgotten
by any of those who keep themselves well instructed in the details
of the peerage. Griselda Grantly had married Lord Dumbello, the
eldest son of the Marquis of Hartletop, – than whom no English
nobleman was more puissant, if broad acres, many castles, high
title, and stars and ribbons are any signs of puissance, – and she
was now, herself, Marchioness of Hartletop, with a little Lord
Dumbello of her own. The daughter's visits to the parsonage of her
father were of necessity rare, such necessity having come from her
own altered sphere of life. A Marchioness of Hartletop has special
duties which will hardly permit her to devote herself frequently to
the humdrum society of a clerical father and mother. That it would
be so, father and mother had understood when they sent the
fortunate girl forth to a higher world. But, now and again, since her
august marriage, she had laid her coroneted head upon one of the
old rectory pillows for a night or so, and on such occasions all the
Plumsteadians had been loud in praise of her condescension. Now
it happened that when this second and more aggravated blast of the
evil wind reached the rectory, – the renewed waft of the tidings as
to Major Grantly's infatuation regarding Miss Grace Crawley,
which, on its renewal, seemed to bring with it something of
confirmation, – it chanced, I say, that at that moment Griselda,
Marchioness of Hartletop, was gracing the paternal mansion. It
need hardly be said that the father was not slow to invoke such a
daughter's counsel, and such a sister's aid.

I am not quite sure that the mother would have been equally
quick to ask her daughter's advice, had she been left in the matter
entirely to her own propensities. Mrs Grantly had ever loved her
daughter dearly, and had been very proud of that great success in

life which Griselda had achieved; but in late years, the child had become, as a woman, separate from the mother, and there had arisen, not unnaturally, a break of that close confidence which in early years had existed between them. Griselda, Marchioness of Hartletop, was more than ever a daughter to the archdeacon, even though he might never see her. Nothing could rob him of the honour of such a progeny, – nothing, even though there had been actual estrangement between them. But it was not so with Mrs Grantly. Griselda had done very well, and Mrs Grantly had rejoiced; but she had lost her child. Now the major, who had done well also, though in a much lesser degree, was still her child, moving in the same sphere of life with her, still dependent in a great degree upon his father's bounty, a neighbour in the county, a frequent visitor at the parsonage, and a visitor who could be received without any of that trouble which attended the unfrequent comings of Griselda, the marchioness, to the home of her youth. And for this reason Mrs Grantly, terribly put out as she was at the idea of a marriage between her son and one standing so poorly in the world's esteem as Grace Crawley, would not have brought forward the matter before her daughter, had she been left to her own desires. A marchioness in one's family is a tower of strength, no doubt; but there are counsellors so strong that we do not wish to trust them, lest in the trusting we ourselves be overwhelmed by their strength. Now Mrs Grantly was by no means willing to throw her influence into the hands of her titled daughter.

But the titled daughter was consulted and gave her advice. On the occasion of the present visit to Plumstead she had consented to lay her head for two nights on the parsonage pillows, and on the second evening her brother the major was to come over from Cosby Lodge to meet her. Before his coming the affair of Grace Crawley was discussed.

'It would break my heart, Griselda,' said the archdeacon, piteously—'and your mother's.'

'There is nothing against the girl's character,' said Mrs Grantly, 'and the father and mother are gentlefolks by birth; but such a marriage for Henry would be very unseemly.'

'To make it worse, there is this terrible story about him,' said the archdeacon.

'I don't suppose there is much in that,' said Mrs Grantly.

'I can't say. There is no knowing. They told me to-day in Barchester that Soames is pressing the case against him.'

'Who is Soames, papa?' asked the marchioness.

'He is Lord Lufton's man of business, my dear.'

'Oh, Lord Lufton's man of business!' There was something of a sneer in the tone of the lady's voice as she mentioned Lord Lufton's name.

'I am told,' continued the archdeacon, 'that Soames declares the cheque was taken from a pocket-book which he left by accident in Crawley's house.'

'You don't mean to say, archdeacon, that you think that Mr Crawley – a clergyman – stole it!' said Mrs Grantly.

'I don't say anything of the kind, my dear. But supposing Mr Crawley to be as honest as the sun, you wouldn't wish Henry to marry his daughter.'

'Certainly not,' said the mother. 'It would be an unfitting marriage. The poor girl has had no advantages.'

'He is not able even to pay his baker's bill. I always thought Arabin was very wrong to place such a man in such a parish as Hogglestock. Of course the family could not live there.' The Arabin here spoken of was Dr Arabin, dean of Barchester. The dean and the archdeacon had married sisters, and there was much intimacy between the families.

'After all it is only a rumour as yet,' said Mrs Grantly.

'Fothergill told me only yesterday, that he sees her almost every day,' said the father. 'What are we to do, Griselda? You know how headstrong Henry is.' The marchioness sat quite still; looking at the fire, and made no immediate answer to this address.

'There is nothing for it, but that you should tell him what you think,' said the mother.

'If his sister were to speak to him, it might do much,' said the archdeacon. To this Mrs Grantly said nothing; but Mrs Grantly's daughter understood very well that her mother's confidence in her was not equal to her father's. Lady Hartletop said nothing, but still sat, with impassive face, and eyes fixed upon the fire. 'I think that if you were to speak to him, Griselda, and tell him that he would disgrace his family, he would be ashamed to go on with such a marriage,' said the father. 'He would feel, connected as he is with Lord Hartletop—'

'I don't think he would feel anything about that,' said Mrs Grantly.

'I dare say not,' said Lady Hartletop.

'I am sure he ought to feel it,' said the father. They were all silent, and sat looking at the fire.

'I suppose, papa, you allow Henry an income,' said Lady Hartletop, after a while.

'Indeed I do, – eight hundred a year.'

'Then I think I should tell him that that must depend upon his conduct. Mamma, if you won't mind ringing the bell, I will send for Cecile, and go upstairs and dress.' Then the marchioness went upstairs to dress, and in about an hour the major arrived in his dog-cart. He also was allowed to go upstairs to dress before anything was said to him about his great offence.

'Griselda is right,' said the archdeacon, speaking to his wife out of his dressing-room. 'She always was right. I never knew a young woman with more sense than Griselda.'

'But you do not mean to say that in any event you would stop Henry's income?' Mrs Grantly also was dressing, and made reply out of her bedroom.

'Upon my word, I don't know. As a father I would do anything to prevent such a marriage as that.'

'But if he did marry her in spite of the threat? And he would if he had once said so.'

'Is a father's word, then, to go for nothing; and a father who allows his son eight hundred a year? If he told the girl that he would be ruined she couldn't hold him to it.'

'My dear, they'd know as well as I do, that you would give way after three months.'

'But why should I give way? Good heavens— !'

'Of course you'd give way, and of course we should have the young woman here, and of course we should make the best of it.'

The idea of having Grace Crawley as a daughter at the Plumstead Rectory was too much for the archdeacon, and he resented it by additional vehemence in the tone of his voice, and a nearer personal approach to the wife of his bosom. All unaccoutred as he was,* he stood in the doorway between the two rooms, and thence fulminated at his wife his assurances that he would never allow himself to be immersed in such a depth of humility as that she had suggested. 'I can tell you this, then, that if ever she comes here, I shall take care to be away. I will never receive her here. You can do as you please.'

'That is just what I cannot do. If I could do as I pleased, I would put a stop to it at once.'

'It seems to me that you want to encourage him. A child about sixteen years of age!'

'I am told she is nineteen.'

'What does it matter if she was fifty-nine? Think of what her bringing up has been. Think what it would be to have all the Crawleys in our house for ever, and all their debts, and all their disgrace!'

'I do not know that they have ever been disgraced.'

'You'll see. The whole county has heard of the affair of this twenty pounds. Look at that dear girl upstairs, who has been such

a comfort to us. Do you think it would be fit that she and her
husband should meet such a one as Grace Crawley at our table?'

'I don't think it would do them a bit of harm,' said Mrs Grantly.
'But there would be no chance of that, seeing that Griselda's
husband never comes to us.'

'He was here the year before last.'

'And I never was so tired of a man in all my life.'

'Then you prefer the Crawleys, I suppose. This is what you get
from Eleanor's teaching.' Eleanor was the dean's wife, and Mrs
Grantly's younger sister. 'It has always been a sorrow to me that I
ever brought Arabin into the diocese.'

'I never asked you to bring him, archdeacon. But nobody was so
glad as you when he proposed to Eleanor.'

'Well, the long and the short of it is this, I shall tell Henry tonight
that if he makes a fool of himself with this girl, he must not look to
me any longer for an income. He has about six hundred a year of
his own, and if he chooses to throw himself away, he had better go
and live in the south of France, or in Canada, or where he pleases.
He shan't come here.'

'I hope he won't marry the girl, with all my heart,' said Mrs
Grantly.

'He had better not. By heavens, he had better not!'

'But if he does, you'll be the first to forgive him.'

On hearing this the archdeacon slammed the door, and retired to
his washing apparatus. At the present moment he was very angry
with his wife, but then he was so accustomed to such anger, and
was so well aware that it in truth meant nothing, that it did not
make him unhappy. The archdeacon and Mrs Grantly had now
been man and wife for more than a quarter of a century, and had
never in truth quarrelled. He had the most profound respect for her
judgment, and the most implicit reliance on her conduct. She had
never yet offended him, or caused him to repent the hour in which
he had made her Mrs Grantly. But she had come to understand that
she might use a woman's privilege with her tongue; and she used
it, – not altogether to his comfort. On the present occasion he was
the more annoyed because he felt that she might be right. 'It would
be a positive disgrace, and I never would see him again,' he said to
himself. And yet as he said it, he knew that he would not have the
strength of character to carry him through a prolonged quarrel with
his son. 'I never would see her, – never, never!' he said to himself.
'And then such an opening as he might have at his sister's house.'

Major Grantly had been a successful man in life, – with the one
exception of having lost the mother of his child within a twelvemonth of his marriage and within a few hours of that child's birth.

He had served in India as a very young man, and had been decorated with the Victoria Cross. Then he had married a lady with some money, and had left the active service of the army, with the concurring advice of his own family and that of his wife. He had taken a small place in his father's county, but the wife for whose comfort he had taken it had died before she was permitted to see it. Nevertheless he had gone to reside there, hunting a good deal and farming a little, making himself popular in the district, and keeping up the good name of Grantly in a successful way, till – alas, – it had seemed good to him to throw those favouring eyes on poor Grace Crawley. His wife had now been dead just two years, and as he was still under thirty, no one could deny it would be right that he should marry again. No one did deny it. His father had hinted that he ought to do so, and had generously whispered that if some little increase to the major's present income were needed, he might possibly be able to do something. 'What is the good of keeping it ?' the archdeacon had said in liberal after-dinner warmth; 'I only want it for your brother and yourself.' The brother was a clergyman.

And the major's mother had strongly advised him to marry again without loss of time. 'My dear Henry,' she had said, 'you'll never be younger, and youth does go for something. As for dear little Edith, being a girl, she is almost no impediment. Do you know those two girls at Chaldicotes ?'

'What, Mrs Thorne's nieces ?'

'No; they are not her nieces but her cousins. Emily Dunstable is very handsome; – and as for money— !'

'But what about birth, mother ?'

'One can't have everything, my dear.'

'As far as I am concerned, I should like to have everything or nothing,' the major had said laughing. Now for him to think of Grace Crawley who had no money, and no particular birth, and not even beauty itself, – so at least Mrs Grantly said, – who had not even enjoyed the ordinary education of a lady, was too bad. Nothing had been wanting to Emily Dunstable's education, and it was calculated that she would have at least twenty thousand pounds on the day of her marriage.

The disappointment to the mother would be the more sore because she had gone to work upon her little scheme with reference to Miss Emily Dunstable, and had at first, as she thought, seen her way to success, – to success in spite of the disparaging words which her son had spoken to her. Mrs Thorne's house at Chaldicotes, – or Dr Thorne's house as it should, perhaps, be more properly called, for Dr Thorne was the husband of Mrs Thorne, – was in these days the pleasantest house in Barsetshire. No one saw so much company as the Thornes, or spent so much money in so pleasant a way. The great county families, the Pallisers and the De Courcys, the Luftons and the Greshams, were no doubt grander, and some of them were perhaps richer than the Chaldicote Thornes, – as they were called to distinguish them from the Thornes of Ullathorne; but none of these people were so pleasant in their ways, so free in their hospitality, or so easy in their modes of living, as the doctor and his wife. When first Chaldicotes, a very old country seat, had by the chances of war fallen into their hands and been newly greenhoused and hot-watered by them, many of the county people had turned up their noses at them. Dear old Lady Lufton had done so, and had been greatly grieved, – saying nothing, however, of her grief, when her son and daughter-in-law had broken away from her, and submitted themselves to the blandishments of the doctor's wife. And the Grantlys had stood aloof, partly influenced, no doubt, by their dear and intimate old friend Miss Monica Thorne of Ullathorne, a lady of the very old school, who, though good as gold and kind as charity, could not endure that an interloping Mrs Thorne, who never had a grandfather, should come to honour and glory* in the county, simply because of her riches. Miss Monica Thorne stood out, but Mrs Grantly gave way, and having once given way found that Dr Thorne, and Mrs Thorne, and Emily Dunstable, and Chaldicote House together, were very charming. And the major had been once there with her, and had made himself very pleasant, and there had certainly been some little passage of incipient love between him and Miss Dunstable, as to which Mrs Thorne, who managed everything, seemed to be well pleased. This had been after the first mention made by Mrs Grantly to her son of Emily Dunstable's name, but before she had heard any faintest whispers of his fancy for Grace Crawley; and she had therefore been justified in hoping, – almost in expecting, that Emily Dunstable would be her daughter-in-law, and was therefore the more aggrieved when this terrible Crawley peril first opened itself before her eyes.

CHAPTER 3

The archdeacon's threat

The dinner-party at the rectory comprised none but the Grantly family. The marchioness had written to say that she preferred to have it so. The father had suggested that the Thornes of Ullathorne, very old friends, might be asked, and the Greshams from Boxall Hill, and had even promised to endeavour to get old Lady Lufton over to the rectory, Lady Lufton having in former years been Griselda's warm friend. But Lady Hartletop had preferred to see her dear father and mother in privacy. Her brother Henry she would be glad to meet, and hoped to make some arrangement with him for a short visit to Hartlebury, her husband's place in Shropshire, – as to which latter hint, it may, however, be at once said, that nothing further was spoken after the Crawley alliance had been suggested. And there had been a very sore point mooted by the daughter in a request made by her to her father that she might not be called upon to meet her grandfather, her mother's father, Mr Harding, a clergyman of Barchester, who was now stricken in years. – 'Papa would not have come,' said Mrs Grantly, 'but I think, – I do think—' Then she stopped herself.

'Your father has odd ways sometimes, my dear. You know how fond I am of having him here myself.'

'It does not signify,' said Mrs Grantly. 'Do not let us say anything more about it. Of course we cannot have everything. I am told the child does her duty in her sphere of life,* and I suppose we ought to be contented.' Then Mrs Grantly went up to her own room, and there she cried. Nothing was said to the major on the unpleasant subject of the Crawleys before dinner. He met his sister in the drawing-room, and was allowed to kiss her noble cheek. 'I hope Edith is well, Henry,' said the sister. 'Quite well; and little Dumbello is the same, I hope?' 'Thank you, yes; quite well.' Then there seemed to be nothing more to be said between the two. The major never made inquiries after the august family, or would allow it to appear that he was conscious of being shone upon by the wife of a marquis. Any adulation which Griselda received of that kind came from her family, and, therefore, unconsciously she had learned to think that her father was better bred than the other members of her family, and more fitted by nature to move in that sacred circle to which she herself had been exalted. We need not dwell upon the dinner, which was but a dull affair. Mrs Grantly strove to carry on the family party exactly as it would have been carried on had her daughter married the son of some neighbouring squire; but she herself was conscious of the struggle, and the fact of there being a struggle produced failure. The rector's servants treated the daughter of the house with special awe, and the marchioness herself moved, and spoke, and ate, and drank with a cold magnificence, which I think had become a second nature with her, but which was not on that account the less oppressive. Even the archdeacon, who enjoyed something in that which was so disagreeable to his wife, felt a relief when he was left alone after dinner with his son. He felt relieved as his son got up to open the door for his mother and sister, but was aware at the same time that he had before him a most difficult and possibly a most disastrous task. His dear son Henry was not a man to be talked smoothly out of, or into, any propriety. He had a will of his own, and having hitherto been a successful man, who in youth had fallen into few youthful troubles, – who had never justified his father in using stern parental authority, – was not now inclined to bend his neck. 'Henry,' said the archdeacon, 'what are you drinking? That's '34 port, but it's not just what it should be. Shall I send for another bottle?'

'It will do for me, sir. I shall only take a glass.'

'I shall drink two or three glasses of claret. But you young fellows have become so desperately temperate.'

'We take our wine at dinner, sir.'

'By-the-by, how well Griselda is looking.'

'Yes, she is. It's always easy for women to look well when they're rich.' How would Grace Crawley look, then, who was poor as poverty itself, and who should remain poor, if his son was fool enough to marry her? That was the train of thought which ran through the archdeacon's mind. 'I do not think much of riches,' said he, 'but it is always well that a gentleman's wife or a gentleman's daughter should have a sufficiency to maintain her position in life.'

'You may say the same, sir, of everybody's wife and everybody's daughter.'

'You know what I mean, Henry.'

'I am not quite sure that I do, sir.'

'Perhaps I had better speak out at once. A rumour has reached your mother and me, which we don't believe for a moment, but which, nevertheless, makes us unhappy even as a report. They say that there is a young woman living in Silverbridge to whom you are becoming attached.'

'Is there any reason why I should not become attached to a young woman in Silverbridge? – though I hope any young woman to whom I may become attached will be worthy at any rate of being called a young lady.'

'I hope so, Henry; I hope so. I do hope so.'

'So much I will promise, sir; but I will promise nothing more.'

The archdeacon looked across into his son's face, and his heart sank within him. His son's voice and his son's eyes seemed to tell him two things. They seemed to tell him, firstly, that the rumour about Grace Crawley was true; and, secondly, that the major was resolved not to be talked out of his folly. 'But you are not engaged to any one, are you?' said the archdeacon. The son did not at first make any answer, and then the father repeated the question. 'Considering our mutual positions, Henry, I think you ought to tell me if you are engaged.'

'I am not engaged. Had I become so, I should have taken the first opportunity of telling either you or my mother.'

'Thank God. Now, my dear boy, I can speak out more plainly. The young woman whose name I have heard is daughter to that Mr Crawley who is perpetual curate at Hogglestock. I knew that there could be nothing in it.'

'But there is something in it, sir.'

'What is there in it? Do not keep me in suspense, Henry. What is it you mean?'

'It is rather hard to be cross-questioned in this way on such a subject. When you express yourself as thankful that there is nothing in the rumour, I am forced to stop you, as otherwise it is possible that hereafter you may say that I have deceived you.'

'But you don't mean to marry her?'

'I certainly do not mean to pledge myself not to do so.'

'Do you mean to tell me, Henry, that you are in love with Miss Crawley?' Then there was another pause, during which the archdeacon sat looking for an answer; but the major said never a word. 'Am I to suppose that you intend to lower yourself by marrying a young woman who cannot possibly have enjoyed any of the advantages of a lady's education? I say nothing of the imprudence of the thing; nothing of her own want of fortune; nothing of your having to maintain a whole family steeped in poverty; nothing of the debts and character of the father, upon whom, as I understand, at this moment there rests a very grave suspicion of – of – of – what I'm afraid I must call downright theft.'

'Downright theft, certainly, if he were guilty.'

'I say nothing of all that; but looking at the young woman herself—'

'She is simply the best educated girl whom it has ever been my lot to meet.'

'Henry, I have a right to expect that you will be honest with me.'

'I am honest with you.'

'Do you mean to ask this girl to marry you ?'

'I do not think that you have any right to ask me that question, sir.'

'I have a right at any rate to tell you this, that if you so far disgrace yourself and me, I shall consider myself bound to withdraw from you all the sanction which would be conveyed by my – my – my continued assistance.'

'Do you intend me to understand that you will stop my income ?'

'Certainly I should.'

'Then, sir, I think you would behave to me most cruelly. You advised me to give up my profession.'

'Not in order that you might marry Grace Crawley.'

'I claim the privilege of a man of my age to do as I please in such a matter as marriage. Miss Crawley is a lady. Her father is a clergyman, as is mine. Her father's oldest friend is my uncle. There is nothing on earth against her except her poverty. I do not think I ever heard of such cruelty on a father's part.'

'Very well, Henry.'

'I have endeavoured to do my duty by you, sir, always ; and by my mother. You can treat me in this way, if you please, but it will not have any effect on my conduct. You can stop my allowance to-morrow, if you like it. I had not as yet made up my mind to make an offer to Miss Crawley, but I shall now do so to-morrow morning.'

This was very bad indeed, and the archdeacon was extremely unhappy. He was by no means at heart a cruel man. He loved his children dearly. If this disagreeable marriage were to take place, he would doubtless do exactly as his wife had predicted. He would not stop his son's income for a single quarter ; and, though he went on telling himself that he would stop it, he knew in his own heart that any such severity was beyond his power. He was a generous man in money matters, – having a dislike for poverty which was not generous, – and for his own sake could not have endured to see a son of his in want. But he was terribly anxious to exercise the power which the use of the threat might give him. 'Henry,' he said, 'you are treating me badly, very badly. My anxiety has always been for the welfare of my children. Do you think that Miss Crawley would be a fitting sister-in-law for that dear girl upstairs?'

'Certainly I do, or for any other dear girl in the world; excepting that Griselda, who is not clever, would hardly be able to appreciate Miss Crawley, who is clever.'

'Griselda not clever! Good heavens!' Then there was another pause, and as the major said nothing, the father continued his entreaties. 'Pray, pray think of what my wishes are, and your mother's. You are not committed as yet. Pray think of us while there is time. I would rather double your income if I saw you marry any one that we could name here.'

'I have enough as it is, if I may only be allowed to know that it will not be capriciously withdrawn.' The archdeacon filled his glass unconsciously, and sipped his wine, while he thought what further he might say. Perhaps it might be better that he should say nothing further at the present moment. The major, however, was indiscreet, and pushed the question. 'May I understand, sir, that your threat is withdrawn, and that my income is secure?'

'What, if you marry this girl?'

'Yes, sir; will my income be continued to me if I marry Miss Crawley?'

'No, it will not.' Then the father got up hastily, pushed the decanter back angrily from his hand, and without saying another word walked away into the drawing-room. That evening at the rectory was very gloomy. The archdeacon now and again said a word or two to his daughter, and his daughter answered him in monosyllables. The major sat apart moodily, and spoke to no one. Mrs Grantly, understanding well what had passed, knew that nothing could be done at the present moment to restore family comfort; so she sat by the fire and knitted. Exactly at ten they all went to bed.

'Dear Henry,' said the mother to her son the next morning; 'think much of yourself, and of your child, and of us, before you take any great step in life.'

'I will, mother,' said he. Then he went out and put on his wrapper, and got into his dog-cart, and drove himself off to Silverbridge. He had not spoken to his father since they were in the dining-room on the previous evening. When he started, the marchioness had not yet come downstairs; but at eleven she breakfasted, and at twelve she also was taken away. Poor Mrs Grantly had not had much comfort from her children's visits.

CHAPTER 4

The clergyman's house at Hogglestock

Mrs Crawley had walked from Hogglestock to Silverbridge on the occasion of her visit to Mr Walker, the attorney, and had been kindly sent back by that gentleman in his wife's little open carriage. The tidings she brought home with her to her husband were very grievous. The magistrates would sit on the next Thursday, – it was then Friday, – and Mr Crawley had better appear before them to answer the charge made by Mr Soames. He would be served with a summons, which he could obey of his own accord. There had been many points very closely discussed between Walker and Mrs Crawley, as to which there had been great difficulty in the choice of words which should be tender enough to convey to her the very facts as they stood. Would Mr Crawley come, or must a policeman be sent to fetch him? The magistrates had already issued a warrant for his apprehension. Such in truth was the fact, but they had agreed with Mr Walker, that as there was no reasonable ground for anticipating any attempt at escape on the part of the reverend gentleman, the lawyer might use what gentle means he could for ensuring the clergyman's attendance. Could Mrs Crawley undertake to say that he would appear? Mrs Crawley did undertake either that her husband should appear on the Thursday, or else that she would send over in the early part of the week and declare her inability to ensure his appearance. In that case it was understood the policeman must come. Then Mr Walker had suggested that Mr Crawley had better employ a lawyer. Upon this Mrs Crawley had looked beseechingly up into Mr Walker's face, and had asked him to undertake the duty. He was of course obliged to explain that he was already employed on the other side. Mr Soames had secured his services, and though he was willing to do all in his power to mitigate the sufferings of the family, he could not abandon the duty he had undertaken. He named another attorney, however, and then sent the poor woman home in his wife's carriage. 'I fear that unfortunate man is guilty. I fear he is,' Mr Walker had said to his wife within ten minutes of the departure of the visitor.

Mrs Crawley would not allow herself to be driven up to the garden gate before her own house, but had left the carriage some three hundred yards off down the road, and from thence she walked home. It was now quite dark. It was nearly six in the evening on a wet December night, and although cloaks and shawls had been supplied to her, she was wet and cold when she reached her house. But at such a moment, anxious as she was to prevent the additional evil which would come to them all from illness to herself, she could not pass through to her room till she had spoken to her husband. He was sitting in the one sitting-room on the left side of the passage as the house was entered, and with him was their daughter Jane, a girl now nearly sixteen years of age. There was no light in the room, and hardly more than a spark of fire showed itself in the grate. The father was sitting on one side of the hearth, in an old arm-chair, and there he had sat for the last hour without speaking. His daughter had been in and out of the room, and had endeavoured to gain his attention now and again by a word, but he had never answered her, and had not even noticed her presence. At the moment when Mrs Crawley's step was heard upon the gravel which led to the door, Jane was kneeling before the fire with a hand upon her father's arm. She had tried to get her hand into his, but he had either been unaware of the attempt, or had rejected it.

'Here is mamma, at last,' said Jane, rising to her feet as her mother entered the house.

'Are you all in the dark?' said Mrs Crawley, striving to speak in a voice that should not be sorrowful.

'Yes, mamma; we are in the dark. Papa is here. Oh, mamma, how wet you are!'

'Yes, dear. It is raining. Get a light out of the kitchen, Jane, and I will go upstairs in two minutes.' Then, when Jane was gone, the wife made her way in the dark over to her husband's side, and spoke a word to him. 'Josiah,' she said, 'will you not speak to me?'

'What should I speak about? Where have you been?'

'I have been to Silverbridge. I have been to Mr Walker. He, at any rate, is very kind.'

'I don't want his kindness. I want no man's kindness. Mr Walker is the attorney, I believe. Kind, indeed!'

'I mean considerate. Josiah, let us do the best we can in this trouble. We have had others as heavy before.'

'But none to crush me as this will crush me. Well; what am I to do? Am I to go to prison – to-night?' At this moment his daughter returned with a candle, and the mother could not make her answer at once. It was a wretched, poverty-stricken room. By degrees the carpet had disappeared, which had been laid down some nine or ten years since, when they had first come to Hogglestock, and which even then had not been new. Now nothing but a poor fragment of it remained in front of the fire-place. In the middle of the room there was a table which had once been large; but one flap of it was gone altogether, and the other flap sloped grievously towards the floor, the weakness of old age having fallen into its legs. There were two or three smaller tables about, but they stood propped against walls, thence obtaining a security which their own strength would not give them. At the further end of the room there was an ancient piece of furniture, which was always called "papa's secretary," at which Mr Crawley customarily sat and wrote his sermons, and did all work that was done by him within his house. The man who had made it, some time in the last century, had intended it to be a locked guardian for domestic documents, and the receptacle for all that was most private in the house of some paterfamilias. But beneath the hands of Mr Crawley it always stood open; and with the exception of the small space at which he wrote, was covered with dog's-eared books, from nearly all of which the covers had disappeared. There were there two odd volumes of Euripides, a Greek Testament, an Odyssey, a duodecimo Pindar, and a miniature Anacreon. There was half a Horace, – the two first books of the Odes at the beginning, and the De Arte Poetica at the end having disappeared. There was a little bit of a volume of Cicero, and there were Cæsar's Commentaries, in two volumes, so stoutly bound that they had defied the combined ill-usage of time and the Crawley family. All these were piled upon the secretary, with many others, – odd volumes of sermons and the like; but the Greek and Latin lay at the top, and showed signs of most frequent use. There was one arm-chair in the room, a Windsor-chair, as such used to be called, made soft by an old cushion in the back, in which Mr Crawley sat when both he and his wife were in the room, and Mrs Crawley when he was absent. And there was an old horsehair sofa, – now almost denuded of its horsehair, – but that, like the tables, required the assistance of a friendly wall. Then there was half a dozen of other chairs, – all of different sorts, – and they completed the furniture of the room. It was not such a room as one would wish to see inhabited by a beneficial clergyman of the Church of England; but they who know what money will do and what it will not, will understand how easily a man with a family, and with a hundred and thirty pounds a year, may be brought to the need of inhabiting such a chamber. When it is remembered that three pounds of meat a day, at ninepence a pound, will cost over forty pounds a year, there need be no difficulty in understanding that it may be so. Bread for such a family must cost at least twenty-five pounds. Clothes for five persons, of whom one must at any rate wear the raiment of a gentleman, can hardly be found for less than ten pounds a year a head. Then there remains fifteen pounds for tea, sugar, beer, wages, education, amusements, and the like. In such circumtances a gentleman can hardly pay much for the renewal of his furniture!

Mrs Crawley could not answer her husband's question before her daughter, and was therefore obliged to make another excuse for again sending her out of the room. 'Jane, dear,' she said, 'bring my things down to the kitchen and I will change them by the fire. I will be there in two minutes, when I have had a word with your papa.' The girl went immediately and then Mrs Crawley answered her husband's question. 'No, my dear; there is no question of your going to prison.'

'But there will be.'

'I have undertaken that you shall attend before the magistrates at Silverbridge on Thursday next, at twelve o'clock. You will do that?'

'Do it! You mean, I suppose, to say that I must go there. Is anybody to come and fetch me?'

'Nobody will come. Only you must promise that you will be there. I have promised for you. You will go; will you not?' She stood leaning over him, half embracing him, waiting for an answer; but for a while he gave none. 'You will tell me that you will do what I have undertaken for you, Josiah?'

'I think I would rather that they fetched me. I think that I will not go myself.'

'And have policemen come for you into the parish! Mr Walker has promised that he will send over his phaeton. He sent me home in it to-day.'

'I want nobody's phaeton. If I go I will walk. If it were ten times the distance, and though I had not a shoe left to my feet I would walk. If I go there at all, of my own accord, I will walk there.'

'But you will go?'

'What do I care for the parish? What matters it who sees me now? I cannot be degraded worse than I am. Everybody knows it.'

'There is no disgrace without guilt,' said his wife.

'Everybody thinks me guilty. I see it in their eyes. The children know of it, and I hear their whispers in the school, "Mr Crawley has taken some money." I heard the girl say it myself.'

'What matters what the girl says?'

'And yet you would have me go in a fine carriage to Silverbridge, as though to a wedding. If I am wanted there let them take me as they would another. I shall be here for them, – unless I am dead.'

At this moment Jane reappeared, pressing her mother to take off her wet clothes, and Mrs Crawley went with her daughter to the kitchen. The one red-armed young girl who was their only servant was sent away, and then the mother and child discussed how best they might prevail with the head of the family. 'But, mamma, it must come right; must it not?'

'I trust it will. I think it will. But I cannot see my way as yet.'

'Papa cannot have done anything wrong.'

'No, my dear; he has done nothing wrong. He has made great mistakes, and it is hard to make people understand that he has not intentionally spoken untruths. He is ever thinking of other things, about the school, and his sermons, and he does not remember.'

'And about how poor we are, mamma.'

'He has much to occupy his mind, and he forgets things which dwell in the memory with other people. He said that he had got this money from Mr Soames, and of course he thought that it was so.'

'And where did he get it, mamma?'

'Ah, – I wish I knew. I should have said that I had seen every shilling that came into the house; but I know nothing of this cheque, – whence it came.'

'But will not papa tell you?'

'He would tell me if he knew. He thinks it came from the dean.'

'And are you sure it did not?'

'Yes; quite sure; as sure as I can be of anything. The dean told me he would give him fifty pounds, and the fifty pounds came. I had them in my own hands. And he has written to say that it was so.'

'But couldn't this be part of the fifty pounds?'

'No, dear, no.'

'Then where did papa get it? Perhaps he picked it up, and has forgotten?'

To this Mrs Crawley made no reply. The idea that the cheque had been found by her husband, – had been picked up as Jane had said, – had occurred also to Jane's mother. Mr Soames was confident that he had dropped the pocket-book at the parsonage. Mrs Crawley had always disliked Mr Soames, thinking him to be hard, cruel, and vulgar. She would not have hesitated to believe him guilty of a falsehood, or even of direct dishonesty, if by so believing she could in her own mind have found the means of reconciling her husband's possession of the cheque with absolute truth on his part. But she could not do so. Even though Soames had, with devilish premeditated malice, slipped the cheque into her husband's pocket, his having done so would not account for her husband's having used the cheque when he found it there. She was driven to make excuses for him which, valid as they might be with herself, could not be valid with others. He had said that Mr Soames had paid the cheque to him. That was clearly a mistake. He had said that the cheque had been given to him by the dean. That was clearly another mistake. She knew, or thought she knew, that he, being such as he was, might make such blunders as these, and yet be true. She believed that such statements might be blunders and not falsehoods, – so convinced was she that her husband's mind would not act at all times as do the minds of other men. But having such a conviction she was driven to believe also that almost anything might be possible. Soames may have been right, or he might have dropped, not the book, but the cheque. She had no difficulty in presuming Soames to be wrong in any detail, if by so supposing she could make the exculpation of her husband easier to herself. If villany on the part of Soames was needful to her theory, Soames would become to her a villain at once, – of the blackest dye. Might it not be possible that the cheque having thus fallen into her husband's hands, he had come, after a while, to think that it had been sent to him by his friend, the dean? And if it were so, would it be possible to make others so believe? That there was some mistake which would be easily explained were her husband's mind lucid at all points, but which she could not explain because of the darkness of his mind, she was thoroughly convinced. But were she herself to put forward such a defence on her husband's part, she would in doing so be driven to say that he was a lunatic, – that he was incapable of managing the affairs of himself or his family. It seemed to her that she would be compelled to have him proved to be either a thief or a madman. And yet she knew that he was neither. That he was not a thief was as clear to her as the sun at noonday. Could she have lain on the man's bosom for twenty years, and not yet have learned the secrets of the heart beneath? The whole mind of the man was, as she told herself, within her grasp. He might have taken the twenty pounds; he might have taken it and spent it, though it was not his own; but yet he was no thief. Nor was he a madman. No man more sane in preaching the gospel of his Lord, in making intelligible to the ignorant the promises of his Saviour, ever got into a parish pulpit, or taught in a parish school. The intellect of the man was as clear as running water in all things not appertaining to his daily life and its difficulties. He could be logical with a vengeance, – so logical as to cause infinite trouble to his wife, who, with all her good sense, was not logical. And he had Greek at his fingers' ends, – as his daughter knew very well. And even to this day he would sometime recite to them English poetry, lines after lines, stanzas upon stanzas, in a sweet low melancholy voice, on long winter evenings when occasionally the burden of his troubles would be lighter to him than was usual. Books in Latin and in French he read with as much ease as in English, and took delight in such as came to him, when he would condescend to accept such loans from the deanery. And there was at times a lightness of heart about the man. In the course of the last winter he had translated into Greek irregular verse the very noble ballad of Lord Bateman,* maintaining the rhythm and the rhyme, and had repeated it with uncouth glee till his daughter knew it all by heart. And when there had come to him a five-pound note from some admiring magazine editor as the price of the same, – still through the dean's hands, – he had brightened up his heart and had thought for an hour or two that even yet the world would smile upon him. His wife knew well that he was not mad; but yet she knew that there were dark moments with him, in which his mind was so much astray that he could not justly be called to account as to what he might remember and what he might forget. How would it be possible to explain all this to a judge and jury, so that they might neither say that he was dishonest, nor yet that he was mad? 'Perhaps he picked it up, and had forgotten,' her daughter said to her. Perhaps it was so, but she might not as yet admit as much even to her child.

'It is a mystery, dear, as yet, which, with God's aid, will be unravelled. Of one thing we at least may be sure; that your papa has not wilfully done anything wrong.'

'Of course we are sure of that, mamma.'

Mrs Crawley had many troubles during the next four or five days, of which the worst, perhaps, had reference to the services of the Sunday which intervened between the day of her visit to Silverbridge, and the sitting of the magistrates. On the Saturday it was necessary that he should prepare his sermons, of which he preached two on every Sunday, though his congregation consisted only of farmers, brickmakers, and agricultural labourers, who would willingly have dispensed with the second. Mrs Crawley proposed to send over to Mr Robarts, a neighbouring clergyman, for the loan of a curate. Mr Robarts was a warm friend to the Crawleys, and in such an emergency would probably have come himself; but Mr Crawley would not hear of it. The discussion took place early on the Saturday morning, before it was as yet daylight, for the poor woman was thinking day and night of her husband's troubles, and it had this good effect, that immediately after breakfast he seated himself at his desk, and worked at his task as though he had forgotten all else in the world.

And on the Sunday morning he went into his school before the hour of the church service, as had been his wont, and taught there as though everything with him was as usual. Some of the children were absent, having heard of their teacher's tribulation, and having been told probably that he would remit his work; and for these absent ones he sent in great anger. The poor bairns came creeping in, for he was a man who by his manners had been able to secure their obedience in spite of his poverty. And he preached to the people of his parish on that Sunday, as he had always preached; eagerly, clearly, with an eloquence fitted for the hearts of such an audience. No one would have guessed from his tones and gestures and appearance on that occasion, that there was aught wrong with him, – unless there had been there some observer keen enough to perceive that the greater care which he used, and the special eagerness of his words, denoted a special frame of mind.

After that, after those church services were over, he sank again and never roused himself till the dreaded day had come.

CHAPTER 5

What the world thought about it

Opinion in Silverbridge, at Barchester, and throughout the county, was very much divided as to the guilt or innocence of Mr Crawley. Up to the time of Mrs Crawley's visit to Silverbridge, the affair had not been much discussed. To give Mr Soames his due, he had been by no means anxious to press the matter against the clergyman; but he had been forced to go on with it. While the first cheque was missing, Lord Lufton had sent him a second cheque for the money, and the loss had thus fallen upon his lordship. The cheque had of course been traced, and inquiry had of course been made as to Mr Crawley's possession of it. When that gentleman declared that he had received it from Mr Soames, Mr Soames had been forced to contradict and to resent such an assertion. When Mr Crawley had afterwards said that the money had come to him from the dean, and when the dean had shown that this also was untrue, Mr Soames, confident as he was that he had dropped the pocket-book at Mr Crawley's house, could not but continue the investigation. He had done so with as much silence as the nature of the work admitted. But by the day of the magistrates' meeting at Silverbridge the subject had become common through the county, and men's minds were very much divided.

All Hogglestock believed their parson to be innocent; but then all Hogglestock believed him to be mad. At Silverbridge the tradesmen with whom he had dealt, and to whom he had owed, and still owed, money, all declared him to be innocent. They knew something of the man personally, and could not believe him to be a thief. All the ladies in Silverbridge, too, were sure of his innocence. It was to them impossible that such a man should have stolen twenty pounds. 'My dear,' said the eldest Miss Prettyman to poor Grace Crawley, 'in England, where the laws are good, no gentleman is ever made out to be guilty when he is innocent; and your papa, of course, is innocent. Therefore you should not trouble yourself.' 'It will break papa's heart,' Grace had said, and she did trouble herself. But the gentlemen in Silverbridge were made of sterner stuff, and believed the man to be guilty, clergyman and gentleman though he was. Mr Walker, who among the lights in Silverbridge was the leading light, would not speak a word upon the subject to anybody ; and then everybody, who was anybody, knew that Mr Walker was convinced of the man's guilt. Had Mr Walker believed him to be innocent, his tongue would have been ready enough. John Walker, who was in the habit of laughing at his father's good nature, had no doubt upon the subject. Mr Winthrop, Mr Walker's partner, shook his head. People did not think much of Mr Winthrop ; excepting certain unmarried ladies ; for Mr Winthrop was a bachelor, and had plenty of money. People did not think much of Mr Winthrop ; but still on this subject he might know something, and when he shook his head he manifestly intended to indicate guilt. And Dr Tempest, the rector of Silverbridge, did not hesitate to declare his belief in the guilt of the incumbent of Hogglestock. No man reverences a clergyman, as a clergyman, so slightly as a brother clergyman. To Dr Tempest it appeared to be neither very strange nor very terrible that Mr Crawley should have stolen twenty pounds. 'What is a man to do,' he said, 'when he sees his children starving ? He should not have married on such a preferment as that.' Mr Crawley had married, however, long before he got the living of Hogglestock.

There were two Lady Luftons, – mother-in-law and daughter-in-law, – who at this time were living together at Framley Hall, Lord Lufton's seat in the county of Barset, and they were both thoroughly convinced of Mr Crawley's innocence. The elder lady had lived much among clergymen, and could hardly, I think, by any means have been brought to believe in the guilt of any man who had taken upon himself the orders of the Church of England. She had also known Mr Crawley personally for some years, and was one of those who could not admit to herself that any one was vile who had been near to herself. She believed intensely in the wickedness of the outside world, of the world which was far away from herself, and of which she never saw anything ; but they who were near to her, and who had even become dear to her, or who even had been respected by her, were made, as it were, saints in her imagination. They were brought into the inner circle, and could hardly be expelled. She was an old woman who thought all evil of those she did not know, and all good of those whom she did know ; and as she did know Mr Crawley, she was quite sure he had not stolen Mr Soames's twenty pounds. She did know Mr Soames also ; and thus there was a mystery for the unravelling of which she was very anxious. And the young Lady Lufton was equally sure, and perhaps with better reason for such certainty. She had, in truth, known more of Mr Crawley personally, than had any one in the county, unless it was the dean. The younger Lady Lufton, the present Lord Lufton's wife, had sojourned at one time in Mr Crawley's house, amidst the Crawley poverty, living as they lived, and nursing Mrs Crawley through an illness which had well nigh been fatal to her; and the younger Lady Lufton believed in Mr Crawley, – as Mr Crawley also believed in her.

'It is quite impossible, my dear,' the old woman said to her daughter-in-law.

'Quite impossible, my lady.' The dowager was always called 'my lady,' both by her own daughter and by her son's wife, except in the presence of their children, when she was addressed as 'grand-mamma.' 'Think how well I knew him. It's no use talking of evidence. No evidence would make me believe it.'

'Nor me; and I think it a great shame that such a report should be spread about.'

'I suppose Mr Soames could not help himself?' said the younger lady, who was not herself very fond of Mr Soames.

'Ludovic says that he has only done what he was obliged to do.' The Ludovic spoken of was Lord Lufton.

This took place in the morning, but in the evening the affair was again discussed at Framley Hall. Indeed, for some days, there was hardly any other subject held to be worthy of discussion in the county. Mr Robarts, the clergyman of the parish and the brother of the younger Lady Lufton, was dining at the hall with his wife, and the three ladies had together expressed their perfect conviction of the falseness of the accusation. But when Lord Lufton and Mr Robarts were together after the ladies had left them there was much less of this certainty expressed. 'By Jove,' said Lord Lufton, 'I don't know what to think of it. I wish with all my heart that Soames had said nothing about it, and that the cheque had passed without remark.'

'That was impossible. When the banker sent to Soames, he was obliged to take the matter up.'

'Of course he was. But I'm sorry that it was so. For the life of me I can't conceive how the cheque got into Crawley's hands.'

'I imagine that it had been lying in the house, and that Crawley had come to think that it was his own.'

'But, my dear Mark,' said Lord Lufton, 'excuse me if I say that that's nonsense. What do we do when a poor man has come to think that another man's property is his own? We send him to prison for making the mistake.'

'I hope they won't send Crawley to prison.'

'I hope so too; but what is a jury to do?'

'You think it will go to a jury, then?'

'I do,' said Lord Lufton. 'I don't see how the magistrates can save themselves from committing him. It is one of those cases in which every one concerned would wish to drop it if it were only possible. But it is not possible. On the evidence, as one sees it at present, one is bound to say that it is a case for a jury.'

'I believe that he is mad,' said the brother parson.

'He always was, as far as I could learn,' said the lord. 'I never knew him, myself. You do, I think?'

'Oh, yes. I know him.' And the vicar of Framley became silent and thoughtful as the memory of a certain interview between himself and Mr Crawley* came back upon his mind. At that time the waters had nearly closed over his head and Mr Crawley had given him some assistance. When the gentlemen had again found the ladies, they kept their own doubts to themselves; for at Framley Hall, as at present tenanted, female voices and female influences predominated over those which came from the other sex.

At Barchester, the cathedral city of the county in which the Crawleys lived, opinion was violently against Mr Crawley. In the city Mrs Proudie, the wife of the bishop, was the leader of opinion in general, and she was very strong in her belief of the man's guilt. She had known much of clergymen all her life, as it behoved a bishop's wife to do, and she had none of that mingled weakness and ignorance which taught so many ladies in Barsetshire to suppose that an ordained clergyman could not become a thief. She hated old Lady Lufton with all her heart, and old Lady Lufton hated her as warmly. Mrs Proudie would say frequently that Lady Lufton was a conceited old idiot, and Lady Lufton would declare as frequently that Mrs Proudie was a vulgar virago. It was known at the palace in Barchester, that kindness had been shown to the Crawleys by the family at Framley Hall, and this alone would have been sufficient to make Mrs Proudie believe that Mr Crawley could have been guilty of any crime. And as Mrs Proudie believed, so did the bishop believe. 'It is a terrible disgrace to the diocese,' said the bishop, shaking his head, and patting his apron as he sat by his study fire.

'Fiddlestick!' said Mrs Proudie.

'But, my dear, – a beneficed clergyman!'

'You must get rid of him; that's all. You must be firm whether he be acquitted or convicted.'

'But if he be acquitted, I cannot get rid of him, my dear.'

'Yes, you can, if you are firm. And you must be firm. Is it not true that he has been disgracefully involved in debt ever since he has been there; that you have been pestered by letters from unfortunate tradesmen who cannot get their money from him?'

'That is true, my dear, certainly.'

'And is that kind of thing to go on? He cannot come to the palace as all clergymen should do, because he has got no clothes to come in. I saw him once about the lanes, and I never set my eyes on such an object in my life! I would not believe that the man was a clergyman till John told me. He is a disgrace to the diocese, and he must be got rid of. I feel sure of his guilt, and I hope he will be convicted. One is bound to hope that a guilty man should be convicted. But if he escape conviction, you must sequestrate the living because of the debts. The income is enough to get an excellent curate. It would just do for Thumble.' To all of which the bishop made no further reply, but simply nodded his head and patted his apron. He knew that he could not do exactly what his wife required of him; but if it should so turn out that poor Crawley was found to be guilty, then the matter would be comparatively easy.

'It should be an example to us, that we should look to our own steps, my dear,' said the bishop.

'That's all very well,' said Mrs Proudie, 'but it has become your duty, and mine too, to look to the steps of other people; and that duty we must do.'

'Of course, my dear; of course.' That was the tone in which the question of Mr Crawley's alleged guilt was discussed at the palace.

We have already heard what was said on the subject at the house of Archdeacon Grantly. As the days passed by, and as other tidings came in, confirmatory of those which had before reached him, the archdeacon felt himself unable not to believe in the man's guilt. And the fear which he entertained as to his son's intended marriage with Grace Crawley, tended to increase the strength of his belief. Dr Grantly had been a very successful man in the world, and on all ordinary occasions had been able to show that bold front with which success endows a man. But he still had his moments of weakness, and feared greatly lest anything of misfortune should touch him, and mar the comely roundness of his prosperity. He was very wealthy. The wife of his bosom had been to him all that a wife should be. His reputation in the clerical world stood very high. He had lived all his life on terms of equality with the best of the gentry around him. His only daughter had made a splendid marriage. His two sons had hitherto done well in the world, not only as regarded their happiness, but as to marriage also, and as to social standing. But how great would be the fall if his son should at last marry the daughter of a convicted thief! How would the Proudies rejoice over him, – the Proudies who had been crushed to the ground by the success of the Hartletop alliance; and how would the low-church curates who swarmed in Barsetshire, gather together and scream in delight over his dismay! 'But why should we say that he is guilty?' said Mrs Grantly.

'It hardly matters as far as we are concerned, whether they find him guilty or not,' said the archdeacon; 'if Henry marries that girl my heart will be broken.'

But perhaps to no one except to the Crawleys themselves had the matter caused so much terrible anxiety as to the archdeacon's son. He had told his father that he had made no offer of marriage to Grace Crawley, and he had told the truth. But there are perhaps few men who make such offers in direct terms without having already said and done that which make such offers simply necessary as the final closing of an accepted bargain. It was so at any rate between Major Grantly and Miss Crawley, and Major Grantly acknowledged to himself that it was so. He acknowledged also to himself that as regarded Grace herself he had no wish to go back from his implied intentions. Nothing that either his father or mother might say would shake him in that. But could it be his duty to bind himself to the family of a convicted thief? Could it be right that he should disgrace his father and his mother and his sister and his one child by such a connection? He had a man's heart, and the poverty of the Crawleys caused him no solicitude. But he shrank from the contamination of a prison.

CHAPTER 6

Grace Crawley

It has already been said that Grace Crawley was at this time living with the two Miss Prettymans, who kept a girls' school at Silverbridge. Two more benignant ladies than the Miss Prettymans never presided over such an establishment. The younger was fat, and fresh, and fair, and seemed to be always running over with the milk of human kindness. The other was very thin and very small, and somewhat afflicted with bad health; – was weak, too, in the eyes, and subject to racking headaches, so that it was considered generally that she was unable to take much active part in the education of the pupils. But it was considered as generally that she did all the thinking, that she knew more than any other woman in Barsetshire, and that all the Prettyman schemes for education emanated from her mind. It was said, too, by those who knew them best, that her sister's good-nature was as nothing to hers; that she was the most charitable, the most loving, and the most conscientious of schoolmistresses. This was Miss Annabella Prettyman, the elder; and perhaps it may be inferred that some portion of her great character for virtue may have been due to the fact that nobody ever saw her out of her own house. She could not even go to church, because the open air brought on neuralgia. She was therefore perhaps taken to be magnificent, partly because she was unknown. Miss Anne Prettyman, the younger, went about frequently to tea-parties, – would go, indeed, to any party to which she might be invited; and was known to have a pleasant taste for pound-cake and sweetmeats. Being seen so much in the outer world, she became common, and her character did not stand so high as did that of her sister. Some people were ill-natured enough to say that she wanted to marry Mr Winthrop; but of what maiden lady that goes out into the world are not such stories told? And all such stories in Silverbridge were told with special reference to Mr Winthrop.

Miss Crawley, at present, lived with the Miss Prettymans, and assisted them in the school. This arrangement had been going on for the last twelve months, since the time in which Grace would have left the school in the natural course of things. There had been no bargain made, and no intention that Grace should stay. She had been invited to fill the place of an absent superintendent, first for one month, then for another, and then for two more months; and when the assistant came back, the Miss Prettymans thought there were reasons why Grace should be asked to remain a little longer. But they took great care to let the fashionable world of Silverbridge know that Grace Crawley was a visitor with them, and not a teacher. 'We pay her no salary, or anything of that kind,' said Miss Anne Prettyman; a statement, however, which was by no means true, for during those four months the regular stipend had been paid to her; and twice since then, Miss Annabella Prettyman, who managed all the money matters, had called Grace into her little room, and had made a little speech, and had put a little bit of paper into her hand. 'I know I ought not to take it,' Grace had said to her friend Anne. 'If I was not here, there would be no one in my place.' Nonsense, my dear,' Anne Prettyman had said; 'it is the greatest comfort to us in the world. And you should make yourself nice, you know, for his sake. All the gentlemen like it.' Then Grace had been very angry, and had sworn that she would give the money back again. Nevertheless, I think she did make herself as nice as she knew how to do. And from all this it may be seen that the Miss Prettymans had hitherto quite approved of Major Grantly's attentions.

But when this terrible affair came on about the cheque which had been lost and found and traced to Mr Crawley's hands, Miss Anne Prettyman said nothing further to Grace Crawley about Major Grantly. It was not that she thought that Mr Crawley was guilty, but she knew enough of the world to be aware that suspicion of such guilt might compel such a man as Major Grantly to change his mind. 'If he had only popped,' Anne said to her sister, 'it would have been all right. He would never have gone back from his word.' 'My dear,' said Annabella, 'I wish you would not talk about popping. It is a terrible word.' 'I shouldn't, to any one except you,' said Anne.

There had come to Silverbridge some few months since, on a visit to Mrs Walker, a young lady from Allington, in the neighbouring county, between whom and Grace Crawley there had grown up from circumstances a warm friendship. Grace had a cousin in London, – a clerk high up and well-to-do in a public office, a nephew of her mother's, – and this cousin was, and for years had been, violently smitten in love for this young lady. But the young lady's tale had been sad, and though she acknowledged feelings of most affectionate friendship for the cousin, she could not bring herself to acknowledge more. Grace Crawley had met the young lady at Silverbridge, and words had been spoken about the cousin; and though the young lady from Allington was some years older than Grace, there had grown up to be a friendship, and, as is not uncommon between young ladies, there had been an agreement that they would correspond. The name of the lady was Miss Lily Dale, and the name of the well-to-do cousin in London was Mr John Eames.

At the present moment Miss Dale was at home with her mother at Allington, and Grace Crawley in her terrible sorrow wrote to her friend, pouring out her whole heart. As Grace's letter and Miss Dale's answer will assist us in our story, I will venture to give them both.

Silverbridge, – December, 186–.

Dearest Lily,

I hardly know how to tell you what has happened, it is so very terrible. But perhaps you will have heard it already, as everybody is talking of it here. It has got into the newspapers, and therefore it cannot be kept secret. Not that I should keep anything from you; only this is so very dreadful that I hardly know how to write it. Somebody says, – a Mr Soames, I believe it is, – that papa has taken some money that does not belong to him, and he is to be brought before the magistrates and tried. Of course, papa has done nothing wrong. I do think he would be the last man in the world to take a penny that did not belong to him. You know how poor he is; what a life he has had! But I think he would almost sooner see mamma starving; – I am sure he would rather be starved himself, than even borrow a shilling which he could not pay. To suppose that he would take money (she had tried to write the word 'steal', but she could not bring her pen to form the letters) is monstrous. But, somehow, the circumstances have been made to look bad against him, and they say that he must come over here to the magistrates. I often think that of all men in the world papa is the most unfortunate. Everything seems to go against him, and yet he is so good! Poor mamma has been over here, and she is distracted. I never saw her so wretched before. She had been to your friend, Mr Walker, and came to me afterwards for a minute. Mr Walker has got something to do with it, though mamma says she thinks he is quite friendly to papa. I wonder whether you could find out, through Mr Walker, what he thinks about it. Of course, mamma knows that papa has done nothing wrong; but she says that the whole thing is most mysterious, and that she does not know how to account for the money. Papa, you know, is not like other people. He forgets things; and is always thinking, thinking, thinking of his great misfortunes. Poor papa! My heart bleeds so when I remember all his sorrows, that I hate myself for thinking about myself.

When mamma left me, – and it was then I first knew that papa would really have to be tried, – I went to Miss Annabella, and told her that I would go home. She asked me why, and I said I would not disgrace her house by staying in it. She got up and took me in her arms, and there came a tear out of both her dear old eyes, and she said that if anything evil came to papa, – which she would not believe, as she knew him to be a good man, – there should be a home in her house not only for me, but for mamma and Jane. Isn't she a wonderful woman? When I think of her, I sometimes think she must be an angel already. Then she became very serious, – for just before, through her tears, she had tried to smile, – and she told me to remember that all people could not be like her, who had nobody to look to but herself and her sister; and that at present I must task myself not to think of that which I had been thinking of before. She did not mention anybody's name, but of course I understood very well what she meant; and I suppose she is right. I said nothing in answer to her, for I could not speak. She was holding my hand, and I took hers up and kissed it, to show her, if I could, that I knew that she was right; but I could not have spoken about it for all the world. It was not ten days since that she herself, with all her prudence, told me that she thought I ought to make up my mind what answer I would give him. And then I did not say anything; but of course she knew. And after that Miss Anne spoke quite freely about it, so that I had to beg her to be silent even before the girls. You know how imprudent she is. But it is all over now. Of course Miss Annabella is right. He has got a great many people to think of; his father and mother, and his darling little Edith, whom he brought here twice, and left her with us once for two days, so that she got to know me quite well; and I took such a love for her, that I could not bear to part with her. But I think sometimes that all our family are born to be unfortunate, and then I tell myself that I will never hope for anything again.

Pray write to me soon. I feel as though nothing on earth could comfort me, and yet I shall like to have your letter. Dear, dear Lily, I am not even yet so wretched but what I shall rejoice to be told good news of you. If it only could be as John wishes it! And why should it not? It seems to me that nobody has a right or a reason to be unhappy except us. Good-by, dearest Lily,

Your affectionate friend,
Grace Crawley.

P.S. – I think I have made up my mind that I will go back to Hogglestock at once if the magistrates decide against papa. I think I should be doing the school harm if I were to stay here.

The answer to this letter did not reach Miss Crawley till after the magistrates' meeting on the Thursday, but it will be better for our story that it should be given here than postponed until the result of that meeting shall have been told. Miss Dale's answer was as follows : –

Allington, – December, 186 – .

Dear Grace,

Your letter has made me very unhappy. If it can at all comfort you to know that mamma and I sympathize with you altogether, in that you may at any rate be sure. But in such troubles nothing will give comfort. They must be borne, till the fire of misfortune burns itself out.

I had heard about the affair a day or two before I got your note. Our clergyman, Mr Boyce, told us of it. Of course we all know that the charge must be altogether unfounded, and mamma says that the truth will be sure to show itself at last. But that conviction does not cure the evil, and I can well understand that your father should suffer grievously ; and I pity your mother quite as much as I do him.

As for Major Grantly, if he be such a man as I took him to be from the little I saw of him, all this would make no difference to him. I am sure that it ought to make none. Whether it should not make a difference in you is another question. I think it should ; and I think your answer to him should be that you could not even consider any such proposition while your father was in so great trouble. I am so much older than you, and seem to have had so much experience, that I do not scruple, as you will see, to come down upon you with all the weight of my wisdom.

About that other subject I had rather say nothing. I have known your cousin all my life, almost ; and I regard no one more kindly than I do him. When I think of my friends, he is always one of the dearest. But when one thinks of going beyond friendship, even if one tries to do so, there are so many barriers !

Your affectionate friend,
Lily Dale.

Mamma bids me say that she would be delighted to have you here whenever it might suit you to come ; and I add to this message my entreaty that you will come at once. You say that you think you ought to leave Miss Prettyman's for a while. I can well understand your feeling; but as your sister is with your mother, surely you had better come to us, – I mean quite at once. I will not scruple to tell you what mamma says, because I know your good sense. She says that as the interest of the school may possibly be concerned, and as you have no regular engagement, she thinks you ought to leave Silverbridge; but she says that it will be better that you come to us than that you should go home. If you went home, people might say that you had left in some sort of disgrace. Come to us, and when all this has been put right, then you go back to Silverbridge; and then, if a certain person speaks again, you can make a different answer. Mamma quite understands that you are to come; so you have only got to ask your own mamma, and come at once.

This letter, as the reader will understand, did not reach Grace Crawley till after the all-important Thursday; but before that day had come round, Grace had told Miss Prettyman, – had told both the Miss Prettymans – that she was resolved to leave them. She had done this without even consulting her mother, driven to it by various motives. She knew that her father's conduct was being discussed by the girls in the school, and that things were said of him which it could not but be for the disadvantage of Miss Prettyman that any one should say of a teacher in her establishment. She felt, too, that she could not hold up her head in Silverbridge in these days, as it would become her to do if she retained her position. She did struggle gallantly, and succeeded much more nearly than she was herself aware. She was all but able to carry herself as though no terrible accusation was being made against her father. Of the struggle, however, she was not herself the less conscious, and she told herself that on that account also she must go. And then she must go also because of Major Grantly. Whether he was minded to come and speak to her that one other needed word, or whether he was not so minded, it would be better that she should be away from Silverbridge. If he spoke it she could only answer him by a negative; and if he were minded not to speak it, would it not be better that she should leave herself the power of thinking that his silence had been caused by her absence, and not by his coldness or indifference ?

She asked, therefore, for an interview with Miss Prettyman, and was shown into the elder sister's room, at eleven o'clock on the Tuesday morning. The elder Miss Prettyman never came into the school herself till twelve, but was in the habit of having interviews with the young ladies, – which were sometimes very awful in their nature, – for the two previous hours. During these interviews an immense amount of business was done, and the fortunes in life of some girls were said to have been there made or marred; as when, for instance, Miss Crimpton had been advised to stay at home with her uncle in England, instead of going out with her sisters to India, both of which sisters were married within three months of their landing at Bombay. The way in which she gave her counsel on such occasions was very efficacious. No one knew better than Miss Prettyman that a cock can crow most effectively in his own farmyard, and therefore all crowing intended to be effective was done by her within the shrine of her own peculiar room.

'Well, my dear, what is it?' she said to Grace. 'Sit in the arm-chair, my dear, and we can then talk comfortably.' The teachers, when they were closeted with Miss Prettyman, were always asked to sit in the arm-chair, whereas a small, straight-backed, uneasy chair was kept for the use of the young ladies. And there was, too, a stool of repentance,* out against the wall, very uncomfortable indeed for young ladies who had not behaved themselves so prettily as young ladies generally do.

Grace seated herself, and then began her speech very quickly. 'Miss Prettyman,' she said, 'I have made up my mind that I will go home, if you please.'

'And why should you go home, Grace? Did I not tell you that you should have a home here?' Miss Prettyman had weak eyes, and was very small, and had never possessed any claim to be called good-looking. And she assumed nothing of majestical awe from any adornment or studied amplification of the outward woman by means of impressive trappings. The possessor of an unobservant eye might have called her a mean-looking, little old woman. And certainly there would have been nothing awful in her to any one who came across her otherwise than as a lady having authority in her own school. But within her own precincts, she did know how to surround herself with a dignity which all felt who approached her there. Grace Crawley, as she heard the simple question which Miss Prettyman had asked, unconsciously acknowledged the strength of the woman's manner. She already stood rebuked for having proposed a plan so ungracious, so unnecessary, and so unwise.

'I think I ought to be with mamma at present,' said Grace.

'Your mother has your sister with her.'

'Yes, Miss Prettyman; Jane is there.'

'If there be no other reason, I cannot think that that can be held to be a reason now. Of course your mother would like to have you always; unless you should be married, – but then there are reasons why this should not be so.'

'Of course there are.'

'I do not think, – that is, if I know all that there is to be known,

– I do not think, I say, that there can be any good ground for your leaving us now, – just now.'

Then Grace sat silent for a moment, gathering her courage, and collecting her words; and after that she spoke. 'It is because of papa, and because of this charge—'

'But Grace—'

'I know what you are going to say, Miss Prettyman; – that is, I think I know.'

'If you will hear me, you may be sure that you know.'

'But I want you to hear me for one moment first. I beg your pardon, Miss Prettyman; I do indeed, but I want to say this before you go on. I must go home, and I know I ought. We are all disgraced, and I won't stop here to disgrace the school. I know papa has done nothing wrong; but nevertheless we are disgraced. The police are to bring him in here on Thursday, and everybody in Silverbridge will know it. It cannot be right that I should be here teaching in the school, while it is all going on; – and I won't. And, Miss Prettyman, I couldn't do it, – indeed I couldn't. I can't bring myself to think of anything I am doing. Indeed I can't; and then, Miss Prettyman, there are other reasons.' By the time that she had proceeded thus far, Grace Crawley's words were nearly choked by her tears.

'And what are the other reasons, Grace?'

'I don't know,' said Grace, struggling to speak through her tears.

'But I know,' said Miss Prettyman. 'I know them all. I know all your reasons, and I tell you that in my opinion you ought to remain where you are, and not go away. The very reasons which to you are reasons for your going, to me are reasons for your remaining here.'

'I can't remain. I am determined to go. I don't mind you and Miss Anne, but I can't bear to have the girls looking at me, – and the servants.'

Then Miss Prettyman paused awhile, thinking what words of wisdom would be most appropriate in the present conjuncture. But words of wisdom did not seem to come easily to her, having for the moment been banished by tenderness of heart. 'Come here, my love,' she said at last. 'Come here, Grace.' Slowly Grace got up from her seat and came round, and stood by Miss Prettyman's elbow. Miss Prettyman pushed her chair a little back, and pushed herself a little forward, and stretching out one hand, placed her arm round Grace's waist, and with the other took hold of Grace's hand, and thus drew her down and kissed the girl's forehead and lips. And then Grace found herself kneeling at her friend's feet. 'Grace,' she said, 'do you not know that I love you? Do you not know that I love you dearly?' In answer to this, Grace kissed the withered hand she held in hers, while the warm tears trickled down upon Miss Prettyman's knuckles. 'I love you as though you were my own,' exclaimed the schoolmistress; 'and will you not trust me, that I know what is best for you?'

'I must go home,' said Grace.

'Of course you shall, if you think it right at last; but let us talk of it. No one in this house, you know, has the slightest suspicion that your father has done anything that is in the least dishonourable.'

'I know that you have not.'

'No, nor has Anne.' Miss Prettyman said this as though no one in that house beyond herself and her sister had a right to have any opinion on any subject.

'I know that,' said Grace.

'Well, my dear. If we think so—'

'But the servants, Miss Prettyman?'

'If any servant in this house says a word to offend yu, I'll – I'll—'

'They don't say anything, Miss Prettyman, but they look. Indeed I'd better go home. Indeed I had!'

'Do not you think your mother has cares enough upon her, and burden enough, without having another mouth to feed, and another head to shelter. You haven't thought of that, Grace!'

'Yes, I have.'

'And as for the work, whilst you are not quite well you shall not be troubled with teaching. I have some old papers that want copying and settling, and you shall sit here and do that just for an employment. Anne knows that I've long wanted to have it done, and I'll tell her that you've kindly promised to do it for me.'

'No; no; no,' said Grace; 'I must go home.' She was still kneeling at Miss Prettyman's knee, and still holding Miss Prettyman's hand. And then, at that moment, there came a tap at the door, gentle but yet not humble, a tap which acknowledged, on the part of the tapper, the supremacy in that room of the lady who was sitting there, but which still claimed admittance almost as a right. The tap was well known by both of them to be the tap of Miss Anne. Grace immediately jumped up, and Miss Prettyman settled herself in her chair with a motion which almost seemed to indicate some feeling of shame as to her late position.

'I suppose I may come in?' said Miss Anne, opening the door and inserting her head.

'Yes, you may come in, – if you have anything to say,' said Miss Prettyman, with an air which seemed to be intended to assert her supremacy. But, in truth, she was simply collecting the wisdom and dignity which had been somewhat dissipated by her tenderness.

'I did not know that Grace Crawley was here,' said Miss Anne.

'Grace Crawley is here,' said Miss Prettyman.

'What is the matter, Grace?' said Miss Anne, seeing the tears.

'Never mind now,' said Miss Prettyman.

'Poor dear, I'm sure I'm sorry as though she were my own sister,' said Anne. 'But, Annabella, I want to speak to you especially.'

'To me, in private?'

'Yes, to you; in private, if Grace won't mind?'

Then Grace prepared to go. But as she was going, Miss Anne, upon whose brow a heavy burden of thought was lying, stopped her suddenly. 'Grace, my dear,' she said, 'go upstairs into your room, will you? – not across the hall to the school.'

'And why shouldn't she go to the school?' said Miss Prettyman.

Miss Anne paused a moment, and then answered, – unwillingly, as though driven to make a reply which she knew to be indiscreet. 'Because there is somebody in the hall.'

'Go to your room, dear,' said Miss Prettyman. And Grace went to her room, never turning an eye down towards the hall. 'Who is it?' said Miss Prettyman.

'Major Grantly is here, asking to see you,' said Miss Anne.

CHAPTER 7

Miss Prettyman's private room

Major Grantly, when threatened by his father with pecuniary punishment, should he demean himself by such a marriage as that he had proposed to himself, had declared that he would offer his hand to Miss Crawley on the next morning. This, however, he had not done. He had not done it, partly because he did not quite believe his father's threat, and partly because he felt that that threat was almost justified, – for the present moment, – by the circumstances in which Grace Crawley's father had placed himself. Henry Grantly acknowledged, as he drove himself home on the morning after his dinner at the rectory, that in this matter of his marriage he did owe much to his family. Should he marry at all, he owed it to them to marry a lady. And Grace Crawley, – so he told himself, – was a lady. And he owed it to them to bring among them as his wife a woman who should not disgrace him or them by her education, manners, or even by her personal appearance. In all these respects Grace Crawley was, in his judgment, quite as good as they had a right to expect her to be, and in some respects a great deal superior to that type of womanhood with which they had been most generally conversant. 'If everybody had her due, my sister isn't fit to hold a candle to her,' he said to himself. It must be acknowledged, therefore, that he was really in love with Grace Crawley; and he declared to himself, over and over again, that his family had no right to demand that he should marry a woman with money. The archdeacon's son by no means despised money. How could he, having come forth as a bird fledged from such a nest as the rectory at Plumstead Episcopi? Before he had been brought by his better nature and true judgment to see that Grace Crawley was the greater woman of the two, he had nearly submitted himself to the twenty thousand pounds of Miss Emily Dunstable, – to that, and her good-humour and rosy freshness combined. But he regarded himself as the well-to-do son of a very rich father. His only child was amply provided for; and he felt that, as regarded money, he had a right to do as he pleased. He felt this with double strength after his father's threat.

But he had no right to make a marriage by which his family would be disgraced. Whether he was right or wrong in supposing that he would disgrace his family were he to marry the daughter of a convicted thief, it is hardly necessary to discuss here. He told himself that it would be so, – telling himself also that, by the stern laws of the world, the son and the daughter must pay for the offence of the father and the mother. Even among the poor, who would willingly marry the child of a man who had been hanged? But he carried the argument beyond this, thinking much of the matter, and endeavouring to think of it not only justly, but generously. If the accusation against Crawley were false, – if the man were being injured by an unjust charge, – even if he, Grantly, could make himself think that the girl's father had not stolen the money, then he would dare everything and go on. I do not know that his argument was good, or that his mind was logical in the matter. He ought to have felt that his own judgment as to the man's guilt was less likely to be correct than that of those whose duty it was and would be to form and to express a judgment on the matter; and as to Grace herself, she was equally innocent whether her father were guilty or not guilty. If he were to be debarred from asking her for her hand by his feelings for her father and mother, he should hardly have trusted to his own skill in ascertaining the real truth as to the alleged theft. But he was not logical, and thus, meaning to be generous, he became unjust.

He found that among those in Silverbridge whom he presumed to be best informed on such matters, there was a growing opinion that Mr Crawley had stolen the money. He was intimate with all the Walkers, and was able to find out that Mrs Walker knew that her husband believed in the clergyman's guilt. He was by no means alone in his willingness to accept Mr Walker's opinion as the true opinion. Silverbridge, generally, was endeavouring to dress itself in Mr Walker's glass, and to believe as Mr Walker believed. The ladies of Silverbridge, including the Miss Prettymans, were aware that Mr Walker had been very kind both to Mr and Mrs Crawley, and argued from this that Mr Walker must think the man to be innocent. But Henry Grantly, who did not dare to ask a direct question of the solicitor, went cunningly to work, and closeted himself wih Mrs Walker, – with Mrs Walker, who knew well of the good fortune which was hovering over Grace's head and was so nearly settling itself upon her shoulders. She would have given a finger to be able to whitewash Mr Crawley in the major's estimation. Nor must it be supposed that she told the major in plain words that her husband had convinced himself of the man's guilt. In plain words no question was asked between them, and in plain words no opinion was expressed. But there was the look of sorrow in the woman's eye, there was the absence of reference to her husband's assurance that the man was innocent, there was the air of settled grief which told of her own conviction; and the major left her, convinced that Mrs Walker believed Mr Crawley to be guilty.

Then he went to Barchester; not open-mouthed with inquiry, but rather with open ears, and it seemed to him that all men in Barchester were of one mind. There was a county-club in Barchester, and at this county-club nine men out of every ten were talking about Mr Crawley. It was by no means necessary that a man should ask questions on the subject. Opinion was expressed so freely that no such asking was required; and opinion in Barchester, – at any rate in the county-club, – seemed now to be all of one mind. There had been every disposition at first to believe Mr Crawley to be innocent. He had been believed to be innocent, even after he had said wrongly that the cheque had been paid to him by Mr Soames; but he had since stated that he had received it from Dean Arabin, and that statement was also shown to be false. A man who has a cheque changed on his own behalf is bound at least to show where he got the cheque. Mr Crawley had not only failed to do this, but had given two false excuses. Henry Grantly, as he drove home to Silverbridge on the Sunday afternoon, summed up all the evidence in his own mind, and brought in a verdict of Guilty against the father of the girl whom he loved.

On the following morning he walked into Silverbridge and called at Miss Prettyman's house. As he went along his heart was warmer towards Grace than it had ever been before. He had told himself that he was now bound to abstain, for his father's sake, from doing that which he had told his father that he would certainly do. But he knew also, that he had said that which, though it did not bind him to Miss Crawley, gave her a right to expect that he would so bind himself. And Miss Prettyman could not but be aware of what his intention had been, and could not but expect that he should now be explicit. Had he been a wise man altogether, he would probably have abstained from saying anything at the present moment, – a wise man, that is, in the ways and feelings of the world in such matters. But, as there are men who will allow themselves all imaginable latitude in their treatment of women, believing that the world will condone any amount of fault of that nature, so are there other men, and a class of men which on the whole is the more numerous of the two, who are tremblingly alive to the danger of censure on this head, – and to the danger of censure not only from others, but from themselves also. Major Grantly had done that which made him think it imperative upon him to do something further, and to do that something at once.

Therefore he started off on the Monday morning after breakfast and walked to Silverbridge, and as he walked he built various castles in the air. Why should he not marry Grace, – if she would have him, – and take her away beyond the reach of her father's calamity? Why should he not throw over his own people altogether, money, position, society, and all, and give himself up to love? Were he to do so, men might say that he was foolish, but no one could hint that he was dishonourable. His spirit was high enough to teach him to think that such conduct on his part would have in it something of magnificence; but, yet, such was not his purpose. In going to Miss Prettyman it was his intention to apologize for not doing this magnificent thing. His mind was quite made up. Nevertheless he built those castles in the air.

It so happened that he encountered the younger Miss Prettyman in the hall. It would not at all have suited him to reveal to her the purport of his visit, or ask her either to assist his suit or to receive his apologies. Miss Anne Prettyman was too common a personage in the Silverbridge world to be fit for such employment. Miss Anne Prettyman was, indeed, herself submissive to him, and treated him with the courtesy which is due to a superior being. He therefore simply asked her whether he could be allowed to see her sister.

'Surely, Major Grantly; – that is, I think so. It is a little early, but I think she can receive you.'

'It is early, I know; but as I want to say a word or two on business—'

'Oh, on business. I am sure she will see you on business; she will only be too proud. If you will be kind enough to step in here for two minutes.' Then Miss Anne, having deposited the major in the little parlour, ran upstairs with her message to her sister. 'Of course it's about Grace Crawley,' she said to herself as she went. 'It can't be about anything else. I wonder what it is he's going to say. If he's going to pop, and the father in all this trouble, he's the finest fellow that ever trod.' Such were her thoughts as she tapped at the door and announced in the presence of Grace that there was somebody in the hall.

'It's Major Grantly,' whispered Anne, as soon as Grace had shut the door behind her.

'So I supposed by your telling her not to go into the hall. What has he come to say?'

'How on earth can I tell you that, Annabella? But I suppose he can have only one thing to say after all that has come and gone. He can only have come with one object.'

'He wouldn't have come to me for that. He would have asked to see herself.'

'But she never goes out now, and he can't see her.'

'Or he would have gone to them over at Hogglestock,' said Miss Prettyman. 'But of course he must come up now he is here. Would you mind telling him ? or shall I ring the bell ?'

'I'll tell him. We need not make more fuss than necessary, with the servants, you know. I suppose I'd better not come back with him ?'

There was a tone of supplication in the younger sister's voice as she made the last suggestion, which ought to have melted the heart of the elder; but it was unavailing. 'As he has asked to see me, I think you had better not,' said Annabella. Miss Anne Prettyman bore her cross meekly, offered no argument on the subject, and returning to the little parlour where she had left the major, brought him upstairs and ushered him into her sister's room without even entering it again, herself.

Major Grantly was as intimately acquainted with Miss Anne Prettyman as a man under thirty may well be with a lady nearer fifty than forty, who is not specially connected with him by any family tie; but of Miss Prettyman he knew personally very much less. Miss Prettyman, as has before been said, did not go out, and was therefore not common to the eyes of the Silverbridgians. She did occasionally see her friends in her own house, and Grace Crawley's lover, as the major had come to be called, had been there on more than one occasion; but of real personal intimacy between them there had hitherto existed none. He might have spoken, perhaps, a dozen words to her in his life. He had now more than a dozen to speak to her, but he hardly knew how to commence them.

She had got up and curtseyed, and had then taken his hand and asked him to sit down. 'My sister tells me that you want to see me,' she said, in her softest, mildest voice.

'I do, Miss Prettyman. I want to speak to you about a matter that troubles me very much, – very much indeed.'

'Anything that I can do, Major Grantly—'

'Thank you, yes. I know that you are very good, or I should not have ventured to come to you. Indeed I shouldn't trouble you now, of course, if it was only about myself. I know very well what a great friend you are to Miss Crawley.'

'Yes, I am. We love Grace dearly here.'

'So do I,' said the major, bluntly; 'I love her dearly, too.' Then he paused, as though he thought that Miss Prettyman ought to take up the speech. But Miss Prettyman seemed to think differently, and he was obliged to go on. 'I don't know whether you have ever heard about it, or noticed it, or – or – or—' He felt that he was very awkward, and he blushed. Major as he was, he blushed as he sat before the old woman, trying to tell his story, but not knowing how to tell it. 'The truth is, Miss Prettyman, I have done all but ask her to be my wife, and now has come this terrible affair about her father.'

'It is a terrible affair, Major Grantly; very terrible.'

'By Jove, you may say that!'

'Of course Mr Crawley is as innocent in the matter as you or I are.'

'You think so, Miss Prettyman?'

'Think so! I feel quite sure of it. What; a clergyman of the Church of England, a pious, hard-working country clergyman, whom we have known among us by his good works for years, suddenly turn thief, and pilfer a few pounds! It is not possible, Major Grantly. And the father of such a daughter, too! It is not possible. It may do for men of business to think so, lawyers and such like, who are obliged to think in accordance with the evidence, as they call it; but to my mind the idea is monstrous. I don't know how he got it, and I don't care; but I'm quite sure he did not steal it. Whoever heard of anybody becoming so base as that all at once?'

The major was startled by her eloquence, and by the indignant tone of voice in which it was expressed. It seemed to tell him that she would give him no sympathy in that which he had come to say to her, and to upbraid him already in that he was not prepared to do the magnificent thing of which he had thought when he had been building his castles in the air. Why should he not do the magnificent thing? Miss Prettyman's eloquence was so strong that it half convinced him that the Barchester Club and Mr Walker had come to a wrong conclusion after all.

'And how does Miss Crawley bear it?' he asked, desirous of postponing for a while any declaration of his own purpose.

'She is very unhappy, of course. Not that she thinks evil of her father.'

'Of course she does not think him guilty.'

'Nobody thinks him so in this house, Major Grantly,' said the little woman, very imperiously. 'But Grace is, naturally enough, very sad; – very sad indeed. I do not think I can ask you to see her to-day.'

'I was not thinking of it,' said the major.

'Poor, dear girl! it is a great trial for her. Do you wish me to give her any message, Major Grantly?'

The moment had now come in which he must say that which he had come to say. The little woman waited for an answer, and as he was there, within her power as it were, he must speak. I fear that what he said will not be approved by any strong-minded reader. I fear that our lover will henceforth be considered by such a one as being but a weak, wishy-washy man, who had hardly any mind of his own to speak of; – that he was a man of no account, as the poor people say. 'Miss Prettyman, what message ought I to send to her?' he said.

'Nay, Major Grantly, how can I tell you that? How can I put words into your mouth?'

'It isn't the words,' he said; 'but the feelings?'

'And how can I tell the feelings of your heart?'

'Oh, as for that, I know what my feelings are. I do love her with all my heart; – I do, indeed. A fortnight ago I was only thinking whether she would accept me when I asked her, – wondering whether I was too old for her, and whether she would mind having Edith to take care of.'

'She is very fond of Edith, – very fond indeed.'

'Is she?' said the major, more distracted than ever. Why should he not do the magnificent thing after all? 'But it is a great charge for a young girl when she marries.'

'It is a great charge; – a very great charge. It is for you to think whether you should entrust so great a charge to one so young.'

'I have no fear about that at all.'

'Nor should I have any, – as you ask me. We have known Grace well, thoroughly, and are quite sure that she will do her duty in that state of life to which it may please God to call her.'*

The major was aware when this was said to him that he had not come to Miss Prettyman for a character of the girl he loved; and yet he was not angry at receiving it. He was neither angry, nor even indifferent. He accepted the character almost gratefully, though he felt that he was being led away from his purpose. He consoled himself for this, however, by remembering that the path by which Miss Prettyman was now leading him, led to the magnificent, and to those pleasant castles in the air which he had been building as he walked into Silverbridge. 'I am quite sure that she is all that you say,' he replied. 'Indeed I had made up my mind about that long ago.'

'And what can I do for you, Major Grantly?'

'You think I ought not to see her?'

'I will ask herself, if you please. I have such trust in her judgment that I should leave her altogether to her own discretion.'

The magnificent thing must be done, and the major made up his mind accordingly. Something of regret came over his spirit as he thought of a father-in-law disgraced and degraded, and of his own father broken-hearted. But now there was hardly an alternative left to him. And was it not the manly thing for him to do? He had loved the girl before this trouble had come upon her, and was he not bound to accept the burden which his love had brought with it? 'I will see her,' he said, 'at once, if you will let me, and ask her to be my wife. But I must see her alone.'

Then Miss Prettyman paused. Hitherto she had undoubtedly been playing her fish cautiously, or rather her young friend's fish, – perhaps I may say cunningly. She had descended to artifice on behalf of the girl whom she loved, admired, and pitied. She had seen some way into the man's mind, and had been partly aware of his purpose, – of his infirmity of purpose, of his double purpose. She had perceived that a word from her might help Grace's chance, and had led the man on till he had committed himself, at any rate to her. In doing this she had been actuated by friendship rather than by abstract principle. But now, when the moment had come in which she must decide upon some action, she paused. Was it right, for the sake of either of them, that an offer of marriage should be made at such a moment as this? It might be very well, in regard to some future time, that the major should have so committed himself. She saw something of the man's spirit, and believed that, having gone so far, – having so far told his love, he would return to his love hereafter, let the result of the Crawley trial be what it might. But, – but, this could be no proper time for love-making. Though Grace loved the man, as Miss Prettyman knew well, – though Grace loved the child, having allowed herself to long to call it her own, though such a marriage would be the making of Grace's fortune as those who loved her could hardly have hoped that it should ever have been made, she would certainly refuse the man, if he were to propose to her now. She would refuse him, and then the man would be free; – free to change his mind if he thought fit. Considering all these things, craftily in the exercise of her friendship, too cunningly, I fear, to satisfy the claims of a high morality, she resolved that the major had better not see Miss Crawley at the present moment. Miss Prettyman paused before she replied, and, when she did speak, Major Grantly had risen from his chair and was standing with his back to the fire. 'Major Grantly,' she said, 'you shall see her if you please, and if she pleases; but I doubt whether her answer at such a moment as this would be that which you would wish to receive.'

'You think she would refuse me.'

'I do not think that she would accept you now. She would feel, –
I am sure she would feel, that these hours of her father's sorrow are
not hours in which love should be either offered or accepted. You
shall, however, see her if you please.'

The major allowed himself a moment for thought; and as he
thought he sighed. Grace Crawley became more beautiful in his
eyes than ever, was endowed by these words from Miss Prettyman
with new charms and brighter virtues than he had seen before. Let
come what might he would ask her to be his wife on some future
day, if he did not so ask her now. For the present, perhaps, he had
better be guided by Miss Prettyman. 'Then I will not see her,' he
said.

'I think that will be the wiser course.'

'Of course you knew before this that I – loved her ?'

'I thought so, Major Grantly.'

'And that I intended to ask her to be my wife ?'

'Well; since you put the question to me so plainly, I must confess
that as Grace's friend I should not quite have let things go on as
they have gone, – though I am not at all disposed to interfere with
any girl whom I believe to be pure and good as I know her to be, –
but still I should hardly have been justified in letting things go as
they have gone, if I had not believed that such was your purpose.'

'I wanted to set myself right with you, Miss Prettyman.'

'You are right with me, – quite right;' and she got up and gave
him her hand. 'You are a fine, noble-hearted gentleman, and I hope
that our Grace may live to be your happy wife, and the mother of
your darling child, and the mother of other children. I do not see
how a woman could have a happier lot in life.'

'And will you give Grace my love ?'

'I will tell her at any rate that you have been here, and that you
have inquired after her with the greatest kindness. She will under-
tand what that means without any word of love.'

'Can I do anything for her, – or for her father; I mean in the way
of – money ? I don't mind mentioning it to you, Miss Prettyman.'

'I will tell her that you are ready to do it, if anything can be done.
For myself I feel no doubt that the mystery will be cleared up at
last; and then, if you will come here, we shall be so glad to see you.
– I shall, at least.'

Then the major went, and Miss Prettyman herself actually
descended with him into the hall, and bade him farewell most
affectionately before her sister and two of the maids who came out
to open the door. Miss Anne Prettyman, when she saw the great
friendship with which the major was dismissed, could not contain

herself, but asked most impudent questions, in a whisper indeed, but in such a whisper that any sharp-eared maid-servant could hear and understand them. 'Is it settled,' she asked when her sister had ascended only the first flight of stairs; – 'has he popped?' The look with which the elder sister punished and dismayed the younger, I would not have borne for twenty pounds. She simply looked, and said nothing, but passed on. When she had regained her room she rang the bell, and desired the servant to ask Miss Crawley to be good enough to step to her. Poor Miss Anne retired discomforted into the solitude of one of the lower rooms, and sat for some minutes all alone, recovering from the shock of her sister's anger. 'At any rate, he hasn't popped,' she said to herself, as she made her way back to the school.

After that Miss Prettyman and Miss Crawley were closeted together for about an hour. What passed between them need not be repeated here word for word; but it may be understood that Miss Prettyman said no more than she ought to have said, and that Grace understood all that she ought to have understood.

'No man ever behaved with more considerate friendship, or more like a gentleman,' said Miss Prettyman.

'I am sure he is very good, and I am so glad he did not ask to see me,' said Grace. Then Grace went away, and Miss Prettyman sat awhile in thought, considering what she had done, not without some stings of conscience.

Major Grantly, as he walked home, was not altogether satisfied with himself, though he gave himself credit for some diplomacy which I do not think he deserved. He felt that Miss Prettyman and the world in general, should the world in general ever hear anything about it, would give him credit for having behaved well; and that he had obtained this credit without committing himself to the necessity of marrying the daughter of a thief, should things turn out badly in regard to the father. But, – and this but robbed him of all the pleasure which comes from real success, – but he had not treated Grace Crawley with the perfect generosity which love owes, and he was in some degree ashamed of himself. He felt, however, that he might probably have Grace, should he choose to ask for her when this trouble should have passed by. 'And I will,' he said to himself, as he entered the gate of his own paddock, and saw his child in her perambulator before the nurse. 'And I will ask her, sooner or later, let things go as they may.' Then he took the perambulator under his own charge for half-an-hour, to the satisfaction of the nurse, of the child, and of himself.

CHAPTER 8

Mr Crawley is taken to Silverbridge

It had become necessary on the Monday morning that Mrs Crawley should obtain from her husband an undertaking that he would present himself before the magistrates at Silverbridge on the Thursday. She had been made to understand that the magistrates were sinning against the strict rule of the law in not issuing a warrant at once for Mr Crawley's apprehension; and that they were so sinning at the instance of Mr Walker, – at whose instance they would have committed almost any sin practicable by a board of English magistrates, so great was their faith in him; and she knew that she was bound to answer her engagement. She had also another task to perform – that, namely, of persuading him to employ an attorney for his defence; and she was prepared with the name of an attorney, one Mr Mason, also of Silverbridge, who had been recommended to her by Mr Walker. But when she came to the performance of these two tasks on the Monday morning, she found that she was unable to accomplish either of them. Mr Crawley first declared that he would have nothing to do with any attorney. As to that he seemed to have made up his mind beforehand, and she saw at once that she had no hope of shaking him. But when she found that he was equally obstinate in the other matter, and that he declared that he would not go before the magistrates unless he were made to do so, – unless the policemen came and fetched him, then she almost sank beneath the burden of her troubles, and for a while was disposed to let things go as they would. How could she strive to bear a load that was so manifestly too heavy for her shoulders?

On the Sunday the poor man had exerted himself to get through his Sunday duties, and he had succeeded. He had succeeded so well that his wife had thought that things might yet come right with him, that he would remember, before it was too late, the true history of that unhappy bit of paper, and that he was rising above that half madness which for months past had afflicted him. On the

Sunday evening, when he was tired with his work, she thought it best to say nothing to him about the magistrates and the business of Thursday. But on the Monday morning she commenced her task, feeling that she owed it to Mr Walker to lose no more time. He was very decided in his manners and made her understand that he would employ no lawyer on his own behalf. 'Why should I want a lawyer? I have done nothing wrong,' he said. Then she tried to make him understand that many who may have done nothng wrong require a lawyer's aid. 'And who is to pay him?' he asked. To this she replied, unfortunately, that there would be no need of thinking of that at once. 'And I am to get further into debt!' he said. 'I am to put myself right before the world by incurring debts which I know I can never pay? When it has been a question of food for the children I have been weak, but I will not be weak in such a matter as this. I will have no lawyer.' She did not regard this denial on his part as very material, though she would fain have followed Mr Walker's advice had she been able; but when, later in the day, he declared that the police should fetch him, then her spirit gave way. Early in the morning he had seemed to assent to the expediency of going into Silverbridge on the Thursday, and it was not till after he had worked himself into a rage about the proposed attorney, that he utterly refused to make the journey. During the whole day, however, his state was such as almost to break his wife's heart. He would do nothing. He would not go to the school, nor even stir beyond the house-door. He would not open a book. He would not eat, nor would he even sit at table or say the accustomed grace when the scanty mid-day meal was placed upon the table. 'Nothing is blessed to me,' he said, when his wife pressed him to say the words for their child's sake. 'Shall I say that I thank God when my heart is thankless? Shall I serve my child by a lie?' Then for hours he sat in the same position, in the old arm-chair, hanging over the fire speechless, sleepless, thinking ever, as she well knew, of the injustice of the world. She hardly dared to speak to him, so great was the bitterness of his words when he was goaded to reply. At last, late in the evening, feeling that it would be her duty to send in to Mr Walker early on the following morning, she laid her hand gently on his shoulder and asked him for his promise. 'I may tell Mr Walker that you will be there on Thursday?'

'No,' he said, shouting at her. 'No. I will have no such message sent.' She started back, trembling. Not that she was accustomed to tremble at his ways, or to show that she feared him in his paroxysms, but that his voice had been louder than she had before known it. 'I will hold no intercourse with them at Silverbridge in this matter. Do you hear me, Mary?'

'I hear you, Josiah; but I must keep my word to Mr Walker. I promised that I would send to him.'

'Tell him, then, that I will not stir a foot out of this house on Thursday, of my own accord. On Thursday I shall be here; and here I will remain all day, – unless they take me hence by force.'

'But, Josiah—'

'Will you obey me, or I shall walk into Silverbridge myself and tell the man that I will not come to him.' Then he arose from his chair and stretched forth his hand to his hat as though he were going forth immediately, on his way to Silverbridge. The night was now pitch dark, and the rain was falling, and abroad he would encounter all the severity of the pitiless winter. Still it might have been better that he should have gone. The exercise and the fresh air, even the wet and the mud, would have served to bring back his mind to reason. But his wife thought of the misery of the journey, of his scanty clothing, of his worn boots, of the need there was to preserve the raiment which he wore; and she remembered that he was fasting, – that he had eaten nothing since the morning, and that he was not fit to be alone. She stopped him, therefore, before he could reach the door.

'Your bidding shall be done,' she said, – 'of course.'

'Tell them, then, that they must seek me here if they want me.'

'But, Josiah, think of the parish, – of the people who respect you, – for their sakes let it not be said that you were taken away by policemen.'

'Was St Paul not bound in prison?* Did he think of what the people might see?'

'If it were necessary, I would encourage you to bear it without a murmur.'

'It is necessary, whether you murmur, or do not murmur. Murmur, indeed! Why does not your voice ascend to heaven with one loud wail against the cruelty of man?' Then he went forth from the room into an empty chamber on the other side of the passage; and his wife, when she followed him there after a few minutes, found him on his knees, with his forehead against the floor, and with his hands clutching at the scanty hairs of his head. Often before had she seen him so, on the same spot, half grovelling, half prostrate in prayer, reviling in his agony all things around him, – nay, nearly all things above him, – and yet striving to reconcile himself to his Creator by the humiliation of confession.

It might be better with him now, if only he could bring himself to some softness of heart. Softly she closed the door, and placing the candle on the mantel-shelf, softly she knelt beside him, and softly touched his hand with hers. He did not stir nor utter a word, but seemed to clutch at his thin locks more violently than before. Then she kneeling there, aloud, but with low voice, with her thin hands clasped, uttered a prayer in which she asked her God to remove from her husband the bitterness of that hour. He listened till she had finished, and then he rose slowly to his feet. 'It is in vain,' said he. 'It is all in vain. It is all in vain.' Then he returned back to the parlour, and seating himself again in the arm-chair, remained there without speaking till past midnight. At last, when she told him that she herself was very cold, and reminded him that for the last hour there had been no fire, still speechless, he went up with her to their bed.

Early on the following morning she contrived to let him know that she was about to send a neighbour's son over with a note to Mr Walker, fearing to urge him further to change his mind; but hoping that he might express his purpose of doing so when he heard that the letter was to be sent; but he took no notice whatever of her words. At this moment he was reading Greek with his daughter, or rather rebuking her because she could not be induced to read Greek.

'Oh, papa,' the poor girl said, 'don't scold me now. I am so unhappy because of all this.'

'And am not I unhappy?' he said, as he closed the book. 'My God, what have I done against thee, that my lines should be cast in such terrible places?'*

The letter was sent to Mr Walker. 'He knows himself to be innocent,' said the poor wife, writing what best excuse she knew how to make, 'and thinks that he should take no step himself in such a matter. He will not employ a lawyer, and he says that he should prefer that he should be sent for, if the law requires his presence at Silverbridge on Thursday.' All this she wrote, as though she felt that she ought to employ a high tone in defending her husband's purpose; but she broke down altogether in the few words of the postscript. 'Indeed, indeed I have done what I could!' Mr Walker understood it all, both the high tone and the subsequent fall.

On the Thursday morning, at about ten o'clock, a fly stopped at the gate of the Hogglestock Parsonage, and out of it there came two men. One was dressed in ordinary black clothes, and seemed from his bearing to be a respectable man of the middle class of life. He was, however, the superintendent of police for the Silverbridge district. The other man was a policeman, pure and simple, with the helmet-looking hat which has lately become common, and all the ordinary half-military and wholly disagreeable outward adjuncts of the profession. 'Wilkins,' said the superintendent, 'likely enough I shall want you, for they tell me the gent is uncommon strange. But if I don't call you when I come out, just open the door like a servant, and mount up on the box when we're in. And don't speak nor say nothing.' Then the senior policeman entered the house.

He found Mrs Crawley sitting in the parlour with her bonnet and shawl on, and Mr Crawley in the arm-chair, leaning over the fire. 'I suppose we had better go with you,' said Mrs Crawley directly the door was opened; for of course she had seen the arrival of the fly from the window.

'The gentleman had better come with us if he'll be so kind,' said Thompson. 'I've brought a close carriage for him.'

'But I may go with him?' said the wife, with frightened voice. 'I may accompany my husband. He is not well, sir, and wants assistance.'

Thompson thought about it for a moment before he spoke. There was room in the fly for only two, or if for three, still he knew his place better than to thrust himself inside together with his prisoner and his prisoner's wife. He had been specially asked by Mr Walker to be very civil. Only one could sit on the box with the driver, and if the request was conceded the poor policeman must walk back. The walk, however, would not kill the policeman. 'All right, ma'am,' said Thompson; – 'that is, if the gentleman will just pass his word not to get out till I ask him.'

'He will not! He will not!' said Mrs Crawley.

'I will pass my word for nothing,' said Mr Crawley.

Upon hearing this, Thompson assumed a very long face, and shook his head as he turned his eyes first towards the husband and then towards the wife, and shrugged his shoulders, and compressing his lips, blew out his breath, as though in this way he might blow off some of the mingled sorrow and indignation with which the gentleman's words afflicted him.

Mrs Crawley rose and came close to him. 'You may take my word for it, he will not stir. You may indeed. He thinks it incumbent on him not to give any undertaking himself, because he feels himself to be so harshly used.'

'I don't know about the harshness,' said Thompson, brindling up. 'A close carriage brought, and—'

'I will walk. If I am made to go, I will walk,' shouted Mr Crawley.

'I did not allude to you, – or to Mr Walker,' said the poor wife. 'I know you have been most kind. I meant the harshness of the circumstances. Of course he is innocent, and you must feel for him.'

'Yes, I feel for him, and for you too, ma'am.'

'That is all I meant. He knows his own innocence, and therefore he is unwilling to give way in anything.'

'Of course he knows hisself, that's certain. But he'd better come in the carriage, if only because of the dirt and slush.'

'He will go in the carriage ; and I will go with him. There will be room there for you, sir.'

Thompson looked up at the rain, and told himself that it was very cold. Then he remembered Mr Walker's injunction, and bethought himself that Mrs Crawley, in spite of her poverty, was a lady. He conceived even unconsciously the idea that something was due to her because of her poverty. 'I'll go with the driver,' said he, 'but he'll only give hisself a deal of trouble if he attempts to get out.'

'He won't ; he won't,' said Mrs Crawley. 'And I thank you with all my heart.'

'Come along, then,' said Thompson.

She went up to her husband, hat in hand, and looking round to see that she was not watched, put the hat on his head, and then lifted him as it were from his chair. He did not refuse to be led, and allowed her to throw round his shoulders the old cloak which was hanging in the passage, and then he passed out, and was the first to seat himself in the Silverbridge fly. His wife followed him, and did not hear the blandishments with which Thompson instructed his myrmidon to follow through the mud on foot. Slowly they made their way through the lanes, and it was nearly twelve when the fly was driven into the yard of the 'George and Vulture' at Silverbridge.

Silverbridge, though it was blessed with a mayor and corporation, and was blessed also with a Member of Parliament all to itself, was not blessed also with any court-house. The magistrates were therefore compelled to sit in the big room at the 'George and Vulture,' in which the county balls were celebrated, and the meeting of the West Barsetshire freemasons was held. That part of the country was, no doubt, very much ashamed of its backwardness in this respect, but as yet nothing had been done to remedy the evil. Thompson and his fly were therefore driven into the yard of the Inn, and Mr and Mrs Crawley were ushered by him up into a little bed-chamber close adjoining to the big room in which the magistrates were already assembled. 'There's a bit of fire here,' said Thompson, 'and you can make yourselves a little warm.' He himself was shivering with the cold. 'When the gents is ready in there, I'll just come and fetch you.'

'I may go in with him ?' said Mrs Crawley.

'I'll have a chair for you at the end of the table, just nigh to him,' said Thompson. 'You can slip into it and say nothing to nobody.' Then he left them and went away to the magistrates.

Mr Crawley had not spoken a word since he had entered the

vehicle. Nor had she said much to him, but had sat with him holding his hand in hers. Now he spoke to her, — 'Where is it that we are?' he asked.

'At Silverbridge, dearest.'

'But what is this chamber? And why are we here?'

'We are to wait here till the magistrates are ready. They are in the next room.'

'But this is the Inn?'

'Yes, dear, it is the Inn.'

'And I see crowds of people about.' There were crowds of people about. There had been men in the yard, and others standing about on the stairs, and the public room was full of men who were curious to see the clergyman who had stolen twenty pounds, and to hear what would be the result of the case before the magistrates. He must be committed; so, at least, said everybody; but then there would be the question of bail. Would the magistrates let him out on bail, and who would be the bailsmen?' 'Why are the people here?' said Mr Crawley.

'I suppose it is the custom when the magistrates are sitting,' said his wife.

'They have come to see the degradation of a clergyman,' said he; — 'and they will not be disappointed.'

'Nothing can degrade but guilt,' said his wife.

'Yes, — misfortune can degrade, and poverty. A man is degraded when the cares of the world press so heavily upon him that he cannot rouse himself. They have come to look at me as though I were a hunted beast.'

'It is but their custom always on such days.'

'They have not always a clergyman before them as a criminal.' Then he was silent for a while, while she was chafing his cold hands. 'Would that I were dead, before they had brought me to this! Would that I were dead!'

'Is it not right, dear, that we should all bear what He sends us?'

'Would that I were dead!' he repeated. 'The load is too heavy for me to bear, and I would that I were dead!'

The time seemed to be very long before Thompson returned and asked them to accompany him into the big room. When he did so, Mr Crawley grasped hold of his chair as though he had resolved that he would not go. But his wife whispered a word to him, and he obeyed her. 'He will follow me,' she said to the policeman. And in that way they went from the small room into the large one. Thompson went first; Mrs Crawley with her veil down came next; and the wretched man followed his wife, with his eyes fixed upon the ground and his hands clasped together upon his breast. He

could at first have seen nothing, and could hardly have known
where he was when they placed him in a chair. She, with a better
courage, contrived to look round through her veil, and saw that
there was a long board or table covered with green cloth, and that
six or seven gentlemen were sitting at one end of it, while there
seemed to be a crowd standing along the sides and about the room.
Her husband was seated at the other end of the table, near the
corner, and round the corner, – so that she might be close to him, –
the chair had been placed. On the other side of him there was
another chair, now empty, intended for any professional gentleman
whom he might choose to employ.

There were five magistrates sitting there. Lord Lufton from
Framley, was in the chair; – a handsome man, still young, who was
very popular in the county. The cheque which had been cashed had
borne his signature, and he had consequently expressed his intention
of not sitting at the board; but Mr Walker, desirous of having him
there, had overruled him, showing him that the loss was not his
loss. The cheque, if stolen, had not been stolen from him. He was
not the prosecutor. 'No, by Jove,' said Lord Lufton, 'if I could
quash the whole thing, I'd do it at once!'

'You can't do that, my lord, but you may help us at the board,'
said Mr Walker.

Then there was the Hon. George De Courcy, Lord De Courcy's
brother, from Castle Courcy. Lord De Courcy did not live in the
county, but his brother did so, and endeavoured to maintain the
glory of the family by the discretion of his conduct. He was not,
perhaps, among the wisest of men, but he did very well as a country
magistrate, holding his tongue, keeping his eyes open, and, on such
occasions as this, obeying Mr Walker in all things. Dr Tempest was
also there, the rector of the parish, he being both magistrate and
clergyman. There were many in Silverbridge who declared that Dr
Tempest would have done far better to stay away when a brother
clergyman was thus to be brought before the bench; but it had been
long since Dr Tempest had cared what was said about him in
Silverbridge. He had become so accustomed to the life he led as to
like to be disliked, and to be enamoured of unpopularity. So when
Mr Walker had ventured to suggest to him that, perhaps, he might
not choose to be there, he had laughed Mr Walker to scorn. 'Of
course I shall be there,' he said. 'I am interested in the case, – very
much interested. Of course I shall be there.' And had not Lord
Lufton been present he would have made himself more conspicuous
by taking the chair. Mr Fothergill was the fourth. Mr Fothergill
was man of business to the Duke of Omnium, who was the great
owner of property in and about Silverbridge, and he was the most

active magistrate in that part of the county. He was a sharp man, and not at all likely to have any predisposition in favour of a clergyman. The fifth was Dr Thorne, of Chaldicotes, a gentleman whose name has been already mentioned in these pages. He had been for many years a medical man practising in a little village in the further end of the county; but it had come to be his fate, late in life, to marry a great heiress, with whose money the ancient house and domain of Chaldicotes had been purchased from the Sowerbys. Since then Dr Thorne had done his duty well as a country gentleman, – not, however, without some little want of smoothness between him and the duke's people.

Chaldicotes lay next to the duke's territory, and the duke had wished to buy Chaldicotes. When Chaldicotes slipped through the duke's fingers and went into the hands of Dr Thorne, – or of Dr Thorne's wife, – the duke had been very angry with Mr Fothergill. Hence it had come to pass that there had not always been smoothness between the duke's people and the Chaldicotes people. It was now rumoured that Dr Thorne intended to stand for the county on the next vacancy, and that did not tend to make things smoother. On the right hand of Lord Lufton sat Lord George and Mr Fothergill, and beyond Mr Fothergill sat Mr Walker, and beyond Mr Walker sat Mr Walker's clerk. On the left hand of the chairman were Dr Tempest and Dr Thorne, and a little lower down was Mr Zachary Winthrop, who held the situation of clerk to the magistrates. Many people in Silverbridge said that this was all wrong, as Mr Winthrop was partner with Mr Walker, who was always employed before the magistrates if there was any employment going for an attorney. For this, however, Mr Walker cared very little. He had so much of his own way in Silverbridge, that he was supposed to care nothing for anybody.

There were many other gentlemen in the room, and some who knew Mr Crawley with more or less intimacy. He, however, took notice of no one, and when one friend, who had really known him well, came up behind and spoke to him gently leaning over his chair, the poor man hardly recognized his friend.

'I'm sure your husband won't forget me,' said Mr Robarts, the clergyman of Framley, as he gave his hand to that lady across the back of Mr Crawley's chair.

'No, Mr Robarts, he does not forget you. But you must excuse him if at this moment he is not quite himself. It is a trying situation for a clergyman.'

'I can understand all that; but I'll tell you why I have come. I suppose this inquiry will finish the whole affair, and clear up whatever may be the difficulty. But should it not do so, it may be just possible, Mrs Crawley, that something may be said about bail. I don't understand much about it, and I daresay you do not either; but if there should be anything of that sort, let Mr Crawley name me. A brother clergyman will be best, and I'll have some other gentleman with me.' Then he left her, not waiting for any answer.

At the same time there was a conversation going on between Mr Walker and another attorney standing behind him, Mr Mason. 'I'll go to him,' said Walker, 'and try to arrange it.' So Mr Walker seated himself in the empty chair beside Mr Crawley, and endeavoured to explain to the wretched man, that he would do well to allow Mr Mason to assist him. Mr Crawley seemed to listen to all that was said, and then turned upon the speaker sharply: 'I will have no one to assist me,' he said so loudly that every one in the room heard the words. 'I am innocent. Why should I want assistance? Nor have I money to pay for it.' Mr Mason made a quick movement forward, intending to explain that that consideration need offer no impediment, but was stopped by further speech from Mr Crawley. 'I will have no one to help me,' said he, standing upright, and for the first time removing his hat from his head. 'Go on, and do what it is you have to do.' After that he did not sit down till the proceedings were nearly over, though he was invited more than once by Lord Lufton to do so.

We need not go through all the evidence that was brought to bear upon the question. It was proved that money for the cheque was paid to Mr Crawley's messenger, and that this money was given to Mr Crawley. When there occurred some little delay in the chain of evidence necessary to show that Mr Crawley had signed and sent the cheque and got the money, he became impatient. 'Why do you trouble the man?' he said. 'I had the cheque, and I sent him; I got the money. Has any one denied it, that you should strive to drive a poor man like that beyond his wits?' Then Mr Soames and the manager of the bank showed what inquiry had been made as soon as the cheque came back from the London bank; how at first they had both thought that Mr Crawley could of course explain the matter, and how he had explained it by a statement which was manifestly untrue. Then there was evidence to prove that the cheque could not have been paid to him by Mr Soames, and as this was given, Mr Crawley shook his head and again became impatient. 'I erred in that,' he exclaimed. 'Of course I erred. In my haste I thought it was so, and in my haste I said so. I am not good at reckoning money and remembering sums; but I saw that I had been wrong when my error was shown to me, and I acknowledged at once that I had been wrong.'

Up to this point he had behaved not only with so much spirit, but with so much reason, that his wife began to hope that the importance of the occasion had brought back the clearness of his mind, and that he would, even now, be able to place himself right as the inquiry went on. Then it was explained that Mr Crawley had stated that the cheque had been given to him by Dean Arabin, as soon as it was shown that it could not have been given to him by Mr Soames. In reference to this, Mr Walker was obliged to explain that application had been made to the dean, who was abroad, and that the dean had stated that he had given fifty pounds to his friend. Mr Walker explained also that the very notes of which this fifty pounds had consisted had been traced back to Mr Crawley, and that they had had no connection with the cheque or with the money which had been given for the cheque at the bank.

Mr Soames stated that he had lost the cheque with a pocket-book; that he had certainly lost it on the day on which he had called on Mr Crawley at Hogglestock; and that he missed his pocket-book on his journey back from Hogglestock to Barchester. At the moment of missing it he remembered that he had taken the book out from his pocket in Mr Crawley's room, and, at that moment, he had not doubted but that he had left it in Mr Crawley's house. He had written and sent to Mr Crawley to inquire, but had been assured that nothing had been found. There had been no other property of value in the pocket-book, – nothing but a few visiting cards and a memorandum, and he had therefore stopped the cheque at the London bank, and thought no more about it.

Mr Crawley was then asked to explain in what way he came possessed of the cheque. The question was first put by Lord Lufton; but it soon fell into Mr Walker's hands, who certainly asked it with all the kindness with which such an inquiry could be made. Could Mr Crawley at all remember by what means that bit of paper had come into his possession, or how long he had had it? He answered the last question first. 'It had been with him for months.' And why had he kept it? He looked round the room sternly, almost savagely, before he answered, fixing his eyes for a moment upon almost every face around him as he did so. Then he spoke. 'I was driven by shame to keep it, – and then by shame to use it.' That this statement was true, no one in the room doubted.

And then the other question was pressed upon him; and he lifted up in his hands, and raised his voice, and swore by the Saviour in whom he trusted, that he knew not from whence the money had come to him. Why then had he said that it had come from the dean? He had thought so. The dean had given him money, covered up, in an enclosure, 'so that the touch of the coin might not add to my disgrace in taking his alms,' said the wretched man, thus speaking openly and freely in his agony of the shame which he had striven so persistently to hide. He had not seen the dean's monies as they had been given, and he had thought that the cheque had been with them. Beyond that he could tell them nothing.

Then there was a conference between the magistrates and Mr Walker, in which Mr Walker submitted that the magistrates had no alternative but to commit the gentleman. To this Lord Lufton demurred, and with him Dr Thorne.

'I believe, as I am sitting here,' said Lord Lufton, 'that he has told the truth, and that he does not know any more than I do from whence the cheque came.'

'I am quite sure he does not,' said Dr Thorne.

Lord George remarked that it was the 'queerest go he had ever come across.' Dr Tempest merely shook his head. Mr Fothergill pointed out that even supposing the gentleman's statement to be true, it by no means went towards establishing the gentleman's innocence. The cheque had been traced to the gentleman's hands, and the gentleman was bound to show how it had come into his possession. Even supposing that the gentleman had found the cheque in his house, which was likely enough, he was not thereby justified in changing it, and applying the proceeds to his own purposes. Mr Walker told them that Mr Fothergill was right, and that the only excuse to be made for Mr Crawley was that he was out of his senses.

'I don't see it,' said Lord Lufton. 'I might have a lot of paper money by me, and not know from Adam where I got it.'

'But you would have to show where you got it, my lord, when inquiry was made,' said Mr Fothergill.

Lord Lufton, who was not particularly fond of Mr Fothergill, and was very unwilling to be instructed by him in any of the duties of a magistrate, turned his back at once upon the duke's agent; but within three minutes afterwards he had submitted to the same instructions from Mr Walker.

Mr Crawley had again seated himself, and during this period of the affair was leaning over the table with his face buried on his arms. Mrs Crawley sat by his side, utterly impotent as to any assistance, just touching him with her hand, and waiting behind her veil till she should be made to understand what was the decision of the magistrates. This was at last communicated to her, – and to him, – in a whisper by Mr Walker. Mr Crawley must understand that he was committed to take his trial at Barchester, at the next assizes, which would be held in April, but that bail would be taken; – his own bail in five hundred pounds, and that of two others in two hundred and fifty pounds each. And Mr Walker explained further that he and the bailmen were ready, and that the bail-bond was prepared. The bailmen were to be the Revd Mr Robarts, and Major Grantly. In five minutes the bond was signed and Mr Crawley was at liberty to go away, a free man, – till the Barchester Assizes should come round in April.

Of all that was going on at this time Mr Crawley knew little or nothing, and Mrs Crawley did not know much. She did say a word of thanks to Mr Robarts, and begged that the same might be said to – the other gentleman. If she had heard the major's name she did not remember it. Then they were led out back into the bed-room, where Mrs Walker was found, anxious to do something, if she only knew what, to comfort the wretched husband and the wretched wife. But what comfort or consolation could there be within their reach? There was tea made ready for them, and sandwiches cut from the Inn larder. And there was sherry in the Inn decanter. But no such comfort as that was possible for either of them.

They were taken home again in the fly, returning without the escort of Mr Thompson, and as they went some few words were spoken by Mrs Crawley. 'Josiah,' she said, 'there will be a way out of this, even yet, if you will only hold up your head and trust.'

'There is a way out of it,' he said. 'There is a way. There is but one way.' When he had so spoken she said no more, but resolved that her eye should never be off him, no, – not for a moment. Then, when she had gotten him once more into that front parlour, she threw her arms round him and kissed him.

CHAPTER 9

Grace Crawley goes to Allington

The tidings of what had been done by the magistrates at their petty sessions* was communicated the same night to Grace Crawley by Miss Prettyman. Miss Anne Prettyman had heard the news within five minutes of the execution of the bail-bond, and had rushed to her sister with information as to the event. 'They have found him guilty; they have, indeed. They have convicted him, – or whatever it is, because he couldn't say where he got it.' 'You do not mean that they have sent him to prison?' 'No; – not to prison; not as yet, that is. I don't understand it altogether; but he's to be tried again at the assizes. In the meantime he's to be out on bail. Major Grantly is to be the bail, – he and Mr Robarts. That, I think, was very nice of him.' It was undoubtedly the fact that Miss Anne Prettyman had received an accession of pleasurable emotion when she learned that Mr Crawley had not been sent away scatheless, but had been condemned, as it were, to a public trial at the assizes. And yet she would have done anything in her power to save Grace Crawley, or even to save her father. And it must be explained that Miss Anne Prettyman was supposed to be specially efficient in teaching Roman history to her pupils, although she was so manifestly ignorant of the course of law in the country in which she lived. 'Committed him,' said Miss Prettyman, correcting her sister with scorn. 'They have not convicted him. Had they convicted him, there could be no question of bail.' 'I don't know how all that is, Annabella, but at any rate Major Grantly is to be the bailsman, and there is to be another trial at Barchester.' 'There cannot be more than one trial in a criminal case,' said Miss Prettyman, 'unless the jury should disagree, or something of that kind. I suppose he has been committed, and that the trial will take place at the assizes.' 'Exactly, – that's just it.' Had Lord Lufton appeared as lictor, and had Thompson carried the fasces,* Miss Anne would have known more about it.

The sad tidings were not told to Grace till the evening. Mrs

Crawley, when the inquiry was over before the magistrates, would fain have had herself driven to the Miss Prettyman's school, that she might see her daughter; but she felt that to be impossible while her husband was in her charge. The father would of course have gone to his child, had the visit been suggested to him; but that would have caused another terrible scene; and the mother, considering it all in her mind, thought it better to abstain. Miss Prettyman did her best to make poor Grace think that the affair had gone so far favourably, – did her best, that is, without saying anything which her conscience told her to be false. 'It is to be settled at the assizes in April,' she said.

'And in the meantime what will become of papa?'

'Your papa will be at home, just as usual. He must have some one to advise him. I dare say it would have been all over now if he would have employed an attorney.'

'But it seems so hard that an attorney should be wanted.'

'My dear Grace, things in this world are hard.'

'But they are always harder for papa and mamma than for anybody else.' In answer to this, Miss Prettyman made some remarks intended to be wise and kind at the same time. Grace, whose eyes were laden with tears, made no immediate reply to this, but reverted to her former statement, that she must go home. 'I cannot remain, Miss Prettyman; I am so unhappy.'

'Will you be more happy at home?'

'I can bear it better there.'

The poor girl soon learned from the intended consolations of those around her, from the ill-considered kindness of the pupils, and from words which fell from the servants, that her father had in fact been judged to be guilty, as far as judgment had as yet gone. 'They do say, miss, it's only because he hadn't a lawyer,' said the housekeeper. And if men so kind as Lord Lufton and Mr Walker had made him out to be guilty, what could be expected from a stern judge down from London, who would know nothing about her poor father and his peculiarities, and from twelve jurymen who would be shopkeepers out of Barchester. It would kill her father, and then it would kill her mother; and after that it would kill her also. And there was no money in the house at home. She knew it well. She had been paid three pounds a month for her services at the school, and the money for the last two months had been sent to her mother. Yet, badly as she wanted anything that she might be able to earn, she knew that she could not go on teaching. It had come to be acknowledged by both the Miss Prettymans that any teaching on her part for the present was impossible. She would go home and perish with the rest of them. There was no room left for hope to her, or to any of her family. They had accused her father of being a common thief, – her father whom she knew to be so nobly honest, her father whom she believed to be among the most devoted of God's servants. He was accused of a paltry theft, and the magistrates and lawyers and policemen among them had decided that the accusation was true! How could she look the girls in the face after that, or attempt to hold her own among the teachers!

On the next morning there came the letter from Miss Lily Dale, and with that in her hand she again went to Miss Prettyman. She must go home, she said. She must at any rate see her mother. Could Miss Prettyman be kind enough to send her home. 'I haven't sixpence to pay for anything,' she said, bursting out into tears; 'and I haven't a right to ask for it.' Then the statements which Miss Prettyman made in her eagerness to cover this latter misfortune were decidedly false. There was so much money owing to Grace, she said; money for this, money for that, money for anything or nothing! Ten pounds would hardly clear the account. 'Nobody owes me anything; but if you'll lend me five shillings!' said Grace, in her agony. Miss Prettyman, as she made her way through this difficulty, thought of Major Grantly and his love. It would have been of no use, she knew. Had she brought them together on that Monday, Grace would have said nothing to him. Indeed such a meeting at such a time would have been improper. But, regarding Major Grantly, as she did, in the light of a millionaire, – for the wealth of the archdeacon was notorious, – she could not but think it a pity that poor Grace should be begging for five shillings. 'You need not at any rate trouble yourself about money, Grace,' said Miss Prettyman. 'What is a pound or two more or less beween you and me? It is almost unkind of you to think about it. Is that letter in your hand anything for me to see, my dear?' Then Grace explained that she did not wish to show Miss Dale's letter, but that Miss Dale had asked her to go to Allington. 'And you will go,' said Miss Prettyman. 'It will be the best thing for you, and the best thing for your mother.'

It was at last decided that Grace should go to her friend at Allington, and to Allington she went. She returned home for a day or two, and was persuaded by her mother to accept the invitation that had been given her. At Hogglestock, while she was there, new troubles came up, of which something shall shortly be told; but they were troubles in which Grace could give no assistance to her mother, and which, indeed, though they were in truth troubles, as will be seen, were so far beneficent that they stirred her father up to a certain action which was in itself salutary. 'I think it will be better that you should be away, dearest,' said the mother, who now, for the first time, heard plainly all that poor Grace had to tell about Major Grantly; – Grace having, heretofore, barely spoken, in most ambiguous words, of Major Grantly as a gentleman whom she had met at Framley, and whom she had described as being 'very nice.'

In old days, long ago, Lucy Robarts, the present Lady Lufton, sister of the Rev. Mark Robarts, the parson of Framley, had sojourned for a while under Mr Crawley's roof at Hogglestock. Peculiar circumstances, which need not, perhaps, be told here, had given occasion for this visit. She had then resolved, – for her future destiny had been known to her before she left Mrs Crawley's house, – that she would in coming days do much to befriend the family of her friend; but the doing of much had been very difficult. And the doing of anything had come to be very difficult through a certain indiscretion on Lord Lufton's part. Lord Lufton had offered assistance, pecuniary assistance, to Mr Crawley, which Mr Crawley had rejected with outspoken anger. What was Lord Lufton to him that his lordship should dare to come to him with his paltry money in his hand? But after a while, Lady Lufton, exercising some cunning in the operations of her friendship, had persuaded her sister-in-law at the Framley parsonage to have Grace Crawley over there as a visitor, – and there she had been during the summer holidays previous to the commencement of our story. And there, at Framley, she had become acquainted with Major Grantly, who was staying with Lord Lufton at Framley Court. She had then said something to her mother about Major Grantly, something ambiguous, something about his being 'very nice,' and the mother had thought how great was the pity that her daughter, who was 'nice' too in her estimation, should have so few of those adjuncts to assist her which come from full pockets. She had thought no more about it then; but now she felt herself constrained to think more. 'I don't quite understand why he should have come to Miss Prettyman on Monday,' said Grace, 'because he hardly knows her at all.'

'I suppose it was on business,' said Mrs Crawley.

'No, mamma, it was not on business.'

'How can you tell, dear?'

'Because Miss Prettyman said it was, – it was – to ask after me. Oh, mamma, I must tell you. I know he did like me.'

'Did he ever say so to you, dearest?'

'Yes, mamma.'

'And what did you tell him?'

'I told him nothing, mamma.'

'And did he ask to see you on Monday?'

'No, mamma; I don't think he did. I think he understood it all too well, for I could not have spoken to him then.'

Mrs Crawley pursued the cross-examination no further, but made up her mind that it would be better that her girl should be away from her wretched home during this period of her life. If it were written in the book of fate that one of her children should be exempted from the series of misfortunes which seemed to fall, one after another, almost as a matter of course, upon her husband, upon her, and upon her family; if so great good fortune were in store for her Grace as such a marriage as this which seemed to be so nearly offered to her, it might probably be well that Grace should be as little at home as possible. Mrs Crawley had heard nothing but good of Major Grantly; but she knew that the Grantlys were proud rich people, – who lived with their heads high up in the county, – and it could hardly be that a son of the archdeacon would like to take his bride direct from Hogglestock parsonage.

It was settled that Grace should go to Allington as soon as a letter could be received from Miss Dale in return to Grace's note, and on the third morning after her arrival at home she started. None but they who have themselves been poor gentry, – gentry so poor as not to know how to raise a shilling, – can understand the peculiar bitterness of the trials which such poverty produces. The poverty of the normal poor does not approach it; or, rather, the pangs arising from such poverty are altogether of a different sort. To be hungry and have no food, to be cold and have no fuel, to be threatened with distraint for one's few chairs and tables, and with the loss of the roof over one's head, – all these miseries, which, if they do not positively reach, are so frequently near to reaching the normal poor, are, no doubt, the severest of the trials to which humanity is subjected. They threaten life, – or, if not life, then liberty, – reducing the abject one to a choice between captivity and starvation. By hook or crook, the poor gentleman or poor lady, – let the one or the other be ever so poor, – does not often come to the last extremity of the workhouse. There are such cases, but they are exceptional. Mrs Crawley, through all her sufferings, had never yet found her cupboard to be absolutely bare, or the bread-pan to be actually empty. But there are pangs to which, at the time, starvation itself would seem to be preferable. The angry eyes of unpaid tradesmen, savage with an anger which one knows to be justifiable; the taunt of the poor servant who wants her wages; the gradual relinquishment of habits which the soft nurture of earlier, kinder years had made second nature; the wan cheeks of the wife whose malady demands wine; the rags of the husband whose outward occupations demand decency; the neglected children, who are learning not to be the children of gentlefolk; and, worse than all, the alms and doles of half-generous friends, the waning pride, the pride that will not wane, the growing doubt whether it be not better to bow the head, and acknowledge to all the world that nothing of the pride of station is left, – that the hand is open to receive and ready to touch the cap, that the fall from the upper to the lower level has been accomplished, – these are the pangs of poverty which drive the Crawleys of the world to the frequent entertaining of that idea of the bare bodkin.* It was settled that Grace should go to Allington; – but how about her clothes? And then, whence was to come the price of her journey?

'I don't think they'll mind about my being shabby at Allington. They live very quietly there.'

'But you say that Miss Dale is so very nice in all her ways.'

'Lily is very nice, mamma; but I shan't mind her so much as her mother, because she knows it all. I have told her everything.'

'But you have given me all your money, dearest.'

'Miss Prettyman told me I was to come to her,' said Grace, who had already taken some small sum from the schoolmistress, which at once had gone into her mother's pocket, and into household purposes. 'She said I should be sure to go to Allington, and that of course I should go to her, as I must pass through Silverbridge.'

'I hope papa will not ask about it,' said Mrs Crawley. Luckily papa did not ask about it, being at the moment occupied much with other thoughts and other troubles, and Grace was allowed to return by Silverbridge, and to take what was needed from Miss Prettyman. Who can tell of the mending and patching, of the weary wearing midnight hours of needlework which were accomplished before the poor girl went, so that she might not reach her friend's house in actual rags? And when the work was ended, what was there to show for it? I do not think that the idea of the bare bodkin, as regarded herself, ever flitted across Mrs Crawley's brain, – she being one of those who are very strong to endure; but it must have occurred to her very often that the repose of the grave is sweet, and that there cometh after death a levelling and making even of things, which would at last cure all her evils.

Grace no doubt looked forward to a levelling and making even of things, – or perhaps even to something more prosperous than that, which should come to her relief on this side of the grave. She could not but have high hopes in regard to her future destiny. Although, as has been said, she understood no more than she ought to have understood from Miss Prettyman's account of the conversation with Major Grantly, still, innocent as she was, she had understood much. She knew that the man loved her, and she knew also that she loved the man. She thoroughly comprehended that the present could be to her no time for listening to speeches of love, or for giving kind answers; but still I think that she did look for relief on this side of the grave.

'Tut, tut,' said Miss Prettyman as Grace in vain tried to conceal her tears up in the private sanctum. 'You ought to know me by this time, and to have learned that I can understand things.' The tears had flown in return not only for the five gold sovereigns which Miss Prettyman had pressed into her hand, but on account of the prettiest, soft, grey merino frock that ever charmed a girl's eye. 'I should like to know how many girls I have given dresses to, when they have been going out visiting. Law, my dear; they take them, many of them, from us old maids, almost as if we were only paying our debts in giving them.' And then Miss Anne gave her a cloth cloak, very warm, with pretty buttons and gimp trimmings, – just such a cloak as any girl might like to wear who thought that she would be seen out walking by her Major Grantly on a Christmas morning. Grace Crawley did not expect to be seen out walking by her Major Grantly, but nevertheless she liked the cloak. By the power of her practical will, and by her true sympathy, the older Miss Prettyman had for a while conquered the annoyance which, on Grace's part, was attached to the receiving of gifts, by the consciousness of her poverty; and when Miss Anne, with some pride in the tone of her voice, expressed a hope that Grace would think the cloak pretty, Grace put her arms pleasantly round her friend's neck, and declared that it was very pretty, – the prettiest cloak in all the world!

Grace was met at the Guestwick railway-station by her friend Lilian Dale, and was driven over to Allington in a pony carriage belonging to Lilian's uncle, the squire of the parish. I think she will be excused in having put on her new cloak, not so much because of the cold as with a view of making the best of herself before Mrs Dale. And yet she knew that Mrs Dale would know all the circumstances of her poverty, and was very glad that it should be so. 'I am so glad that you have come, dear,' said Lily. 'It will be such a comfort.'

'I am sure you are very good,' said Grace.

'And mamma is so glad. From the moment that we both talked ourselves into eagerness about it, – while I was writing my letter, you know, we resolved that it must be so.'

'I'm afraid I shall be a great trouble to Mrs Dale.'

'A trouble to mamma! Indeed you will not. You shall be a trouble to no one but me. I will have all the trouble myself, and the labour I delight in shall physic my pain.'*

Grace Crawley could not during the journey be at home and at ease even wth her friend Lily. She was going to a strange house under strange circumsances. Her father had not indeed been tried and found guilty of theft, but the charge of theft had been made against him, and the magistrates before whom it had been made had thought that the charge was true. Grace knew that all the local newspapers had told the story, and was of course aware that Mrs Dale would have heard it. Her own mind was full of it, and though she dreaded to speak of it, yet she could not be silent. Miss Dale, who understood much of this, endeavoured to talk her friend into easiness; but she feared to begin upon the one subject, and before the drive was over they were, both of them, too cold for much conversation. 'There's mamma,' said Miss Dale as they drove up, turning out of the street of the village to the door of Mrs Dale's house. 'She always knows, by instinct, when I am coming. You must understand now that you are among us, that mamma and I are not mother and daughter, but two loving old ladies, living together in peace and harmony. We do have our quarrels, – whether the chicken shall be roast or boiled, but never anything beyond that. Mamma, here is Grace, starved to death; and she says if you don't give her some tea she will go back at once.'

'I will give her some tea,' said Mrs Dale.

'And I am worse than she is, because I've been driving. It's all up with Bernard and Mr Green for the next week at least. It is freezing as hard as it can freeze, and they might as well try to hunt in Lapland as here.'

'They'll console themselves with skating,' said Mrs Dale.

'Have you ever observed, Grace,' said Miss Dale, 'how much amusement gentlemen require, and how imperative it is that some other game should be provided when one game fails?'

'Not particularly,' said Grace.

'Oh, but it is so. Now, with women, it is supposed that they can amuse themselves or live without amusement. Once or twice in a year, perhaps something is done for them. There is an arrow-shooting party, or a ball, or a picnic. But the catering for men's sport is never-ending, and is always paramount to everything else. And yet the pet game of the day never goes off properly. In partridge time, the partridges are wild, and won't come to be killed. In hunting time the foxes won't run straight, – the wretches. They show no spirit, and will take to ground to save their brushes. Then comes a nipping frost, and skating is proclaimed; but the ice is always rough, and the woodcocks have deserted the country. And as for salmon, – when the summer comes round I do really believe that they suffer a great deal about the salmon. I'm sure they never catch any. So they go back to their clubs and their cards, and their billiards, and abuse their cooks and blackball their friends. That's about it, mamma; is it not?'

'You know more about it than I do, my dear.'

'Because I have to listen to Bernard, as you never will do. We've got such a Mr Green down here, Grace. He's such a duck of a man, – such top-boots and all the rest of it. And yet they whisper to me that he doesn't ride always to hounds. And to see him play billiards is beautiful, only he never can make a stroke. I hope you play billiards, Grace, because Uncle Christopher has just had a new table put up.'

'I never saw a billard-table yet,' said Grace.

'Then Mr Green shall teach you. He'll do anything that you ask him. If you don't approve the colour of the ball, he'll go to London to get you another one. Only you must be very careful about saying that you like anything before him, as he'll be sure to have it for you the next day. Mamma happened to say that she wanted a four-penny postage-stamp, and he walked off to Guestwick to get it for her instantly, although it was lunch-time.'

'He did nothing of the kind, Lily,' said her mother. 'He was going to Guestwick, and was very good-natured, and brought me back a postage-stamp that I wanted.'

'Of course he's good-natured, I know that. And there's my cousin Bernard. He's Captain Dale, you know. But he prefers to be called Mr Dale, because he has left the army, and has set up as junior squire of the parish. Uncle Christopher is the real squire; only Bertram does all the work. And now you know all about us. I'm afraid you'll find us dull enough, – unless you can take a fancy to Mr Green.'

'Does Mr Green live here?' asked Grace.

'No; he does not live here. I never heard of his living anywhere. He was something once, but I don't know what; and I don't think he's anything now in particular. But he's Bernard's friend, and like most men, as one sees them, he never has much to do. Does Major Grantly ever go forth to fight his country's battles?' This last question she asked in a low whisper, so that the words did not reach her mother. Grace blushed up to her eyes, however, as she answered,—

'I think that Major Grantly has left the army.'

'We shall get her round in a day or two, mamma,' said Lily Dale to her mother that night. 'I'm sure it will be the best thing to force her to talk of her troubles.'

'I would not use too much force, my dear.'

'Things are better when they're talked about. I'm sure they are. And it will be good to make her accustomed to speak of Major

Grantly. From what Mary Walker tells me, he certainly means it. And if so, she should be ready for it when it comes.'

'Do not make her ready for what may never come.'

'No, mamma; but she is at present such a child that she knows nothing of her own powers. She should be made to understand that it is possible that even a Major Grantly may think himself fortunate in being allowed to love her.'

'I should leave all that to Nature, if I were you,' said Mrs Dale.

CHAPTER 10

Dinner at Framley Court

Lord Lufton, as he drove home to Framley after the meeting of the magistrates at Silverbridge, discussed the matter with his brother-in-law, Mark Robarts, the clergyman. Lord Lufton was driving a dog-cart, and went along the road at the rate of twelve miles an hour. 'I'll tell you what it is, Mark,' he said, 'that man is innocent; but if he won't employ lawyers at his trial, the jury will find him guilty.'

'I don't know what to think about it,' said the clergyman.

'Were you in the room when he protested so vehemently that he didn't know where he got the money?'

'I was in the room all the time.'

'And did you not believe him when he said that?'

'Yes, – I think I did.'

'Anybody must have believed him, – except old Tempest, who never believes anybody, and Fothergill, who always suspects everybody. The truth is, that he had found the cheque and put it by, and did not remember anything about it.'

'But, Lufton, surely that would amount to stealing it.'

'Yes, if it wasn't that he is such a poor, cracked, crazy creature, with his mind all abroad. I think Soames did drop his book in his house. I'm sure Soames would not say so unless he was quite confident. Somebody has picked it up, and in some way the cheque has got into Crawley's hand. Then he has locked it up and has forgotten all about it; and when that butcher threatened him, he has put his hand upon it, and he has thought, or believed, that it had come from Soames or from the dean, or from heaven, if you will. When a man is so crazy as that, you can't judge of him as you do of others.'

'But a jury must judge of him as it would of others.'

'And therefore there should be a lawyer to tell the jury what to do. They should have somebody up out of the parish to show that he is beside himself half his time. His wife would be the best person, only it would be hard lines on her.'

'Very hard. And after all he would only escape by being shown to be mad.'

'And he is mad.'

'Mrs Proudie would come upon him in such a case as that, and sequester his living.'

'And what will Mrs Proudie do when he's a convicted thief? Simply unfrock him, and take away his living altogether. Nothing on earth should induce me to find him guilty if I were on a jury.'

'But you have committed him.'

'Yes, – I've been one, at least, in doing so. I simply did that which Walker told us we must do. A magistrate is not left to himself as a juryman is. I'd eat the biggest pair of boots in Barchester before I found him guilty. I say, Mark, you must talk it over with the women, and see what can be done for them. Lucy tells me that they're so poor, that if they have bread to eat, it's as much as they have.'

On this evening Archdeacon Grantly and his wife dined and slept at Framley Court, there having been a very long family friendship between old Lady Lufton and the Grantlys, and Dr Thorne with his wife, from Chaldicotes, also dined at Framley. There was also there another clergyman from Barchester, Mr Champion, one of the prebends of the cathedral. There were only three now who had houses in the city since the retrenchments of the ecclesiastical commission had come into full force. And this Mr Champion was dear to the Dowager Lady Lufton, because he carried on worthily the clerical war against the bishop which had raged in Barsetshire ever since Dr Proudie had come there, – which war old Lady Lufton, good and pious and charitable as she was, considered that he was bound to keep up, even to the knife, till Dr Proudie and all his satellites should have been banished into outer darkness. As the light of the Proudies still shone brightly, it was probable that poor old Lady Lufton might die before her battle was accomplished. She often said that it would be so, but when so saying, always expressed a wish that the fight might be carried on after her death. 'I shall never, never rest in my grave,' she had once said to the archdeacon, 'while that woman sits in your father's palace.' For the archdeacon's father had been Bishop of Barchester before Dr Proudie. What mode of getting rid of the bishop or his wife Lady Lufton proposed to herself, I am unable to say; but I think she lived in hopes that in some way it might be done. If only the bishop could have been found to have stolen a cheque for twenty pounds instead of poor Mr Crawley, Lady Lufton would, I think, have been satisfied.

In the course of these battles Framley Court would sometimes assume a clerical aspect, – have a prevailing hue, as it were, of black coats, which was not altogether to the taste of Lord Lufton, and as to which he would make complaint to his wife, and to Mark Robarts, himself a clergyman. 'There's more of this than I can stand,' he'd say to the latter. 'There's a deuced deal more of it than you like yourself, I know.'

'It's not for me to like or dislike. It's a great thing having your mother in the parish.'

'That's all very well; and of course she'll do as she likes. She may ask whom she pleases here, and I shan't interfere. It's the same as though it was her own house. But I shall take Lucy to Lufton.' Now Lord Lufton had been building his house at Lufton for the last seven years, and it was not yet finished, – or nearly finished, if all that his wife and mother said was true. And if they could have their way, it never would be finished. And so, in order that Lord Lufton might not be actually driven away by the turmoils of ecclesiastical contest, the younger Lady Lufton would endeavour to moderate both the wrath and the zeal of the elder one, and would struggle against the coming clergyman. On this day, however, three sat at the board at Framley, and Lady Lufton, in her justification to her son, swore that the invitation had been given by her daugther-in-law. 'You know, my dear,' the dowager said to Lord Lufton, 'something must be done for these poor Crawleys; and as the dean is away, Lucy wants to speak to the archdeacon about them.'

'And the archdeacon could not subscribe his ten-pound note without having Mr Champion to back him?'

'My dear Ludovic, you do put it in such a way.'

'Never mind, mother. I've no special dislike to Champion; only as you are not paid five thousand a year for your trouble, it is rather hard that you should have to do all the work of opposition bishop in the diocese.'

It was felt by them all, – including Lord Lufton himself, who became so interested in the matter as to forgive the black coats before the evening was over, – that this matter of Mr Crawley's committal was very serious, and demanded the full energies of their party. It was known to them all that the feeling at the palace was inimical to Mr Crawley. 'That she-Beelzebub hates him for his poverty, and because Arabin brought him into the diocese,' said the archdeacon, permitting himself to use very strong language in his allusion to the bishop's wife. It must be recorded on his behalf that he used the phrase in the presence only of the gentlemen of the party. I think he might have whispered the word into the ear of his confidential friend old Lady Lufton, and perhaps have given no offence; but he would not have ventured to use such words aloud in the presence of ladies.

'You forget, archdeacon,' said Dr Thorne, laughing, 'that the she-Beelzebub is my wife's particular friend.'

'Not a bit of it,' said the archdeacon. 'Your wife knows better than that. You tell her what I call her, and if she complains of the name, I'll unsay it.' It may therefore be supposed that Dr Thorne, and Mrs Thorne, and the archdeacon, knew each other intimately, and understood each other's feelings on these matters.

It was quite true that the palace party was inimical to Mr Crawley. Mr Crawley undoubtedly was poor, and had not been so submissive to episcopal authority as it behoves any clergyman to be whose loaves and fishes are scanty. He had raised his back more than once against orders emanating from the palace in a manner that had made the hairs on the head of the bishop's wife to stand almost on end, and had taken as much upon himself as though his living had been worth twelve hundred a year. Mrs Proudie, almost as energetic in her language as the archdeacon, had called him a beggarly perpetual curate. 'We must have perpetual curates, my dear,' the bishop had said. 'They should know their places then. But what can you expect of a creature from the deanery? All that ought to be altered. The dean should have no patronage in the diocese. No dean should have any patronage. It is an abuse from the beginning to the end. Dean Arabin, if he had any conscience, would be doing the duty at Hogglestock himself.' How the bishop strove to teach his wife, with mildest words, what really ought to be a dean's duty, and how the wife rejoined by teaching her husband, not in the mildest words, what ought to be a bishop's duty, we will not further inquire here. The fact that such dialogues took place at the palace is recorded simply to show that the palatial feeling in Barchester ran counter to Mr Crawley.

And this was cause enough, if no other cause existed, for partiality to Mr Crawley at Framley Court. But, as has been partly explained, there existed, if possible, even stronger ground than this for adherence to the Crawley cause. The younger Lady Lufton had known the Crawleys intimately, and the elder Lady Lufton had reckoned them among the neighbouring clerical families of her acquaintance. Both these ladies were therefore staunch in their defence of Mr Crawley. The archdeacon himself had his own reasons, – reasons which for the present he kept altogether within his own bosom, – for wishing that Mr Crawley had never entered the diocese. Whether the perpetual curate should or should not be declared to be a thief, it would be terrible to him to have to call the child of that perpetual curate his daughter-in-law. But not the less on this occasion was he true to his order, true to his side in the diocese, true to his hatred of the palace.

'I don't believe it for a moment,' he said, as he took his place on the rug before the fire in the drawing-room when the gentlemen came in from their wine. The ladies understood at once what it was that he couldn't believe. Mr Crawley had for the moment so usurped the county that nobody thought of talking of anything else.

'How is it, then,' said Mrs Thorne, 'that Lord Lufton, and my husband, and the other wiseacres at Silverbridge, have committed him for trial?'

'Because we were told to do so by the lawyer,' said Dr Thorne.

'Ladies will never understand that magistrates must act in accordance with the law,' said Lord Lufton.

'But you all say he's not guilty,' said Mrs Robarts.

'The fact is, that the magistrates cannot try the question,' said the archdeacon; 'they only hear the primary evidence. In this case I don't believe Crawley would ever have been committed if he had employed an attorney, instead of speaking for himself.'

'Why didn't somebody make him have an attorney?' said Lady Lufton.

'I don't think any attorney in the world could have spoken for him better than he spoke for himself,' said Dr Thorne.

'And yet you committed him,' said his wife. 'What can we do for him? Can't we pay the bail, and send him off to America?'

'A jury will never find him guilty,' said Lord Lufton.

'And what is the truth of it?' asked the younger Lady Lufton.

Then the whole matter was discussed again, and it was settled among them all that Mr Crawley had undoubtedly appropriated the cheque through temporary obliquity of judgment, – obliquity of judgment and forgetfulness as to the source from whence the cheque had come to him. 'He has picked it up about the house, and then has thought that it was his own,' said Lord Lufton. Had they come to the conclusion that such an appropriation of money had been made by one of the clergy of the palace, by one of the Proudeian party, they would doubtless have been very loud and very bitter as to the iniquity of the offender. They would have said much as to the weakness of the bishop and the wickedness of the bishop's wife, and would have declared the appropriator to have been as very a thief as ever picked a pocket or opened a till; – but they were unanimous in their acquittal of Mr Crawley. It had not been his intention, they said, to be a thief, and a man should be judged only by his intention. It must now be their object to induce a Barchester jury to look at the matter in the same light.

'When they come to understand how the land lies,' said the

archdeacon, 'they will be all right. There's not a tradesman in the city who does not hate that woman as though she were—'

'Archdeacon,' said his wife, cautioning him to repress his energy.

'Their bills are all paid by this new chaplain they've got, and he is made to claim discount on every leg of mutton,' said the archdeacon. Arguing from which fact, – or from which assertion, he came to the conclusion that no Barchester jury would find Mr Crawley guilty.

But it was agreed on all sides that it would not be well to trust to the unassisted friendship of the Barchester tradesmen. Mr Crawley must be provided with legal assistance, and this must be furnished to him whether he should be willing or unwilling to receive it. That there would be a difficulty was acknowledged. Mr Crawley was known to be a man not easy of persuasion, with a will of his own, with a great energy of obstinacy on points which he chose to take up as being of importance to his calling, or to his own professional status. He had pleaded his own cause before the magistrates, and it might be that he would insist on doing the same thing before the judge. At last Mr Robarts, the clergyman of Framley, was deputed from the knot of Crawleian advocates assembled in Lady Lufton's drawing-room, to undertake the duty of seeing Mr Crawley, and of explaining to him that his proper defence was regarded as a matter appertaining to the clergy and gentry generally of that part of the country, and that for the sake of the clergy and gentry the defence must of course be properly conducted. In such circumstances the expense of the defence would of course be borne by the clergy and gentry concerned. It was thought that Mr Robarts could put the matter to Mr Crawley with such a mixture of the strength of manly friendship and the softness of clerical persuasion, as to overcome the recognized difficulties of the task.

CHAPTER 11

The bishop sends his inhibition

Tidings of Mr Crawley's fate reached the palace at Barchester on the afternoon of the day on which the magistrates had committed him. All such tidings travel very quickly, conveyed by imperceptible wires, and distributed by indefatigable message boys whom Rumour seems to supply for the purpose. Barchester is twenty miles from Silverbridge by road, and more than forty by railway. I doubt whether any one was commissioned to send the news along the actual telegraph, and yet Mrs Proudie knew it before four o'clock. But she did not know it quite accurately. 'Bishop,' she said, standing at her husband's study door. 'They have committed that man to gaol. There was no help for them unless they had forsworn themselves.'

'Not forsworn themselves, my dear,' said the bishop, striving, as was usual with him, by some meek and ineffectual word to teach his wife that she was occasionally led by her energy into error. He never persisted in the lessons when he found, as was usual, that they were taken amiss.

'I say forsworn themselves!' said Mrs Proudie; 'and now what do you mean to do? This is Thursday, and of course the man must not be allowed to desecrate the church of Hogglestock by performing the Sunday service.'

'If he has been committed, my dear, and is in prison,—'

'I said nothing about prison, bishop.'

'Gaol, my dear.'

'I say they have committed him to gaol. So my information tells me. But of course all the Plumstead and Framley set will move heaven and earth to get him out, so that he may be there as a disgrace to the diocese. I wonder how the dean will feel when he hears of it! I do, indeed. For the dean, though he is an idle, useless man, with no church principles, and no real piety, still he has a conscience. I think he has a conscience.'

'I'm sure he has, my dear.'

'Well; – let us hope so. And if he has a conscience, what must be his feelings when he hears that this creature whom he brought into the diocese has been committed to gaol along with common felons.'

'Not with felons, my dear ; at least, I should think not.'

'I say with common felons! A downright robbery of twenty pounds, just as though he had broken into the bank! And so he did, with sly artifice, which is worse in such hands than a crowbar. And now what are we to do? Here is Thursday, and something must be done before Sunday for the souls of those poor benighted creatures at Hogglestock.' Mrs Proudie was ready for the battle, and was even now sniffing the blood afar-off.* 'I believe it's a hundred and thirty pounds a year,' she said, before the bishop had collected his thoughts sufficiently for a reply.

'I think we must find out, first of all, whether he is really to be shut up in prison,' said the bishop.

'And suppose he is not to be shut up. Suppose they have been weak, or untrue to their duty – and from what we know of the magistrates of Barsetshire, there is too much reason to suppose that they will have been so ; suppose they have let him out, is he to go about like a roaring lion – among the souls of the people ?'*

The bishop shook in his shoes. When Mrs Proudie began to talk of the souls of the people he always shook in his shoes. She had an eloquent way of raising her voice over the word souls that was qualified to make any ordinary man shake in his shoes. The bishop was a conscientious man, and well knew that poor Mr Crawley, even though he might have become a thief under terrible temptation, would not roar at Hogglestock to the injury of any man's soul. He was aware that this poor clergyman had done his duty laboriously and efficiently, and he was also aware that though he might have been committed by the magistrates, and then let out upon bail, he should not be regarded now, in these days before his trial, as a convicted thief. But to explain all this to Mrs Proudie was beyond his power. He knew well that she would not hear a word in mitigation of Mr Crawley's presumed offence. Mr Crawley belonged to the other party, and Mrs Proudie was a thorough-going partisan. I know a man, – an excellent fellow, who, being himself a strong politician, constantly expresses a belief that all politicians opposed to him are thieves, child-murderers, parricides, lovers of incest, demons upon the earth. He is a strong partisan, but not, I think, so strong as Mrs Proudie. He says that he believes all evil of his opponents ; but she really believed the evil. The archdeacon had called Mrs Proudie a she-Beelzebub ; but that was a simple ebullition of mortal hatred. He believed her to be simply a vulgar, interfering, brazen-faced virago. Mrs Proudie in truth believed that the archdeacon was an actual emanation from Satan, sent to those parts to devour souls, – as she would call it, – and that she herself was an emanation of another sort, sent from another source expressly to Barchester, to prevent such devouring, as far as it might possibly be prevented by a mortal agency. The bishop knew it all, – understood it all. He regarded the archdeacon as a clergyman belonging to a party opposed to his party, and he disliked the man. He knew that from his first coming into the diocese he had been encountered with enmity by the archdeacon and the archdeacon's friends. If left to himself he could feel and to a certain extent could resent such enmity. But he had no faith in his wife's doctrine of emanation. He had no faith in many things which she believed religiously; – and yet what could he do? If he attempted to explain, she would stop him before he had got through the first half of his first sentence.

'If he is out on bail—,' commenced the bishop.

'Of course he will be out on bail.'

'Then I think he should feel—'

'Feel! such men never feel! What feeling can one expect from a convicted thief?'

'Not convicted as yet, my dear,' said the bishop.

'A convicted thief,' repeated Mrs Proudie; and she vociferated the words in such a tone that the bishop resolved that he would for the future let the word convicted pass without notice. After all she was only using the phrase in a peculiar sense given to it by herself.

'It won't be proper, certainly, that he should do the services,' suggested the bishop.

'Proper! It would be a scandal to the whole diocese. How could he raise his head as he pronounced the eighth commandment?* That must be at least prevented.'

The bishop, who was seated, fretted himself in his chair, moving about with little movements. He knew that there was a misery coming upon him; and, as far as he could see it, it might become a great misery, – a huge blistering sore upon him. When miseries came to him, as they did not unfrequently, he would unconsciously endeavour to fathom them and weigh them, and then, with some gallantry, resolve to beat them, if he could find that their depth and weight were not too great for his powers of endurance. He would let the cold wind whistle by him, putting up the collar of his coat, and would encounter the winter weather without complaint. And he would be patient under the hot sun, knowing well that tranquillity is best for those who have to bear tropical heat. But when the storm threatened to knock him off his legs, when the earth beneath him became too hot for his poor tender feet, – what could he do then? There had been with him such periods of misery, during which he had wailed inwardly and had confessed to himself that the wife of his bosom was too much for him. Now the storm seemed to be coming very roughly. It would be demanded of him that he should exercise certain episcopal authority which he knew did not belong to him. Now, episcopal authority admits of being stretched or contracted according to the character of the bishop who uses it. It is not always easy for a bishop himself to know what he may do, and what he may not do. He may certainly give advice to any clergyman in his diocese, and he may give it in such form that it will have in it something of authority. Such advice coming from a dominant bishop to a clergyman with a submissive mind, has in it very much of authority. But Bishop Proudie knew that Mr Crawley was not a clergyman with a submissive mind, and he feared that he himself, as regarded from Mr Crawley's point of view, was not a dominant bishop. And yet he could only act by advice. 'I will write to him,' said the bishop, 'and will explain to him that as he is circumstanced he should not appear in the reading desk.'

'Of course he must not appear in the reading desk. That scandal must at any rate be inhibited.' Now the bishop did not at all like the use of the word inhibited, understanding well that Mrs Proudie intended it to be understood as implying some episcopal command against which there should be no appeal; – but he let it pass.

'I will write to him, my dear, to-night.'

'And Mr Thumble can go over with the letter the first thing in the morning.'

'Will not the post be better?'

'No, bishop; certainly not.'

'He would get it sooner, if I write to-night, my dear.'

'In either case he will get it to-morrow morning. An hour or two will not signify, and if Mr Thumble takes it himself we shall know how it is received. It will be well that Thumble should be there in person as he will want to look for lodgings in the parish.'

'But, my dear—'

'Well, bishop?'

'About lodgings? I hardly think that Mr Thumble, if we decide that Mr Thumble shall undertake the duty—'

'We have decided that Mr Thumble should undertake the duty. That is decided.'

'But I do not think he should trouble himself to look for lodgings at Hogglestock. He can go over on the Sundays.'

'And who is to do the parish work? Would you have that man, a convicted thief, to look after the schools, and visit the sick, and perhaps attend the dying ?'

'There will be a great difficulty; there will indeed,' said the bishop, becoming very unhappy, and feeling that he was driven by circumstances either to assert his own knowledge or teach his wife something of the law with reference to his position as a bishop. 'Who is to pay Mr Thumble ?'

'The income of the parish must be sequestrated, and he must be paid out of that. Of course he must have the income while he does the work.'

'But, my dear, I cannot sequestrate the man's income.'

'I don't believe it, bishop. If the bishop cannot sequestrate, who can ? But you are always timid in exercising the authority put into your hands for wise purposes. Not sequestrate the income of a man who has been proved to be a thief ! You leave that to us, and we will manage it.' The 'us' here named comprised Mrs Proudie and the bishop's managing chaplain.

Then the bishop was left alone for an hour to write the letter which Mr Thumble was to carry over to Mr Crawley, – and after a while he did write it. Before he commenced the task, however, he sat for some moments in his arm-chair close by the fire-side, asking himself whether it might not be possible for him to overcome his enemy in this matter. How would it go with him suppose he were to leave the letter unwritten, and send in a message by his chaplain to Mrs Proudie, saying that as Mr Crawley was out on bail, the parish might be left for the present without episcopal interference ? She could not make him interfere. She could not force him to write the letter. So, at least, he said to himself. But as he said it, he almost thought that she could do these things. In the last thirty years, or more, she had ever contrived by some power latent in her to have her will effected. But what would happen if now, even now, he were to rebel ? That he would personally become very uncomfortable, he was well aware, but he thought that he could bear that. The food would become bad, – mere ashes between his teeth, the daily modicum of wine would lose its flavour, the chimneys would all smoke, the wind would come from the east, and the servants would not answer the bell. Little miseries of that kind would crowd upon him. He had arrived at a time of his life in which such miseries make such men very miserable; but yet he thought that he could endure them. And what other wretchedness would come to him ? She would scold him, – frightfully, loudly, scornfully, and worse than all, continually. But of this he had so much habitually, that anything added might be borne also; – if only he could be sure that the scoldings should go on in private, that the world of the palace should not be allowed to hear the revilings to which he would be subjected. But to be scolded publicly was the great evil which he dreaded beyond all evils. He was well aware that the palace would know his misfortune, that it was known, and freely discussed by all, from the examining chaplain down to the palace boot-boy; — nay, that it was known to all the diocese; but yet he could smile upon those around him, and look as though he held his own like other men, — unless when open violence was displayed. But when that voice was heard aloud along the corridors of the palace, and when he was summoned imperiously by the woman, calling for her bishop, so that all Barchester heard it, and when he was compelled to creep forth from his study, at the sound of that summons, with distressed face, and shaking hands, and short hurrying steps, — a being to be pitied even by a deacon, — not venturing to assume an air of masterdom should he chance to meet a housemaid on the stairs, — then, at such moments as that, he would feel that any submission was better than the misery which he suffered. And he well knew that should he now rebel, the whole house would be in a turmoil. He would be bishoped here, and bishoped there, before the eyes of all palatial men and women, till life would be a burden to him. So he got up from his seat over the fire, and went to his desk and wrote the letter. The letter was as follows: —

The Palace, Barchester, — December, 186–.

Reverend Sir, — (he left out the dear, because he knew that if he inserted it he would be compelled to write the letter over again.)

I have heard to-day with the greatest trouble of spirit, that you have been taken before a bench of magistrates assembled at Silverbridge, having been previously arrested by the police in your parsonage house at Hogglestock, and that the magistrates of Silverbridge have committed you to take your trial at the next assizes at Barchester, on a charge of theft.

Far be it from me to prejudge the case. You will understand, reverend sir, that I express no opinion whatever as to your guilt or innocence in this matter. If you have been guilty, may the Lord give you grace to repent of your great sin and to make such amends as may come from immediate acknowledgment and confession. If you are innocent, may He protect you, and make your innocence to shine before all men. In either case may the Lord be with you and keep your feet from further stumbling.

But I write to you now as your bishop, to explain to you that circumstanced as you are, you cannot with decency perform the church services of your parish. I have that confidence in you that I doubt not you will agree with me in this, and will be grateful to me for relieving you so far from the immediate perplexities of your position. I have, therefore, appointed the Rev. Caleb Thumble to perform the duties of incumbent of Hogglestock till such time as a jury shall have decided upon your case at Barchester; and in order that you may at once become acquainted with Mr Thumble, as will be most convenient that you should do, I will commission him to deliver this letter into your hand personally to-morrow, trusting that you will receive him with that brotherly spirit in which he is sent upon this painful mission.

Touching the remuneration to which Mr Thumble will become entitled for his temporary ministrations in the parish of Hogglestock, I do not at present lay down any strict injunction. He must, at any rate, be paid at a rate not less than that ordinarily afforded for a curate.

I will once again express my fervent hope that the Lord may bring you to see the true state of your own soul, and that he may fill you with the grace of repentance, so that the bitter waters of the present hour may not pass over your head and destroy you.

I have the honour to be,
Reverend Sir,
Your faithful servant in Christ,
T. Barnum.*

The bishop had hardly finished his letter when Mrs Proudie returned to the study, followed by the Rev. Caleb Thumble. Mr Thumble was a little man, about forty years of age, who had a wife and children living in Barchester, and who existed on such chance clerical crumbs as might fall from the table of the bishop's patronage. People in Barchester said that Mrs Thumble was a cousin of Mrs Proudie's; but as Mrs Proudie stoutly denied the connection, it may be supposed that the people of Barchester were wrong. And, had Mr Thumble's wife in truth been a cousin, Mrs Proudie would surely have provided for him during the many years in which the diocese had been in her hands. No such provision had been made, and Mr Thumble, who had now been living in the diocese for three years, had received nothing else from the bishop than such chance employment as this which he was now to undertake at Hogglestock. He was a humble, mild-voiced man, when within the palace precincts, and had so far succeeded in making his way among his brethren in the cathedral city as to be employed not unfrequently

---

* Baronum Castrum having been the old Roman name from which the modern Barchester is derived, the bishops of the diocese have always signed themselves Barnum.

for absent minor canons in chanting the week-day services, being remunerated for his work at the rate of about two shillings and sixpence a service.

The bishop handed his letter to his wife, observing in an off-hand kind of way that she might as well see what he said. 'Of course I shall read it,' said Mrs Proudie. And the bishop winced visibly, because Mr Thumble was present. 'Quite right,' said Mrs Proudie, 'quite right to let him know that you knew that he had been arrested, – actually arrested by the police.'

'I thought it proper to mention that, because of the scandal,' said the bishop.

'Oh, it has been terrible in the city,' said Mr Thumble.

'Never mind, Mr Thumble,' said Mrs Proudie. 'Never mind that at present.' Then she continued to read the letter. 'What's this? Confession! That must come out, bishop. It will never do that you should recommend confession to anybody, under any circumstances.'

'But, my dear—'

'It must come out, bishop.'

'My lord has not meant auricular confession,'* suggested Mr Thumble. Then Mrs Proudie turned round and looked at Mr Thumble, and Mr Thumble nearly sank amidst the tables and chairs. 'I beg your pardon, Mrs Proudie,' he said. 'I didn't mean to intrude.'

'The word must come out, bishop,' repeated Mrs Proudie. 'There should be no stumbling-blocks prepared for feet that are only too ready to fall.' And the word did come out.

'Now, Mr Thumble,' said the lady, as she gave the letter to her satellite, 'the bishop and I wish you to be at Hogglestock early to-morrow. You should be there not later than ten, certainly.' Then she paused until Mr Thumble had given the required promise. 'And we request that you will be very firm in the mission which is confided to you, a mission which, as of course you see, is of a very delicate and important nature. You must be firm.'

'I will endeavour,' said Mr Thumble.

'The bishop and I both feel that this most unfortunate man must not under any circumstances be allowed to perform the services of the Church while this charge is hanging over him, – a charge as to the truth of which no sane man can entertain a doubt.'

'I'm afraid not, Mrs Proudie,' said Mr Thumble.

'The bishop and I therefore are most anxious that you should make Mr Crawley understand at once, – at once,' and the lady, as she spoke, lifted up her left hand with an eloquent violence which had its effect upon Mr Thumble, 'that he is inhibited,' – the bishop shook in his shoes, – 'inhibited from the performance of any of his sacred duties.' Thereupon, Mr Thumble promised obedience and went his way.

CHAPTER 12

Mr Crawley seeks for sympathy

Matters went very badly indeed in the parsonage house at Hogglestock. On the Friday morning, the morning of the day after his committal, Mr Crawley got up very early, long before the daylight, and dressing himself in the dark, groped his way downstairs. His wife having vainly striven to persuade him to remain where he was, followed him into the cold room below with a lighted candle. She found him standing with his hat on and with his old cloak, as though he were prepared to go out. 'Why do you do this?' she said. 'You will make youself ill with the cold and the night air; and then you, and I too, will be worse than we now are.'

'We cannot be worse. You cannot be worse, and for me it does not signify. Let me pass.'

'I will not let you pass, Josiah. Be a man and bear it. Ask God for strength, instead of seeking it in an over-indulgence of your own sorrow.'

'Indulgence!'

'Yes, love; – indulgence. It is indulgence. You will allow your mind to dwell on nothing for a moment but your own wrongs.'

'What else have I that I can think of? Is not all the world against me?'

'Am I against you?'

'Sometimes I think you are. When you accuse me of self-indulgence you are against me, – me, who for myself have desired nothing but to be allowed to do my duty, and to have bread enough to keep me alive, and clothes enough to make me decent.'

'Is it not self-indulgence, this giving way to grief? Who would know so well as you how to teach the lesson of endurance to others? Come, love. Lay down your hat. It cannot be fitting that you should go out into the wet and cold of the raw morning.'

For a moment he hesitated, but as she raised her hand to take his cloak from him he drew back from her, and would not permit it. 'I shall find those up whom I want to see,' he said. 'I must visit my flock, and I dare not go through the parish by daylight lest they hoot after me as a thief.'

'Not one in Hogglestock would say a word to insult you.'

'Would they not? The very children in the school whisper at me. Let me pass, I say. It has not as yet come to that, that I should be stopped in my egress and ingress. They have – bailed me; and while their bail lasts, I may go where I will.'

'Oh, Josiah, what words to me! Have I ever stopped your liberty? Would I not give my life to secure it?'

'Let me go, then, now. I tell you that I have business in hand.'

'But I will go with you? I will be ready in an instant.'

'You go! Why should you go? Are there not the children for you to mind?'

'There is only Jane.'

'Stay with her, then. Why should you go about the parish?' She still held him by the cloak, and looked anxiously up into his face. 'Woman,' he said, raising his voice, 'what is it that you dread? I command you to tell me what is it that you fear?' He had now taken hold of her by the shoulder, slightly thrusting her from him, so that he might see her face by the dim light of the single candle. 'Speak, I say. What is that you think that I shall do?'

'Dearest, I know that you will be better at home, better with me, than you can be on such a morning as this out in the cold damp air.'

'And is that all?' He looked hard at her, while she returned his gaze with beseeching loving eyes. 'Is there nothing behind, that you will not tell me?'

She paused for a moment before she replied. She had never lied to him. She could not lie to him. 'I wish you knew my heart towards you,' she said, 'with all and everything in it.'

'I know your heart well, but I want to know your mind. Why would you persuade me not to go out among my poor?'

'Because it will be bad for you to be out alone in the dark lanes, in the mud and wet, thinking of your sorrow. You will brood over it till you will lose your senses through the intensity of your grief. You will stand out in the cold air, forgetful of everything around you, till your limbs will be numbed, and your blood chilled,—'

'And then— ?'

'Oh, Josiah, do not hold me like that, and look at me so angrily.'

'And even then I will bear my burden till the Lord in his mercy shall see fit to relieve me. Even then I will endure, though a bare bodkin or a leaf of hemlock* would put an end to it. Let me pass on; you need fear nothing.'

She did let him pass without another word, and he went out of
the house, shutting the door after him noiselessly, and closing the
wicket-gate of the garden. For a while she sat herself down on the
nearest chair, and tried to make up her mind how she might best
treat him in his present state of mind. As regarded the present
morning her heart was at ease. She knew that he would do now
nothing of that which she had apprehended. She could trust him
not to be false in his word to her, though she could not before have
trusted him not to commit so much heavier a sin. If he would really
employ himself from morning till night among the poor, he would
be better so, – his trouble would be easier of endurance, – than
with any other employment which he could adopt. What she most
dreaded was that he should sit idle over the fire and do nothing.
When he was so seated she could read his mind, as though it was
open to her as a book. She had been quite right when she had
accused him of over-indulgence in his grief. He did give way to it
till it became a luxury to him, – a luxury which she would not have
had the heart to deny him, had she not felt it to be of all luxuries
the most pernicious. During these long hours, in which he would sit
speechless, doing nothing, he was telling himself from minute to
minute that of all God's creatures he was the most heavily afflicted,
and was revelling in the sense of the injustice done to him. He was
recalling all the facts of his life, his education, which had been
costly, and, as regarded knowledge, successful; his vocation to the
church, when in his youth he had determined to devote himself to
the service of his Saviour, disregarding promotion or the favour of
men; the short, sweet days of his early love, in which he had
devoted himself again, – thinking nothing of self, but everything of
her; his diligent working, in which he had ever done his very
utmost for the parish in which he was placed, and always his best
for the poorest; the success of other men who had been his
compeers, and, as he too often told himself, intellectually his
inferiors; then of his children, who had been carried off from his
love to the churchyard, – over whose graves he himself had stood,
reading out the pathetic words of the funeral service with unswerv-
ing voice and a bleeding heart; and then of his children still living,
who loved their mother so much better than they loved him. And
he would recall all the circumstances of his poverty, – how he had
been driven to accept alms, to fly from creditors, to hide himself, to
see his chairs and tables seized before the eyes of those over whom
he had been set as their spiritual pastor. And in it all, I think, there
was nothing so bitter to the man as the derogation from the
spiritual grandeur of his position as priest among men, which came
as one necessary result from his poverty. St Paul could go forth

without money in his purse or shoes to his feet or two suits to his back, and his poverty never stood in the way of his preaching, or hindered the veneration of the faithful. St Paul, indeed, was called upon to bear stripes, was flung into prison, encountered terrible dangers. But Mr Crawley, – so he told himself, – could have encountered all that without flinching. The stripes and scorn of the unfaithful would have been nothing to him, if only the faithful would have believed in him, poor as he was, as they would have believed in him had he been rich! Even they whom he had most loved treated him almost with derision, because he was now different from them. Dean Arabin had laughed at him because he had persisted in walking ten miles through the mud instead of being conveyed in the dean's carriage; and yet, after that, he had been driven to accept the dean's charity! No one respected him. No one! His very wife thought that he was a lunatic. And now he had been publicly branded as a thief; and in all likelihood would end his days in a gaol! Such were always his thoughts as he sat idle, silent, moody, over the fire; and his wife well knew their currents. It would certainly be better that he should drive himself to some employment, if any employment could be found possible to him.

When she had been alone for a few minutes, Mrs Crawley got up from her chair, and going into the kitchen, lighted the fire there, and put the kettle over it, and began to prepare such breakfast for her husband as the means in the house afforded. Then she called the sleeping servant-girl, who was little more than a child, and went into her own girl's room, and then she got into bed with her daughter.

'I have been up with your papa, dear, and I am cold.'

'Oh, mamma, poor mamma! Why is papa up so early?'

'He has gone out to visit some of the brickmakers before they go to their work. It is better for him to be employed.'

'But, mamma, it is pitch dark.'

'Yes, dear, it is still dark. Sleep again for a while, and I will sleep too. I think Grace will be here to-night, and then there will be no room for me here.'

Mr Crawley went forth and made his way with rapid steps to a portion of his parish nearly two miles distant from his house, through which was carried a canal, affording water communication in some intricate way both to London and Bristol. And on the brink of this canal there had sprung up a colony of brickmakers, the nature of the earth in those parts combining with the canal to make brickmaking a suitable trade. The workmen there assembled were not, for the most part, native-born Hogglestockians, or folk descended from Hogglestockian parents. They had come thither from unknown regions, as labourers of that class do come when they are needed. Some young men from that and neighbouring parishes had joined themselves to the colony, allured by wages, and disregarding the menaces of the neighbouring farmers; but they were all in appearance and manners nearer akin to the race of navvies than to ordinary rural labourers. They had a bad name in the country; but it may be that their name was worse than their deserts. The farmers hated them, and consequently they hated the farmers. They had a beershop, and a grocer's shop, and a huxter's shop for their own accommodation, and were consequently vilified by the small old-established tradesmen around them. They got drunk occasionally, but I doubt whether they drank more than did the farmers themselves on market-day. They fought among themselves sometimes, but they forgave each other freely, and seemed to have no objection to black eyes. I fear that they were not always good to their wives, nor were their wives always good to them; but it should be remembered that among the poor, especially when they live in clusters, such misfortunes cannot be hidden as they may be amidst the decent belongings of more wealthy people. That they worked very hard was certain; and it was certain also that very few of their number ever came upon the poor rates. What became of the old brickmakers no one knew. Who ever sees a worn-out aged navvie?

Mr Crawley, ever since his first coming into Hogglestock, had been very busy among these brickmakers, and by no means without success. Indeed the farmers had quarrelled with him because the brickmakers had so crowded the narrow parish church, as to leave but scant room for decent people. 'Doo they folk pay tithes? That's what I want 'un to tell me?' argued one farmer, – not altogether unnaturally, believing as he did that Mr Crawley was paid by tithes out of his own pocket. But Mr Crawley had done his best to make the brickmakers welcome at the church, scandalizing the farmers by causing them to sit or stand in any portion of the church which was hitherto unappropriated. He had been constant in his personal visits to them, and had felt himself to be more a St Paul with them than with any other of his neighbours around him.

It was a cold morning, but the rain of the preceding evening had given way to frost, and the air, though sharp, was dry. The ground under the feet was crisp, having felt the wind and frost, and was no longer clogged with mud. In his present state of mind the walk was good for our poor pastor, and exhilarated him; but still, as he went, he thought always of his injuries. His own wife believed that he was about to commit suicide, and for so believing he was very angry with her; and yet, as he well knew, the idea of making away with himself had flitted through his own mind a dozen times. Not from his own wife could he get real sympathy. He would see what he could do with a certain brickmaker of his acquaintance.

'Are you here, Dan?' he said, knocking at the door of a cottage which stood alone, close to the towing-path of the canal, and close also to a forlorn corner of the muddy, watery, ugly, disordered brickfield. It was now just past six o'clock, and the men would be rising, as in midwinter they commenced their work at seven. The cottage was an unalluring, straight brick-built tenement, seeming as though intended to be one of a row which had never progressed beyond Number One. A voice answered from the interior, inquiring who was the visitor, to which Mr Crawley replied by giving his name. Then the key was turned in the lock, and Dan Morris, the brickmaker, appeared with a candle in his hand. He had been engaged in lighting the fire, with a view to his own breakfast. 'Where is your wife, Dan?' asked Mr Crawley. The man answered by pointing with a short poker, which he held in his hand, to the bed, which was half screened from the room by a ragged curtain, which hung from the ceiling half-way down to the floor. 'And are the Darvels here?' asked Mr Crawley. Then Morris, again using the poker, pointed upwards showing that the Darvels were still in their own allotted abode upstairs.

'You're early out, Muster Crawley,' said Morris, and then he went on with his fire. 'Drat the sticks, if they bean't as wet as the old 'un hisself. Get up, old woman, and do you do it, for I can't. They wun't kindle for me, nohow.' But the old woman, having well noted the presence of Mr Crawley, thought it better to remain where she was.

Mr Crawley sat himself down by the obstinate fire, and began to arrange the sticks. 'Dan, Dan,' said a voice from the bed, 'sure you wouldn't let his reverence trouble himself with the fire.'

'How be I to keep him from it, if he chooses? I didn't ax him.' Then Morris stood by and watched, and after a while Mr Crawley succeeded in his attempt.

'How could it burn when you had not given the small spark a current of air to help it?' said Mr Crawley.

'In course not,' said the woman, 'but he be such a stupid.'

The husband said no word in acknowledgment of this compliment, nor did he thank Mr Crawley for what he had done, nor appear as though he intended to take any notice of him. He was going on with his work when Mr Crawley again interrupted him.

'How did you get back from Silverbridge yesterday, Dan?'

'Footed it, – all the blessed way.'

'It's only eight miles.'

'And I footed it there, and that's sixteen. And I paid one-and-sixpence for beer and grub; – s'help me, I did.'

'Dan!' said the voice from the bed, rebuking him for the impropriety of his language.

'Well; I beg pardon, but I did. And they guv' me two bob; – just two plain shillings, by—'

'Dan!'

'And I'd 've arned three-and-six here at brickmaking easy; that's what I would. How's a poor man to live that way? They'll not cotch me at Barchester 'Sizes at that price; they may be sure of that. Look there, – that's what I've got for my day.' And he put his hand into his breeches'-pocket and fetched out a sixpence. 'How's a man to fill his belly out of that? Damnation!'

'Dan!'

'Well, what did I say? Hold your jaw, will you, and not be halloaing at me that way? I know what I'm a saying of, and what I'm a doing of.'

'I wish they'd given you something more with all my heart,' said Crawley.

'We knows that,' said the woman from the bed. 'We is sure of that, your reverence.'

'Sixpence!' said the man, scornfully. 'If they'd have guv me nothing at all but the run of my teeth at the public-house, I'd 've taken it better. But sixpence!'

Then there was a pause. 'And what have they given to me?' said Mr Crawley, when the man's ill-humour about his sixpence had so far subsided as to allow of his busying himself again about the premises.

'Yes, indeed; – yes, indeed,' said the woman. 'Yes, yes, we feel that; we do indeed, Mr Crawley.'

'I tell you what, sir; for another sixpence I'd 've sworn you'd never guv' me the paper at all; and so I will now, if it bean't too late; – sixpence or no sixpence. What do I care? d – them.'

'Dan!'

'And why shouldn't I? They hain't got brains enough among them to winny the truth from the lies, – not among the lot of 'em. I'll swear afore the judge that you didn't give it me at all, if that'll do any good.'

'Man, do you think I would have you perjure yourself, even if that would do me a service? And do you think that any man was ever served by a lie?'

'Faix, among them chaps it don't do to tell them too much of the truth. Look at that!' And he brought out the sixpence again from his breeches'-pocket. 'And look at your reverence. Only that they've let you out for a while, they've been nigh as hard on you as though you were one of us.'

'If they think that I stole it, they have been right,' said Mr Crawley.

'It's been along of that chap, Soames,' said the woman. 'The lord would've paid the money out of his own pocket and never said not a word.'

'If they think that I've been a thief, they've done right,' repeated Mr Crawley. 'But how can they think so? How can they think so? Have I lived like a thief among them?'

'For the matter o' that, if a man ain't paid for his work by them as is his employers, he must pay hisself. Them's my notions. Look at that!' Whereupon he again pulled out the sixpence, and held it forth in the palm of his hand.

'You believe, then,' said Mr Crawley, speaking very slowly, 'that I did steal the money. Speak out, Dan; I shall not be angry. As you go you are honest men, and I want to know what such of you think about it.'

'He don't think nothing of the kind,' said the woman, almost getting out of bed in her energy. 'If he'd athought the like o' that in his head, I'd read 'un such a lesson he'd never think again the longest day he had to live.'

'Speak out, Dan,' said the clergyman, not attending to the woman. 'You can understand that no good can come of a lie.' Dan Morris scratched his head. 'Speak out, man, when I tell you,' said Crawley.

'Drat it all,' said Dan, 'where's the use of so much jaw about it?'

'Say you know his reverence is as innocent as the babe as isn't born,' said the woman.

'No; I won't, – say nothing of the kind,' said Dan.

'Speak out the truth,' said Crawley.

'They do say, among 'em,' said Dan, 'that you picked it up, and then got a woolgathering in your head till you didn't rightly know where it come from.' Then he paused. 'And after a bit you guv' it me to get the money. Didn't you, now?'

'I did.'

'And they do say if a poor man had done it, it'd been stealing, for sartain.'

'And I'm a poor man, – the poorest in all Hogglestock; and, therefore, of course, it is stealing. Of course I am a thief. Yes; of course I am a thief. When did not the world believe the worst of the poor?' Having so spoken, Mr Crawley rose from his chair and hurried out of the cottage, waiting no further reply from Dan Morris or his wife. And as he made his way slowly home, not going there by the direct road, but by a long circuit, he told himself that there could be no sympathy for him anywhere. Even Dan Morris, the brickmaker, thought that he was a thief.

'And am I a thief?' he said to himself, standing in the middle of the road, with his hands up to his forehead.

CHAPTER 13

The bishop's angel

It was nearly nine before Mr Crawley got back to his house, and found his wife and daughter waiting breakfast for him. 'I should not wonder if Grace were over here to-day,' said Mrs Crawley. 'She'd better remain where she is,' said he. After this the meal passed almost without a word. When it was over, Jane, at a sign from her mother, went up to her father and asked him whether she should read with him. 'Not now,' he said, 'not just now. I must rest my brain before it will be fit for any work.' Then he got into the chair over the fire, and his wife began to fear that he would remain there all the day.

But the morning was not far advanced, when there came a visitor who disturbed him, and by disturbing him did him real service. Just at ten there arrived at the little gate before the house a man on a pony, whom Jane espied, standing there by the pony's head and looking about for some one to relieve him from the charge of his steed. This was Mr Thumble, who had ridden over to Hogglestock on a poor spavined brute belonging to the bishop's stable, and which had once been the bishop's cob. Now it was the vehicle by which Mrs Proudie's episcopal messages were sent backwards and forwards through a twelve-miles ride round Barchester; and so many were the lady's requirements, that the poor animal by no means eat the hay of idleness.* Mr Thumble had suggested to Mrs Proudie, after their interview with the bishop and the giving up of the letter to the clerical messenger's charge, that before hiring a gig from the Dragon of Wantley, he should be glad to know, – looking as he always did to 'Mary Anne and the children,' – whence the price of the gig was to be returned to him. Mrs Proudie had frowned at him, – not with all the austerity of frowning which she could use when really angered, but simply with a frown which gave her some little time for thought, and would enable her to continue the rebuke if, after thinking, she should find that rebuke was needed. But

mature consideration showed her that Mr Thumble's caution was
not without reason. Were the bishop energetic, – or even the
bishop's managing chaplain as energetic as he should be, Mr
Crawley might, as Mrs Proudie felt assured, be made in some way
to pay for a conveyance for Mr Thumble. But the energy was
lacking, and the price of the gig, if the gig were ordered, would
certainly fall ultimately upon the bishop's shoulders. This was very
sad. Mrs Proudie had often grieved over the necessary expenditure
of episcopal surveillance, and had been heard to declare her opinion
that a liberal allowance for secret service should be made in every
diocese. What better could the Ecclesiastical Commissioners do
with all those rich revenues which they had stolen from the
bishops ?* But there was no such liberal allowance at present, and,
therefore, Mrs Proudie, after having frowned at Mr Thumble for
some seconds, desired him to take the grey cob. Now, Mr Thumble
had ridden the grey cob before, and would much have preferred a
gig. But even the grey cob was better than a gig at his own cost.

'Mamma, there's a man at the gate wanting to come in,' said
Jane. 'I think he's a clergyman.'

Mr Crawley immediately raised his head, though he did not at
once leave his chair. Mrs Crawley went to the window, and
recognized the reverend visitor. 'My dear, it is that Mr Thumble,
who is so much with the bishop.'

'What does Mr Thumble want with me ?'

'Nay, my dear; he will tell you that himself.' But Mrs Crawley,
though she answered him with a voice intended to be cheerful,
greatly feared the coming of this messenger from the palace. She
perceived at once that the bishop was about to interfere with her
husband in consequence of that which the magistrates had done
yesterday.

'Mamma, he doesn't know what to do with his pony,' said Jane.

'Tell him to tie it to the rail,' said Mr Crawley. 'If he has expected
to find menials here, as he has them at the palace, he will be wrong.
If he wants to come in here, let him tie the beast to the rail.' So Jane
went out and sent a message to Mr Thumble by the girl, and Mr
Thumble did tie the pony to the rail, and followed the girl into the
house. Jane in the meantime had retired out by the back door to the
school, but Mrs Crawley kept her ground. She kept her ground
although she almost believed that her husband would prefer to have
the field to himself. As Mr Thumble did not at once enter the room,
Mr Crawley stalked to the door, and stood with it open in his hand.
Though he knew Mr Thumble's person, he was not acquainted with
him, and therefore he simply bowed to the visitor, bowing more
than once or twice with a cold courtesy, which did not put Mr

Thumble altogether at his ease. 'My name is Mr Thumble,' said the
visitor, – 'The Reverend Caleb Thumble,' and he held the bishop's
letter in his hand. Mr Crawley seemed to take no notice of the
letter, but motioned Mr Thumble with his hand into the room.

'I suppose you have come over from Barchester this morning?'
said Mrs Crawley.

'Yes, madam, – from the palace.' Mr Thumble, though a humble
man in positions in which he felt that humility would become him,
– a humble man to his betters, as he himself would have expressed
it, – had still about him something of that pride which naturally
belonged to those clergymen who were closely attached to the
palace at Barchester. Had he been sent on a message to Plumstead,
– could any such message from Barchester palace have been
possible, he would have been properly humble in his demeanour to
the archdeacon, or to Mrs Grantly had he been admitted to the
august presence of that lady; but he was aware that humility would
not become him on his present mission; he had been expressly
ordered to be firm by Mrs Proudie, and firm he meant to be; and
therefore, in communicating to Mrs Crawley the fact that he had
come from the palace, he did load the tone of his voice with
something of dignity which Mr Crawley might perhaps be excused
for regarding as arrogance.

'And what does the "palace" want with me?' said Mr Crawley.
Mrs Crawley knew at once that there was to be a battle. Nay, the
battle had begun. Nor was she altogether sorry; for though she
could not trust her husband to sit alone all day in his arm-chair
over the fire, she could trust him to carry on a disputation with any
other clergyman on any subject whatever. 'What does the palace
want with me?' And as Mr Crawley asked the question he stood
erect, and looked Mr Thumble full in the face. Mr Thumble called
to mind the fact, that Mr Crawley was a very poor man indeed, –
so poor that he owed money all round the country to butchers and
bakers, and the other fact, that he, Mr Thumble himself, did not
owe any money to any one, his wife luckily having a little income
of her own; and, strengthened by these remembrances, he endeavoured to bear Mr Crawley's attack with gallantry.

'Of course, Mr Crawley, you are aware that this unfortunate
affair at Silverbridge—'

'I am not prepared, sir, to discuss the unfortunate affair at
Silverbridge with a stranger. If you are the bearer of any message to
me from the Bishop of Barchester, perhaps you will deliver it.'

'I have brought a letter,' said Mr Thumble. Then Mr Crawley
stretched out his hand without a word, and taking the letter with
him to the window, read it very slowly. When he had made himself

master of its contents, he refolded the letter, placed it again in the envelope, and returned to the spot where Mr Thumble was standing. 'I will answer the bishop's letter,' he said; 'I will answer it of course, as it is fitting that I should do. Shall I ask you to wait for my reply, or shall I send it by course of post?'

'I think, Mr Crawley, as the bishop wishes me to undertake the duty—'

'You will not undertake the duty, Mr Thumble. You need not trouble yourself, for I shall not surrender my pulpit to you.'

'But the bishop—'

'I care nothing for the bishop in this matter.' So much he spoke in anger, and then he corrected himself. 'I crave the bishop's pardon, and yours as his messenger, if in the heat occasioned by my strong feelings I have said aught which may savour of irreverence towards his lordship's office. I respect his lordship's high position as bishop of this diocese, and I bow to his commands in all things lawful. But I must not bow to him in things unlawful, nor must I abandon my duty before God at his bidding, unless his bidding be given in accordance with the canons of the Church and the laws of the land. It will be my duty, on the coming Sunday, to lead the prayers of my people in the church of my parish, and to preach to them from my pulpit; and that duty, with God's assistance, I will perform. Nor will I allow any clergyman to interfere with me in the performance of those sacred offices, – no, not though the bishop himself should be present with the object of enforcing his illegal command.' Mr Crawley spoke these words without hesitation, even with eloquence, standing upright, and with something of a noble anger gleaming over his poor wan face; and, I think, that while speaking them, he was happier than he had been for many a long day.

Mr Thumble listened to him patiently, standing with one foot a little in advance of the other, with one hand folded over the other, with his head rather on one side, and with his eyes fixed on the corner where the wall and ceiling joined each other. He had been told to be firm, and he was considering how he might best display firmness. He thought that he remembered some story of two parsons fighting for one pulpit, and he thought also that he should not himself like to incur the scandal of such a proceeding in the diocese. As to the law in the matter he knew nothing himself; but he presumed that a bishop would probably know the law better than a perpetual curate. That Mrs Proudie was intemperate and imperious, he was aware. Had the message come from her alone, he might have felt that even for her sake he had better give way. But as the despotic arrogance of the lady had been in this case backed by the timid presence and hesitating words of her lord, Mr Thumble thought that he must have the law on his side. 'I think you will find, Mr Crawley,' said he, 'that the bishop's inhibition is strictly legal.' He had picked up the powerful word from Mrs Proudie and flattered himself that it might be of use to him in carrying his purpose.

'It is illegal,' said Mr Crawley, speaking somewhat louder than before, 'and will be absolutely futile. As you pleaded to me that you yourself and your own personal convenience were concerned in this matter, I have made known my intentions to you, which otherwise I should have made known only to the bishop. If you please, we will discuss the subject no further.'

'Am I to understand, Mr Crawley, that you refuse to obey the bishop?'

'The bishop has written to me, sir; and I will make known my intention to the bishop by a written answer. As you have been the bearer of the bishop's letter to me, I am bound to ask you whether I shall be indebted to you for carrying back my reply, or whether I shall send it by course of post?' Mr Thumble considered for a moment, and then made up his mind that he had better wait, and carry back the epistle. This was Friday, and the letter could not be delivered by post till the Saturday morning. Mrs Proudie might be angry with him if he should be the cause of loss of time. He did not, however, at all like waiting, having perceived that Mr Crawley, though with language courteously worded, had spoken of him as a mere messenger.

'I think,' he said, 'that I may, perhaps, best further the object which we must all have in view, that namely of providing properly for the Sunday services of the church of Hogglestock, by taking your reply personally to the bishop.'

'That provision is my care and need trouble no one else,' said Mr Crawley, in a loud voice. Then, before seating himself at his old desk, he stood awhile, pondering, with his back turned to his visitor. 'I have to ask your pardon, sir,' said he, looking round for a moment, 'because, by reason of the extreme poverty of this house, my wife is unable to offer to you that hospitality which is especially due from one clergyman to another.'

'Oh, don't mention it,' said Mr Thumble.

'If you will allow me, sir, I would prefer that it should be mentioned.' Then he seated himself at his desk, and commenced his letter.

Mr Thumble felt himself to be awkwardly placed. Had there been no third person in the room he could have sat down in Mr Crawley's arm-chair, and waited patiently till the letter should be finished. But Mrs Crawley was there, and of course he was bound to speak to her. In what strain could he do so? Even he, little as he was given to indulge in sentiment, had been touched by the man's appeal to his own poverty, and he felt, moreover, that Mrs Crawley must have been deeply moved by her husband's position with reference to the bishop's order. It was quite out of the question that he should speak of that, as Mr Crawley would, he was well aware, immediately turn upon him. At last he thought of a subject, and spoke with a voice intended to be pleasant. 'That was the school-house I passed, probably, just as I came here?' Mrs Crawley told him that it was the school-house. 'Ah, yes, I thought so. Have you a certified teacher here?' Mrs Crawley explained that no Government aid had ever reached Hogglestock. Besides themselves, they had only a young woman whom they themselves had instructed. 'Ah, that is a pity,' said Mr Thumble.

'I, – I am the certified teacher,' said Mr Crawley, turning round upon him from his chair.

'Oh, ah, yes,' said Mr Thumble; and after that Mr Thumble asked no more questions about the Hogglestock school. Soon afterwards Mrs Crawley left the room, seeing the difficulty under which Mr Thumble was labouring, and feeling sure that her presence would not now be necessary. Mr Crawley's letter was written quickly, though every now and then he would sit for a moment with his pen poised in the air, searching his memory for a word. But the words came to him easily, and before an hour was over he had handed his letter to Mr Thumble. The letter was as follows: –

The Parsonage, Hogglestock, Dec. 186–

Right Reverend Lord,

I have received the letter of yesterday's date which your lordship has done me the honour of sending to me by the hands of the Reverend Mr Thumble, and I avail myself of that gentleman's kindness to return to you an answer by the same means, moved thus to use his patience chiefly by the consideration that in this way my reply to your lordship's injunctions may be in your hands with less delay than would attend the regular course of the mail-post.

It is with deep regret that I feel myself constrained to inform your lordship that I cannot obey the command which you have laid upon me with reference to the services of my church in this parish. I cannot permit Mr Thumble, or any other delegate from your lordship, to usurp my place in my pulpit. I would not have you to think, if I can possibly dispel such thoughts from your mind, that I disregard your high office, or that I am deficient in that respectful obedience to the bishop set over me, which is due to the authority of the Crown as the head of the church in these realms; but in this, as in all questions of obedience, he who is required to obey must examine the extent of the authority exercised by him who demands obedience. Your lordship might possibly call upon me, using your voice as bishop of the diocese, to abandon altogether the freehold rights which are now mine in this perpetual curacy. The judge of assize, before whom I shall soon stand for my trial, might command me to retire to prison without a verdict given by the jury. The magistrates who committed me so lately as yesterday, upon whose decision in that respect your lordship has taken action against me so quickly, might have equally strained their authority. But in no case, in this land, is he that is subject bound to obey, further than where the law gives authority and exacts obedience. It is not in the power of the Crown itself to inhibit me from the performance of my ordinary duties in this parish by any such missive as that sent to me by your lordship. If your lordship think it right to stop my mouth as a clergyman in your diocese, you must proceed to do so in an ecclesiastical court in accordance with the laws, and will succeed in your object, or fail, in accordance with the evidences as to ministerial fitness or unfitness, which may be produced respecting me before the proper tribunal.

I will allow that much attention is due from a clergyman to pastoral advice given to him by his bishop. On that head I must first express to your lordship my full understanding that your letter has not been intended to convey advice, but an order; – an inhibition, as your messenger, the Reverend Mr Thumble, has expressed it. There might be a case certainly in which I should submit myself to counsel, though I should resist command. No counsel, however, has been given, – except indeed that I should receive your messenger in a proper spirit, which I hope I have done. No other advice has been given me, and therefore there is now no such case as that I have imagined. But in this matter, my lord, I could not have accepted advice from living man, no, not though the hands of the apostles themselves had made him bishop who tendered it to me, and had set him over me for my guidance. I am in a terrible straight. Trouble, and sorrow, and danger are upon me and mine. It may well be, as your lordship says, that the bitter waters of the present hour may pass over my head and destroy me. I thank your lordship for telling me whither I am to look for assistance. Truly I know not whether there is any to be found for me on earth. But the deeper my troubles, the greater my sorrow, the more pressing my danger, the stronger is my need that I should carry myself in these days with that outward respect of self which will teach those around me to know that, let who will condemn me, I have not condemned myself. Were I to abandon my pulpit, unless forced to do so by legal means, I should in doing so be putting a plea of guilty against myself upon the record. This, my lord, I will not do.

> I have the honour to be, my lord,
> Your lordship's most obedient servant,
> Josiah Crawley.

When he had finished writing his letter he read it over slowly, and then handed it to Mr Thumble. The act of writing, and the current of the thoughts through his brain, and the feeling that in every word written he was getting the better of the bishop, – all this joined to a certain manly delight in warfare against authority, lighted up the man's face and gave to his eyes an expression which had been long wanting to them. His wife at that moment came into the room and he looked at her with an air of triumph as he handed the letter to Mr Thumble. 'If you will give that to his lordship with an assurance of my duty to his lordship in all things proper, I will thank you kindly, craving your pardon for the great delay to which you have been subjected.'

'As to the delay, that is nothing,' said Mr Thumble.

'It has been much; but you as a clergyman will feel that it has been incumbent on me to speak my mind fully.'

'Oh, yes; of course.' Mr Crawley was standing up, as also was Mrs Crawley. It was evident to Mr Thumble that they both expected that he should go. But he had been specially enjoined to be firm, and he doubted whether hitherto he had been firm enough. As far as this morning's work had as yet gone, it seemed to him that Mr Crawley had had the play all to himself, and that he, Mr Thumble, had not had his innings. He, from the palace, had been, as it were, cowed by this man, who had been forced to plead his own poverty. It was certainly incumbent upon him, before he went, to speak up, not only for the bishop, but for himself also. 'Mr Crawley,' he said, 'hitherto I have listened to you patiently.'

'Nay,' said Mr Crawley, smiling, 'you have indeed been patient, and I thank you; but my words have been written, not spoken.'

'You have told me that you intend to disobey the bishop's inhibition.'

'I have told the bishop so certainly.'

'May I ask you now to listen to me for a few minutes?'

Mr Crawley, still smiling, still having in his eyes the unwonted triumph which had lighted them up, paused a moment, and then answered him. 'Reverend sir, you must excuse me if I say no, – not on this subject.'

'You will not let me speak?'

'No; not on this matter, which is very private to me. What should you think if I went into your house and inquired of you as to those things which were particularly near to you?'

'But the bishop sent me.'

'Though ten bishops had sent me, – a council of archbishops if you will!' Mr Thumble started back, appalled at the energy of the words used to him. 'Shall a man have nothing of his own; – no sorrow in his heart, no care in his family, no thought in his breast so private and special to him, but that, if he happen to be a clergyman, the bishop may touch it with his thumb?'

'I am not the bishop's thumb,'* said Mr Thumble, drawing himself up.

I intended not to hint anything personally objectionable to yourself. I will regard you as one of the angels of the church.'* Mr Thumble, when he heard this, began to be sure that Mr Crawley was mad; he knew of no angels that could ride about the Barsetshire lanes on grey ponies. 'And as such I will respect you; but I cannot discuss with you the matter of the bishop's message.'

'Oh, very well. I will tell his lordship.'

'I will pray you to do so.'

'And his lordship, should he so decide, will arm me with such power on my next coming as will enable me to carry out his lordship's wishes.'

'His lordship will abide by the law, as will you also.' In speaking these last words he stood with the door in his hand, and Mr Thumble, not knowing how to increase or even to maintain his firmness, thought it best to pass out, and mount his grey pony and ride away.

'The poor man thought that you were laughing at him when you called him an angel of the church,' said Mrs Crawley, coming up to him and smiling on him.

'Had I told him he was simply a messenger, he would have taken it worse; – poor fool! When they have rid themselves of me they may put him here, in my church; but not yet, – not yet. Where is Jane? Tell her that I am ready to commence the Seven against Thebes* with her.' Then Jane was immediately sent for out of the school, and the Seven against Thebes was commenced with great energy. Often during the next hour and a half Mrs Crawley from the kitchen would hear him reading out, or rather saying by rote, with sonorous, rolling voice, great passages from some chorus, and she was very thankful to the bishop who had sent over to them a

message and a messenger which had been so salutary in their effect
upon her husband. 'In truth an angel of the church,' she said to
herself as she chopped up the onions for the mutton-broth; and
ever afterwards she regarded Mr Thumble as an 'angel.'

CHAPTER 14

Major Grantly consults a friend

Grace Crawley passed through Silverbridge on her way to Allington on the Monday, and on the Tuesday morning Major Grantly received a very short note from Miss Prettyman, telling him that she had done so. 'Dear Sir, – I think you will be glad to learn that our friend Miss Crawley went from us yesterday on a visit to her friend, Miss Dale, at Allington. – Yours truly, Annabella Prettyman.' The note said no more than that. Major Grantly was glad to get it, obtaining from it that satisfaction which a man always feels when he is presumed to be concerned in the affairs of the lady with whom he is in love. And he regarded Miss Prettyman with favourable eyes, – as a discreet and friendly woman. Nevertheless, he was not altogether happy. The very fact that Miss Prettyman should write to him on such a subject made him feel that he was bound to Grace Crawley. He knew enough of himself to be sure that he could not give her up without making himself miserable. And yet, as regarded her father, things were going from bad to worse. Everybody now said that the evidence was so strong against Mr Crawley as to leave hardly a doubt of his guilt. Even the ladies in Silverbridge were beginning to give up his cause, acknowledging that the money could not have come rightfully into his hands, and excusing him on the plea of partial insanity. 'He has picked it up and put it by for months, and then thought that it was his own.' The ladies of Silverbridge could find nothing better to say for him than that; and when young Mr Walker remarked that such little mistakes were the customary causes of men being taken to prison, the ladies of Silverbridge did not know how to answer him. It had come to be their opinion that Mr Crawley was affected with a partial lunacy, which ought to be forgiven in one to whom the world had been so cruel; and when young Mr Walker endeavoured to explain to them that a man must be sane altogether or mad altogether, and that Mr Crawley must, if sane, be locked up as a thief, and if mad, locked up as a madman, they sighed, and were convinced that until the world should have been improved by a new infusion of romance, and a stronger feeling of poetic justice, Mr John Walker was right.

And the result of this general opinion made its way out to Major Grantly, and made its way, also, to the archdeacon at Plumstead. As to the major, in giving him his due, it must be explained that the more certain he became of the father's guilt, the more certain also he became of the daugher's merits. It was very hard. The whole thing was cruelly hard. It was cruelly hard upon him that he should be brought into this trouble, and be forced to take upon himself the armour of a knight-errant for the redress of the wrong on the part of the young lady. But when alone in his house, or with his child, he declared to himself that he would do so. It might well be that he could not live in Barsetshire after he had married Mr Crawley's daughter. He had inherited from his father enough of that longing for ascendancy among those around him to make him feel that in such circumstances he would be wretched. But he would be made more wretched by the self-knowledge that he had behaved badly to the girl he loved; and the world beyond Barsetshire was open to him. He would take her with him to Canada, to New Zealand, or to some other far-away country, and there begin his life again. Should his father choose to punish him for so doing by disinheriting him, they would be poor enough; but, in his present frame of mind, the major was able to regard such poverty as honourable and not altogether disagreeable.

He had been out shooting all day at Chaldicotes, with Dr Thorne and a party who were staying in the house there, and had been talking about Mr Crawley, first with one man and then with another. Lord Lufton had been there, and young Gresham from Greshamsbury, and Mr Robarts the clergyman, and news had come among them of the attempt made by the bishop to stop Mr Crawley from preaching. Mr Robarts had been of opinion that Mr Crawley should have given way; and Lord Lufton, who shared his mother's intense dislike of everything that came from the palace, had sworn that he was right to resist. The sympathy of the whole party had been with Mr Crawley; but they had all agreed that he had stolen the money.

'I fear he'll have to give way to the bishop at last,' Lord Lufton had said.

'And what on earth will become of his children?' said the doctor. 'Think of the fate of that pretty girl; for she is a very pretty girl. It will be ruin to her. No man will allow himself to fall in love with her when her father shall have been found guilty of stealing a cheque for twenty pounds.'

'We must do something for the whole family,' said the lord. 'I say, Thorne, you haven't half the game here that there used to be in poor old Sowerby's time.'

'Haven't I?' said the doctor. 'You see Sowerby had been at it all his days, and never did anything else. I only began late in life.'

The major had intended to stay and dine at Chaldicotes, but when he heard what was said about Grace, his heart became sad, and he made some excuse as to his child, and returned home. Dr Thorne had declared that no man could allow himself to fall in love with her. But what if a man had fallen in love with her beforehand? What if a man had not only fallen in love, but spoken of his love? Had he been alone with the doctor, he would, I think, have told him the whole of his trouble; for in all the county there was no man whom he would sooner have trusted with his secret. This Dr Thorne was known far and wide for his soft heart, his open hand, and his well-sustained indifference to the world's opinions on most of those social matters with which the world meddles; and therefore the words which he had spoken had more weight with Major Grantly than they would have had from other lips. As he drove home he almost made up his mind that he would consult Dr Thorne upon the matter. There were many younger men with whom he was very intimate, – Frank Gresham, for instance, and Lord Lufton himself; but this was an affair which he hardly knew how to discuss with a young man. To Dr Thorne he thought that he could bring himself to tell the whole story.

In the evening there came to him a messenger from Plumstead, with a letter from his father and some present for the child. He knew at once that the present had been thus sent as an excuse for the letter. His father might have written by the post, of course; but that would have given to his letter a certain air and tone which he had not wished it to bear. After some message from the major's mother, and some allusion to Edith, the archdeacon struck off upon the matter that was near his heart.

'I fear it is all up with that unfortunate man at Hogglestock,' he said. 'From what I hear of the evidence which came out before the magistrates, there can, I think, be no doubt as to his guilt. Have you heard that the bishop sent over on the following day to stop him from preaching? He did so, and sent again on the Sunday. But Crawley would not give way, and so far I respect the man; for, as a matter of course, whatever the bishop did, or attempted to do, he would do with an extreme of bad taste, probably with gross ignorance as to his own duty and as to the duty of the man under him. I am told that on the first day Crawley turned out of his house the messenger sent to him, – some stray clergyman whom Mrs

Proudie keeps about the house; and that on the Sunday the stairs to the reading-desk and pulpit were occupied by a lot of brickmakers, among whom the parson from Barchester did not venture to attempt to make his way, although he was fortified by the presence of one of the cathedral vergers and by one of the palace footmen. I can hardly believe about the verger and the footman. As for the rest, I have no doubt it is all true. I pity Crawley from my heart. Poor, unfortunate man! The general opinion seems to be that he is not in truth responsible for what he has done. As for his victory over the bishop, nothing on earth could be better.

'Your mother particularly wishes you to come over to us before the end of the week, and to bring Edith. Your grandfather will be here, and he is becoming so infirm that he will never come to us for another Christmas. Of course you will stay over the new year.'

Though the letter was full of Mr Crawley and his affairs there was not a word in it about Grace. This, however, was quite natural. Major Grantly perfectly well understood his father's anxiety to carry his point without seeming to allude to the disagreeable subject. 'My father is very clever,' he said to himself, 'very clever. But he isn't so clever but one can see how clever he is.'

On the next day he went into Silverbridge, intending to call on Miss Prettyman. He had not quite made up his mind what he would say to Miss Prettyman; nor was he called upon to do so, as he never got as far as that lady's house. While walking up the High Street he saw Mrs Thorne in her carriage, and, as a matter of course, he stopped to speak to her. He knew Mrs Thorne quite as intimately as he did her husband, and liked her quite as well. 'Major Grantly,' she said, speaking out loud to him, half across the street; 'I was very angry with you yesterday. Why did you not come up to dinner? We had a room ready for you and everything.'

'I was not quite well, Mrs Thorne.'

'Fiddlestick. Don't tell me of not being well. There was Emily breaking her heart about you.'

'I'm sure Miss Dunstable—'

'To tell you the truth, I think she'll get over it. It won't be mortal with her. But do tell me, Major Grantly, what are we to think about this poor Mr Crawley? It was so good of you to be one of his bailsmen.'

'He would have found twenty in Silverbridge, if he had wanted them.'

'And do you hear that he has defied the bishop? I do so like him for that. Not but what poor Mrs Proudie is the dearest friend I have in the world, and I'm always fighting a battle with old Lady Lufton on her behalf. But one likes to see one's friends worsted sometimes, you know.'

'I don't quite understand what did happen at Hogglestock on Sunday,' said the major.

'Some say he had the bishop's chaplain put under the pump. I don't believe that; but there is no doubt that when the poor fellow tried to get into the pulpit, they took him and carried him neck and heels out of the church. But, tell me, Major Grantly, what is to become of the family?'

'Heaven knows!'

'Is it not sad? And that eldest girl is so nice! They tell me that she is perfect, – not only in beauty, but in manners and accomplishments. Everybody says that she talks Greek just as well as she does English, and that she understands philosophy from the top to the bottom.'

'At any rate, she is so good and so lovely that one cannot but pity her now,' said the major.

'You know her, then, Major Grantly? By-the-by, of course you do, as you were staying with her at Framley.'

'Yes, I know her.'

'What is to become of her? I'm going your way. You might as well get into the carriage, and I'll drive you home. If he is sent to prison, – and they say he must be sent to prison, – what is to become of them?' Then Major Grantly did get into the carriage, and, before he got out again, he had told Mrs Thorne the whole story of his love.

She listened to him with the closest attention; only interrupting him now and then with little words, intended to signify her approval. He, as he told his tale, did not look her in the face, but sat with his eyes fixed upon her muff. 'And now,' he said, glancing up at her almost for the first time as he finished his speech, 'and now, Mrs Thorne, what am I to do?'

'Marry her, of course,' said she, raising her hand aloft and bringing it down heavily upon his knee as she gave her decisive reply.

'H – sh – h,' he exclaimed, looking back in dismay towards the servants.

'Oh, they never hear anything up there. They're thinking about the last pot of porter they had, or the next they're to get. Deary me, I am so glad! Of course you'll marry her.'

'You forget my father.'

'No, I don't. What has a father to do with it? You're old enough to please yourself without asking your father. Besides, Lord bless me, the archdeacon isn't the man to bear malice. He'll storm and threaten and stop the supplies for a month or so. Then he'll double them, and take your wife to his bosom, and kiss her and bless her, and all that kind of thing. We all know what parental wrath means in such cases as that.'

'But my sister—'

'As for your sister, don't talk to me about her. I don't care two straws about your sister. You must excuse me, Major Grantly, but Lady Hartletop is really too big for my powers of vision.'

'And Edith, – of course, Mrs Thorne, I can't be blind to the fact that in many ways such a marriage would be injurious to her. No man wishes to be connected with a convicted thief.'

'No, Major Grantly ; but a man does wish to marry the girl that he loves. At least, I suppose so. And what man ever was able to give a more touching proof of his affection than you can do now ? If I were you, I'd be at Allington before twelve o'clock to-morrow, – I would indeed. What does it matter about the trumpery cheque ? Everybody knows it was a mistake, if he did take it. And surely you would not punish her for that.'

'No, – no ; but I don't suppose she'd think it a punishment.'

'You go and ask her, then. And I'll tell you what. If she hasn't a house of her own to be married from, she shall be married from Chaldicotes. We'll have such a breakfast ! And I'll make as much of her as if she were the daughter of my old friend, the bishop himself, – I will indeed.'

This was Mrs Thorne's advice. Before it was completed, Major Grantly had been carried half-way to Chaldicotes. When he left his impetuous friend he was too prudent to make any promise, but he declared that what she had said should have much weight with him.

'You won't mention it to anybody ?' said the major.

'Certainly not, without your leave,' said Mrs Thorne. 'Don't you know that I'm the soul of honour ?'

CHAPTER 15

Up in London

Some kind and attentive reader may perhaps remember that Miss Grace Crawley, in a letter written by her to her friend Miss Lily Dale, said a word or two of a certain John. 'If it can only be as John wishes it!' And the same reader, if there be one so kind and attentive, may also remember that Miss Lily Dale had declared, in reply, that 'about that other subject she would rather say nothing,' – and then she had added, 'When one thinks of going beyond friendship, – even if one tries to do so, – there are so many barriers!' From which words the kind and attentive reader, if such reader be in such matters intelligent as well as kind and attentive, may have learned a great deal with reference to Miss Lily Dale.

We will now pay a visit to the John in question, – a certain Mr John Eames, living in London, a bachelor, as the intelligent reader will certainly have discovered, and cousin to Miss Grace Crawley. Mr John Eames at the time of our story was a young man, some seven or eight and twenty years of age, living in London, where he was supposed by his friends in the country to have made his mark, and to be something a little out of the common way. But I do not know that he was very much out of the common way, except in the fact that he had had some few thousand pounds left him by an old nobleman, who had been in no way related to him; but who had regarded him with great affection, and who had died some two years since. Before this, John Eames had not been a very poor man, as he filled the comfortable official position of private secretary to the Chief Commissioner of the Income-tax Board, and drew a salary of three hundred and fifty pounds a year from the resources of his country; but when, in addition to this source of official wealth, he became known as the undoubted possessor of a hundred and twenty-eight shares in one of the most prosperous joint-stock banks in the metropolis, which property had been left to him free of legacy duty by the lamented nobleman above named, then Mr John Eames rose very high indeed as a young man in the estimation of those who knew him, and was supposed to be something a good deal out of the common way. His mother, who lived in the country, was obedient to his slightest word, never venturing to impose upon him any sign of parental authority; and to his sister, Mary Eames, who lived with her mother, he was almost a god upon earth. To sisters who have nothing of their own, – not even some special god for their own individual worship, – generous, affectionate, unmarried brothers, with sufficient incomes, are gods upon earth.

And even up in London Mr John Eames was somebody. He was so especially at his office; although, indeed, it was remembered by many a man how raw a lad he had been when he first came there, not so very many years ago; and how they had laughed at him and played him tricks; and how he had customarily been known to be without a shilling for the last week before pay-day, during which period he would borrow sixpence here and a shilling there with great energy, from men who now felt themselves to be honoured when he smiled upon them. Little stories of his former days would often be told of him behind his back; but they were not told with ill-nature, because he was very constant in referring to the same matters himself. And it was acknowledged by every one at the office, that neither the friendship of the nobleman, nor the fact of the private secretaryship, nor the acquisition of his wealth, had made him proud to his old companions or forgetful of old friend-ships. To the young men, lads who had lately been appointed, he was perhaps a little cold; but then it was only reasonable to conceive that such a one as Mr John Eames was now could not be expected to make an intimate acquaintance with every new clerk that might be brought into the office. Since competitive examin-ations had come into vogue, there was no knowing who might be introduced; and it was understood generally through the establish-ment, – and I may almost say by the civil service at large, so wide was his fame, – that Mr Eames was very averse to the whole theory of competition. The 'Devil take the hindmost' scheme, he called it; and would then go on to explain that hindmost candidates were often the best gentlemen, and that, in this way, the Devil got the pick of the flock. And he was respected the more for this opinion, because it was known that on this subject he had fought some hard battles with the chief commissioner. The chief commissioner was a great believer in competition, wrote papers about it, which he read aloud to various bodies of the civil service, – not at all to their delight, – which he got to be printed here and there, and which he sent by post all over the kingdom. More than once this chief commissioner had told his private secretary that they must part company, unless the private secretary could see fit to alter his view, or could, at least, keep his views to himself. But the private secretary would do neither; and, nevertheless, there he was, still private secretary. 'It's because Johnny has got money,' said one of the young clerks, who was discussing this singular state of things with his brethren at the office. 'When a chap has got money, he may do what he likes. Johnny has got lots of money, you know.' The young clerk in question was by no means on intimate terms with Mr Eames, but there had grown up in the office a way of calling him Johnny behind his back, which had probbaly come down from the early days of his scrapes and his poverty.

Now the entire life of Mr John Eames was pervaded by a great secret; and although he never, in those days, alluded to the subject in conversation with any man belonging to the office, yet the secret was known to them all. It had been historical for the last four or five years, and was now regarded as a thing of course. Mr John Eames was in love, and his love was not happy. He was in love, and had long been in love, and the lady of his love was not kind to him. The little history had grown to be very touching and pathetic, having received, no doubt, some embellishments from the imaginations of the gentlemen of the Income-tax Office. It was said of him that he had been in love from his early boyhood, that at sixteen he had been engaged, under the sanction of the nobleman now deceased and of the young lady's parents, that contracts of betrothals had been drawn up, and things done very unusual in private families in these days, and that then there had come a stranger into the neighbourbood just as the young lady was beginning to reflect whether she had a heart of her own or not, and that she had thrown her parents, and the noble lord, and the contract, and poor Johnny Eames to the winds, and had—Here the story took different directions, as told by different men. Some said the lady had gone off with the stranger, and that there had been a clandestine marriage, which afterwards turned out to be no marriage at all; others, that the stranger suddenly took himself off, and was no more seen by the young lady; others that he owned at last to having another wife, – and so on. The stranger was very well known to be one Mr Crosbie, belonging to another public office; and there were circumstances in his life, only half known, which gave rise to these various rumours. But there was one thing certain, one point as to which no clerk in the Income-tax Office had a doubt, one fact which had conduced much to the high position which Mr John Eames now held in the estimation of his brother clerks, – he had given this Mr Crosbie such a thrashing that no man had ever received such treatment before and had lived through it. Wonderful stories were told about that thrashing, so that it was believed, even by the least enthusiastic in such matters, that the poor victim had only dragged on a crippled existence since the encounter. 'For nine weeks he never said a word or ate a mouthful,' said one young clerk to a younger clerk who was just entering the office; 'and even now he can't speak above a whisper, and has to take all his food in pap.' It will be seen, therefore, that Mr John Eames had about him much of the heroic.

That he was still in love, and in love with the same lady, was known to every one in the office. When it was declared of him that in the way of amatory expressions he had never in his life opened his mouth to another woman, there were those in the office who knew that this was an exaggeration. Mr Cradell, for instance, who in his early years had been very intimate with John Eames, and who still kept up the old friendship, – although, being a domestic man, with a wife and six young children, and living on a small income, he did not go much out among his friends, – could have told a very different story; for Mrs Cradell herself had, in days before Cradell had made good his claim upon her, been not unadmired by Cradell's fellow-clerk. But the constancy of Mr Eames's present love was doubted by none who knew him. It was not that he went about with his stockings ungartered, or any of the old acknowledged signs of unrequited affection.* In his manner he was rather jovial than otherwise, and seemed to live a happy, somewhat luxurious life, well contented with himself and the world around him. But still he had this passion within his bosom, and I am inclined to think that he was a little proud of his own constancy.

It might be presumed that when Miss Dale wrote to her friend Grace Crawley about going beyond friendship, pleading that there were so many 'barriers,' she had probably seen her way over most of them. But this was not so; nor did John Eames himself at all believe that the barriers were in a way to be overcome. I will not say that he had given the whole thing up as a bad job, because it was the law of his life that the thing never should be abandoned as long as hope was possible. Unless Miss Dale should become the wife of somebody else, he would always regard himself as affianced to her. He had so declared to Miss Dale herself and to Miss Dale's mother, and to all the Dale people who had ever been interested in the matter. And there was an old lady living in Miss Dale's neighbourhood, the sister of the lord who had left Johnny Eames the bank shares, who always fought his battles for him, and kept a close look-out, fully resolved that John Eames should be rewarded at last. This old lady was connected with the Dales by family ties, and therefore had means of close observation. She was in constant correspondence with John Eames, and never failed to acquaint him when any of the barriers were, in her judgment, giving way. The nature of some of the barriers may possibly be made intelligible to my readers by the following letter from Lady Julia De Guest to her young friend.

Guestwick Cottage,—December, 186–.

My dear John, –

I am much obliged to you for going to Jones's. I send stamps for two shillings and fourpence, which is what I owe you. It used only to be two shillings and twopence, but they say everything has got to be dearer now, and I suppose pills as well as other things. Only think of Pritchard coming to me, and saying she wanted her wages raised, after living with me for twenty years! I was *very* angry, and scolded her roundly; but as she acknowledged she had been wrong, and cried and begged my pardon, I did give her two guineas a year more.

I saw dear Lily just for a moment on Sunday, and upon my word I think she grows prettier every year. She had a young friend with her, – a Miss Crawley, – who, I believe, is the cousin I have heard you speak of. What is this sad story about her father, the clergyman? Mind you tell me all about it.

It is quite true what I told you about the De Courcys. Old Lady De Courcy is in London, and Mr Crosbie is going to law with her about his wife's money. He has been at it in one way or the other ever since poor Lady Alexandrina died. I wish she had lived, with all my heart. For though I feel sure that our Lily will never willingly see him again, yet the tidings of her death disturbed her, and set her thinking of things that were fading from her mind. I rated her soundly, not mentioning your name, however; but she only kissed me, and told me in her quiet drolling way that I didn't mean a word of what I said.

You can come here whenever you please after the tenth of January. But if you come early in January you must go to your mother first, and come to me for the last week of your holiday. Go to Blackie's in Regent Street, and bring me down all the colours in wool that I ordered. I said you would call. And tell them at Dolland's the last spectacles don't suit at all, and I won't keep them. They had better send me down, by you, one or two more pairs to try. And you had better see Smithers and Smith, in Lincoln's Inn Fields, No 57 – but you have been there before, – and beg them to let me know how my poor dear brother's matters are to be settled at last. As far as I can see I shall be dead before I shall know what income I have got to spend. As to my cousins at the manor, I never see them; and as to talking to them about business, I should not dream of it. She hasn't come to me since she first called, and she may be *quite sure* I shan't go to her till she does. Indeed I think we shall like each other apart quite as much as we should together. So let me know when you're coming, and *pray* don't forget to call at Blackie's; nor yet at Dolland's, which is much more important than the wool, because of my eyes getting so weak. But what I want you specially to remember is about Smithers and Smith. How is a woman to live if she doesn't know how much she has got to spend?

> Believe me to be, my dear John,
> Your most sincere friend,
> Julia De Guest

Lady Julia always directed her letters for her young friend to his office, and there he received the one now given to the reader. When he had read it he made a memorandum as to the commissions, and then threw himself back in his arm-chair to think over the tidings communicated to him. All the facts stated he had known before; that Lady De Courcy was in London, and that her son-in-law, Mr Crosbie, whose wife, – Lady Alexandrina, – had died some twelve months since at Baden Baden, was at variance with her respecting money which he supposed to be due to him. But there was that in Lady Julia's letter which was wormwood to him. Lily Dale was again thinking of this man, whom she had loved in old days, and who had treated her with monstrous perfidy! It was all very well for Lady Julia to be sure that Lily Dale would never desire to see Mr Crosbie again; but John Eames was by no means equally certain that it would be so. 'The tidings of her death disturbed her!' said Johnny, repeating to himself certain words out of the old lady's letter. 'I know they disturbed me. I wish she could have lived for ever. If he ever ventures to show himself within ten miles of Allington, I'll see if I cannot do better than I did the last time I met him!' Then there came a knock at the door, and the private secretary, finding himself to be somewhat annoyed by the disturbance at such a moment, bade the intruder enter in angry voice. 'Oh, it's you, Cradell, is it? What can I do for you?' Mr Cradell, who now entered, and who, as before said, was an old ally of John Eames, was a clerk of longer standing in the department than his friend. In age he looked to be much older, and he had left with him none of that appearance of the gloss of youth which will stick for many years to men who are fortunate in their worldly affairs. Indeed it may be said that Mr Cradell was almost shabby in his outward appearance, and his brow seemed to be laden with care, and his eyes were dull and heavy.

'I thought I'd just come in and ask you how you are,' said Cradell.

'I'm pretty well, thank you; and how are you?'

'Oh, I'm pretty well, – in health, that is. You see one has so many things to think of when one has a large family. Upon my word, Johnny, I think you've been lucky to keep out of it.'

'I have kept out of it, at any rate; haven't I?'

'Of course; living with you as much as I used to do, I know the whole story of what has kept you single.'

'Don't mind about that, Cradell; what is it you want?'

'I mustn't let you suppose, Johnny, that I'm grumbling about my lot. Nobody knows better than you what a trump I got in my wife.'

'Of course you did; – an excellent woman.'

'And if I cut you out a little there, I'm sure you never felt malice against me for that.'

'Never for a moment, old fellow.'

'We all have our luck, you know.'

'Your luck has been a wife and family. My luck has been to be a bachelor.'

'You may say a family,' said Cradell. 'I'm sure that Amelia does the best she can; but we are desperately pushed some times, – desperately pushed. I never was so bad, Johnny, as I am now.'

'So you said the last time.'

'Did I? I don't remember it. I didn't think I was so bad then. But, Johnny, if you can let me have one more fiver now I have made arrangements with Amelia how I'm to pay you off by thirty shillings a month, – as I get my salary. Indeed I have. Ask her else.'

'I'll be shot if I do.'

'Don't say that, Johnny.'

'It's no good your Johnnying me, for I won't be Johnnyed out of another shilling. It comes too often, and there's no reason why I should do it. And what's more, I can't afford it. I've people of my own to help.'

'But oh, Johnny, we all know how comfortable you are. And I'm sure no one rejoiced as I did when the money was left to you. If it had been myself I could hardly have thought more of it. Upon my solemn word and honour if you'll let me have it this time, it shall be the last.'

'Upon my word and honour then, I won't. There must be an end to everything.'

Although Mr Cradell would probably, if pressed, have admitted the truth of this last assertion, he did not seem to think that the end had as yet come to his friend's benevolence. It certainly had not come to his own importunity. 'Don't say that, Johnny; pray don't.'

'But I do say it.'

'When I told Amelia yesterday evening that I didn't like to go to you again, because of course a man has feelings, she told me to mention her name. "I'm sure he'd do it for my sake," she said.'

'I don't believe she said anything of the kind.'

'Upon my word she did. You ask her.'

'And if she did, she oughtn't to have said it.'

'Oh, Johnny, don't speak in that way of her. She's my wife, and you know what your own feelings were once. But look here, – we are in that state at home at this moment, that I must get money somewhere before I go home. I must, indeed. If you'll let me have three pounds this once, I'll never ask you again. I'll give you a written promise if you like, and I'll pledge myself to pay it back by thirty shillings a time out of the two next months' salary. I will, indeed.' And then Mr Cradell began to cry. But when Johnny at last took out his cheque-book and wrote a cheque for three pounds, Mr Cradell's eyes glistened with joy. 'Upon my word I am so much obliged to you! You are the best fellow that ever lived. And Amelia will say the same when she hears of it.'

'I don't believe she'll say anything of the kind, Cradell. If I remember anything of her, she has a stouter heart than that.' Cradell admitted that his wife had a stouter heart than himself, and then made his way back to his own part of the office.

This little interruption to the current of Mr Eames's thoughts was, I think, for the good of the service, as, immediately on his friend's departure, he went to his work; whereas, had not he been thus called away from his reflections about Miss Dale, he would have sat thinking about her affairs probably for the rest of the morning. As it was, he really did write a dozen notes in answer to as many private letters addressed to his chief, Sir Raffle Buffle, in all of which he made excellently-worded false excuses for the non-performance of various requests made to Sir Raffle by the writers. 'He's about the best hand at it that I know,' said Sir Raffle, one day, to the secretary; 'otherwise you may be sure I shouldn't keep him there.' 'I will allow that he is clever,' said the secretary. 'It isn't cleverness, so much as tact. It's what I call tact. I hadn't been long in the service before I mastered it myself; and now that I've been at the trouble to teach him I don't want to have the trouble to teach another. But upon my word he must mind his *p*'s and *q*'s; upon my word he must; and you had better tell him so.' 'The fact is, Mr Kissing,' said the private secretary the next day to the secretary, – Mr Kissing was at that time secretary to the board of commissioners for the receipt of income tax – 'The fact is, Mr Kissing, Sir Raffle should never attempt to write a letter himself. He doesn't know how to do it. He always says twice too much, and yet not half enough. I wish you'd tell him so. He won't believe me.' From which it will be seen Mr Eames was proud of his special accomplishment, but did not feel any gratitude to the master who assumed to himself the glory of having taught him. On the present occasion John Eames wrote all his letters before he thought again of Lily Dale, and was able to write them without interruption, as the chairman was absent for the day at the Treasury, – or perhaps at his club. Then, when he had finished, he rang his bell, and ordered some sherry and soda-water, and stretched himself before the fire, – as though his exertions in the public service had been very great, – and seated himself comfortably in his arm-chair, and lit a cigar, and again took out Lady Julia's letter.

As regarded the cigar, it may be said that both Sir Raffle and Mr Kissing had given orders that on no account should cigars be lit within the precincts of the Income-tax Office. Mr Eames had taken upon himself to understand that such orders did not apply to a private secretary, and was well aware that Sir Raffle knew his habit. To Mr Kissing, I regret to say, he put himself in opposition whenever and wherever opposition was possible; so that men in the office said that one of the two must go at last. 'But Johnny can do anything, you know, because he has got money.' That was too frequently the opinion finally expressed among the men.

So John Eames sat down, and drank his soda-water, and smoked his cigar, and read his letter; or rather, simply that paragraph of the letter which referred to Miss Dale. 'The tidings of her death have disturbed her, and set her thinking again of things that were fading from her mind.' He understood it all. And yet how could it possibly be so? How could it be that she should not despise a man, – despise him if she did not hate him, – who had behaved as this man had behaved to her? It was now four years since this Crosbie had been engaged to Miss Dale, and had jilted her so heartlessly as to incur the disgust of every man in London who had heard the story. He had married an earl's daughter, who had left him within a few months of their marriage, and now Mr Crosbie's noble wife was dead. The wife was dead, and simply because the man was free again, he, John Eames, was to be told that Miss Dale's mind was 'disturbed,' and that her thoughts were going back to things which had faded from her memory, and which should have been long since banished altogether from such holy ground.

If Lily Dale were now to marry Mr Crosbie, anything so perversely cruel as the fate of John Eames would never yet have been told in romance. That was his own idea on the matter as he sat smoking his cigar. I have said that he was proud of his constancy, and yet, in some sort, he was also ashamed of it. He acknowledged the fact of his love, and believed himself to have out-Jacobed Jacob;* but he felt that it was hard for a man who had risen in the world as he had done to be made a plaything of by a foolish passion. It was now four years ago, – that affair of Crosbie, – and Miss Dale should have accepted him long since. Half-a-dozen times he had made up his mind to be very stern to her; and he had written somewhat sternly, – but the first moment that he saw her he was conquered again. 'And now that brute will reappear, and everything will be wrong again,' he said to himself. If the brute did reappear, something should happen of which the world should hear the tidings. So he lit another cigar, and began to think what that something should be.

As he did so he heard a loud noise, as of harsh, rattling winds in the next room, and he knew that Sir Raffle had come back from the Treasury. There was a creaking of boots, and a knocking of chairs, and a ringing of bells, and then a loud angry voice, – a voice that was very harsh, and on this occasion very angry. Why had not his twelve-o'clock letters been sent up to him to the West End? Why not? Mr Eames knew all about it. Why did Mr Eames know all about it? Why had not Mr Eames sent them up? Where was Mr Eames? Let Mr Eames be sent to him. All which Mr Eames heard standing with the cigar in his mouth and his back to the fire. 'Somebody has been bullying old Buffle, I suppose. After all he has been at the Treasury to-day,' said Eames to himself. But he did not stir till the messenger had been to him, nor even then, at once. 'All right, Rafferty,' he said; 'I'll go in just now.' Then he took half-a-dozen more whiffs from the ciagar, threw the remainder into the fire, and opened the door which communicated between his room and Sir Raffle's.

The great man was standing with two unopened epistles in his hand. 'Eames,' said he, 'here are letters—' Then he stopped himself, and began upon another subject. 'Did I not give express orders that I would have no smoking in the office?'

'I think Mr Kissing said something about it, sir.'

'Mr Kissing! It was not Mr Kissing at all. It was I. I gave the order myself.'

'You'll find it began with Mr Kissing.'

'It did not begin with Mr Kissing; it began and ended with me. What are you going to do, sir?' John Eames had stepped towards the bell, and his hand was already on the bell-pull.

'I was going to ring for the papers, sir.'

'And who told you to ring for the papers? I don't want the papers. The papers won't show anything. I suppose my word may be taken without the papers. Since you're so fond of Mr Kissing—'

'I'm not fond of Mr Kissing at all.'

'You'll have to go back to him, and let somebody come here who will not be too independent to obey my orders. Here are two most important letters have been lying here all day, instead of being sent up to me at the Treasury.'

'Of course they have been lying there. I thought you were at the club.'

'I told you I should go to the Treasury. I have been there all the morning with the chancellor,' – when Sir Raffle spoke officially of the - chancellor he was not supposed to mean the Lord Chancellor – ' and here I find letters which I particularly wanted lying upon my desk now. I must put an end to this kind of thing. I must, indeed. If you like the outer office better say so at once, and you can go.'

'I'll think about it, Sir Raffle.'

'Think about it! What do you mean by thinking about it? But I can't talk about that now. I'm very busy, and shall be here till past seven. I suppose you can stay?'

'All night, if you wish it, sir.'

'Very well. That will do for the present. – I wouldn't have had these letters delayed for twenty pounds.'

'I don't suppose it would have mattered one straw if both of them remained unopened till next week.' This last little speech, however, was not made aloud to Sir Raffle, but by Johnny to himself in the solitude of his own room.

Very soon after that he went away, Sir Raffle having discovered that one of the letters in question required his immediate return to the West End. 'I've changed my mind about staying. I shan't stay now. I should have done if these letters had reached me as they ought.'

'Then I suppose I can go?'

'You can do as you like about that,' said Sir Raffle.

Eames did do as he liked, and went home, or to his club; and as he went he resolved that he would put an end, and at once, to the present trouble of his life. Lily Dale should accept him or reject him; and, taking either the one or the other alternative, she should hear a bit of his mind plainly spoken.

CHAPTER 16

Down at Allington

It was Christmas-time down at Allington, and at three o'clock on Christmas Eve, just as the darkness of the early winter evening was coming on, Lily Dale and Grace Crawley were seated together, one above the other, on the steps leading up to the pulpit in Allington Church. They had been working all day at the decorations of the church, and they were now looking round them at the result of their handiwork. To an eye unused to the gloom the place would have been nearly dark; but they could see every corner turned by the ivy sprigs, and every line on which the holly-leaves were shining. And the greeneries of the winter had not been stuck up in the old-fashioned, idle way, a bough just fastened up here and a twig inserted there; but everything had been done with some meaning, with some thought towards the original architecture of the building. The Gothic lines had been followed, and all the lower arches which it had been possible to reach with an ordinary ladder had been turned as truly with the laurel cuttings as they had been turned originally with the stone.

'I wouldn't tie another twig,' said the elder girl, 'for all the Christmas pudding that was ever boiled.'

'It's lucky then that there isn't another twig to tie.'

'I don't know about that. I see a score of places where the work has been scamped. This is the sixth time I have done the church, and I don't think I'll ever do it again. When we first began it, Bell and I, you know, – before Bell was married, – Mrs Boyce, and the Boycian establishment generally, used to come and help. Or rather we used to help her. Now she hardly ever looks after it at all.'

'She is older, I suppose.'

'She's a little older, and a deal idler. How idle people do get! Look at him. Since he has had a curate he hardly ever stirs round the parish. And he is getting so fat that—H – sh! Here she is herself, – come to give her judgment upon us.' Then a stout lady, the wife of the vicar, walked slowly up the aisle. 'Well, girls,' she said, 'you have worked hard, and I am sure Mr Boyce will be very much obliged to you.'

'Mr Boyce, indeed!' said Lily Dale. 'We shall expect the whole parish to rise from their seats and thank us. Why didn't Jane and Bessy come and help us?'

'They were so tired when they came in from the coal club. Besides, they don't care for this kind of thing, – not as you do.'

'Jane is utilitarian* to the backbone, I know,' said Lily, 'and Bessy doesn't like getting up ladders.'

'As for ladders,' said Mrs Boyce, defending her daughter, 'I am not quite sure that Bessy isn't right. You don't mean to say that you did all those in the capitals yourself?'

'Every twig, with Hopkins to hold the ladder and cut the sticks; and as Hopkins is just a hundred and one years old, we could have done it pretty nearly as well alone.'

'I do not think that,' said Grace.

'He has been grumbling all the time,' said Lily, 'and swears he never will have the laurels so robbed again. Five or six years ago he used to declare that death would certainly save him from the pain of such another desecration before the next Christmas; but he has given up that foolish notion now, and talks as though he meant to protect the Allington shrubs at any rate to the end of this century.'

'I am sure we gave our share from the parsonage,' said Mrs Boyce, who never understood a joke.

'All the best came from the parsonage, as of course they ought,' said Lily. 'But Hopkins had to make up the deficiency. And as my uncle told him to take the haycart for them instead of the hand-barrow, he is broken-hearted.'

'I am sure he was very good-natured,' said Grace.

'Nevertheless he is broken-hearted; and I am very good-natured too, and I am broken-backed. Who is going to preach to-morrow morning, Mrs Boyce?'

'Mr Swanton will preach in the morning.'

'Tell him not to be long, because of the children's pudding. Tell Mr Boyce if he is long, we won't any of us come next Sunday.'

'My dear, how can you say such wicked things! I shall not tell him anything of the kind.'

'That's not wicked, Mrs Boyce. If I were to say I had eaten so much lunch that I didn't want any dinner, you'd understand that. If Mr Swanton will preach for three-quarters of an hour once—'

'He only preached for three-quarters of an hour once, Lily.'

'He has been over the half-hour every Sunday since he has been here. His average is over forty minutes, and I say it's a shame.'

'It is not a shame at all, Lily,' said Mrs Boyce, becoming very serious.

'Look at my uncle; he doesn't like to go to sleep, and he has to suffer a purgatory in keeping himself awake.'

'If your uncle is heavy, how can Mr Swanton help it? If Mr Dale's mind were on the subject he would not sleep.'

'Come, Mrs Boyce; there's somebody else sleeps sometimes besides my uncle. When Mr Boyce puts up his finger and just touches his nose, I know as well as possible why he does it.'

'Lily Dale, you have no business to say so. It is not true. I don't know how you can bring yourself to talk in that way of your own clergyman. If I were to tell your mamma she would be shocked.'

'You won't be so ill-natured, Mrs Boyce, – after all that I've done for the church.'

'If you'd think more about the clergyman, Lily, and less about the church,' said Mrs Boyce very sententiously, 'more about the matter and less about the manner, more of the reality and less of the form, I think you'd find that your religion would go further with you. Miss Crawley is the daughter of a clergyman, and I'm sure she'll agree with me.'

'If she agrees with anybody in scolding me I'll quarrel with her.'

'I didn't mean to scold you, Lily.'

'I don't mind it from you, Mrs Boyce. Indeed, I rather like it. It is a sort of pastoral visitation; and as Mr Boyce never scolds me himself, of course I take it as coming from him by attorney.' Then there was silence for a minute or two, during which Mrs Boyce was endeavouring to discover whether Miss Dale was laughing at her or not. As she was not quite certain, she thought at last that she would let the suspected fault pass unobserved. 'Don't wait for us, Mrs Boyce,' said Lily. 'We must remain till Hopkins has sent Gregory to sweep the church out and take away the rubbish. We'll see that the key is left at Mrs Giles's.'

'Thank you, my dear. Then I may as well go. I thought I'd come in and see that it was all right. I'm sure Mr Boyce will be very much obliged to you and Miss Crawley. Good-night, my dear.'

'Good-night, Mrs Boyce; and be sure you don't let Mr Swanton be long to-morrow.' To this parting shot Mrs Boyce made no rejoinder; but she hurried out of the church somewhat the quicker for it, and closed the door after her with something of a slam.

Of all persons clergymen are the most irreverent in the handling of things supposed to be sacred, and next to them clergymen's wives, and after them those other ladies, old or young, who take upon themselves semi-clerical duties. And it is natural that it should be so; for is it not said that familiarity does breed contempt? When a parson takes his lay friend over his church on a week day, how much less of the spirit of genuflexion and head-uncovering the clergyman will display than the layman! The parson pulls about the woodwork and knocks about the stonework, as though it were mere wood and stone; and talks aloud in the aisle, and treats even the reading-desk as a common thing; whereas the visitor whispers gently, and carries himself as though even in looking at a church he was bound to regard himself as performing some service that was half divine. Now Lily Dale and Grace Crawley were both accustomed to churches, and had been so long at work in this church for the last two days, that the building had lost to them much of its sacredness, and they were almost as irreverent as though they were two curates.

'I am so glad she has gone,' said Lily. 'We shall have to stop here for the next hour, as Gregory won't know what to take away and what to leave. I was so afraid she was going to stop and see us off the premises.'

'I don't know why you should dislike her.'

'I don't dislike her. I like her very well,' said Lily Dale. 'But don't you feel that there are people whom one knows very intimately, who are really friends, – for whom if they were dying one would grieve, whom if they were in misfortune one would go far to help, but with whom for all that one can have no sympathy. And yet they are so near to one that they know all the events of one's life, and are justified by unquestioned friendship in talking about things which should never be mentioned except where sympathy exists.'

'Yes; I understand that.'

'Everybody understands it who has been unhappy. That woman sometimes says things to me that make me wish, – wish that they'd make him bishop of Patagonia. And yet she does it all in friendship, and mamma says that she is quite right.'

'I liked her for standing up for her husband.'

'But he does go to sleep, – and then he scratches his nose to show that he's awake. I shouldn't have said it, only she is always hinting at Uncle Christopher. Uncle Christopher certainly does go to sleep when Mr Boyce preaches, and he hasn't studied any scientific little movements during his slumbers to make the people believe that he's all alive. I gave him a hint one day, and he got so angry with me!'

'I shouldn't have thought he could have been angry with you. It seems to me from what you say that you may do whatever you please with him.'

'He is very good to me. If you knew it all, – if you could understand how good he has been! I'll try and tell you some day. It is not what he has done that makes me love him so, – but what he has thoroughly understood, and what, so understanding, he has not done, and what he has not said. It is a case of sympathy. If ever there was a gentleman Uncle Christopher is one. And I used to dislike him so, at one time!'

'And why?'

'Chiefly because he would make me wear brown frocks when I wanted to have them pink or green. And he kept me for six months from having them long, and up to this day he scolds me if there is half an inch on the ground for him to tread upon.'

'I shouldn't mind that if I were you.'

'I don't, – not now. But it used to be serious when I was a young girl. And we thought, Bell and I, that he was cross to mamma. He and mamma didn't agree at first, you know, as they do now. It is quite true that he did dislike mamma when we first came here.'

'I can't think how anybody could ever dislike Mrs Dale.'

'But he did. And then he wanted to make up a marriage between Bell and my cousin Bernard. But neither of them cared a bit for the other, and then he used to scold them, – and then, – and then, – and then – Oh, he was so good to me! Here's Gregory at last. Gregory, we've been waiting this hour and a half.'

'It ain't ten minutes since Hopkins let me come with the barrows, miss.'

'Then Hopkins is a traitor. Never mind. You'd better begin now, – up there at the steps. It'll be quite dark in a few minutes. Here's Mrs Giles with her broom. Come, Mrs Giles; we shall have to pass the night here if you don't make haste. Are you cold, Grace?'

'No; I'm not cold. I'm thinking what they are doing now in the church at Hogglestock.'

'The Hogglesock church is not pretty; – like this?'

'Oh, no. It is a very plain brick building, with something like a pigeon-house for a belfry. And the pulpit is over the reading-desk, and the reading-desk over the clerk, so that papa, when he preaches, is nearly up to the ceiling. And the whole place is divided into pews, in which the farmers hide themselves when they come to church.'

'So that nobody can see whether they go to sleep or no. Oh, Mrs Giles, you mustn't pull that down. That's what we have been putting up all day.'

'But it be in the way, miss; so that the minister can't budge in or out o' the door.'

'Never mind. Then he must stay one side or the other. That would be too much after all our trouble!' And Miss Dale hurried across the chancel to save some prettily arching boughs, which, in the judgment of Mrs Giles, encroached too much on the vestry door. 'As if it signified which side he was,' she said in a whisper to Grace.

'I don't suppose they'll have anything in the church at home,' said Grace.

'Somebody will stick up a wreath or two, I daresay.'

'Nobody will. There never is anybody at Hogglestock to stick up wreaths, or to do anything for the prettinesses of life. And now there will be less done than ever. How can mamma look after holly-leaves in her present state ? And yet she will miss them, too. Poor mamma sees very little that is pretty ; but she has not forgotten how pleasant pretty things are.'

'I wish I knew your mother, Grace.'

'I think it would be impossible for any one to know mamma now, – for any one who had not known her before. She never makes even a new acquaintance. She seems to think that there is nothing left for her in the world but to try and keep papa out of misery. And she does not succeed in that. Poor papa !'

'Is he very unhappy about this wicked accusation ?'

'Yes ; he is very unhappy. But, Lily, I don't know about its being wicked.'

'But you know that it is untrue.'

'Of course I know that papa did not mean to take anything that was not his own. But, you see, nobody knows where it came from ; and nobody except mamma and Jane and I understand how very absent papa can be. I'm sure he doesn't know the least in the world how he came by it himself, or he would tell mamma. Do you know, Lily, I think I have been wrong to come away.'

'Don't say that, dear. Remember how anxious Mrs Crawley was that you should come.'

'But I cannot bear to be comfortable here while they are so wretched at home. It seems such a mockery. Every time I find myself smiling at what you say to me, I think I must be the most heartless creature in the world.'

'Is it so very bad with them, Grace ?'

'Indeed it is bad. I don't think you can imagine what mamma has to go through. She has to cook all that is eaten in the house, and then, very often, there is no money in the house to buy anything. If you were to see the clothes she wears, even that would make your heart bleed. I who have been used to being poor all my life, – even I, when I am at home, am dismayed by what she has to endure.'

'What can we do for her, Grace ?'

'You can do nothing, Lily. But when things are like that at home you can understand what I feel in being here.'

Mrs Giles and Gregory had now completed their task, or had so nearly done so as to make Miss Dale think that she might safely leave the church. 'We will go in now,' she said; 'for it is dark and cold, and what I call creepy. Do you ever fancy that perhaps you will see a ghost some day?'

'I don't think I shall ever see a ghost; but all the same I should be half afraid to be here alone in the dark.'

'I am often here alone in the dark, but I am beginning to think I shall never see a ghost now. I am losing all my romance, and getting to be an old woman. Do you know, Grace, I do so hate myself for being such an old maid.'

'But who says you're an old maid, Lily?'

'I see it in people's eyes, and hear it in their voices. And they all talk to me as if I were very steady, and altogether removed from anything like fun and frolic. It seems to be admitted that if a girl does not want to fall in love, she ought not to care for any other fun in the world. If anybody made out a list of the old ladies in these parts, they'd put down Lady Julia, and mamma, and Mrs Boyce, and me, and old Mrs Hearne. The very children have an awful respect for me, and give over playing directly they see me. Well, mamma, we've done at last, and I have had such a scolding from Mrs Boyce.'

'I daresay you deserved it, my dear.'

'No, I did not, mamma. Ask Grace if I did.'

'Was she not saucy to Mrs Boyce, Miss Crawley?'

'She said that Mr Boyce scratches his nose in church,' said Grace.

'So he does; and goes to sleep, too.'

'If you told Mrs Boyce that, Lily, I think she was quite right to scold you.'

Such was Miss Lily Dale, with whom Grace Crawley was staying; – Lily Dale with whom Mr John Eames, of the Income-tax Office; had been so long and so steadily in love, that he was regarded among his fellow-clerks as a miracle of constancy, – who had, herself, in former days been so unfortunate in love as to have been regarded among her friends in the country as the most ill-used of women. As John Eames had been able to be comfortable in life, – that is to say, not utterly a wretch, – in spite of his love, so had she managed to hold up her head, and live as other young women live, in spite of her misfortune. But as it may be said also that his constancy was true constancy, although he knew how to enjoy the good things of the world, so also had her misfortune been a true misfortune, although she had been able to bear it without much outer show of shipwreck. For a few days, – for a week or two, when the blow first struck her, she had been knocked down, and the friends who were nearest to her had thought that she would never again stand erect upon her feet. But she had been very strong, stout at heart, of a fixed purpose, and capable of resistance against oppression. Even her own mother had been astonished, and sometimes almost dismayed, by the strength of her will. Her mother knew well how it was with her now; but they who saw her frequently, and who did not know her as her mother knew her, – the Mrs Boyces of her acquaintance, – whispered among themselves that Lily Dale was not so soft of heart as people used to think.

On the next day, Christmas Day, as the reader will remember, Grace Crawley was taken up to dine at the big house with the old squire. Mrs Dale's eldest daughter, with her husband, Dr Crofts, was to be there; and also Lily's old friend, who was also especially the old friend of Johnny Eames, Lady Julia De Guest. Grace had endeavoured to be excused from the party, pleading many pleas. But the upshot of all her pleas was this, – that while her father's position was so painful she ought not to go out anywhere. In answer to this, Lily Dale, corroborated by her mother, assured her that for her father's sake she ought not to exhibit any such feeling; that in doing so, she would seem to express a doubt as to her father's innocence. Then she allowed herself to be persuaded, telling her friend, however, that she knew the day would be very miserable to her. 'It will be very humdrum, if you please,' said Lily. 'Nothing can be more humdrum than Christmas at the Great House. Nevertheless, you must go.'

Coming out of church, Grace was introduced to the old squire. He was a thin, old man, with grey hair, and the smallest possible grey whiskers, with a dry, solemn face; not carrying in his outward gait much of the customary jollity of Christmas. He took his hat off to Grace, and said some word to her as to hoping to have the pleasure of seeing her at dinner. It sounded very cold to her, and she became at once afraid of him. 'I wish I was not going,' she said to Lily, again. 'I know he thinks I ought not to go. I shall be so thankful if you will but let me stay.'

'Don't be foolish, Grace. It all comes from your not knowing him, or understanding him. And how should you understand him? I give you my word that I would tell you if I did not know that he wishes you to go.'

She had to go. 'Of course I haven't a dress fit. How should I?' she said to Lily. 'How wrong it is of me to put myself up to such a thing as this.'

'Your dress is beautiful, child. We are none of us going in evening dresses. Pray believe that I will not make you do wrong. If you won't trust me, can't you trust mamma?'

Of course she went. When the three ladies entered the drawing-room of the Great House they found that Lady Julia had arrived just before them. Lady Julia immediately took hold of Lily, and led her apart, having a word or two to say about the clerk in the Income-tax Office. I am not sure but what the dear old woman sometimes said a few more words than were expedient, with a view to the object which she had so closely at heart. 'John is to be with us the first week in February,' she said. 'I suppose you'll see him before that, as he'll probably be with his mother a few days before he comes to me.'

'I daresay we shall see him quite in time, Lady Julia,' said Lily.

'Now, Lily, don't be ill-natured.'

'I'm the most good-natured young woman alive, Lady Julia, and as for Johnny, he is always made as welcome at the Small House as violets in March. Mamma purrs about him when he comes, asking all manner of flattering questions as though he were a cabinet minister at least, and I always admire some little knicknack that he has got, a new ring, or a stud, or a button. There isn't another man in all the world whose buttons I'd look at.'

'It isn't his buttons, Lily.'

'Ah, that's just it. I can go as far as his buttons. But come, Lady Julia, this is Christmas-time, and Christmas should be a holiday.'

In the meantime Mrs Dale was occupied with her married daughter and her son-in-law, and the squire had attached himself to poor Grace. 'You have never been in this part of the country before, Miss Crawley,' he said.

'No, sir.'

'It is rather pretty just about here, and Guestwick Manor is a fine place in its way, but we have not so much natural beauty as you have in Barsetshire. Chaldicote Chase is, I think, as pretty as anything in England.'

'I never saw Chaldicote Chase, sir. It isn't pretty at all at Hogglestock, where we live.'

'Ah, I forgot. No; it is not very pretty at Hogglestock. That's where the bricks come from.'

'Papa is clergyman at Hogglestock.'

'Yes, yes; I remember. Your father is a great scholar. I have often heard of him. I am so sorry he should be distressed by this charge they have made. But it will all come right at the assizes. They always get at the truth there. I used to be intimate with a clergyman in Barsetshire of the name of Grantly;' – Grace felt that her ears were tingling, and that her face was red; – 'Archdeacon Grantly. His father was bishop of the diocese.'

'Yes, sir. Archdeacon Grantly lives at Plumstead.'

'I was staying once with an old friend of mine, Mr Thorne of

Ullathorne, who lives close to Plumstead, and saw a good deal of them. I remember thinking Henry Grantly was a very nice lad. He married afterwards.'

'Yes, sir; but his wife is dead now, and he has got a little girl, – Edith Grantly.'

'Is there no other child?'

'No, sir; only Edith.'

'You know him, then?'

'Yes, sir; I know Major Grantly, – and Edith. I never saw Archdeacon Grantly.'

'Then, my dear, you never saw a very famous pillar of the church. I remember when people used to talk a great deal about Archdeacon Grantly; but when his time came to be made a bishop, he was not sufficiently new-fangled; and so he got passed by. He is much better off as he is, I should say. Bishops have to work very hard, my dear.'

'Do they, sir?'

'So they tell me. And the archdeacon is a wealthy man. So Henry Grantly has got an only daughter? I hope she is a nice child, for I remember liking him well.'

'She is a very nice child, indeed, Mr Dale. She could not be nicer. And she is so lovely.' Then Mr Dale looked into his young companion's face, struck by the sudden animation of her words, and perceived for the first time that she was very pretty.

After this Grace became accustomed to the strangeness of the faces round her, and managed to eat her dinner without much perturbation of spirit. When after dinner the squire proposed to her that they should drink the health of her papa and mamma, she was almost reduced to tears, and yet she liked him for doing it. It was terrible to her to have them mentioned, knowing as she did that every one who mentioned them must be aware of their misery, – for the misfortune of her father had become notorious in the country; but it was almost more terrible to her that no allusion should be made to them; for then she would be driven to think that her father was regarded as a man whom the world could not afford to mention. 'Papa and mamma,' she just murmured, raising her glass to her lips. 'Grace, dear,' said Lily from across the table, 'here's papa and mamma, and the young man at Marlborough who is carrying everything before him.' 'Yes; we won't forget the young man at Marlborough,' said the squire. Grace felt this to be good-natured, because her brother at Marlborough was the one bright spot in her family, – and she was comforted.

'And we will drink the health of my friend, John Eames,' said Lady Julia.

'John Eames's health,' said the squire, in a low voice.

'Johnny's health,' said Mrs Dale; but Mrs Dale's voice was not very brisk.

'John's health,' said Dr Crofts and Mrs Crofts in a breath.

'Here's the health of Johnny Eames,' said Lily; and her voice was the clearest and the boldest of them all. But she made up her mind that if Lady Julia could not be induced to spare her for the future, she and Lady Julia must quarrel. 'No one can understand,' she said to her mother that evening, 'how dreadful it is, – this being constantly told before one's family and friends that one ought to marry a certain young man.'

'She didn't say that, my dear.'

'I should much prefer that she should, for then I could get up on my legs and answer her off the reel.'* Of course everybody there understood what she meant, – including old John Bates, who stood at the sideboard and coolly drank the toast himself.

'He always does that to all the family toasts on Christmas Day. Your uncle likes it.'

'That wasn't a family toast, and John Bates had no right to drink it.'

After dinner they all played cards, – a round game, – and the squire put in the stakes. 'Now, Grace,' said Lily, 'you are the visitor and you must win, or else Uncle Christopher won't be happy. He always likes a young lady visitor to win.'

'But I never played a game of cards in my life.'

'Go and sit next to him and he'll teach you. Uncle Christopher, won't you teach Grace Crawley? She never saw a Pope Joan board* in her life before.'

'Come here, my dear, and sit next to me. Dear, dear, dear; fancy Henry Grantly having a little girl. What a handsome lad he was. And it seems only yesterday.' If it was so that Lily had said a word to her uncle about Grace and the major, the old squire had become on a sudden very sly. Be that as it may, Grace Crawley thought that he was a pleasant old man; and though, while talking to him about Edith, she persisted in not learning to play Pope Joan, so that he could not contrive that she should win, nevertheless the squire took to her very kindly, and told her to come up with Lily and see him sometimes while she was staying at the Small House. The squire in speaking of his sister-in-law's cottage always called it the Small House.

'Only think of my winning,' said Lady Julia, drawing together her wealth. 'Well, I'm sure I want it bad enough, for I don't at all know whether I've got any income of my own. It's all John Eames's fault, my dear, for he won't go and make those people settle it in Lincoln's Inn Fields.' Poor Lily, who was standing on the hearth-rug, touched her mother's arm. She knew that Johnny's name was lugged in with reference to Lady Julia's money altogether for her benefit. 'I wonder whether she ever had a Johnny of her own,' she said to her mother, 'and, if so, whether she liked it when her friends sent the town-crier round to talk about him.'

'She means to be good-natured,' said Mrs Dale.

'Of course she does. But it is such a pity when people won't understand.'

'My uncle didn't bite you after all, Grace,' said Lily to her friend as they were going home at night, by the pathway which led from the garden of one house to the garden of the other.

'I like Mr Dale very much,' said Grace. 'He was very kind to me.'

'There is some queer-looking animal of whom they say that he is better than he looks, and I always think of that saying when I think of my uncle.'

'For shame, Lily,' said her mother. 'Your uncle, for his age, is as good a looking man as I know. And he always looks like just what he is, – an English gentleman.'

'I didn't mean to say a word against his dear old face and figure, mamma; but his heart, and mind, and general disposition, as they come out in experience and days of trial, are so much better than the samples of them which he puts out on the counter for men and women to judge by. He wears well, and he washes well, – if you know what I mean, Grace.'

'Yes; I think I know what you mean.'

'The Apollos of the world, – I don't mean in outward looks, mamma, – but the Apollos in heart, the men – and the women too, – who are so full of feeling, so soft-natured, so kind, who never say a cross word, who never get out of bed on the wrong side in the morning, – it so often turns out that they won't wash.'

Such was the expression of Miss Lily Dale's experience.

CHAPTER 17

Mr Crawley is summoned to Barchester

The scene which occurred in Hogglestock church on the Sunday after Mr Thumble's first visit to that parish had not been described with absolute accuracy either by the archdeacon in his letter to his son, or by Mrs Thorne. There had been no footman from the palace in attendance on Mr Thumble, nor had there been a battle with the brickmakers; neither had Mr Thumble been put under the pump. But Mr Thumble had gone over, taking his gown and surplice with him, on the Sunday morning, and had intimated to Mr Crawley his intention of performing the service. Mr Crawley, in answer to this, had assured Mr Thumble that he would not be allowed to open his mouth in the church; and Mr Thumble, not seeing his way to any further successful action, had contented himself with attending the services in his surplice, making thereby a silent protest that he, and not Mr Crawley, ought to have been in the reading-desk and the pulpit.

When Mr Thumble reported himself and his failure at the palace, he strove hard to avoid seeing Mrs Proudie, but not successfully. He knew something of the palace habits, and did manage to reach the bishop alone on the Sunday evening, justifying himself to his lordship for such an interview by the remarkable circumstances of the case and the importance of his late mission. Mrs Proudie always went to church on Sunday evenings, making a point of hearing three services and three sermons every Sunday of her life. On weekdays she seldom heard any, having an idea that week-day services were an invention of the High Church enemy, and that they should therefore be vehemently discouraged. Services on saints' days she regarded as rank papacy, and had been known to accuse a clergyman's wife, to her face, of idolatry, because the poor lady had dated a letter, St John's Eve. Mr Thumble, on this Sunday evening, was successful in finding the bishop at home, and alone, but he was not lucky enough to get away before Mrs Proudie returned. The bishop, perhaps, thought that the story of the failure had better reach his wife's ears from Mr Thumble's lips than from his own.

'Well, Mr Thumble?' said Mrs Proudie, walking into the study, armed in her full Sunday-evening winter panoply, in which she had just descended from her carriage. The church which Mrs Proudie attended in the evening was nearly half a mile from the palace, and the coachman and groom never got a holiday on Sunday night. She was gorgeous in a dark brown silk dress of awful stiffness and terrible dimensions; and on her shoulders she wore a short cloak of velvet and fur, very handsome withal, but so swelling in its proportions on all sides as necessarily to create more of dismay than of admiration in the mind of any ordinary man. And her bonnet was a monstrous helmet with the beaver up, displaying the awful face of the warrior, always ready for combat, and careless to guard itself from attack. The large contorted bows which she bore were as a grisly crest upon her casque, beautiful, doubtless, but majestic and fear-compelling. In her hand she carried her armour all complete, a prayer-book, a bible, and a book of hymns. These the footman had brought for her to the study door, but she had thought fit to enter her husband's room with them in her own custody.

'Well, Mr Thumble!' she said.

Mr Thumble did not answer at once, thinking, probably, that the bishop might choose to explain the circumstances. But, neither did the bishop say any thing.

'Well, Mr Thumble?' she said again; and then she stood looking at the man who had failed so disastrously.

'I have explained to the bishop,' said he. 'Mr Crawley has been contumacious, – very contumacious indeed.'

'But you preached at Hogglestock?'

'No, indeed, Mrs Proudie. Nor would it have been possible, unless I had had the police to assist me.'

'Then you should have had the police. I never heard of anything so mismanaged in all my life, – never in all my life.' And she put her books down on the study table, and turned herself round from Mr Thumble towards the bishop. 'If things go on like this, my lord,' she said, 'your authority in the diocese will very soon be worth nothing at all.' It was not often that Mrs Proudie called her husband my lord, but when she did do so, it was a sign that terrible times had come; – times so terrible that the bishop would know that he must either fight or fly. He would almost endure anything rather than descend into the arena for the purpose of doing battle with his wife, but occasions would come now and again when even the alternative of flight was hardly left to him.

'But, my dear,—' began the bishop.

'Am I to understand that this man has professed himself to be altogether indifferent to the bishop's prohibition?' said Mrs Proudie, interrupting her husband and addressing Mr Thumble.

'Quite so. He seemed to think that the bishop had no lawful power in the matter at all,' said Mr Thumble.

'Do you hear that, my lord?' said Mrs Proudie.

'Nor have I any,' said the bishop, almost weeping as he spoke.

'No authority in your own diocese!'

'None to silence a man merely by my own judgment. I thought, and still think, that it was for this gentleman's own interest, as well as for the credit of the Church, that some provision should be made for his duties during his present, – present – difficulties.'

'Difficulties indeed! Everybody knows that the man has been a thief.'

'No, my dear; I do not know it.'

'You never know anything, bishop.'

'I mean to say that I do not know it officially. Of course I have heard the sad story; and, though I hope it may not be the—'

'There is no doubt about its truth. All the world knows it. He has stolen twenty pounds, and yet he is to be allowed to desecrate the Church, and imperil the souls of the people!' The bishop got up from his chair and began to walk backwards and forwards through the room with short quick steps. 'It only wants five days to Christmas Day,' continued Mrs Proudie, 'and something must be done at once. I say nothing as to the propriety or impropriety of his being out on bail, as it is no affair of ours. When I heard that he had been bailed by a beneficed clergyman of this diocese, of course I knew where to look for the man who would act with so much impropriety. Of course I was not surprised when I found that that person belonged to Framley. But, as I have said before, that is no business of ours. I hope, Mr Thumble, that the bishop will never be found interfering with the ordinary laws of the land. I am very sure that he will never do so by my advice. But when there comes a question of inhibiting a clergyman who has committed himself as this clergyman unfortunately has done, then I say that that clergyman ought to be inhibited.' The bishop walked up and down the room throughout the whole of this speech, but gradually his steps became quicker, and his turns became shorter. 'And now here is Christmas Day upon us, and what is to be done?' With these words Mrs Proudie finished her speech.

'Mr Thumble,' said the bishop, 'perhaps you had better now retire. I am very sorry that you should have had so thankless and so disagreeable a task.'

'Why should Mr Thumble retire?' asked Mrs Proudie.

'I think it better,' said the bishop. 'Mr Thumble, good night.' Then Mr Thumble did retire, and Mrs Proudie stood forth in her full panoply of armour, silent and awful, with her helmet erect, and vouchsafed no recognition whatever of the parting salutation with which Mr Thumble greeted her. 'My dear, the truth is, you do not understand the matter,' said the bishop as soon as the door was closed. 'You do not know how limited is my power.'

'Bishop, I understand it a great deal better than some people; and I understand also what is due to myself and the manner in which I ought to be treated by you in the presence of the subordinate clergy of the diocese. I shall not, however, remain here to be insulted either in the presence or in the absence of any one.' Then the conquered amazon collected together the weapons which she had laid upon the table, and took her departure with majestic step, and not without the clang of arms. The bishop, when he was left alone, enjoyed for a few moments the triumph of his victory.

But then he was left so very much alone! When he looked round about him upon his solitude after the departure of his wife, and remembered that he should not see her again till he should encounter her on ground that was all her own, he regretted his own success, and was tempted to follow her and to apologize. He was unable to do anything alone. He would not even know how to get his tea, as the very servants would ask questions, if he were to do so unaccustomed a thing as to order it to be brought up to him in his solitude. They would tell him that Mrs Proudie was having tea in her little sitting-room upstairs, or else that the things were laid in the drawing-room. He did wander forth to the latter apartment, hoping that he might find his wife there; but the drawing-room was dark and deserted, and so he wandered back again. It was a grand thing certainly to have triumphed over his wife, and there was a crumb of comfort in the thought that he had vindicated himself before Mr Thumble; but the general result was not comforting, and he knew from of old how short-lived his triumph would be.

But wretched as he was during that evening he did employ himself with some energy. After much thought he resolved that he would again write to Mr Crawley, and summon him to appear at the palace. In doing this he would at any rate be doing something. There would be action. And though Mr Crawley would, as he thought, decline to obey the order, something would be gained even by that disobedience. So he wrote his summons, – sitting very comfortless and all alone on that Sunday evening, – dating his letter, however, for the following day: –

Palace, December 20, 186–

Reverend Sir,

I have just heard from Mr Thumble that you have declined to
accede to the advice which I thought it my duty to tender to you as
the bishop who has been set over you by the Church, and that you
yesterday insisted on what you believed to be your right, to
administer the services in the parish church of Hogglestock. This
has occasioned me the deepest regret. It is, I think, unavailing that I
should further write to you my mind upon the subject, as I possess
such strong evidence that my written word will not be respected by
you. I have, therefore, no alternative now but to invite you to come
to me here; and this I do, hoping that I may induce you to listen to
that authority which I cannot but suppose you acknowledge to be
vested in the office which I hold.

I shall be glad to see you on to-morrow, Tuesday, as near the
hour of two as you can make it convenient to yourself to be here,
and I will take care to order that refreshment shall be provided for
yourself and your horse.

I am, Reverend Sir,
&c. &c. &c.,
Thos. Barnum.

'My dear,' he said, when he did again encounter his wife that
night, 'I have written to Mr Crawley, and I thought I might as well
bring up the copy of my letter.'

'I wash my hands of the whole affair,' said Mrs Proudie – 'of the
whole affair!'

'But you will look at the letter?'

'Certainly not. Why should I look at the letter? My word goes
for nothing. I have done what I could, but in vain. Now let us see
how you will manage it yourself.'

The bishop did not pass a comfortable night; but in the morning
his wife did read his letter, and after that things went a little
smoother with him. She was pleased to say that, considering all
things; seeing, as she could not help seeing, that the matter had
been dreadfully mismanaged, and that great weakness had been
displayed; – seeing that these faults had already been committed,
perhaps no better step could now be taken than that proposed in
the letter.

'I suppose he will not come,' said the bishop.

'I think he will,' said Mrs Proudie, 'and I trust that we may be
able to convince him that obedience will be his best course. He will
be more humble-minded here than at Hogglestock.' In saying this

the lady showed some knowledge of the general nature of clergymen and of the world at large. She understood how much louder a cock can crow in its own farmyard than elsewhere, and knew that episcopal authority, backed by all the solemn awe of palatial grandeur, goes much further than it will do when sent under the folds of an ordinary envelope. But though she understood ordinary human nature, it may be that she did not understand Mr Crawley's nature.

But she was at any rate right in her idea as to Mr Crawley's immediate reply. The palace groom who rode over to Hogglestock returned with an immediate answer.

My Lord – said Mr Crawley.

I will obey your lordship's summons, and, unless impediments should arise, I will wait upon your lordship at the hour you name to-morrow. I will not trespass on your hospitality. For myself, I rarely break bread in any house but my own; and as to the horse, I have none.

I have the honour to be,

> My Lord, &c. &c.,
>   Josiah Crawley.

'Of course I shall go,' he had said to his wife as soon as he had had time to read the letter, and make known to her the contents. 'I shall go if it be possible for me to get there. I think that I am bound to comply with the bisop's wishes in so much as that.'

'But how will you get there, Josiah?'

'I will walk, – with the Lord's aid.'

Now Hogglestock was fifteen miles from Barchester, and Mr Crawley was, as his wife well knew, by no means fitted in his present state for great physical exertion. But from the tone in which he had replied to her, she well knew that it would not avail for her to remonstrate at the moment. He had walked more than thirty miles in a day since they had been living at Hogglestock, and she did not doubt but that it might be possible for him to do it again. Any scheme, which she might be able to devise for saving him from so terrible a journey in the middle of winter, must be pondered over silently, and brought to bear, if not slyly, at least deftly, and without discussion. She made no reply therefore when he declared that on the following day he would walk to Barchester and back, – with the Lord's aid; nor did she see, or ask to see the note which he sent to the bishop. When the messenger was gone, Mr Crawley was all alert, looking forward with evident glee to his encounter with the bishop, – snorting like a racehorse at the expected triumph of the coming struggle. And he read much Greek with Jane on that afternoon, pouring into her young ears, almost with joyous rapture, his appreciation of the glory and the pathos and the humanity, as also of the awful tragedy, of the story of Oedipus.* His very soul was on fire at the idea of clutching the weak bishop in his hand, and crushing him with his strong grasp.

In the afternoon Mrs Crawley slipped out to a neighbouring farmer's wife, and returned in an hour's time with a little story which she did not tell with any appearance of eager satisfaction. She had learned well what were the little tricks necessary to the carrying of such a matter as that which she had now in hand. Mr Mangle, the farmer, as it happened, was going to-morrow morning in his tax-cart as far as Framley Mill, and would be delighted if Mr Crawley would take a seat. He must remain at Framley the best part of the afternoon, and hoped that Mr Crawley would take a seat back again. Now Framley Mill was only half a mile off the direct road to Barchester, and was almost half way from Hogglestock parsonage to the city. This would, at any rate, bring the walk within a practicable distance. Mr Crawley was instantly placed upon his guard, like an animal that sees the bait and suspects the trap. Had he been told that farmer Mangle was going all the way to Barchester, nothing would have induced him to get into the cart. He would have felt sure that farmer Mangle had been persuaded to pity him in his poverty and his strait, and he would sooner have started to walk to London than have put a foot upon the step of the cart. But this lift half way did look to him as though it were really fortuitous. His wife could hardly have been cunning enough to persuade the farmer to go to Framley, conscious that the trap would have been suspected had the bait been made more full. But I fear, – I fear the dear good woman had been thus cunning, – had understood how far the trap might be baited, and had thus succeeded in catching her prey.

On the following morning he consented to get into farmer Mangle's cart, and was driven as far as Framley Mill. 'I wouldn't think nowt, your reverence, of running you over into Barchester, – that I wouldn't. The powny is so mortial good,' said farmer Mangle in his foolish good-nature.

'And how about your business here?' said Mr Crawley. The farmer scratched his head, remembering all Mrs Crawley's injunctions, and awkwardly acknowledged that to be sure his own business with the miller was very pressing. Then Mr Crawley descended, terribly suspicious, and went on his journey.

'Anyways, your reverence will call for me coming back?' said farmer Mangle. But Mr Crawley would make no promise. He bade the farmer not wait for him. If they chanced to meet together on the road he might get up again. If the man really had business at Framley, how could he have offered to go on to Barchester? Were they deceiving him? The wife of his bosom had deceived him in such matters before now. But his trouble in this respect was soon dissipated by the pride of his anticipated triumph over the bishop. He took great glory from the thought that he would go before the bishop with dirty boots, – with boots necessarily dirty, – with rusty pantaloons, that he would be hot and mud-stained with his walk, hungry, and an object to be wondered at by all who should see him, because of the misfortunes which had been unworthily heaped upon his head; whereas the bishop would be sleek and clean and well-fed, – pretty with all the prettinesses that are becoming to a bishop's outward man. And he, Mr Crawley, would be humble, whereas the bishop would be very proud. And the bishop would be in his own arm-chair, – the cock in his own farmyard, while he, Mr Crawley, would be seated afar off, in the cold extremity of the room, with nothing of outward circumstances to assist him, – a man called thither to undergo censure. And yet he would take the bishop in his grasp and crush him, – crush him, – crush him! As he thought of this he walked quickly through the mud, and put out his long arm and his great hand, far before him out into the air, and, there and then, he crushed the bishop in his imagination. Yes, indeed! He thought it very doubtful whether the bishop would ever send for him a second time. As all this passed through his mind, he forgot his wife's cunning, and farmer Mangle's sin, and for the moment he was happy.

As he turned a corner round by Lord Lufton's park paling, who should he meet but his old friend Mr Robarts, the parson of Framley, – the parson who had committed the sin of being bail for him, – the sin, that is, according to Mrs Proudie's view of the matter. He was walking with his hand still stretched out, – still crushing the bishop, when Mr Robarts was close upon him.

'What Crawley! upon my word I am very glad to see you; you are coming up to me, of course?'

'Thank you, Mr Robarts; no, not to-day. The bishop has summoned me to his presence, and I am on my road to Barchester.'

'But how are you going?'

'I shall walk.'

'Walk to Barchester. Impossible!'

'I hope not quite impossible, Mr Robarts. I trust I shall get as far before two o'clock; but to do so I must be on my road.' Then he showed signs of a desire to go on upon his way without further parley.

'But, Crawley, do let me send you over. There is the horse and gig doing nothing.'

'Thank you, Mr Robarts; no. I should prefer to walk to-day.'

'And you have walked from Hogglestock?'

'No; – not so. A neighbour coming hither, who happened to have business at your mill, – he brought me so far in his cart. The walk home will be nothing, – nothing. I shall enjoy it. Good morning, Mr Robarts.'

But Mr Robarts thought of the dirty road, and of the bishop's presence, and of his own ideas of what would be becoming for a clergyman, – and persevered. 'You will find the lanes so very muddy; and our bishop, you know, is apt to notice such things. Do be persuaded.'

'Notice what things?' demanded Mr Crawley, in an indignant tone.

'He, or perhaps she rather, will say how dirty your shoes were when you came to the palace.'

'If he, or she, can find nothing unclean about me but my shoes, let them say their worst. I shall be very indifferent. I have long ceased, Mr Robarts, to care much what any man or woman may say about my shoes. Good morning.' Then he stalked on, clutching and crushing in his hand the bishop, and the bishop's wife, and the whole diocese, – and all the Church of England. Dirty shoes, indeed! Whose was the fault that there were in the church so many feet soiled by unmerited poverty, and so many hands soiled by undeserved wealth? If the bishop did not like his shoes, let the bishop dare to tell him so! So he walked on through the thick of the mud, by no means picking his way.

He walked fast, and he found himself in the close half an hour before the time named by the bishop. But on no account would he have rung the palace bell one minute before two o'clock. So he walked up and down under the towers of the cathedral, and cooled himself, and looked up at the pleasant plate-glass in the windows of the house of his friend the dean, and told himself how, in their college days, he and the dean had been quite equal, – quite equal, except that by the voices of all qualified judges in the university, he, Mr Crawley, had been acknowledged to be the riper scholar. And now the Mr Arabin of those days was Dean of Barchester, – travelling abroad luxuriously at this moment for his delight, while he, Crawley, was perpetual curate at Hogglestock, and had now walked into Barchester at the command of the bishop, because he was suspected of having stolen twenty pounds! When he had fully imbued his mind with the injustice of all this, his time was up, and he walked boldly to the bishop's gate, and boldly rang the bishop's bell.

CHAPTER 18

The Bishop of Barchester is crushed

Who inquires why it is that a little greased flour rubbed in among the hair on a footman's head, – just one dab here and another there, – gives such a tone of high life to the family ? And seeing that the thing is so easily done, why do not more people attempt it ? The tax on hair-powder is but thirteen shillings a year. It may, indeed, be that the slightest dab in the world justifies the wearer in demanding hot meat three times a day, and wine at any rate on Sundays. I think, however, that a bishop's wife may enjoy the privilege without such heavy attendant expense ; otherwise the man who opened the bishop's door to Mr Crawley would hardly have been so ornamented.

The man asked for a card. 'My name is Mr Crawley,' said our friend. 'The bishop has desired me to come to him at his hour. Will you be pleased to tell him that I am here.' The man again asked for a card. 'I am not bound to carry with me my name printed on a ticket,' said Mr Crawley. 'If you cannot remember it, give me pen and paper, and I will write it.' The servant, somewhat awed by the stranger's manner, brought the pen and paper, and Mr Crawley wrote his name : –

The Rev. Joshua Crawley, M.A.,
Perpetual Curate of Hogglestock.

He was then ushered into a waiting-room, but, to his disappointment, was not kept there waiting long. Within three minutes he was ushered into the bishop's study, and into the presence of the two great luminaries of the diocese. He was at first somewhat disconcerted by finding Mrs Proudie in the room. In the imaginary conversation with the bishop which he had been preparing on the road, he had conceived that the bishop would be attended by a chaplain, and he had suited his words to the joint discomfiture of the bishop and of the lower clergyman ; – but now the line of his battle must be altered. This was no doubt an injury, but he trusted

to his courage and readiness to enable him to surmount it. He had
left his hat behind him in the waiting-room, but he kept his old
short cloak still upon his shoulders; and when he entered the
bishop's room his hands and arms were hid beneath it. There was
something lowly in this constrained gait. It showed at least that he
had no idea of being asked to shake hands with the august persons
he might meet. And his head was somewhat bowed, though his
great, bald, broad forehead showed itself so prominent, that neither
the bishop nor Mrs Proudie could drop it from their sight during
the whole interview. He was a man who when seen could hardly be
forgotten. The deep angry remonstrant eyes, the shaggy eyebrows,
telling tales of frequent anger, – of anger frequent but generally
silent, – the repressed indignation of the habitual frown, the long
nose and large powerful mouth, the deep furrows on the cheek, and
the general look of thought and suffering, all combined to make the
appearance of the man remarkable, and to describe to the beholders
at once his true character. No one ever on seeing Mr Crawley took
him to be a happy man, or a weak man, or an ignorant man, or a
wise man.

'You are very punctual, Mr Crawley,' said the bishop. Mr
Crawley simply bowed his head, still keeping his hands beneath his
cloak. 'Will you not take a chair nearer to the fire?' Mr Crawley
had not seated himself, but had placed himself in front of a chair at
the extreme end of the room, – resolved that he would not use it
unless he were duly asked.

'Thank you, my lord,' he said, 'I am warm with walking, and, if
you please, will avoid the fire.'

'You have not walked, Mr Crawley?'

'Yes, my lord. I have been walking.'

'Not from Hogglestock!'

Now this was a matter which Mr Crawley certainly did not mean
to discuss with the bishop. It might be well for the bishop to
demand his presence in the palace, but it could be no part of the
bishop's duty to inquire how he got there. 'That, my lord, is a
matter of no moment,' said he. 'I am glad at any rate that I have
been enabled to obey your lordship's order in coming hither on this
morning.'

Hitherto Mrs Proudie had not said a word. She stood back in the
room, near the fire, – more backward a good deal than she was
accustomed to do when clergymen made their ordinary visits. On
such occasions she would come forward and shake hands with
them graciously, – graciously even, if proudly; but she had felt that
she must do nothing of that kind now; there must be no shaking
hands with a man who had stolen a cheque for twenty pounds! It

might probably be necessary to keep Mr Crawley at a distance, and therefore she had remained in the background. But Mr Crawley seemed to be disposed to keep himself in the background, and therefore she could speak. 'I hope your wife and children are well, Mr Crawley,' she said.

'Thank you, madam, my children are well, and Mrs Crawley suffers no special ailment at present.'

'That is much to be thankful for, Mr Crawley.' Whether he were or were not thankful for such mercies as these was no business of the bishop or of the bishop's wife. That was between him and his God. So he would not even bow to this civility, but sat with his head erect, and with a great frown on his heavy brow.

Then the bishop rose from his chair to speak, intending to take up a position on the rug. But as he did so Mr Crawley, who had seated himself on an intimation that he was expected to sit down, rose also, and the bishop found that he would thus lose his expected vantage. 'Will you not be seated, Mr Crawley?' said the bishop. Mr Crawley smiled, but stood his ground. Then the bishop returned to his armchair, and Mr Crawley also sat down again. 'Mr Crawley,' began the bishop, 'this matter which came the other day before the magistrates at Silverbridge has been a most unfortunate affair. It has given me, I can assure you, the most sincere pain.'

Mr Crawley had made up his mind how far the bishop should be allowed to go without a rebuke. He had told himself that it would only be natural, and would not be unbecoming, that the bishop should allude to the meeting of the magistrates and to the alleged theft, and that therefore such allusion should be endured with patient humility. And, moreover, the more rope he gave the bishop, the more likely the bishop would be to entangle himself. It certainly was Mr Crawley's wish that the bishop should entangle himself. He, therefore, replied very meekly, 'It has been most unfortunate, my lord.'

'I have felt for Mrs Crawley very deeply,' said Mrs Proudie. Mr Crawley had now made up his mind that as long as it was possible he would ignore the presence of Mrs Proudie altogether; and, therefore, he made no sign that he had heard the latter remark.

'It has been most unfortunate,' continued the bishop. 'I have never before had a clergyman in my diocese placed in so distressing a position.'

'That is a matter of opinion, my lord,' said Mr Crawley, who at that moment thought of a crisis which had come in the life of another clergyman in the diocese of Barchester, with the circumstances of which he had by chance been made acquainted.

'Exactly,' said the bishop. 'And I am expressing my opinion.' Mr

Crawley, who understood fighting, did not think that the time had yet come for striking a blow, so he simply bowed again. 'A most unfortunate position, Mr Crawley,' continued the bishop. 'Far be it from me to express an opinion upon the matter, which will have to come before a jury of your countrymen. It is enough for me to know that the magistrates assembled at Silverbridge, gentlemen to whom no doubt you must be known, as most of them live in your neighbourhood, have heard evidence upon the subject—'

'Most convincing evidence,' said Mrs Proudie, interrupting her husband. Mr Crawley's black brow became a little blacker as he heard the word, but still he ignored the woman. He not only did not speak, but did not turn his eye upon her.

'They have heard the evidence on the subject,' continued the bishop, 'and they have thought it proper to refer the decision as to your innocence or your guilt to a jury of your countrymen.'

'And they were right,' said Mr Crawley.

'Very possibly. I don't deny it. Probably,' said the bishop, whose eloquence was somewhat disturbed by Mr Crawley's ready acquiescence.

'Of course they were right,' said Mrs Proudie.

'At any rate it is so,' said the bishop. 'You are in the position of a man amenable to the criminal laws of the land.'

'There are no criminal laws, my lord,' said Mr Crawley; 'but to such laws as there are we are all amenable, – your lordship and I alike.'

'But you are so in a very particular way. I do not wish to remind you what might be your condition now, but for the interposition of private friends.'

'I should be in the condition of a man not guilty before the law; – guiltless, as far as the law goes, – but kept in durance, not for faults of his own, but because otherwise, by reason of laches in the police, his presence at the assizes might not be ensured. In such a position a man's reputation is made to hang for awhile on the trust which some friends or neighbours may have in it. I do not say that the test is a good one.'

'You would have been put in prison, Mr Crawley, because the magistrates were of opinion that you had taken Mr Soames's cheque,' said Mrs Proudie. On this occasion he did look at her. He turned one glance upon her from under his eyebrows, but he did not speak.

'With all that I have nothing to do,' said the bishop.

'Nothing whatever, my lord,' said Mr Crawley.

'But, bishop, I think that you have,' said Mrs Proudie. 'The judgment formed by the magistrates as to the conduct of one of your clergymen makes it imperative upon you to act in the matter.'

'Yes, my dear, yes; I am coming to that. What Mrs Proudie says is perfectly true. I have been constrained most unwillingly to take action in this matter. It is undoubtedly the fact that you must at the next assizes surrender yourself at the court-house yonder, to be tried for this offence against the laws.'

'That is true. If I be alive, my lord, and have strength sufficient, I shall be there.'

'You must be there,' said Mrs Proudie. 'The police will look to that, Mr Crawley.' She was becoming very angry in that the man would not answer her a word. On this occasion again he did not even look at her.

'Yes; you will be there,' said the bishop. 'Now that is, to say the least of it, an unseemly position for a beneficed clergyman.'

'You said before, my lord, that it was an unfortunate position, and the word, methinks, was better chosen.'

'It is very unseemly, very unseemly indeed,' said Mrs Proudie; 'nothing could possibly be more unseemly. The bishop might very properly have used a much stronger word.'

'Under these circumstances,' continued the bishop, 'looking to the welfare of your parish, to the welfare of the diocese, and allow me to say, Mr Crawley, to the welfare of yourself also—'

'And especially to the souls of the people,' said Mrs Proudie.

The bishop shook his head. It is hard to be impressively eloquent when one is interrupted at every best turned period, even by a supporting voice. 'Yes; – and looking of course to the religious interests of your people, Mr Crawley, I came to the conclusion that it would be expedient that you should cease your ministrations for awhile.' The bishop paused, and Mr Crawley bowed his head. 'I, therefore, sent over to you a gentleman with whom I am well acquainted, Mr Thumble, with a letter from myself, in which I endeavoured to impress upon you, without the use of any severe language, what my convictions were.'

'Severe words are often the best mercy,' said Mrs Proudie. Mr Crawley had raised his hand, with his finger out, preparatory to answering the bishop. But as Mrs Proudie had spoken he dropped his finger and was silent.

'Mr Thumble brought me back your written reply,' continued the bishop, 'by which I was grieved to find that you were not willing to submit yourself to my counsel in the matter.'

'I was most unwilling, my lord. Submission to authority is at times a duty; – and at times opposition to authority is a duty also.'

'Opposition to just authority cannot be a duty, Mr Crawley.'

'Opposition to usurped authority is an imperative duty,' said Mr Crawley.

'And who is to be the judge?' demanded Mrs Proudie. Then there was silence for a while; when, as Mr Crawley made no reply, the lady repeated her question. 'Will you be pleased to answer my question, sir? Who, in such a case, is to be the judge?' But Mr Crawley did not please to answer her question. 'The man is obstinate,' said Mrs Proudie.

'I had better proceed,' said the bishop. 'Mr Thumble brought me back your reply, which grieved me greatly.'

'It was contumacious and indecent,' said Mrs Proudie.

The bishop again shook his head and looked so unutterably miserable that a smile came across Mr Crawley's face. After all, others besides himself had their troubles and trials. Mrs Proudie saw and understood the smile, and became more angry than ever. She drew her chair close to the table, and began to fidget with her fingers among the papers. She had never before encountered a clergyman so contumacious, so indecent, so unreverend, – so upsetting. She had had to do with men difficult to manage; – the archdeacon for instance; but the archdeacon had never been so impertinent to her as this man. She had quarrelled once openly with a chaplain of her husband's, a clergyman whom she herself had introduced to her husband, and who had treated her very badly; – but not so badly, not with such unscrupulous violence, as she was now encountering from this ill-clothed beggarly man, this perpetual curate, with his dirty broken boots, this already half-convicted thief! Such was her idea of Mr Crawley's conduct to her, while she was fingering the papers, – simply because Mr Crawley would not speak to her.

'I forget where I was,' said the bishop. 'Oh. Mr Thumble came back, and I received your letter; – of course I received it. And I was surprised to learn from that, that in spite of what had occurred at Silverbridge, you were still anxious to continue the usual Sunday ministrations in your church.'

'I was determined that I would do my duty at Hogglestock, as long as I might be left there to do it,' said Mr Crawley.

'Duty!' said Mrs Proudie.

'Just a moment, my dear,' said the bishop. 'When Sunday came, I had no alternative but to send Mr Thumble over again to Hogglestock. It occurred to us, – to me and Mrs Proudie, – '

'I will tell Mr Crawley just now what has occurred to me,' said Mrs Proudie.

'Yes; – just so. And I am sure that he will take it in good part. It occurred to me, Mr Crawley, that your first letter might have been written in haste.'

'It was written in haste, my lord; your messenger was waiting.'

'Yes; – just so. Well; so I sent him again, hoping that he might be accepted as a messenger of peace. It was a most disagreeable mission for any gentleman, Mr Crawley.'

'Most disagreeable, my lord.'

'And you refused him permission to obey the instructions which I had given him! You would not let him read from your desk, or preach from your pulpit.'

'Had I been Mr Thumble,' said Mrs Proudie, 'I would have read from that desk and I would have preached from that pulpit.'

Mr Crawley waited a moment, thinking that the bishop might perhaps speak again; but as he did not, but sat expectant as though he had finished his discourse, and now expected a reply, Mr Crawley got up from his seat and drew near to the table. 'My lord,' he began, 'it has all been just as you have said. I did answer your first letter in haste.'

'The more shame for you,' said Mrs Proudie.

'And therefore, for aught I know, my letter to your lordship may be so worded as to need some apology.'

'Of course it needs an apology,' said Mrs Proudie.

'But for the matter of it, my lord, no apology can be made, nor is any needed. I did refuse to your messenger permission to perform the services of my church, and if you send twenty more, I shall refuse them all, – till the time may come when it will be your lordship's duty, in accordance with the laws of the Church, – as borne out and backed by the laws of the land, to provide during my constrained absence for the spiritual wants of those poor people at Hogglestock.'

'Poor people, indeed,' said Mrs Proudie. 'Poor wretches!'

'And, my lord, it may well be, that it shall soon by your lordship's duty to take due and legal steps for depriving me of my benefice at Hogglestock; – nay, probably, for silencing me altogether as to the exercise of my sacred profession!'

'Of course it will, sir. Your gown will be taken from you,' said Mrs Proudie. The bishop was looking with all his eyes up at the great forehead and great eyebrows of the man, and was so fascinated by the power that was exercised over him by the other man's strength that he hardly now noticed his wife.

'It may well be so,' continued Mr Crawley. 'The circumstances are strong against me; and, though your lordship has altogether misunderstood the nature of the duty performed by the magistrates in sending my case for trial, – although, as it seems to me, you have come to conclusions in this matter in ignorance of the very theory of our laws,—'

'Sir !' said Mrs Proudie.

'Yet I can foresee the probability that a jury may discover me to have been guilty of theft.'

'Of course the jury will do so,' said Mrs Proudie.

'Should such verdict be given, then, my lord, your interference will be legal, proper, and necessary. And you will find that, even if it be within my power to oppose obstacles to your lordship's authority, I will oppose no such obstacle. There is, I believe, no appeal in criminal cases.'

'None at all,' said Mrs Proudie. 'There is no appeal against your bishop. You should have learned that before.'

'But till that time shall come, my lord, I shall hold my own at Hogglestock as you hold your own here at Barchester. Nor have you more power to turn me out of my pulpit by your mere voice, than I have to turn you out of your throne by mine. If you doubt me, my lord, your lordship's ecclesiastical court is open to you. Try it there.'

'You defy us, then ?' said Mrs Proudie.

'My lord, I grant your authority as bishop to be great, but even a bishop can only act as the law allows him.'

'God forbid that I should do more,' said the bishop.

'Sir, you will find that your wicked threats will fall back upon your own head,' said Mrs Proudie.

'Peace, woman,' Mr Crawley said, addressing her at last. The bishop jumped out of his chair at hearing the wife of his bosom called a woman. But he jumped rather in admiration than in anger. He had already begun to perceive that Mr Crawley was a man who had better be left to take care of the souls at Hogglestock, at any rate till the trial should come on.

'Woman !' said Mrs Proudie, rising to her feet as though she really intended some personal encounter.

'Madam,' said Mr Crawley, 'you should not interfere in these matters. You simply debase your husband's high office. The distaff were more fitting for you. My lord, good morning.' And before either of them could speak again, he was out of the room, and through the hall, and beyond the gate, and standing beneath the towers of the cathedral. Yes, he had, he thought, in truth crushed the bishop. He had succeeded in crumpling the bishop up within the clutch of his fist.

He started in a spirit of triumph to walk back on his road towards Hogglestock. He did not think of the long distance before him for the first hour of his journey. He had had his victory, and the remembrance of that braced his nerves and gave elasticity to his sinews, and he went stalking along the road with rapid strides, muttering to himself from time to time as he went along some word about Mrs Proudie and her distaff. Mr Thumble would not, he thought, come to him again, – not, at any rate, till the assizes were drawing near. And he had resolved what he would do then. When the day of his trial was near, he would himself write to the bishop, and beg that provision might be made for his church, in the event of the verdict going against him. His friend, Dean Arabin, was to be home before that time, and the idea had occurred to him of asking the dean to see to this; but now the other would be the more independent course, and the better. And there was a matter as to which he was not altogether well pleased with the dean, although he was so conscious of his own peculiarities as to know that he could hardly trust himself for a judgment. But, at any rate, he would apply to the bishop, – to the bishop whom he had just left prostrate in his palace, – when the time of his trial should be close at hand.

Full of such thoughts as these he went along almost gaily, nor felt the fatigue of the road till he had covered the first five miles out of Barchester. It was nearly four o'clock, and the thick gloom of the winter evening was making itself felt. And then he began to be fatigued. He had not as yet eaten since he had left his home in the morning, and he now pulled a crust out of his pocket and leaned against a gate as he crunched it. There were still ten miles before him, and he knew that such an addition to the work he had already done would task him very severely. Farmer Mangle had told him that he would not leave Framley Mill till five, and he had got time to reach Framley Mill by that time. But he had said that he would not return to Framley Mill, and he remembered his suspicion that his wife and farmer Mangle between them had cozened him. No; he would persevere and walk, – walk, though he should drop upon the road. He was now nearer fifty than forty years of age, and hardships as well as time had told upon him. He knew that though his strength was good for the commencement of a hard day's work, it would not hold out for him as it used to do. He knew that the last four miles in the dark night would be very sad with him. But still he persevered, endeavouring, as he went, to cherish himself with the remembrance of his triumph.

He passed the turning going down to Framley with courage, but when he came to the further turning, by which the cart would return from Framley to the Hogglestock road, he looked wistfully down the road for farmer Mangle. But farmer Mangle was still at the mill, waiting in expectation that Mr Crawley might come to him. But the poor traveller paused here barely for a minute, and then went on, stumbling through the mud, striking his ill-covered feet against the rough stones in the dark, sweating in his weakness, almost tottering at times, and calculating whether his remaining strength would serve to carry him home. He had almost forgotten the bishop and his wife before at last he grasped the wicket gate leading to his own door.

'Oh, mamma, here is papa!'

'But where is the cart? I did not hear the wheels,' said Mrs Crawley.

'Oh, mamma, I think papa is ill.' Then the wife took her drooping husband by both arms and strove to look him in the face. 'He has walked all the way, and he is ill,' said Jane.

'No, my dear, I am very tired, but not ill. Let me sit down, and give me some bread and tea, and I shall recover myself.' Then Mrs Crawley, from some secret hoard, got him a small modicum of spirits, and gave him meat and tea, and he was docile; and, obeying her behests, allowed himself to be taken to his bed.

'I do not think the bishop will send for me again,' he said, as she tucked the clothes around him.

CHAPTER 19

Where did it come from?

When Christmas morning came no emissary from the bishop appeared at Hogglestock to interfere with the ordinary performance of the day's services. 'I think we need fear no further disturbance,' Mr Crawley said to his wife, – and there was no further disturbance.

On the day after his walk from Framley to Barchester, and from Barchester back to Hogglestock, Mr Crawley had risen not much the worse for his labour, and had gradually given to his wife a full account of what had taken place. 'A poor weak man,' he said, speaking of the bishop. 'A poor weak creature, and much to be pitied.'

'I have always heard that she is a violent woman.'

'Very violent, and very ignorant; and most intrusive withal.'

'And you did not answer her a word?'

'At last my forbearance with her broke down, and I bade her mind her distaff.'

'What; – really? Did you say those words to her?'

'Nay; as for my exact words I cannot remember them. I was thinking more of the words with which it might be fitting that I should answer the bishop. But I certainly told her that she had better mind her distaff.'

'And how did she behave then?'

'I did not wait to see. The bishop had spoken, and I had replied; and why should I tarry to behold the woman's violence? I had told him that he was wrong in law, and that I at least would not submit to usurped authority. There was nothing to keep me longer, and so I went without much ceremony of leave-taking. There had been little ceremony of greeting on their part, and there was less in the making of adieux on mine. They had told me that I was a thief—'

'No, Josiah, – surely not so? They did not use that very word?'

'I say the did; – they did use the very word. But stop. I am wrong. I wrong his lordship, and I crave pardon for having done so. If my memory serve me, no expression so harsh escaped from the bishop's mouth. He gave me, indeed, to understand more than once that the action taken by the magistrates was tantamount to a conviction, and that I must be guilty because they had decided that there was evidence sufficient to justify a trial. But all that arose from my lord's ignorance of the administration of the laws of his country. He was very ignorant, – puzzle-pated, as you may call it, – led by the nose by his wife, weak as water, timid, and vacillating. But he did not wish, I think, to be insolent. It was Mrs Proudie who told me to my face that I was a – thief.'

'May she be punished for the cruel word!' said Mrs Crawley. 'May the remembrance that she has spoken it come, some day, heavily upon her heart!'

'"Vengeance is mine. I will repay," saith the Lord,'* answered Mr Crawley. 'We may safely leave all that alone, and rid our minds of such wishes, if it be possible. It is well, I think, that violent offences, when committed, should be met by instant rebuke. To turn the other cheek instantly to the smiter can hardly be suitable in these days, when the hands of so many are raised to strike. But the return blow should be given only while the smart remains. She hurt me then; but what is it to me now, that she called me a thief to my face? Do I not know that, all the country round, men and women are calling me the same behind my back?'

'No, Josiah, you do not know that. They say that the thing is very strange, – so strange that it requires a trial; but no one thinks you have taken that which was not your own.'

'I think I did. I myself think I took that which was not my own. My poor head suffers so; – so many grievous thoughts distract me, that I am like a child, and know not what I do.' As he spoke thus he put both hands up to his head, leaning forward as though in anxious thought, – as though he were striving to bring his mind to bear with accuracy upon past events. 'It could not have been mine, and yet—' Then he sat silent, and made no effort to continue his speech.

'And yet?' – said his wife, encouraging him to proceed. If she could only learn the real truth, she thought that she might perhaps yet save him, with assistance from their friends.

'When I said that I had gotten it from that man I must have been mad.'

'From which man, love?'

'From the man Soames, – he who accuses me. And yet, as the Lord hears me, I thought so then. The truth is, that there are times when I am not – sane. I am not a thief, – not before God; but I am – mad at times.' These last words he spoke very slowly, in a whisper, — without any excitement, — indeed with a composure which was horrible to witness. And what he said was the more terrible because she was so well convinced of the truth of his words. Of course he was no thief. She wanted no one to tell her that. As he himself had expressed it, he was no thief before God, however the money might have come into his possession. That there were times when his reason, once so fine and clear, could not act, could not be trusted to guide him right, she had gradually come to know with fear and trembling. But he himself had never before hinted his own consciousness of this calamity. Indeed he had been so unwilling to speak of himself and of his own state, that she had been unable even to ask him a question about the money, — lest he should suspect that she suspected him. Now he was speaking, — but speaking with such heartrending sadness that she could hardly urge him to go on.

'You have sometimes been ill, Josiah, as any of us may be,' she said, 'and that has been the cause.'

'There are different kinds of sickness. There is sickness of the body, and sickness of the heart, and sickness of the spirit; — and then there is sickness of the mind, the worst of all.'

'With you, Josiah, it has chiefly been the first.'

'With me, Mary, it has been all of them, — every one! My spirit is broken, and my mind has not been able to keep its even tenour amidst the ruins. But I will strive. I will strive. I will strive still. And if God helps me, I will prevail.' Then he took up his hat and cloak, and went forth among the lanes; and on this occasion his wife was glad that he should go alone.

This occurred a day or two before Christmas, and Mrs Crawley during those days said nothing more to her husband on the subject which he had so unexpectedly discussed. She asked him no questions about the money, or as to the possibility of his exercising his memory, nor did she counsel him to plead that the false excuses given by him for his possession of the cheque had been occasioned by the sad slip to which sorrow had in those days subjected his memory and his intellect. But the matter had always been on her mind. Might it not be her paramount duty to do something of this at the present moment? Might it not be that his acquittal or conviction would depend on what she might now learn from him? It was clear to her that he was brighter in spirit since his encounter with the Proudies than he had ever been since the accusation had been first made against him. And she knew well that his present mood would not be of long continuance. He would fall again into his moody silent ways, and then the chance of learning aught from him would be past, and perhaps, for ever.

He performed the Christmas services with nothing of special despondency in his tone or manner, and his wife thought that she had never heard him give the sacrament with more impressive dignity. After the service he stood awhile at the churchyard gate, and exchanged a word of courtesy as to the season with such of the families of the farmers as had stayed for the Lord's supper.

'I waited at Framley for your reverence till after six, – so I did,' said farmer Mangle.

'I kept the road, and walked the whole way,' said Mr Crawley. 'I think I told you that I should not return to the mill. But I am not the less obliged by your great kindness.'

'Say nowt o' that,' said the farmer. 'No doubt I had business at the mill, – lots to do at the mill.' Nor did he think that the fib he was telling was at all incompatible with the Holy Sacrament in which he had just taken a part.

The Christmas dinner at the parsonage was not a repast that did much honour to the season, but it was a better dinner than the inhabitants of that house usually saw on the board before them. There was roast pork and mince-pies, and a bottle of wine. As Mrs Crawley with her own hand put the meat upon the table, and then, as was her custom in their house, proceeded to cut it up, she looked at her husband's face to see whether he was scrutinizing the food with painful eye. It was better that she should tell the truth at once than that she should be made to tell it, in answer to a question. Everything on the table, except the bread and potatoes, had come in a basket from Framley Court. Pork had been sent instead of beef, because people in the country, when they kill their pigs, do sometimes give each other pork, – but do not exchange joints of beef, when they slay their oxen. All this was understood by Mrs Crawley, but she almost wished that beef had been sent, because beef would have attracted less attention. He said, however, nothing to the meat; but when his wife proposed to him that he should eat a mince-pie he resented it. 'The bare food,' said he, 'is bitter enough, coming, as it does; but that would choke me.' She did not press it, but eat one herself, as otherwise her girl would have been forced also to refuse the dainty.

That evening, as soon as Jane was in bed, she resolved to ask him some further questions. 'You will have a lawyer, Josiah, – will you not?' she said.

'Why should I have a lawyer?'

'Because he will know what questions to ask, and how questions on the other side should be answered.'

'I have no questions to ask, and there is only one way in which questions should be answered. I have no money to pay a lawyer.'

'But, Josiah, in such a case as this, where your honour, and our very life depend upon it – '

'Depend on what?'

'On your acquittal.'

'I shall not be acquitted. It is as well to look it in the face at once. Lawyer, or no lawyer, they will say that I took the money. Were I upon the jury, trying the case myself, knowing all that I know now,' – and as he said this he struck forth with his hands into the air, – 'I think that I should say so myself. A lawyer will do no good. It is here. It is here.' And again he put his hands up to his head.

So far she had been successful. At this moment it had in truth been her object to induce him to speak of his own memory, and not of the aid that a lawyer might give. The proposition of the lawyer had been brought in to introduce the subject.

'But, Josiah, – '

'Well?'

It was very hard for her to speak. She could not bear to torment him by any allusion to his own deficiencies. She could not endure to make him think that she suspected him of any frailty either in intellect or thought. Wifelike, she desired to worship him, and that he should know that she worshipped him. But if a word might save him! 'Josiah, where did it come from?'

'Yes,' said he; 'yes; that is the question. Where did it come from?' – and he turned sharp upon her, looking at her with all the power of his eyes. 'It is because I cannot tell you where it came from that I ought to be, – either in Bedlam, as a madman, or in the county gaol as a thief.' The words were so dreadful to her that she could not utter at the moment another syllable. 'How is a man – to think himself – fit – for a man's work, when he cannot answer his wife such a plain question as that?' Then he paused again. 'They should take me to Bedlam at once, – at once, – at once. That would not disgrace the children as the gaol will do.'

Mrs Crawley could ask no further questions on that evening.

CHAPTER 20

What Mr Walker thought about it

It had been suggested to Mr Robarts, the parson of Framley, that he should endeavour to induce his old acquaintance, Mr Crawley, to employ a lawyer to defend him at his trial, and Mr Robarts had not forgotten the commission which he had undertaken. But there were difficulties in the matter of which he was well aware. In the first place Mr Crawley was a man whom it had not at any time been easy to advise on matters private to himself; and, in the next place, this was a matter on which it was very hard to speak to the man implicated, let him be who he would. Mr Robarts had come round to the generally accepted idea that Mr Crawley had obtained possession of the cheque illegally, – acquitting his friend in his own mind of theft, simply by supposing that he was wool-gathering when the cheque came in his way. But in speaking to Mr Crawley, it would be necessary, – so he thought, – to pretend a conviction that Mr Crawley was as innocent in fact as in intention.

He had almost made up his mind to dash at the subject when he met Mr Crawley walking through Framley to Barchester, but he had abstained, chiefly because Mr Crawley had been too quick for him, and had got away. After that he resolved that it would be almost useless for him to go to work unless he should be provided with a lawyer ready and willing to undertake the task; and as he was not so provided at present, he made up his mind that he would go into Silverbridge, and see Mr Walker, the attorney there. Mr Walker always advised everybody in those parts about everything, and would be sure to know what would be the proper thing to be done in this case. So Mr Robarts got into his gig, and drove himself into Silverbridge, passing very close to Mr Crawley's house on his road. He drove at once to Mr Walker's office, and on arriving there found that the attorney was not at that moment within. But Mr Winthrop was within. Would Mr Robarts see Mr Winthrop? Now, seeing Mr Winthrop was a very different thing from seeing Mr

Walker, although the two gentlemen were partners. But still Mr
Robarts said that he would see Mr Winthrop. Perhaps Mr Walker
might return while he was there.

'Is there anything I can do for you, Mr Robarts?' asked Mr
Winthrop. Mr Robarts said that he had wished to see Mr Walker
about that poor fellow Crawley. 'Ah, yes; very sad case! So much
sadder being a clergyman, Mr Robarts. We are really quite sorry
for him; – we are indeed. We wouldn't have touched the case
ourselves if we could have helped ourselves. We wouldn't indeed.
But we are obliged to take all that business here. At any rate he'll
get nothing but fair usage from us.'

'I am sure of that. You don't know whether he has employed any
lawyer as yet to defend him?'

'I can't say. We don't know, you know. I should say he had, –
probably some Barchester attorney. Borleys and Bonstock in Barchester are very good people, – very good people indeed; – for that
sort of business I mean, Mr Robarts. I don't suppose they have
much county property in their hands.'

Mr Robarts knew that Mr Winthrop was a fool, and that he
could get no useful advice from him. So he suggested that he would
take his gig down to the inn, and call back again before long.
'You'll find that Walker knows no more than I do about it,' said
Mr Winthrop, 'but of course he'll be glad to see you if he happens
to come in.' So Mr Robarts went to the inn, put up his horse, and
then, as he sauntered back up the street, met Mr Walker coming
out of the private door of his house.

'I've been at home all the morning,' he said, 'but I've had a stiff
job of work on hand, and told them to say in the office that I was
not in. Seen Winthrop, have you? I don't suppose he did know that
I was here. The clerks often know more than the partners. About
Mr Crawley is it? Come into my dining-room, Mr Robarts, where
we shall be alone. Yes; – it is a bad case; a very bad case. The pity
is that anybody should ever have said anything about it. Lord bless
me, if I'd been Soames I'd have let him have the twenty pounds.
Lord Lufton would never have allowed Soames to lose it.'

'But Soames wanted to find out the truth.'

'Yes; – that was just it. Soames couldn't bear to think that he
should be left in the dark, and then, when the poor man said that
Soames had paid the cheque to him in the say of business, – it was
not odd that Soames' back should have been up, was it? But, Mr
Robarts, I should have thought a deal about it before I should have
brought such a man as Mr Crawley before a bench of magistrates
on that charge.'

'But between you and me, Mr Walker, did he steal the money?'

'Well, Mr Robarts, you know how I'm placed.'

'Mr Crawley is my friend, and of course I want to assist him. I was under a great obligation to Mr Crawley once, and I wish to befriend him, whether he took the money or not. But I could act so much better if I felt sure one way or the other.'

'If you ask me, I think he did take it.'

'What ! – stole it ?'

'I think he knew it was not his own when he took it. You see I don't think he meant to use it when he took it. He perhaps had some queer idea that Soames had been hard on him, or his lordship, and that the money was fairly his due. Then he kept the cheque by him till he was absolutely badgered out of his life by the butcher up the street there. That was about the long and the short of it, Mr Robarts.'

'I suppose so. And now what had he better do ?'

'Well; if you ask me,—He is in very bad health, isn't he ?'

'No ; I should say not. He walked to Barchester and back the other day.'

'Did he ? But he's very queer, isn't he ?'

'Very odd-mannered indeed.'

'And does and says all manner of odd things ?'

'I think you'd find the bishop would say so after that interview.'

'Well; if it would do any good, you might have the bishop examined.'

'Examined for what, Mr Walker ?'

'If you could show, you know, that Crawley has got a bee in his bonnet; that the mens sana* is not there, in short; – I think you might manage to have the trial postponed.'

'But then somebody must take charge of his living.'

'You parsons could manage that among you; – you and the dean and the archdeacon. The archdeacon has always got half-a-dozen curates about somewhere. And then, – after the assizes, Mr Crawley might come to his senses; and I think, – mind it's only an idea, – but I think the committal might be quashed. It would have been temporary insanity, and, though mind I don't give my word for it, I think he might go on and keep his living. I think so, Mr Robarts.'

'That has never occurred to me.'

'No; – I daresay not. You see the difficulty is this. He's so stiff-necked, – will do nothing himself. Well, that will do for one proof of temporary insanity. The real truth is, Mr Robarts, he is as mad as a hatter.'

'Upon my word I've often thought so.'

'And you wouldn't mind saying so in evidence, – would you ?

Well, you see, there is no helping such a man in any other way. He won't even employ a lawyer to defend him.'

'That was what I had come to you about.'

'I'm told he won't. Now a man must be mad who won't employ a lawyer when he wants one. You see, the point we should gain would be this, – if we tried to get him through as being a little touched in the upper story, – whatever we could do for him, we could do against his own will. The more he opposed us the stronger our case would be. He would swear he was not mad at all, and we should say that that was the greatest sign of his madness. But when I say we, of course I mean you. I must not appear in it.'

'I wish you could, Mr Walker.'

'Of course I can't; but that won't make any difference.'

'I suppose he must have a lawyer?'

'Yes, he must have a lawyer; – or rather his friends must.'

'And who should employ him, ostensibly?'

'Ah; – there's the difficulty. His wife wouldn't do it, I suppose? She couldn't do him a better turn.'

'He would never forgive her. And she would never consent to act against him.'

'Could you interfere?'

'If necessary, I will; – but I hardly know him well enough.'

'Has he no father or mother, or uncles or aunts? He must have somebody belonging to him,' said Mr Walker.

Then it occurred to Mr Robarts that Dean Arabin would be the proper person to interfere. Dean Arabin and Mr Crawley had been intimate friends in early life, and Dean Arabin knew more of him than did any man, at least in those parts. All this Mr Robarts explained to Mr Walker, and Mr Walker agreed with him that the services of Dean Arabin should if possible be obtained. Mr Robarts would at once write to Dean Arabin and explain at length all the circumstances of the case. 'The worst of it is, he will hardly be home in time,' said Mr Walker. 'Perhaps he would come a little sooner if you were to press it?'

'But we could act in his name in his absence, I suppose? – of course with his authority?'

'I wish he could be here a month before the assizes, Mr Robarts. It would be better.'

'And in the meantime shall I say anything to Mr Crawley, myself, about employing a lawyer?'

'I think I would. If he turns upon you, as like enough he may, and abuses you, that will help us in one way. If he should consent, and perhaps he may, that would help us in the other way. I'm told he's been over and upset the whole coach at the palace.'

'I shouldn't think the bishop got much out of him,' said the parson.

'I don't like Crawley the less for speaking his mind free to the bishop,' said the attorney, laughing. 'And he'll speak it free to you too, Mr Robarts.'

'He won't break any of my bones. Tell me, Mr Walker, what lawyer shall I name to him?'

'You can't have a better man than Mr Mason, up the street there.'

'Winthrop proposed Borleys at Barchester.'

'No, no, no. Borleys and Bonstock are capital people to push a fellow through on a charge of horse-stealing, or to squeeze a man for a little money; but they are not the people for Mr Crawley in such a case as this. Mason is a better man; and then Mason and I know each other.' In saying which Mr Walker winked.

There was then a discussion between them whether Mr Robarts should go at once to Mr Mason; but it was decided at last that he should see Mr Crawley and also write to the dean before he did so. The dean might wish to employ his own lawyer, and if so the double expense should be avoided. 'Always remember, Mr Robarts, that when you go into an attorney's office door, you will have to pay for it, first or last. In here, you see, the dingy old mahogany, bare as it is, makes you safe. Or else it's the salt-cellar, which will not allow itself to be polluted by six-and-eightpenny consider-ations.* But there is the other kind of tax to be paid. You must go up and see Mrs Walker, or you won't have her help in this matter.'

Mr Walker returned to his work, either to some private den within the house, or to his office, and Mr Robarts was taken upstairs to the drawing-room. There he found Mrs Walker and her daughter, and Miss Anne Prettyman, who had just looked in, full of the story of Mr Crawley's walk to Barchester. Mr Thumble had seen one of Dr Tempest's curates, and had told the whole story – he, Mr Thumble, having heard Mrs Proudie's version of what had occurred, and having, of course, drawn his own deductions from her premises. And it seemed that Mr Crawley had been watched as he passed through the close out of Barchester. A minor canon had seen him, and had declared that he was going at the rate of a hunt, swinging his arms on high and speaking very loud, though, – as the minor canon said with regret, – the words were hardly audible. But there had been no doubt as to the man. Mr Crawley's old hat, and short rusty cloak, and dirty boots, had been duly observed and chronicled by the minor canon; and Mr Thumble had been enabled to put together a not altogether false picture of what had occurred. As soon as the greetings between Mr Robarts and the ladies had been made, Miss Anne Prettyman broke out again, just where she had left off when Mr Robarts came in. 'They say that Mrs Proudie declared that she will have him sent to Botany Bay !'

'Luckily Mrs Proudie won't have much to do in the matter,' said Miss Walker, who ranged herself, as to church matters, in ranks altogether opposed to those commanded by Mrs Proudie.

'She will have nothing to do with it, my dear,' said Mrs Walker; 'and I daresay Mrs Proudie was not foolish enough to say anything of the kind.'

'Mamma, she would be fool enough to say anything. Would she not, Mr Robarts ?'

'You forget, Miss Walker, that Mrs Proudie is in authority over me.'

'So she is, for the matter of that,' said the young lady; 'but I know very well what you all think of her, and say of her too, at Framley. Your friend, Lady Lufton, loves her dearly. I wish I could have been hidden behind a curtain in the palace, to hear what Mr Crawley said to her.'

'Mr Smillie declares,' said Miss Anne Prettyman, 'that the bishop has been ill ever since. Mr Smillie went over to his mother's at Barchester for Christmas, and took part of the cathedral duty, and we had Mr Spooner over here in his place. So Mr Smillie of course heard all about it. Only fancy, poor Mr Crawley walking all the way from Hogglestock to Barchester and back; – and I am told he hardly had a shoe to his foot ! Is it not a shame, Mr Robarts ?'

'I don't think it was quite so bad as you say, Miss Prettyman; but, upon the whole, I do think it is a shame. But what can we do ?'

'I suppose there are tithes at Hogglestock. Why are they not given up to the church, as they ought to be ?'

'My dear Miss Prettyman, that is a very large subject, and I am afraid it cannot be settled in time to relieve our poor friend from his distress.' Then Mr Robarts escaped from the ladies in Mr Walker's house, who, as it seemed to him, were touching upon dangerous ground, and went back to the yard of the George Inn for his gig, – the George and Vulture it was properly called, and was the house in which the magistrates had sat when they committed Mr Crawley for trial.

'Footed it every inch of the way, blowed if he didn't,' the ostler was saying to a gentleman's groom, whom Mr Robarts recognized to be the servant of his friend, Major Grantly; and Mr Robarts knew that they also were talking about Mr Crawley. Everybody in the county was talking about Mr Crawley. At home, at Framley, there was no other subject of discourse. Lady Lufton, the dowager, was full of it, being firmly convinced that Mr Crawley was innocent, because the bishop was supposed to regard him as guilty. There had been a fmily conclave held at Framley Court over that basket of provisions which had been sent for the Christmas cheer of the Hogglestock parsonage, each of the three ladies, the two Lady Luftons and Mrs Robarts, having special views of their own. How the pork had been substituted for the beef by old Lady Lufton, young Lady Lufton thinking that after all the beef would be less dangerous, and how a small turkey had been rashly suggested by Mrs Robarts, and how certain small articles had been inserted in the bottom of the basket which Mrs Crawley had never shewn to her husband, need not here be told at length. But Mr Robarts, as he heard the two grooms talking about Mr Crawley, began to feel that Mr Crawley had achieved at least celebrity.

The groom touched his hat as Mr Robarts walked up. 'Has the major returned home yet?' Mr Robarts asked. The groom said that his master was still at Plumstead, and that that he was to go over to Plumstead to fetch the major and Miss Edith in a day or two. Then Mr Robarts got into his gig, and as he drove out of the yard he heard the words of the men as they returned to the same subject. 'Footed it all the way,' said one. 'And yet he's a gen'leman, too,' said the other. Mr Robarts thought of this as he drove on, intending to call at Hogglestock on that very day on his way home. It was undoubtedly the fact that Mr Crawley was recognized to be a gentleman by all who knew him, high or low, rich or poor, by those who thought well of him and by those who thought ill. These grooms, who had been telling each other that this parson, who was to be tried as a thief, had been constrained to walk from Hogglestock to Barchester and back, because he could not afford to travel in any other way, and that his boots were cracked and his clothes ragged, had still known him to be a gentleman! Nobody doubted it; not even they who thought he had stolen the money. Mr Robarts himself was certain of it, and told himself that he knew it by evidences which his own education made clear to him. But how was it that the grooms knew it? For my part I think that there are no better judges of the article than the grooms.

Thinking still of all which he had heard, Mr Robarts found himself at Mr Crawley's gate at Hogglestock.

CHAPTER 21

Mr Robarts on his embassy

Mr Robarts was not altogether easy in his mind as he approached Mr Crawley's house. He was aware that the task before him was a very difficult one, and he had not confidence in himself, – that he was exactly the man fitted for the performance of such a task. He was a little afraid of Mr Crawley, acknowledging tacitly to himself that the man had a power of ascendancy with which he would hardly be able to cope successfully. In old days he had once been rebuked by Mr Crawley, and had been cowed by the rebuke; and though there was no touch of rancour in his heart on this account, no slightest remaining venom, – but rather increased respect and friendship, – still he was unable to overcome the remembrance of the scene in which the perpetual curate of Hogglestock had undoubtedly had the mastery of him. So, when two dogs have fought and one has conquered, the conquered dog will always show an unconscious submission to the conqueror.

He hailed a boy on the road as he drew near to the house, knowing that he would find no one at the parsonage to hold his horse for him, and was thus able without delay to walk through the garden and knock at the door. 'Papa was not at home,' Jane said. 'Papa was at the school. But papa could certainly be summoned. She herself would run across to the school if Mr Robarts would come in.' So Mr Robarts entered, and found Mrs Crawley in the sitting-room. Mr Crawley would be in directly, she said. And then, hurrying on to the subject with confused haste, in order that a word or two might be spoken before her husband came back, she expressed her thanks and his for the good things which had been sent to them at Christmas-tide.

'It's old Lady Lufton's doings,' said Mr Robarts, trying to laugh the matter over.

'I knew that it came from Framley, Mr Robarts, and I know how good you all are there. I have not written to thank Lady Lufton. I thought it better not to write. Your sister will understand why, if no one else does. But you will tell them from me, I am sure, that it was, as they intended, a comfort to us. Your sister knows too much of us for me to suppose that our great poverty can be secret from her. And, as far as I am concerned, I do not now much care who knows it.'

'There is no disgrace in not being rich,' said Mr Robarts.

'No; and the feeling of disgrace which does attach itself to being so poor as we are is deadened by the actual suffering which such poverty brings with it. At least it has become so with me. I am not ashamed to say that I am very grateful for what you all have done for us at Framley. But you must not say anything to him about that.'

'Of course I will not, Mrs Crawley.'

'His spirit is higher than mine, I think, and he suffers more from the natural disinclination which we all have to receiving alms. Are you going to speak to him about this affair of the – cheque, Mr Robarts?'

'I am going to ask him to put his case into some lawyer's hands.'

'Oh! I wish he would!'

'And will he not?'

'It is very kind of you, your coming to ask him, but—'

'Has he so strong an objection?'

'He will tell you that he has no money to pay a lawyer.'

'But, surely, if he were convinced that it was absolutely necessary for the vindication of his innocence, he would submit to charge himself with an expense so necessary, not only for himself, but for his family?'

'He will say it ought not to be necessary. You know, Mr Robarts, that in some respects he is not like other men. You will not let what I say of him set you against him?'

'Indeed, no.'

'It is most kind of you to make the attempt. He will be here directly, and when he comes I will leave you together.'

While she was yet speaking his step was heard along the gravel-path, and he hurried into the room with quick steps. 'I crave your pardon, Mr Robarts,' he said, 'that I should keep you waiting.' Now Mr Robarts had not been there ten minutes, and any such asking of pardon was hardly necessary. And, even in his own house, Mr Crawley affected a mock humility, as though, either through his own debasement, or because of the superior station of the other clergyman, he were not entitled to put himself on an equal footing with his visitor. He would not have shaken hands with Mr Robarts, – intending to indicate that he did not presume to do so while the present accusation was hanging over him, – had not the action been forced upon him. And then there was something of a protest in his manner, as though remonstrating aainst a thing that was unbecoming to him. Mr Robarts, without analysing it, understood it all, and knew that behind the humility there was a crushing pride, – a pride which, in all probability, would rise up and crush him before he could get himself out of the room again. It was, perhaps, after all, a question whether the man was not served rightly by the extremities to which he was reduced. There was something radically wrong within him, which had put him into antagonism with all the world, and which produced these never-dying grievances. There were many clergymen in the country with incomes as small as that which had fallen to the lot of Mr Crawley, but they managed to get on without displaying their sores as Mr Crawley displayed his. They did not wear their old rusty cloaks with all that ostentatious bitterness of poverty which seemed to belong to the garment when displayed on Mr Crawley's shoulders. Such, for a moment, were Mr Robarts' thoughts, and he almost repented himself of his present mission. But then he thought of Mrs Crawley, and remembering that her sufferings were at any rate undeserved, determined that he would persevere.

Mrs Crawley disappeared almost as soon as her husband appeared, and Mr Robarts found himself standing in front of his friend, who remained fixed on the spot, with his hands folded over each other and his neck slightly bent forward, in token also of humility. 'I regret,' he said, 'that your horse should be left there, exposed to the inclemency of the weather; but—'

'The horse won't mind it a bit,' said Mr Robarts. 'A parson's horse is like a butcher's, and knows that he mustn't be particular about waiting in the cold.'

'I never have had one myself,' said Mr Crawley. Now Mr Robarts had had more horses than one before now, and had been thought by some to have incurred greater expense than was befitting in his stable comforts. The subject, therefore, was a sore one, and he was worried a little. 'I just wanted to say a few words to you, Crawley,' he said, 'and if I am not occupying too much of your time—'

'My time is altogether at your disposal. Will you be seated?'

Then Mr Robarts sat down, and, swinging his hat between his legs, bethought himself how he should begin his work. 'We had the archdeacon over at Framley the other day,' he said. 'Of course you know the archdeacon?'

'I never had the advantage of any acquaintance with Dr Grantly. Of course I know him well by name, and also personally, – that is, by sight.'

'And by character?'

'Nay; I can hardly say so much as that. But I am aware that his name stands high with many of his order.'

'Exactly; that is what I mean. You know that his judgment is thought more of in clerical matters than that of any other clergyman in the county.'

'By a certain party, Mr Robarts.'

'Well, yes. They don't think much of him, I suppose, at the palace. But that won't lower him in your estimation.'

'I by no means wish to derogate from Dr Grantly's high position in his own archdeaconry, – to which, as you are aware, I am not attached, – nor to criticize his conduct in any respect. It would be unbecoming in me to do so. But I cannot accept it as a point in a clergyman's favour, that he should be opposed to his bishop.'

Now this was too much for Mr Robarts. After all that he had heard of the visit paid by Mr Crawley to the palace, – of the venom displayed by Mrs Proudie on that occasion, and of the absolute want of subordination to episcopal authority which Mr Crawley himself was supposed to have shown, – Mr Robarts did feel it hard that his friend the archdeacon should be snubbed in this way because he was deficient in reverence for his bishop! 'I thought, Crawley,' he said, 'that you yourself were inclined to dispute orders coming to you from the palace. The world at least says as much concerning you.'

'What the world says of me I have learned to disregard very much, Mr Robarts. But I hope that I shall never disobey the authority of the Church when properly and legally exercised.'

'I hope with all my heart you never will; nor I either. And the archdeacon, who knows, to the breadth of a hair, what a bishop ought to do and what he ought not, and what he may do and what he may not, will, I should say, be the last man in England to sin in that way.'

'Very probably. I am far from contradicting you there. Pray understand, Mr Robarts, that I bring no accusation against the archdeacon. Why should I?'

'I didn't mean to discuss him at all.'

'Nor did I, Mr Robarts.'

'I only mentioned his name, because, as I said, he was over with us the other day at Framley, and we were all talking about your affair.'

'My affair!' said Mr Crawley. And then came a frown upon his brow, and a gleam of fire into his eyes, which effectually banished that look of extreme humility which he had assumed. 'And may I ask why the archdeacon was discussing – my affair?'

'Simply from the kindness which he bears to you.'

'I am grateful for the archdeacon's kindness, as a man is bound to be for any kindness, whether displayed wisely or unwisely. But it seems to me that my affair, as you call it, Mr Robarts, is of that nature that they who wish well to me will better further their wishes by silence than by any discussion.'

'Then I cannot agree with you.' Mr Crawley shrugged his shoulders, opened his hands a little and then closed them, and bowed his head. He could not have declared more clearly by any words that he differed altogether from Mr Robarts, and that as the subject was one so peculiarly his own he had a right to expect that his opinion should be allowed to prevail against that of any other person. 'If you come to that, you know, how is anybody's tongue to be stopped?'

'That vain tongues cannot be stopped, I am well aware. I do not expect that people's tongues should be stopped. I am not saying what men will do, but what good wishes should dictate.'

'Well, perhaps you'll hear me out for a minute.' Mr Crawley again bowed his head. 'Whether we were wise or unwise, we were discussing this affair.'

'Whether I stole Mr Soames's money?'

'No; nobody supposed for a moment you had stolen it.'

'I cannot understand how they should suppose anything else, knowing, as they do, that the magistrates have committed me for the theft. This took place at Framley, you say, and probably in Lord Lufton's presence.'

'Exactly.'

'And Lord Lufton was chairman at the sitting of the magistrates at which I was committed. How can it be that he should think otherwise?'

'I am sure he has not an idea that you were guilty. Nor yet has Dr Thorne, who was also one of the magistrates. I don't suppose one of them then thought so.'

'Then their action, to say the least of it, was very strange.'

'It was all because you had nobody to manage it for you. I thoroughly believe that if you had placed the matter in the hands of a good lawyer, you would never have heard a word more about it. That seems to be the opinion of everybody I speak to on the subject.'

'Then in this country a man is to be punished or not, according to his ability to fee a lawyer!'

'I am not talking about punishment.'

'And presuming an innocent man to have the ability and not the will to do so, he is to be punished, to be ruined root and branch, self and family, character and pocket, simply because, knowing his own innocence, he does not choose to depend on the mercenary skill of a man whose trade he abhors for the establishment of that which should be clear as the sun at noon-day! You say I am innocent, and yet you tell me I am to be condemned as a guilty man, have my gown taken from me, be torn from my wife and children, be disgraced before the eyes of all men, and be made a byword and a thing horrible to be mentioned, because I will not fee an attorney to fee another man to come and lie on my behalf, to browbeat witnesses, to make false appeals, and perhaps shed false tears in defending me. You have come to me asking me to do this, if I understand you, telling me that the archdeacon would so advise me.'

'That is my object.' Mr Crawley, as he had spoken, had in his vehemence risen from his seat, and Mr Robarts was also standing.

'Then tell the archdeacon,' said Mr Crawley, 'that I will have none of his advice. I will have no one there paid by me to obstruct the course of justice or to hoodwink a jury. I have been in courts of law, and know what is the work for which these gentlemen are hired. I will have none of it, and I will thank you to tell the archdeacon so, with my respectful acknowledgments of his consideration and condescension. I say nothing as to my own innocence, or my own guilt. But I do say that if I am dragged before that tribunal, an innocent man, and am falsely declared to be guilty, because I lack money to bribe a lawyer to speak for me, then the laws of this country deserve but little of that reverence which we are accustomed to pay to them. And if I be guilty—'

'Nobody supposes you to be guilty.'

'And if I be guilty,' continued Mr Crawley, altogether ignoring the interruption, except by the repetition of his words, and a slight raising of his voice, 'I will not add to my guilt by hiring any one to prove a falsehood or to disprove a truth.'

'I'm sorry that you should say so, Mr Crawley.'

'I speak according to what light I have, Mr Robarts; and if I have been over-warm with you, – and I am conscious that I have been in fault in that direction, – I must pray you to remember that I am somewhat hardly tried. My sorrows and troubles are so great that they rise against me and disturb me, and drive me on, – whither I would not be driven.'

'But, my friend, is not that just the reason why you should trust in this matter to some one who can be more calm than yourself?'

'I cannot trust to any one, – in a matter of conscience. To do as you would have me is to me wrong. Shall I do wrong because I am unhappy?'

'You should cease to think it wrong when so advised by persons you can trust.'

'I can trust no one with my own conscience; – not even the archdeacon, great as he is.'

'The archdeacon has meant only well to you.'

'I will presume so. I will believe so. I do think so. Tell the archdeacon from me that I humbly thank him; – that, in a matter of church question, I might probably submit my judgment to his; even though he might have no authority over me, knowing as I do that in such matters his experience has been great. Tell him also, that though I would fain that this unfortunate affair might burden the tongue of none among my neighbours, – at least till I shall have stood before the-judge to receive the verdict of the jury, and, if needful, his lordship's sentence – still I am convinced that in what he has spoken, as also in what he has done, he has not yielded to the idleness of gossip, but has exercised his judgment with intended kindness.'

'He has certainly intended to do you a service; and as for its not being talked about, that is out of the question.'

'And for yourself, Mr Robarts, whom I have ever regarded as a friend since circumstances brought me into your neighbourhood, – for you, whose sister I love tenderly in memory of past kindness, though now she is removed so far above my sphere, as to make it unfit that I should call her my friend—'

'She does not think so at all.'

'For yourself, as I was saying, pray believe me that though from the roughness of my manner, being now unused to social inter-course, I seem to be ungracious and forbidding, I am grateful and mindful, and that in the tablets of my heart I have written you down as one in whom I could trust, – were it given to me to trust in men and women.' Then he turned round with his face to the wall and his back to his visitor, and so remained till Mr Robarts had left him. 'At any rate I wish you well through your trouble,' said Robarts; and as he spoke he found that his own words were nearly choked by a sob that was rising in his throat.

He went away without another word, and got out to his gig without seeing Mrs Crawley. During one period of the interview he had been very angry with the man, – so angry as to make him almost declare to himself that he would take no more trouble on is behalf. Then he had been brought to acknowledge that Mr Walker was right, and that Crawley was certainly mad. He was so mad, so far removed from the dominion of sound sense, that no jury could say that he was guilty and that he ought to be punished for his guilt. And, as he so resolved, he could not but ask himself the question, whether the charge of the parish ought to be left in the hands of such a man? But at last, just before he went, these feelings and these convictions gave way to pity, and he remembered simply the troubles which seemed to have been heaped on the head of this poor victim of misfortune. As he drove home he resolved that there was nothing left for him to do, but to write to the dean. It was known to all who knew them both, that the dean and Mr Crawley had lived together on the closest intimacy at college, and that that friendship had been maintained through life; – though, from the peculiarity of Mr Crawley's character, the two had not been much together of late years. Seeing how things were going now, and hearing how pitiful was the plight in which Mr Crawley was placed, the dean would, no doubt, feel it to be his duty to hasten his return to England. He was believed to be at this moment in Jerusalem, and it would be long before a letter could reach him; but there still wanted three months to the assizes, and his return might be probably effected before the end of February.

'I never was so distressed in my life,' Mark Robarts said to his wife.

'And you think you have done no good?'

'Only this, that I have convinced myself that the poor man is not responsible for what he does, and that for her sake as well as for his own, some person should be enabled to interfere for his protection.' Then he told Mrs Robarts what Mr Walker had said; also the message which Mr Crawley had sent to the archdeacon. But they both agreed that that message need not be sent on any further.

CHAPTER 22

Major Grantly at home

Mrs Thorne had spoken very plainly in the advice which she had given to Major Grantly. 'If I were you, I'd be at Allington before twelve o'clock to-morrow.' That had been Mrs Thorne's advice; and though Major Grantly had no idea of making the journey so rapidly as the lady had proposed, still he thought that he would make it before long, and follow the advice in spirit if not to the letter. Mrs Thorne had asked him if it was fair that the girl should be punished because of the father's fault; and the idea had been sweet to him that the infliction or non-infliction of such punishment should be in his hands. 'You go and ask her,' Mrs Thorne had said. Well; – he would go and ask her. If it should turn out at last that he had married the daughter of a thief, and that he was disinherited for doing so, – an arrangement of circumstances which he had to teach himself to regard as very probable, – he would not love Grace the less on that account, or allow himself for one moment to repent what he had done. As he thought of all this he became somewhat in love with a small income, and imagined to himself what honours would be done to him by the Mrs Thornes of the county, when they should come to know in what way he had sacrificed himself to his love. Yes; – they would go and live at Pau. He thought Pau would do. He would have enough of income for that; – and Edith would get lessons cheaply, and would learn to talk French fluently. He certainly would do it. He would go down to Allington, and ask Grace to be his wife; and bid her understand that if she loved him she could not be justified in refusing him by the circumstances of her father's position.

But he must go to Plumstead before he could go to Allington. He was engaged to spend his Christmas there, and must go now at once. There was not time for the journey to Allington before he was due at Plumstead. And, moreover, though he could not bring himself to resolve that he would tell his father what he was going to do; – 'It would seem as though I were asking his leave !' he said to himself; – he thought that he would make a clean breast of it to his mother. It made him sad to think that he should cut the rope which fastened his own boat among the other boats in the home harbour at Plumstead, and that he should go out all alone into strange waters, – turned adrift altogether, as it were, from the Grantly fleet. If he could only get the promise of his mother's sympathy for Grace it would be something. He understood, – no one better than he, – the tendency of all his family to an uprising in the world, which tendency was almost as strong in his mother as in his father. And he had been by no means without a similar ambition himself, though with him the ambition had been only fitful, not enduring. He had a brother, a clergyman, a busy, stirring, eloquent London preacher, who got churches built, and was heard of far and wide as a rising man, who had married a certain Lady Anne, the daughter of an earl, and who was already mentioned as a candidate for high places. How his sister was the wife of a marquis, and a leader in the fashionable world, the reader already knows. The archdeacon himself was a rich man, so powerful that he could afford to look down upon a bishop ; and Mrs Grantly, though there was left about her something of an old softness of nature, a touch of the former life which had been hers before the stream of her days had run gold, yet she, too, had taken kindly to wealth and high standing, and was by no means one of those who construe literally that passage of scripture which tells us of the camel and the needle's eye.* Our Henry Grantly, our major, knew himself to be his mother's favourite child, – knew himself to have become so since something of coolness had grown up between her and her august daughter. The augustness of the daughter had done much to reproduce the old freshness of which I have spoken in the mother's heart, and had specially endeared to her the son who, of all her children, was the least subject to the family failing. The clergyman, Charles Grantly, – he who had married the Lady Anne, – was his father's darling in these days. The old archdeacon would go up to London and be quite happy in his son's house. He met there the men whom he loved to meet, and heard the talk which he loved to hear. It was very fine, having the Marquis of Hartletop for his son-in-law, but he had never cared to be much at Lady Hartletop's house. Indeed, the archdeacon cared to be in no house in which those around him were supposed to be bigger than himself. Such was the little family fleet from out of which Henry Grantly was now proposing to sail alone with his little boat, – taking Grace Crawley with him at the helm. 'My father is a just man at the bottom,' he said to himself, 'and though he may not forgive me, he will not punish Edith.'

But there was still left one of the family, – not a Grantly, indeed, but one so nearly allied to them as to have his boat moored in the same harbour, – who, as the major well knew, would thoroughly sympathize with him. This was old Mr Harding, his mother's father, – the father of his mother and of his aunt Mrs Arabin, – whose home was now at the deanery. He was also to be at Plumstead during this Christmas, and he at any rate would give a ready assent to such a marriage as that which the major was proposing for himself. But then poor old Mr Harding had been thoroughly deficient in that ambition which had served to aggrandize the family into which his daughter had married. He was a poor old man who, in spite of good friends, – for the late bishop of the diocese had been his dearest friend, – had never risen high in his profession, and had fallen even from the moderate altitude which he had attained. But he was a man whom all loved who knew him; and it was much to the credit of his son-in-law, the archdeacon, that, with all his tendencies to love rising suns, he had ever been true to Mr Harding.

Major Grantly took his daughter with him, and on his arrival at Plumstead she of course was the first object of attention. Mrs Grantly declared that she had grown immensely. The archdeacon complimented her red cheeks, and said that Cosby Lodge was as healthy a place as any in the county, while Mr Harding, Edith's great-grandfather, drew slowly from his pocket sundry treasures with which he had come prepared for the delight of the little girl. Charles Grantly and Lady Anne had no children, and the heir of all the Hartletops was too august to have been trusted to the embraces of her mother's grandfather. Edith, therefore, was all that he had in that generation, and of Edith he was prepared to be as indulgent as he had been, in their time, of his grandchildren the Grantlys, and still was of his grandchildren the Arabins, and had been before that of his own daughters. 'She's more like Eleanor than any one else,' said the old man in a plaintive tone. Now Eleanor was Mrs Arabin, the dean's wife, and was at this time, – if I were to say over forty I do not think I should be uncharitable. No one else saw the special likeness, but no one else remembered, as Mr Harding did, what Eleanor had been when she was three years old.

'Aunt Nelly is in France,' said the child.

'Yes, my darling, Aunt Nelly is in France, and I wish she were at home. Aunt Nelly has been away a long time.'

'I suppose she'll stay till the dean picks her up on his way home?' said Mrs Grantly.

'So she says in her letters. I heard from her yesterday, and I brought the letter, as I thought you'd like to see it.' Mrs Grantly took the letter and read it, while her father still played with the child. The archdeacon and the major were standing together on the rug discussing the shooting at Chaldicotes, as to which the archdeacon had a strong opinion. 'I'm quite sure that a man with a place like that does more good by preserving than by leaving it alone. The better head of game he has the richer the county will be generally. It is just the same with pheasants as it is with sheep and bullocks. A pheasant doesn't cost more than he's worth any more than a barn-door fowl. Besides, a man who preserves is always respected by the poachers, and the man who doesn't is not.'

'There's something in that, sir, certainly,' said the major.

'More than you think for, perhaps. Look at poor Sowerby, who went on there for years without a shilling. How he was respected, because he lived as the people around him expected a gentleman to live. Thorne will have a bad time of it, if he tries to change things.'

'Only think,' exclaimed Mrs Grantly, 'when Eleanor wrote she had not heard of that affair of poor Mr Crawley's.'

'Does she say anything about him?' asked the major.

'I'll read what she says. "I see in Galignani* that a clergyman in Barsetshire has been committed for theft. Pray tell me who it is. Not the bishop, I hope, for the credit of the diocese?"'

'I wish it were,' said the archdeacon.

'For shame, my dear,' said his wife.

'No shame at all. If we are to have a thief among us, I'd sooner find him in a bad man than a good one. Besides we should have a change at the palace, which would be a great thing.'

'But is it not odd that Eleanor should have heard nothing of it?' said Mrs Grantly.

'It's odd that you should not have mentioned it yourself.'

'I did not, certainly; nor you, papa, I suppose?'

Mr Harding acknowledged that he had not spoken of it, and then they calculated that perhaps she might not have received any letter from her husband written since the news had reached him. 'Besides, why should he have mentioned it?' said the major. 'He only knows as yet of the injury about the cheque, and can have heard nothing of what was done by the magistrates.'

'Still it seems so odd that Eleanor should not have known of it, seeing that we have been talking of nothing else for the last week,' said Mrs Grantly.

For two days the major said not a word of Grace Crawley to any one. Nothing could be more courteous and complaisant than was his father's conduct to him. Anything that he wanted for Edith was to be done. For himself there was no trouble which would not be taken. His hunting, and his shooting, and his fishing seemed to have become matters of paramount consideration to his father. And then the archdeacon became very confidential about money matters, – not offering anything to his son, which, as he well knew, would have been seen through as palpable bribery and corruption, – but telling him of this little scheme and of that, of one investment and of another; – how he contemplated buying a small property here, and spending a few thousands on building there. 'Of course it is all for you and your brother,' said the archdeacon, with that benevolent sadness which is used habitually by fathers on such occasions; 'and I like you to know what it is that I am doing. I told Charles about the London property the last time I was up,' said the archdeacon, 'and there shall be no difference between him and you, if all goes well.' This was very good-natured on the archdeacon's part, and was not strictly necessary, as Charles was the eldest son; but the major understood it perfectly. 'There shall be an elysium opened to you, if only you will not do that terrible thing of which you spoke when last here.' The archdeacon uttered no such words as these, and did not even allude to Grace Crawley; but the words were as good as spoken, and had they been spoken ever so plainly the major could not have understood them more clearly. He was quite awake to the loveliness of the elysium opened before him. He had had his moment of anxiety, whether his father would or would not make an elder son of his brother Charles. The whole thing was now put before him plainly. Give up Grace Crawley, and you shall share alike with your brother. Disgrace yourself by marrying her, and your brother shall have everything. There was the choice, and it was still open to him to take which side he pleased. Were he never to go near Grace Crawley again no one would blame him, unless it were Miss Prettyman or Mrs Thorne. 'Fill your glass, Henry,' said the archdeacon. 'You'd better, I tell you, for there is no more of it left.' Then the major filled his glass and sipped the wine, and swore to himself that he would go down to Allington at once. What! Did his father think to bribe him by giving him '20 port? He would certainly go down to Allington, and he would tell his mother to-morrow morning, or certainly on the next day, what he was going to do. 'Pity it should be all gone; isn't it, sir?' said the archdeacon to his father-in-law. 'It has lasted my time,' said Mr Harding, 'and I'm very much obliged to it. Dear, dear; how well I remember your father giving the order for it! There were two pipes, and somebody said it was a heady wine. "If the prebendaries and rectors can't drink it," said your father, "the curates will."'

'Curates indeed!' said the archdeacon. 'It's too good for a bishop, unless one of the right sort.'

'Your father used to say those things, but with him the poorer the guest the better the cheer. When he had a few clergymen round him, how he loved to make them happy!'

'Never talked shop to them, – did he?' said the archdeacon.

'Not after dinner, at any rate. Goodness gracious, when one thinks of it! Do you remember how we used to play cards?'

'Every night regularly; – threepenny points, and sixpence on the rubber,' said the archdeacon.

'Dear, dear! How things are changed! And I remember when the clergymen did more of the dancing in Barchester than all the other young men in the city put together.'

'And a good set they were; – gentlemen every one of them. It's well that some of them don't dance now; – that is, for the girls' sake.'

'I sometimes sit and wonder,' said Mr Harding, 'whether your father's spirit ever comes back to the old house and sees the changes, – and if so whether he approves them.'

'Approves them!' said the archdeacon.

'Well; – yes. I think he would, upon the whole. I'm sure of this: he would not disapprove, because the new ways are changed from his ways. He never thought himself infallible. And do you know, my dear, I am not sure that it isn't all for the best. I sometimes think that some of us were very idle when we were young. I was, I know.'

'I worked hard enough,' said the archdeacon.

'Ah, yes; you. But most of us took it very easily. Dear, dear! When I think of it, and see how hard they work now, and remember what pleasant times we used to have, – I don't feel sometimes quite sure.'

'I believe the work was done a great deal better than it is now,' said the archdeacon. 'There wasn't so much fuss, but there was more reality. And men were men, and clergymen were gentlemen.

'Yes; – they were gentlemen.'

'Such a creature as that old woman at the palace couldn't have held his head up among us. That's what has come from Reform. A reformed House of Commons makes Lord Brock Prime Minister, and then your Prime Minister makes Dr Proudie a bishop! Well; – it will last my time, I suppose.'

'It has lasted mine, – like the wine,' said Mr Harding.

'There's one glass more, and you shall have it, sir.' Then Mr Harding drank the last glass of the 1820 port, and they went into the drawing-room.

On the next morning after breakfast the major went out for a walk by himself. His father had suggested to him that he should go over to shoot at Framley, and had offered him the use of everything the archdeaconry possessed in the way or horses, dogs, guns and carriages. But the major would have none of these things. He would go out and walk by himself. 'He's not thinking of her; is he?' said the archdeacon to his wife, in a whisper. 'I don't know. I think he is,' said Mrs Grantly. 'It will be so much the better for Charles, if he does,' said the archdeacon grimly; and the look of his face as he spoke was by no means pleasant. 'You will do nothing unjust, archdeacon,' said his wife. 'I will do as I like with my own,' said he. And then he also went out and took a walk by himself.

That evening after dinner, there was no 1820 port, and no recollections of old days. They were rather dull, the three of them, as they sat together, – and dulness is always more unendurable than sadness. Old Mr Harding went to sleep and the archdeacon was cross. 'Henry,' he said, 'you haven't a word to throw to a dog.' 'I've got rather a headache this evening, sir,' said the major. The archdeacon drank two glasses of wine, one after another, quickly. Then he woke his father-in-law gently, and went off. 'Is there anything the matter?' asked the old man. 'Nothing particular. My father seems to be a little cross.' 'Ah! I've been to sleep and I oughtn't. It's my fault. We'll go in and smooth him down.' But the archdeacon wouldn't be smoothed down on that occasion. He would let his son see the difference between a father pleased, and a father displeased, – or rather between a father pleasant, and a father unpleasant. 'He hasn't said anything to you, has he?' said the archdeacon that night to his wife. 'Not a word; – as yet.' 'If he does it without the courage to tell us, I shall think him a cur,' said the archdeacon. 'But he did tell you,' said Mrs Grantly, standing up for her favourite son; 'and, for the matter of that, he has courage enough for anything. If he does it, I shall always say that he has been driven to it by your threats.'

'That's sheer nonsense,' said the archdeacon.

'It's not nonsense at all,' said Mrs Grantly.

'Then I suppose I was to hold my tongue and say nothing?' said the archdeacon; and as he spoke he banged the door between his dressing-room and Mrs Grantly's bedroom.

On the first day of the new year Major Grantly spoke his mind to his mother. The archdeacon had gone into Barchester, having in vain attempted to induce his son to go with him. Mr Harding was in the library reading a little and sleeping a little, and dreaming of old days and old friends, and perhaps, sometimes, of the old wine. Mrs Grantly was alone in a small sitting-room which she frequented upstairs, when suddenly her son entered the room. 'Mother,' he said, 'I think it better to tell you that I am going to Allington.'

'To Allington, Henry?' She knew very well who was at Allington, and what must be the business which would take him there.

'Yes, mother. Miss Crawley is there, and there are circumstances which make it incumbent on me to see her without delay.'

'What circumstances, Henry?'

'As I intend to ask her to be my wife, I think it best to do so now. I owe it to her and to myself that she should not think that I am deterred by her father's position.'

'But would it not be reasonable that you should be deterred by her father's position?'

'No, I think not. I think it would be dishonest as well as ungenerous. I cannot bring myself to brook such delay. Of course I am alive to the misfortune which has fallen upon her, – upon her and me, too, should she ever become my wife. But it is one of those burdens which a man should have shoulders broad enough to bear.'

'Quite so, if she were your wife, or even if you were engaged to her. Then honour would require it of you, as well as affection. As it is, your honour does not require it, and I think you should hesitate, for all our sakes, and especially for Edith's.'

'It will do Edith no harm; and, mother, if you alone were concerned, I think you would feel that it would not hurt you.'

'I was not thinking of myself, Henry.'

'As for my father, the very threats which he has used make me conscious that I have only to measure the price. He has told me that he will stop my allowance.'

'But that may not be the worst. Think how you are situated. You are the younger son of a man who will be held to be justified in making an elder son, if he thinks fit to do so.'

'I can only hope that he will be fair to Edith. If you will tell him that from me, it is all that I will ask you to do.'

'But you will see him yourself?'

'No, mother; not till I have been to Allington. Then I will see him again or not, just as he pleases. I shall stop at Guestwick, and will write to you a line from thence. If my father decides on doing anything, let me know at once, as it will be necessary that I should get rid of the lease of my house.'

'Oh, Henry!'

I have thought a great deal about it, mother, and I believe I am right. Whether I am right or wrong, I shall do it. I will not ask you now for any promise or pledge; but should Miss Crawley become my wife, I hope that you at least will not refuse to see her as your daughter.' Having so spoken, he kissed his mother, and was about to leave the room; but she held him by his arm, and he saw that her eyes were full of tears. 'Dearest mother, if I grieve you I am sorry indeed.'

'Not me, not me, not me,' she said.

'For my father, I cannot help it. Had he not threatened me I should have told him also. As he has done so, you must tell him. But give him my kindest love.'

'Oh, Henry; you will be ruined. You will, indeed. Can you not wait? Remember how headstrong your father is, and yet how good; – and how he loves you! Think of all that he has done for you. When did he refuse you anything?'

'He has been good to me, but in this I cannot obey him. He should not ask me.'

'You are wrong. You are indeed. He has a right to expect that you will not bring disgrace upon the family.'

'Nor will I; – except such disgrace as may attend upon poverty. Good-by, mother. I wish you could have said one kind word to me.'

'Have I not said a kind word?'

'Not as yet, mother.'

'I would not for worlds speak unkindly to you. If it were not for your father I would bid you bring whom you pleased home to me as your wife; and I would be as a mother to her. And if this girl should become your wife – '

'It shall not be my fault if she does not.'

'I will try to love her – some day.'

Then the major went, leaving Edith at the rectory, as requested by his mother. His own dog-cart and his servant were at Plumstead, and he drove himself home to Cosby Lodge.

When the archdeacon returned the news was told to him at once. 'Henry has gone to Allington to propose to Miss Crawley,' said Mrs Grantly.

'Gone, – without speaking to me!'

'He left his love, and said that it was useless his remaining, as he knew he should only offend you.'

'He has made his bed, and he must lie upon it,' said the archdeacon. And then there was not another word said about Grace Crawley on that occasion.

CHAPTER 23

Miss Lily Dale's resolution

The ladies at the Small House at Allington breakfasted always at nine, – a liberal nine; and the postman whose duty it was to deliver letters in that village at half-past eight, being also liberal in his ideas as to time, always arrived punctually in the middle of breakfast, so that Mrs Dale expected her letters, and Lily hers, just before their second cup of tea, as though the letters formed a part of the morning meal. Jane, the maid-servant, always brought them in, and handed them to Mrs Dale, – for Lily had in these days come to preside at the breakfast-table; and then there would be an examination of the outsides before the envelopes were violated, and as each knew pretty well all the circumstances of the correspondence of the other, there would be some guessing as to what this or that epistle might contain; and after that a reading out loud of passages, and not unfrequently of the entire letter. But now, at the time of which I am speaking, Grace Crawley was at the Small House, and therefore the common practice was somewhat in abeyance.

On one of the first days of the new year Jane brought in the letters as usual, and handed them to Mrs Dale. Lily was at the time occupied with the teapot, but still she saw the letters, and had not her hands so full as to be debarred from the expression of her usual anxiety. 'Mamma, I'm sure I see two there for me,' she said. 'Only one for you, Lily,' said Mrs Dale. Lily instantly knew from the tone of the voice that some letter had come, which by the very aspect of the handwriting had disturbed her mother. 'There is one for you, my dear,' said Mrs Dale, throwing a letter across the table to Grace. 'And one for you, Lily, from Bell. The others are for me.' 'And whom are yours from, mamma?' asked Lily. 'One is from Mrs Jones; the other, I think, is a letter on business.' Then Lily said nothing further, but she observed that her mother only opened one of her letters at the breakfast-table. Lily was very patient; – not by nature, I think, but by exercise and practice. She had, once in her

life, been too much in a hurry; and having then burned herself
grievously, she now feared the fire. She did not therefore follow her
mother after breakfast, but sat with Grace over the fire, hemming
diligently at certain articles of clothing which were intended for use
in the Hogglestock parsonage. The two girls were making a set of
new shirts for Mr Crawley. 'But I know he will ask where they
come from,' said Grace; 'and then mamma will be scolded.' 'But I
hope he'll wear them,' said Lily. 'Sooner or later he will,' said
Grace; 'because mamma manages generally to have her way at
last.' Then they went on for an hour or so, talking about the home
affairs at Hogglestock. But during the whole time Lily's mind was
intent upon her mother's letter.

Nothing was said about it at lunch, and nothing when they
walked out after lunch, for Lily was very patient. But during the
walk Mrs Dale became aware that her daughter was uneasy. These
two watched each other unconsciously with a closeness which
hardly allowed a glance of the eye, certainly not a tone of the voice,
to pass unobserved. To Mrs Dale it was everything in the world
that her daughter should be, if not happy at heart, at least tranquil;
and to Lily, who knew that her mother was always thinking of her,
and of her alone, her mother was the only human divinity now
worthy of adoration. But nothing was said about the letter during
the walk.

When they came home it was nearly dusk, and it was their habit
to sit up for a while without candles, talking, till the evening had in
truth set in and the unmistakable and enforced idleness of remaining
without candles was apparent. During this time, Lily, demanding
patience of herself all the while, was thinking what she would do,
or rather what she would say, about the letter. That nothing could
be done or said in the presence of Grace Crawley was a matter of
course, nor would she do or say anything to get rid of Grace. She
would be very patient; but she would, at last, ask her mother about
the letter.

And then, as luck would have it, Grace Crawley got up and left
the room. Lily still waited for a few minutes, and, in order that her
patience might be thoroughly exercised, she said a word or two
about her sister Bell; how the eldest child's whooping-cough was
nearly well, and how the baby was doing wonderful things with its
first tooth. But as Mrs Dale had already seen Bell's letter, all this
was not intensely interesting. At last Lily came to the point and
asked her question. 'Mamma, from whom was that other letter
which you got this morning?'

Our story will perhaps be best told by communicating the letter

to the reader before it was discussed with Lily. The letter was as
follows: –

General Committee Office, – January, 186–

I should have said that Mrs Dale had not opened the letter till
she had found herself in the solitude of her own bedroom; and that
then, before doing so, she had examined the handwriting with
anxious eyes. When she first received it she thought she knew the
writer, but was not sure. Then she had glanced at the impression
over the fastening, and had known at once from whom the letter
had come. It was from Mr Crosbie, the man who had brought so
much trouble into her house, who had jilted her daughter; the only
man in the world whom she had a right to regard as a positive
enemy to herself. She had no doubt about it, as she tore the
envelope open; and yet, when the address given made her quite
sure, a new feeling of shivering came upon her, and she asked
herself whether it might not be better that she should send his letter
back to him without reading it. But she read it.

Madam, the letter began, –

You will be very much surprised to hear from me, and I am quite
aware that I am not entitled to the ordinary courtesy of an
acknowledgment from you, should you be pleased to throw my
letter on one side as unworthy of your notice. But I cannot refrain
from addressing you, and must leave it to you to reply to me or not,
as you may think fit.

I will not refer to that episode of my life with which you are
acquainted, for the sake of acknowledging my great fault and of
assuring you that I did not go unpunished. It would be useless for
me now to attempt to explain to you the circumstances which led
me into that difficulty which ended in so great a blunder; but I will
ask you to believe that my folly was greater than my sin.

But I will come to my point at once. You are, no doubt, aware
that I married a daughter of Lord De Courcy, and that I was
separated from my wife a few weeks after our unfortunate marriage.
It is now something over twelve months since she died at Baden-
Baden in her mother's house. I never saw her since the day we first
parted. I have not a word to say against her. The fault was mine in
marrying a woman whom I did not love and had never loved. When
I married Lady Alexandrina I loved, not her, but your daughter.

I believe I may venture to say to you that your daughter once
loved me. From the day on which I last wrote to you that terrible
letter which told you of my fate, I have never mentioned the name
of Lily Dale to human ears. It has been too sacred for my mouth, –

too sacred for the intercourse of any friendship with which I have been blessed. I now use it for the first time to you, in order that I may ask whether it be possible that her old love should ever live again. Mine has lived always, – has never faded for an hour, making me miserable during the years that have passed since I saw her, but capable of making me very happy, if I may be allowed to see her again.

You will understand my purpose now as well as though I were to write pages. I have no scheme formed in my head for seeing your daughter again. How can I dare to form a scheme, when I am aware that the chance of success must be so strong against me? But if you will tell me that there can be a gleam of hope, I will obey any commands that you can put upon me in any way that you may point out. I am free again, – and she is free. I love her with all my heart, and seem to long for nothing in the world but that she should become my wife. Whether any of her old love may still abide with her, you will know. If it do, it may even yet prompt her to forgive one who, in spite of falseness of conduct, has yet been true to her in heart.

> I have the honour to be, Madam,
> Your most obedient servant,
> Adolphus Crosbie.

This was the letter which Mrs Dale had received, and as to which she had not as yet said a word to Lily, or even made up her mind whether she would say a word or not. Dearly as the mother and daughter loved each other, thorough as was the confidence between them, yet the name of Adolphus Crosbie had not been mentioned between them oftener, perhaps, than half-a-dozen times since the blow had been struck. Mrs Dale knew that their feelings about the man were altogether different. She, herself, not only condemned him for what he had done, believing it to be impossible that any shadow of excuse could be urged for his offence, thinking that the fault had shown the man to be mean beyond redemption, – but she had allowed herself actually to hate him. He had in one sense murdered her daughter, and she believed that she could never forgive him. But Lily, as her mother well knew, had forgiven this man altogether, had made excuses for him which cleansed his sin of all its blackness in her own eyes, and was to this day anxious as ever for his welfare and his happiness. Mrs Dale feared that Lily did in truth love him still. If it was so, was she not bound to show her this letter? Lily was old enough to judge for herself, – old enough, and wise enough too. Mrs Dale told herself half-a-score of times that morning that she could not be justified in keeping the letter from her daughter.

But yet she much wished that the letter had never been written, and would have given very much to be able to put it out of the way without injustice to Lily. To her thinking it would be impossible that Lily should be happy in marrying such a man. Such a marriage now would be, as Mrs Dale thought, a degradation to her daughter. A terrible injury had been done to her; but such reparations as this would, in Mrs Dale's eyes, only make the injury deeper. And yet Lily loved the man; and, loving him, how could she resist the temptation of his offer? 'Mamma, from whom was that letter which you got this morning?' Lily asked. For a few moments Mrs Dale remained silent. 'Mamma,' continued Lily, 'I think I know whom it was from. If you tell me to ask nothing further, of course I will not.'

'No, Lily; I cannot tell you that.'

'Then, mamma, out with it at once. What is the use of shivering on the brink?'

'It was from Mr Crosbie.'

'I knew it. I cannot tell you why, but I knew it. And now, mamma; – am I to read it?'

'You shall do as you please, Lily.'

'Then I please to read it.'

'Listen to me a moment first. For myself, I wish that the letter had never been written. It tells badly for the man, as I think of it. I cannot understand how any man could have brought himself to address either you or me, after having acted as he acted.'

'But, mamma, we differ about all that, you know.'

'Now he has written, and there is the letter, – if you choose to read it.'

Lily had it in her hand, but she still sat motionless, holding it. 'You think, mamma, I ought not to read it?'

'You must judge for yourself, dearest.'

'And if I do not read it, what shall you do, mamma?'

'I shall do nothing; – or, perhaps, I should in such a case acknowledge it, and tell him that we have nothing more to say to him.'

'That would be very stern.'

'He has done that which makes some sternness necessary.'

Then Lily was again silent, and still she sat motionless, with the letter in her hand. 'Mamma,' she said, at last, 'if you tell me not to read it, I will give it you back unread. If you bid me exercise my own judgment, I shall take it upstairs and read it.'

'You must exercise your own judgment,' said Mrs Dale. Then

Lily got up from her chair and walked slowly out of the room, and went to her mother's chamber. The thoughts which passed through Mrs Dale's mind while her daughter was reading the letter were very sad. She could find no comfort anywhere. Lily, she told herself, would surely give way to this man's renewed expressions of affection, and she, Mrs Dale herself, would be called upon to give her child to a man whom she could neither love nor respect; – whom, for aught she knew, she could never cease to hate. And she could not bring herself to believe that Lily would be happy with such a man. As for her own life, desolate as it would be, – she cared little for that. Mothers know that their daughters will leave them. Even widowed mothers, mothers with but one child left, – such a one as was this mother, – are aware that they will be left alone, and they can bring themselves to welcome the sacrifice of themselves with something of satisfaction. Mrs Dale and Lily had, indeed, of late become bound together especially, so that the mother had been justified in regarding the link which joined them as being firmer than that by which most daughters are bound to their mothers; – but in all that she would have found no regret. Even now, in these very days, she was hoping that Lily might yet be brought to give herself to John Eames. But she could not, after all that was come and gone, be happy in thinking that Lily should be given to Adolphus Crosbie.

When Mrs Dale went upstairs to her own room before dinner Lily was not there; nor were they alone together again that evening, except for a moment, when Lily, as was usual, went into her mother's room when she was undressing. But neither of them then said a word about the letter. Lily during dinner and throughout the evening had borne herself well, giving no sign of special emotion, keeping to herself entirely her own thoughts about the proposition made to her. And afterwards she had progressed diligently with the fabrication of Mr Crawley's shirts, as though she had no such letter in her pocket. And yet there was not a moment in which she was not thinking of it. To Grace, just before she went to bed, she did say one word. 'I wonder whether it can ever come to a person to be so placed that there can be no doing right, let what will be done; – that, do or not do, as you may, it must be wrong?'

'I hope you are not in such a condition,' said Grace.

'I am something near it,' said Lily, 'but perhaps if I look long enough I shall see the light.'

'I hope it will be a happy light at last,' said Grace, who thought that Lily was referring only to John Eames.

At noon on the next day Lily had still said nothing to her mother about the letter ; and then what she said was very little. 'When must you answer Mr Crosbie, mamma ?'

'When, my dear ?'

'I mean how long may you take ? It need not be to-day.'

'No; – certainly not to-day.'

'Then I will talk over it with you to-morrow. It wants some thinking; – does it not, mamma ?'

'It would not want much with me, Lily.'

'But then, mamma, you are not I. Believing as I believe, feeling as I feel, it wants some thinking. That's what I mean.'

'I wish I could help you, my dear.'

'You shall help me, – to-morrow.' The morrow came and Lily was still very patient; but she had prepared herself, and had prepared the time also, so that in the hour of the gloaming she was alone with her mother, and sure that she might remain alone with her for an hour or so. 'Mamma, sit there,' she said, 'I will sit down here, and then I can lean against you and be comfortable. You can bear as much of me as that, – can't you, mamma ?' Then Mrs Dale put her arm over Lily's shoulder, and embraced her daughter. 'And now, mamma, we will talk about this wonderful letter.'

'I do not know, dear, that I have anything to say about it.'

'But you must have something to say about it, mamma. You must bring yourself to have something to say, – to have a great deal to say.'

'You know what I think as well as though I talked for a week.'

'That won't do, mamma. Come, you must not be hard with me.'

'Hard, Lily !'

'I don't mean that you will hurt me, or not give me any food, – or that you will not go on caring about me more than anything else in the whole world ten times over;—' And Lily as she spoke tightened the embrace of her mother's arms and round her neck. 'I'm not afraid you'll be hard in that way. But you must soften your heart so as to be able to mention his name and talk about him, and tell me what I ought to do. You must see with my eyes, and hear with my ears, and feel with my heart; – and then, when I know that you have done that, I must judge with your judgment.'

'I wish you to use your own.'

'Yes; – because you won't see with my eyes and hear with my ears. That's what I call being hard. Though you should feed me with blood from your breast, I should call you a hard pelican, unless you could give me also the sympathy which I demand from you. You see, mamma, we have never allowed ourselves to speak of this man.'

'What need has there been, dearest ?'

'Only because we have been thinking of him. Out of the full heart the mouth speaketh;* – that is, the mouth does so when the full heart is allowed to have its own way comfortably.'

'There are things which should be forgotten.'

'Forgotten, mamma !'

'The memory of which should not be fostered by much talking.'

'I have never blamed you, mamma; never, even in my heart. I have known how good and gracious and sweet you have been. But I have often accused myself of cowardice because I have not allowed his name to cross my lips either to you or to Bell. To talk of forgetting such an accident as that is a farce. And as for fostering the memory of it—! Do you think that I have ever spent a night from that time to this without thinking of him? Do you imagine that I have ever crossed our own lawn, or gone down through the garden-path there, without thinking of the time when he and I walked there together? There needs no fostering for such memories as those. They are weeds which will grow rank and strong though nothing be done to foster them. There is the earth and the rain, and that is enough for them. You cannot kill them if you would, and they certainly will not die because you are careful not to hoe and rake the ground.'

'Lily, you forget how short the time has been as yet.'

'I have thought it very long; but the truth is, mamma, that this non-fostering of memories, as you call it, has not been the real cause of our silence. We have not spoken of Mr Crosbie because we have not thought alike about him. Had you spoken you would have spoken with anger, and I could not endure to hear him abused. That has been it.'

'Partly so, Lily.'

'Now you must talk of him, and you must not abuse him. We must talk of him, because something must be done about his letter. Even if it be left unanswered, it cannot be so left without discussion. And yet you must say no evil of him.'

'Am I to think that he behaved well?'

'No, mamma; you are not to think that; but you are to look upon his fault as a fault that has been forgiven.'

'It cannot be forgotten, dear.'

'But, mamma, when you go to heaven—'

'My dear !'

'But you will go to heaven, mamma, and why should I not speak of it? You will go to heaven, and yet I suppose you have been very wicked, because we are all very wicked. But you won't be told of your wickedness there. You won't be hated there, because you were this or that when you were here.'

'I hope not, Lily; but isn't your argument almost profane?'

'No; I don't think so. We ask to be forgiven just as we forgive. That is the way in which we hope to be forgiven, and therefore it is the way in which we ought to forgive. When you say that prayer at night, mamma, do you ever ask yourself whether you have forgiven him?'

'I forgive him as far as humanity can forgive. I would do him no injury.'

'But if you and I are forgiven only after that fashion we shall never get to heaven.' Lily paused for some further answer from her mother, but as Mrs Dale was silent she allowed that portion of the subject to pass as completed. 'And now, mamma, what answer do you think we ought to send to his letter?'

'My dear, how am I to say? You know I have said already that if I could act on my own judgment, I would send none.'

'But that was said in the bitterness of gall.'

'Come, Lily, say what you think yourself. We shall get on better when you have brought yourself to speak. Do you think that you wish to see him again?'

'I don't know, mamma. Upon the whole, I think not.'

'Then in heaven's name let me write and tell him so.'

'Stop a moment, mamma. There are two persons here to be considered, – or rather, three.'

'I would not have you think of me in such a question.'

'I know you would not; but never mind, and let me go on. The three of us are concerned, at any rate; you, and he, and I. I am thinking of him now. We have all suffered, but I do believe that hitherto he has had the worst of it.'

'And who has deserved the worst?'

'Mamma, how can you go back in that way? We have agreed that that should be regarded as done and gone. He has been very unhappy, and now we see what remedy he proposes to himself for his misery. Do I flatter myself if I allow myself to look at it in that way?'

'Perhaps he thinks he is offering a remedy for your misery.'

As this was said Lily turned round slowly and looked up into her mother's face. 'Mamma,' she said, 'that is very cruel. I did not think you could be so cruel. How can you, who believe him to be so selfish, think that?'

'It is very hard to judge of men's motives. I have never supposed him to be so black that he would not wish to make atonement for the evil he has done.'

'If I thought that there certainly could be but one answer.'

'Who can look into a man's heart and judge all the sources of his actions? There are mixed feelings there, no doubt. Remorse for what he has done; regret for what he has lost; — something, perhaps, of the purity of love.'

'Yes, something, — I hope something, — for his sake.'

'But when a horse kicks and bites, you know his nature and do not go near him. When a man has cheated you once, you think he will cheat you again, and you do not deal with him. You do not look to gather grapes from thistles,* after you have found that they are thistles.'

'I still go for the roses though I have often torn my hand with thorns in looking for them.'

'But you do not pluck those that have become cankered in the blowing.'

'Because he was once at fault, will he be cankered always?'

'I would not trust him.'

'Now, mamma, see how different we are; or, rather, how different it is when one judges for oneself or for another. If it were simply myself, and my own future fate in life, I would trust him with it all to-morrow, without a word. I should go to him as a gambler goes to the gambling-table, knowing that if I lost everything I could hardly be poorer than I was before. But I should have a better hope than the gambler is justified in having. That, however, is not my difficulty. And when I think of him I can see a prospect of success for the gambler. I think so well of myself that, loving him, as I do; — yes, mamma, do not be uneasy; — loving him, as I do, I believe I could be a comfort to him. I think that he might be better with me than without me. That is, he would be so, if he could teach himself to look back upon the past as I can do, and to judge of me as I can judge of him.'

'He had nothing, at least, for which to condemn you.'

'But he would have, were I to marry him now. He would condemn me because I had forgiven him. He would condemn me because I had borne what he had done to me, and had still loved him — loved him through it all. He would feel and know the weakness; — and there is weakness. I have been weak in not being able to rid myself of him altogether. He would recognize this after awhile, and would despise me for it. But he would not see what there is of devotion to him in my being able to bear the taunts of the world in going back to him, and your taunts, and my own taunts. I should have to bear his also, — not spoken aloud, but to be seen in his face and heard in his voice, — and that I could not endure. If he despised me, and he would, that would make us both unhappy. Therefore, mamma, tell him not to come; tell him that he can never come; but, if it be possible, tell him this tenderly.' Then she got up and walked away, as though she were going out of the room; but her mother had caught her before the door was opened.

'Lily,' she said, 'if you think you can be happy with him, he shall come.'

'No, mamma, no. I have been looking for the light ever since I read his letter, and I think I see it. And now, mamma, I will make a clean breast of it. From the moment in which I heard that that poor woman was dead, I have been in a state of flutter. It has been weak of me, and silly, and contemptible. But I could not help it. I kept on asking myself whether he would ever think of me now. Well; he has answered the question; and has so done it that he has forced upon me the necessity of a resolution. I have resolved, and I believe that I shall be the better for it.'

The letter which Mrs Dale wrote to Mr Crosbie, was as follows: —

'Mrs Dale presents her compliments to Mr Crosbie, and begs to assure him that it will not now be possible that he should renew the relations which were broken off three years ago, between him and Mrs Dale's family.' It was very short, certainly, and it did not by any means satisfy Mrs Dale. But she did not know how to say more without saying too much. The object of her letter was to save him the trouble of a futile perseverance, and them from the annoyance of persecution; and this she wished to do without mentioning her daughter's name. And she was determined that no word should escape her in which there was any touch of severity, any hint of an accusation. So much she owed to Lily in return for all that Lily was prepared to abandon. 'There is my note,' she said at last, offering it to her daughter. 'I did not mean to see it,' said Lily, 'and, mamma, I will not read it now. Let it go. I know you have been good and have not scolded him.' 'I have not scolded him, certainly,' said Mrs Dale. And then the letter was sent.

CHAPTER 24

Mrs Dobbs Broughton's dinner-party

Mr John Eames, of the Income-tax Office, had in these days risen
so high in the world that people in the west-end of town, and very
respectable people too, – people living in South Kensington, in
neighbourhoods not far from Belgravia, and in very handsome
houses round Bayswater, – were glad to ask him out to dinner.
Money had been left to him by an earl, and rumour had of course
magnified that money. He was a private secretary, which is in itself
a great advance on being a mere clerk. And he had become the
particularly intimate friend of an artist who had pushed himself
into high fashion during the last year or two, – one Conway
Dalrymple, whom the rich English world was beginning to pet and
pelt with gilt sugar-plums, and who seemed to take very kindly to
petting and gilt sugar-plums. I don't know whether the friendship
of Conway Dalrymple had not done as much to secure John Eames
his position at the Bayswater dinner-tables, as had either the private
secretaryship, or the earl's money; and yet, when they had first
known each other, now only two or three years ago, Conway
Dalrymple had been the poorer man of the two. Some chance had
brought them together, and they had lived in the same rooms for
nearly two years. This arrangement had been broken up, and the
Conway Dalrymple of these days had a studio of his own, somewhere near Kensington Palace, where he painted portraits of young
countesses, and in which he had even painted a young duchess. It
was the peculiar merit of his pictures, – so at least said the art-
loving world, – that though the likeness was always good, the
stiffness of the modern portrait was never there. There was also
ever some story told in Dalrymple's pictures over and above the
story of the portraiture. This countess was drawn as a fairy with
wings, that countess as a goddess with a helmet. The thing took for
a time, and Conway Dalrymple was picking up his gilt sugar-plums
with considerable rapidity.

On a certain day he and John Eames were to dine out together at a certain house in that Bayswater district. It was a large mansion, if not made of stone yet looking very stony, with thirty windows at least, all of them with cut-stone frames, requiring, let me say, at least four thousand a year for its maintenance. And its owner, Dobbs Broughton, a man very well known both in the City and over the grass in Northamptonshire, was supposed to have a good deal more than four thousand a year. Mrs Dobbs Broughton, a very beautiful woman, who certainly was not yet thirty-five, let her worst enemies say what they might, had been painted by Conway Dalrymple as a Grace. There were, of course, three Graces in the picture, but each Grace was Mrs Dobbs Broughton repeated. We all know how Graces stand sometimes; two Graces looking one way, and one the other. In this picture, Mrs Dobbs Broughton as centre Grace looked you full in the face. The same lady looked away from you, displaying her left shoulder as one side Grace, and displaying her right shoulder as the other side Grace. For this pretty toy Mr Conway Dalrymple had picked up a gilt sugar-plum to the tune of six hundred pounds, and had, moreover, won the heart both of Mr and Mrs Dobbs Broughton. 'Upon my word, Johnny,' Dalrymple had said to his friend, 'he's a deuced good fellow, has really a good glass of claret, – which is getting rarer and rarer every day, – and will mount you for a day, whenever you please, down at Market Harboro'. Come and dine with them.' Johnny Eames condescended, and did go and dine with Mr Dobbs Broughton. I wonder whether he remembered, when Conway Dalrymple was talking of the rarity of good claret, how much beer the young painter used to drink when they were out together in the country, as they used to be occasionally, three years ago; and how the painter had then been used to complain that bitter beer cost threepence a glass, instead of twopence, which had hitherto been the recognized price of the article. In those days the sugar-plums had not been gilt, and had been much rarer.

Johnny Eames and his friend went together to the house of Mr Dobbs Broughton. As Dalrymple lived close to the Broughtons, Eames picked him up in a cab. 'Filthy things, these cabs are,' said Dalrymple, as he got into the Hansom.

'I don't know about that,' said Johnny. 'They're pretty good, I think.'

'Foul things,' said Conway. 'Don't you feel what a draught comes in here because the glass is cracked. I'd have one of my own, only I should never know what to do with it.'

'The greatest nuisance on earth, I should think,' said Johnny.

'If you could always have it standing ready round the corner,' said the artist, 'it would be delightful. But one would want half a dozen horses, and two or three men for that.'

'I think the stands are the best,' said Johnny.

They were a little late, – a little later than they should have been had they considered that Eames was to be introduced to his new acquaintances. But he had already lived long enough before the world to be quite at his ease in such circumstances, and he entered Mrs Broughton's drawing-room with his pleasantest smile upon his face. But as he entered he saw a sight which made him look serious in spite of his efforts to the contrary. Mr Adolphus Crosbie, secretary to the Board at the General Committee Office, was standing on the rug before the fire.

'Who will be there?' Eames had asked of his friend, when the suggestion to go and dine with Dobbs Broughton had been made to him.

'Impossible to say,' Conway had replied. 'A certain horrible fellow of the name of Musselboro, will almost certainly be there. He always is when they have anything of a swell dinner-party. He is a sort of partner of Broughton's in the city. He wears a lot of chains, and has elaborate whiskers, and an elaborate waistcoat, which is worse; and he doesn't wash his hands as often as he ought to do.'

'An objectionable party, rather, I should say,' said Eames.

'Well, yes; Musselboro is objectionable. He's very good-humoured you know, and good-looking in a sort of way, and goes everywhere; that is among people of this sort. Of course he's not hand-and-glove with Lord Derby; and I wish he could be made to wash his hands. They haven't any other standing dish, and you may meet anybody. They always have a Member of Parliament; they generally manage to catch a Baronet; and I have met a Peer there. On that august occasion Musselboro was absent.'

So instructed, Eames, on entering the room, looked round at once for Mr Musselboro. 'If I don't see the whiskers and chain,' he had said, 'I shall know there's a Peer.' Mr Musselboro was in the room, but Eames had descried Mr Crosbie long before he had seen Mr Musselboro.

There was no reason for confusion on his part in meeting Crosbie. They had both loved Lily Dale. Crosbie might have been successful, but for his own fault. Eames had on one occasion been thrown into contact with him, and on that occasion had quarrelled with him and had beaten him, giving him a black eye, and in this way obtaining some mastery over him. There was no reason why he should be ashamed of meeting Crosbie; and yet, when he saw him, the blood mounted all over his face, and he forgot to make any further search for Mr Musselboro.

'I am so much obliged to Mr Dalrymple for bringing you,' said Mrs Dobbs Broughton very sweetly, 'only he ought to have come sooner. Naughty man! I know it was his fault. Will you take Miss Demolines down? Miss Demolines, – Mr Eames.'

Mr Dobbs Broughton was somewhat sulky and had not welcomed our hero very cordially. He was beginning to think that Conway Dalrymple gave himself airs and did not sufficiently understand that a man who had horses at Market Harboro' and '41 Lafitte was at any rate as good as a painter who was pelted with gilt sugar-plums for painting countesses. But he was a man whose ill-humour never lasted long, and he was soon pressing his wine on Johnny Eames as though he loved him dearly.

But there was yet a few minutes before they went down to dinner, and Johnny Eames, as he endeavoured to find something to say to Miss Demolines, – which was difficult, as he did not in the least know Miss Demolines' line of conversation, – was aware that his efforts were impeded by thoughts of Mr Crosbie. The man looked older than when he had last seen him, – so much older that Eames was astonished. He was bald, or becoming bald; and his whiskers were grey, or were becoming grey, and he was much fatter. Johnny Eames, who was always thinking of Lily Dale, could not now keep himself from thinking of Adolphus Crosbie. He saw at a glance that the man was in mourning, though there was nothing but his shirt-studs by which to tell it; and he knew that he was in mourning for his wife. 'I wish she might have lived for ever,' Johnny said to himself.

He had not yet been definitely called upon by the entrance of the servant to offer his arm to Miss Demolines, when Crosbie walked across to him from the rug and addressed him.

'Mr Eames,' said he, 'it is some time since we met.' And he offered his hand to Johnny.

'Yes, it is,' said Johnny, accepting the proffered salutation. 'I don't know exactly how long, but ever so long.'

'I am very glad to have the opportunity of shaking hands with you,' said Crosbie; and then he retired, as it had become his duty to wait with his arm ready for Mrs Dobbs Broughton. Having married an earl's daughter he was selected for that honour. There was a barrister in the room, and Mrs Dobbs Broughton ought to have known better. As she professed to be guided in such matters by the rules laid down by the recognized authorities, she ought to have been aware that a man takes no rank from his wife. But she was entitled I think to merciful consideration for her error. A woman situated as was Mrs Dobbs Broughton cannot altogether ignore these terrible rules. She cannot let her guests draw lots for precedence. She must select some one for the honour of her own arm. And amidst the intricacies of rank how is it possible for a woman to learn and to remember everything? If Providence would only send Mrs Dobbs Broughton a Peer for every dinner-party, the thing would go more easily; but what woman will tell me, off-hand, which should go out of a room first; a CB, an Admiral of the Blue, the Dean of Barchester, or the Dean of Arches?* Who is to know who was everybody's father? How am I to remember that young Thompson's progenitor was made a baronet and not a knight when he was Lord Mayor? Perhaps Mrs Dobbs Broughton ought to have known that Mr Crosbie could have gained nothing by his wife's rank, and the barrister may be considered to have been not immoderately severe when he simply spoke of her afterwards as the silliest and most ignorant old woman he had ever met in his life. Eames with the lovely Miss Demolines on his arm was the last to move before the hostess. Mr Dobbs Broughton had led the way energetically with old Lady Demolines. There was no doubt about Lady Demolines, – as his wife had told him, because her title marked her. Her husband had been a physician in Paris, and had been knighted in consequence of some benefit supposed to have been done to some French scion of royalty, – when such scions in France were royal and not imperial. Lady Demolines' rank was not much, certainly; but it served to mark her, and was beneficial.

As he went downstairs Eames was still thinking of his meeting with Crosbie, and had as yet hardly said a word to his neighbour, and his neighbour had not said a word to him. Now Johnny understood dinners quite well enough to know that in a party of twelve, among whom six are ladies, everything depends on your next neighbour, and generally on the next neighbour who specially belongs to you; and as he took his seat he was a little alarmed as to his prospect for the next two hours. On his other hand sat Mrs Ponsonby, the barrister's wife, and he did not much like the look of Mrs Ponsonby. She was fat, heavy, and good-looking; with a broad space between her eyes, and light smooth hair; – a youthful British matron every inch of her, of whom any barrister with a young family of children might be proud. Now Miss Demolines, though she was hardly to be called beautiful, was at any rate remarkable. She had large, dark, well-shaped eyes, and very dark hair, which she wore tangled about in an extraordinary manner, and she had an expressive face, – a face made expressive by the owner's will. Such power of expression is often attained by dint of labour, – though it never reaches to the expression of anything in particular.

She was almost sufficiently good-looking to be justified in considering herself to be a beauty.

But Miss Demolines, though she had said nothing as yet, knew
her game very well. A lady cannot begin conversation to any good
purpose in the drawing-room, when she is seated and the man is
standing; – nor can she know then how the table may subsequently
arrange itself. Powder may be wasted, and often is wasted, and the
spirit rebels against the necessity of commencing a second enterprise. But Miss Demolines, when she found herself seated, and
perceived that on the other side of her was Mr Ponsonby, a married
man, commenced her enterprise at once, and our friend John Eames
was immediately aware that he would have no difficulty as to
conversation.

'Don't you like winter dinner-parties?' began Miss Demolines.
This was said just as Johnny was taking his seat, and he had time
to declare that he liked dinner-parties at all periods of the year if
the dinner was good and the people pleasant before the host had
muttered something which was intended to be understood to be a
grace. 'But I mean especially in winter,' continued Miss Demolines.
'I don't think daylight should ever be admitted at a dinner-table;
and though you may shut out the daylight, you can't shut out the
heat. And then there are always so many other things to go to in
May and June and July. Dinners should be stopped by Act of
Parliament for those three months. I don't care what people do
afterwards, because we always fly away on the first of August.'

'That is good-natured on your part.'

'I'm sure what I say would be for the good of society; – but at
this time of the year a dinner is warm and comfortable.'

'Very comfortable, I think.'

'And people get to know each other;' – in saying which Miss
Demolines looked very pleasantly up into Johnny's face.

'There is a great deal in that,' said he. 'I wonder whether you and
I will get to know each other?'

'Of course we shall; – that is, if I'm worth knowing.'

'There can be no doubt about that, I should say.'

'Time alone can tell. But, Mr Eames, I see that Mr Crosbie is a
friend of yours.'

'Hardly a friend.'

'I know very well that men are friends when they step up and
shake hands with each other. It is the same as when women kiss.'

'When I see women kiss, I always think that there is deep hatred
at the bottom of it.'

'And there may be deep hatred between you and Mr Crosbie for
anything I know to the contrary,' said Miss Demolines.

'The very deepest,' said Johnny, pretending to look grave.

'Ah; then I know he is your bosom friend, and that you will tell him anything I say. What a strange history that was of his marriage!'

'So I have heard; – but he is not quite bosom friend enough with me to have told me all the particulars. I know that his wife is dead.'

'Dead; oh, yes; she has been dead these two years I should say.'

'Not so long as that, I should think.'

'Well, – perhaps not. But it's ever so long ago; – quite long enough for him to be married again. Did you know her?'

'I never saw her in my life.'

'I knew her, – not well indeed; but I am intimate with her sister, Lady Amelia Gazebee, and I have met her there. None of that family have married what you may call well. And now, Mr Eames, pray look at the menu and tell me what I am to eat. Arrange for me a little dinner of my own, out of the great bill of fare provided. I always expect some gentleman to do that for me. Mr Crosbie, you know, only lived with his wife for one month.'

'So I've been told.'

'And a terrible month they had of it. I used to hear of it. He doesn't look that sort of man, does he?'

'Well; – no. I don't think he does. But what sort of man do you mean?'

'Why, such a regular Bluebeard! Of course you know how he treated another girl before he married Lady Alexandrina. She died of it, – with a broken heart; absolutely died;; and there he is, indifferent as possible; – and would treat me in the same way to-morrow if I would let him.'

Johnny Eames, finding it impossible to talk to Miss Demolines about Lily Dale, took up the card of the dinner and went to work in earnest, recommending his neighbour what to eat and what to pass by. 'But you've skipped the pâté,' she said, with energy.

'Allow me to ask you to choose mine for me instead. You are much more fit to do it.' And she did choose his dinner for him.

They were sitting at a round table, and in order that the ladies and gentlemen should alternate themselves properly, Mr Mussel-boro was opposite to the host. Next to him on his right was old Mrs Van Siever, the widow of a Dutch merchant, who was very rich. She was a ghastly thing to look at, as well from the quantity as from the nature of the wiggeries which she wore. She had not only a false front, but long false curls, as to which it cannot be conceived that she would suppose that any one would be ignorant as to their falseness. She was very thin, too, and very small, and putting aside her wiggeries, you would think her to be all eyes. She was a ghastly old woman to the sight, and not altogether pleasant in her mode of talking. She seemed to know Mr Musselboro very well, for she called him by his name without any prefix. He had, indeed, begun life as a clerk in her husband's office.

'Why doesn't What's-his-name have real silver forks?' she said to him. Now Mrs What's-his-name, – Mrs Dobbs Broughton we will call her, – was sitting on the other side of Mr Musselboro, between him and Mr Crosbie; and, so placed, Mr Musselboro found it rather hard to answer the question, more especially as he was probably aware that other questions would follow.

'What's the use?' said Mr Musselboro. 'Everybody has these plated things now. What's the use of a lot of capital lying dead?'

'Everybody doesn't. I don't. You know as well as I do, Musselboro, that the appearance of the thing goes for a great deal. Capital isn't lying dead as long as people know that you've got it.'

Before answering this Mr Musselboro was driven to reflect that Mrs Dobbs Broughton would probably hear his reply. 'You won't find that there is any doubt on that head in the City as to Broughton,' he said.

'I shan't ask in the City, and if I did, I should not believe what people told me. I think there are sillier folks in the City than anywhere else. What did he give for that picture upstairs which the young man painted?'

'What, Mrs Dobbs Broughton's portrait?'

'You don't call that a portrait, do you? I mean the one with the three naked women?' Mr Musselboro glanced round with one eye, and felt sure that Mrs Dobbs Broughton had heard the question. But the old woman was determined to have an answer. 'How much did he give for it, Musselboro?'

'Six hundred pounds, I believe,' said Mr Musselboro, looking straight before him as he answered, and pretending to treat the subject with perfect indifference.

'Did he indeed, now? Six hundred pounds! And yet he hasn't got silver spoons. How things are changed! Tell me, Musselboro, who was that young man who came in with the painter?'

Mr Musselboro turned round and asked Mrs Broughton. 'A Mr John Eames, Mrs Van Siever,' said Mrs Broughton, whispering across the front of Mr Musselboro. 'He is private secretary to Lord – Lord – Lord – I forget who. Some one of the Ministers, I know. And he had a great fortune left him the other day by Lord – Lord – Lord somebody else.'

'All among the lords, I see,' said Mrs Van Siever. Then Mrs Dobbs Broughton drew herself back, remembering some little attack which had been made on her by Mrs Van Siever when she herself had had the real lord to dine with her.

There was a Miss Van Siever there also, sitting between Crosbie and Conway Dalrymple. Conway Dalrymple had been specially brought there to sit next to Miss Van Siever. 'There's no knowing how much she'll have,' said Mrs Dobbs Broughton, in the warmth of her friendship. 'But it's all real. It is, indeed. The mother is awfully rich.'

'But she's awful in another way, too,' said Dalrymple.

'Indeed she is, Conway.' Mrs Dobbs Broughton had got into a way of calling her young friend by his Christian name. 'All the world calls him Conway,' she had said to her husband once when her husband caught her doing so. 'She is awful. Her husband made the business in the City, when things were very different from what they are now, and I can't help having her. She has transactions of business with Dobbs. But there's no mistake about the money.'

'She needn't leave it to her daughter, I suppose?'

'But why shouldn't she? She has nobody else. You might offer to paint her, you know. She'd make an excellent picture. So much character. You come and see her.'

Conway Dalrymple had expressed his willingness to meet Miss Van Siever, saying something, however, as to his present position being one which did not admit of any matrimonial speculation. Then Mrs Dobbs Broughton had told him, with much seriousness, that he was altogether wrong, and that were he to forget himself, or commit himself, or misbehave himself, there must be an end to their pleasant intimacy. In answer to which, Mr Dalrymple had said that his Grace was surely of all Graces the least gracious. And now he had come to meet Miss Van Siever, and was seated next to her at table.

Miss Van Siever, who at this time had perhaps reached her twenty-fifth year, was certainly a handsome young woman. She was fair and large, bearing no likeness whatever to her mother. Her features were regular, and her full, clear eyes had a brilliance of their own, looking at you always steadfastly and boldly, though very seldom pleasantly. Her mouth would have been beautiful had it not been too strong for feminine beauty. Her teeth were perfect, – too perfect, – looking like miniature walls of carved ivory. She knew the fault of this perfection, and shewed her teeth as little as she could. Her nose and chin were finely chiselled, and her head stood well upon her shoulders. But there was something hard about it all which repelled you. Dalrymple, when he saw her, recoiled from her, not outwardly, but inwardly. Yes, she was handsome, as may be a horse or a tiger; but there was about her nothing of feminine softness. He could not bring himself to think of taking Clara Van Siever as the model that was to sit before him for the rest of his life. He certainly could make a picture of her, as had been suggested by his friend, Mrs Broughton, but it must be as Judith with the dissevered head, or as Jael using her hammer over the temple of Sisera.* Yes, – he thought she would do as Jael; and if Mrs Van Siever would throw him a sugar-plum, – for he would want the sugar-plum, seeing that any other result was out of the question, – the thing might be done. Such was the idea of Mr Conway Dalrymple respecting Miss Van Siever, – before he led her down to dinner.

At first he found it hard to talk to her. She answered him, and not with monosyllables. But she answered him without sympathy, or apparent pleasure in talking. Now the young artist was in the habit of being flattered by ladies, and expected to have his small talk made very easy for him. He liked to give himself little airs, and was not generally disposed to labour very hard at the task of making himself agreeable.

'Were you ever painted yet?' he asked her after they had both been sitting silent for two or three minutes.

'Was I ever – ever painted? In what way?'

'I don't mean rouged, or enamelled, or got up by Madame Rachel;* but have you ever had your portrait taken?'

'I have been photographed, – of course.'

'That's why I asked you if you had been painted, – so as to make some little distinction between the two. I am a painter by profession, and do portraits.'

'So Mrs Broughton told me.'

'I am not asking for a job, you know.'

'I am quite sure of that.'

'But I should have thought you would have been sure to have sat to somebody.'

'I never did. I never thought of doing so. One does those things at the instigation of one's intimate friends, – fathers, mothers, uncles, and aunts, and the like.'

'Or husbands, perhaps, – or lovers?'

'Well, yes; my intimate friend is my mother, and she would never dream of such a thing. She hates pictures.'

'Hates pictures!'

'And especially portraits. And I'm afraid, Mr Dalrymple, she hates artists.'

'Good heavens; how cruel! I suppose there is some story attached to it. There has been some fatal likeness, – some terrible picture, – something in her early days?'

'Nothing of the kind, Mr Dalrymple. It is merely the fact that her sympathies are with ugly things, rather than with pretty things. I think she loves the mahogany dinner-table better than anything else in the house; and she likes to have everything dark, and plain, and solid.

'And good?'

'Good of its kind, certainly.'

'If everybody was like your mother, how would the artists live?'

'There would be none.'

'And the world, you think, would be none the poorer?'

'I did not speak of myself. I think the world would be very much the poorer. I am very fond of the ancient masters, though I do not suppose that I understand them.'

'They are easier understood than the modern, I can tell you. Perhaps you don't care for modern pictures?'

'Not in comparison, certainly. If that is uncivil, you have brought it on yourself. But I do not in truth mean anything derogatory to the painters of the day. When their pictures are old, they, – that is the good ones among them, – will be nice also.'

'Pictures are like wine, and want age, you think?'

'Yes, and statues too, and buildings above all things. The colours of new paintings are so glaring, and the faces are so bright and self-conscious, that they look to me when I go to the exhibition like coloured prints in a child's new picture-book. It is the same thing with buildings. One sees all the points, and nothing is left to the imagination.'

'I find I have come across a real critic.'

'I hope, at any rate, I am not a sham one;' and Miss Van Siever as she said this looked very savage.

'I shouldn't take you to be a sham in anything.'

'Ah, that would be saying a great deal for myself. Who can undertake to say that he is not a sham in anything?'

As she said this the ladies were getting up. So Miss Van Siever also got up, and left Mr Conway Dalrymple to consider whether he could say or could think of himself that he was not a sham in anything. As regarded Miss Clara Van Siever, he began to think that he should not object to paint her portrait, even though there might be no sugar-plum. He would certainly do it as Jael; and he would, if he dared, insert dimly in the background some idea of the face of the mother, half-appearing, half-vanishing, as the spirit of the sacrifice. He was composing his picture, while Mr Dobbs Broughton was arranging himself and his bottles.

'Musselboro,' he said, 'I'll come up between you and Crosbie. Mr Eames, though I run away from you, the claret shall remain;

or, rather, it shall flow backwards and forwards as rapidly as you will.'

'I'll keep it moving,' said Johnny.

'Do; there's a good fellow. It's a nice glass of wine, isn't it? Old Ramsby, who keeps as good a stock of stuff as any wine-merchant in London, gave me a hint, three or four years ago, that he'd a lot of tidy Bordeaux. It's '41, you know. He had ninety dozen, and I took it all.'

'What was the figure, Broughton?' said Crosbie, asking the question which he knew was expected.

'Well, I only gave one hundred and four for it then; it's worth a hundred and twenty now. I wouldn't sell a bottle of it for any money. Come, Dalrymple, pass it round; but fill your glass first.'

'Thank you, no; I don't like it. I'll drink sherry.'

'Don't like it!' said Dobbs Broughton.

'It's strange, isn't it? but I don't.'

'I thought you particularly told me to drink his claret?' said Johnny to his friend afterwards.

'So I did,' said Conway; 'and wonderfully good wine it is. But I make it a rule never to eat or drink anything in a man's house when he praises it himself and tells me the price of it.'

'And I make it a rule never to cut the nose off my own face,' said Johnny.

Before they went, Johnny Eames had been specially invited to call on Lady Demolines, and had said that he would do so. 'We live in Porchester Gardens,' said Miss Demolines. 'Upon my word, I believe that the farther London stretches in that direction, the farther mamma will go. She thinks the air so much better. I know it's a long way.'

'Distance is nothing to me,' said Johnny; 'I can always set off over night.'

Conway Dalrymple did not get invited to call on Mrs Van Siever, but before he left the house he did say a word or two more to his friend Mrs Broughton as to Clara Van Siever. 'She is a fine young woman,' he said; 'she is indeed.'

'You have found it out, have you?'

'Yes, I have found it out. I do not doubt that some day she'll murder her husband or her mother, or startle the world by some newly-invented crime; but that only makes her the more interesting.'

'And when you add to that all the old woman's money,' said Mrs Dobbs Broughton, 'you think that she might do?'

'For a picture, certainly. I'm speaking of her simply as a model. Could we not manage it? Get her once here, without her mother

knowing it, or Broughton, or any one. I've got the subject, – Jael
and Sisera, you know. I should like to put Musselboro in as Sisera,
with the nail half driven in.' Mrs Dobbs Broughton declared that
the scheme was a great deal too wicked for her participation, but at
last she promised to think of it.

'You might as well come up and have a cigar,' Dalrymple said, as
he and his friend left Mr Broughton's house. Johnny said that he
would go up and have a cigar or two. 'And now tell me what you
think of Mrs Dobbs Broughton and her set,' said Conway.

'Well; I'll tell you what I think of them. I think they stink of
money, as the people say; but I'm not sure that they've got any all
the same.'

'I should suppose he makes a large income.'

'Very likely, and perhaps spends more than he makes. A good
deal of it looked to me like make-believe. There's no doubt about
the claret, but the champagne was execrable. A man is a criminal to
have such stuff handed round to his guests. And there isn't the ring
of real gold about the house.'

'I hate the ring of the gold, as you call it,' said the artist.

'So do I, – I hate it like poison; but if it is there, I like it to be
true. There is a sort of persons going now, – and one meets them
out here and there every day of one's life, – who are downright
Brummagem to the ear and to the touch and to the sight, and we
recognize them as such at the very first moment. My honoured lord
and master, Sir Raffle, is one such. There is no mistaking him. Clap
him down upon the counter, and he rings dull and untrue at once.
Pardon me, my dear Conway, if I say the same of your excellent
friend Mr Dobbs Broughton.'

'I think you go a little too far, but I don't deny it. What you mean
is, that he's not a gentleman.'

'I mean a great deal more than that. Bless you, when you come
to talk of a gentleman, who is to define the word? How do I know
whether or no I'm a gentleman myself. When I used to be in Burton
Crescent, I was hardly a gentleman then, – sitting at the same table
with Mrs Roper and the Lupexes; – do you remember them, and
the lovely Amelia?'

'I suppose you were a gentleman, then, as well as now.'

'You, if you had been painting duchesses then, with a studio in
Kensington Gardens, would not have said so, if you had happened
to come across me. I can't define a gentleman, even in my own
mind; – but I can define the sort of man with whom I think I can
live pleasantly.'

'And poor Dobbs doesn't come within the line?'

'N – o, not quite; a very nice fellow, I'm quite sure, and I'm very much obliged to you for taking me there.'

'I never will take you to any house again. And what did you think of his wife?'

'That's a horse of another colour altogether. A pretty woman with such a figure as hers has got a right to be anything she pleases. I see you are a great favourite.'

'No, I'm not; – not especially. I do like her. She wants to make up a match between me and that Miss Van Siever. Miss Van is to have gold by the ingot, and jewels by the bushel, and a hatful of bank shares, and a whole mine in Cornwall, for her fortune.'

'And is very handsome into the bargain.'

'Yes; she's handsome.'

'So is her mother,' said Johnny. 'If you take the daughter, I'll take the mother, and see if I can't do you out of a mine or two. Good-night, old fellow. I'm only joking about old Dobbs. I'll go and dine there again to-morrow, if you like it.'

CHAPTER 25

Miss Madalina Demolines

'I don't think you care two straws about her,' Conway Dalrymple said to his friend John Eames, two days after the dinner-party at Mrs Dobbs Broughton's. The painter was at work in his studio, and the private secretary from the Income-tax Office, who was no doubt engaged on some special mission to the West End on the part of Sir Raffle Buffle, was sitting in a lounging-chair and smoking a cigar.

'Because I don't go about with my stockings cross-gartered,* and do that kind of business?'

'Well, yes; because you don't do that kind of business, more or less.'

'It isn't in my line, my dear fellow. I know what you mean, very well. I daresay, artistically speaking, – '

'Don't be an ass, Johnny.'

'Well then, poetically, or romantically, if you like that better, – I daresay that poetically or romantically I am deficient. I eat my dinner very well, and I don't suppose I ought to do that; and, if you'll believe me, I find myself laughing sometimes.'

'I never knew a man who laughed so much. You're always laughing.'

'And that, you think, is a bad sign?'

'I don't believe you really care about her. I think you are aware that you have got a love-affair on hand, and that you hang on to it rather persistently, having in some way come to a resolution that you would be persistent. But there isn't much heart in it. I daresay there was once.'

'And that is your opinion?'

'You are just like some of those men who for years past have been going to write a book on some new subject. The intention has been sincere at first, and it never altogether dies away. But the would-be author, though he still talks of his work, knows that it will never be executed, and is very patient under the disappointment. All enthusiasm about the thing is gone, but he is still known as the man who is going to do it some day. You are the man who means to marry Miss Dale in five, ten, or twenty years' time.'

'Now, Conway, all that is thoroughly unfair. The would-be author talks of his would-be book to everybody. I have never talked of Miss Dale to any one but you, and one or two very old family friends. And from year to year, and from month to month, I have done all that has been in my power to win her. I don't think I shall ever succeed, and yet I am as determined about it as I was when I first began it, – or rather much more so. If I do not marry Lily, I shall never marry at all, and if anybody were to tell me to-morrow that she had made up her mind to have me, I should well nigh go mad for joy. But I am not going to give up all my life for love. Indeed the less I can bring myself to give up for it, the better I shall think of myself. Now I'll go away and call on old Lady Demolines.'

'And flirt with her daughter.'

'Yes; – flirt with her daughter, if I get the opportunity. Why shouldn't I flirt with her daughter?'

'Why not, if you like it?'

'I don't like it, – not particularly, that is; because the young lady is not very pretty, nor yet very graceful, nor yet very wise.'

'She is pretty after a fashion,' said the artist, 'and if not wise, she is at any rate clever.'

'Nevertheless, I do not like her,' said John Eames.

'Then why do you go there?'

'One has to be civil to people though they are neither pretty nor wise. I don't mean to insinuate that Miss Demolines is particularly bad, or indeed that she is worse than young ladies in general. I only abused her because there was an insinuation in what you said, that I was going to amuse myself with Miss Demolines in the absence of Miss Dale. The one thing has nothing to do with the other thing. Nothing that I shall say to Miss Demolines will at all militate against my loyalty to Lily.'

'All right, old fellow; – I didn't mean to put you on your purgation. I want you to look at that sketch. Do you know for whom it is intended?' Johnny took up a scrap of paper, and having scrutinized it for a minute or two declared that he had not the slightest idea who was represented. 'You know the subject, – the story that is intended to be told?' said Dalrymple.

'Upon my word I don't. There's some old fellow seems to be catching it over the head; but it's all so confused I can't make much of it. The woman seems to be uncommon angry.'

'Do you ever read your Bible?'

'Ah, dear! not as often as I ought to do. Ah, I see; it's Sisera. I never could quite believe that story. Jael might have killed Captain Sisera in his sleep, – for which, by-the-by, she ought to have been hung, and she might possibly have done it with a hammer and a nail. But she could not have driven it through, and staked him to the ground.'

'I've warrant enough for putting it into a picture, at any rate. My Jael there is intended for Miss Van Siever.'

'Miss Van Siever! Well, it is like her. Has she sat for it?'

'O dear, no; not yet. I mean to get her to do so. There's a strength about her, which would make her sit the part admirably. And I fancy she would like to be driving a nail into a fellow's head. I think I shall take Musselboro for a Sisera.'

'You're not in earnest?'

'He would just do for it. But of course I shan't ask him to sit, as my Jael would not like it. She would not consent to operate on so base a subject. So you really are going down to Guestwick?'

'Yes; I start to-morrow. Good-by, old fellow. I'll come and sit for Sisera if you'll let me; – only Miss Van Jael shall have a blunted nail, if you please.'

Then Johnny left the artist's room and walked across from Kensington to Lady Demolines' house. As he went he partly accused himself, and partly excused himself in that matter of his love for Lily Dale. There were moments of his life in which he felt that he would willingly die for her, – that life was not worth having without her, – in which he went about inwardly reproaching fortune for having treated him so cruelly. Why should she not be his? He half believed that she loved him. She had almost told him so. She could not surely still love that other man who had treated her with such vile falsehood? As he considered the question in all its bearings he assured himself over and over again that there would be now no fear of that rival; – and yet he had such fears, and hated Crosbie almost as much as ever. It was a thousand pities, certainly, that the man should have been made free by the death of his wife. But it could hardly be that he should seek Lily again, or that Lily, if so sought, should even listen to him. But yet there he was, free once more, – an odious being, whom Johnny was determined to sacrifice to his vengeance, if cause for such sacrifice should occur. And thus thinking of the real truth of his love, he endeavoured to excuse himself to himself from that charge of vagueness and laxness which his friend Conway Dalrymple had brought against him. And then again he accused himself of the same sin. If he had been positively in earnest, with downright manly earnestness, would he have allowed the thing to drag itself on with a weak uncertain life, as it had done for the last two or three years? Lily Dale had been a dream to him in his boyhood; and he had made a reality of his dream as soon as he had become a man. But before he had been able, as a man, to tell his love to the girl whom he had loved as a child, another man had intervened, and his prize had been taken from him. Then the wretched victor had thrown his treasure away, and he, John Eames, had been content to stoop to pick it up, – was content to do so now. But there was something which he felt to be unmanly in the constant stooping. Dalrymple had told him that he was like a man who is ever writing a book and yet never writes it. He would make another attempt to get his book written, – an attempt into which he would throw all his strength and all his heart. He would do his very best to make Lily his own. But if he failed now, he would have done with it. It seemed to him to be below his dignity as a man to be always coveting a thing which he could not obtain.

Johnny was informed by the boy in buttons, who opened the door for him at Lady Demolines', that the ladies were at home, and he was shown up into the drawing-room. Here he was allowed full ten minutes to explore the knicknacks on the table, and open the photograph book, and examine the furniture, before Miss Demolines made her appearance. When she did come, her hair was tangled more marvellously even than when he saw her at the dinner-party, and her eyes were darker, and her cheeks thinner. 'I'm afraid mamma won't be able to come down,' said Miss Demolines. 'She will be so sorry; but she is not quite well to-day. The wind is in the east, she says, and when she says the wind is in the east she always refuses to be well.'

'Then I should tell her it was in the west.'

'But it is in the east.'

'Ah, there I can't help you, Miss Demolines. I never know which is east, and which west; and if I did, I shouldn't know from which point the wind blew.'

'At any rate mamma can't come downstairs, and you must excuse her. What a very nice woman Mrs Dobbs Broughton is.' Johnny acknowledged that Mrs Dobbs Broughton was charming. 'And Mr Broughton is so good-natured!' Johnny again assented. 'I like him of all things,' said Miss Demolines. 'So do I,' said Johnny; – 'I never liked anybody so much in my life. I suppose one is bound to say that kind of thing.' 'Oh, you ill-natured man,' said Miss Demolines. 'I suppose you think that poor Mr Broughton is a little – just a little, – you know what I mean.'

'Not exactly,' said Johnny.

'Yes, you do; you know very well what I mean. And of course he is. How can he help it?'

'Poor fellow, – no. I don't suppose he can help it, or he would; – wouldn't he ?'

'Of course Mr Broughton had not the advantage of birth or much early education. All his friends know that, and make allowance accordingly. When she married him, she was aware of his deficiency, and made up her mind to put up with it.'

'It was very kind of her; don't you think so ?'

'I knew Maria Clutterbuck for years before she was married. Of course she was very much my senior, but, nevertheless, we were friends. I think I was hardly more then twelve years old when I first began to correspond with Maria. She was then past twenty. So you see, Mr Eames, I make no secret of my age.'

'Why should you ?'

'But never mind that. Everybody knows that Maria Clutterbuck was very much admired. Of course I'm not going to tell you or any other gentleman all her history.'

'I was in hopes you were.'

'Then certainly your hopes will be frustrated, Mr Eames. But undoubtedly when she told us that she was going to take Dobbs Broughton, we were a little disappointed. Maria Clutterbuck had been used to a better kind of life. You understand what I mean, Mr Eames ?'

'Oh, exactly, – and yet it's not a bad kind of life, either.'

'No, no; that is true. It has its attractions. She keeps her carriage, sees a good deal of company, has an excellent house, and goes abroad for six weeks every year. But you know, Mr Eames, there is, perhaps, a little uncertainty about it.'

'Life is always uncertain, Miss Demolines.'

'You're quizzing now, I know. But don't you feel now, really, that City money is always very chancy ? It comes and goes so quick.'

'As regards the going, I think that's the same with all money,' said Johnny.

'Not with land, or the funds. Mamma has every shilling laid out in a first-class mortgage on land at four per cent. That does make one feel so secure ! The land can't run away.'

'But you think poor Broughton's money may ?'

'It's all speculation, you know. I don't believe she minds it; I don't indeed. She lives that kind of fevered life now that she likes excitement. Of course we all know that Mr Dobbs Broughton is not what we can call an educated gentleman. His manners are against him, and he is very ignorant. Even dear Maria would admit that.'

'One would perhaps let that pass without asking her opinion at all.'

'She has acknowledged it to me, twenty times. But he is very good-natured, and lets her do pretty nearly anything that she likes. I only hope she won't trespass on his good-nature. I do, indeed.'

'You mean, spend too much money?'

'No; I didn't mean that exactly. Of course she ought to be moderate, and I hope she is. To that kind of fevered existence profuse expenditure is perhaps necessary. But I was thinking of something else. I fear she is a little giddy.'

'Dear me! I should have thought she was too – too – too – '

'You mean too old for anything of that kind. Maria Broughton must be thirty-three if she's a day.'

'That would make you just twenty-five,' said Johnny, feeling perfectly sure as he said so that the lady whom he was addressing was at any rate past thirty!

'Never mind my age, Mr Eames; whether I am twenty-five, or a hundred-and-five, has nothing to do with poor Maria Clutterbuck. But now I'll tell you why I mention all this to you. You must have seen how foolish she is about your friend Mr Dalrymple?'

'Upon my word, I haven't.'

'Nonsense, Mr Eames; you have. If she were your wife, would you like her to call a man Conway? Of course you would not. I don't mean to say that there's anything in it. I know Maria's principles too well to suspect that. It's merely because she's flighty and fevered.'

'That fevered existence accounts for it all,' said Johnny.

'No doubt it does,' said Miss Demolines, with a nod of her head which was intended to show that she was willing to give her friend the full benefit of any excuse which could be offered for her. 'But don't you think you could do something, Mr Eames.'

'I do something?'

'Yes, you. You and Mr Dalrymple are such friends! If you were just to point out to him you know—'

'Point out what? Tell him that he oughtn't to be called Conway? Because, after all, I suppose that's the worst of it. If you mean to say that Dalrymple is in love with Mrs Broughton, you never made a greater mistake in your life.'

'Oh, no; not in love. That would be terrible, you know.' And Miss Demolines shook her head sadly. 'But there may be so much mischief done without anything of that kind! Thoughtlessness, you know, Mr Eames, – pure thoughtlessness! Think of what I have said, and if you can speak a word to your friend, do. And now I want to ask you something else. I'm so glad you are come, because circumstances have seemed to make it necessary that you and I should know each other. We may be of so much use if we put our heads together.' Johnny bowed when he heard this, but made no immediate reply. 'Have you heard anything about a certain picture that is being planned?' Johnny did not wish to answer this question, but Miss Demolines paused so long, and looked so earnestly into his face, that he found himself forced to say something.

'What picture?'

'A certain picture that is – , or, perhaps, that is not to be, painted by Mr Dalrymple?'

'I hear so much about Dalrymple's pictures! You don't mean the portrait of Lady Glencora Palliser? That is nearly finished, and will be in the Exhibition this year.'

'I don't mean that at all. I mean a picture that has not yet been begun.'

'A portrait, I suppose?'

'As to that I cannot quite say. It is at any rate to be a likeness. I am sure you have heard of it. Come, Mr Eames; it would be better that we should be candid with each other. You remember Miss Van Siever, of course?'

'I remember that she dined at the Broughtons'.'

'And you have heard of Jael, I suppose, and Sisera?'

'Yes; in a general way, – in the Bible.'

'And now will you tell me whether you have not heard the names of Jael and Miss Van Siever coupled together? I see you know all about it.'

'I have heard of it, certainly.'

'Of course you have. So have I, as you perceive. Now, Mr Eames,' – and Miss Demolines' voice became tremulously eager as she addressed him, – 'it is your duty, and it is my duty, to take care that that picture shall never be painted.'

'But why should it not be painted?'

'You don't know Miss Van Siever, yet.'

'Not in the least.'

'Nor Mrs Van Siever.'

'I never spoke a word to her.'

'I do. I know them both, – well.' There was something almost grandly tragic in Miss Demolines' voice as she thus spoke. 'Yes, Mr Eames, I know them well. If that scheme be continued, it will work terrible mischief. You and I must prevent it.'

'But I don't see what harm it will do.'

'Think of Conway Dalrymple passing so many hours in Maria's sitting-room upstairs! The picture is to be painted there, you know.'

'But Miss Van Siever will be present. Won't that make it all right? What is there wrong about Miss Van Siever?'

'I won't deny that Clara Van Siever has a certain beauty of her own. To me she is certainly the most unattractive woman that I ever came near. She is simply repulsive!' Hereupon Miss Demolines held up her hand as though she were banishing Miss Van Siever for ever from her sight, and shuddered slightly. 'Men think her handsome, and she is handsome. But she is false, covetous, malicious, cruel, and dishonest.'

'What a fiend in petticoats!'

'You may say that, Mr Eames. And then her mother! Her mother is not so bad. Her mother is very different. But the mother is an odious woman, too. It was an evil day for Maria Clutterbuck when she first saw either the mother or the daughter. I tell you that in confidence.'

'But what can I do?' said Johnny, who began to be startled and almost interested by the eagerness of the woman.

'I'll tell you what you can do. Don't let your friend go to Mr Broughton's house to paint the picture. If he does do it, there will mischief come of it. Of course you can prevent him.'

'I should not think of trying to prevent him unless I knew why.'

'She's a nasty proud minx, and it would set her up ever so high, – to think that she was being painted by Mr Dalrymple! But that isn't the reason. Maria would get into terrible trouble about it, and there would be no end of mischief. I must not tell you more now, and if you do not believe me, I cannot help it. Surely, Mr Eames, my word may be taken as going for something? And when I ask you to help me in this, I do expect that you will not refuse me.' By this time Miss Demolines was sitting close to him, and had more than once put her hand upon his arm in the energy of her eloquence. Then as he remembered that he had never seen Miss Demolines till the other day, or Miss Van Siever, or even Mrs Dobbs Broughton, he bethought himself that it was all very droll. Nevertheless he had no objection to Miss Demolines putting her hand upon his arm.

'I never like to interfere in anything that does not seem to be my own business,' said Johnny.

'Is not your friend's business your own business? What does friendship mean if it is not so? And when I tell you that it is my business, mine of right, does that go for nothing with you? I thought I might depend upon you, Mr Eames; I did indeed.' Then again she put her hand upon his arm, and as he looked into her eyes he began to think that after all she was good-looking in a certain way. At any rate she had fine eyes, and there was something picturesque about the entanglement of her hair. 'Think of it, and then come back and talk to me again,' said Miss Demolines.

'But I am going out of town to-morrow.'

'For how long?'

'For ten days.'

'Nothing can be done during that time. Clara Van Siever is going away in a day, and will not be back for three weeks. I happen to know that; so we have plenty of time for working. It would be very desirable that she should never even hear of it; but that cannot be hoped, as Maria has such a tongue! Couldn't you see Mr Dalrymple to-night?'

'Well, no; I don't think I could.'

'Mind, at least, that you come to me as soon as ever you return.'

Before he got out of the house, which he did after a most affectionate farewell, Johnny felt himself compelled to promise that he would come to Miss Demolines again as soon as he got back to town; and as the door was closed behind him by the boy in buttons, he made up his mind that he certainly would call as soon as he returned to London. 'It's as good as a play,' he said to himself. Not that he cared in the least for Miss Demolines, or that he would take any steps with the intention of preventing the painting of the picture. Miss Demolines had some battle to fight, and he would leave her to fight it with her own weapons. If his friend chose to paint a picture of Jael, and take Miss Van Siever as a model, it was no business of his. Nevertheless he would certainly go and see Miss Demolines again, because, as he said, she was as good as a play.

CHAPTER 26

The picture

On that same afternoon Conway Dalrymple rolled up his sketch of
Jael and Sisera, put it into his pocket, dressed himself with some
considerable care, putting on a velvet coat which he was in the
habit of wearing out of doors when he did not intend to wander
beyond Kensington Gardens and the neighbourhood and which was
supposed to become him well, yellow gloves, and a certain Spanish
hat of which he was fond, and slowly sauntered across to the house
of his friend Mrs Dobbs Broughton. When the door was opened to
him he did not ask if the lady were at home, but muttering some
word to the servant, made his way through the hall, upstairs, to a
certain small sitting-room looking to the north, which was much
used by the mistress of the house. It was quite clear that Conway
Dalrymple had arranged his visit beforehand, and that he was
expected. He opened the door without knocking, and, though the
servant had followed him, he entered without being announced.
'I'm afraid I'm late,' he said, as he gave his hand to Mrs Broughton;
'but for the life I could not get away sooner.'

'You are quite in time,' said the lady, 'for any good that you are
likely to do.'

'What does that mean?'

'It means this, my friend, that you had better give the idea up. I
have been thinking of it all day, and I do not approve of it.'

'What nonsense!'

'Of course you will say so, Conway. I have observed of late that
whatever I say to you is called nonsense. I suppose it is the new
fashion that gentlemen should so express themselves, but I am not
quite sure that I like it.'

'You know what I mean. I am very anxious about this picture,
and I shall be much disappointed if it cannot be done now. It was
you put it into my head first.'

'I regret it very much, I can assure you ; but it will not be generous in you to urge that against me.'

'But why shouldn't it succeed ?'

'There are many reasons, – some personal to myself.'

'I do not know what they can be. You hinted at something which I only took as having been said in joke.'

'If you mean about Miss Van Siever and yourself, I was quite in earnest, Conway. I do not think you could do better, and I should be glad to see it of all things. Nothing would please me more than to bring Miss Van Siever and you together.'

'And nothing would please me less.'

'But why so ?'

'Because, – because—. I can do nothing but tell you the truth, carina ; because my heart is not free to present itself at Miss Van Siever's feet.'

'It ought to be free, Conway, and you must make it free. It will be well that you should be married, and well for others besides yourself. I tell you so as your friend, and you have no truer friend. Sit where you are, if you please. You can say nothing you have to say without stalking about the room.'

'I was not going to stalk, – as you call it.'

'You will be safer and quieter while you are sitting. I heard a knock at the door, and I do not doubt that it is Clara. She said she would be here.'

'And you have told her of the picture ?'

'Yes ; I have told her. She said that it would be impossible, and that her mother would not allow it. Here she is.' Then Miss Van Siever was shown into the room, and Dalrymple perceived that she was a girl the peculiarity of whose complexion bore daylight better even than candlelight. There was something in her countenance which seemed to declare that she could bear any light to which it might be subjected without flinching from it. And her bonnet, which was very plain, and her simple brown morning gown, suited her well. She was one who required none of the circumstances of studied dress to carry off aught in her own appearance. She could look her best when other women look their worst, and could dare to be seen at all times. Dalrymple, with an artist's eye, saw this at once, and immediately confessed to himself that there was something great about her. He could not deny her beauty. But there was ever present to him that look of hardness which had struck him when he first saw her. He could not but fancy that though at times she might be playful, and allow the fur of her coat to be stroked with good-humour, – she would be a dangerous plaything, using her claws unpleasantly when the good-humour should have passed away. But not the less was she beautiful, and – beyond that and better than that, for his purpose, – she was picturesque.

'Clara,' said Mrs Broughton, 'here is this mad painter, and he says that he will have you on his canvas, either with your will or without it.'

'Even if he could do that, I am sure he would not,' said Miss Van Siever.

'To prove to you that I can, I think I need only show you the sketch,' said Dalrymple, taking the drawing out of his pocket. 'As regards the face, I know it so well by heart already, that I feel certain I could produce a likeness without even a sitting. What do you think of it, Mrs Broughton ?'

'It is clever,' she said, looking at it with all the enthusiasm which women are able to throw into their eyes on such occasions ; 'very clever. The subject would just suit her. I have never doubted that.'

'Eames says that it is confused,' said the artist.

'I don't see that at all,' said Mrs Broughton.

'Of course a sketch must be rough. This one has been rubbed about and altered, – but I think there is something in it.'

'An immense deal,' said Mrs Broughton. 'Don't you think so, Clara ?'

'I am not a judge.'

'But you can see the woman's fixed purpose ; and her stealthiness as well ; – and the man sleeps like a log. What is that dim outline ?'

'Nothing in particular,' said Dalrymple. But the dim outline was intended to represent Mrs Van Siever.

'It is very good, – unquestionably good,' said Mrs Dobbs Broughton. 'I do not for a moment doubt that you would make a great picture of it. It is just the subject for you, Conway ; so much imagination, and yet such a scope for portraiture. It would be full of action, and yet such perfect repose. And the lights and shadows would be exactly in your line. I can see at a glance how you would manage the light in the tent, and bring it down just on the nail. And then the pose of the woman would be so good, so much strength, and yet such grace ! You should have the bowl he drank the milk out of, so as to tell the whole story. No painter living tells a story so well as you do, Conway.' Conway Dalrymple knew that the woman was talking nonsense to him, and yet he liked it, and liked her for talking it.

'But Mr Dalrymple can paint his Sisera without making me a Jael,' said Miss Van Siever.

'Of course he can,' said Mrs Broughton.

'But I never will,' said the artist. 'I conceived the subject as connected with you, and I will never disjoin the two ideas.'

'I think it no compliment, I can assure you,' said Miss Van Siever.

'And none was intended. But you may observe that artists in all ages have sought for higher types of models in painting women who have been violent or criminal, than have sufficed for them in their portraitures of gentleness and virtue. Look at all the Judiths, and the Lucretias, and the Charlotte Cordays;* how much finer the women are than the Madonnas and the Saint Cecilias.'

'After that, Clara, you need not scruple to be a Jael,' said Mrs Broughton.

'But I do scruple, – very much; so strongly that I know I never shall do it. In the first place I don't know why Mr Dalrymple wants it.'

'Want it !' said Conway. 'I want to paint a striking picture.'

'But you can do that without putting me into it.'

'No; – not this picture. And why should you object? It is the commonest thing in the world for ladies to sit to artists in that manner.'

'People would know it.'

'Nobody would know it, so that you need care about it. What would it matter if everybody knew it? We are not proposing anything improper; – are we, Mrs Broughton?'

'She shall not be pressed if she does not like it,' said Mrs Broughton. 'You know I told you before Clara came in, that I was afraid it could not be done.'

'And I don't like it,' said Miss Van Siever, with some little hesitation in her voice.

'I don't see anything improper in it, if you mean that,' said Mrs Broughton.

'But, mamma !'

'Well, yes; that is the difficulty, no doubt. The only question is, whether your mother is not so very singular, as to make it impossible that you should comply with her in everything.'

'I am afraid that I do not comply with her in very much,' said Miss Van Siever in her gentlest voice.

'Oh, Clara !'

'You drive me to say so, as otherwise I should be a hypocrite. Of course I ought not to have said it before Mr Dalrymple.'

'You and Mr Dalrymple will understand all about that, I daresay, before the picture is finished,' said Mrs Broughton.

It did not take much persuasion on the part of Conway Dalrymple to get the consent of the younger lady to be painted, or of the elder to allow the sitting to go on in her room. When the question of easels and other apparatus came to be considered Mrs Broughton was rather flustered, and again declared with energy that the whole thing must fall to the ground; but a few more words from the painter restored her, and at last the arrangements were made. As Mrs Dobbs Broughton's dear friend, Madalina Demolines had said, Mrs Dobbs Broughton liked a fevered existence. 'What will Dobbs say?' she exclaimed more than once. And it was decided at last that Dobbs should know nothing about it as long as it could be kept from him. 'Of course he shall be told at last,' said his wife. 'I wouldn't keep anything from the dear fellow for all the world. But if he knew it at first it would be sure to get through Musselboro to your mother.'

'I certainly shall beg that Mr Broughton may not be taken into confidence if Mr Musselboro is to follow,' said Clara. 'And it must be understood that I must cease to sit immediately, whatever may be the inconvenience, should mamma speak to me about it.'

This stipulation was made and conceded, and then Miss Van Siever went away, leaving the artist with Mrs Dobbs Broughton. 'And now, if you please, Conway, you had better go too,' said the lady, as soon as there had been time for Miss Van Siever to get downstairs and out of the hall-door.

'Of course you are in a hurry to get rid of me.'

'Yes, I am.'

'A little while ago I improperly said that some suggestion of yours was nonsense and you rebuked me for my blunt incivility. Might not I rebuke you now with equal justice?'

'Do so, if you will; – but leave me. I tell you, Conway, that in these matters you must either be guided by me, or you and I must cease to see each other. It does not do that you should remain here with me longer than the time usually allowed for a morning call. Clara has come and gone, and you also must go. I am sorry to disturb you, for you seem to be so very comfortable in that chair.'

'I am comfortable, – and I can look at you. Come; – there can be no harm in saying that, if I say nothing else. Well; – there, now I am gone.' Whereupon he got up from his arm-chair.

'But you are not gone while you stand there.'

'And you would really wish me to marry that girl?'

'I do, – if you can love her.'

'And what about her love?'

'You must win it, of course. She is to be won, like any other woman. The fruit won't fall into your mouth merely because you open your lips. You must climb the tree.'

'Still climbing trees in the Hesperides,'* said Conway. 'Love does that, you know; but it is hard to climb the trees without the love. It seems to me that I have done my climbing, – have clomb as high as I knew how, and that the boughs are breaking with me, and that I am likely to get a fall. Do you understand me?'

'I would rather not understand you.'

'That is no answer to my question. Do you understand that at this moment I am getting a fall which will break every bone in my skin and put any other climbing out of the question as far as I am concerned? Do you understand that?'

'No; I do not,' said Mrs Broughton, in a tremulous voice.

'Then I'll go and make love at once to Clara Van Siever. There's enough of pluck left in me to ask her to marry me, and I suppose I could manage to go through the ceremony if she accepted me.'

'But I want you to love her,' said Mrs Dobbs Broughton.

'I daresay I should love her well enough after a bit; – that is, if she didn't break my head or comb my hair.* I suppose there will be no objection to my saying that you sent me when I ask her?'

'Conway, you will of course not mention my name to her. I have suggested to you a marriage which I think would tend to make you happy, and would give you a stability in life which you want. It is perhaps better that I should be explicit at once. As an unmarried man I cannot continue to know you. You have said words of late which have driven me to this conclusion. I have thought about it much, – too much, perhaps, and I know that I am right. Miss Van Siever has beauty and wealth and intellect, and I think that she would appreciate the love of such a man as you are. Now go.' And Mrs Dobbs Broughton, standing upright, pointed to the door. Conway Dalrymple slowly took his Spanish hat from off the marble slab on which he had laid it, and left the room without saying a word. The interview had been quite long enough, and there was nothing else which he knew how to say with effect.

Croquet is a pretty game out of doors, and chess is delightful in a drawing-room. Battledore and shuttlecock and hunt-the-slipper have also their attractions. Proverbs are good, and cross questions with crooked answers may be made very amusing. But none of these games are equal to the game of love-making, – providing that the players can be quite sure that there shall be no heart in the matter. Any touch of heart not only destroys the pleasure of the game, but makes the player awkward and incapable and robs him of his skill. And thus it is that there are many people who cannot play the game at all. A deficiency of some needed internal physical strength prevents the owners of the heart from keeping a proper control over its valves, and thus emotion sets in, and the pulses are accelerated, and feeling supervenes. For such a one to attempt a game of love-making, is as though your friend with the gout should insist on playing croquet. A sense of the ridiculous, if nothing else, should in either case deter the afflicted one from the attempt. There was no such absurdity with our friend Mrs Dobbs Broughton and Conway Dalrymple. Their valves and pulses were all right. They could play the game without the slightest danger of any inconvenient result; – of any inconvenient result, that is, as regarded their own feelings. Blind people cannot see and stupid people cannot understand, – and it might be that Mr Dobbs Broughton, being both blind and stupid in such matters, might perceive something of the playing of the game and not know that it was only a game of skill.

When I say that as regarded these two lovers there was nothing of love between them, and that the game was therefore so far innocent, I would not be understood as asserting that these people had no hearts within their bosoms. Mrs Dobbs Broughton probably loved her husband in a sensible, humdrum way, feeling him to be a bore, knowing him to be vulgar, aware that he often took a good deal more wine than was good for him, and that he was almost as uneducated as a hog. Yet she loved him, and showed her love by taking care that he should have things for dinner which he liked to eat. But in this alone there were to be found none of the charms of a fevered existence, and therefore Mrs Dobbs Broughton, requiring those charms for her comfort, played her little game with Conway Dalrymple. And as regarded the artist himself, let no reader presume him to have been heartless because he flirted with Mrs Dobbs Broughton. Doubtless he will marry some day, will have a large family for which he will work hard, and will make a good husband to some stout lady who will be careful in looking after his linen. But on the present occasion he fell into some slight trouble in spite of the innocence of his game. As he quitted his friend's room he heard the hall-door slammed heavily; then there was a quick step on the stairs, and on the landing-place above the first flight he met the master of the house, somewhat flurried, as it seemed, and not looking comfortable, either as regarded his person or his temper. 'By George, he's been drinking!' Conway said to himself, after the first glance. Now it certainly was the case that poor Dobbs Broughton would sometimes drink at improper hours.

'What the devil are you doing here?' said Dobbs Broughton to his friend the artist. 'You're always here. You're here a doosed sight more than I like.' Husbands when they have been drinking are very apt to make mistakes as to the purport of the game.

'Why, Dobbs,' said the painter, 'there's something wrong with you.'

'No, there ain't. There's nothing wrong; and if there was, what's that to you? I shan't ask you to pay anything for me, I suppose.'

'Well; – I hope not.'

'I won't have you here, and let that be an end of it. It's all very well when I choose to have a few friends to dinner, but my wife can do very well without your fal-ladding here all day. Will you remember that, if you please ?'

Conway Dalrymple, knowing that he had better not argue any question with a drunken man, took himself out of the house, shrugging his shoulders as he thought of the misery which his poor dear play-fellow would now be called upon to endure.

CHAPTER 27

A hero at home

On the morning after his visit to Miss Demolines John Eames found himself at the Paddington station asking for a ticket for Guestwick, and as he picked up his change another gentleman also demanded a ticket for the same place. Had Guestwick been as Liverpool or Manchester, Eames would have thought nothing about it. It is a matter of course that men should always be going from London to Liverpool and Manchester; but it seemed odd to him that two men should want first-class tickets for so small a place as Guestwick at the same moment. And when, afterwards, he was placed by the guard in the same carriage with this other traveller, he could not but feel some little curiosity. The man was four or five years Johnny's senior, a good-looking fellow, with a pleasant face, and the outward appurtenances of a gentleman. The intelligent reader will no doubt be aware that the stranger was Major Grantly; but the intelligent reader has in this respect had much advantage over John Eames, who up to this time had never even heard of his cousin Grace Crawley's lover. 'I think you were asking for a ticket for Guestwick,' said Johnny; – whereupon the major owned that such was the case. 'I lived at Guestwick the greater part of my life,' said Johnny, 'and it's the dullest, dearest little town in all England.' 'I never was there before,' said the major, 'and indeed I can hardly say I am going there now. I shall only pass through it.' Then he got out his newspaper, and Johnny also got out his, and for a time there was no conversation between them. John remembered how holy was the errand upon which he was intent, and gathered his thoughts together, resolving that having so great a matter on his mind he would think about nothing else and speak about nothing at all. He was going down to Allington to ask Lily Dale for the last time whether she would be his wife; to ascertain whether he was to be successful or unsuccessful in the one great wish of his life; and, as such was the case with him, – as he had in hand a thing so vital, it could be nothing to him whether the chance companion of his voyage was an agreeable or a disagreeable person. He himself, in any of the ordinary circumstances of life, was prone enough to talk with any one he might meet. He could have travelled for twelve hours together with an old lady, and could listen to her or make her listen to him without half an hour's interruption. But this journey was made on no ordinary occasion, and it behoved him to think of Lily. Therefore, after the first little almost necessary effort at civility, he fell back into gloomy silence. He was going to do his best to win Lily Dale, and this doing of his best would require all his thought and all his energy.

And probably Major Grantly's mind was bent in the same direction. He, too, had this work before him, and could not look upon his work as a thing that was altogether pleasant. He might probably get that which he was intent upon obtaining. He knew, – he almost knew, – that he had won the heart of the girl whom he was seeking. There had been that between him and her which justified him in supposing that he was dear to her, although no expression of affection had ever passed from her lips to his ears. Men may know all that they require to know on that subject without any plainly spoken words. Grace Crawley had spoken no word, and yet he had known, – at any rate had not doubted, that he could have the place in her heart of which he desired to be the master. She would never surrender herself altogether till she had taught herself to be sure of him to whom she gave herself. But she had listened to him with silence that had not rebuked him, and he had told himself that he might venture, without fear of that rebuke as to which the minds of some men are sensitive to a degree which other men cannot even understand. But for all this Major Grantly could not be altogether happy as to his mission. He would ask Grace Crawley to be his wife; but he would be ruined by his own success. And the remembrance that he would be severed from all his own family by the thing that he was doing, was very bitter to him. In generosity he might be silent about this to Grace, but who can endure to be silent on such a subject to the woman who is to be his wife? And then it would not be possible for him to abstain from explanation. He was now following her down to Allington, a step which he certainly would not have taken but for the misfortune which had befallen her father, and he must explain to her in some sort why he did so. He must say to her, – if not in so many words, still almost as plainly as words could speak, – I am here now to ask you to be my wife, because you specially require the protection and countenance of the man who loves you, in the present circumstances of your father's affairs. He knew that he was doing right; – perhaps had some idea that he was doing nobly; but this very appreciation of his own good qualities made the task before him the more difficult.

Major Grantly had The Times, and John Eames had the Daily News, and they exchanged papers. One had the last Saturday, and the other the last Spectator,* and they exchanged those also. Both had the Pall Mall Gazette,* of which enterprising periodical they gradually came to discuss the merits and demerits, thus falling into conversation at last, in spite of the weight of the mission on which each of them was intent. Then, at last, when they were within half-an-hour of the end of their journey, Major Grantly asked his companion what was the best inn at Guestwick. He had at first been minded to go on to Allington at once, – to go on to Allington and get his work done, and then return home or remain there, or find the nearest inn with a decent bed, as circumstances might direct him. But on reconsideration, as he drew nearer to the scene of his future operations, he thought that it might be well for him to remain that night at Guestwick. He did not quite know how far Allington was from Guestwick, but he did know that it was still mid-winter, and that the days were very short. 'The Magpie' was the best inn, Johnny said. Having lived at Guestwick all his life, and having a mother living there now, he had never himself put up at 'The Magpie,' but he believed it to be a good country inn. They kept post-horses there, he knew. He did not tell the stranger that his late old friend, Lord De Guest, and his present old friend, Lady Julia, always hired post-horses from 'The Magpie,' but he grounded his ready assertion on the remembrance of that fact. 'I think I shall stay there to-night,' said the major. 'You'll find it pretty comfortable, I don't doubt,' said Johhny. 'Though, indeed, it always seems to me that a man alone at an inn has a very bad time of it. Reading is all very well, but one gets tired of it at last. And then I hate horse-hair chairs.' 'It isn't very delightful,' said the major, 'but beggars mustn't be choosers.' Then there was a pause, after which the major spoke again. 'You don't happen to know which way Allington lies?'

'Allington!' said Johnny.

'Yes, Allington. Is there not a village called Allington?'

'There is a village called Allington, certainly. It lies over there.' And Johnny pointed with his finger through the window. 'As you do not know the country you can see nothing, but I can see the Allington trees at this moment.'

'I suppose there is no inn at Allington?'

'There's a public-house, with a very nice clean bedroom. It is called the "Red Lion." Mrs Forrard keeps it. I would quite as soon stay there as "The Magpie." Only if they don't expect you, they wouldn't have much for dinner.'

'Then you know the village of Allington?'

'Yes, I know the village of Allington very well. I have friends living there. Indeed, I may say I know everybody in Allington.'

'Do you know Mrs Dale?'

'Mrs Dale?' said Johnny. 'Yes, I know Mrs Dale. I have known Mrs Dale pretty nearly all my life.' Who could this man be who was going down to see Mrs Dale, – Mrs Dale, and consequently; Lily Dale? He thought that he knew Mrs Dale so well, that she could have no visitor of whom he would not be entitled to have some knowledge. But Major Grantly had nothing more to say at the moment about Mrs Dale. He had never seen Mrs Dale in his life, and was now going to her home, not to see her, but a friend of hers. He found that he could not very well explain this to a stranger, and therefore at the moment he said nothing further. But Johnny would not allow the subject to be dropped. 'Have you known Mrs Dale long?' he asked.

'I have not the pleasure of knowing her at all,' said the major.

'I thought, perhaps, by your asking after her—'

'I intend to call upon her, that is all. I suppose they will have an omnibus here from "The Magpie?"' Eames said that there no doubt would be an omnibus from 'The Magpie,' and then they were at their journey's end.

For the present we will follow John Eames, who went at once to his mother's house. It was his intention to remain there for two or three days, and then go over to the house, or rather to the cottage, of his great ally Lady Julia, which lay just beyond Guestwick Manor, and somewhat nearer to Allington than to the town of Guestwick. He had made up his mind that he would not himself go over to Allington till he could do so from Guestwick Cottage, as it was called, feeling that, under certain untoward circumstances, – should untoward circumstances arise, – Lady Julia's sympathy might be more endurable than that of his mother. But he would take care that it should be known at Allington that he was in the neighbourhood. He understood the necessary strategy of his campaign too well to suppose that he could startle Lily into acquiescence.

With his own mother and sister, John Eames was in these days quite a hero. He was a hero with them now, because in his early boyish days there had been so little about him that was heroic. Then there had been a doubt whether he would ever earn his daily bread, and he had been a very heavy burden on the slight family resources in the matter of jackets and trousers. The pride taken in our Johnny had not been great, though the love felt for him had been warm. But gradually things had changed, and John Eames had become heroic in his mother's eyes. A chance circumstance had endeared him to Earl De Guest, and from that moment things had gone well with him. The earl had given him a watch and had left him a fortune, and Sir Raffle Buffle had made him a private secretary. In the old days, when Johnny's love for Lily Dale was first discussed by his mother and sister, they had thought it impossible that Lily should ever bring herself to regard with affection so humble a suitor; – for the Dales have ever held their heads up in the world. But now there is no misgivings on that score with Mrs Eames and her daughter. Their wonder is that Lily Dale should be such a fool as to decline the love of such a man. So Johnny was received with the respect due to a hero, as well as with the affection belonging to a son; – by which I mean it to be inferred that Mrs Eames had got a little bit of fish for dinner as well as a leg of mutton.

'A man came down in the train with me who says he is going over to Allington,' said Johnny. 'I wonder who he can be. He is staying at "The Magpie."'

'A friend of Captain Dale's, probably,' said Mary. Captain Dale was the squire's nephew and his heir.

'But this man was not going to the squire's. He was going to the Small House.'

'Is he going to stay there?'

'I suppose not, as he asked about the inn.' Then Johnny reflected that the man might probably be a friend of Crosbie's, and became melancholy in consequence. Crosbie might have thought it expedient to send an ambassador down to prepare the ground for him before he should venture again upon the scene himself. If it were so, would it not be well that he, John Eames, should get over to Lily as soon as possible, and not wait till he should be staying with Lady Julia?

It was at any rate incumbent upon him to call upon Lady Julia the next morning, because of his commission. The Berlin wool* might remain in his portmanteau till his portmanteau should go with him to the cottage; but he would take the spectacles at once, and he must explain to Lady Julia what the lawyers had told him about the income. So he hired a saddle-horse from 'The Magpie' and started after breakfast on the morning after his arrival. In his unheroic days he would have walked, – as he had done, scores of times, over the whole distance from Guestwick to Allington. But now, in these grander days, he thought about his boots and the mud, and the formal appearance of the thing. 'Ah dear,' he said to himself, as the nag walked slowly out of the town, 'it used to be better with me in the old days. I hardly hoped that she would ever accept me, but at least she had never refused me. And then that brute had not as yet made his way down to Allington !'

He did not go very fast. After leaving the town he trotted on for a mile or so. But when he got to the palings of Guestwick Manor he let the animal walk again, and his mind ran back over the incidents of his life which were connected with the place. He remembered a certain long ramble which he had taken in those woods after Lily had refused him. That had been subsequent to the Crosbie episode in his life, and Johnny had been led to hope by certain of his friends, – especially by Lord De Guest and his sister, – that he might then be successful. But he had been unsuccessful, and had passed the bitterest hour of his life wandering about in those woods. Since that he had been unsuccessful again and again ; but the bitterness of failure had not been so strong with him as on that first occasion. He would try again now, and if he failed, he would fail for the last time. As he was thinking of all this, a gig overtook him on the road, and on looking round he saw that the occupant of the gig was the man who had travelled with him on the previous day in the train. Major Grantly was alone in the gig, and as he recognized John Eames he stopped his horse. 'Are you also going to Allington ?' he asked. John Eames, with something of scorn in his voice, replied that he had no intention of going to Allington on that day. He still thought that this man might be an emissary from Crosbie, and therefore resolved that but scant courtesy was due to him. 'I am on my way there now,' said Grantly, 'and am going to the house of your friend. May I tell her that I travelled with you yesterday ?'

'Yes, sir,' said Johnny. 'You may tell her that you came down with John Eames.'

'And are you John Eames ?' asked the major.

'If you have no objection,' said Johnny. 'But I can hardly suppose you have ever heard my name before ?'

'It is familiar to me, because I have the pleasure of knowing a cousin of yours, Miss Grace Crawley.'

'My cousin is at present staying at Allington with Mrs Dale,' said Johnny.

'Just so,' said the major, who now began to reflect that he had been indiscreet in mentioning Grace Crawley's name. No doubt every one connected with the family, all the Crawleys, all the Dales, and all the Eames's, would soon know the business which had brought him down to Allington ; but he need not have taken the trouble of beginning the story against himself. John Eames, in truth, had never even heard Major Grantly's name, and was quite unaware of the fortune which awaited his cousin. Even after what he had now been told, he still suspected the stranger of being an emissary from his enemy; but the major, not giving him credit for his ignorance, was annoyed with himself for having told so much of his own history. 'I will tell the ladies that I had the pleasure of meeting you,' he said; 'that is, if I am lucky enough to see them.' And then he drove on.

'I know I should hate that fellow if I were to meet him anywhere again,' said Johnny to himself as he rode on. 'When I take an aversion to a fellow at first sight, I always stick to it. It's instinct, I suppose.' And he was still giving himself credit for the strength of his instincts when he reached Lady Julia's cottage. He rode at once into the stable-yard, with the privilege of an accustomed friend of the house, and having given up his horse, entered the cottage by the back door. 'Is my lady at home, Jemima?' he said to the maid.

'Yes, Mr John; she is in the drawing-room, and friends of yours are with her.' Then he was announced, and found himself in the presence of Lady Julia, Lily Dale, and Grace Crawley.

He was very warmly received. Lady Julia really loved him dearly, and would have done anything in her power to bring about a match between him and Lily. Grace was his cousin, and though she had not seen him often, she was prepared to love him dearly as Lily's lover. And Lily, – Lily loved him dearly too, – if only she could have brought herself to love him as he wished to be loved! To all of them Johnny Eames was something of a hero. At any rate in the eyes of all of them he possessed those virtues which seemed to them to justify them in petting him and making much of him.

'I am so glad you've come, – that is, if you've brought my spectacles,' said Lady Julia.

'My pockets are crammed with spectacles,' said Johnny.

'And when are you coming to me?'

'I was thinking of Tuesday.'

'No; don't come till Wednesday. But I mean Monday. No; Monday won't do. Come on Tuesday, – early, and drive me out. And now tell us the news.'

Johnny swore that there was no news. He made a brave attempt to be gay and easy before Lily; but he failed, and he knew that he failed, – and he knew that she knew that he failed. 'Mamma will be so glad to see you,' said Lily. 'I suppose you haven't seen Bell yet?'

'I only got to Guestwick yesterday afternoon,' said he.

'And it will be so nice having Grace at the Small House; – won't it? Uncle Christopher has quite taken a passion for Grace, – so that I am hardly anybody now in the Allington world.'

'By-the-by,' said Johnny, 'I came down here with a friend of yours, Grace.'

'A friend of mine ?' said Grace.

'So he says, and he is at Allington at this moment. He passed me in a gig going there.'

'And what was his name ?' Lily asked.

'I have not the remotest idea,' said Johnny. 'He is a man about my age, very good-looking, and apparently very well able to take care of himself. He is short-sighted, and holds a glass in one eye when he looks out of a carriage-window. That's all that I know about him.'

Grace Crawley's face had become suffused with blushes at the first mention of the friend and the gig ; but then Grace blushed very easily. Lily knew all about it at once; – at once divined who must be the friend in the gig, and was almost beside herself with joy. Lady Julia, who had heard no more of the major than had Johnny, was still clever enough to perceive that the friend must be a particular friend, – for she had noticed Miss Crawley's blushes. And Grace herself had no doubt as to the man. The picture of her lover, with the glass in his eye as he looked out of the window, had been too perfect to admit of a doubt. In her distress she put out her hand and took hold of Lily's dress.

'And you say he is at Allington now ?' said Lily.

'I have no doubt he is at the Small House at this moment,' said Johnny.

CHAPTER 28

Showing how Major Grantly took a walk

Major Grantly drove his gig into the yard of the 'Red Lion' at Allington, and from thence walked away at once to Mrs Dale's house. When he reached the village he had hardly made up his mind as to the way in which he would begin his attack; but now, as he went down the street, he resolved that he would first ask for Mrs Dale. Most probably he would find himself in the presence of Mrs Dale and her daughter, and of Grace also, at his first entrance; and if so, his position would be awkward enough. He almost regretted now that he had not written to Mrs Dale, and asked for an interview. His task would be very difficult if he should find all the ladies together. But he was strong in the feeling that when his purpose was told it would meet the approval at any rate of Mrs Dale; and he walked boldly on, and bravely knocked at the door of the Small House, as he had already learned that Mrs Dale's residence was called by all the neighbourhood. Nobody was at home, the servant said; and then, when the visitor began to make further inquiry, the girl explained that the two young ladies had walked as far as Guestwick Cottage, and that Mrs Dale was at this moment at the Great House with the squire. She had gone across soon after the young ladies had started. The maid, however, was interrupted before she had finished telling all this to the major, by finding her mistress behind her in the passage. Mrs Dale had returned, and had entered the house from the lawn.

'I am here now, Jane,' said Mrs Dale, 'if the gentleman wishes to see me.'

Then the major announced himself. 'My name is Major Grantly,' said he; and he was blundering on with some words about his own intrusion, when Mrs Dale begged him to follow her into the drawing-room. He had muttered something to the effect that Mrs Dale would not know who he was; but Mrs Dale knew all about him, and had heard the whole of Grace's story from Lily. She and

Lily had often discussed the question whether, under existing circumstances, Major Grantly should feel himself bound to offer his hand to Grace, and the mother and daughter had differed somewhat on the matter. Mrs Dale had held that he was not so bound, urging that the unfortunate position in which Mr Crawley was placed was so calamitous to all connected with him, as to justify any man, not absolutely engaged, in abandoning the thoughts of such a marriage. Mrs Dale had spoken of Major Grantly's father and mother and brother and sister, and had declared her opinion that they were entitled to consideration. But Lily had opposed this idea very stoutly, asserting that in an affair of love a man should think neither of father or brother or mother or sister. 'If he is worth anything,' Lily had said, 'he will come to her now, – now in her trouble; and will tell her that she at least has got a friend who will be true to her. If he does that, then I shall think that there is something of the poetry and nobleness of love left.' In answer to this Mrs Dale had replied that women had no right to expect from men such self-denying nobility as that. 'I don't expect it, mamma,' said Lily. 'And I am sure that Grace does not. Indeed I am quite sure that Grace does not expect even to see him ever again. She never says so, but I know that she has made up her mind about it. Still I think he ought to come.' 'It can hardly be that a man is bound to do a thing, the doing of which, as you confess, would be almost more than noble,' said Mrs Dale. And so the matter had been discussed between them. But now, as it seemed to Mrs Dale, the man had come to do this noble thing. At any rate he was there in her drawing-room, and before either of them had sat down he had contrived to mention Grace. 'You may not probably have heard my name,' he said, 'but I am acquainted with your friend, Miss Crawley.'

'I know your name very well, Major Grantly. My brother-in-law who lives over yonder, Mr Dale, knows your father very well, – or he did some years ago. And I have heard him say that he remembers you.'

'I recollect. He used to be staying at Ullathorne. But that is a long time ago. Is he at home now?'

'Mr Dale is almost always at home. He very rarely goes away, and I am sure would be glad to see you.'

Then there was a little pause in the conversation. They had managed to seat themselves, and Mrs Dale had said enough to put her visitor fairly at his ease. If he had anything special to say to her, he must say it, – any request or proposition to make as to Grace Crawley, he must make it. And he did make it at once. 'My object in coming to Allington,' he said, 'was to see Miss Crawley.'

'She and my daughter have taken a long walk to call on a friend, and I am afraid they will stay for lunch; but they will certainly be home between three and four, if that is not too long for you to remain at Allington.'

'O dear, no,' said he. 'It will not hurt me to wait.'

'It certainly will not hurt me, Major Grantly. Perhaps you will lunch with me?'

'I'll tell you what, Mrs Dale; if you'll permit me, I'll explain to you why I have come here. Indeed, I have intended to do so all through, and I can only ask you to keep my secret, if after all it should require to be kept.'

'I will certainly keep any secret that you may ask me to keep,' said Mrs Dale, taking off her bonnet.

'I hope there may be no need of one,' said Major Grantly. 'The truth is, Mrs Dale, that I have known Miss Crawley for some time, – nearly two years now, and – I may as well speak it out at once, – I have made up my mind to ask her to be my wife. That is why I am here.' Considering the nature of the statement, which must have been embarrassing, I think that it was made with fluency and simplicity.

'Of course, Major Grantly, you know that I have no authority with our young friend,' said Mrs Dale. 'I mean that she is not connected with us by family ties. She has a father and mother, living, as I believe, in the same county with yourself.'

'I know that, Mrs Dale.'

'And you may, perhaps, understand that, as Miss Crawley is now staying with me, I owe it in a measure to her friends to ask you whether they are aware of your intention.'

'They are not aware of it.'

'I know that at the present moment they are in great trouble.'

Mrs Dale was going on, but she was interrupted by Major Grantly. 'That is just it,' he said. 'There are circumstances at present which make it almost impossible that I should go to Mr Crawley and ask his permission to address his daughter. I do not know whether you have heard the whole story?'

'As much, I believe, as Grace could tell me.'

'He is, I believe, in such a state of mental distress as to be hardly capable of giving me a considerate answer. And I should not know how to speak to him, or how not to speak to him, about this unfortunate affair. But, Mrs Dale, you will, I think, perceive that the same circumstances make it imperative upon me to be explicit to Miss Crawley. I think I am the last man to boast of a woman's regard, but I had learned to think that I was not indifferent to Grace. If that be so, what must she think of me if I stay away from her now?'

'She understands too well the weight of the misfortune which has fallen upon her father, to suppose that any one not connected with her can be bound to share it.'

'That is just it. She will think that I am silent for that reason. I have determined that that shall not keep me silent, and, therefore, I have come here. I may, perhaps, be able to bring comfort to her in her trouble. As regards my worldly position, – though, indeed, it will not be very good, – as hers is not good either, you will not think yourself bound to forbid me to see her on that head.'

'Certainly not. I need hardly say that, as I fully understand that, as regards money, you are offering everything where you can get nothing.'

'And you understand my feeling ?'

'Indeed, I do, – and appreciate the great nobility of your love for Grace. You shall see her here, if you wish it, – and to-day, if you choose to wait.' Major Grantly said that he would wait and would see Grace on that afternoon. Mrs Dale again suggested that he should lunch with her, but this he declined. She then proposed that he should go across and call upon the squire, and thus consume his time. But to this he also objected. He was not exactly in the humour, he said, to renew so old and so slight an acquaintance at that time. Mr Dale would probably have forgotten him, and would be sure to ask what had brought him to Allington. He would go and take a walk, he said, and come again exactly at half-past three. Mrs Dale again expressed her certainty that the young ladies would be back by that time, and Major Grantly left the house.

Mrs Dale when she was left alone could not but compare the good fortune which was awaiting Grace, with the evil fortune which had fallen on her own child. Here was a man who was at all points a gentleman. Such, at least, was the character which Mrs Dale at once conceded to him. And Grace had chanced to come across this man, and to please his eye, and satisfy his taste, and be loved by him. And the result of that chance would be that Grace would have everything given to her that the world has to give worth acceptance. She would have a companion for her life whom she could trust, admire, love, and of whom she could be infinitely proud. Mrs Dale was not at all aware whether Major Grantly might have five hundred a year to spend, or five thousand, – or what sum intermediate between the two, – nor did she give much of her thoughts at the moment to that side of the subject. She knew without thinking of it, – or fancied that she knew, that there were means sufficient for comfortable living. It was solely the nature and character of the man that was in her mind, and the sufficiency that was to be found in them for a wife's happiness. But her daughter, her Lily, had come across a man who was a scoundrel, and, as the consequence of that meeting, all her life was marred! Could any credit be given to Grace for her success, or any blame attached to Lily for her failure. Surely not the latter! How was her girl to have guarded herself from a love so unfortunate, or have avoided the rock on which her vessel had been shipwrecked? Then many bitter thoughts passed through Mrs Dale's mind, and she almost envied Grace Crawley her lover. Lily was contented to remain as she was, but Lily's mother could not bring herself to be satisfied that her child should fill a lower place in the world than other girls. It had ever been her idea, – an idea probably never absolutely uttered even to herself, but not the less practically conceived, – that it is the business of a woman to be married. That her Lily should have been won and not worn, had been, and would be, a trouble to her for ever.

Major Grantly went back to the inn and saw his horse fed, and smoked a cigar, and then, finding that it was still only just one o'clock, he started for a walk. He was careful not to go out of Allington by the road he had entered it, as he had no wish to encounter Grace and her friend on their return into the village; so he crossed a little brook which runs at the bottom of the hill on which the chief street of Allington is built, and turned into a field-path to the left as soon as he had got beyond the houses. Not knowing the geography of the place he did not understand that by taking that path he was making his way back to the squire's house; but it was so; and after sauntering on for about a mile and crossing back again over the stream, of which he took no notice, he found himself leaning across a gate, and looking into a paddock on the other side of which was the high wall of a gentleman's garden. To avoid this he went on a little further and found himself on a farm road, and before he could retrace his steps so as not to be seen, he met a gentleman whom he presumed to be the owner of the house. It was the squire surveying his home farm, as was his daily custom; but Major Grantly had not perceived that the house must of necessity be Allington House, having been aware that he had passed the entrance to the place, as he entered the village on the other side. 'I'm afraid I'm intruding,' he said, lifting his hat. 'I came up the path yonder, not knowing that it would lead me so close to a gentleman's house.'

'There is a right of way through the fields on to the Guestwick road,' said the squire, 'and therefore you are not trespassing in any sense; but we are not particular about such things down here, and you would be very welcome if there were no right of way. If you are a stranger, perhaps you would like to see the outside of the old house. People think it picturesque.'

Then Major Grantly became aware that this must be the squire, and he was annoyed with himself for his own awkwardness in having thus come upon the house. He would have wished to keep himself altogether unseen if it had been possible, – and especially unseen by this old gentleman, to whom, now that he had met him, he was almost bound to introduce himself. But he was not absolutely bound to do so, and he determined that he would still keep his peace. Even if the squire should afterwards hear of his having been there, what would it matter? But to proclaim himself at the present moment would be disagreeable to him. He permitted the squire, however, to lead him to the front of the house, and in a few moments was standing on the terrace hearing an account of the architecture of the mansion.

'You can see the date still in the brickwork of one of the chimneys, – that is, if your eyes are very good you can see it, – 1617. It was completed in that year, and very little has been done to it since. We think the chimneys are pretty.'

'They are very pretty,' said the major. 'Indeed, the house altogether is as graceful as it can be.'

'Those trees are old, too,' said the squire, pointing to two cedars which stood at the side of the house. 'They say they are older than the house, but I don't feel sure of it. There was a mansion here before, very nearly, though not quite, on the same spot.'

'Your own ancestors were living here before that, I suppose?' said Grantly, meaning to be civil.

'Well, yes; two or three hundred years before it, I suppose. If you don't mind coming down to the churchyard, you'll get an excellent view of the house; – by far the best that there is. By-the-by, would you like to step in and take a glass of wine?'

'I'm very much obliged,' said the major, 'but indeed I'd rather not.' Then he followed the squire down to the churchyard, and was shown the church as well as the view of the house, and the vicarage, and a view over to Allington woods from the vicarage gate, of which the squire was very fond, and in this way he was taken back on to the Guestwick side of the village, and even down on to the road by which he had entered it, without in the least knowing where he was. He looked at his watch and saw that it was past two. 'I'm very much obliged to you, sir,' he said, again taking off his hat to the squire, 'and if I shall not be intruding I'll make my way back to the village.'

'What village?' said the squire.

'To Allington,' said Grantly.

'This is Allington,' said the squire; and as he spoke, Lily Dale and Grace Crawley turned a corner from the Guestwick road and came close upon them. 'Well, girls, I did not expect to see you,' said the squire; 'your mamma told me you wouldn't be back till it was nearly dark, Lily.'

'We have come back earlier than we intended,' said Lily. She of course had seen the stranger with her uncle, and knowing the ways of the squire in such matters had expected to be introduced to him. But the reader will be aware that no introduction was possible. It never occurred to Lily that this man could be the Major Grantly of whom she and Grace had been talking during the whole length of the walk home. But Grace and her lover had of course known each other at once, and Grantly, though he was abashed, and almost dismayed by the meeting, of course came forward and gave his hand to his friend. Grace in taking it did not utter a word.

'Perhaps I ought to have introduced myself to you as Major Grantly?' said he, turning to the squire.

'Major Grantly! Dear me! I had no idea that you were expected in these parts.'

'I have come without being expected.'

'You are very welcome, I'm sure. I hope your father is well? I used to know him some years ago, and I daresay he has not forgotten me.' Then, while the girls stood by in silence, and while Grantly was endeavouring to escape, the squire invited him very warmly to send his portmanteau up to the house. 'We'll have the ladies up from the house below, and make it as little dull for you as possible.' But this would not have suited Grantly, – at any rate would not suit him till he should know what answer he was to have. He excused himself therefore, pleading a positive necessity to be at Guestwick that evening, and then, explaining that he had already seen Mrs Dale, he expressed his intention of going back to the Small House in company with the ladies, if they would allow him. The squire, who did not as yet quite understand it all, bade him a formal adieu, and Lily led the way home down behind the churchyard wall and through the bottom of the gardens belonging to the Great House. She of course knew now who the stranger was, and did all in her power to relieve Grace of her embarrassment. Grace had hitherto not spoken a single word since she had seen her lover, nor did she say a word to him in their walk to the house. And, in truth, he was not much more communicative than Grace. Lily did all the talking, and with wonderful female skill contrived to have some words ready for use till they all found themselves together in Mrs Dale's drawing-room. 'I have caught a major, mamma, and landed him,' said Lily laughing, 'but I'm afraid, from what I hear, that you had caught him first.'

CHAPTER 29

Miss Lily Dale's logic

Lady Julia De Guest always lunched at one exactly, and it was not much past twelve when John Eames made his appearance at the cottage. He was of course told to stay, and of course said that he would stay. It had been his purpose to lunch with Lady Julia; but then he had not expected to find Lily Dale at the cottage. Lily herself would have been quite at her ease, protected by Lady Julia, and somewhat protected also by her own powers of fence, had it not been that Grace was there also. But Grace Crawley, from the moment that she had heard the description of the gentleman who looked out of the window with his glass in his eye, had by no means been at her ease. Lily saw at once that she could not be brought to join in any conversation, and both John and Lady Julia, in their ignorance of the matter in hand, made matters worse.

'So that was Major Grantly?' said John. 'I have heard of him before, I think. He is a son of the old archdeacon, is he not?'

'I don't know about old archdeacon,' said Lady Julia. 'The archdeacon is the son of the old bishop, whom I remember very well. And it is not so very long since the bishop died, either.'

'I wonder what he's doing at Allington?' said Johnny.

'I think he knows my uncle,' said Lily.

'But he's going to call on your mother,' he said. Then Johnny remembered that the major had said something as to knowing Miss Crawley, and for the moment he was silent.

'I remember when they talked of making the son a bishop also,' said Lady Julia.

'What; – this same man who is now a major?' said Johnny.

'No, you goose. He is not the son; he is the grandson. They were going to make the archdeacon a bishop, and I remember hearing that he was terribly disappointed. He is getting to be an old man now, I suppose; and yet, dear me, how well I remember his father.'

'He didn't look like a bishop's son,' said Johnny.

'How does a bishop's son look?' Lily asked.

'I suppose he ought to have some sort of clerical tinge about him; but this fellow had nothing of that kind.'

'But then this fellow, as you call him,' said Lily, 'is only the son of an archdeacon.'

'That accounts for it, I suppose,' said Johnny.

But during all this time Grace did not say a word, and Lily perceived it. Then she bethought herself as to what she had better do. Grace, she knew, could not be comfortable where she was. Nor, indeed, was it probable that Grace would be very comfortable in returning home. There could not be much ease for Grace till the coming meeting between her and Major Grantly should be over. But it would be better that Grace should go back to Allington at once; and better also, perhaps, for Major Grantly that it should be so. 'Lady Julia,' she said, 'I don't think we'll mind stopping for lunch to-day.'

'Nonsense, my dear; you promised.'

'I think we must break our promise; I do indeed. You mustn't be angry with us.' And Lily looked at Lady Julia, as though there were something which Lady Julia ought to understand, which she, Lily, could not quite explain. I fear that Lily was false, and intended her old friend to believe that she was running away because John Eames had come there.

'But you will be famished,' said Lady Julia.

'We shall live through it,' said Lily.

'It is out of the question that I should let you walk all the way here from Allington and all the way back without taking something.'

'We shall just be home in time for lunch if we go now,' said Lily. 'Will not that be best, Grace?'

Grace hardly knew what would be best. She only knew that Major Grantly was at Allington, and that he had come thither to see her. The idea of hurrying back after him was unpleasant to her, and yet she was so flurried that she felt thankful to Lily for taking her away from the cottage. The matter was compromised at last. They remained for half an hour, and ate some biscuits and pretended to drink a glass of wine, and then they started. John Eames, who in truth believed that Lily Dale was running away from him, was by no means well pleased, and when the girls were gone, did not make himself so agreeable to his old friend as he should have done. 'What a fool I am to come here at all,' he said, throwing himself into an armchair as soon as the front door was closed.

'That's very civil to me, John!'

'You know what I mean, Lady Julia. I am a fool to come near

her, until I can do so without thinking more of her than I do of any other girl in the county.'

'I don't think you have anything to complain of as yet,' said Lady Julia, who had in some sort perceived that Lily's retreat had been on Grace's account, and not on her own. 'It seems to me that Lily was very glad to see you, and when I told her that you were coming to stay here, and would be near them for some days, she seemed to be quite pleased; – she did indeed.'

'Then why did she run away the moment I came in ?' said Johnny.

'I think it was something you said about that man who has gone to Allington.'

'What difference can the man make to her ? The truth is, I despise myself; – I do indeed, Lady Julia. Only think of my meeting Crosbie at dinner the other day, and his having the impertinence to come up and shake hands with me.'

'I suppose he didn't say anything about what happened at the Paddington Station ?'

'No ; he didn't speak about that. I wish I knew whether she cares for him still. If I thought she did, I would never speak another word to her, – I mean about myself. Of course I am not going to quarrel with them. I am not such a fool as that.' Then Lady Julia tried to comfort him, and succeeded so far that he was induced to eat the mince veal that had been intended for the comfort and support of the two young ladies who had run away.

'Do you think it is he ?' were the first words which Grace said when they were fairly on their way back together.

'I should think it must be. What other man can there be, of that sort, who would be likely to come to Allington to see you ?'

'His coming is not likely. I cannot understand that he should come. He let me leave Silverbridge without seeing me, – and I thought that he was quite right.

'And I think he is quite right to come here. I am very glad he has come. It shows that he has really something like a heart inside him. Had he not come, or sent, or written, or taken some step before the trial comes on, to make you know that he was thinking of you, I should have said that he was as hard, – as hard as any other man that I ever heard of. Men are so hard ! But I don't think he is, now. I am beginning to regard him as the one chevalier sans peur et sans reproche,* and to fancy that you ought to go down on your knees before him, and kiss his highness's shoebuckle. In judging of men one's mind vacillates so quickly between the scorn which is due to a false man and the worship which is due to a true man.' Then she was silent for a moment, but Grace said nothing, and Lily continued, 'I tell you fairly, Grace, that I shall expect very much from you now.'

'Much in what way, Lily?'

'In the way of worship. I shall not be content that you should merely love him. If he has come here, as he must have done, to say that the moment of the world's reproach is the moment he has chosen to ask you to be his wife, I think that you will owe him more than love.'

'I shall owe him more than love, and I will pay him more than love,' said Grace. There was something in the tone of her voice as she spoke which made Lily stop her and look up into her face. There was a smile there which Lily had never seen before, and which gave a beauty to her which was wonderful to Lily's eyes. Surely this lover of Grace's must have seen her smile like that, and therefore had loved her and was giving such wonderful proof of his love. 'Yes,' continued Grace, standing and looking at her friend, 'you may stare at me, Lily, but you may be sure that I will do for Major Grantly all the good that I can do for him.'

'What do you mean, Grace?'

'Never mind what I mean. You are very imperious in managing your own affairs, and you must let me be so equally in mine.'

'But I tell you everything.'

'Do you suppose that if – if – if in real truth it can possibly be the case that Major Grantly shall have come here to offer me his hand when we are all ground down into the dust, as we are, do you think that I will let him sacrifice himself? Would you?'

'Certainly. Why not? There will be no sacrifice. He will be asking for that which he wishes to get; and you will be bound to give it to him.'

'If he wants it, where is his nobility? If it be as you say, he will have shown himself noble, and his nobility will have consisted in this, that he has been willing to take that which he does not want, in order that he may succour one whom he loves. I also will succour one whom I love, as best I know how.' Then she walked on quickly before her friend, and Lily stood for a moment thinking before she followed her. They were now on a field-path, by which they were enabled to escape the road back to Allington for the greater part of the distance, and Grace had reached a stile, and had clambered over it before Lily had caught her.

'You must not go away by yourself,' said Lily.

'I don't wish to go away by myself.'

'I want you to stop a moment and listen to me. I am sure you are wrong in this, – wrong for both your sakes. You believe that he loves you?'

'I thought he did once; and if he has come here to see me, I suppose he does still.'

'If that be the case, and if you also love him—'

'I do. I make no mystery about that to you. I do love him with all my heart. I love him to-day, now that I believe him to be here, and that I suppose I shall see him, perhaps this very afternoon. And I loved him yesterday, when I thought that I should never see him again. I do love him. I do. I love him so well that I will never do him an injury.'

'That being so, if he makes you an offer you are bound to accept it. I do not think that you have an alternative.'

'I have an alternative, and I shall use it. Why don't you take my cousin John?'

'Because I like somebody else better. If you have got as good a reason I won't say another word to you.'

'And why don't you take that other person?'

'Because I cannot trust his love; that is why. It is not very kind of you, opening my sores afresh, when I am trying to heal yours.'

'Oh, Lily, am I unkind, – unkind to you, who have been so generous to me?'

'I'll forgive you all that and a deal more if you will only listen to me and try to take my advice. Because this major of yours does a generous thing, which is for the good of you both, – the infinite good of both of you, – you are to emulate his generosity by doing a thing which will be for the good of neither of you. That is about it. Yes, it is, Grace. You cannot doubt that he has been meaning this for some time past; and of course, if he looks upon you as his own, – and I daresay, if the whole truth is to be told, he does—'

'But I am not his own.'

'Yes, you are, in one sense; you have just said so with a great deal of energy. And if it is so, – let me see, where was I?'

'Oh, Lily, you need not mind where you were.'

'But I do mind, and I hate to be interrupted in my arguments. Yes, just that. If he saw his cow sick, he'd try to doctor the cow in her sickness. He sees that you are sick, and of course he comes to your relief.'

'I am not Major Grantly's cow.'

'Yes, you are.'

'Nor his dog, nor his ox, nor his ass, nor anything that is his,* except – except, Lily, the dearest friend that he has on the face of the earth. He cannot have a friend that will go further for him than I will. He will never know how far I will go to serve him. You don't know his people. Nor do I know them. But I know what they are. His sister is married to a marquis.'

'What has that to do with it?' said Lily, sharply. 'If she were married to an archduke, what difference would that make?'

'And they are proud people – all of them – and rich; and they live with high persons in the world.'

'I didn't care though they lived with the royal family, and had the Prince of Wales for their bosom friend. It only shows how much better he is than they are.'

'But think what my family is, – how we are situated. When my father was simply poor I did not care about it, because he has been born and bred a gentleman. But now he is disgraced. Yes, Lily, he is. I am bound to say so, at any rate to myself, when I am thinking of Major Grantly; and I will not carry that disgrace into a family which would feel it so keenly as they would do.' Lily, however, went on with her arguments, and was still arguing when they turned the corner of the lane, and came upon Lily's uncle and the major himself.

CHAPTER 30

Showing what Major Grantly did after his walk

In going down from the church to the Small House Lily Dale had all the conversation to herself. During some portion of the way the path was only broad enough for two persons, and here Major Grantly walked by Lily's side, while Grace followed them. Then they found their way into the house, and Lily made her little speech to her mother about catching the major. 'Yes, my dear, I have seen Major Grantly before,' said Mrs Dale. 'I suppose he has met you on the road. But I did not expect that any of you would have returned so soon.' Some little explanation followed as to the squire, and as to Major Grantly's walk, and after that the great thing was to leave the two lovers alone. 'You will dine here, of course, Major Grantly,' Mrs Dale said. But this he declined. He had learned, he said, that there was a night-train up to London, and he thought that he would return to town by that. He had intended, when he left London, to get back as soon as possible. Then Mrs Dale, having hesitated for two or three seconds, got up and left the room, and Lily followed. 'It seems very odd and abrupt,' said Mrs Dale to her daughter, 'but I suppose it is best.' 'Of course it is best, mamma. Do as one would be done by, – that's the only rule. It will be much better for her that she should have it over.'

Grace was seated on a sofa, and Major Grantly got up from his chair, and came and stood opposite to her. 'Grace,' he said, 'I hope you are not angry with me for coming down to see you here.'

'No, I am not angry,' she said.

'I have thought a great deal about it, and your friend, Miss Prettyman, knew that I was coming. She quite approves of my coming.'

'She has written to me, but did not tell me of it,' said Grace, not knowing what other answer to make.

'No, – she could not have done that. She had no authority. I only mention her name because it will have weight with you, and because

I have not done that which, under other circumstances, perhaps, I should have been bound to do. I have not seen your father.'

'Poor papa,' said Grace.

'I have felt that at the present moment I could not do so with any success. It has not come of any want of respect either for him or for you. Of course, Grace, you know why I am here?' He paused, and then remembering that he had no right to expect an answer to such a question, he continued, 'I have come here, dearest Grace, to ask you to be my wife, and to be a mother to Edith. I know that you love Edith.'

'I do indeed.'

'And I have hoped sometimes, – though I suppose I ought not to say so, – but I have hoped and almost thought sometimes, that you have been willing to – to love me too. It is better to tell the truth simply, is it not?'

'I suppose so,' said Grace.

'And therefore, and because I love you dearly myself, I have come to ask you to be my wife.' Saying which he opened out his hand, and held it to her. But she did not take it. 'There is my hand, Grace. If your heart is as I would have it you can give me yours, and I shall want nothing else to make me happy.' But still she made no motion towards granting him his request. 'If I have been too sudden,' he said, 'you must forgive me for that. I have been sudden and abrupt but as things are, no other way has been open to me. Can you not bring yourself to give me some answer, Grace?' His hand had now fallen again to his side, but he was still standing before her.

She had said no word to him as yet, except that one in which she had acknowledged her love for his child, and had expressed no surprise, even in her countenance, at his proposal. And yet the idea that he should do such a thing, since the idea that he certainly would do it had become clear to her, had filled her with a world of surprise. No girl ever lived with any beauty belonging to her who had a smaller knowledge of her own possession than Grace Crawley. Nor had she the slightest pride in her own acquirements. That she had been taught in many things more than had been taught to other girls, had come of her poverty and of the desolation of her home. She had learned to read Greek and Italian because there had been nothing else for her to do in that sad house. And, subsequently, accuracy of knowledge had been necessary for the earning of her bread. I think that Grace had at times been weak enough to envy the idleness and almost to envy the ignorance of other girls. Her figure was light, perfect in symmetry, full of grace at all points; but she had thought nothing of her figure, remembering only the poverty of her dress, but remembering also with a brave resolution that she would never be ashamed of it. And as her acquaintance with Major Grantly had begun and had grown, and as she had learned to feel unconsciously that his company was pleasanter to her than that of any other person she knew, she had still told herself that anything like love must be out of the question. But then words had been spoken, and there had been glances in his eye, and a tone in his voice, and a touch upon his fingers, of which she could not altogether refuse to accept the meaning. And others had spoken to her of it, the two Miss Prettymans and her friend Lily. Yet she would not admit to herself that it could be so, and she would not allow herself to confess to herself that she loved him. Then had come the last killing misery to which her father had been subjected. He had been accused of stealing money, and had been committed to be tried for the theft. From that moment, at any rate, any hope, if there had been a hope, must be crushed. But she swore to herself bravely that there had been no such hope. And she assured herself also that nothing had passed which had entitled her to expect anything beyond ordinary friendship from the man of whom she certainly had thought much. Even if those touches and those tones and those glances had meant anything, all such meaning must be annihilated by this disgrace which had come upon her. She might know that her father was innocent; she might be sure at any rate, that he had been innocent in intention; but the world thought differently, and she, her brothers and sister, and her mother and her poor father, must bend to the world's opinion. If those dangerous joys had meant anything, they must be taken as meaning nothing more.

Thus she had argued with herself, and, fortified by such self-teachings, she had come down to Allington. Since she had been with her friends there had come upon her from day to day a clear conviction that her arguments had been undoubtedly true, — a clear conviction which had been very cold to her heart in spite of all her courage. She had expected nothing, hoped for nothing, and yet when nothing came she was sad. She thought of one special half-hour in which he had said almost all that he might have said, — more than he ought to have said; — of a moment during which her hand had remained in his; of a certain pressure with which he had put her shawl upon her shoulders. If he had only written to her one word to tell her that he believed her father was innocent! But no; she had no right to expect anything from him. And then Lily had ceased to talk of him, and she did expect nothing. Now he was there before here, asking her come to him and be his wife. Yes; she would kiss his shoebuckles, only that the kissing of his shoebuckles would bring upon him that injury which he should never suffer from her hands ! He had been generous, and her self-pride was satisfied. But her other pride was touched, and she also would be generous. 'Can you not bring yourself to give me some answer ?' he had said to her. Of course she must give him an answer, but how should she give it ?

'You are very kind,' she said.

'I would be more than kind.'

'So you are. Kind is a cold word when used to such a friend at such a time.'

'I would be everything on earth to you that a man can be to a woman.'

'I know I ought to thank you if I knew how. My heart is full of thanks; it is, indeed.'

'And is there no room for love, there ?'

'There is no room for love in our house, Major Grantly. You have not seen papa.'

'No; but, if you wish it, I will do so at once.'

'It would do no good, – none. I only asked you because you can hardly know how sad is our state at home.'

'But I cannot see that that need deter you, if you can love me.'

'Can you not ? If you saw him, and the house, and my mother, you would not say so. In the Bible it is said of some season that it is not a time for marrying, or for giving in marriage.* And so it is with us.'

'I am not pressing you as to a day. I only ask you to say that you will be engaged to me, – so that I may tell my own people, and let it be known.'

'I understand all that. I know how good you are. But, Major Grantly, you must understand me also when I assure you that it cannot be so.'

'Do you mean that you refuse me altogether ?'

'Yes; altogether.'

'And why ?'

'Must I answer that question ? Ought I to be made to answer it ? But I will tell you fairly, without touching on anything else, that I feel that we are all disgraced, and that I will not take disgrace into another family.'

'Grace, do you love me ?'

'I love no one now, – that is, as you mean. I can love no one. I have no room for any feeling except for my father and mother, and for us all. I should not be here now but that I save my mother the bread that I should eat at home.'

'Is it as bad at that ?'

'Yes; it is as bad as that. It is much worse than that, if you knew it all. You cannot conceive how low we have fallen. And now they tell me that my father will be found guilty, and will be sent to prison. Putting ourselves out of the question, what would you think of a girl who could engage herself to any man under such circumstances? What would you think of a girl who would allow herself to be in love in such a position? Had I been ten times engaged to you I would have broken it off.' Then she got up to leave him.

But he stopped her, holding her by the arm. 'What you have said will make me say what I certainly should never have said without it. I declare that we are engaged.'

'No, we are not,' said Grace.

'You have told me that you loved me.'

'I never told you so.'

'There are other ways of speaking than the voice; and I will boast to you, though to no one else, that you have told me so. I believe you love me. I shall hold myself as engaged to you, and I shall think you false if I hear that you listen to another man. Now, good-by, Grace; – my own Grace.'

'No, I am not your own,' she said, through her tears.

'You are my own, my very own. God bless you, dear, dear, dearest Grace. You shall hear from me in a day or two, and shall see me as soon as this horrid trial is over.' Then he took her in his arms before she could escape from him, and kissed her forehead and her lips, while she struggled in his arms. After that he left the room and the house as quickly as he could, and was seen no more of the Dales upon that occasion.

CHAPTER 31

Showing how Major Grantly returned to Guestwick

Grace, when she was left alone, threw herself upon the sofa, and hid her face in her hands. She was weeping almost hysterically, and had been utterly dismayed and frightened by her lover's impetuosity. Things had gone after a fashion which her imagination had not painted to her as possible. Surely she had the power to refuse the man if she pleased. And yet she felt as she lay there weeping that she did in truth belong to him as part of his goods, and that her generosity had been foiled. She had especially resolved that she would not confess to any love for him. She had made no such confession. She had guarded herself against doing so with all the care which she knew how to use. But he had assumed the fact, and she had been unable to deny it. Could she have lied to him, and have sworn that she did not love him? Could she have so perjured herself, even in support of her generosity? Yes, she would have done so, – so she told herself, – if a moment had been given to her for thought. She ought to have done so, and she blamed herself for being so little prepared for the occasion. The lie would be useless now. Indeed, she would have no opportunity for telling it; for of course she would not answer, – would not even read his letter. Though he might know that she loved him, yet she would not be his wife. He had forced her secret from her, but he could not force her to marry him. She did love him, but he should never be disgraced by her love.

After a while she was able to think of his conduct, and she believed that she ought to be very angry with him. He had taken her roughly in his arms, and had insulted her. He had forced a kiss from her. She had felt his arms warm and close and strong about her, and had not known whether she was in paradise or in purgatory. She was very angry with him. She would send back his letter to him without reading it, – without opening it, if that might be possible. He had done that to her which nothing could justify.

But yet, – yet, – yet how dearly she loved him! Was he not a prince of men? He had behaved badly, of course; but had any man ever behaved so badly before in so divine a way? Was it not a thousand pities that she should be driven to deny anything to a lover who so richly deserved everything that could be given to him? He had kissed her hand as he let her go, and now, not knowing what she did, she kissed the spot on which she had felt his lips. His arm had been round her waist, and the old frock which she wore should be kept by her for ever, because it had been so graced.

What was she now to say to Lily and to Lily's mother? Of one thing there was no doubt. She would never tell them of her lover's wicked audacity. That was a secret never to be imparted to any ears. She would keep her resentment to herself, and not ask the protection of any vicarious wrath. He could never so sin again, that was certain; and she would keep all knowledge and memory of the sin for her own purposes. But how could it be that such a man as that, one so good though so sinful, so glorious though so great a trespasser, should have come to such a girl as her and have asked for her love? Then she thought of her father's poverty and the misery of her own condition, and declared to herself that it was very wonderful.

Lily was the first to enter the room, and she, before she did so, learned from the servant that Major Grantly had left the house. 'I heard the door, miss, and then I saw the top of his hat out of the pantry window.' Armed with this certain information Lily entered the drawing-room, and found Grace in the act of rising from the sofa.

'Am I disturbing you?' said Lily.

'No; not at all. I am glad you have come. Kiss me, and be good to me.' And she twined her arms about Lily and embraced her.

'Am I not always good to you, you simpleton? Has he been good?'

'I don't know what you mean?'

'And have you been good to him?'

'As good as I knew how, Lily.'

'And where is he?'

'He has gone away. I shall never see him any more, Lily.'

Then she hid her face upon her friend's shoulder and broke forth again into hysterical tears.

'But tell me, Grace, what he said; – that is, if you mean to tell me!'

'I will tell you everything; – that is, everything I can.' And Grace blushed as she thought of the one secret which she certainly would not tell.

'Has he, – has he done what I said he would do? Come, speak out boldly. Has he asked you to be his wife?'

'Yes,' said Grace, barely whispering the word.

'And you have accepted him?'

'No, Lily, I have not. Indeed, I have not. I did not know how to speak, because I was surprised; – and he, of course, could say what he liked. But I told him as well as I could, that I would not marry him.'

'And why; – did you tell him why?'

'Yes; because of papa!'

'Then, if he is the man I take him to be, that answer will go for nothing. Of course he knew all that before he came here. He did not think you were an heiress with forty thousand pounds. If he is in earnest, that will go for nothing. And I think he is in earnest.'

'And so was I in earnest.'

'Well, Grace; – we shall see.'

'I suppose I may have a will of my own, Lily.'

'Do not be so sure of that. Women are not allowed to have wills of their own on all occasions. Some man comes in a girl's way, and she gets to be fond of him, just because he does come in her way. Well; when that has taken place, she has no alternative but to be taken if he chooses to take her; or to be left, if he chooses to leave her.'

'Lily, don't say that.'

'But I do say it. A man may assure himself that he will find for himself a wife who shall be learned, or beautiful, or six feet high, if he wishes it, or who has red hair, or red eyes, or red cheeks, – just what he pleases; and he may go about till he finds it, as you can go about and match your worsteds. You are a fool if you buy a colour you don't want. But we can never match our worsteds for that other piece of work, but are obliged to take any colour that comes, – and, therefore, it is that we make such a jumble of it! Here's mamma. We must not be philosophical before her. Mamma, Major Grantly has – skedaddled.'

'Oh, Lily, what a word!'

'But, oh, mamma, what a thing! Fancy his going away and not saying a word to anybody!'

'If he had anything to say to Grace, I suppose he said it.'

'He asked her to marry him, of course. We none of us had any doubt about that. He swore to her that she and none but she should be his wife, – and all that kind of thing. But he seems to have done it in the most prosaic way; – and now he has gone away without saying a word to any of us. I shall never speak to him again, – unles. Grace asks me.'

'Grace, my dear, may I congratulate you?' said Mrs Dale.

Grace did not answer, as Lily was too quick for her. 'Oh, she has refused him, of course. But Major Grantly is a man of too much sense to expect that he should succeed the first time. Let me see; this is the fourteenth. These clocks run fourteen days, and, therefore, you may expect him again about the twenty-eighth. For myself, I think you are giving him an immense deal of unnecessary trouble, and that if he left you in the lurch it would only serve you right; but you have the world with you, I'm told. A girl is supposed to tell a man two fibs before she may tell him one truth.'

'I told him no fib, Lily. I told him that I would not marry him, and I will not.'

'But why not, dear Grace?' said Mrs Dale.

'Because the people say that papa is a thief!' Having said this, Grace walked slowly out of the room, and neither Mrs Dale nor Lily attempted to follow her.

'She's as good as gold,' said Lily, when the door was closed.

'And he; – what of him?'

'I think he is good, too; but she has told me nothing yet of what he has said to her. He must be good, or he would not have come down here after her. But I don't wonder at his coming, because she is so beautiful! Once or twice as we were walking back to-day, I thought her face was the most lovely that I had ever seen. And did you see her just now, as she spoke of her father?'

'Oh, yes; – I saw her.'

'Think what she will be in two or three years' time, when she becomes a woman. She talks French, and Italian, and Hebrew for anything that I know; and she is perfectly beautiful. I never saw a more lovely figure; – and she has spirit enough for a goddess. I don't think that Major Grantly is such a fool after all.'

'I never took him for a fool.'

'I have no doubt all his own people do; – or they will, when they hear of it. But, mamma, she will grow to be big enough to walk atop of all the Lady Hartletops in England. It will all come right at last.'

'You think it will?'

'Oh, yes. Why should it not? If he is worth having, it will; – and I think he is worth having. He must wait till this horrid trial is over. It is clear to me that Grace thinks that her father will be convicted.

'But he cannot have taken the money.'

'I think he took it, and I think it wasn't his. But I don't think he stole it. I don't know whether you can understand the difference.'

'I am afraid a jury won't understand it.'

'A jury of men will not. I wish they could put you and me on it, mamma. I would take my best boots and eat them down to the heels, for Grace's sake, and for Major Grantly's. What a good-looking man he is !'

'Yes, he is.'

'And so like a gentleman ! I'll tell you what, mamma ; we won't say anything to her about him for the present. Her heart will be so full she will be driven to talk, and we can comfort her better in that way.' The mother and daughter agreed to act upon these tactics, and nothing more was said to Grace about her lover on that evening.

Major Grantly walked from Mrs Dale's house to the inn and ordered his gig, and drove himself out of Allington, almost without remembering where he was or whither he was going. He was thinking solely of what had just occurred, and of what, on his part, should follow as the result of that meeting. Half at least of the noble deeds done in this world are due to emulation, rather than to the native nobility of the actors. A young man leads a forlorn hope because another young man has offered to do so. Jones in the hunting-field rides at an impracticable fence because he is told that Smith took it three years ago. And Walker puts his name down for ten guineas at a charitable dinner, when he hears Thompson's read out for five. And in this case the generosity and self-denial shown by Grace warmed and cherished similar virtues within her lover's breast. Some few weeks ago Major Grantly had been in doubt as to what his duty required of him in reference to Grace Crawley ; but he had no doubt whatsoever now. In the fervour of his admiration he would have gone straight to the archdeacon, had it been possible, and have told him what he had done and what he intended to do. Nothing now should stop him ; – no consideration, that is, either as regarded money or position. He had pledged himself solemnly, and he was very glad that he had pledged himself. He would write to Grace and explain to her that he trusted altogether in her father's honour and innocence, but that no consideration as to that ought to influence either him or her in any way. If, independently of her father, she could bring herself to come to him and be his wife, she was bound to do so now, let the position of her father be what it might. And thus, as he drove his gig back towards Guestwick, he composed a very pretty letter to the lady of his love.

And as he went, at the corner of the lane which led from the main road up to Guestwick cottage, he again came upon John Eames, who was also returning to Guestwick. There had been a few words spoken between Lady Julia and Johnny respecting Major Grantly after the girls had left the cottage, and Johnny had been persuaded that the strange visitor to Allington could have no connection with his arch-enemy. 'And why has he gone to Allington?' John demanded, somewhat sternly, of his hostess.

'Well; if you ask me, I think he has gone there to see your cousin, Grace Crawley.'

'He told me that he knew Grace,' said John, looking as though he were conscious of his own ingenuity in putting two and two together very cleverly.

'Your cousin Grace is a very pretty girl,' said Lady Julia.

'It's a long time since I've seen her,' said Johnny.

'Why, you saw her just this minute,' said Lady Julia.

'I didn't look at her,' said Johnny. Therefore, when he again met Major Grantly, having continued to put two and two together with great ingenuity, he felt quite sure that the man had nothing to do with the arch-enemy, and he determined to be gracious. 'Did you find them at home at Allington?' he said, raising his hat.

'How do you do again?' said the major. 'Yes, I found your friend Mrs Dale at home.'

'But not her daughter, or my cousin? They were up there; – where I've come from. But, perhaps, they had got back before you left.'

'I saw them both. They found me on the road with Mr Dale.'

'What, – the squire? Then you have seen everybody?'

'Everybody I wished to see at Allington.'

'But you wouldn't stay at the "Red Lion?"'

'Well, no. I remembered that I wanted to get back to London; and as I had seen my friends, I thought I might as well hurry away.'

'You knew Mrs Dale before, then?'

'No, I didn't. I never saw her in my life before. But I knew the old squire when I was a boy. However, I should have said friend. I went to see one friend, and I saw her.'

John Eames perceived that his companion put a strong emphasis on the word 'her,' as though he were determined to declare boldly that he had gone to Allington solely to see Grace Crawley. He had not the slightest objection to recognizing in Major Grantly a suitor for his cousin's hand. He could only reflect what an unusually fortunate girl Grace must be if such a thing could be true. Of those poor Crawleys he had only heard from time to time that their misfortunes were as numerous as the sands on the sea-shore, and as unsusceptible of any fixed and permanent arrangement. But, as regarded Grace, here would be a very permanent arrangement. Tidings had reached him that Grace was a great scholar, but he had never heard much of her beauty. It must probably be the case that Major Grantly was fond of Greek. There was, he reminded himself, no accounting for tastes; but as nothing could be more respectable than such an alliance, he thought that it would become him to be civil to the major.

'I hope you found her quite well. I had barely time to speak to her myself.'

'Yes, she was very well. This is a sad thing about her father.'

'Very sad,' said Johnny. Perhaps the major had heard about the accusation for the first time to-day, and was going to find an escape on that plea. If such was the case, it would not be so well to be particularly civil.

'I believe Mr Crawley is a cousin of yours?' said the major.

'His wife is my mother's first-cousin. Their mothers were sisters.'

'She is an excellent woman.'

'I believe so. I don't know much about them myself, — that is, personally. Of course I have heard of this charge that has been made against him. It seems to me to be a great shame.'

'Well, I can't exactly say that it is a shame. I do not know that there has been anything done with a feeling of persecution or of cruelty. It is a great mystery, and we must have it cleared up if we can.'

'I don't suppose he can have been guilty,' said Johnny.

'Certainly not in the ordinary sense of the word. I heard all the evidence against him.'

'Oh, you did?'

'Yes,' said the major. 'I live near them in Barsetshire, and I am one of his bailsmen.'

'Then you are an old friend, I suppose?'

'Not exactly that; but circumstances make me very much interested about them. I fancy that the cheque was left in his house by accident, and that it got into his hands he didn't know how, and that when he used it he thought it was his.'

'That's queer,' said Johnny.

'He is very odd, you know.'

'But it's a kind of oddity that they don't like at the assizes.'

'The great cruelty is,' said the major, 'that whatever may be the result, the punishment will fall so heavily upon his wife and daughters. I think the whole county ought to come forward and take them by the hand. Well, good-by. I'll drive on, as I'm a little in a hurry.'

'Good-by,' said Johnny. 'I'm very glad to have had the pleasure of meeting you.' 'He's a good sort of fellow after all,' he said to himself when the gig had passed on. 'He wouldn't have talked in that way if he had meant to hang back.'

CHAPTER 32

Mr Toogood

Mr Crawley had declared to Mr Robarts, that he would summon
no legal aid to his assistance at the coming trial. The reader may,
perhaps, remember the impetuosity with which he rejected the
advice on this subject which was conveyed to him by Mr Robarts
with all the authority of Archdeacon Grantly's name. 'Tell the
archdeacon,' he had said, 'that I will have none of his advice.' And
then Mr Robarts had left him, fully convinced that any further
interference on his part could be of no avail. Nevertheless, the
words which had then been spoken were not without effect. This
coming trial was ever present to Mr Crawley's mind, and though,
when driven to discuss the subject, he would speak of it with high
spirit, as he had done both to the bishop and to Mr Robarts, yet in
his long hours of privacy, or when alone with his wife, his spirit
was anything but high. 'It will kill me,' he would say to her. 'I shall
get salvation thus. Death will relieve me, and I shall never be called
upon to stand before those cruel eager eyes.' Then would she try to
say words of comfort, sometimes soothing him as though he were a
child, and at others bidding him be a man, and remember that as a
man he should have sufficient endurance to bear the eyes of any
crowd that might be there to look at him.

'I think I will go up to London,' he said to her one evening, very
soon after the day of Mr Robarts's visit.

'Go up to London, Josiah!' Mr Crawley had not been up to
London once since they had been settled at Hogglestock, and this
sudden resolution on his part frightened his wife. 'Go up to London,
dearest! and why?'

'I will tell you why. They all say that I should speak to some man
of the law whom I may trust about this coming trial. I trust no one
in these parts. Not, mark you, that I say that they are untrust-
worthy. God forbid that I should so speak or even so think of men
whom I know not. But the matter has become so common in men's

mouths at Barchester and at Silverbridge, that I cannot endure to go among them and to talk of it. I will go up to London, and I will see your cousin, Mr John Toogood, of Gray's Inn.' Now in this scheme there was an amount of everyday prudence which startled Mrs Crawley almost as much as did the prospect of the difficulties to be overcome if the journey were to be made. Her husband, in the first place, had never once seen Mr John Toogood; and in days very long back, when he and she were making their first gallant struggle, – for in those days it had been gallant, – down in their Cornish curacy, he had reprobated certain Toogood civilities, – professional civilities, – which had been proffered, perhaps, with too plain an intimation that on the score of relationship the professional work should be done without payment. The Mr Toogood of those days, who had been Mrs Crawley's uncle, and the father of Mrs Eames and grandfather of our friend Johnny Eames, had been much angered by some correspondence which had grown up between him and Mr Crawley, and from that day there had been a cessation of all intercourse between the families. Since those days that Toogood had been gathered to the ancient Too-goods of old, and the son reigned on the family throne in Ray-mond's Buildings. The present Toogood was therefore first-cousin to Mrs Crawley. But there had been no intimacy between them. Mrs Crawley had not seen her cousin since her marriage, – as indeed she had seen none of her relations, having been estranged from them by the singular bearing of her husband. She knew that her cousin stood high in his profession, the firm of Toogood and Crump, – Crump and Toogood it should have been properly called in these days, – having always held its head up high above all dirty work; and she felt that her husband could look for advice from no better source. But how would such a one as he manage to tell his story to a stranger? Nay, how would he find his way alone into the lawyer's room, to tell his story at all, – so strange was he to the world? And then the expense! 'If you do not wish me to apply to your cousin, say so, and there shall be an end of it,' said Mr Crawley in an angry tone.

'Of course I would wish it. I believe him to be an excellent man, and a good lawyer.'

'Then why should I not go to his chambers? In forma pauperis* I must go to him, and must tell him so. I cannot pay him for the labour of his counsel, nor for such minutes of his time as I shall use.'

'Oh, Josiah, you need not speak of that.'

'But I must speak of it. Can I go to a professional man, who keeps as it were his shop open for those who may think fit to come, and purchase of him, and take of his goods, and afterwards, when the goods have been used, tell him that I have not the price in my hand? I will not do that, Mary. You think that I am mad, that I know not what I do. Yes, – I see it in your eyes; and you are sometimes partly right. But I am not so mad but that I know what is honest. I will tell your cousin that I am sore straitened, and brought down into the very dust by misfortune. And I will beseech him, for what of ancient feeling of family he may bear to you, to listen to me for a while. And I will be very short, and, if need be, will bide his time patiently, and perhaps he may say a word to me that may be of use.'

There was certainly very much in this to provoke Mrs Crawley. It was not only that she knew well that her cousin would give ample and immediate attention, and lend himself thoroughly to the matter without any idea of payment, – but that she could not quite believe that her husband's humility was true humility. She strove to believe it, but knew that she failed. After all it was only a feeling on her part. There was no argument within herself about it. An unpleasant taste came across the palate of her mind, as such a savour will sometimes, from some unexpected source, come across the palate of the mouth. Well; she could only gulp at it, and swallow it and excuse it. Among the salad that comes from your garden a bitter leaf will now and then make its way into your salad-bowl. Alas, there were so many bitter leaves ever making their way into her bowl! 'What I mean is, Josiah, that no long explanation will be needed. I think, from what I remember of him, that he would do for us anything that he could do.'

'Then I will go to the man, and will humble myself before him. Even that, hard as it is to me, may be a duty that I owe.' Mr Crawley as he said this was remembering the fact that he was a clergyman of the Church of England, and that he had a rank of his own in the country, which, did he ever do such a thing as go out to dinner in company, would establish for him a certain right of precedence; whereas this attorney, of whom he was speaking, was, so to say, nobody in the eyes of the world.

'There need be no humbling, Josiah, other than that which is due from man to man in all circumstances. But never mind; we will not talk about that. If it seems good to you, go to Mr Toogood. I think that it is good. May I write to him and say that you will go?'

'I will write myself; it will be more seemly.'

Then the wife paused before she asked the next question, – paused for some minute or two, and then asked it with anxious doubt, – 'And may I go with you, Josiah?'

'Why should two go when one can do the work?' he answered sharply. 'Have we money so much at command?'

'Indeed, no.'

'You should go and do it all, for you are wiser in these things than I am, were it not that I may not dare to show — that I submit myself to my wife.'

'Nay, my dear!'

'But it is ay, my dear. It is so. This is a thing such as men do; not such as women do, unless they be forlorn and unaided of men. I know that I am weak where you are strong; that I am crazed where you are clear-witted.'

'I meant not that, Josiah. It was of your health that I thought.'

'Nevertheless it is as I say; but, for all that, it may not be that you should do my work. There are those watching me who would say, "Lo! he confesses himself incapable." And then some one would whisper something of a madhouse. Mary, I fear that worse than a prison.'

'May God in His mercy forbid such cruelty!'

'But I must look to it, my dear. Do you think that that woman, who sits there at Barchester in high places, disgracing herself and that puny ecclesiastical lord who is her husband, — do you think that she would not immure me if she could? She is a she-wolf, — only less reasonable than the dumb brute as she sharpens her teeth in malice coming from anger, and not in malice coming from hunger as do the utter wolves of the forest. I tell you, Mary, that if she had a colourable ground for her action, she would swear to-morrow that I am mad.'

'You shall go alone to London.'

'Yes, I will go alone. They shall not say that I cannot yet do my own work as a man should do it. I stood up before him, the puny man who is called a bishop, and before her who makes herself great by his littleness, and I scorned them both to their faces. Though the shoes which I had on were all broken, as I myself could not but see when I stood, yet I was greater than they were with all their purple and fine linen.'

'But, Josiah, my cousin will not be harsh to you.'

'Well, — and if he be not?'

'Ill-usage you can bear; and violent ill-usage, such as that which Mrs Proudie allowed herself to exhibit, you can repay with interest; but kindness seems to be too heavy a burden for you.'

'I will struggle. I will endeavour. I will speak but little, and, if possible, I will listen much. Now, my dear, I will write to this man, and you shall give me the address that is proper to him.' Then he wrote the letter, not accepting a word in the way of dictation from his wife, but 'craving the great kindness of a short interview, for which he ventured to become a solicitor, urged thereto by his wife's assurance that one with whom he was connected by family ties would do as much as this for the possible preservation of the honour of the family.' In answer to this, Mr Toogood wrote back as follows: – 'Dear Mr Crawley, I will be at my office all Thursday morning next from ten to two, and will take care that you shan't be kept waiting for me above ten minutes. You parsons never like waiting. But hadn't you better come and breakfast with me and Maria at nine? then we'd have a talk as we walk to the office. Yours always, THOMAS TOOGOOD.' And the letter was dated from the attorney's private house in Tavistock Square.

'I am sure he means to be kind,' said Mrs Crawley.

'Doubtless he means to be kind. But his kindness is rough; – I will not say unmannerly, as the word would be harsh. I have never even seen the lady whom he calls Maria.'

'She is his wife!'

'So I would venture to suppose; but she is unknown to me. I will write again, and thank him, and say that I will be with him at ten to the moment.'

There were still many things to be settled before the journey could be made. Mr Crawley, in his first plan, proposed that he should go up by night mail train, travelling in the third class, having walked over to Silverbridge to meet it; that he should then walk about London from 5 A.M. to 10 A.M., and afterwards come down by an afternoon train to which a third class was also attached. But at last his wife persuaded him that such a task as that, performed in the middle of the winter, would be enough to kill any man, and that, if attempted, it would certainly kill him; and he consented at last to sleep the night in town, – being specially moved thereto by discovering that he could, in conformity with this scheme, get in and out of the train at a station considerably nearer to him than Silverbridge, and that he could get a return-ticket at a third-class fare. The whole journey, he found, could be done for a pound, allowing him seven shillings for his night's expenses in London; and out of the resources of the family there were produced two sovereigns, so that in the event of accident he would not utterly be a castaway from want of funds.

So he started on his journey after an early dinner, almost hopeful through the new excitement of a journey to London, and his wife walked with him nearly as far as the station. 'Do not reject my cousin's kindness,' were the last words she spoke.

'For his professional kindness, if he will extend it to me, I will be most thankful,' he replied. She did not dare to say more; nor had she dared to write privately to her cousin, asking for any special help, lest by doing so she should seem to impugn the sufficiency and stability of her husband's judgment. He got up to town late at night, and having made inquiry of one of the porters, he hired a bed for himself in the neighbourhood of the railway station. Here he had a cup of tea and a morsel of bread-and-butter, and in the morning he breakfasted again on the same fare. 'No, I have no luggage,' he had said to the girl at the public-house, who had asked him as to his travelling gear. 'If luggage be needed as a certificate of respectability, I will pass on elsewhere,' said he. The girl stared, and assured him that she did not doubt his respectability. 'I am a clergyman of the Church of England,' he had said, 'but my circumstances prevent me from seeking a more expensive lodging.' They did their best to make him comfortable, and, I think, almost disappointed him in not heaping further misfortunes on his head.

He was in Raymond's Building at half-past nine, and for half an hour walked up and down the umbrageous pavement, – it used to be umbrageous, but perhaps the trees have gone now, – before the doors of the various chambers. He could hear the clock strike from Gray's Inn; and the moment that it had struck he was turning in, but was encountered in the passage by Mr Toogood, who was equally punctual with himself. Strange stories about Mr Crawley had reached Mr Toogood's household, and that Maria, the mention of whose Christian name had been so offensive to the clergyman, had begged her husband not to be a moment late. Poor Mr Toogood, who on ordinary days did perhaps take a few minutes' grace, was thus hurried away almost with his breakfast in his throat, and, as we have seen, just saved himself. 'Perhaps, sir, you are Mr Crawley?' he said in a good-humoured, cheery voice. He was a good-humoured, cheery-looking man, about fifty years of age, with grizzled hair and sunburnt face, and large whiskers. Nobody would have taken him to be a partner in any of those great houses of which we have read in history, – the Quirk, Gammon and Snaps of the profession, or the Dodson and Foggs,* who are immortal.

'That is my name, sir,' said Mr Crawley, taking off his hat, and bowing low, 'and I am here by appointment to meet Mr Toogood, the solicitor, whose name I see affixed upon the door-post.'

'I am Mr Toogood, the solicitor, and I hope I see you quite well, Mr Crawley.' Then the attorney shook hands with the clergyman and preceded him upstairs to the front room on the first floor. 'Here we are, Mr Crawley, and pray take a chair. I wish you could have made it convenient to come and see us at home. We are rather long,

as my wife says, – long in family, she means, and therefore are not
very well off for spare beds—'

'Oh, sir.'

'I've twelve of 'em living, Mr Crawley, – from eighteen years, the
eldest, – a girl, down to eighteen months the youngest, – a boy, and
they go in and out, boy and girl, boy and girl, like the cogs of a
wheel. They ain't such far away distant cousins from your own
young ones – only first, once, as we call it.'

'I am aware that there is a family tie, or I should not have
ventured to trouble you.'

'Blood is thicker than water; isn't it? I often say that. I heard of
one of your girls only yesterday. She is staying somewhere down in
the country, not far from where my sister lives – Mrs Eames, the
widow of poor John Eames, who never did any good in this world.
I daresay you've heard of her?'

'The name is familiar to me, Mr Toogood.'

'Of course it is. I've a nephew down there just now, and he saw
your girl the other day; – very highly he spoke of her too. Let me
see; – how many is it you have?'

'Three living, Mr Toogood.'

'I've just four times three; – that's the difference. But I comfort
myself with the text about the quiver* you know; and I tell them
that when they've eat up all the butter, they'll have to take their
bread dry.'

'I trust the young people take your teaching in a proper spirit.'

'I don't know much about spirit. There's spirit enough. My
second girl, Lucy, told me that if I came home to-day without
tickets for the pantomime I shouldn't have any dinner allowed me.
That's the way they treat me. But we understand each other at
home. We're all pretty good friends there, thank God. And there
isn't a sick chick among the boiling.'

'You have many mercies for which you should indeed be thankful,' said Mr Crawley, gravely.

'Yes, yes, yes; that's true. I think of that sometimes, though
perhaps not so much as I ought to do. But the best way to be
thankful is to use the goods the gods provide you. "The lovely
Thais sits beside you. Take the goods the gods provide you."* I
often say that to my wife, till the children have got to calling her
Thais. The children have it pretty much their own way with us, Mr
Crawley.'

By this time Mr Crawley was almost beside himself, and was
altogether at a loss how to bring in the matter on which he wished
to speak. He had expected to find a man who in the hurry of
London business might perhaps just manage to spare him five

minutes, – who would grapple instantly with the subject that was to be discussed between them, would speak to him half-a-dozen hard words of wisdom, and would then dismiss him and turn on the instant to other matters of important business; – but here was an easy familiar fellow, who seemed to have nothing on earth to do, and who at this first meeting had taken advantage of a distant family connexion to tell him everything about the affairs of his own household. And then how peculiar were the domestic traits which he told! What was Mr Crawley to say to a man who had taught his own children to call their mother Thais? Of Thais Mr Crawley did know something, and he forgot to remember that perhaps Mr Toogood knew less. He felt it, however, to be very difficult to submit the details of his case to a gentleman who talked in such a strain about his own wife and children.

But something must be done. Mr Crawley, in his present frame of mind, could not sit and talk about Thais all day. 'Sir,' he said 'the picture of your home is very pleasant, and I presume that plenty abounds there.'

'Well, you know, pretty toll-loll for that. With twelve of 'em, Mr Crawley, I needn't tell you they are not going to have castles and parks of their own, unless they can get 'em off their own bats. But I pay upwards of a hundred a year each for my eldest three boys' schooling, and I've been paying eighty for the girls. Put that and that together and see what it comes to. Educate, educate, educate; that's my word.'

'No better word can be spoken, sir.'

'I don't think there's a girl in Tavistock Square that can beat Polly, – she's the eldest, called after her mother, you know; – that can beat her at the piano. And Lucy has read Lord Byron and Tom Moore* all through, every word of 'em. By Jove, I believe she knows most of Tom Moore by heart. And the young uns are coming on just as well.'

'Perhaps, sir, as your time is, no doubt, precious—'

'Just at this time of the day we don't care so much about it, Mr Crawley; and one doesn't catch a new cousin every day, you know.'

'However, if you will allow me,—'

'We'll tackle to? Very well; so be it. Now, Mr Crawley, let me hear what it is that I can do for you.' Of a sudden, as Mr Toogood spoke these last words, the whole tone of his voice seemed to change, and even the position of his body became so much altered as to indicate a different kind of man. 'You just tell your story in your own way, and I won't interrupt you till you've done. That's always the best.'

'I must first crave your attention to an unfortunate preliminary,' said Mr Crawley.

'And what is that?'

'I come before you in forma pauperis.' Here Mr Crawley paused and stood up before the attorney with his hands crossed one upon the other, bending low, as though calling attention to the poorness of his raiment. 'I know that I have no justification for my conduct. I have nothing of reason to offer why I should trespass upon your time. I am a poor man, and cannot pay you for your services.'

'Oh, bother!' said Mr Toogood, jumping up out of his chair.

'I do not know whether your charity will grant me that which I ask—'

'Don't let's have any more of this,' said the attorney. 'We none of us like this kind of thing at all. If I can be of any service to you, you're as welcome to it as flowers in May; and as for billing my first-cousin, which your wife is, I should as soon think of sending in an account to my own.'

'But, Mr Toogood,—'

'Do you go on now with your story; I'll put the rest all right.'

'I was bound to be explicit, Mr Toogood.'

'Very well; now you have been explicit with a vengeance, and you may heave a-head. Let's hear the story, and if I can help you I will. When I've said that, you may be sure I mean it. I've heard something of it before; but let me hear it all from you.'

Then Mr Crawley began and told the story. Mr Toogood was actually true to his promise and let the narrator go on with his narrative without interruption. When Mr Crawley came to his own statement that the cheque had been paid to him by Mr Soames, and went on to say that that statement had been false, – 'I told him that, but I told him so wrongly,' and then paused, thinking that the lawyer would ask some question, Mr Toogood simply said, 'Go on; go on. I'll come back to all that when you've done.' And he merely nodded his head when Mr Crawley spoke of his second statement, that the money had come from the dean. 'We had been bound together by close ties of early familiarity,' said Mr Crawley, 'and in former years our estates in life were the same. But he has prospered and I have failed. And when creditors were importunate, I consented to accept relief in money which had previously been often offered. And I must acknowledge, Mr Toogood, while saying this, that I have known, – have known with heartfelt agony, – that at former times my wife has taken that from my friend Mr Arabin, with hand half-hidden from me, which I have refused. Whether it be better to eat – the bread of charity, – or not to eat bread at all, I, for myself, have no doubt,' he said; 'but when the want strikes one's wife and children, and the charity strikes only oneself, then there is a doubt.' When he spoke thus, Mr Toogood got up, and thrusting his hands into his waistcoat pockets walked about the room, exclaiming, 'By George, by George, by George!' But he still let the man go on with his story, and heard him out at last to the end.

'And they committed you for trial at the next Barchester assizes?' said the lawyer.

'They did.'

'And you employed no lawyer before the magistrates?'

'None; – I refused to employ any one.'

'You were wrong there, Mr Crawley. I must be allowed to say that you were wrong there.'

'I may possibly have been so from your point of view, Mr Toogood; but permit me to explain. I—'

'It's no good explaining now. Of course you must employ a lawyer for your defence, – an attorney who will put the case into the hands of counsel.'

'But that I cannot do, Mr Toogood.'

'You must do it. If you don't do it, your friends should do it for you. If you don't do it, everybody will say you're mad. There isn't a single solicitor you could find within half a mile of you at this moment who wouldn't give you the same advice, – not a single man, either, who has got a head on his shoulders worth a turnip.'

When Mr Crawley was told that madness would be laid to his charge if he did not do as he was bid, his face became very black, and assumed something of that look of determined obstinacy which it had worn when he was standing in the presence of the bishop and Mrs Proudie. 'It may be so,' he said. 'It may be as you say, Mr Toogood. But these neighbours of yours, as to whose collected wisdom you speak with so much certainty, would hardly recommend me to indulge in a luxury for which I have no means of paying.'

'Who thinks about paying under such circumstances as these?'

'I do, Mr Toogood.'

'The wretchedest costermonger that comes to grief has a barrister in a wig and gown to give him his chance of escape.'

'But I am not a costermonger, Mr Toogood, – though more wretched perhaps than any costermonger now in existence. It is my lot to have to endure the sufferings of poverty, and at the same time not to be exempt from those feelings of honour to which poverty is seldom subject. I cannot afford to call in legal assistance for which I cannot pay, – and I will not do it.'

'I'll carry the case through for you. It certainly is not just my line of business, – but I'll see it carried through for you.'

'Out of your own pocket?'

'Never mind; when I say I'll do a thing, I'll do it.'

'No, Mr Toogood; this thing you can not do. But do not suppose I am the less grateful.'

'What is it I can do then? Why do you come to me if you won't take my advice?'

After this the conversation went on for a considerable time without touching on any point which need be brought palpably before the reader's eye. The attorney continued to beg the clergyman to have his case managed in the usual way, and went so far as to tell him that he would be ill-treating his wife and family if he continued to be obstinate. But the clergyman was not shaken from his resolve, and was at last able to ask Mr Toogood what he had better do, – how he had better attempt to defend himself, – on the understanding that no legal aid was to be employed. When this question was at last asked in such a way as to demand an answer, Mr Toogood sat for a moment or two in silence. He felt that an answer was not only demanded, but almost enforced; and yet there might be much difficulty in giving it.

'Mr Toogood,' said Mr Crawley, seeing the attorney's hesitation, 'I declare to you before God, that my only object will be to enable the jury to know about this sad matter all that I know myself. If I could open my breast to them I should be satisfied. But then a prisoner can say nothing; and what he does say is ever accounted false.'

'That is why you should have legal assistance.'

'We had already come to a conclusion on that matter, as I thought,' said Mr Crawley.

Mr Toogood paused for another moment or two, and then dashed at his answer; or rather, dashed at a counter question. 'Mr Crawley, where did you get the cheque? You must pardon me, you know; or, if you wish it, I will not press the question. But so much hangs on that, you know.'

'Every thing would hang on it, – if I only knew.'

'You mean that you forget?'

'Absolutely; totally. I wish, Mr Toogood, I could explain to you the toilsome perseverance with which I have cudgelled my poor brains, endeavouring to extract from them some scintilla of memory that would aid me.'

'Could you have picked it up in the house?'

'No; – no; that I did not do. Dull as I am, I know so much. It was mine of right, from whatever source it came to me. I know myself as no one else can know me, in spite of the wise man's motto.* Had I picked up a cheque in my house, or on the road, I should not have slept till I had taken steps to restore it to the seeming owner. So much I can say. But, otherwise, I am in such matters so shandy-pated, that I can trust myself to be sure of nothing. I thought, – I certainly thought—'

'You thought what?'

'I thought that it had been given to me by my friend the dean. I remember well that I was in his library at Barchester, and I was somewhat provoked in spirit. There were lying on the floor hundreds of volumes, all glittering with gold, and reeking with new leather from the binders. He asked me to look at his toys. Why should I look at them? There was a time, but the other day it seemed, when he had been glad to borrow from me such treasures as I had. And it seemed to me that he was heartless in showing me these things. Well; I need not trouble you with all that.'

'Go on; – go on. Let me hear it all and I shall learn something.'

'I know now how vain, how vile I was. I always know afterwards how low the spirit has grovelled. I had gone to him then because I had resolved to humble myself, and, for my wife's sake, to ask my friend – for money. With words which were very awkward, – which no doubt were ungracious – I had asked him, and he had bid me follow him from his hall into his library. There he left me awhile, and on returning told me with a smile that he had sent for money, – and, if I can remember, the sum he named was fifty pounds.'

'But it has turned out, as you say, that you have payed fifty pounds with his money, – besides the cheque.'

'That is true; – that is quite true. There is no doubt of that. But as I was saying, – then he fell to talking about the books, and I was angered. I was very sore in my heart. From the moment in which the words of beggary had passed from my lips, I had repented. And he had laughed and had taken it gaily. I turned upon him and told him that I had changed my mind. I was grateful, but I would not have his money. And so I prepared to go. But he argued with me, and would not let me go, – telling me of my wife and of my children, and while he argued there came a knock at the door, and something was handed in, and I knew that it was the hand of his wife.'

'It was the money, I suppose?'

'Yes, Mr Toogood; it was the money. And I became the more uneasy, because she herself is rich. I liked it the less because it seemed to come from her hand. But I took it. What could I do when he reminded me that I could not keep my parish unless certain sums were paid? He gave me a little parcel in a cover, and I took it, –

and left him sorrowing. I had never before come quite to that; – though, indeed, it had in fact been often so before. What was the difference whether the alms were given into my hands or into my wife's?'

'You are too touchy about it all, Mr Crawley.'

'Of course I am. Do you try it, and see whether you will be touchy. You have worked hard at your profession, I daresay.'

'Well, yes; pretty well. To tell the truth, I have worked hard. By George, yes! It's not so bad now as it used to be.'

'But you have always earned your bread; bread for yourself, and bread for your wife and little ones. You can buy tickets for the play.'

'I couldn't always buy tickets, mind you.'

'I have worked as hard, and yet I cannot get bread. I am older than you, and I cannot earn my bare bread. Look at my clothes. If you had to go and beg from Mr Crump, would not you be touchy?'

'As it happens, Crump isn't so well off as I am.'

'Never mind. But I took it, and went home, and for two days I did not look at it. And then there came an illness upon me, and I know not what passed. But two men who had been hard on me came to the house when I was out, and my wife was in a terrible state; and I gave her the money, and she went into Silverbridge and paid them.'

'And this cheque was with what you gave her?'

'No; I gave her money in notes, – just fifty pounds. When I gave it her, I thought I gave it all; and yet afterwards I thought I remembered that in my illness I had found the cheque with the dean's money. But it was not so.'

'You are sure of that?'

'He has said that he put five notes of 10*l* each into the cover, and such notes I certainly gave to my wife.'

'Where then did you get the cheque?' Mr Crawley again paused before he answered. 'Surely, if you will exert your mind, you will remember,' said the lawyer. 'Where did you get the cheque?'

'I do not know.'

Mr Toogood threw himself back in his chair, took his knee up into his lap to nurse it, and began to think of it. He sat thinking of it for some minutes without a word, – perhaps for five minutes, though the time seemed to be much longer to Mr Crawley, who was, however, determined that he would not interrupt him. And Mr Toogood's thoughts were at variance with Mr Toogood's former words. Perhaps, after all, this scheme of Mr Crawley's, – or rather the mode of defence on which he had resolved without any scheme, – might be the best of which the case admitted. It might be well that he should go into court without a lawyer. 'He has convinced me of his innocence,' Mr Toogood said to himself, 'and why should he not convince a jury? He has convinced me, not because I am specially soft, or because I love the man, – for as to that I dislike him rather than otherwise; – but because there is either real truth in his words, or else so well-feigned a show of truth that no jury can tell the difference. I think it is true. By George, I think he did get the twenty pounds honestly, and that he does not this moment know where he got it. He may have put his finger into my eye; but, if so, why not also into the eyes of a jury?' Then he released his leg, and spoke something of his thoughts aloud. 'It's a sad story,' he said; 'a very sad story.'

'Well, yes, it's sad enough. If you could see my house, you'd say so.'

'I haven't a doubt but what you're as innocent as I am.' Mr Toogood, as he said this, felt a little twinge of conscience. He did believe Mr Crawley to be innocent, but he was not so sure of it as his words would seem to imply. Nevertheless he repeated the words again; – 'as innocent as I am.'

'I don't know,' said Mr Crawley. 'I don't know. I think I am; but I don't know.'

'I believe you are. But you see the case is a very distressing one. A jury has a right to say that the man in possession of a cheque for twenty pounds should account for his possession of it. If I understand the story aright, Mr Soames will be able to prove that he brought the cheque into your house, and, as far as he knows, never took it out again.'

'I suppose so; all the same, if he brought it in, then did he also take it out again.'

'I am saying what he will prove, – or, in other words, what he will state upon oath. You can't contradict him. You can't get into the box* to do it, – even if that would be of any avail; and I am glad that you cannot, as it would be of no avail. And you can put no one else into the box who can do so.'

'No; no.'

'That is to say, we think you cannot do so. People can do so many things that they don't think they can do; and can't do so many things that they think that they can do! When will the dean be home?'

'I don't know.'

'Before the trial?'

'I don't know. I have no idea.'

'It's almost a toss-up whether he'd do more harm or good if he were there.'

'I wish he might be there if he has anything to say, whether it might be for harm or good.'

'And Mrs Arabin; – she is with him?'

'They tell me she is not. She is in Europe. He is in Palestine.'

'In Palestine, is he?'

'So they tell me. A dean can go where he likes. He has no cure of souls to stand in the way of his pleasures.'

'He hasn't, – hasn't he? I wish I were a dean; that is, if I were not a lawyer. Might I write a line to the dean, – and to Mrs Dean, if it seemed fit? You wouldn't mind that? As you have come to see your cousin at last, – and very glad I am that you have, – you must leave him a little discretion. I won't say anything I oughtn't to say.' Mr Crawley opposed this scheme for some time, but at last consented to the proposition. 'And I'll tell you what, Mr Crawley; I am very fond of cathedrals, I am indeed; and I have long wanted to see Barchester. There's a very fine what-you-may-call-em; isn't there? Well; I'll just run down at the assizes. We have nothing to do in London when the judges are in the country, – of course.' Mr Toogood looked into Mr Crawley's eyes as he said this, to see if his iniquity were detected, but the perpetual curate was altogether innocent in these matters. 'Yes; I'll just run down for a mouthful of fresh air. Of course I shan't open my mouth in court. But I might say one word to the dean, if he's there; – and one word to Mr Soames. Who is conducting the prosecution?' Mr Crawley said that Mr Walker was doing so. 'Walker, Walker, Walker? Oh, – yes; Walker and Winthrop, isn't it? A decent sort of man, I suppose?'

'I have heard nothing to his discredit, Mr Toogood.'

'And that's saying a great deal for a lawyer. Well, Mr Crawley, if nothing else comes out between this and that, – nothing, that is, that shall clear your memory about that unfortunate bit of paper, you must simply tell your story to the jury as you've told it to me. I don't think any twelve men in England would convict you; – I don't indeed.'

'You think they would not?'

'Of course I've only heard one side, Mr Crawley.'

'No, – no, – no, that is true.'

'But judging as well as I can judge from one side, I don't think a jury can convict you. At any rate I'll see you at Barchester, and I'll write a line or two before the trial, just to find out anything than can be found out. And you're sure you won't come and take a bit of mutton with us in the Square? The girls would be delighted to see you, and so would Maria.' Mr Crawley said that he was quite sure he could not do that, and then having tendered reiterated thanks to his new friend in words which were touching in spite of their old-fashioned gravity, he took his leave, and walked back again to the public-house at Paddington.

He returned home to Hogglestock on the same afternoon, reaching that place at nine in the evening. During the whole of the day after leaving Raymond's Buildings he was thinking of the lawyer, and of the words which the lawyer had spoken. Although he had been disposed to quarrel with Mr Toogood on many points, although he had been more than once disgusted by the attorney's bad taste, shocked by his low morality, and almost insulted by his easy familiarity, still, when the interview was over, he liked the attorney. When first Mr Toogood had begun to talk, he regretted very much that he had subjected himself to the necessity of discussing his private affairs with such a windbag of a man; but when he left the chamber he trusted Mr Toogood altogether, and was very glad that he had sought his aid. He was tired and exhausted when he reached home, as he had eaten nothing but a biscuit or two since his breakfast; but his wife got him food and tea, and then asked him as to his success. 'Was my cousin kind to you?'

'Very kind, – more than kind, – perhaps somewhat too pressing in his kindness. But I find no fault. God forbid that I should. He is, I think, a good man, and certainly has been good to me.'

'And what is to be done?'

'He will write to the dean.'

'I am glad of that.'

'And he will be at Barchester.'

'Thank God for that.'

'But not as my lawyer.'

'Nevertheless, I thank God that some one will be there who will know how to give you assistance and advice.'

CHAPTER 33

The Plumstead foxes

The letters had been brought into the breakfast-parlour at Plumstead Rectory one morning, and the archdeacon had inspected them all, and then thrown over to his wife her share of the spoil, – as was the custom of the house. As to most of Mrs Grantly's letters, he never made any further inquiry. To letters from her sister, the dean's wife, he was profoundly indifferent, and rarely made any inquiry as to those which were directed in writing with which he was not familiar. But there were others as to which, as Mrs Grantly knew, he would be sure to ask her questions if she did not show them. No note ever reached her from Lady Hartletop as to which he was not curious, and yet Lady Hartletop's notes very seldom contained much that was of interest. Now, on this morning, there came a letter which, as a matter of course, Mrs Grantly read at breakfast, and which, she knew, would not be allowed to disappear without inquiry. Nor, indeed, did she wish to keep the letter from her husband. It was too important to be so treated. But she would have been glad to gain time to think in what spirit she would discuss the contents of the letter, – if only such time might be allowed to her. But the archdeacon would allow her no time. 'What does Henry say, my dear?' he asked, before the breakfast things had been taken away.

'What does he say? Well; he says—. I'll give you his letter to read by-and-by.'

'And why not now?'

'I thought I'd read it again myself, first.'

'But if you have read it, I suppose you know what's in it?'

'Not very clearly, as yet. However, there it is.' She knew very well that when she had once been asked for it, no peace would be allowed to her till he had seen it. And, alas! there was not much probability of peace in the house for some time after he should see it.

The archdeacon read the three or four first lines in silence, – and then he burst out. 'He has, has he? Then, by heavens—'

'Stop, dearest; stop,' said his wife, rising from her chair and coming over to him; 'do not say words which you will surely repent.'

'I will say words which shall make him repent. He shall never have from me a son's portion.'

'Do not make threats in anger. Do not! You know that it is wrong. If he has offended you, say nothing about it, – even to yourself, – as to threatened punishments, till you can judge of the offence in cool blood.'

'I am cool,' said the archdeacon.

'No, my dear; no; you are angry. And you have not even read his letter through.'

'I will read his letter.'

'You will see that the marriage is not imminent. It may be that even yet it will never take place. The young lady has refused him.'

'Psha!'

'You will see that she has done so. He tells us so himself. And she has behaved very properly.'

'Why has she refused him?'

'There can be no doubt about the reason. She feels that, with this charge hanging over her father, she is not in a position to become the wife of any gentleman. You cannot but respect her for that.'

Then the archdeacon finished his son's letter, uttering sundry interjections and ejaculations as he did so.

'Of course; I knew it. I understood it all,' he said at last. 'I've nothing to do with the girl. I don't care whether she be good or bad.'

'Oh, my dear!'

'I care not at all, – with reference to my own concerns. Of course I would wish that the daughter of a neighbouring clergyman, – that the daughter of any neighbour, – that the daughter of any one whatsoever, – should be good rather than bad. But as regards Henry and me, and our mutual relation, her goodness can make no difference. Let her be another Grizel,* and still such a marriage must estrange him from me, and me from him.'

'But she has refused him.'

'Yes; and what does he say? – that he has told her that he will not accept her refusal. Of course we know what it all means. The girl I am not judging. The girl I will not judge. But my own son, to whom I have ever done a father's duty with a father's affectionate indulgence, – him I will judge. I have warned him, and he declares himself to be careless of my warning. I shall take no notice of this letter. I shall neither write to him about it, or speak to him about it. But I charge you to write to him, and tell him that if he does this thing he shall not have a child's portion from me. It is not that I will shorten that which would have been his; but he shall have – nothing !' Then, having spoken these words with a solemnity which for the moment silenced his wife, he got up and left the room. He left the room and closed the door, but, before he had gone half the length of the hall towards his own study, he returned and addressed his wife again. 'You understand my instructions, I hope ?'

'What instructions ?'

'That you write to Henry and tell him what I say.'

'I will speak again to you about it by-and-by.'

'I will speak no more about it, – not a word more. Let there be not a word said, but oblige me by doing as I ask you.'

Then he was again about to leave the room, but she stopped him. 'Wait a moment, my dear.'

'Why should I wait ?'

'That you may listen to me. Surely you will do that, when I ask you. I will write to Henry, of course, if you bid me ; and I will give him your message, whatever it may be ; but not to-day, my dear.'

'Why not to-day ?'

'Because the sun shall go down upon your wrath* before I become its messenger. If you choose to write to-day yourself, I cannot help it. I cannot hinder you. If I am to write to him on your behalf I will take my instructions from you to-morrow morning. When to-morrow morning comes you will not be angry with me because of the delay.'

The archdeacon was by no means satisfied ; but he knew his wife too well, and himself too well, and the world too well, to insist on the immediate gratification of his passion. Over his bosom's mistress he did exercise a certain marital control, – which was, for instance, quite sufficiently fixed to enable him to look down with thorough contempt on such a one as Bishop Proudie ; but he was not a despot who could exact a passive obedience to every fantasy. His wife would not have written the letter for him on that day, and he knew very well that she would not do so. He knew also that she was right ; – and yet he regretted his want of power. His anger at the present moment was very hot, – so hot that he wished to wreak it. He knew that it would cool before the morrow ; – and, no doubt, knew also theoretically, that it would be most fitting that it should cool. But not the less was it a matter of regret to him that so much good hot anger should be wasted, and that he could not have his will of his disobedient son while it lasted. He might, no doubt, have written himself, but to have done so would not have suited him.

Even in his anger he could not have written to his son without using the ordinary terms of affection, and in his anger he could not bring himself to use those terms. 'You will find that I shall be of the same mind to-morrow, – exactly,' he said to his wife. 'I have resolved about it long since; and it is not likely that I shall change in a day.' Then he went out, about his parish, intending to continue to think of his son's iniquity, so that he might keep his anger hot, – red hot. Then he remembered that the evening would come, and that he would say his prayers; and he shook his head in regret, – in a regret of which he was only half conscious, though it was very keen, and which he did not attempt to analyze, – as he reflected that his rage would hardly be able to survive that ordeal. How common with us it is to repine that the devil is not stronger over us than he is.

The archdeacon, who was a very wealthy man, had purchased a property in Plumstead, contiguous to the glebe-land, and had thus come to exercise in the parish the double duty of rector and squire. And of this estate in Barsetshire, which extended beyond the confines of Plumstead into the neighbouring parish of Eiderdown, and which comprised also an outlying farm in the parish of Stogpingum, – Stoke Pinguium would have been the proper name had not barbarous Saxon tongues clipped it of its proper proportions, – he had always intended that his son Charles should enjoy the inheritance. There was other property, both in land and in money, for his elder son, and other again for the maintenance of his wife, – for the archdeacon's father had been for many years Bishop of Barchester, and such a bishopric as that of Barchester had been in those days was worth money. Of his intention in this respect he had never spoken in plain language to either of his sons; but the major had for the last year or two enjoyed the shooting of the Barsetshire covers, giving what orders he pleased about the game; and the father had encouraged him to take something like the management of the property into his hands. There might be some fifteen hundred acres of it altogether, and the archdeacon had rejoiced over it with his wife scores of times, saying that there was many a squire in the county whose elder son would never find himself half so well placed as would his own younger son. Now there was a string of narrow woods called Plumstead Coppices which ran from a point near the church right across the parish, dividing the archdeacon's land from the Ullathorne estate, and these coppices, or belts of woodland, belonged to the archdeacon. On the morning of which we are speaking, the archdeacon, mounted on his cob, still thinking of his son's iniquity and of his own fixed resolve to punish him as he had said that he would punish him, opened with his whip a woodland gate, from which a green muddy lane led through the trees up to the house of his gamekeeper. The man's wife was ill, and in his ordinary way of business the archdeacon was about to call and ask after her health. At the door of the cottage he found the man, who was woodman as well as game-keeper, and was responsible for fences and faggots, as well as for foxes and pheasants' eggs.

'How's Martha, Flurry?' asked the archdeacon.

'Thanking your reverence, she be a deal improved since the mistress was here, – last Tuesday it was, I think.'

'I'm glad of that. It was only rheumatism, I suppose?'

'Just a tich of fever with it, your reverence, the doctor said.'

'Tell her I was asking after it. I won't mind getting down to-day, as I am rather busy. She has had what she wanted from the house?'

'The mistress has been very good in that way. She always is, God bless her!'

'Good-day to you, Flurry. I'll ask Mr Sims to come and read to her a bit this afternoon, or to-morrow morning.' The archdeacon kept two curates, and Mr Sims was one of them.

'She'll take it very kindly, your reverence. But while you are here, sir, there's just a word I'd like to say. I didn't happen to catch Mr Henry when he was here the other day.'

'Never mind Mr Henry; what is it you have to say?'

'I do think, I do indeed, sir, that Mr Thorne's man ain't dealing fairly along of the foxes. I wouldn't say a word about it, only that Mr Henry is so particular.'

'What about the foxes? What is he doing with the foxes?'

'Well, sir, he's a trapping on 'em. He is, indeed, your reverence. I wouldn't speak if I warn't well nigh mortial sure.'

Now the archdeacon had never been a hunting man, though in his early days many a clergyman had been in the habit of hunting without losing his clerical character by doing so; but he had lived all his life among gentlemen in a hunting county, and had his own very strong ideas about the trapping of foxes. Foxes first, and pheasants afterwards, had always been the rule with him as to any land of which he himself had had the management. And no man understood better than he did how to deal with keepers as to this matter of fox-preserving, or knew better that keepers will in truth obey not the words of their employers, but their sympathies. 'Wish them to have foxes, and pay them, and they will have them,' Mr Sowerby of Chaldicotes used to say, and he in his day was reckoned to be the best preserver of foxes in Barsetshire. 'Tell them to have them, and don't wish it, and pay them well, and you won't have a fox to interfere with your game. I don't care what a man says to me, I can read it all like a book when I see his covers drawn.' That was what poor Mr Sowerby of Chaldicotes used to say, and the archdeacon had heard him say it a score of times, and had learned the lesson. But now his heart was not with the foxes, — and especially not with the foxes on behalf of his son Henry. 'I can't have any meddling with Mr Thorne,' he said; 'I can't, and I won't.'

'But I don't suppose it can be Mr Thorne's order, your reverence; and Mr Henry is so particular.'

'Of course it isn't Mr Thorne's order. Mr Thorne has been a hunting man all his life.'

'But he have guv' up now, your reverence. He ain't a hunted these two years.'

'I'm sure he wouldn't have the foxes trapped.'

'Not if he knowed it, he wouldn't, your reverence. A gentleman of the likes of him, who's been a hunting over fifty years, wouldn't do the likes of that; but the foxes is trapped, and Mr Henry 'll be a putting it on me if I don't speak out. They is Plumstead foxes, too; and a vixen was trapped just across the field yonder, in Goshall Springs, no later than yesterday morning.' Flurry was now thoroughly in earnest; and, indeed, the trapping of a vixen in February is a serious thing.

'Goshall Springs don't belong to me,' said the archdeacon.

'No, your reverence; they're on the Ullathorne property. But a word from your reverence would do it. Mr Henry thinks more of the foxes than anything. The last word he told me was that it would break his heart if he saw the coppices drawn blank.'

'Then he must break his heart.' The words were pronounced, but the archdeacon had so much command over himself as to speak them in such a voice that the man should not hear them. But it was incumbent on him to say something that the man should hear. 'I will have no meddling in the matter, Flurry. Whether there are foxes or whether there are not, is matter of no great moment. I will not have a word said to annoy Mr Thorne.' Then he rode away, back through the wood and out on to the road, and the horse walked with him leisurely on, whither the archdeacon hardly knew, — for he was thinking, thinking, thinking. 'Well; — if that ain't the darn'dest thing that ever was,' said Flurry; 'but I'll tell the squire about Thorne's man, — darned if I don't.' Now 'the squire' was young Squire Gresham, the master of the East Barsetshire hounds.

But the archdeacon went on thinking, thinking, thinking. He could have heard nothing of his son to stir him more in his favour than this strong evidence of his partiality for foxes. I do not mean it to be understood that the archdeacon regarded foxes as better than active charity, or a contented mind, or a meek spirit, or than self-denying temperance. No doubt all these virtues did hold in his mind their proper place, altogether beyond contamination of foxes. But he had prided himself on thinking that his son should be a country gentleman, and, probably nothing doubting as to the major's active charity and other virtues, was delighted to receive evidence of those tastes which he had ever wished to encourage in his son's character. Or rather, such evidence would have delighted him at any other time than the present. Now it only added more gall to his cup. 'Why should he teach himself to care for such things, when he has not the spirit to enjoy them,' said the archdeacon to himself. 'He is a fool, – a fool. A man that has been married once, to go crazy after a little girl, that has hardly a dress to her back, and who never was in a drawing-room in her life! Charles is the eldest, and he shall be the eldest. It will be better to keep it together. It is the way in which the country has become what it is.' He was out nearly all day, and did not see his wife till dinner-time. Her father, Mr Harding, was still with them, but had breakfasted in his own room. Not a word, therefore, was said about Henry Grantly between the father and mother on that evening.

Mrs Grantly was determined that, unless provoked, she would say nothing to him till the following morning. He should sleep upon his wrath before she spoke to him again. And he was equally unwilling to recur to the subject. Had she permitted it, the next morning would have passed away, and no word would have been spoken. But this would not have suited her. She had his orders to write, and she had undertaken to obey these orders, – with the delay of one day. Were she not to write at all, – or in writing to send no message from the father, there would be cause for further anger. And yet this, I think, was what the archdeacon wished.

'Archdeacon,' she said, 'I shall write to Henry to-day.'

'Very well.'

'And what am I to say from you?'

'I told you yesterday what are my intentions.'

'I am not asking about that now. We hope there will be years and years to come, in which you may change them, and shape them as you will. What shall I tell him now from you?'

'I have nothing to say to him, – nothing; not a word. He knows what he has to expect from me, for I have told him. He is acting with his eyes open, and so am I. If he marries Miss Crawley, he must live on his own means. I told him that myself so plainly, that he can want no further intimation.' Then Mrs Grantly knew that she was absolved from the burden of yesterday's message, and she plumed herself on the prudence of her conduct. On the same morning the archdeacon wrote the following note: –

Dear Thorne, –

My man tells me that foxes have been trapped on Darvell's farm, just outside the coppices. I know nothing of it myself, but I am sure you'll look to it.

Yours always,
T. Grantly.

CHAPTER 34

Mrs Proudie sends for her lawyer

There was great dismay in Barchester Palace after the visit paid to the bishop and Mrs Proudie by that terrible clerical offender, Mr Crawley. It will be remembered, perhaps, how he had defied the bishop with spoken words, and how he had defied the bishop's wife by speaking no words to her. For the moment, no doubt, Mr Crawley had the best of it. Mrs Proudie acknowledged to herself that this was the case; but as she was a woman who had never yet succumbed to an enemy, who had never, – if on such an occasion I may be allowed to use a schoolboy's slang, – taken a licking from any one, it was not likely that Mr Crawley would be long allowed to enjoy his triumph in peace. It would be odd if all the weight of the palace would not be able to silence a wretch of a perpetual curate who had already been committed to take his trial for thieving; – and Mrs Proudie was determined that all the weight of the palace should be used. As for the bishop, though he was not as angry as his wife, he was quite as unhappy, and therefore quite as hostile to Mr Crawley; and was fully conscious that there could be no peace for him now until Mr Crawley should be crushed. If only the assizes would come at once, and get him condemned out of the way, what a blessed thing it would be! But unluckily it still wanted three months to the assizes, and during those three months Mr Crawley would be at large and subject only to episcopal authority. During that time he could not be silenced by the arm of the civil law. His wife was not long in expressing her opinion after Mr Crawley had left the palace. 'You must proceed against him in the Court of Arches,* – and that at once,' said Mrs Proudie. 'You can do that, of course? I know that it will be expensive. Of course it will be expensive. I suppose it may cost us some hundreds of pounds; but duty is duty, my lord, and in such a case as this your duty as a bishop is paramount.'

The poor bishop knew that it was useless to explain to her the various mistakes which she made, – which she was ever making, – as to the extent of his powers and the modes of procedure which were open to him. When he would do so she would only rail at him for being lukewarm in his office, poor in spirit, and afraid of dealing roundly with those below him. On the present occasion he did say a word, but she would not even hear him to the end. 'Don't tell me about rural deans, as if I didn't know. The rural dean has nothing to do with such a case. The man has been committed for trial. Send for Mr Chadwick at once, and let steps be taken before you are an hour older.'

'But, my dear, Mr Chadwick can do nothing.'

'Then I will see Mr Chadwick.' And in her anger she did sit down and write a note to Mr Chadwick, begging him to come over to her at the palace.

Mr Chadwick was a lawyer, living in Barchester, who earned his bread from ecclesiastical business. His father, and his uncle, and his grandfather and granduncles, had all been concerned in the affairs of the diocese of Barchester. His uncle had been bailiff to the episcopal estates, or steward as he had been called, in Bishop Grantly's time, and still contrived to draw his income in some shape from the property of the see. The nephew had also been the legal assistant of the bishop in his latter days, and had been continued in that position by Bishop Proudie, not from love, but from expediency. Mr John Chadwick was one of those gentlemen, two or three of whom are to be seen in connection with every see, – who seem to be hybrids – half-lay, half-cleric. They dress like clergymen, and affect that mixture of clerical solemnity and clerical waggishness which is generally to be found among minor canons and vicar chorals* of a cathedral. They live, or at least have their offices, half in the Close and half out of it, – dwelling as it were just on the borders of holy orders. They always wear white neck-handkerchiefs and black gloves; and would be altogether clerical in their appearance, were it not that as regards the outward man they impinge somewhat on the characteristics of the undertaker. They savour of the church, but the savour is of the church's exterior. Any stranger thrown into chance contact with one of them would, from instinct, begin to talk of things ecclesiastical without any reference to things theological or things religious. They are always most worthy men, much respected in the society of the Close, and I never heard of one of them whose wife was not comfortable or whose children were left without provision.

Such a one was Mr John Chadwick, and as it was a portion of his duties to accompany the bishop to consecrations and ordinations, he knew Dr Proudie very well. Having been brought up, as it were, under the very wing of Bishop Grantly, it could not well be that he should love Bishop Grantly's successor. The old bishop and the new bishop had been so different that no man could like, or even esteem, them both. But Mr Chadwick was a prudent man, who knew well the source from which he earned his bread, and he had never quarrelled with Bishop Proudie. He knew Mrs Proudie also, – of necessity, – and when I say of him that he had hitherto avoided any open quarrel with her, it will I think be allowed that he was a man of prudence and sagacity.

But he had sometimes been sorely tried, and he felt when he got her note that he was now about to encounter a very sore trial. He muttered something which might have been taken for an oath, were it not that the outward signs of the man gave warranty that no oath could proceed from such a one. Then he wrote a short note presenting his compliments to Mrs Proudie, and saying that he would call at the palace at eleven o'clock on the following morning.

But, in the meantime, Mrs Proudie, who could not be silent on the subject for a moment, did learn something of the truth from her husband. The information did not come to her in the way of instruction, but was teased out of the unfortunate man. 'I know that you can proceed against him in the Court of Arches, under the "Church Discipline Act," '* she said.

'No, my dear; no;' said the Bishop, shaking his head in his misery.

'Or in the Consistorial Court.* It's all the same thing.'

'There must be an inquiry first, – by his brother clergy. There must indeed. It's the only way of proceeding.'

'But there has been an inquiry, and he has been committed.'

'That doesn't signify, my dear. That's the Civil Law.'

'And if the Civil Law condemns him, and locks him up in prison; – as it most certainly will do?'

'But it hasn't done so yet, my dear. I really think that as it has gone so far, it will be best to leave it as it is till he has taken his trial.'

'What; leave him there after what occurred this morning in this palace?' The palace with Mrs Proudie was always a palace, and never a house. 'No; no; ten thousand times, no. Are you not aware that he insulted you, and grossly, most grossly insulted me? I was never treated with such insolence by any clergyman before, since I first came to this palace; – never, never. And we know the man to be a thief; – we absolutely know it. Think, my lord, of the souls of his people!'

'Oh, dear; oh, dear; oh, dear,' said the bishop.

'Why do you fret yourself in that way?'

'Because you will get me into trouble. I tell you the only thing to be done is to issue a commission with the rural dean at the head of it.'

'Then issue a commission.'

'And they will take three months.'

'Why should they take three months? Why should they take more than three days, – or three hours. It is all plain sailing.'

'These things are never plain sailing, my dear. When a bishop has to oppose any of his clergy, it is always made as difficult as possible.'

'More shame for them who make it so.'

'But it is so. If I were to take legal proceedings against him, it would cost, – oh, dear, – more than a thousand pounds, I should say.'

'If it costs two, you must do it.' Mrs Proudie's anger was still very hot, or she would not have spoken of an unremunerative outlay of money in such language as that.

In this manner she did come to understand, before the arrival of Mr Chadwick, that her husband could take no legal steps towards silencing Mr Crawley until a commission of clergymen had been appointed to inquire into the matter, and that that commission should be headed by the rural dean within the limits of whose rural deanery the parish of Hogglestock was situated, or by some beneficed parochial clergyman of repute in the neighbourhood. Now the rural dean was Dr Tempest of Silverbridge, – who had held that position before the coming of Dr Proudie to the diocese; and there had grown up in the bosom of Mrs Proudie a strong feeling that undue mercy had been shown to Mr Crawley by the magistrates of Silverbridge, of whom Dr Tempest had been one. 'These magistrates had taken bail for his appearance at the assizes, instead of committing him to prison at once, – as they were bound to do, when such an offence as that had been committed by a clergyman. But, no; – even though there was a clergyman among them, they had thought nothing of the souls of the poor people !' In such language Mrs Proudie had spoken of the affair at Silverbridge, and having once committed herself to such an opinion, of course she thought that Dr Tempest would go through fire and water, – would omit no stretch of what little judicial power might be committed to his hands, – with the view of opposing his bishop and maintaining the culprit in his position. 'In such a case as this, can not you name an acting rural dean yourself? Dr Tempest, you know, is very old.' 'No, my dear; no; I cannot.' 'You can ask Mr Chadwick, at any rate, and then you could name Mr Thumble.' 'But Mr Thumble doesn't even hold a living in the diocese. Oh, dear; oh, dear; oh, dear!' And so the matter rested until Mr Chadwick came.

Mrs Proudie had no doubt intended to have Mr Chadwick all to herself, – at any rate so to encounter him in the first instance. But having been at length convinced that the inquiry by the rural dean was really necessary as a preliminary, and having also slept upon the question of expenditure, she gave directions that the lawyer should be shown into the bishop's study, and she took care to be absent at the moment of his arrival. Of course she did not intend that Mr Chadwick should leave the palace without having heard what she had to say, but she thought that it would be well that he should be made to conceive that though the summons had been written by her, it had really been intended on the part of the bishop. 'Mr Chadwick will be with you at eleven bishop,' she said, as she got up from the breakfast-table, at which she left his lordship with two of his daughters and with a married son-in-law, a clergyman who was staying in the house. 'Very well, my dear,' said the bishop, with a smile, – for he was anxious not to betray any vexation at his wife's interference before his daughter or the Rev. Mr Tickler. But he understood it all. Mr Chadwick had been sent for with reference to Mr Crawley, and he was driven, – absolutely driven, to propose to his lawyer that this commission of inquiry should be issued.

Punctually at eleven Mr Chadwick came, wearing a very long face as he entered the palace door, – for he felt that he would in all probability be now compelled to quarrel with Mrs Proudie. Much he could bear, but there was a limit to his endurance. She had never absolutely sent for him before, though she had often interfered with him. 'I shall have to tell her a bit of my mind,' he said, as he stepped across the Close, habited in his best suit of black, with most exact white cravat, and yet looking not quite like a clergyman, – with some touch of the undertaker in his gait. When he found that he was shown into the bishop's room, and that the bishop was there, – and the bishop only, – his mind was relieved. It would have been better that the bishop should have written himself, or that the chaplain should have written in his lordship's name; that, however, was a trifle.

But the bishop did not know what to say to him. If he intended to direct an inquiry to be made by the rural dean, it would be by no means becoming that he should consult Mr Chadwick as to doing so. It might be well, or if not well at any rate not improper, that he should make the application to Dr Tempest through Mr Chadwick; but in that case he must give the order at once, and he still wished to avoid it if it were possible. Since he had been in the diocese no case so grave as this had been pushed upon him. The intervention of the rural dean in an ordinary way he had used, – had been made to use, – more than once, by his wife. A vicar had been absent a little too long from one parish, and there had been rumours about brandy-and-water in another. Once he had been very nearly in deep water because Mrs Proudie had taken it in dudgeon that a certain young rector, who had been left a widower, had a very pretty governess for his children; and there had been that case, sadly notorious in the diocese at the time, of our excellent friend Mr Robarts of Framley, when the bailiffs were in his house because he couldn't pay his debts, – or rather, the debts of his friend for whom he had signed bills. But in all these cases some good fortune had intervened, and he had been saved from the terrible necessity of any ulterior process. But now, – now he was being driven beyond himself, and all to no purpose. If Mrs Proudie would only wait three months the civil law would do it all for him. But here was Mr Chadwick in the room, and he knew that it would be useless for him to attempt to talk to Mr Chadwick about other matters, and so dismiss him. The wife of his bosom would be down upon them before Chadwick could be out of the room.

'H – m – ha. How d'ye do, Mr Chadwick – won't you sit down?' Mr Chadwick thanked his lordship, and sat down. 'It's very cold, isn't it, Mr Chadwick?'

'A hard frost, my lord, but a beautiful day.'

'Won't you come near the fire?' The bishop knew that Mrs Proudie was on the road, and had an eye to the proper strategical position of his forces. Mrs Proudie would certainly take up her position in a certain chair from whence the light enabled her to rake her husband thoroughly. What advantage she might have from this he could not prevent; – but he could so place Mr Chadwick, that the laywer should be more within the reach of his eye than that of his wife. So the bishop pointed to an arm-chair opposite to himself and near the fire, and Mr Chadwick seated himself accordingly.

'This is a very sad affair about Mr Crawley,' said the bishop.

'Very sad indeed,' said the lawyer. 'I never pitied a man so much in my life, my lord.'

This was not exactly the line which the bishop was desirous of taking. 'Of course he is to be pitied; – of course he is. But from all I hear, Mr Chadwick, I am afraid, – I am afraid we must not acquit him.'

'As to that, my lord, he has to stand his trial, of course.'

'But, you see, Mr Chadwick, regarding him as a beneficed clergyman, – with a cure of souls, – the question is whether I should be justified in leaving him where he is till his trial shall come on.'

'Of course your lordship knows best about that, but—'

'I know there is a difficulty. I know that. But I am inclined to think that in the interests of the parish I am bound to issue a commission of inquiry.'

'I believe your lordship has attempted to silence him, and that he has refused to comply.'

'I thought it better for everybody's sake, – especially for his own, that he should for a while be relieved from his duties; but he is an obstinate man, a very obstinate man. I made the attempt with all consideration for his feelings.'

'He is hard put to it, my lord. I know the man and his pride. The dean has spoken of him to me more than once, and nobody knows him so well as the dean. If I might venture to offer an opinion—'

'Good morning, Mr Chadwick,' Mrs Proudie, coming into the room and taking her accustomed seat. 'No thank you, no; I will stay away from the fire, if you please. His lordship has spoken to you no doubt about this unfortunate, wretched man?'

'We are speaking of him now, my dear.'

'Something must of course be done to put a stop to the crying disgrace of having such a man preaching from a pulpit in this diocese. When I think of the souls of the people in that poor village, my hair literally stands on end. And then he is disobedient!'

'That is the worst of it,' said the bishop. 'It would have been so much better for himself if he would have allowed me to provide quietly for the services till the trial be over.'

'I could have told you, my lord, that he would not do that, from what I knew of him,' said Mr Chadwick.

'But he must do it,' said Mrs Proudie. 'He must be made to do it.'

'His lordship will find it difficult,' said Mr Chadwick.

'I can issue a commission, you know, to the rural dean,' said the bishop mildly.

'Yes, you can do that. And Dr Tempest in two months' time will have named his assessors—'

'Dr Tempest must not name them; the bishop must name them,' said Mrs Proudie.

'It is customary to leave that to the rural dean,' said Mr Chadwick. 'The bishop no doubt can object to any one named.'

'And can specially select any clergyman he pleased from the arch-deaconry,' said the bishop. 'I have known it done.'

'The rural dean in such case has probably been an old man, and not active,' said the lawyer.

'And Dr Tempest is a very old man,' said Mrs Proudie, 'and in such a matter not at all trustworthy. He was one of the magistrates who took bail.'

'His lordship could hardly set him aside,' said the lawyer. 'At any rate I would not recommend him to try. I think you might suggest a commission of five, and propose two of the number yourself. I do not think that in such a case Dr Tempest would raise any question.'

At last it was settled in this way. Mr Chadwick was to prepare a letter to Dr Tempest, for the bishop's signature, in which the doctor should be requested, as the rural dean to whom Mr Crawley was subject, to hold a commission of five to inquire into Mr Crawley's conduct. The letter was to explain to Dr Tempest that the bishop, moved by his solicitude for the souls of the people of Hogglestock, had endeavoured, 'in a friendly way,' to induce Mr Crawley to desist from his ministrations; but that having failed through Mr Crawley's obstinacy, he had no alternative but to proceed in this way. 'You had better say that his lordship, as bishop of the diocese, can take no heed of the coming trial,' said Mrs Proudie. 'I think his lordship had better say nothing at all about the trial,' said Mr Chadwick. 'I think that will be best,' said the bishop.

'But if they report against him,' said Mr Chadwick, 'you can only then proceed in the ecclesiastical court, – at your own expense.'

'He'll hardly be so obstinate as that,' said the bishop.

'I'm afraid you don't know him, my lord,' said the lawyer. The bishop, thinking of the scene which had taken place in that very room only yesterday, felt that he did know Mr Crawley, and felt also that the hope which he had just expressed was one in which he himself put no trust. But something might turn up; and it was devoutly to be hoped that Dr Tempest would take a long time over his inquiry. The assizes might come on as soon as it was terminated, or very shortly afterwards; and then everything might be well. 'You won't find Dr Tempest very ready at it,' said Mr Chadwick. The bishop in his heart was comforted by the words. 'But he must be made to be ready to do his duty,' said Mrs Proudie, imperiously. Mr Chadwick shrugged his shoulders, then got up, spoke his farewell little speeches, and left the palace.

CHAPTER 35

Lily Dale writes two words in her book

John Eames saw nothing more of Lily Dale till he packed up his portmanteau, left his mother's house, and went to stay for a few days with his old friend Lady Julia; and this did not happen till he had been above a week at Guestwick. Mrs Dale repeatedly said that it was odd that Johnny did not come to see them; and Grace, speaking of him to Lily, asked why he did not come. Lily, in her funny way, declared that he would come soon enough. But even while she was joking there was something of half-expressed consciousness in her words, — as though she felt it to be foolish to speak of his coming as she might of that of any other young man, before people who knew her whole story. 'He'll come quick enough. He knows, and I know, that his coming will do no good. Of course I shall be glad to see him. Why shouldn't I be glad to see him? I've known him and liked him all my life. I liked him when there did not seem to be much about him to like, and now that he is clever, and agreeable, and good-looking, — which he never was as a lad, — why shouldn't I go on liking him? he's more like a brother to me than anybody else I've got. James,' — James was her brother-in-law, Dr Crofts, — 'thinks of nothing but his patients and his babies, and my cousin Bernard is much too grand a person for me to take the liberty of loving him. I shall be very glad to see Johnny Eames.' From all which Mrs Dale was led to believe that Johnny's case was still hopeless. And how should it not be hopeless? Had Lily not confessed within the last week or two that she still loved Adolphus Crosbie?

Mrs Eames also, and Mary, were surprised that John did not go over to Allington. 'You haven't seen Mrs Dale yet, or the squire?' said his mother.

'I shall see them, when I am at the cottage.'

'Yes; — no doubt. But it seems strange that you should be here so long without going to them.'

'There's time enough,' said he. 'I shall have nothing else to do when I'm at the cottage.' Then, when Mary had spoken to him again in private, expressing a hope that there was 'nothing wrong,' he had been very angry with his sister. 'What do you mean by wrong? What rubbish you girls talk! and you never have any delicacy of feeling to make you silent.'

'Oh, John, don't say such hard things as that of me!'

'But I do say them. You'll make me swear among you some day that I will never see Lily Dale again. As it is, I wish I never had seen her, — simply because I am so dunned about it.' In all of which I think that Johnny was manifestly wrong. When the humour was on him he was fond enough of talking about Lily Dale. Had he not taught her to do so, I doubt whether his sister would ever have mentioned Lily's name to him. 'I did not mean to dun you, John,' said Mary, meekly.

But at last he went to Lady Julia's, and was no sooner there than he was ready to start for Allington. When Lady Julia spoke to him about Lily, he did not venture to snub her. Indeed, of all his friends, Lady Julia was the one with whom on this subject he allowed himself the most unrestricted confidence. He came over one day, just before dinner, and declared his intention of walking over to Allington immediately after breakfast on the following morning. 'It's the last time, Lady Julia,' he said.

'So you say, Johnny.'

'And so I mean it! What's the good of a man frittering away his life? What's the good of wishing for what you can't get?'

'Jacob was not in such a hurry when he wished for Rachel.'

'That was all very well for an old patriarch who had seven or eight hundred years to live.'

'My dear John, you forget your Bible. Jacob did not live half as long as that.'

'He lived long enough, and slowly enough, to be able to wait fourteen years; — and then he had something to comfort him in the meantime. And after all, Lady Julia, it's more than seven years since I first thought Lily was the prettiest girl I ever saw.'

'How old are you now?'

'Twenty-seven, — and she's twenty-four.'

'You've time enough yet, if you'll only be patient.'

'I'll be patient for to-morrow, Lady Julia, but never again. Not that I mean to quarrel with her. I'm not such a fool as to quarrel with a girl because she can't like me. I know how it all is. If that scoundrel had not come across my path just when he did, — in that very nick of time, all might have been right betwixt her and me. I couldn't have offered to marry her before, when I hadn't as much income as would have found her in bread-and-butter. And then, just as better times came to me, he stepped in! I wonder whether it will be expected of me that I should forgive him?'

'As far as that goes, you have no right to be angry with him.'

'But I am, – all the same.'

'And so was I, – but not for stepping in, as you call it.'

'You and I are different, Lady Julia. I was angry with him for stepping in; but I couldn't show it. Then he stepped out, and I did manage to show it. And now I shouldn't wonder if he doesn't step in again. After all, why should he have such a power? It was simply the nick of time which gave it to him.' That John Eames should be able to find some consolation in this consideration is devoutly to be hoped by us all.

There was nothing said about Lily Dale the next morning at breakfast. Lady Julia observed that John was dressed a little more neatly than usual; – though the change was not such as to have called for her special observation, had she not known the business on which he was intent.

'You have nothing to send to the Dales?' he said, as he got up from the table.

'Nothing but my love, Johnny.'

'No worsted or embroidery work, – or a pot of special jam for the squire?'

'No, sir, nothing; though I should like to make you carry a pair of panniers, if I could.'

'They would become me well,' said Johnny, 'for I am going on an ass's errand.' Then, without waiting for the word of affection which was on the old woman's lips, he got himself out of the room, and started on his journey.

The walk was only three miles and the weather was dry and frosty, and he had come to the turn leading up to the church and the squire's house almost before he remembered that he was near Allington. Here he paused for a moment to think. If he continued his way down by the 'Red Lion' and through Allington Street, he must knock at Mrs Dale's door, and ask for admission by means of the servant, – as would be done by any ordinary visitor. But he could make his way on to the lawn by going up beyond the wall of the churchyard and through the squire's garden. He knew the path well, – very well; and he thought that he might take so much liberty as that, both with the squire and with Mrs Dale, although his visits to Allington were not so frequent now as they used to be in the days of his boyhood. He did not wish to be admitted by the servant, and therefore he went through the gardens. Luckily he did not see the squire, who would have detained him, and he escaped from

Hopkins, the old gardener, with little more than a word. 'I'm going down to see the ladies, Hopkins; I suppose I shall find them?' And then, while Hopkins was arranging his spade so that he might lean upon it for a little chat, Johnny was gone and had made his way into the other garden. He had thought it possible that he might meet Lily out among the walks by herself, and such a meeting as this would have suited him better than any other. And as he crossed the little bridge which separated the gardens he thought of more than one such meeting, – of one especial occasion on which he had first ventured to tell her in plain words that he loved her. But before that day Crosbie had come there, and at the moment in which he was speaking of his love she regarded Crosbie as an angel of light upon the earth. What hope could there have been for him then? What use was there in his telling such a tale of love at that time? When he told it, he knew that Crosbie had been before him. He knew that Crosbie was at that moment the angel of light. But as he had never before been able to speak of his love, so was he then unable not to speak of it. He had spoken, and of course had been simply rebuked. Since that day Crosbie had ceased to be an angel of light, and he, John Eames, had spoken often. But he had spoken in vain, and now he would speak once again.

He went through the garden and over the lawn belonging to the Small House and saw no one. He forgot, I think, that ladies do not come out to pick roses when the ground is frozen, and that croquet is not often in progress with the hoar-frost on the grass. So he walked up to the little terrace before the drawing-room, and looking in saw Mrs Dale, and Lily, and Grace at their morning work. Lily was drawing, and Mrs Dale was writing, and Grace had her needle in her hand. As it happened, no one at first perceived him, and he had time to feel that after all he would have managed better if he had been announced in the usual way. As, however, it was not necessary that he should announce himself, he knocked at the window, and they all immediately looked up and saw him. 'It's my cousin John,' said Grace. 'Oh, Johnny, how are you at last?' said Mrs Dale. But it was Lily who, without speaking, opened the window for him, who was the first to give him her hand, and who led him through into the room.

'It's a great shame my coming in this way,' said John, 'and letting all the cold air in upon you.'

'We shall survive it,' said Mrs Dale. 'I suppose you have just come down from my brother-in-law?'

'No; I have not seen the squire as yet. I will do so before I go back, of course. But it seemed such a commonplace sort of thing to go round by the village.'

'We are very glad to see you, by whatever way you come; – are we not, mamma?' said Lily.

'I'm not so sure of that. We were only saying yesterday that as you had been in the country a fortnight without coming to us, we did not think we would be at home when you did come.'

'But I have caught you, you see,' said Johnny.

And so they went on, chatting of old times and of mutual friends very comfortably for full an hour. And there was some serious conversation about Grace's father and his affairs, and John declared his opinion that Mr Crawley ought to go to his uncle, Thomas Toogood, not at all knowing at that time that Mr Crawley himself had come to the same opinion. And John gave them an elaborate description of Sir Raffle Buffle, standing up with his back to the fire with his hat on his head, and speaking with a loud harsh voice, to show them the way in which he declared that that gentleman received his inferiors; and then bowing and scraping and rubbing his hands together and simpering with would-be softness, – declaring that after that fashion Sir Raffle received his superiors. And they were very merry, – so that no one would have thought that Johnny was a despondent lover, now bent on throwing the dice for his last stake; or that Lily was aware that she was in the presence of one lover, and that she was like to fall to the ground between two stools, – having two lovers, neither of whom could serve her turn.

'How can you consent to serve him if he's such a man as that?' said Lily, speaking of Sir Raffle.

'I do not serve him. I serve the Queen, – or rather the public. I don't take his wages, and he does not play his tricks with me. He knows that he can't. He has tried it, and has failed. And he only keeps me where I am because I've had some money left me. He thinks it fine to have a private secretary with a fortune. I know that he tells people all manner of lies about it, making it out to be five times as much as it is. Dear old Huffle Snuffle. He is such an ass; and yet he's had wit enough to get to the top of the tree, and to keep himself there. He began the world without a penny. Now he has got a handle to his name, and he'll live in clover all his life. It's very odd, isn't it, Mrs Dale?'

'I suppose he does his work?'

'When men get so high as that, there's no knowing whether they work or whether they don't. There isn't much for them to do, as far as I can see. They have to look beautiful, and frighten the young ones.'

'And does Sir Raffle look beautiful?' Lily asked.

'After a fashion, he does. There is something imposing about such a man till you're used to it, and can see through it. Of course it's all padding. There are men who work, no doubt. but among the bigwigs, and bishops and cabinet ministers, I fancy that the looking beautiful is the chief part of it. Dear me, you don't mean to say it's luncheon time ?'

But it was luncheon time, and not only had he not as yet said a word of all that which he had come to say, but had not as yet made any move towards getting it said. How was he to arrange that Lily should be left alone with him ? Lady Julia had said that she should not expect him back till dinner-time, and he had answered her lackadaisically, 'I don't suppose I shall be there above ten minutes. Ten minutes will say all I've got to say, and do all I've got to do. And then I suppose I shall go and cut names about upon bridges, – eh, Lady Julia ?' Lady Julia understood his words ; for once, upon a former occasion, she had found him cutting Lily's name on the rail of a wooden bridge in her brother's grounds. But he had now been a couple of hours at the Small House, and had not said a word of that which he had come to say.

'Are you going to walk out with us after lunch ?' said Lily.

'He will have had walking enough,' said Mrs Dale.

'We'll convoy him back part of the way,' said Lily.

'I'm not going yet,' said Johnny, 'unless you turn me out.'

'But we must have our walk before it is dark,' said Lily.

'You might go up with him to your uncle,' said Mrs Dale. 'Indeed, I promised to go up myself, and so did you, Grace, to see the microscope. I heard Mr Dale give orders that one of those long-legged reptiles should be caught on purpose for your inspection.'

Mrs Dale's little scheme for bringing the two together was very transparent, but it was not the less wise on that account. Schemes will often be successful, let them be ever so transparent. Little intrigues become necessary, not to conquer unwilling people, but people who are willing enough, who, nevertheless, cannot give way except under the machinations of an intrigue.

'I don't think I'll mind looking at the long-legged creature to-day,' said Johnny.

'I must go, of course,' said Grace.

Lily said nothing at the moment, either about the long-legged creature or the walk. That which must be, must be. She knew well why John Eames had come there. She knew that the visits to his mother and to Lady Julia would never have been made, but that he might have this interview. And he had a right to demand, at any rate, as much as that. That which must be, must be. And therefore when both Mrs Dale and Grace stoutly maintained their purpose of going up to the squire, Lily neither attempted to persuade John to accompany them, nor said that she would do so herself.

'I will convoy you home myself,' she said, 'and Grace, when she has done with the beetle, shall come and meet me. Won't you Grace?'

'Certainly.'

'We are not helpless young ladies in these parts, nor yet timorous,' continued Lily. 'We can walk about without being afraid of ghosts, robbers, wild bulls, young men, or gipsies. Come the field path, Grace. I will go as far as the big oak with him, and then I shall turn back, and I shall come in by the stile opposite the church gate, and through the garden. So you can't miss me.'

'I daresay he'll come back with you,' said Grace.

'No, he won't. He will do nothing of the kind. He'll have to go on and open Lady Julia's bottle of port wine for his own drinking.'

All this was very good on Lily's part, and very good also on the part of Mrs Dale; and John was of course very much obliged to them. But there was a lack of romance in it all, which did not seem to him to argue well as to his success. He did not think much about it, but he felt that Lily would not have been so ready to arrange their walk had she intended to yield to his entreaty. No doubt in these latter days plain good sense had become the prevailing mark of her character, – perhaps, as Johnny thought, a little too strongly prevailing; but even with all her plain good sense and determination to dispense with the absurdities of romance in the affairs of her life, she would not have proposed herself as his companion for a walk across the fields merely that she might have an opportunity of accepting his hand. He did not say all this to himself, but he instinctively felt that it was so. And he felt also that it should have been his duty to arrange the walk, or the proper opportunity for the scene that was to come. She had done it instead, – she and her mother between them, thereby forcing upon him a painful conviction that he himself had not been equal to the occasion. 'I always make a mull of it,' he said to himself, when the girls went up to get their hats.

They went down together through the garden, and parted where the paths led away, one to the great house and the other towards the church. 'I'll certainly come and call upon the squire before I go back to London,' said Johnny.

'We'll tell him so,' said Mrs Dale. 'He would be sure to hear that you had been with us, even if we said nothing about it.'

'Of course he would,' said Lily; 'Hopkins has seen him.' Then they separated, and Lily and John Eames were together.

Hardly a word was said, perhaps not a word, till they had crossed the road and got into the field opposite to the church. And in this first field there was more than one path, and the children of the village were often there, and it had about it something of a public nature. John Eames felt that it was by no means a fitting field to say that which he had to say. In crossing it, therefore, he merely remarked that the day was very fine for walking. Then he added one special word, 'And it is good of you, Lily, to come with me.'

'I am very glad to come with you. I would do more than that, John, to show how glad I am to see you.' Then they had come to the second little gate, and beyond that the fields were really fields, and there were stiles instead of wicket-gates, and the business of the day must be begun.

'Lily, whenever I come here you say you are glad to see me?'

'And so I am, – very glad. Only you would take it as meaning what it does not mean, I would tell you, that of all my friends living away from the reach of my daily life, you are the one whose coming is ever the most pleasant to me.'

'Oh, Lily !'

'It was, I think, only yesterday that I was telling Grace that you are more like a brother to me than any one else. I wish it might be so. I wish we might swear to be brother and sister. I'd do more for you then than walk across the fields with you to Guestwick Cottage. Your prosperity would then be the thing in the world for which I should be most anxious. And if you should marry—'

'It can never be like that between us,' said Johnny.

'Can it not ? I think it can. Perhaps not this year, or next year ; perhaps not in the next five years. But I make myself happy with thinking that it may be so some day. I shall wait for it patiently, very patiently, even though you should rebuff me again and again, – as you have done now.'

'I have not rebuffed you.'

'Not maliciously, or injuriously, or offensively. I will be very patient, and take little rebuffs without complaining. This is the worst stile of all. When Grace and I are here together we can never manage it without tearing ourselves all to pieces. It is much nicer to have you to help me.'

'Let me help you always,' he said, keeping her hands in his after he had aided her to jump from the stile to the ground.

'Yes, as my brother.'

'That is nonsense, Lily.'

'Is it nonsense ? Nonsense is a hard word.'

'It is nonsense as coming from you to me. Lily, I sometimes think that I am persecuting you, writing to you, coming after you, as I am doing now, – telling the same whining story, – asking, asking, and asking for that which you say you will never give me. And then I feel ashamed of myself, and swear that I will do it no more.

'Do not be ashamed of yourself; but yet do it no more.'

'And then,' he continued, without minding her words, 'at other times I feel that it must be my own fault; that if I only persevered with sufficient energy I must be successful. At such times I swear that I will never give it up.'

'Oh, John, if you could only know how little worthy of such pursuit it is.'

'Leave me to judge of that, dear. When a man has taken a month, or perhaps only a week, or perhaps not more than half an hour, to make up his mind, it may be very well to tell him that he doesn't know what he is about. I've been in the office now for over seven years, and the first day I went I put an oath into a book that I would come back and get you for my wife when I had got enough to live upon.'

'Did you, John?'

'Yes. I can show it you. I used to come and hover about the place in the old days, before I went to London, when I was such a fool that I couldn't speak to you if I met you. I am speaking of a time long before, – before that man came down here.'

'Do not speak of him, Johnny.'

'I must speak of him. A man isn't to hold his tongue when everything he has in the world is at stake. I suppose he loved you after a fashion, once.'

'Pray, pray do not speak ill of him.'

'I am not going to abuse him. You can judge of him by his deeds. I cannot say anything worse of him than what they say. I suppose he loved you; but he certainly did not love you as I have done. I have at any rate been true to you. Yes, Lily, I have been true to you. I am true to you. He did not know what he was about. I do. I am justified in saying that I do. I want you to be my wife. It is no use your talking about it as though I only half wanted it.'

'I did not say that.'

'Is not a man to have any reward? Of course if you had married him there would have been an end of it. He had come in between me and my happiness, and I must have borne it, as other men bear such sorrows. But you have not married him; and, of course, I cannot but feel that I may yet have a chance. Lily, answer me this. Do you believe that I love you?' But she did not answer him. 'You can at any rate tell me that. Do you think that I am in earnest?'

'Yes, I think you are in earnest.'

'And do you believe that I love you with all my heart and all my strength and all my soul?'*

'Oh, John!'

'But do you?'

'I think you love me.'

'Think! what am I to say or to do to make you understand that my only idea of happiness is the idea that sooner or later I may get you to be my wife? Lily, will you say that it shall be so? Speak, Lily. There is no one that will not be glad. Your uncle will consent, – has consented. Your mother wishes it. Bell wishes it. My mother wishes it. Lady Julia wishes it. You would be doing what everybody about you wants you to do. And why should you not do it? It isn't that you dislike me. You wouldn't talk about being my sister, if you had not some kind of regard for me.'

'I have a regard for you.'

'Then why will you not be my wife? Oh, Lily, say the word now, here, at once. Say the word, and you'll make me the happiest fellow in all England.' As he spoke he took her by both arms, and held her fast. She did not struggle to get away from him, but stood quite still, looking into his face, while the first sparkle of a salt tear formed itself in each eye. 'Lily, one little word will do it, – half a word, a nod, a smile. Just touch my arm with your hand and I will take it for a yes.' I think that she almost tried to touch him; that the word was in her throat, and that she almost strove to speak it. But there was no syllable spoken, and her fingers did not loose themselves to fall upon his sleeve. 'Lily, Lily, what can I say to you?'

'I wish I could,' she whispered; – but the whisper was so hoarse that he hardly recognized the voice.

'And why can you not? What is there to hinder you? There is nothing to hinder you, Lily.'

'Yes, John; there is that which must hinder me.'

'And what is it?'

'I will tell you. You are so good and so true, and so excellent, – such a dear, dear, dear friend, that I will tell you everything, so that you may read my heart. I will tell you as I tell mamma, – you and her and no one else; – for you are the choice friend of my heart. I cannot be your wife because of the love I bear for another man.'

'And that man is he, – he who came here?'

'Of course it is he. I think, Johnny, you and I are alike in this, that when we have loved we cannot bring ourselves to change. You will not change, though it would be so much better you should do so.'

'No; I will never change.'

'Nor can I. When I sleep I dream of him. When I am alone I cannot banish him from my thoughts. I cannot define what it is to love him. I want nothing from him, – nothing, nothing. But I move about through my little world thinking of him, and I shall do so to the end. I used to feel proud of my love, though it made me so wretched that I thought it would kill me. I am not proud of it any longer. It is a foolish poor-spirited weakness, – as though my heart had been only half formed in the making. 'Do you be stronger, John. A man should be stronger than a woman.'

'I have none of that sort of strength.'

'Nor have I. What can we do but pity each other, and swear that we will be friends, – dear friends. There is the oak-tree and I have got to turn back. We have said everything that we can say, – unless you will tell me that you will be my brother.'

'No ; I will not tell you that.'

'Good-by, then, Johnny.'

He paused, holding her by the hand and thinking of another question which he longed to put to her, – considering whether he would ask her that question or not. He hardly knew whether we were entitled to ask it; – whether or no the asking of it would be ungenerous. She had said that she would tell him everything, – as she had told everything to her mother. 'Of course,' he said, 'I have no right to expect to know anything of your future intentions ?'

'You may know them, all, – as far as I know them myself. I have said that you should read my heart.'

'If this man, whose name I cannot bear to mention, should come again—'

'If he were to come again he would come in vain, John.' She did not say that he had come again. She could tell her own secret, but not that of another person.

'You would not marry him, now that he is free ?'

She stood and thought a while before she answered him. 'No, I should not marry him now. I think not.' Then she paused again. 'Nay, I am sure I would not. After what has passed I could not trust myself to do it. There is my hand on it. I will not.'

'No, Lily, I do not want that.'

'But I insist. I will not marry Mr Crosbie. But you must not misunderstand me, John. There; – all that is over for me now. All those dreams about love, and marriage, and a house of my own, and children, – and a cross husband, and a wedding-ring growing always tighter as I grow fatter and older. I have dreamed of such things as other girls do, – more perhaps than other girls, more than I should have done. And now I accept the thing as finished. You wrote something in your book, you dear John, – something that could not be made to come true. Dear John, I wish for your sake it was otherwise. I will go home and I will write in my book, this very day, Lilian Dale, Old Maid. If ever I make that false, do you come and ask me for the page.'

'Let it remain there till I am allowed to tear it out.'

'I will write it, and it shall never be torn out. You I cannot marry. Him I will not marry. You may believe me, Johnny, when I say there can never be a third.'

'And is that to be the end of it?'

'Yes; – that is to be the end of it. Not the end of our friendship. Old maids have friends.'

'It shall not be the end of it. There shall be no end of it with me.'

'But, John—'

'Do not suppose that I will trouble you again, – at any rate not for a while. In five years time perhaps,—'

'Now, Johnny, you are laughing at me. And of course it is the best way. If there is not Grace, and she has caught me before I have turned back. Good-by, dear, dear John. God bless you. I think you the finest fellow there is in the world. I do, and so does mamma. Remember always that there is a temple at Allington in which your worship is never forgotten.' Then she pressed his hand and turned away from him to meet Grace Crawley. John did not stop to speak a word to his cousin, but pursued his way alone.

'That cousin of yours,' said Lily, 'is simply the dearest, warmest-hearted, finest creature that ever was seen in the shape of a man.'

'Have you told him that you think him so?' said Grace.

'Indeed, I have,' said Lily.

'But have you told this finest, warmest, dearest creature that he shall be rewarded with the prize he covets?'

'No, Grace. I have told him nothing of the kind. I think he understands it all now. If he does not, it is not for the want of my telling him. I don't suppose any lady was ever more open-spoken to a gentleman than I have been to him.'

'And why have you sent him away disappointed? You know you love him.'

'You see, my dear,' said Lily, 'you allow yourself, for the sake of your argument, to use a word in a double sense, and you attempt to confound me by doing so. But I am a great deal too clever for you, and have thought too much about it, to be taken in in that way. I certainly love your cousin John; and so I do love Mr Boyce, the vicar.'

'You love Johnny much better than you do Mr Boyce.'

'True; very much better; but it is the same sort of love. However, it is a great deal too deep for you to understand. You're too young, and I shan't try to explain it. But the long and the short of it is, – I am not going to marry your cousin.'

'I wish you were,' said Grace, 'with all my heart.'

John Eames as he returned to the cottage was by no means able to fall back upon those resolutions as to his future life, which he had formed for himself and communicated to his friend Dalrymple, and which he had intended to bring at once into force in the event of his being again rejected by Lily Dale. 'I will cleanse my mind of it altogether,' he had said, 'and though I may not forget her, I will live as though she were forgotten. If she declines my proposal again, I will accept her word as final. I will not go about the world any longer as a stricken deer,* – to be pitied or else bullied by the rest of the herd.' On his way down to Guestwick he had sworn twenty times that it should be so. He would make one more effort, and then he would give it up. But now, after his interview with Lily, he was as little disposed to give it up as ever.

He sat upon a gate in a paddock through which there was a back entrance into Lady Julia's garden, and there swore a thousand oaths that he would never give her up. He was, at any rate, sure that she would never become the wife of any one else. He was equally sure that he would never become the husband of any other wife. He could trust her. Yes; he was sure of that. But could he trust himself? Communing with himself, he told himself that after all he was but a poor creature. Circumstances had been very good to him, but he had done nothing for himself. He was vain, and foolish, and unsteady. So he told himself while sitting upon the gate. But he had, at any rate, been constant to Lily, and constant he would remain.

He would never more mention her name to any one, – unless it were to Lady Julia to-night. To Dalrymple he would not open his mouth about her, but would plainly ask his friend to be silent on that subject if her name should be mentioned by him. But morning and evening he would pray for her, and in his prayers he would always think of her as his wife. He would never speak to another girl without remembering that he was bound to Lily. He would go nowhere into society without recalling to mind the fact that he was bound by the chains of a solemn engagement. If he knew himself he would be constant to Lily.

And then he considered in what manner it would be best and most becoming that he should still prosecute his endeavour and repeat his offer. He thought that he would write to her every year, on the same day of the year, year after year, it might be for the next twenty years. And his letters should be very simple. Sitting there on the gate he planned the wording of his letters; – of his first letter, and of his second, and of his third. They should be very like to each other, – should hardly be more than a repetition of the same words. 'If now you are ready for me, then, Lily, am I, as ever, still ready for you.' And then 'if now' again, and again 'if now; – and still if now.' When his hair should be grey, and the wrinkles on his cheeks,

– ay, though they should be on hers, he would still continue to tell her from year to year that he was ready to take her. Surely some day that 'if now' would prevail. And should it never prevail, the merit of his constancy should be its own reward.

Such letters as those she would surely keep. Then he looked forward, down into the valley of coming years, and fancied her as she might sit reading them in the twilight of some long evening, – letters which had been written all in vain. He thought that he could look forward with some satisfaction towards the close of his own career, in having been the hero of such a love-story. At any rate, if such a story were to be his story, the melancholy attached to it should arise from no fault of his own. He would still press her to be his wife. And then as he remembered that he was only twenty-seven and that she was twenty-four, he began to marvel at the feeling of grey old age which had come upon him, and tried to make himself believe that he would have her yet before the bloom was off her cheek.

He went into the cottage and made his way at once into the room in which Lady Julia was sitting. She did not speak at first, but looked anxiously into his face. And he did not speak, but turned to a table near the window and took up a book, – though the room was too dark for him to see to read the words. 'John,' at last said Lady Julia.

'Well, my lady?'

'Have you nothing to tell me, John?'

'Nothing on earth, – except the same old story, which has now become a matter of course.'

'But, John, will you not tell me what she has said?'

'Lady Julia, she has said no; simply no. It is a very easy word to say, and she has said it so often that it seems to come from her quite naturally.' Then he got a candle and sat down over the fire with a volume of a novel. It was not yet past five, and Lady Julia did not go upstairs to dress till six, and therefore there was an hour during which they were together. John had at first been rather grand to his old friend, and very uncommunicative. But before the dressing bell had rung he had been coaxed into a confidential strain and had told everything. 'I suppose it is wrong and selfish,' he said. 'I suppose I am a dog in a manger. But I do own that there is a consolation to me in the assurance that she will never be the wife of that scoundrel.'

'I could never forgive her if she were to marry him now,' said Lady Julia.

'I could never forgive him. But she has said that she will not, and I know that she will not forswear herself. I shall go on with it, Lady

Julia. I have made up my mind to that. I suppose it will never come to anything, but I shall stick to it. I can live an old bachelor as well as another man. At any rate I shall stick to it.' Then the good silly old woman comforted him and applauded him as though he were a hero among men, and did reward him, as Lily had predicted, by one of those now rare bottles of superexcellent port which had come to her from her brother's cellar.

John Eames stayed out his time at the cottage, and went over more than once again to Allington, and called on the squire, on one occasion dining with him and meeting the three ladies from the Small House; and he walked with the girls, comporting himself like any ordinary man. But he was not again alone with Lily Dale, nor did he learn whether she had in truth written those two words in her book. But the reader may know that she did write them there on the evening of the day on which the promise was made. 'Lilian, Dale, – Old Maid.'

And when John's holiday was over, he returned to his duties at the elbow of Sir Raffle Buffle.

CHAPTER 36

Grace Crawley returns home

About this time Grace Crawley received two letters, the first of them reaching her while John Eames was still at the cottage, and the other immediately after his return to London. They both help to tell our story, and our reader shall, therefore, read them if he so pleases, – or, rather, he shall read the first and as much of the second as is necessary for him. Grace's answer to the first letter he shall see also. Her answer to the second will be told in a very few words. The first was from Major Grantly, and the task of answering that was by no means easy to Grace.

Cosby Lodge, – February, 186–.

Dearest Grace,

I told you when I parted from you, that I should write to you, and I think it best to do so at once, in order that you may fully understand me. Spoken words are soon forgotten, – I shall never forget his words, Grace said to herself as she read this; – and are not always as plain as they might be. Dear Grace, I suppose I ought not to say so, but I fancied when I parted from you at Allington, that I had succeeded in making myself dear to you. I believe you to be so true in spirit, that you were unable to conceal from me the fact that you love me. I shall believe that this is so, till I am deliberately and solemnly assured by yourself that it is not so; – and I conjure you to think what is due both to yourself and to myself, before you allow yourself to think of making such an assurance unless it be strictly true.

I have already told my own friends that I have asked you to be my wife. I tell you this, in order that you may know how little effect your answer to me has had towards inducing me to give you up. What you said about your father and your family has no weight with me, and ought ultimately to have none with you. This business of your father's is a great misfortune, – so great that, probably, had we not known each other before it happened, it might have prevented our becoming intimate when we changed to meet. But we had met before it happened, and before it happened I had determined to ask you to be my wife. What should I have to think of myself if I allowed my heart to be altered by such a cause as that?

I have only further to say that I love you better than any one in the world, and that it is my best hope that you will be my wife. I will not press you till this affair of your father's has been settled; but when that is over I shall look for my reward without reference to its result. Not that I doubt the result if there be anything like justice in England; but that your debt to me, if you owe me any debt, will be altogether irrespective of that. If, as I suppose, you will remain at Allington for some time longer, I shall not see you till after the trial is over. As soon as that is done, I will come to you wherever you are. In the meantime I shall look for an answer to this; and if it be true that you love me dear, dear Grace, pray have the courage to tell me so.

Most affectionately your own,
Henry Grantly.

When the letter was given to Grace across the breakfast-table, both Mrs Dale and Lily suspected that it came from Major Grantly, but not a word was spoken about it. When Grace with hesitating hand broke the envelope, neither of her friends looked at her. Lily had a letter of her own, and Mrs Dale opened the newspaper. But still it was impossible not to perceive that her face became red with blushes, and then they knew that the letter must be from Major Grantly. Grace herself could not read it, though her eye ran down over the two pages catching a word here and a word there. She had looked at the name at once, and had seen the manner of his signature. 'Most affectionately your own!' What was she to say to him? Twice, thrice, as she sat at the breakfast-table she turned the page of the letter, and at each turning she read the signature. And she read the beginning, 'Dearest Grace.' More than that she did not really read till she had got the letter away with her into the seclusion of her own room.

Not a word was said about the letter at breakfast. Poor Grace went on eating or pretending to eat, but could not bring herself to utter a word. Mrs Dale and Lily spoke of various matters, which were quite indifferent to them; but even with them the conversation was so difficult that Grace felt it to be forced, and was conscious that they were thinking about her and her lover. As soon as she could make an excuse she left the room, and hurrying upstairs took the letter from her pocket and read it in earnest.

'That was from Major Grantly, mamma,' said Lily.

'I daresay it was, my dear.'

'And what had we better do; or what had we better say?'

'Nothing, – I should say. Let him fight his own battle. If we interfere, we may probably only make her more stubborn in clinging to her old idea.'

'I think she will cling to it.'

'For a time she will, I daresay. And it will be best that she should. He himself will respect her for it afterwards.' Thus it was agreed between them that they should say nothing to Grace about the letter unless Grace should first speak to them.

Grace read her letter over and over again. It was the first love-letter she had ever had; – the first letter she had ever received from any man except her father and brother, – the first, almost, that had ever been written to her by any other than her own old special friends. The words of it were very strange to her ear. He had told her when he left her that he would write to her, and therefore she had looked forward to the event which had now come; but she had thought that it would be much more distant, – and she had tried to make herself believe that when it did come it would be very different from this letter which she now possessed. 'He will tell me that he has altered his mind. He ought to do so. It is not proper that he should still think of me when we are in such disgrace.' But now the letter had come, and she acknowledged the truth of his saying that written words were clearer in their expression than those simply spoken. 'Not that I could ever forget a syllable that he said.' Yet, as she held the letter in her hand she felt that it was a possession. It was a thing at which she could look in coming years, when he and she might be far apart, – a thing at which she could look with pride in remembering that he had thought her worthy of it.

Neither on that day nor on the next day did she think of her answer, nor on the third or the fourth with any steady thinking. She knew that an answer would have to be written, and she felt that the sooner it was written the easier might be the writing; but she felt also that it should not be written too quickly. A week should first elapse, she thought, and therefore a week was allowed to elapse, and then the day for writing her answer came. She had spoken no word about it either to Mrs Dale or to Lily. She had longed to do so, but had feared. Even though she should speak to Lily she could not be led by Lily's advice. Her letter, whatever it might be, must be her own letter. She would admit of no dictation.

She must say her own say, let her say it ever so badly. As to the manner of saying it, Lily's aid would have been invaluable; but she feared that she could not secure that aid without compromising her own power of action, – her own individuality; and therefore she said no word about the letter either to Lily or to Lily's mother.

On a certain morning she fixed herself at her desk to write her letter. She had known that the task would be difficult, but she had little known how difficult it would be. On that day of her first attempt she did not get it written at all. How was she to begin? He had called her 'Dearest Grace;' and this mode of beginning seemed as easy as it was sweet. 'It is very easy for a gentleman,' she said to herself, 'because he may say just what he pleases.' She wrote the words, 'Dearest Henry,' on a scrap of paper, and immediately tore it into fragments as though she were ashamed of having written them. She knew that she would not dare to let such words in her own handwriting remain within the recesses of her own little desk. 'Dear Major Grantly,' she began at length. It seemed to her to be very ugly, but after much consideration she believed it to be correct. On the second day the letter was written as follows: –

Allington, Thursday.

My dear Major Grantly, –

I do not know how I ought to answer your kind letter, but I must tell you that I am very much flattered by your great goodness to me. I cannot understand why you should think so much of me, but I suppose it is because you have felt for all our misfortunes. I will not say anything about what might have happened, if it had not been for papa's sorrow and disgrace; and as far as I can help it, I will not think of it; but I am sure that I ought not to think about loving any one, that is, in the way you mean, while we are in such trouble at home. I should not dare to meet any of your great friends, knowing that I had brought nothing with me but disgrace. And I should feel that I was doing an injury to *dear* Edith, which would be worse to me than anything.

Pray believe that I am quite in earnest about this. I know that a gentleman ought not to marry any girl to do himself and his family an injury by it; and I know that if I were to make such a marriage I should be unhappy ever afterwards, even though I loved the man ever so dearly, with all my heart.' These last words she had underscored at first, but the doing so had been the unconscious expression of her own affection, and had been done with no desire on her part to convey that expression to him. But on reading the words she discovered their latent meaning, and wrote it all again.

'Therefore I know that it will be best that I should wish you good-by, and I do so, thanking you again and again for your goodness to me.

Believe me to be,
Yours very sincerely,
Grace Crawley.

The letter when it was written was hateful to her; but she had tried her hand at it again and again, and had found that she could do nothing better. There was much in his letter that she had not attempted to answer. He had implored her to tell him whether or not she did in truth love him. Of course she loved him. He knew that well enough. Why should she answer any such question? There was a way of answering it indeed which might serve her turn, – or rather serve his, of which she was thinking more than of her own. She might say that she did not love him. It would be a lie, and he would know that it would be a lie. But still it might serve the turn. She did not like the idea of writing such a lie as that, but nevertheless she considered the matter. It would be very wicked; but still, if it would serve the turn, might it not be well to write it. But at last she reflected that, after all, the doing of the thing was in her own hands. She could refuse to marry this man without burdening her conscience with any lie about it. It only required that she should be firm. She abstained, therefore, from the falsehood, and left her lover's question unanswered. So she put up her letter and directed it, and carried it herself to the village post-office.

On the day after this she got the second letter, and that she showed immediately to Mrs Dale. It was from her mother, and was written to tell her that her father was seriously ill. 'He went up to London to see a lawyer about this weary work of the trial,' said Mrs Crawley. 'The fatigue was very great, and on the next day he was so weak that he could not leave his bed. Dr Turner, who has been very kind, says that we need not frighten ourselves, but he thinks it must be some time before he can leave the house. He has a low fever on him, and wants nourishment. His mind has wandered once or twice, and he has asked for you, and I think it will be best, love, that you should come home. I know you will not mind it when I say that I think he would like to have you here. Dr Turner says that the illness is chiefly owing to his not having proper food.'

Of course she would go at once. 'Dear Mrs Dale,' she said, 'I must go home. Can you send me to the station?' Then Mrs Dale read the letter. Of course they would send her. Would she go on that day, or on the next? Might it not be better to write first, and say that she was going? But Grace would go at once. 'I know it will be a comfort to mamma; and I know that he is worse than mamma says.' Of course there was no more to be said, and she was despatched to the station. Before she went Mrs Dale asked after her purse. 'If there is any trouble about money, – for your journey, or anything, you will not scruple to come to me as to an old friend.' But Grace assured her that there was no trouble about money – for her journey. Then Lily took her aside and produced two clean new five-pound notes. 'Grace, dear, you won't be ill-natured. You know I have a little fortune of my own. You know I can give them without missing them.' Grace threw herself into her friend's arms and wept, but would have none of her money. 'Buy a present from me for your mother, – whom I love though I do not know her.' 'I will give her your love,' Grace said, 'but nothing else.' And then she went.

CHAPTER 37

Hook Court

Mr Dobbs Broughton and Mr Musselboro were sitting together on a certain morning at their office in the City discussing the affairs of their joint business. The City office was a very poor place indeed, in comparison with the fine house which Mr Dobbs occupied at the West End; but then City offices are poor places, and there are certain City occupations which seem to enjoy the greater credit the poorer are the material circumstances by which they are surrounded. Turning out of a lane which turns out of Lombard Street, there is a desolate, forlorn-looking, dark alley, which is called Hook Court. The entrance to this alley is beneath the first-floor of one of the houses in the lane, and in passing under this covered way the visitor to the place finds himself in a small paved square court, at the two further corners of which there are two open doors; for in Hook Court there are only two houses. There is No. 1, Hook Court, and No. 2, Hook Court. The entire premises indicated by No 1, are occupied by a firm of wine and spirit merchants, in connexion with whose trade one side and two angles of the court are always lumbered with crates, hampers, and wooden cases. And nearly in the middle of the court, though somewhat more to the wine-merchants' side than to the other, there is always gaping open a trap-door, leading down to vaults below; and over the trap there is a great board with a bright advertisement in very large letters: –

BURTON AND BANGLES.
HIMALAYA WINES,
22s. 6d. per dozen.

And this notice is so bright and so large, and the trap-door is so conspicuous in the court, that no visitor, even to No. 2, even afterwards can quite divest his memory of those names, Burton and Bangles, Himalaya wines. It may therefore be acknowledged that Burton and Bangles have achieved their object in putting up the notice. The house No. 2, small as it seems to be, standing in the jamb of a corner, is divided among different occupiers, whose names are painted in small letters upon the very dirty posts of the doorway. Nothing can be more remarkable than the contrast between Burton and Bangles and these other City gentlemen in the method taken by them in declaring their presence to visitors in the court. The names of Dobbs Broughton and of A. Musselboro, – the Christian name of Mr Musselboro was Augustus, – were on one of those dirty posts, not joined together by any visible 'and,' so as to declare boldly that they were partners; but in close vicinity, – showing at least that the two gentlemen would be found in apartments very near to each other. And on the first-floor of this house Dobbs Broughton and his friend did occupy three rooms, – or rather two rooms and a closet – between them. The larger and front room was tenanted by an old clerk, who sat within a rail in one corner of it. And there was a broad, short counter which jutted out from the wall into the middle of the room, intended for the use of such of the public as might come to transact miscellaneous business with Dobbs Broughton or Augustus Musselboro. But any one accustomed to the look of offices might have seen with half an eye that very little business was ever done on that counter. Behind this large room was a smaller one, belonging to Dobbs Broughton, in the furnishing and arrangement of which some regard had been paid to comfort. The room was carpeted, and there was a sofa in it, though a very old one, and two arm-chairs and a mahogany office-table, and a cellaret, which was generally well supplied with wine which Dobbs Broughton did not get out of the vaults of his neighbours, Burton and Bangles. Behind this again, but with a separate entrance from the passage, was the closet; and this closet was specially devoted to the use of Mr Musselboro. Closet as it was, – or cupboard as it might almost have been called, – it contained a table and two chairs; and it had a window of its own, which opened out upon a blank wall which was distant from it not above four feet. As the house to which this wall belonged was four stories high, it would sometimes happen that Mr Musselboro's cupboard was rather dark. But this mattered the less as in these days Mr Musselboro seldom used it. Mr Musselboro, who was very constant at his place of business, – much more constant than his friend, Dobbs Broughton, – was generally to be found in his friend's room. Only on some special occasions, on which it was thought expedient that the commercial world should be made to understand that Mr Augustus Musselboro had an individual existence of his own, did that gentleman really seat himself in the dark closet. Mr Dobbs Broughton, had he been asked what was his trade, would have said that he was a stockbroker; and he would have answered truly, for he was a stockbroker. A man may be a stockbroker though he never sells any stock; as he may be a barrister though he has no practice at the bar. I do not say that Mr Broughton never sold any stock; but the buying and selling of stock for other people was certainly not his chief business. And had Mr Musselboro been asked what was his trade, he would have probably given an evasive answer. At any rate in the City, and among people who understood City matters, he would not have said that he was a stockbroker. Both Mr Broughton and Mr Musselboro bought and sold a good deal, but it was chiefly on account. The shares which were bought and sold very generally did not pass from hand to hand; but the difference in the price of the shares did do so. And then they had another little business between them. They lent money on interest. And in this business there was a third partner, whose name did not appear on the dirty door-post. That third partner was Mrs Van Siever, the mother of Clara Van Siever whom Mr Conway Dalrymple intended to portray as Jael driving a nail into Sisera's head.

On a certain morning Mr Broughton and Mr Musselboro were sitting together in the office which has been described. They were in Mr Broughton's room, and occupied each an arm-chair on the different sides of the fire. Mr Musselboro was sitting close to the table, on which a ledger was open before him, and he had a pen and ink before him, as though he had been at work. Dobbs Broughton had a small betting-book in his hand, and was seated with his feet up against the side of the fireplace. Both men wore their hats, and the aspect of the room was not the aspect of a place of business. They had been silent for some minutes when Broughton took his cigar-case out of his pocket, and nibbled off the end of a cigar, preparatory to lighting it.

'You had better not smoke here this morning, Dobbs,' said Musselboro.

'Why shouldn't I smoke in my own room?'

'Because she'll be here just now.'

'What do I care? If you think I'm going to be afraid of Mother Van, you're mistaken. Let come what may, I'm not going to live under her thumb.' So he lighted his cigar.

'All right,' said Musselboro, and he took up his pen and went to work at his book.

'What is she coming here for this morning?' asked Broughton.

'To look after her money. What should she come for?'

'She gets her interest. I don't suppose there's better paid money in the City.'

'She hasn't got what was coming to her at Christmas yet.'

'And this is February. What would she have? She had better put her dirty money into the three per cents, if she is frightened at having to wait a week or two.'

'Can she have it to-day?'

'What, the whole of it? Of course she can't. You know that as well as I do. She can have four hundred pounds, if she wants it. But seeing all she gets out of the concern, she has no right to press for it in that way. She is the—old usurer I ever came across in my life.'

'Of course she likes her money.'

'Likes her money! By George she does; her own and anybody else's that she can get hold of. For a downright leech, recommend me always to a woman. When a woman does go in for it, she is much more thorough than any man.' Then Broughton turned over the little pages of his book, and Musselboro pondered over the big pages of his book, and there was silence for a quarter of an hour.

'There's something about nine hundred and fifteen pounds due to her,' said Musselboro.

'I daresay there is.'

'It would be a very good thing to let her have it if you've got it. The whole of it this morning, I mean.'

'If! yes, if!' said Broughton.

'I know there's more than that at the bank.'

'And I'm to draw out every shilling that there is! I'll see Mother Van – further first. She can have 500*l*. if she likes it, – and the rest in a fortnight. Or she can have my note-of-hand for it all at fourteen days.'

'She won't like that at all,' said Musselboro.

'Then she must lump it. I'm not going to bother myself about her. I've pretty nearly as much money in it as she has, and we're in a boat together. If she comes here bothering, you'd better tell her so.'

'You'll see her yourself?'

'Not unless she comes within the next ten minutes. I must go down to the court.* I said I'd be there by twelve. I've got somebody I want to see.'

'I'd stay if I were you.'

'Why should I stay for her? If she thinks that I'm going to make myself her clerk, she's mistaken. It may be all very well for you, Mussy, but it won't do for me. I'm not dependent on her, and I don't want to marry her daughter.'

'It will simply end in her demanding to have her money back again.'

'And how will she get it?' said Dobbs Broughton. 'I haven't a doubt in life but she'd take it to-morrow if she could put her hands upon it. And then, after a bit, when she began to find that she didn't like four per cent, she'd bring it back again. But nobody can do business after such a fashion as that. For the last three years she's drawn close upon two thousand a year for less than eighteen thousand pounds. When a woman wants to do that, she can't have her money in her pocket every Monday morning.'

'But you've done better than that yourself, Dobbs.'

'Of course I have. And who has made the connexion : and who has done the work ? I suppose she doesn't think that I'm to have all the sweat and that she is to have all the profit.'

'If you talk of work, Dobbs, it is I that have done the most of it.' This Mr Musselboro said in a very serious voice, and with a look of much reproach.

'And you've been paid for what you've done. Come, Mussy, you'd better not turn against me. You'll never get your change out of that. Even if you marry the daughter, that won't give you the mother's money. She'll stick to every shilling of it till she dies ; and she'd take it with her then, if she knew how.' Having said this, he got up from his chair, put his little book into his pocket, and walked out of the office. He pushed his way across the court, which was more than ordinarily crowded with the implements of Burton and Bangles' trade, and as he passed under the covered way he encountered at the entrance an old woman getting out of a cab. The old woman was, of course, Mother Van, as her partner, Mr Dobbs Broughton, irreverently called her. 'Mrs Van Siever, how d'ye do ? Let me give you a hand. Fare from South Kensington ? I always give the fellows three shillings.'

'You don't mean to tell me it's six miles !' And she tendered a florin to the man.

'Can't take that, ma'am,' said the cabman.

'Can't take it ! But you must take it. Broughton, just get a policeman, will you ?' Dobbs Broughton satisfied the driver out of his own pocket, and the cab was driven away. 'What did you give him ?' said Mrs Van Siever.

'Just another sixpence. There never is a policeman anywhere about here.'

'It'll be out of your own pocket, then,' said Mrs Van. 'But you're not going away ?'

'I must be at Capel Court by half-past twelve ; — I must, indeed. If it wasn't real business, I'd stay.'

'I told Musselboro I should be here.'

'He's up there, and he knows all about the business just as well as I do. When I found that I couldn't stay for you, I went through the account with him, and it's all settled. Good morning. I'll see

you at the West End in a day or two.' Then he made his way out
into Lombard Street, and Mrs Van Siever picked her steps across
the yard, and mounted the stairs, and made her way into the room
in which Mr Musselboro was sitting.

'Somebody's been smoking, Gus,' she said, almost as soon as she
had entered the room.

'That's nothing new here,' he replied, as he got up from his chair.

'There's no good being done when men sit and smoke over their
work. Is it you, or he, or both of you?'

'Well; – it was Broughton was smoking just now. I don't smoke
of a morning myself.'

'What made him get up and run away when I came?'

'How can I tell, Mrs Van Siever,' said Musselboro, laughing. 'If
he did run away when you came, I suppose it was because he didn't
want to see you.'

'And why shouldn't he want to see me? Gus, I expect the truth
from you. How are things going on here?' To this question Mr
Musselboro made no immediate answer; but tilted himself back in
his chair and took his hat off, and put his thumbs into the arm-
holes of his waistcoat, and looked his patroness full in the face.
'Gus,' she said again, 'I do expect the truth from you. How are
things going on here?'

'There'd be a good business, – if he'd only keep things together.'

'But he's idle. Isn't he idle?'

'Confoundedly idle,' said Musselboro.

'And he drinks; – don't he drink in the day?'

'Like the mischief, – some days. But that isn't the worst of it.'

'And what is the worst of it?'

'Newmarket; – that's the rock he's going to pieces on.'

'You don't mean to say he takes the money out of the business
for that?' And Mrs Van Siever's face, as she asked the question,
expressed almost a tragic horror. 'If I thought that I wouldn't give
him an hour's mercy.'

'When a man bets he doesn't well know what money he uses. I
can't say that he takes money that is not his own. Situated as I am,
I don't know what is his own and what isn't. If your money was in
my name I could keep a hand on it; – but as it is not I can do
nothing. I can see that what is put out is put out fairly well; and
when I think of it, Mrs Van Siever, it is quite wonderful that we've
lost so little. It has been next to nothing. That has been my doing;
– and that's about all that I can do.'

'You must know whether he has used my money for his own
purposes or not.'

'If you ask me, I think he has,' said Mr Musselboro.

'Then I'll go into it, and I'll find it out, and if it is so, as sure as my name's Van Siever, I'll sew him up.' Having uttered which terrible threat, the old woman drew a chair to the table and seated herself fairly down, as though she were determined to go through all the books of the office before she quitted that room. Mrs Van Siever in her present habiliments was not a thing so terrible to look at as she has been in her wiggeries at Mrs Dobbs Broughton's dinner-table. Her curls were laid aside altogether, and she wore simply a front beneath her close bonnet, – and a very old front, too, which was not loudly offensive because it told no lies. Her eyes were as bright, and her little wizen face was as sharp, as ever; but the wizen face and the bright eyes were not so much amiss as seen together with the old dark brown silk dress which she now wore, as they had been with the wiggeries and the evening finery. Even now, in her morning costume, in her work-a-day business dress, as we may call it, she looked to be very old, – so old that nobody could guess her age. People attempting to guess would say that she must be at least over eighty. And yet she was wiry, and strong, and nimble. It was not because she was feeble that she was thought to be so old. They who so judged of her were led to their opinion by the extreme thinness of her face, and by the brightness of her eyes, joined to the depth of the hollows in which they lay, and the red margin by which they were surrounded. It was not really the fact that Mrs Van Siever was so very aged, for she had still some years to live before she would reach eighty, but that she was such a weird old woman, so small, so ghastly and so ugly! 'I'll sew him up, if he's been robbing me,' she said. 'I will, indeed.' And she stretched out her hand to grab at the ledger which Musselboro had been using.

'You won't understand anything from that,' said he, pushing the book over to her.

'You can explain it to me.'

'That's all straight sailing, that is.'

'And where does he keep the figures that ain't straight sailing? That's the book I want to see.'

'There is no such book.'

'Look here, Gus, – if I find you deceiving me I'll throw you overboard as sure as I'm a living woman. I will indeed. I'll have no mercy. I've stuck to you, and made a man of you, and I expect you to stick to me.'

'Not much of a man,' said Musselboro, with a touch of scorn in his voice.

'You've never had a shilling yet but what I gave you.'

'Yes; I have. I've had what I've worked for, – and worked confounded hard too.'

'Look here, Musselboro; if you're going to throw me over, just tell me so, and let us begin fair.'

'I'm not going to throw you over. I've always been on the square with you. Why don't you trust me out and out, and then I could do a deal better for you. You ask me now about your money. I don't know about your money, Mrs Van Siever. How am I to know anything about your money, Mrs Van Siever? You don't give me any power of keeping a hand upon Dobbs Broughton. I suppose you have security from Dobbs Broughton, but I don't know what security you have, Mrs Van Siever. He owes you now 915*l*. 16*s*. 2*d*. on last year's account!'

'Why doesn't he give me a cheque for the money?'

'He says he can't spare it. You may have 500*l*., and the rest when he can give it you. Or he'll give you his note-of-hand at fourteen days for the whole.'

'Bother his note-of-hand. Why should I take his note-of-hand?'

'Do as you like, Mrs Van Siever.'

'It's the interest on my own money. Why don't he give it me? I suppose he has had it.'

'You must ask him that, Mrs Van Siever. You're in partnership with him, and he can tell you. Nobody else knows anything about it. If you were in partnership with me, then of course I could tell you. But you're not. You've never trusted me, Mrs Van Siever.'

The lady remained there closeted with Mr Musselboro for an hour after that, and did, I think, at length learn something more as to the details of her partner's business, than her faithful servant Mr Musselboro had at first found himself able to give to her. And at last they came to friendly and confidential terms, in the midst of which the personal welfare of Mr Dobbs Broughton was, I fear, somewhat forgotten. Not that Mr Musselboro palpably and plainly threw his friend overboard. He took his friend's part, – alleging excuses for him, and pleading some facts. 'Of course, you know, a man like that is fond of pleasure, Mrs Van Siever. He's been at it more or less all his life. I don't suppose he ever missed a Derby or an Oaks, or the cup at Ascot, or the Goodwood in his life.' 'He'll have to miss them before long, I'm thinking,' said Mrs Van Siever. 'And as to not cashing up, you must remember, Mrs Van Siever, that ten per cent. won't come in quite as regularly as four or five. When you go for high interest, there must be hitches here and there. There must, indeed, Mrs Van Siever.' 'I know all about it,' said Mrs Van Siever. 'If he gave it me as soon as he got it himself, I shouldn't complain. Never mind. He's only got to give me my little bit of money out of the business, and then he and I will be all square. You come and see Clara this evening, Gus.'

Then Mr Musselboro put Mrs Van Siever into another cab, and went out upon 'Change, – hanging about the Bank, and standing in Threadneedle Street, talking to other men just like himself. When he saw Dobbs Broughton he told that gentleman that Mrs Van Siever had been in her tantrums, but that he had managed to pacify her before she left Hook Court. 'I'm to take her the cheque for the five hundred to-night,' he said.

CHAPTER 38

Jael

On the first of March, Conway Dalrymple's easel was put up in Mrs Dobbs Broughton's boudoir upstairs, the canvas was placed upon it on which the outlines of Jael and Sisera had been already drawn, and Mrs Broughton and Clara Van Siever and Conway Dalrymple were assembled with the view of steady art-work. But before we see how they began their work together, we will go back for a moment to John Eames on his return to his London lodgings. The first thing every man does when he returns home after an absence, is to look at his letters, and John Eames looked at his. There were not very many. There was a note marked immediate, from Sir Raffle Buffle, in which Sir R. had scrawled in four lines a notification that he should be driven to an extremity of inconvenience if Eames were not at his post at half-past nine on the following morning. 'I think I see myself there at that hour,' said John. There was a notification of a house dinner, which he was asked to join, at his club, and a card for an evening gathering at Lady Glencora Palliser's, – procured for him by his friend Conway, – and an invitation to dinner at the house of his uncle, Mr Toogood; and there was a scented note in the handwriting of a lady, which he did not recognize. 'My nearest and dearest friend, M.D.M.,' he said, as he opened the note and looked at the signature. Then he read the letter from Miss Demolines.

My dear Mr Eames,

Pray come to me at once. I know that you are to be back to-morrow. Do not lose an hour if you can help it. I shall be at home at half-past five. I fear what you know of has been begun. But it certainly shall not go on. In one way or another it must be prevented. I won't say another word till I see you, but pray come at once.

Yours always,

Thursday.

M.D.M.

Poor mamma isn't very well, so you had better ask for me.

Beautiful!' said Johnny, as he read the note. 'There's nothing I like so much as a mystery, – especially if it's about nothing. I wonder why she is so desperately anxious that the picture should not be painted. I'd ask Dalrymple, only I should spoil the mystery.' Then he sat himself down, and began to think of Lily. There could be no treason to Lily in his amusing himself with the freaks of such a woman as Miss Demolines.

At eleven o'clock on the morning of the 1st of March, – the day following that on which Miss Demolines had written her note, – the easel was put up and the canvas was placed on it in Mrs Broughton's room. Mrs Broughton and Clara were both there, and when they had seen the outlines as far as it had been drawn, they proceeded to make arrangements for their future operations. The period of work was to begin always at eleven, and was to be continued for an hour and a half or for two hours on the days on which they met. I fear that there was a little improper scheming in this against the two persons whom the ladies were bound to obey. Mr Dobbs Broughton invariably left his house soon after ten in the morning. It would sometimes happen, though not frequently, that he returned home early in the day, – at four perhaps, or even before that; and should he chance to do so while the picture was going on, he would catch them at their work if the work were postponed till after luncheon. And then again, Mrs Van Siever would often go out in the morning, and when she did so, would always go without her daughter. On such occasions she went into the city, or to other resorts of business, at which, in some manner quite unintelligible to her daughter, she looked after her money. But when she did not go out in the morning, she did go out in the afternoon, and she would then require her daughter's company. There was some place to which she always went on a Friday morning, and at which she stayed for two or three hours. Friday therefore was a fitting day on which to begin the work at Mrs Broughton's house. All this was explained between the three conspirators. Mrs Dobbs Broughton declared that if she entertained the slightest idea that her husband would object to the painting of the picture in her room, nothing on earth would induce her to lend her countenance to it; but yet it might be well not to tell him just at first, perhaps not till the sittings were over, – perhaps not till the picture was finished; as, otherwise, tidings of the picture might get round to ears which were not intended to hear it. 'Poor dear Dobbs is so careless with a secret.' Miss Van Siever explained her motives in a very different way. 'I know mamma would not let me do it if she knew it;

and therefore I shall not tell her. 'My dear Clara,' said Mrs Broughton with a smile, 'you are so outspoken!' 'And why not?' said Miss Van Siever. 'I am old enough to judge for myself. If mamma does not want to be deceived, she ought not to treat me like a child. Of course she'll find it out sooner or later; but I don't care about that.' Conway Dalrymple said nothing as the two ladies were thus excusing themselves. 'How delightful it must be not to have a master,' said Mrs Broughton, addressing him. 'But then a man has to work for his own bread,' said he. 'I suppose it comes about equal in the long run.'

Very little drawing or painting was done on that day. In the first place it was necessary that the question of costume should be settled, and both Mrs Broughton and the artist had much to say on the subject. It was considered proper that Jael should be dressed as a Jewess, and there came to be much question how Jewesses dressed themselves in those very early days. Mrs Broughton had prepared her jewels and raiment of many colours, but the painter declared that the wife of Heber the Kenite would have no jewels. But when Mrs Broughton discovered from her Bible that Heber had been connected by family ties with Moses, she was more than ever sure that Heber's wife would have in her tent much of the spoilings of the Egyptians. And when Clara Van Siever suggested that at any rate she would not have worn them in a time of confusion when soldiers were loose, flying about the country, Mrs Broughton was quite confident that she would have put them on before she invited the captain of the enemy's host into her tent. The artist at last took the matter into his own hand by declaring that Miss Van Siever would sit the subject much better without jewels, and therefore all Mrs Broughton's gewgaws were put back into their boxes. And then on four different times the two ladies had to retire into Mrs Broughton's room in order that Jael might be arrayed in various costumes, – and in each costume she had to kneel down, taking the hammer in her hand, and holding the pointed stick which had been prepared to do duty as the nail, upon the forehead of a dummy Sisera. At last it was decided that her raiment should be altogether white, and that she should wear, twisted round her head and falling over her shoulder, a Roman silk scarf of various colours. 'Where Jael could have gotten it I don't know,' said Clara. 'You may be sure that there were lots of such things among the Egyptians,' said Mrs Broughton, 'and that Moses brought away all the best for his own family.'

'And who is to be Sisera?' asked Mrs Broughton in one of the pauses in their work.'

'I'm thinking of asking my friend John Eames to sit.'

'Of course we cannot sit together,' said Miss Van Siever.

'There's no reason why you should,' said Dalrymple. 'I can do the second figure in my own room.' Then there was a bargain made that Sisera should not be a portrait. 'It would never do,' said Mrs Broughton, shaking her head very gravely.

Though there was really very little done to the picture on that day, the work was commenced; and Mrs Broughton who had at first objected strongly to the idea, and who had said twenty times that it was quite out of the question that it should be done in her house, became very eager in her delight about it. Nobody should know anything of the picture till it should be exhibited. That would be best. And it should be the picture of the year! She was a little heart-broken when Dalrymple assured her that it could not possibly be finished for exhibition in that May; but she came to again when he declared that he meant to put out all his strength upon it. 'There will be five or six months' work on it,' he said. 'Will there, indeed? And how much work was there in "The Graces?"' 'The Graces,' as will perhaps be remembered, was the triple portrait of Mrs Dobbs Broughton herself. This question the artist did not answer with absolute accuracy, but contented himself with declaring that with such a model as Mrs Broughton the picture had been comparatively easy.

Mrs Broughton, having no doubt that ultimate object of which she had spoken to her friend Conway steadily in view, took occasion before the sitting was over to leave the room, so that the artist might have an opportunity of speaking a word in private to his model, – if he had any such word to speak. And Mrs Broughton, as she did this, felt that she was doing her duty as a wife, a friend, and a Christian. She was doing her duty as a wife because she was giving the clearest proof in the world, – the clearest at any rate to herself, – that the intimacy between herself and her friend Conway had in it nothing that was improper. And she was doing her duty as a friend, because Clara Van Siever, with her large expectations, would be an eligible wife. And she was doing her duty as a Christian, because the whole thing was intended to be moral. Miss Demolines had declared that her friend Maria Clutterbuck, – as Miss Demolines delighted to call Mrs Broughton, in memory of dear old innocent days, – and high principles; and the reader will see that she was justified in her declaration. 'It will be better so,' said Mrs Broughton, as she sat upon her bed and wiped a tear from the corner of her eye. 'Yes; it will be better so. There is a pang. Of course there's a pang. But it will be better so.' Acting upon this high principle, she allowed Conway Dalrymple five minutes to say what he had to say to Clara Van Siever. Then she allowed herself to indulge in some very savage feelings in reference to her husband, – accusing her husband in her thoughts of great cruelty, – nay, of brutality, because of certain sharp words that he had said as to Conway Dalrymple. 'But of course he can't understand,' said Mrs Broughton to herself. 'How is it to be expected that he should understand?'

But she allowed her friend on this occasion only five minutes, thinking probably that so much time might suffice. A woman, when she is jealous, is apt to attribute to the other woman with whom her jealousy is concerned, both weakness and timidity, and to the man both audacity and strength. A woman who has herself taken perhaps twelve months in the winning, will think that another woman is to be won in five minutes. It is not to be supposed that Mrs Dobbs Broughton had ever been won by any one except by Mr Dobbs Broughton. At least, let it not be supposed that she had ever acknowledged a spark of love for Conway Dalrymple. But neverthe-less there was enough of jealousy in her present mood to make her think poorly of Miss Van Siever's capacity for standing a siege against the artist's eloquence. Otherwise, having left the two together with the object which she had acknowledged to herself, she would hardly have returned to them after so very short an interval.

'I hope you won't dislike the trouble of all this?' said Dalrymple to his model, as soon as Mrs Broughton was gone.

'I cannot say that I like it very much,' said Miss Van Siever.

'I'm afraid it will be a bore; – but I hope you'll go through with it.'

'I shall if I am not prevented,' said Miss Van Siever. 'When I've said that I'll do a thing, I like to do it.'

There was a pause in the conversation which took up a consider-able portion of the five minutes. Miss Van Siever was not holding her nail during these moments, but was sitting in a commonplace way on her chair, while Dalrymple was scraping his palette. 'I wonder what it was that first induced you to sit?' said he.

'Oh, I don't know. I took a fancy for it.'

'I'm very glad you did take the fancy. You'll make an excellent model. If you won't mind posing again for a few minutes – I will not weary you to-day. Your right arm a little more forward.'

'But I should tumble down.'

'Not if you lean well on to the nail.'

'But that would have woken Sisera before she had struck a blow.'

'Never mind that. Let us try it.' Then Mrs Broughton returned, with that pleasant feeling in her bosom of having done her duty as a wife, a friend, and a Christian. 'Mrs Broughton,' continued the painter, 'just steady Miss Van Siever's shoulder with your hand; and now bring the arm and the elbow a little more forward.'

'But Jael did not have a friend to help her in that way,' said Miss Van Siever.

At the end of an hour and a half the two ladies retired, and Jael disrobed herself, and Miss Van Siever put on her customary raiment. It was agreed among them that they had commenced their work auspiciously, and that they would meet again on the following Monday. The artist begged to be allowed an hour to go on with his work in Mrs Broughton's room, and the hour was conceded to him. It was understood that he could not take the canvas backwards and forwards with him to his own house, and he pointed out that no progress whatever could be made, unless he were occasionally allowed some such grace as this. Mrs Broughton doubted and hesitated, made difficulties, and lifted up her hands in despair. 'It is easy for you to say, Why not? but I know very well why not.' But at last she gave way. 'Honi soit qui mal y pense,'* she said; 'that must be my protection.' So she followed Miss Van Siever downstairs, leaving Mr Dalrymple in possession of her boudoir. 'I shall give you just one hour,' she said, 'and then I shall come and turn you out.' So she went down, and, as Miss Van Siever would not stay to lunch with her, she ate her lunch by herself, sending a glass of sherry and a biscuit up to the poor painter at his work.

Exactly at the end of the hour she returned to him. 'Now, Conway, you must go,' she said.

'But why in such a hurry?'

'Because I say that it must be so. When I say so, pray let that be sufficient.' But still Dalrymple went on working. 'Conway,' she said, 'how can you treat me with so much disdain?'

'Disdain, Mrs Broughton!'

'Yes, disdain. Have I not begged you to understand that I cannot allow you to remain here, and yet you pay no attention to my wishes.'

'I have done now;' and he began to put his brushes and paints together. 'I suppose all these things may remain here?'

'Yes; they may remain. They must do so, of course. There; if you will put the easel in the corner, with the canvas behind it, they will not be seen if he should chance to come into the room.'

'He would not be angry, I suppose, if he saw them?'

'There is no knowing. Men are so unreasonable. All men are, I think. All those are whom I have had the fortune to know. Women generally say that men are selfish. I do not complain so much that they are selfish as that they are thoughtless. They are headstrong and do not look forward to results. Now you, – I do not think you would willingly do me an injury ?'

'I do not think I would.'

'I am sure you would not; – but yet you would forget to save me from one.'

'What injury ?'

'Oh, never mind. I am not thinking of anything in particular. From myself, for instance. But we will not talk about that. That way madness lies.* Tell me, Conway; – what do you think of Clara Van Siever ?'

'She is very handsome, certainly.'

'And clever ?'

'Decidedly clever. I should think she has a temper of her own.'

'What woman is there worth a straw that has not ? If Clara Van Siever were ill-used, she would resent it. I do not doubt that for a moment. I should not like to be the man who would do it.'

'Nor I, either,' said Conway.

'But there is plenty of feminine softness in that character, if she were treated with love and kindness. Conway, if you will take my advice you will ask Clara Van Siever to be your wife. But perhaps you have already.'

'Who; I ?'

'Yes; you.'

'I have not done it yet, certainly, Mrs Broughton.'

'And why should you not do it ?'

'There are two or three reasons; – but perhaps none of any great importance. Do you know of none, Mrs Broughton ?'

'I know of none,' said Mrs Broughton in a very serious, – in almost a tragic tone; – 'of none that should weigh for a moment. As far as I am concerned, nothing would give me more pleasure.'

'That is so kind of you !'

'I mean to be kind. I do, indeed, Conway. I know it will be better for you that you should be settled, – very much better. And it will be better for me. I do not mind admitting that; – though in saying so I trust greatly to your generosity to interpret my words properly.'

'I shall not flatter myself, if you mean that.'

'There is no question of flattery, Conway. The question is simply of truth and prudence. Do you not know that it would be better that you should be married ?'

'Not unless a certain gentleman were to die first,' said Conway Dalrymple, as he deposited the last of his painting paraphernalia in the recess which had been prepared for them by Mrs Broughton.

'Conway, how can you speak in that wicked, wicked way !'

'I can assure you I do not wish the gentleman in question the slightest harm in the world. If his welfare depended on me, he should be as safe as the Bank of England.'

'And you will not take my advice?'

'What advice?'

'About Clara?'

'Mrs Broughton, matrimony is a very important thing.'

'Indeed, it is; – oh, who can say how important! There was a time, Conway, when I thought you had given your heart to Madalina Demolines.

'Heaven forbid!'

'And I grieved, because I thought that she was not worthy of you.'

'There was never anything in that, Mrs Broughton.'

'She thought that there was. At any rate, she said so. I know that for certain. She told me so herself. But let that pass. Clara Van Siever is in every respect very different from Madalina. Clara, I think, is worthy of you. And Conway, – of course it is not for me to dictate to you; but this I must tell you—' Then she paused, as though she did not know how to finish her sentence.

'What must you tell me?'

'I will tell you nothing more. If you cannot understand what I have said, you must be more dull of comprehension than I believe you to be. Now go. Why are you not gone this half-hour?'

'How could I go while you were giving me all this good advice?'

'I have not asked you to stay. Go now, at any rate. And, remember, Conway, if this picture is to go on, I will not have you remaining here after the work is done. Will you remember that?' And she held him by the hand while he declared that he would remember it.

Mrs Dobbs Broughton was no more in love with Conway Dalrymple than she was in love with King Charles on horseback at Charing Cross. And, over and beyond the protection which came to her in the course of nature from unimpassioned feelings in this special phase of her life, – and indeed, I may say, in every phase of her life, – it must be acknowledged on her behalf that she did enjoy that protection which comes from what we call principle, – though the principle was not perhaps very high of its kind. Madalina Demolines had been right when she talked of her friend Maria's principles. Dobbs Broughton had been so far lucky in that jump in the dark which he had made in taking a wife to himself, that he had not fallen upon a really vicious woman, or upon a woman of strong feeling. If it had come to be the lot of Mrs Dobbs Broughton to have six hours' work to do every day of her life, I think that the work would have been done badly, but it would have kept her free from all danger. As it was she had nothing to do. She had no child. She was not given to much reading. She could not sit with a needle in her hand all day. She had no aptitude for May meetings, or the excitement of charitable good works. Life with her was very dull, and she found no amusement within her reach so easy and so pleasant as the amusement of pretending to be in love. If all that she did and all that she said could only have been taken for its worth and for nothing more, by the different persons concerned, there was very little in it to flatter Mr Dalrymple or to give cause for tribulation to Mr Broughton. She probably cared but little for either of them. She was one of those women to whom it is not given by nature to care very much for anybody. But, of the two, she certainly cared the most for Mr Dobbs Broughton, – because Mr Dobbs Broughton belonged to her. As to leaving Mr Dobbs Broughton's house, and putting herself into the hands of another man, – no Imogen* of a wife was ever less likely to take a step so wicked, so dangerous, and so generally disagreeable to all the parties concerned.

But Conway Dalrymple, – though now and again he had got a side glance at her true character with clear-seeing eyes, – did allow himself to be flattered and deceived. He knew that she was foolish and ignorant, and that she often talked wonderful nonsense. He knew also that she was continually contradicting herself, – as when she would strenuously beg him to leave her, while she would continue to talk to him in a strain that prevented the possibility of his going. But, nevertheless, he was flattered, and he did believe that she loved him. As to his love for her, – he knew very well that it amounted to nothing. Now and again, perhaps twice a week, if he saw her as often, he would say something which would imply a declaration of affection. He felt that as much as that was expected from him, and that he ought not to hope to get off cheaper. And now that this little play was going on about Miss Van Siever, he did think that Mrs Dobbs Broughton was doing her very best to overcome an unfortunate attachment. It is so gratifying to a young man's feelings to suppose that another man's wife has conceived an unfortunate attachment for him! Conway Dalrymple ought not to have been fooled by such a woman; but I fear that he was fooled by her.

As he returned home to-day from Mrs Broughton's house to his own lodgings he rambled out for a while into Kensington Gardens, and thought of his position seriously. 'I don't see why I should not marry her,' he said to himself, thinking of course of Miss Van Siever. 'If Maria is not in earnest it is not my fault. And it would be my wish that she should be in earnest. If I suppose her to be so, and take her at her word, she can have no right to quarrel with me. Poor Maria! at any rate it will be better for her, for no good can come of this kind of thing. And, by heavens, with a woman like that, of strong feelings, one never knows what may happen.' And then he thought of the condition he would be in, if he were to find her some fine day in his own rooms, and if she were to tell him that she could not go home again, and that she meant to remain with him!

In the meantime Mrs Dobbs Broughton had gone down into her own drawing-room, had tucked herself up on the sofa, and had fallen fast asleep.

CHAPTER 39

A new flirtation

John Eames sat at his office on the day after his return to London, and answered the various letters which he had found waiting for him at his lodgings on the previous evening. To Miss Demolines he had already written from his club, – a single line, which he considered to be appropriate to the mysterious necessities of the occasion. 'I will be with you at a quarter to six to-morrow. – J. E. Just returned.' There was not another word; and as he scrawled it at one of the club tables while two or three men were talking to him, he felt rather proud of his correspondence. 'It was capital fun,' he said; 'and after all,' – the 'all' on this occasion being Lily Dale, and the sadness of his disappointment at Allington, – 'after all, let a fellow be ever so down in the mouth, a little amusement should do him good.' And he reflected further that the more a fellow be 'down in the mouth,' the more good the amusement would do him. He sent off his note, therefore, with some little inward rejoicing, – and a word or two also spoken rejoicing. 'What fun women are sometimes,' he said to one of his friends, – a friend with whom he was very intimate, calling him always Fred, and slapping his back, but whom he never by any chance saw out of his club.

'What's up now, Johnny? Some good fortune?'

'Good fortune; no. I never have good fortunes of that kind. But I've got hold of a young woman, – or rather a young woman has got hold of me, who insists on having a mystery with me. In the mystery itself there is not the slightest interest. But the mysteriousness of it is charming. I have just written to her three words to settle an appointment for to-morrow. We don't sign our names lest the Postmaster-General should find out all about it.'

'Is she pretty?'

'Well; – she isn't ugly. She has just enough of good looks to make the sort of thing pass off pleasantly. A mystery with a downright ugly young woman would be unpleasant.'

After this fashion the note from Miss Demolines had been received, and answered at once, but the other letters remained in his pocket till he reached his office on the following morning. Sir Raffle had begged him to be there at half-past nine. This he had sworn he would not do; but he did seat himself in his room at ten minutes before ten, finding of course the whole building untenanted at that early hour, – that unearthly hour, as Johnny called it himself. 'I shouldn't wonder if he really is here this morning,' Johnny said, as he entered the building, 'just that he may have an opportunity of jumping on me.' But Sir Raffle was not there, and then Johnny began to abuse Sir Raffle. 'If ever I come here early to meet him again, because he says he means to be here himself, I hope I may be—blessed.' On that especial morning it was twelve before Sir Raffle made his appearance, and Johnny avenged himself, – I regret to have to tell it, – by fib. That Sir Raffle fibbed first, was no valid excuse whatever for Eames.

'I've been at it ever since six o'clock,' said Sir Raffle.

'At what?' said Johnny.

'Work, to be sure; – and very hard work too. I believe the Chancellor of the Exchequer thinks that he can call upon me to any extent that he pleases; – just any extent that he pleases. He doesn't give me credit for a desire to have a single hour to myself.'

'What would he do, Sir Raffle, if you were to get ill, or wear yourself out?'

'He knows I'm not one of the wearing-out sort. You got my note last night?'

'Yes; I got your note.'

'I'm sorry that I troubled you; but I couldn't help it. I didn't expect to get a box full of papers at eleven o'clock last night.'

'You didn't put me out, Sir Raffle; I happened to have business of my own which prevented the possibility of my being here early.'

This was the way in which John Eames avenged himself. Sir Raffle turned his face upon his private secretary, and his face was very black. Johnny bore the gaze without dropping an eyelid. 'I'm not going to stand it, and he may as well know that at once,' Johnny said to one of his friends in the office afterwards. 'If he ever wants any thing really done, I'll do it; – though it should take me twelve hours at a stretch. But I'm not going to pretend to believe all the lies he tells me about the Chancellor of the Exchequer. If that is to be part of the private secretary's business, he had better get somebody else.' But now Sir Raffle was very angry, and his countenance was full of wrath as he looked down upon his subordinate minister. 'If I had come here, Mr Eames, and had found you absent, I should have been very much annoyed, very much annoyed indeed, after having written as I did.'

'You would have found me absent at the hour you named. As I wasn't here then, I think it's only fair to say so.'

'I'm afraid you begrudge your time to the service, Mr Eames.'

'I do begrudge it when the service doesn't want it.'

'At your age, Mr Eames, that's not for you to judge. If I had acted in that way when I was young I should never have filled the position I now hold. I always remembered in those days that as I was the hand and not the head, I was bound to hold myself in readiness whether work might be required from me or not.'

'If I'm wanted as hand now, Sir Raffle, I'm ready.'

'That's all very well; – but why were you not here at the hour I named?'

'Well, Sir Raffle, I cannot say that the Chancellor of the Exchequer detained me; – but there was business. As I've been here for the last two hours, I am happy to think that in this instance the public service will not have suffered from my disobedience.'

Sir Raffle was still standing with his hat on, and with his back to the fire, and his countenance was full of wrath. It was on his tongue to tell Johnny that he had better return to his former work in the outer office. He greatly wanted the comfort of a private secretary who would believe in him – or at least pretend to believe in him. There are men who, though they have not sense enough to be true, have nevertheless sense enough to know that they cannot expect to be really believed in by those who are near enough to them to know them. Sir Raffle Baffle was such a one. He would have greatly delighted in the services of some one who would trust him implicitly, – of some young man who would really believe all that he said of himself and of the Chancellor of the Exchequer; but he was wise enough to perceive that no such young man was to be had; or that any such young man, – could such a one be found, – would be absolutely useless for any purposes of work. He knew himself to be a liar whom nobody trusted. And he knew himself also to be a bully, – though he could not think so low of himself as to believe that he was a bully whom nobody feared. A private secretary was at the least bound to pretend to believe in him. There is a decency in such things, and that decency John Eames did not observe. He thought that he must get rid of John Eames, in spite of certain attractions which belonged to Johnny's appearance and general manners, and social standing, and reputed wealth. But it would not be wise to punish a man on the spot for breaking an appointment which he himself had not kept, and therefore he would wait for another opportunity. 'You had better go to your own room now,' he said. 'I am engaged on a matter connected with the Treasury, in which I will not ask for your assistance.' He knew that Eames would not believe a word as to what he said about the Treasury, – not even some very trifling base of truth which did exist; but the boast gave him the opportunity of putting an end to the interview after his own fashion. Then John Eames went to his own room and answered the letters which he had in his pocket.

To the club dinner he would not go. 'What's the use of paying two guineas for a dinner with fellows you see every day of your life?' he said. To Lady Glencora's he would go, and he wrote a line to his friend Dalrymple proposing that they should go together. And he would dine with his cousin Toogood in Tavistock Square. 'One meets the queerest people in the world there,' he said; 'but Tommy Toogood is such a good fellow himself!' After that he had his lunch. Then he read the paper, and before he went away he wrote a dozen or two of private notes, presenting Sir Raffle's compliments right and left, and giving in no one note a single word of information that could be of any use to any person. Having thus earned his salary by half-past four o'clock he got into a hansom cab and had himself driven to Porchester Terrace. Miss Demolines was at home, of course, and he soon found himself closeted with that interesting young woman.

'I thought you never would have come.' These were the first words she spoke.

'My dear Miss Demolines, you must not forget that I have my bread to earn.'

'Fiddlestick – bread! As if I didn't know that you can get away from your office when you choose.'

'But, indeed, I cannot.'

'What is there to prevent you, Mr Eames?'

'I'm not tied up like a dog, certainly; but who do you suppose will do my work if I do not do it myself? It is a fact, though the world does not believe it, that men in public offices have got something to do.'

'Now you are laughing at me, I know; but you are welcome, if you like it. It's the way of the world just at present that ladies should submit to that sort to thing from gentlemen.'

'What sort of thing, Miss Demolines?'

'Chaff, – as you call it. Courtesy is out of fashion, and gallantry has come to signify quite a different kind of thing from what it used to do.'

'The Sir Charles Grandison* business is done and gone. That's what you mean, I suppose? Don't you think we should find it very heavy if we tried to get it back again?'

'I'm not going to ask you to be a Sir Charles Grandison, Mr Eames. But never mind all that now. Do you know that that girl has absolutely had her first sitting for the picture?'

'Has she, indeed?'

'She has. You may take my word for it. I know it as a fact. What a fool that young man is!'

'Which young man?'

'Which young man! Conway Dalrymple to be sure. Artists are always weak. Of all men in the world they are the most subject to flattery from women; and we all know that Conway Dalrymple is very vain.'

'Upon my word I didn't know it,' said Johnny.

'Yes, you do. You must know it. When a man goes about in a purple velvet coat of course he is vain.'

'I certainly cannot defend a purple velvet coat.'

'That is what he wore when this girl sat to him this morning.'

'This morning was it?'

'Yes; this morning. They little think that they can do nothing without my knowing it. He was there for nearly four hours, and she was dressed up in a white robe as Jael, with a turban on her head. Jael, indeed! I call it very improper, and I am quite astonished that Maria Clutterbuck should have lent herself to such a piece of work. That Maria was never very wise, of course we all know; but I thought that she had principle enough to have kept her from this kind of thing.'

'It's her fevered existence,' said Johnny.

'That is just it. She must have excitement. It is like dram-drinking. And then, you know, they are always living in the crater of a volcano.'

'Who are living in the crater of a volcano?'

'The Dobbs Broughtons are. Of course they are. There is no saying what day a smash may come. These City people get so used to it that they enjoy it. The risk is every thing to them.'

'They like to have a little certainty behind the risk, I fancy.'

'I'm afraid there is very little that's certain with Dobbs Broughton. But about this picture, Mr Eames. I look to you to assist me there. It must be put a stop to. As to that I am determined. It must be – put a – stop to.' And as Miss Demolines repeated these last words with tremendous emphasis she leant with both her elbows on a little table that stood between her and her visitor, and looked with all her eyes into his face. 'I do hope that you agree with me in that,' said she.

'Upon my word I do not see the harm of the picture,' said he.

'You do not?'

'Indeed, no. Why should not Dalrymple paint Miss Van Siever as well as any other lady ? It is his special business to paint ladies.'

'Look here, Mr Eames. – ' And now Miss Demolines, as she spoke, drew her own seat closer to that of her companion and pushed away the little table. 'Do you suppose that Conway Dalrymple, in the usual way of his business, paints pictures of young ladies, of which their mothers know nothing ? Do you suppose that he paints them in ladies' rooms without their husband's knowledge ? And in the common way of his business does he not expect to be paid for his pictures ?'

'But what is all that to you and me, Miss Demolines ?'

'Is the welfare of your friend nothing to you ? Would you like to see him become the victim of the artifice of such a girl as Clara Van Siever ?'

'Upon my word I think he is very well able to take care of himself.'

'And would you wish to see that poor creature's domestic hearth ruined and broken up ?'

'Which poor creature ?'

'Dobbs Broughton, to be sure.'

'I can't pretend that I care very much for Dobbs Broughton,' said John Eames; 'and you see I know so little about his domestic hearth.'

'Oh, Mr Eames !'

'Besides, her principles will pull her through. You told me yourself that Mrs Broughton has high principles.'

'God forbid that I should say a word against Maria Clutterbuck,' said Miss Demolines, fervently. 'Maria Clutterbuck was my early friend, and though words have been spoken which never should have been spoken, and though things have been done which never should have been even dreamed of, still I will not desert Maria Clutterbuck in her hour of need. No, never !'

'I'm sure you're what one may call a trump to your friends, Miss Demolines.'

'I have always endeavoured to be so, and always shall. You will find me so; – that is if you and I ever become intimate enough to feel that sort of friendship.'

'There's nothing on earth I should like better,' said Johnny. As soon as the words were out of his mouth he felt ashamed of himself. He knew that he did not in truth desire the friendship of Miss Demolines, and that any friendship with such a one would mean something different from friendship, – something that would be an injury to Lily Dale. A week had hardly passed since he had sworn a life's constancy to Lily Dale, – and sworn it, not to her only, but to himself; and now he was giving way to a flirtation with this woman, not because he liked it himself, but because he was too weak to keep out of it.

'If that is true—,' said Miss Demolines.

'Oh, yes; it's quite true,' said Johnny.

'Then you must earn my friendship by doing what I ask of you. That picture must not be painted. You must tell Conway Dalrymple as his friend that he must cease to carry on such an intrigue in another man's house.'

'You would hardly call painting a picture an intrigue; would you?'

'Certainly I would when it's kept a secret from the husband by the wife, – and from the mother by the daughter. If it cannot be stopped in any other way, I must tell Mrs Van Siever; – I must, indeed. I have such an abhorrence of the old woman, that I could not bring myself to speak to her, – but I should write to her. That's what I should do.'

'But what's the reason? You might as well tell me the real reason.' Had Miss Demolines been christened Mary, or Fanny, or Jane, I think that John Eames would now have called her by either of those names; but Madalina was such a mouthful that he could not bring himself to use it at once. He had heard that among her intimates she was called Maddy. He had an idea that he had heard Dalrymple in old times talk of her as Maddy Mullins, and just at this moment the idea was not pleasant to him; at any rate he could not call her Maddy as yet. 'How am I to help you,' he said, 'unless I know all about it?'

'I hate that girl like poison!' said Miss Demolines, confidentially, drawing herself very near to Johnny as she spoke.

'But what has she done?'

'What has she done? I can't tell you what she has done. I could not demean myself by repeating it. Of course we all know what she wants. She wants to catch Conway Dalrymple. That's as plain as anything can be. Not that I care about that.'

'Of course not,' said Johnny.

'Not in the least. It's nothing to me. I have known Mr Dalrymple no doubt, for a year or two, and I should be sorry to see a young man who has his good points sacrificed in that sort of way. But it is mere acquaintance between Mr Dalrymple and me, and of course I cannot interfere.'

'She'll have a lot of money, you know.'

'He thinks so; does he? I suppose that is what Maria has told him. Oh, Mr Eames, you don't know the meanness of women; you don't, indeed. Men are so much more noble.'

'Are they, do you think?'

'Than some women. I see women doing things that really disgust me; I do, indeed; – things that I wouldn't do myself, were it ever so; – striving to catch men in every possible way, and for such purposes! I wouldn't have believed it of Maria Clutterbuck. I wouldn't indeed. However, I will never say a word against her, because she has been my friend. Nothing shall ever induce me.'

John Eames before he left Porchester Terrace, had at last succeeded in calling his fair friend Madalina, and had promised that he would endeavour to open the artist's eyes to the folly of painting his picture in Broughton's house without Broughton's knowledge.

CHAPTER 40

Mr Toogood's ideas about society

A day or two after the interview which was described in the last chapter John Eames dined with his uncle Mr Thomas Toogood, in Tavistock Square. He was in the habit of doing this about once a month, and was a great favourite both with his cousins and with their mother. Mr Toogood did not give dinner-parties; always begging those whom he asked to enjoy his hospitality, to take pot luck, and telling young men whom he could treat with familiarity, – such as his nephew, – that if they wanted to be regaled à la Russe* they must not come to number 75, Tavistock Square. 'A leg of mutton and trimmings; that will be about the outside of it,' he would say; but he would add in a whisper, – 'and a glass of port such as you don't get every day of your life.' Polly and Lucy Toogood were pretty girls, and merry withal, and certain young men were well contented to accept the attorney's invitations, – whether attracted by the promised leg of mutton, or the port wine, or the young ladies, I will not attempt to say. I it had so happened that one young man, a clerk from John Eames' office, had partaken so often of the pot luck and port wine that Polly Toogood had conquered him by her charms, and he was now a slave, waiting an appropriate time for matrimonial sacrifice. William Summerkin was the young man's name; and as it was known that Mr Summerkin was to inherit a fortune amounting to five thousand pounds from his maiden aunt, it was considered that Polly Toogood was not doing amiss. 'I'll give you three hundred pounds, my boy, just to put a few sheets on the beds,' said Toogood the father, 'and when the old birds are both dead she'll have a thousand pounds out of the nest. That's the extent of Polly's fortune; – so now you know.' Summerkin was, however, quite contented to have his own money settled on his darling Polly, and the whole thing was looked at with pleasant and propitious eyes by the Toogood connection.

When John Eames entered the drawing-room Summerkin and

Polly were already there. Summerkin blushed up to his eyes, of course, but Polly sat as demurely as though she had been accustomed to having lovers all her life. 'Mamma will be down almost immediately, John,' said Polly as soon as the first greetings were over, 'and papa has come in, I know.'

'Summerkin,' said Johnny, 'I am afraid you left the office before four o'clock.'

'No, I did not,' said Summerkin. 'I deny it.'

'Polly,' said her cousin, 'you should keep him in better order. He will certainly come to grief if he goes on like this. I suppose you could do without him for half an hour.'

'I don't want him, I can assure you,' said Polly.

'I have only been here just five minutes,' said Summerkin, 'and I came because Mrs Toogood asked me to do a commission.'

'That's civil to you, Polly,' said John.

'It's quite as civil as I wish him to be,' said Polly. 'And as for you, John, everybody knows that you're a goose, and that you always were a goose. Isn't he always doing foolish things at the office, William?' But as John Eames was rather a great man at the Income-tax Office, Summerkin would not fall into his sweetheart's joke on this subject, finding it easier and perhaps safer to twiddle the bodkins in Polly's work-basket. Then Toogood and Mrs Toogood entered the room together, and the lovers were able to be alone again during the general greeting with which Johnny was welcomed.

'You don't know the Silverbridge people, – do you?' asked Mr Toogood. Eames said that he did not. He had been at Silverbridge more than once, but did not know very much of the Silverbridgians. 'Because Walker is coming to dine here. Walker is the leading man in Silverbridge.'

'And what is Walker; – besides being leading man in Silverbridge?'

'He's a lawyer. Walker and Winthrop. Everybody knows Walker in Barsetshire. I've been down at Barchester since I saw you.'

'Have you indeed?' said Johnny.

'And I'll tell you what I've been about. You know Mr Crawley; don't you?'

'The Hogglestock clergyman that has come to grief? I don't know him personally. He's a sort of cousin by marriage, you know.'

'Of course he is,' said Mr Toogood. 'His wife is my first-cousin, and your mother's first-cousin. He came here to me the other day; – or rather to the shop. I had never seen the man before in my life, and a very queer fellow he is too. He came to me about this trouble of his, and of course I must do what I can for him. I got myself introduced to Walker, who has the management of the prosecution, and I asked him to come here to dine to-day.'

'And what sort of fellow did you find Crawley, uncle Tom ?'

'Such a queer fish; – so unlike anybody else in the world !'

'But I suppose he did take the money ?' said Johnny.

'I don't know what to say about it. I don't indeed. If he took it he didn't mean to steal it. I'm as sure that man didn't mean to steal twenty pounds as I ever could be of anything. Perhaps I shall get something about it out of Walker after dinner.' Then Mr Walker entered the room. 'This is very kind of you, Mr Walker; very indeed. I take it quite as a compliment, your coming in in this sort of way. It's just pot luck, you know, and nothing else.' Mr Walker of course assured his host that he was delighted. 'Just a leg of mutton and a bottle of old port, Mr Walker,' continued Toogood. 'We never get beyond that in the way of dinner-giving; do we, Maria ?'

But Maria was at this moment descanting on the good luck of the family to her nephew, – and on one special piece of good luck which had just occurred. Mr Summerkin's maiden aunt had declared her intention of giving up the fortune to the young people at once. She had enough to live upon, she said, and would therefore make two lovers happy. 'And they're to be married on the first of May,' said Lucy, – that Lucy of whom her father had boasted to Mr Crawley that she knew Byron by heart, – 'and won't that be jolly ? Mamma is going out to look for a house for them to-morrow. Fancy Polly with a house of her own ! Won't it be stunning ? I wish you were going to be married too, Johnny.'

'Don't be a fool, Lucy.'

'Of course I know that you are in love. I hope you are not going to give over being in love, Johnny, because it is such fun.'

'Wait till you're caught yourself, my girl.'

'I don't mean to be caught till some great swell comes this way. And as great swells never do come into Tavistock Square I shan't have a chance. I'll tell you what I would like; I'd like to have a Corsair, – or else a Giaour; – I think a Giaour would be nicest. Only a Giaour wouldn't be a Giaour here, you know. Fancy a lover "Who thundering comes on blackest steed, With slackened bit and hoof of speed."* Were not those the days to live in ! But all that is over now, you know, and young people take houses in Woburn Place, instead of being locked up, or drowned, or married to a hideous monster behind a veil.* I suppose it's better as it is, for some reasons.'

'I think it must be more jolly, as you call it, Lucy.'

'I'm not quite sure. I know I'd go back and be Medora, if I could.

Mamma is always telling Polly that she must be careful about William's dinner. But Conrad didn't care for his dinner. "Light toil! to cull and dress thy frugal fare! See, I have plucked the fruit that promised best."'*

'And how often do you think Conrad got drunk?'

'I don't think he got drunk at all. There is no reason why he should, any more than William. Come along, and take me down to dinner. After all, papa's leg of mutton is better than Medora's apples, when one is as hungry as I am.'

The leg of mutton on this occasion consisted of soup, fish, and a bit of roast beef, and a couple of boiled fowls. 'If I had only two children instead of twelve, Mr Walker,' said the host, 'I'd give you a dinner à la Russe.'

'I don't begrudge Mrs Toogood a single arrow in her quiver* on that score,' said Mr Walker.

'People are getting to be so luxurious that one can't live up to them at all,' said Mrs Toogood. 'We dined out here with some new comers in the square only last week. We had asked them before, and they came quite in a quiet way, – just like this; and when we got there we found they'd four kinds of ices after dinner!'

'And not a morsel of food on the table fit to eat,' said Toogood. 'I never was so poisoned in my life. As for soup, – it was just the washings of the pastrycook's kettle next door.'

'And how is one to live with such people, Mr Walker?' continued Mrs Toogood. 'Of course we can't ask them back again. We can't give them four kinds of ices.'

'But would that be necessary? Perhaps they haven't got twelve children.'

'They haven't got any,' said Toogood, triumphing; 'not a chick belonging to them. But you see one must do as other people do. I hate anything grand. I wouldn't want more than this for myself, if bank-notes were as plenty as curl-papers.'

'Nobody has any curl-papers now, papa,' said Lucy.

'But I can't bear to be outdone,' said Mr Toogood. 'I think it's very unpleasant, – people living in that sort of way. It's all very well telling me that I needn't live so too; – and of course I don't. I can't afford to have four men in from the confectioner's, dressed a sight better than myself, at ten shillings a head. I can't afford it, and I don't do it. But the worst of it is that I suffer because other people do it. It stands to reason that I must either be driven along with the crowd, or else be left behind. Now, I don't like either. And what's the end of it? Why, I'm half carried away and half left behind.'

'Upon my word, papa, I don't think you're carried away at all,' said Lucy.

'Yes, I am; and I'm ashamed of myself. Mr Walker, I don't dare to ask you to drink a glass of wine with me in my own house, – that's what I don't, – because it's the proper thing for you to wait till somebody brings it you, and then to drink it by yourself. There is no knowing whether I mightn't offend you.' And Mr Toogood as he spoke grasped the decanter at his elbow. Mr Walker grasped another at his elbow, and the two attorney's took their glass of wine together.

'A very queer case this is of my cousin Crawley's,' said Toogood to Walker, when the ladies had left the dining-room.

'A most distressing case. I never knew anything so much talked of in our part of the country.'

'He can't have been a popular man, I should say?'

'No; not popular, – not in the ordinary way; – anything but that. Nobody knew him personally before this matter came up.'

'But a good clergyman, probably? I'm interested in the case, of course, as his wife is my first-cousin. You will under stand, however, that I know nothing of him. My father tried to be civil to him once, but Crawley wouldn't have it at all. We all thought he was mad then. I suppose he has done his duty in his parish?'

'He has quarrelled with the bishop, you know, – out and out.'

'Has he, indeed? But I'm not sure that I think so very much about bishops, Mr Walker.'

'That depends very much on the particular bishop. Some people say ours isn't all that a bishop ought to be, while others are very fond of him.'

'And Mr Crawley belongs to the former set; that's all?' said Mr Toogood.

'No, Mr Toogood; that isn't all. The worst of your cousin is that he has an aptitude to quarrel with everybody. He is one of those men who always think themselves to be ill-used. Now our dean, Dr Arabin, has been his very old friend, – and as far as I can learn, a very good friend; but it seems that Mr Crawley has done his best to quarrel with him too.'

'He spoke of the dean in the highest terms to me.'

'He may do that, – and yet quarrel with him. He'd quarrel with his own right hand, if he had nothing else to quarrel with. That makes the difficulty, you see. He'll take nobody's advice. He thinks that we're all against him.'

'I suppose the world has been heavy on him, Mr Walker?'

'The world has been very heavy on him,' said John Eames, who had now been left free to join the conversation, Mr Summerkin having gone away to his lady-love. 'You must not judge him as you do other men.'

'That is just it,' said Mr Walker. 'And to what result will that bring us?'

'That we ought to stretch a point in his favour,' said Toogood.'

'But why?' asked the attorney from Silverbridge. 'What do we mean when we say that one man isn't to be trusted as another? We simply imply that he is not what we call responsible.'

'And I don't think Mr Crawley is responsible,' said Johnny.

'Then how can he be fit to have charge of a parish?' said Mr Walker. 'You see where the difficulty is. How it embarrasses one all round. The amount of evidence as to the cheque is, I think, sufficient to get a verdict in an ordinary case, and the Crown has no alternative but so to treat it. Then his friends come forward, – and from sympathy with his sufferings, I desire to be ranked among the number, – and say, "Ah, but you should spare this man, because he is not responsible." Were he one who filled no position requiring special responsibility, that might be very well. His friends might undertake to look after him, and the prosecution might perhaps be smothered. But Mr Crawley holds a living, and if he escape he will be triumphant, – especially triumphant over the bishop. Now, if he has really taken this money, and if his only excuse be that he did not know when he took it whether he was stealing or whether he was not, – for the sake of justice that ought not to be allowed.' So spoke Mr Walker.

'You think he certainly did steal the money?' said Johnny.

'You have heard the evidence, no doubt?' said Mr Walker.

'I don't feel quite sure about it, yet,' said Mr Toogood.'

'Quite sure of what?' said Mr Walker.

'That the cheque was dropped in his house.'

'It was at any rate traced to his hands.'

'I have no doubt about that,' said Toogood.

'And he can't account for it,' said Walker.

'A man isn't bound to show where he got his money,' said Johnny. 'Suppose that sovereign is marked,' and Johnny produced a coin from his pocket, 'and I don't know but what it is; and suppose it is proved to have belonged to some one who lost it, and then to be traced to my hands, – how am I to say where I got it? If I were asked, I should simply decline to answer.'

'But a cheque is not a sovereign, Mr Eames,' said Walker. 'It is presumed that a man can account for the possession of a cheque. It may be that a man should have a cheque in his possession and not be able to account for it, and should yet be open to no grave suspicion. In such a case a jury has to judge. Here is the fact: that Mr Crawley has the cheque, and brings it into use some considerable time after it is drawn; and the additional fact that the drawer of the cheque had lost it, as he thought, in Mr Crawley's house, and had looked for it there, soon after it was drawn, and long before it was paid. A jury must judge; but, as a lawyer, I should say that the burden of disproof lies with Mr Crawley.'

'Did you find out anything, Mr Walker,' said Toogood, 'about the man who drove Mr Soames that day?'

'No, – nothing.'

'The trap was from "The Dragon" at Barchester, I think?'

'Yes, – from "The Dragon of Wantly."'

'A respectable sort of house?'

'Pretty well for that, I believe. I've heard that the people are poor,' said Mr Walker.

'Somebody told me that they'd had a queer lot about the house, and that three or four of them left just then. I think I heard that two or three men from the place went to New Zealand together. It just came out in conversation while I was in the inn-yard.'

'I have never heard anything of it,' said Mr Walker.

'I don't say that it can help us.'

'I don't see that it can,' said Mr Walker.

After that there was a pause, and Mr Toogood pushed about the old port, and made some very stinging remarks as to the claret-drinking propensities of the age. 'Gladstone claret* the most of it is, I fancy,' said Mr Toogood. 'I find that port wine which my father bought in the wood five-and-twenty years ago is good enough for me.' Mr Walker said that it was quite good enough for him, almost too good, and that he thought that he had had enough of it. The host threatened another bottle, and was up to draw the cork, – rather to the satisfaction of John Eames, who liked his uncle's port, – but Mr Walker stopped him. 'Not a drop more for me,' he said. 'You are quite sure?' 'Quite sure.' And Mr Walker moved towards the door.

'It's a great pity, Mr Walker,' said Toogood, going back to the old subject, 'that this dean and his wife should be away.'

'I understand that they will both be home before the trial,' said Mr Walker.

'Yes, – but you know how very important it is to learn before-hand exactly what your witnesses can prove and what they can't prove. And moreover, though neither the dean nor his wife might perhaps be able to tell us anything themselves, they might help to put us on the proper scent. I think I'll send somebody after them. I think I will.

'It would be a heavy expense, Mr Toogood.'

'Yes,' said Toogood, mournfully, thinking of the twelve children;

'it would be a heavy expense. But I never like to stick at a thing when it ought to be done. I think I shall send a fellow after them.'

'I'll go,' said Johnny.

'How can you go?'

'I'll make old Snuffle give me leave.'

'But will that lessen the expense?' said Mr Walker.

'Well, yes, I think it will,' said John, modestly.

'My nephew is a rich man, Mr Walker,' said Toogood.

'That alters the case,' said Mr Walker. And thus, before they left the dining-room, it was settled that John Eames should be taught his lesson and should seek both Mrs Arabin and Dr Arabin on their travels.

CHAPTER 41

Grace Crawley at home

On the morning after his return from London Mr Crawley showed symptoms of great fatigue, and his wife implored him to remain in bed. But this he would not do. He would get up, and go out down to the brickfields. He had specially bound himself, – he said, to see that the duties of the parish did not suffer by being left in his hands. The bishop had endeavoured to place them in other hands, but he had persisted in retaining them. As he had done so he could allow no weariness of his own to interfere, – and especially no weariness induced by labours undertaken on his own behalf. The day in the week had come round on which it was his wont to visit the brickmakers, and he would visit them. So he dragged himself out of his bed and went forth amidst the cold storm of a harsh wet March morning. His wife well knew when she heard his first word on that morning that one of those terrible moods had come upon him which made her doubt whether she ought to allow him to go anywhere alone. Latterly there had been some improvement in his mental health. Since the day of his encounter with the bishop and Mrs Proudie, though he had been as stubborn as ever, he had been less apparently unhappy, less depressed in spirits. And the journey to London had done him good. His wife had congratulated herself on finding him able to set about his work like another man, and he himself had experienced a renewal, if not of hope, at any rate, of courage, which had given him a comfort which he had recognized. His common-sense had not been very striking in his interview with Mr Toogood, but yet he had talked more rationally then and had given a better account of the matter in hand than could have been expected from him for some weeks previously. But now that the labour was over, a reaction had come upon him, and he went away from his house having hardly spoken a word to his wife after the speech which he made about his duty to his parish.

I think that at this time nobody saw clearly the working of his mind, – not even his wife, who studied it very closely, who gave him credit for all his high qualities, and who had gradually learned to acknowledge to herself that she must distrust his judgment in many things. She knew that he was good and yet weak, that he was afflicted by false pride and supported by true pride, that his intellect was still very bright, yet so dismally obscured on many sides as almost to justify people in saying that he was mad. She knew that he was almost a saint, and yet almost a castaway through vanity and hatred of those above him. But she did not know that he knew all this of himself also. She did not comprehend that he should be hourly telling himself that people were calling him mad and were so calling him with truth. It did not occur to her that he could see her insight into him. She doubted as to the way in which he had got the cheque, – never imagining, however, that he had wilfully stolen it; – thinking that his mind had been so much astray as to admit of his finding it and using it without wilful guilt, – thinking also, alas, that a man who could so act was hardly fit for such duties as those which were entrusted to him. But she did not dream that this was precisely his own idea of his own state and of his own position; – that he was always inquiring of himself whether he was not mad; whether, if mad, he was not bound to lay down his office; that he was ever taxing himself with improper hostility to the bishop, – never forgetting for a moment his wrath against the bishop and the bishop's wife, still comforting himself with his triumph over the bishop and the bishop's wife, – but, for all that, accusing himself of a heavy sin and proposing to himself to go to the palace and there humbly to relinquish his clerical authority. Such a course of action he was proposing to himself, but not with any realized idea that he would so act. He was as a man who walks along a river's bank thinking of suicide, calculating how best he might kill himself, – whether the river does not offer an opportunity too good to be neglected, telling himself that for many reasons he had better do so, suggesting to himself that the water is pleasant and cool, and that his ears would soon be deaf to the harsh noises of the world, – but yet knowing, or thinking that he knows, that he never will kill himself. So it was with Mr Crawley. Though his imagination pictured to himself the whole scene, – how he would humble himself to the ground as he acknowledged his unfitness, how he would endure the small-voiced triumph of the little bishop, how, from the abjectness of his own humility, even from the ground on which he would be crouching, he would rebuke the loud-mouthed triumph of the bishop's wife; though there was no touch wanting to the picture which he drew, – he did not really propose to himself to commit his professional suicide. His wife, too, had considered whether it might be in truth becoming that he should give up his clerical duties, at any rate for a while; but she had never thought that the idea was present in his mind also.

Mr Toogood had told him that people would say that he was mad; and Mr Toogood had looked at him, when he declared for the second time that he had no knowledge whence the cheque had come to him, as though his words were to be regarded as the words of some sick child. 'Mad!' he said to himself, as he walked home from the station that night. 'Well; yes; and what if I am mad? When I think of all that I have endured my wonder is that I should not have been mad sooner.' And then he prayed, – yes, prayed, that in his madness the Devil might not be too strong for him, and that he might be preserved from some terrible sin of murder or violence. What, if the idea should come to him in his madness that it would be well for him to slay his wife and his children? Only that was wanting to make him of all men the most unfortunate.

He went down among the brickmakers on the following morning, leaving the house almost without a morsel of food, and he remained at Hoggle End for the greater part of the day. There were sick persons there with whom he prayed, and then he sat talking with rough men while they ate their dinners, and he read passages from the Bible to women while they washed their husbands' clothes. And for a while he sat with a little girl in his lap teaching the child her alphabet. If it were possible for him he would do his duty. He would spare himself in nothing, though he might suffer even to fainting. And on this occasion he did suffer, – almost to fainting, for as he returned home in the afternoon he was forced to lean from time to time against the banks on the road-side, while the cold sweat of weakness trickled down his face, in order that he might recover strength to go on a few yards. But he would persevere. If God would but leave to him mind enough for his work, he would go on. No personal suffering should deter him. He told himself that there had been men in the world whose sufferings were sharper even than his own. Of what sort had been the life of the man who had stood for years on the top of a pillar?* But then the man on the pillar had been honoured by all around him. And thus, though he had thought of the man on the pillar to encourage himself by remembering how lamentable had been that man's suffering, he came to reflect that after all his own sufferings were perhaps keener than those of the man on the pillar.

When he reached home, he was very ill. There was no doubt about it then. He staggered to his arm-chair, and stared at his wife first, then smiled at her with a ghastly smile. He trembled all over, and when food was brought to him he could not eat it. Early on the next morning the doctor was by his bedside, and before that evening came he was delirious. He had been at intervals in this state for nearly two days, when Mrs Crawley wrote to Grace, and though she had restrained herself from telling everything, she had written with sufficient strength to bring Grace at once to her father's bedside.

He was not so ill when Grace arrived but that he knew her, and he seemed to receive some comfort from her coming. Before she had been in the house an hour she was reading Greek to him, and there was no wandering in his mind as to the due emphasis to be given to the plaints of the injured heroines, or as to the proper meaning of choruses. And as he lay with his head half buried in the pillows, he shouted out long passages, lines from tragic plays by the score, and for a while seemed to have all the enjoyment of a dear old pleasure placed newly within his reach. But he tired of this after a while, and then, having looked round to see that his wife was not in the room, he began to talk of himself.

'So you have been to Allington, my dear?'

'Yes, papa.'

'Is it a pretty place?'

'Yes, papa; – very pretty.'

'And they were good to you?'

'Yes, papa; – very good.'

'Had they heard anything there about – me; of this trial that is to come on?'

'Yes, papa; they had heard of it.'

'And what did they say? You need not think that you will shock me by telling me. They cannot say worse there than people have said here, – or think worse.'

'They don't think at all badly of you at Allington, papa.'

'But they must think badly of me if the magistrates were right?'

'They suppose that there has been a mistake; – as we all think.'

'They do not try men at the assizes for mistakes.'

'That you have been mistaken, I mean; – and the magistrates mistaken.'

'Both cannot have been mistaken, Grace.'

'I don't know how to explain myself, papa; but we all know that it is very sad, and are quite sure that you have never meant for one moment to do anything that was wrong.'

'But people when they are, – you know what I mean, Grace; when they are not themselves, – do things that are wrong without meaning it.' Then he paused, while she remained standing by him with her hand on the back of his. She was looking at his face, which had been turned towards her while they were reading together, but which now was so far moved that she knew that his eyes could not be fixed upon hers. 'Of course if the bishop orders it, it shall be so,' he said. 'It is quite enough for me that he is the bishop.'

'What has the bishop ordered, papa?'

'Nothing at all. It is she who does it. He has given no opinion about it. Of course not. He has none to give. It is the woman. You go and tell her from me that in such a matter I will not obey the word of any woman living. Go at once, when I tell you.'

Then she knew that he father's mind was wandering, and she knelt down by the bedside, still holding his hand.

'Grace,' he said.

'Yes, papa, I am here.'

'Why do you not do what I tell you?' And he sat upright in his bed. 'I suppose you are afraid of the woman?'

'I should be afraid of her, dear papa.'

'I was not afraid of her. When she spoke to me, I would have nothing to say to her; – not a word; not a word; – not a word.' As he said this he waved his hands about. 'But as for him, – if it must be, it must. I know I'm not fit for it. Of course I am not. Who is? But what has he ever done that he should be a dean? I beat him at everything; almost at everything. He got the Newdegate, and that was about all. Upon my word I think that was all.'

'But Dr Arabin loves you truly, dear papa.'

'Love me! psha! Does he ever come here to tea, as he used to do? No! I remember buttering toast for him down on my knees before the fire, because he liked it, – and keeping all the cream for him. He should have had my heart's blood if he wanted it. But now; – look at his books, Grace. It's the outside of them he cares about. They are all gilt, but I doubt if he ever reads. As for her, – I will not allow any woman to tell me my duty. No; – by my Maker; not even your mother, who is the best of women. And as for her, with her little husband dangling at her apron-strings, as a call-whistle to be blown into when she pleases, – that she would dare to teach me my duty! No! The men in the jury-box may decide it how they will. If they can believe a plain story, let them! If not, – let them do as they please. I am ready to bear it all.'

'Dear papa, you are tired. Will you not try to sleep?'

'Tell Mrs Proudie what I say; and as for Arabin's money, I took it. I know I took it. What would you have had me do? Shall I – see them – all – starve?' Then he fell back upon his bed and did sleep.

The next day he was better, and insisted upon getting out of bed, and on sitting in his old arm-chair over the fire. And the Greek books were again had out; and Grace, not at all unwillingly, was put through her facings. 'If you don't take care, my dear,' he said,

'Jane will beat you yet. She understands the force of the verbs better than you do.'

'I am very glad that she is doing so well, papa. I am sure I shall not begrudge her her superiority.'

'Ah, but you should begrudge it her!' Jane was sitting by at the time, and the two sisters were holding each other by the hand. 'Always to be best; – always to be in advance of others. That should be your motto.'

'But we can't both be best, papa,' said Jane.

'You can both strive to be best. But Grace has the better voice. I remember when I knew the whole of the Antigone by heart. You girls should see which can learn it first.'

'It would take such a long time,' said Jane.

'You are young, and what can you do better with your leisure hours? Fie, Jane! I did not expect that from you. When I was learning it I had eight or nine pupils, and read an hour a day with each of them. But I think that nobody works now as they used to work then. Where is your mamma? Tell her I think I could get out as far as Mrs Cox's, if she would help me to dress.' Soon after this he was in bed again, and his head was wandering; but still they knew that he was better than he had been.

'You are more of a comfort to your papa than I can be,' said Mrs Crawley to her eldest daughter that night as they sat together, when everybody else was in bed.

'Do not say that, mamma. Papa does not think so.'

'I cannot read Greek plays to him as you can do. I can only nurse him in his illness and endeavour to do my duty. Do you know, Grace, that I am beginning to fear that he half doubts me?'

'Oh, mamma!'

'That he half doubts me, and is half afraid of me. He does not think as he used to do, that I am altogether, heart and soul, on his side. I can see it in his eye as he watches me. He thinks that I am tired of him, – tired of his sufferings, tired of his poverty, tired of the evil which men say of him. I am not sure but what he thinks that I suspect him.'

'Of what, mamma?'

'Of general unfitness for the work he has to do. The feeling is not strong as yet, but I fear that he will teach himself to think that he has an enemy of his hearth, – not a friend. It will be the saddest mistake he ever made.'

'He told me to-day that you were the best of women. Those were his very words.'

'Were they, my dear? I am glad at least that he should say so to

you. He has been better since you came; – a great deal better. For
one day I was frightened; but I am sorry now that I sent for you.'

'I am so glad mamma; so very glad.'

'You were happy there, – and comfortable. And if they were glad
to have you, why should I have brought you away?'

'But I was not happy; – even though they were very good to me.
How could I be happy there when I was thinking of you and papa
and Jane here at home? Whatever there is here, I would sooner
share it with you than be anywhere else, – while this trouble lasts.'

'My darling! – it is a great comfort to see you again.'

'Only that I knew that one less in the house would be a saving to
you I should not have gone. When there is unhappiness, people
should stay together; – shouldn't they, mamma?' They were sitting
quite close to each other, on an old sofa in a small upstairs room,
from which a door opened into the larger chamber in which Mr
Crawley was lying. It had been arranged between them that on this
night Mrs Crawley should remain with her husband, and that Grace
should go to her bed. It was now past one o'clock, but she was still
there, clinging to her mother's side, with her mother's arm drawn
round her. 'Mamma,' she said, when they had both been silent for
some ten minutes, 'I have got something to tell you.'

'To-night?'

'Yes, mamma; to-night, if you will let me.'

'But you promised that you would go to bed. You were up all
last night.'

'I am not sleepy, mamma.'

'Of course you shall tell me what you please, dearest. Is it a
secret? Is it something I am not to repeat?'

'You must say how that ought to be, mamma. I shall not tell it to
any one else.'

'Well, dear?'

'Sit comfortably, mamma; – there; like that, and let me have
your hand. It's a terrible story to have to tell.'

'A terrible story, Grace?'

'I mean that you must not draw away from me. I shall want to
feel that you are quite close to me. Mamma, while I was at
Allington, Major Grantly came there.'

'Did he, my dear?'

'Yes, mamma.'

'Did he know them before?'

'No, mamma; not at the Small House. But he came there – to see
me. He asked me – to be his wife. Don't move, mamma.'

'My darling child! I won't move, dearest. Well; and what did
you say to him? God bless him, at any rate. May God bless him,

because he has seen with a true eye, and felt with a noble instinct. It is something, Grace, to have been wooed by such a man at such a time.'

'Mamma, it did make me feel proud; it did.'

'You had known him well before, – of course? I knew that you and he were friends, Grace.'

'Yes, we were friends. I always liked him. I used not to know what to think about him. Miss Anne Prettyman told me that it would be so; and once before I thought so myself.'

'And had you made up your mind what to say to him?'

'Yes, I had then. But I did not say it.'

'Did not say what you had made up your mind to say?'

'That was before all this had happened to papa.'

'I understand you, dearest.'

'When Miss Anne Prettyman told me that I should be ready with my answer, and when I saw that Miss Prettyman herself used to let him come to the house and seemed to wish that I should see him when he came, and when he once was – so very gentle and kind, and when he said that he wanted me to love Edith,— Oh, mamma!'

'Yes, darling, I know. Of course you loved him.'

'Yes, mamma. And I do love him. How could one not love him?'

'I love him, – for loving you.'

'But, mamma, one is bound not to do a harm to any one that one loves. So when he came to Allington I told him that I could not be his wife.'

'Did you, my dear?'

'Yes; I did. Was I not right? Ought I to go to him to bring a disgrace upon all the family, just because he is so good that he asks me? Shall I injure him because he wants to do me a service?'

'If he loves you, Grace, the service he will require will be your love in return.'

'That is all very well, mamma, – in books; but I do not believe it in reality. Being in love is very nice, and in poetry they make it out to be everything. But I do not think I should make Major Grantly happy if when I became his wife his own father and mother would not see him. I know I should be so wretched, myself, that I could not live.

'But would it be so?'

'Yes; – I think it would. And the archdeacon is very rich, and can leave all his money away from Major Grantly if he pleases. Think what I should feel if I were the cause of Edith losing her fortune!'

'But why do you suppose these terrible things?'

'I have a reason for supposing them. This must be a secret. Miss Anne Prettyman wrote to me.'

'I wish Miss Anne Prettyman's hand had been in the fire.'

'No, mamma; no; she was right. Would not I have wished, do you think, to have learned all the truth about the matter before I answered him? Besides, it made no difference. I could have made no other answer while papa is under such a terrible ban. It is no time for us to think of being in love. We have got to love each other. Isn't it so, mamma?' The mother did not answer in words, but slipping down on her knees before her child threw her arms round her girl's body in a close embrce. 'Dear mamma; dearest mamma; this is what I wanted; – that you should love me!'

'Love you, my angel!'

'And trust me; – and that we should understand each other, and stand close by each other. We can do so much to comfort one another; – but we cannot comfort other people.'

'He must know that best himself, Grace; – but what did he say more to you?'

'I don't think he said anything more.'

'He just left you then?'

'He said one thing more.'

'And what was that?'

'He said; – but he had no right to say it.'

'What was it, dear?'

'That he knew I loved him, and that therefore— But, mamma, do not think of that. I will never be his wife, – never, in opposition to his family.'

'But he did not take your answer?'

'He must take it, mamma. He shall take it. If he can be stubborn, so can I. If he knows how to think of me more than himself, I can think of him and Edith more than of myself. That is not quite all, mamma. Then he wrote to me. There is his letter.'

Mrs Crawley read the letter. 'I suppose you answered it?'

'Yes, I answered it. It was very bad, my letter. I should think after that he will never want to have anything more to say to me. I tried for two days, but I could not write a nice letter.'

'But what did you say?'

'I don't in the least remember. It does not in the least signify now, but it was such a bad letter.'

'I daresay it was very nice.'

'It was terribly stiff, and all about a gentleman.'

'All about a gentleman! What do you mean, my dear?'

'Gentleman is such a frightful word to have to use to a gentleman; but I did not know what else to say. Mamma, if you please, we won't talk about it; – not about the letter I mean. As for him,

I'll talk about him for ever if you like it. I don't mean to be a bit broken-hearted.'

'It seems to me that he is a gentleman.'

'Yes, mamma, that he is; and it is that which makes me so proud. When I think of it, I can hardly hold myself. But now I've told you everything, and I'll go away, and go to bed.'

CHAPTER 42

Mr Toogood travels professionally

Mr Toogood paid another visit to Barsetshire, in order that he might get a little further information which he thought would be necessary before despatching his nephew upon the traces of Dean Arabin and his wife. He went down to Barchester after his work was over by an evening train, and put himself up at 'The Dragon of Wantly,' intending to have the whole of the next day for his work. Mr Walker had asked him to come and take a return pot-luck dinner with Mrs Walker at Silverbridge; and this he had said that he would do. After having 'rummaged about for tidings' in Barchester, as he called it, he would take the train for Silverbridge, and would get back to town in time for business on the third day. 'One day won't be much, you know,' he said to his partner, as he made half an apology for absenting himself on business which was not to be in any degree remunerative. 'That sort of thing is very well when one does it without any expense,' said Crump. 'So it is,' said Toogood; 'and the expense won't make it any worse.' He had made up his mind, and it was not probable that anything Mr Crump might say would deter him.

He saw John Eames before he started. 'You'll be ready this day week, will you?' John Eames promised that he would. 'It will cost you some forty pounds, I should say. By George, – if you have to go on to Jerusalem, it will cost you more.' In answer to this, Johnny pleaded that it would be as good as any other tour to him. He would see the world. 'I'll tell you what,' said Toogood; 'I'll pay half. Only you mustn't tell Crump. And it will be quite as well not to tell Maria.' But Johnny would hear nothing of this scheme. He would pay the entire cost of his own journey. He had lots of money, he said, and would like nothing better. 'Then I'll run down,' said Toogood, and 'rummage up what tidings I can. As for writing to the dean, what's the good of writing to a man when you don't know where he is? Business letters always lie at hotels for two months, and then come back with double postage. From all I can hear, you'll stumble on her before you find him. If we do nothing else but bring him back, it will be a great thing to have the support of such a friend in the court. A Barchester jury won't like to find a man guilty who is hand-and-glove with the dean.'

Mr Toogood reached the 'Dragon' about eleven o'clock, and allowed the boots to give him a pair of slippers and a candlestick. But he would not go to bed just at that moment. He would go into the coffee-room first, and have a glass of hot brandy-and-water. So the hot brandy-and-water was brought to him, and a cigar, and as he smoked and drank he conversed with the waiter. The man was a waiter of the ancient class, a gray-haired waiter, with seedy clothes, and a dirty towel under his arm; not a dapper waiter, with black shiny hair, and dressed like a guest for a dinner-party. There are two distinct classes of waiters, and as far as I have been able to perceive, the special status of the waiter in question cannot be decided by observations of the class of waiter to which he belongs. In such a town as Barchester you may find the old waiter with the dirty towel in the head inn, or in the second-class inn, and so you may the dapper waiter. Or you may find both in each, and not know which is senior waiter and which junior waiter. But for service I always prefer the old waiter with the dirty towel, and I find it more easy to satisfy him in the matter of sixpences when my relations with the inn come to an end.

'Have you been here long, John?' said Mr Toogood.

'A goodish many years, sir.'

'So I thought, by the look of you. One can see that you belong in a way to the place. You do a good deal of business here, I suppose, at this time of the year?'

'Well, sir, pretty fair. The house ain't what it used to be, sir.'

'Times are bad at Barchester, – are they?'

'I don't know much about the times. It's the people is worse than the times, I think. They used to like to have a little bit of dinner now and again at a hotel; – and a drop of something to drink after it.'

'And don't they like it now?'

'I think they like it well enough, but they don't do it. I suppose it's their wives as don't let 'em come out and enjoy themselves. There used to be the Goose and Glee club; – that was once a month. They've gone and clean done away with themselves, – that club has. There's old Bumpter in the High Street, – he's the last of the old Geese. They died off, you see, and when Mr Biddle died they wouldn't choose another president. A club for having dinner, sir, ain't nothing without a president.'

'I suppose not.'

'And there's the Freemasons. They must meet, you know, sir, in course, because of the dooties. But if you'll believe me, sir, they don't so much as wet their whistles. They don't indeed. It always used to be a supper, and that was once a month. Now they pays a rent for the use of the room! Who is to get a living out of that, sir? – not in the way of a waiter, that is.'

'If that's the way things are going on I suppose the servants leave their places pretty often?'

'I don't know about that, sir. A man may do a deal worse than "The Dragon of Wantly." Them as goes away to better themselves, often worses themselves, as I call it. I've seen a good deal of that.'

'And you stick to the old shop?'

'Yes, sir; I've been here fifteen year, I think it is. There's a many goes away, as doesn't go out of their own heads, you know, sir.'

'They get the sack, you mean?'

'There's words between them and master, – or more likely, missus. That's where it is. Servants is so foolish. I often tell 'em how wrong folks are to say that soft words butter no parsnips, and hard words break no bones.'

'I think you've lost some of the old hands here since this time last year, John?'

'You knows the house then, sir?'

'Well; – I've been here before.'

'There was four of them went, I think it's just about twelve months back, sir.'

'There was a man in the yard I used to know, and last time I was down here, I found that he was gone.'

'There was one of 'em out of the yard, and two out of the house. Master and them had got to very high words. There was poor Scuttle, who had been post-boy at "The Compasses" before he came here.'

'He went away to New Zealand, didn't he?'

'B'leve he did, sir; or to some foreign parts. And Anne, as was under-chambermaid here; she went with him, fool as she was. They got theirselves married and went off, and he was well nigh as old as me. But seems he'd saved a little money, and that goes a long way with any girl.'

'Was he the man who drove Mr Soames that day the cheque was lost?' Mr Toogood asked this question perhaps a little too abruptly. At any rate he obtained no answer to it. The waiter said he knew nothing about Mr Soames, or the cheque, and the lawyer suspecting that the waiter was suspecting him, finished his brandy-and-water and went to bed.

Early on the following morning he observed that he was specially regarded by a shabby-looking man, dressed in black, but in a black suit that was very old, with a red nose, whom he had seen in the hotel on the preceding day; and he learned that this man was a cousin of the landlord, – one Dan Stringer, – who acted as a clerk in the hotel bar. He took an opportunity also of saying a word to Mr Stringer the landlord, – whom he found to be a somewhat forlorn and gouty individual, seated on cushions in a little parlour behind the bar. After breakfast he went out, and having twice walked round the Cathedral close and inspected the front of the palace and looked up at the windows of the prebendaries' houses, he knocked at the door of the deanery. The dean and Mrs Arabin were on the Continent, he was told. Then he asked for Mr Harding, having learned that Mr Harding was Mrs Arabin's father, and that he lived at the deanery. Mr Harding was at home, but was not very well, the servant said. Mr Toogood, however, persevered, sending up his card, and saying that he wished to have a few minutes' conversation with Mr Harding on very particular business. He wrote a word upon his card before giving it to the servant, – 'about Mr Crawley.' In a few minutes he was shown into the library, and had hardly time, while looking at the shelves, to remember what Mr Crawley had said of his anger at the beautiful bindings, before an old man, very thin and very pale, shuffled into the room. He stooped a good deal, and his black clothes were very loose about his shrunken limbs. He was not decrepit, nor did he seem to be one who had advanced to extreme old age; but yet he shuffled rather than walked, hardly raising his feet from the ground. Mr Toogood, as he came forward to meet him, thought that he had never seen a sweeter face. There was very much of melancholy in it, of that soft sadness of age which seems to acknowledge, and in some sort to regret, the waning oil of life; but the regret to be read in such faces has in it nothing of the bitterness of grief; there is no repining that the end has come, but simply a touch of sorrow that so much that is dear must be left behind. Mr Harding shook hands with his visitor, and invited him to sit down, and then seated himself, folding his hands together over his knees, and he said a few words in a very low voice as to the absence of his daughter and of the dean.

'I hope you will excuse my troubling you,' said Mr Toogood.

'It is no trouble at all, – if I could be of any use. I don't know whether it is proper, but may I ask whether you call as, – as, – as a friend of Mr Crawley's ?'

'Altogether as a friend, Mr Harding.'

'I'm glad of that; though of course I am well aware that the gentlemen engaged on the prosecution must do their duty. Still, – I don't know, – somehow I would rather not hear them speak of this poor gentleman before the trial.'

'You know Mr Crawley, then?'

'Very slightly, – very slightly indeed. He is a gentleman not much given to social habits, and has been but seldom here. But he is an old friend whom my son-in-law loves dearly.'

'I'm glad to hear you say that, Mr Harding. Perhaps before I go any further I ought to tell you that Mrs Crawley and I are first-cousins.'

'Oh, indeed. Then you are a friend.'

'I never saw him in my life till a few days ago. He is very queer you know, – very queer indeed. I'm a lawyer, Mr Harding, practising in London; – an attorney, that is.' At each separate announcement Mr Harding bowed, and when Toogood named his special branch of his profession Mr Harding bowed lower than before, as though desirous of showing that he had great respect for attorneys. 'And of course I'm anxious, if only out of respect for the family, that my wife's cousin should pull through this little difficulty, if possible.'

'And for the sake of the poor man himself too, and for his wife, and his children; – and for the sake of the cloth.'

'Exactly; taking it all together it's such a pity, you know. I think, Mr Harding, he can hardly have intended to steal the money.'

'I'm sure he did not.'

'It's very hard to be sure of anybody, Mr Harding; – very hard.'

'I feel quite sure that he did not. He has been a most pious, hard-working clergyman. I cannot bring myself to think that he is guilty. What does the Latin proverb say? "No one of a sudden becomes most base."'*

'But the temptation, Mr Harding, was very strong. He was awfully badgered about his debts. That butcher in Silverbridge was playing the mischief with him.'

'All the butchers in Barsetshire could not make an honest man steal money, and I think that Mr Crawley is an honest man. You'll excuse me for being a little hot about one of my own order.'

'Why; he's my cousin, – or rather, my wife's. But the fact is, Mr Harding, we must get hold of the dean as soon as possible; and I'm going to send a gentleman after him.'

'To send a gentleman after him?' said Mr Harding, almost in dismay.

'Yes; I think that will be best.'

'I'm afraid he'll have to go a long way, Mr Toogood.'

'The dean, I'm told is in Jerusalem.'

'I'm afraid he is, – or on his journey there. He's to be there for the Easter week, and Sunday week will be Easter Sunday. But why should the gentleman want to go to Jerusalem after the dean ?'

Then Mr Toogood explained as well as he was able that the dean might have something to say on the subject which would serve Mr Crawley's defence. 'We shouldn't leave any stone unturned,' said Mr Toogood. 'As far as I can judge, Crawley still thinks, – or half thinks, – that he got the cheque from your son-in-law.' Mr Harding shook his head sorrowfully. 'I'm not saying he did, you know,' continued Mr Toogood. 'I can't see myself how it is possible; – but still, we ought not to leave any stone unturned. And Mrs Arabin, – can you tell me at all where we shall find her ?'

'Has she anything to do with it, Mr Toogood ?'

'I can't quite say that she has, but it's just possible. As I said before, Mr Harding, we mustn't leave a stone unturned. They're not expected here till the end of April ?'

'About the 25th or 26th, I think.'

'And the assizes are the 28th. The judges come into the city on that day. It will be too late to wait till then. We must have our defence ready you know. Can you say where my friend will find Mrs Arabin ?'

Mr Harding began nursing his knee, patting it and being very tender to it, as he sat meditating with his head on one side, – meditating not so much as to the nature of his answer as to that of the question. Could it be necessary that any emissary from a lawyer's office should be sent after his daughter ? He did not like the idea of his Eleanor being disturbed by questions as to a theft. Though she had been twice married and had a son who was now nearly a man, still she was his Eleanor. But if it was necessary on Mr Crawley's behalf, of course it must be done. 'Her last address was at Paris, sir ; but I think she has gone on to Florence. She has friends there, and she purposes to meet the dean at Venice on his return.' Then Mr Harding turned the table and wrote on a card his daughter's address.

'I suppose Mrs Arabin must have heard of the affair ?' said Mr Toogood.

'She had not done so when she last wrote. I mentioned it to her the other day, before I knew that she had left Paris. If my letters and her sister's letters have been sent on to her, she must know it now.'

Then Mr Toogood got up to take his leave. 'You will excuse me for troubling you, I hope, Mr Harding.'

'Oh, sir, pray do not mention that. It is no trouble, if one could only be of any service.'

'One can always try to be of service. In these affairs so much is to be done by rummaging about, as I always call it. There have been many theatrical managers, you know, Mr Harding, who have usually made up their pieces according to the dresses they have happened to have in their wardrobes.'

.'Have there, indeed, now? I never should have thought of that.'

'And we lawyers have to do the same thing.'

'Not with your clothes, Mr Toogood?'

'Not exactly with our clothes; – but with our information.'

'I do not quite understand you, Mr Toogood.'

'In preparing a defence we have to rummage about and get up what we can. If we can't find anything that suits us exactly, we are obliged to use what we do find as well as we can. I remember, when I was a young man, an ostler was to be tried for stealing some oats in the Borough; and he did steal them too, and sold them at a rag-shop regularly. The evidence against him was a plain as a pike-staff. All I could find out was that on a certain day a horse had trod on the fellow's foot. So we put it to the jury whether the man could walk as far as the rag-shop with a bag of oats when he was dead lame; – and we got him off.'

'Did you though?' said Mr Harding.

'Yes, we did.'

'And he was guilty?'

'He had been at it regularly for months.'

'Dear, dear, dear! Wouldn't it have been better to have had him punished for the fault, – gently; so as to warn him of the consequences of such doings?'

'Our business was to get him off, – and we got him off. It's my business to get my cousin's husband off, if I can, and we must do it, by hook or crook. It's a very difficult piece of work, because he won't let us employ a barrister. However, I shall have one in the court and say nothing to him about it at all. Good-by, Mr Harding. As you say, it would be a thousand pities that a clergyman should be convicted of a theft; – and one so well connected too.'

Mr Harding, when he was left alone, began to turn the matter over in his mind and to reflect whether the thousand pities of which Mr Toogood had spoken appertained to the conviction of the criminal, or the doing of the crime. 'If he did steal the money I suppose he ought to be punished, let him be ever so much a clergyman,' said Mr Harding to himself. But yet, – how terrible it would be! Of clergymen convicted of fraud in London he had often heard; but nothing of the kind had ever disgraced the diocese to which he belonged since he had known it. He could not teach himself to hope that Mr Crawley should be acquitted if Mr Crawley were guilty; – but he could teach himself to believe that Mr Crawley was innocent. Something of a doubt had crept across his mind as he talked to the lawyer. Mr Toogood, though Mrs Crawley was his cousin, seemed to believe that the money had been stolen; and Mr Toogood as a lawyer ought to understand such matters better than an old secluded clergyman in Barchester. But, nevertheless, Mr Toogood might be wrong; and Mr Harding succeeded in satisfying himself at last that he could not be doing harm in thinking that Mr Toogood was wrong. When he had made up his mind on this matter he sat down and wrote the following letter, which he addressed to his daughter at the post-office in Florence: –

Deanery, March – , 186–.

Dearest Nelly, –

When I wrote on Tuesday I told you about poor Mr Crawley, that he was the clergyman in Barsetshire of whose misfortune you read an account in Galignani's Messenger, – and I think Susan must have written about it also, because everybody here is talking of nothing else, and because, of course, we know how strong a regard the dean has for Mr Crawley. But since that something has occurred which makes me write to you again, – at once. A gentleman has just been here, and has indeed only this moment left me, who tells me that he is an attorney in London, and that he is nearly related to Mrs Crawley. He seems to be a very good-natured man, and I daresay he understands his business as a lawyer. His name is Toogood, and he has come down as he says to get evidence to help the poor gentleman on his trial. I cannot understand how this should be necessary, because it seems to me that the evidence should all be wanted on the other side. I cannot for a moment suppose that a clergyman and a gentleman such as Mr Crawley should have stolen money, and if he is innocent I cannot understand why all this trouble should be necessary to prevent a jury finding him guilty.

Mr Toogood came here because he wanted to see the dean, – and you also. He did not explain, as far as I can remember, why he wanted to see you; but he said it would be necessary, and that he was going to send off a messenger to find you first, and the dean afterwards. It has something to do with the money which was given to Mr Crawley last year, and which, if I remember right, was your present. But of course Mr Toogood could not have known anything about that. However, I gave him the address, – poste restante, Florence, – and I daresay that somebody will make you out before long, if you are still stopping at Florence. I did not like letting him go without telling you about it, as I thought that a lawyer's coming to you would startle you.

The bairns are quite well, as I told you in my other letter, and Miss Jones says that little Elly is as good as gold. They are with me every morning and evening, and behave like darling angels, as they are. Posy is my own little jewel always. You may be quite sure I do nothing to spoil them.

God bless you, dearest Nelly,
Your most affectionate father,
Septimus Harding.

After this he wrote another letter to his other daughter, Mrs Grantly, telling her also of Mr Toogood's visit; and then he spent the remainder of the day thinking over the gravity of the occurrence. How terrible would it be if a beneficed clergyman in the diocese should really be found guilty of theft by a jury from the city! And then he had always heard so high a character of this man from his son-in-law. No, – it was impossible to believe that Mr Crawley had in truth stolen a cheque for twenty pounds!

Mr Toogood could get no other information in Barchester, and went on to Silverbridge early in the afternoon. He was half disposed to go by Hogglestock and look up his cousin, whom he had never seen, and his cousin's husband, upon whose business he was now intent; but on reflection he feared that he might do more harm than good. He had quite appreciated the fact that Mr Crawley was not like other men. 'The man's not above half-saved,' he had said to his wife, – meaning thereby to insinuate that the poor clergyman was not in full possession of his wits. And, to tell the truth of Mr Toogood, he was a little afraid of his relative. There was a something in Mr Crawley's manner, in spite of his declared poverty, and in spite also of his extreme humility, which seemed to announce that he expected to be obeyed when he spoke on any point with authority. Mr Toogood had not forgotten the tone in which Mr Crawley had said to him, 'Sir, this thing you cannot do.' And he thought that, upon the whole, he had better not go to Hogglestock on this occasion.

When at Silverbridge, he began at once to 'rummage about.' His chief rummaging was to be done at Mr Walker's table; but before dinner he had time to call upon the magistrate's clerk, and ask a few questions as to the proceedings at the sitting from which Mr Crawley was committed. He found a very taciturn old man, who was nearly as difficult to deal with in any rummaging process as a porcupine. But, nevertheless, at last he reached a state of conversation which was not absolutely hostile. Mr Toogood pleaded that he was the poor man's cousin, – pleaded that, as the family lawyer, he was naturally the poor man's protector at such a time as the present, – pleaded also that as the poor man was so very poor, no one else could come forward on his behalf, – and in this way somewhat softened the hard sharpness of the old porcupine's quills. But after all this, there was very little to be learned from the old porcupine. 'There was not a magistrate on the bench,' he said, 'who had any doubt that the evidence was sufficient to justify them in sending the case to the assizes. They had all regretted,' – the porcupine said in his sofest moment, – 'that the gentleman had come there without a legal adviser.' 'Ah, that's been the mischief of it all!' said Mr Toogood, dashing his hand against the porcupine's mahogany table. 'But the facts were so strong, Mr Toogood!' 'Nobody there to soften 'em down, you know,' said Mr Toogood, shaking his head. Very little more than this was learned from the porcupine; and then Mr Toogood went away, and prepared for Mr Walker's dinner.

Mr Walker had invited Dr Tempest and Miss Anne Prettyman and Major Grantly to meet Mr Toogood, and had explained, in a manner intended to be half earnest and half jocose, that though Mr Toogood was an attorney, like himself, and was at this moment engaged in a noble way on behalf of his cousin's husband, without any idea of receiving back even the money which he would be out of pocket; still he wasn't quite, – not quite, you know – 'not quite so much of a gentleman as I am,' – Mr Walker would have said, had he spoken out freely that which he insinuated. But he contented himself with the emphasis he put upon the 'not quite,' which expressed his meaning fully. And Mr Walker was correct in his opinion of Mr Toogood. As regards the two attorneys I will not venture to say that either of them was not a 'perfect gentleman.' A perfect gentleman is a thing which I cannot define. But undoubtedly Mr Walker was a bigger man in his way than was Mr Toogood in his, and did habitually consort in the county of Barsetshire with men of higher standing than those with whom Mr Toogood associated in London.

It seemed to be understood that Mr Crawley was to be the general subject of conversation, and no one attempted to talk about anything else. Indeed, at this time, very little else was talked about in that part of the county; – not only because of the interest naturally attaching to the question of the suspected guilt of a parish clergyman, but because much had become lately known of Mr Crawley's character, and because it was known also that an internecine feud had arisen between him and the bishop. It had undoubtedly become the general opinion that Mr Crawley had picked up and used a cheque which was not his own; – that he had, in fact, stolen it; but there was, in spite of that belief, a general wish that he might be acquitted and left in his living. And when the tidings of Mr Crawley's victory over the bishop at the palace had become bruited about, popular sympathy went with the victor. The theft was, as it were, condoned, and people made excuses which were not always rational, but which were founded on the instincts of true humanity. And now the tidings of another stage in the battle, as fought against Mr Crawley by the bishop, had gone forth through the county, and men had heard that the rural dean was to be instructed to make inquiries which would be preliminary to proceedings against Mr Crawley in an ecclesiastical court. Dr Tempest, who was now about to meet Mr Toogood at Mr Walker's, was the rural dean to whom Mr Crawley would have to submit himself in any such inquiry; but Dr Tempest had not as yet received from the bishop any official order on the subject.

'We are so delighted to think that you have taken up your cousin's case,' said Mrs Walker to Mr Toogood, almost in a whisper.

'He is not just my cousin, himself,' said Mr Toogood, 'but of course it's all the same thing. And as to taking up his case, you see, my dear madam, he won't let me take it up.'

'I thought you had. I thought you were down here about it?'

'Only on the sly, Mrs Walker. He has such queer ideas that he will not allow a lawyer to be properly employed; and you can't conceive how hard that makes it. Do you know him, Mrs Walker?'

'We know his daughter Grace.' And then Mrs Walker whispered something further, which we may presume to have been an intimation that the gentleman opposite, – Major Grantly, – was supposed by some people to be very fond of Miss Grace Crawley.

'Quite a child, isn't she?' said Toogood, whose own daughter, now about to be married, was three or four years older than Grace.

'She's beyond being a child, I think. Of course she is young.'

'But I suppose this affair will knock all that on the head,' said the lawyer.

'I do not know how that may be; but they do say he is very much attached to her. The major is a man of family, and of course it would be very disagreeable if Mr Crawley were found guilty.'

'Very disagreeable, indeed; but, upon my word, Mrs Walker, I don't know what to say about it.'

'You think it will go against him, Mr Toogood?' Mr Toogood shook his head, and on seeing this, Mrs Walker sighed deeply.

'I can only say that I have heard nothing from the bishop as yet,' said Dr Tempest, after the ladies had left the room. 'Of course, if he thinks well to order it, the inquiry must be made.'

'But how long would it take?' asked Mr Walker.

'Three months, I should think, – or perhaps more. Of course Crawley would do all that he could to delay us, and I am not at all sure that we should be in any very great hurry ourselves.'

'Who are the "we", doctor?' said Mr Walker.

'I cannot make such an inquiry by myself, you know. I suppose the bishop would ask me to select two or four other clergymen to act with me. That's the usual way of doing it. But you may be quite sure of this, Walker; the assizes will be over, and the jury have found their verdict long before we have settled our preliminaries.'

'And what will be the good of your going on after that?'

'Only this good: – if the unfortunate man be convicted—'

'Which he won't,' said Mr Toogood, who thought it expedient to put on a bolder front in talking of the matter to the rural dean, than he had assumed in his whispered conversation with Mrs Walker.

'I hope not, with all my heart,' said the doctor. 'But, perhaps, for the sake of the argument, the supposition may be allowed to pass.'

'Certainly, sir,' said Mr Toogood. 'For the sake of the argument, it may pass.'

'If he be convicted, then, I suppose, there will be an end of the question. He would be sentenced for not less, I should say, than twelve months; and after that—'

'And would be as good a parson of Hogglestock when he came out of prison as when he went in,' said Mr Walker. 'The conviction and judgment in a civil court would not touch his temporality.'

'Certainly not,' said Mr Toogood.'

'Of course not,' said the doctor. 'We all know that; and in the event of Mr Crawley coming back to his parish it would be open to the bishop to raise the question as to his fitness for the duties.'

'Why shouldn't he be as fit as any one else?' said Mr Toogood.

'Simply because he would have been found to be a thief,' said the doctor. 'You must excuse me, Mr Toogood, but it's only for the sake of the argument.'

'I don't see what that has to do with it,' said Mr Toogood. 'He would have undergone his penalty.'

'It is preferable that a man who preaches from a pulpit should not have undergone such a penalty,' said the doctor. 'But in practice, under such circumstances, – which we none of us anticipate, Mr Toogood, – the living should no doubt be vacated. Mr Crawley would probably hardly wish to come back. The jury will do their work before we can do ours, – will do it on a much better base than any we can have; and, when they have done it, the thing ought to be finished. If the jury acquit him, the bishop cannot proceed any further. If he be found guilty I think that the resignation of the living must follow.'

'It is all spite, then, on the bishop's part?' said the major.

'Not at all,' said the doctor. 'The poor man is weak; that is all. He is driven to persecute because he cannot escape persecution himself. But it may really be a question whether his present proceeding is not right. If I were bishop I should wait till the trial was over; that is all.'

From this and from much more that was said during the evening on the same subject Mr Toogood gradually learned the position which Mr Crawley and the question of Mr Crawley's guilt really held in the county, and he returned to town resolved to go on with the case.

'I'll have a barrister down express, and I'll defend him in his own teeth,' he said to his wife. 'There'll be a scene in court, I daresay, and the man will call upon his own counsel to hold his tongue and shut up his brief; and, as far as I can see, counsel in such a case would have no alternative. But there would come an explanation, – how Crawley was too honourable to employ a man whom he could not pay, and there would be a romance, and it would all go down with the jury. One wants sympathy in such a case as that – not evidence.'

'And how much will it cost, Tom?' said Maris, dolefully.

'Only a trifle. We won't think of that yet. There's John Eames is going all the way to Jerusalem, out of his pocket.'

'But Johnny hasn't got twelve children, Tom.'

'One doesn't have a cousin in trouble every day,' said Toogood. 'And then you see there's something very pretty in the case. It's quite a pleasure getting it up.'

CHAPTER 43

Mr Crosbie goes into the City

'I've known the City now for more than ten years, Mr Crosbie, and
I never knew money to be so tight as it is at this moment. The best
commercial bills going can't be done under nine, and any other
kind of paper can't so much as get itself looked at.' Thus spoke Mr
Musselboro. He was seated in Dobbs Broughton's arm-chair in
Dobbs Broughton's room in Hook Court, on the hind legs of which
he was balancing himself comfortably; and he was communicating
his experience in City matters to our old friend, Adolphus Crosbie,
– of whom we may surmise that he would not have been there, at
that moment, in Hook Court, if things had been going well with
him. It was now past eleven o'clock, and he should have been at his
office at the West End. His position in his office was no doubt high
enough to place him beyond the reach of any special inquiry as to
such absences; but it is generally felt that when the Crosbies of the
West End have calls into the City about noon, things in the world
are not going well with them. The man who goes into the City to
look for money is generally one who does not know where to get
money when he wants it. Mr Musselboro on this occasion kept his
hat on his head, and there was something in the way in which he
balanced his chair which was in itself an offence to Mr Crosbie's
personal dignity. It was hardly as yet two months since Mr Dobbs
Broughton had assured him in that very room that there need not
be the slightest anxiety about his bill. Of course it could be renewed,
– the commission being duly paid. As Mr Dobbs Broughton
explained on that occasion, that was his business. There was
nothing he liked so much as renewing bills for such customers as
Mr Crosbie; and he was very candid at that meeting, explaining
how he did this branch of his business, raising money on his own
credit at four or five per cent, and lending it on his own judgment
at eight or nine. Mr Crosbie did not feel himself then called upon
to exclaim that what he was called upon to pay was about twelve,

perfectly understanding the comfort and grace of euphony; but he had turned it over in his mind, considering whether twelve per cent was not more than he ought to be mulcted for the accommodation he wanted. Now, at the moment, he would have been glad to get it from Mr Musselboro, without further words, for twenty.

Things had much changed with Adolphus Crosbie when he was driven to make morning visits to such a one as Mr Musselboro with the view of having a bill renewed for two hundred and fifty pounds. In his early life he had always had the merit of being a careful man as to money. In some other respects he had gone astray very foolishly, – as has been partly explained in our earlier chapters; but up to the date of his marriage with Lady Alexandrina De Courcy he had never had dealings in Hook Court or in any such locality. Money troubles had then come upon him. Lady Alexandrina, being the daughter of a countess, had high ideas; and when, very shortly after his marriage, he had submitted to a separation from his noble wife, he had found himself and his income to be tied up inextricably in the hands of one Mr Mortimer Gazebee, a lawyer who had married one of his wife's sisters. It was not that Mr Gazebee was dishonest; nor did Crosbie suspect him of dishonesty; but the lawyer was so wedded to the interest of the noble family with which he was connected, that he worked for them all as an inferior spider might be supposed to work, which, from the infirmity of its nature, was compelled by its instincts to be catching flies always for superior spiders. Mr Mortimer Gazebee had in this way entangled Mr Crosbie in his web on behalf of those noble spiders, the De Courcys, and our poor friend, in his endeavour to fight his way through the web, had fallen into the hands of the Hook Court firm of Mrs Van Siever, Dobbs Broughton, and Musselboro.

'Mr Broughton told me when I was last here,' said Crosbie, 'that there would be no difficulty about it.'

'And it was renewed then; wasn't it?'

'Of course it was, – for two months. But he was speaking of a continuation of renewal.'

'I'm afraid we can't do it, Mr Crosbie. I'm afraid we can't, indeed. Money is so awful tight.'

'Of course I must pay what you choose to charge me.'

'It isn't that, Mr Crosbie. The bill is out for collection, and must be collected. In times like these we must draw ourselves in a little, you know. Two hundred and fifty pounds isn't a great deal of money, you will say; but every little helps, you know; and, besides, of course we go upon a system. Business is business, and must not be made pleasure of. I should have had a great deal of pleasure in doing this for you, but it can't be done in the way of business.'

'When will Broughton be here?'

'He may be in at any time; – I can't say when. I suppose he's down at the court now.'

'What court?'

'Capel Court.'

'I suppose I can see him there?' said Crosbie.

'If you catch him you can see him, of course. But what good will that do you, Mr Crosbie? I tell you that we can't do it for you. If Broughton was here this moment it couldn't make the slightest difference.'

Now Mr Crosbie had an idea that Mr Musselboro, though he sat in Dobbs Broughton's seat and kept on his hat, and balanced his chair on two legs, was in truth nothing more than a clerk. He did not quite understand the manner in which the affairs of the establishment were worked, though he had been informed that Mrs Van Siever was one of the partners. That Dobbs Broughton was the managing man, who really did the business, he was convinced; and he did not therefore like to be answered peremptorily by such a one as Musselboro. 'I should wish to see Mr Broughton,' he said.

'You can call again, – or you can go down to the court if you like it. But you may take this as an answer from me that the bill can't be renewed by us.' At this moment the door of the room was opened, and Dobbs Broughton himself came into it. His face was not all pleasant, and any one might have seen with half an eye that the money-market was a great deal tighter than he liked it to be. 'Here is Mr Crosbie here, – about that bill,' said Musselboro.

'Mr Crosbie must take up his bill; that's all,' said Dobbs Broughton.

'But it doesn't suit me to take it up,' said Crosbie.

'Then you must take it up without suiting you,' said Dobbs Broughton.

It might have been seen, I said, with half an eye, that Mr Broughton did not like the state of the money-market; and it might also be seen with the other half that he had been endeavouring to mitigate the bitterness of his dislike by alcoholic aid. Musselboro at once perceived that his patron and partner was half drunk, and Crosbie was aware that he had been drinking. But, nevertheless, it was necessary that something more should be said. The bill would be due to-morrow, – was payable at Crosbie's bankers; and, as Mr Crosbie too well knew, there were no funds there for the purpose. And there were other purposes, very needful, for which Mr Crosbie's funds were at the present moment unfortunately by no means sufficient. He stood for a few moments thinking what he would do; – whether he would leave the drunken man and his office and let the bill take its chance, or whether he would make one more effort for an arrangement. He did not for a moment believe that Broughton himself was subject to any pecuniary difficulty. Broughton lived in a big house, as rich men live, and had a name for commercial success. It never occurred to Crosbie that it was a matter of great moment to Dobbs Broughton himself that the bill should be taken up. Crosbie still thought that Musselboro was his special enemy, and that Broughton had joined Musselboro in his hostility simply because he was too drunk to know better. 'You might, at any rate, answer me civilly, Mr Broughton,' he said.

'I know nothing about civility with things as they are at present,' said Broughton. 'Civil by— ! There's nothing so civil as paying money when you owe it. Musselboro, reach me down the decanter and some glasses. Perhaps Mr Crosbie will wet his whistle.'

'He don't want any wine, – nor you either,' said Musselboro.

'What's up now?' said Broughton, staggering across the room towards a cupboard, in which it was his custom to keep a provision of that comfort which he needed at the present moment. 'I suppose I may stand a glass of wine to a fellow in my own room, if I like it.'

'I will take no wine, thank you,' said Crosbie.

'Then you can do the other thing. When I ask a gentleman to take a glass of wine, there is no compulsion. But about the bill there is compulsion. Do you understand that? You may drink, or let it alone; but pay you must. Why, Mussy, what d'ye think? – there's Carter, Ricketts and Carter; – I'm blessed if Carter just now didn't beg for two months, as though two months would be all the world to him, and that for a trumpery five hundred pounds. I never saw money like it is now; never.' To this appeal, Musselboro made no reply, not caring, perhaps, at the present moment to sustain his partner. He still balanced himself in his chair, and still kept his hat on his head. Even Mr Crosbie began to perceive that Mr Musselboro's genius was in the ascendant in Hook Court.

'I can hardly believe,' said Crosbie, 'that things can be so bad that I cannot have a bill for two hundred and fifty pounds renewed when I am willing to pay for the accommodation. I have not done much in the way of bills, but I never had one dishonoured yet.'

'Don't let this be the first,' said Dobbs Broughton.

'Not if I can prevent it,' said Crosbie. 'But, to tell you the truth, Mr Broughton, my bill will be dishonoured unless I can have it renewed. If it does not suit you to do it, I suppose you can recommend me to some one who can make it convenient.'

'Why don't you go to your bankers?' said Musselboro.

'I never did ask my bankers for anything of the kind.'

'Then you should try what your credit with them is worth,' said

Broughton. 'It isn't worth much here, as you can perceive. Ha, ha, ha!'

Crosbie, when he heard this, became very angry; and Mussel-boro, perceiving this, got out of his chair, so that he might be in readiness to prevent any violence, if violence were attempted. 'It really is no good you're staying here,' he said. 'You see that Broughton has been drinking. There's no knowing what he may say or do.'

'You be blowed,' said Broughton, who had taken the arm-chair as soon as Musselboro had left it.

'But you may believe me in the way of business,' continued Musselboro, 'when I tell you that it really does not suit us to renew the bill. We're pressed ourselves, and we must press others.'

'And who will do it for me?' said Crosbie, almost in despair.

'There are Burton and Bangles there, the wine-merchants down in the yard; perhaps they may accommodate you. It's all in their line; but I'm told they charge uncommon dear.'

'I don't know Messrs Burton and Bangles,' said Crosbie.

'That needn't stand in your way. You tell them where you come from, and they'll make inquiry. If they think it's about right, they'll give you the money; and if they don't, they won't.'

Mr Crosbie then left the office without exchanging another word with Dobbs Broughton, and went down into Hook Court. As he descended the stairs he turned over in his mind the propriety of going to Messrs Burton and Bangles with the view of relieving himself from his present difficulty. He knew that it was ruinous. Dealings even with such men as Dobbs Broughton and Musselboro, whom he presumed to be milder in their greed than Burton and Bangles, were, all of them, steps on the road to ruin. But what was he to do? If his bill were dishonoured, the fact would certainly become known at his office, and he might even ultimately be arrested. In the doorway at the bottom of the stairs he stood for some moments, looking over at Burton and Bangles', and he did not at all like the aspect of the establishment. Inside the office he could see a man standing with a cigar in his mouth, very resplendent with a new hat, – with a hat remarkable for the bold upward curve of its rim, and this man was copiously decorated with a chain and seals hanging about widely over his waistcoat. He was leaning with his back against the counter, and was talking to some one on the other side of it. There was something in the man's look and manner that was utterly replusive to Crosbie. He was more vulgar to the eye even than Musselboro, and his voice, which Crosbie could hear as he stood in the other doorway, was almost as detestable as that of Dobbs Broughton in his drunkenness. Crosbie did not doubt that this was either Burton or Bangles, and that the man standing inside was either Bangles or Burton. He could not bring himself to accost these men and tell them of his necessities, and propose to them that they should relieve him. In spite of what Musselboro had just said to him, he could not believe it possible that he should succeed, were he to do so without some introduction. So he left Hook Court and went out into the lane, hearing as he went the loud voice of the man with the turned-up hat and the chain.

But what was he to do? At the outset of his pecuniary troubles, when he first found it necessary to litigate some question with the De Courcy people, and withstand the web which Mortimer Gazebee wove so assiduously, his own attorney had introduced him to Dobbs Broughton, and the assistance which he had needed had come to him, at any rate, without trouble. He did not especially like Mr Broughton; and when Mr Broughton first invited him to come and eat a little bit of dinner, he had told himself with painful remorse that in his early days he had been accustomed to eat his little bits of dinner with people of a different kind. But there had been nothing really painful in this. Since his marriage with a daughter of the De Courcys, – by which marriage he had intended to climb to the highest pinnacle of social eating and drinking, – he had gradually found himself to be falling in the scale of such matters, and could bring himself to dine with a Dobbs Broughton without any violent pain. But now he had fallen so low that Dobbs Broughton had insulted him, and he was in such distress that he did not know where to turn for ten pounds. Mr Gazebee had beaten him at litigation, and his own lawyer had advised him that it would be foolish to try the matter further. In his marriage with the noble daughter of the De Courcys he had allowed the framers of the De Courcy settlement to tie him up in such a way that now, even when chance had done so much for him in freeing him from his wife, he was still bound to the De Courcy faction. Money had been paid away, – on his behalf, as alleged by Mr Gazebee, – like running water; money for furniture, money for the lease of a house, money when he had been separated from his wife, money while she was living abroad. It had seemed to him that he had been made to pay for the entire support of the female moiety of the De Courcy family which had settled itself at Baden-Baden, from the day, and in some respects from before the day, on which his wife had joined that moiety. He had done all in his power to struggle against these payments, but every such struggle had only cost him more money. Mr Gazebee had written to him the civilest notes; but every note seemed to cost him money, – every word of each note seemed to find its way into some bill. His wife had died and her body had been brought back, with all the pomp befitting the body of an earl's daughter, that it might be laid with the old De Courcy dust, – at his expense. The embalming of her dear remains had cost a wondrous sum, and was a terrible blow upon him. All these items were showered upon him by Mr Gazebee with the most courteously worded demands for settlement as soon as convenient. And then, when he applied that Lady Alelxandrina's small fortune should be made over to him, – according to a certain agreement under which he had made over all his possessions to his wife, should she have survived him, – Mr Gazebee expressed a mild opinion that he was wrong in his law, and blandly recommended an amicable lawsuit. The amicable lawsuit was carried on. His own lawyer seemed to throw him over. Mr Gazebee was successful in everything. No money came to him. Money was demanded from him on old scores and on new scores, – and all that he received to console him for what he had lost was a mourning ring with his wife's hair, – for which, with sundry other mourning rings, he had to pay, – and an introduction to Mr Dobbs Broughton. To Mr Dobbs Broughton he owed five hundred pounds; and as regarded a bill for the one-half of that sum which was due to-morrow, Mr Dobbs Broughton had refused to grant him renewal for a single month!

I know no more uncomfortable walking than that which falls to the lot of men who go into the City to look for money, and who find none. Of all the lost steps trodden by men, surely the steps lost after that fashion are the most melancholy. It is not only that they are so vain, but that they are accompanied by so killing a sense of shame! To wait about in dingy rooms, which look on to bare walls, and are approached through some Hook Court; or to keep appointments at a low coffee-house, to which trystings the money-lender will not trouble himself to come unless it pleases him; to be civil, almost suppliant, to a cunning knave whom the borrower loathes; to be refused thrice, and then cheated with his eyes open on the fourth attempt; to submit himself to vulgarity of the foulest kind, and to have to seem to like it; to be badgered, reviled, and at last accused of want of honesty by the most fraudulent of mankind; and at the same time to be clearly conscious of the ruin that is coming, – this is the fate of him who goes into the city to find money, not knowing where it is to be found!

Crosbie went along the lane into Lombard Street, and then he stood still for a moment to think. Though he knew a good deal of affairs in general, he did not quite know what would happen to him if his bill should be dishonoured. That somebody would bring it to him noted, and require him instantly to put his hand into his pocket and bring out the amount of the bill, plus the amount of certain expenses, he thought that he did know. And he knew that were he in trade he would become a bankrupt; and he was well aware that such an occurrence would prove him to be insolvent. But he did not know what his creditors would immediately have the power of doing. That the fact of the bill having been dishonoured would reach the Board under which he served, – and, therefore, also the fact that he had had recourse to such bill transactions, – this alone was enough to fill him with dismay. In early life he had carried his head so high, he had been so much more than a mere Government clerk, that the idea of the coming disgrace almost killed him. Would it not be well that he should put an end to himself, and thus escape? What was there in the world now for which it was worth his while to live? Lily, whom he had once gained, and by that gain had placed himself high in all hopes of happiness and riches, – whom he had then thrown away from him, and who had again seemed to be almost within his reach, – Lily had so refused him that he knew not how to approach her with a further prayer. And, had she not refused him, how could he have told her of his load of debt? As he stood at the corner where the lane runs into Lombard Street, he came for a while to think almost more of Lily than of his rejected bill. Then, as he thought of both his misfortunes together, he asked himself whether a pistol would not conveniently put an end to them together.

At that moment a loud, harsh voice greeted his ear. 'Hallo, Crosbie, what brings you so far east? One does not often see you in the City.' It was the voice of Sir Raffle Buffle, which in former days had been very odious to Crosbie's ears; – for Sir Raffle Buffle had once been the presiding genius of the office to which Crosbie still belonged.

'No, indeed, not very often,' said Crosbie, smiling. Who can tell, who has not felt it, the pain that goes to the forcing of such smiles? But Sir Raffle was not an acutely observant person, and did not see that anything was wrong.

'I suppose you're doing a little business?' said Sir Raffle. 'If a man has kept a trifle of money by him, this certainly is the time for turning it. You have always been wide awake about such things.'

'No, indeed,' said Crosbie. If he could only make up his mind that he would shoot himself, would it not be a pleasant thing to inflict some condign punishment on this odious man before he left the world? But Crosbie knew that he was not going to shoot himself, and he knew also that he had no power of inflicting condign punishment on Sir Raffle Buffle. He could only hate the man, and curse him inwardly.

'Ah, ha!' said Sir Raffle. 'You wouldn't be here unless you knew where a good thing is to be picked up. But I must be off. I'm on the Rocky Mountain Canal Company Directory. I'm not above taking my two guineas a day. Good-by, my boy. Remember me to old Optimist.' And so Sir Raffle passed on, leaving Crosbie still standing at the corner of the lane.

What was he to do? This interruption had at least seemed to drive Lily from his mind, and to send his ideas back to the consideration of his pecuniary difficulties. He thought of his own bank, a West-End establishment at which he was personally known to many of the clerks, and where he had been heretofore treated with great consideration. But of late his balances had been very low, and more than once he had been reminded that he had overdrawn his account. He knew well that the distinguished firm of Bounce, Bounce, and Bounce would not cash a bill for him or lend him money without security. He did not even dare to ask them to do so.

On a sudden he jumped into a cab, and was driven back to his office. A thought had come upon him. He would throw himself upon the kindness of a friend there. Hitherto he had contrived to hold his head so high above the clerks below him, so high before the Commissioners who were above him, that none there suspected him to be a man in difficulty. It not seldom happens that a man's character stands too high for his interest, – so high that it cannot be maintained, and so high that any fall will be dangerous. And so it was with Crosbie and his character at the General Committee Office. The man to whom he was now thinking of applying as his friend, was a certain Mr Butterwell, who had been his predecessor in the secretary's chair, and who now filled the less onerous but more dignified position of a Commissioner. Mr Crosbie had somewhat despised Mr Butterwell, and had of late years not been averse to showing that he did so. He had snubbed Mr Butterwell, and Mr Butterwell, driven to his wits' ends, had tried a fall or two with him. In all these struggles Crosbie had had the best of it, and Butterwell had gone to the wall. Nevertheless, for the sake of official decency, and from certain wise remembrances of the sources of official comfort and official discomfort, Mr Butterwell had always maintained a show of outward friendship with the secretary. They smiled and were gracious, called each other Butterwell and Crosbie, and abstained from all cat-and-dog absurdities. Nevertheless, it was the frequently expressed opinion of every clerk in the office that Mr Butterwell hated Mr Crosbie like poison. This was the man to whom Crosbie suddenly made up his mind that he would have recourse.

As he was driven back to his office he resolved that he would make a plunge at once at the difficulty. He knew that Butterwell was fairly rich, and he knew also that he was good-natured, – with that sort of sleepy good-nature which is not active for philanthropic purposes, but which dislikes to incur the pain of refusing. And then Mr Butterwell was nervous, and if the thing was managed well, he might be cheated out of an asset, before time had been given him in which to pluck up courage for refusing. But Crosbie doubted his own courage also, – fearing that if he gave himself time for hesitation he would hesitate, and that, hesitating, he would feel the terrible disgrace of the thing and not do it. So, without going to his own desk, or ridding himself of his hat, he went at once to Butterwell's room. When he opened the door, he found Mr Butterwell alone, reading The Times. 'Butterwell,' said he, beginning to speak before he had even closed the door, 'I have come to you in great distress. I wonder whether you can help me; I want you to lend me five hundred pounds? It must be for not less than three months.'

Mr Butterwell dropped the paper from his hands, and stared at the secretary over his spectacles.

END OF VOL I.

Volume Two

CHAPTER 44

I suppose I must let you have it

Crosbie had been preparing the exact words with which he assailed Mr Butterwell for the last quarter of an hour, before they were uttered. There is always a difficulty in the choice, not only of the words with which money should be borrowed, but of the fashion after which they should be spoken. There is the slow deliberate manner, in using which the borrower attempts to carry the wished-for lender along with him by force of argument, and to prove that the desire to borrow shows no imprudence on his own part, and that a tendency to lend will show none on the part of the intended lender. It may be said that this mode fails oftener than any other. There is the piteous manner, – the plea for commiseration. 'My dear fellow, unless you will see me through now, upon my word I shall be very badly off.' And this manner may be divided again into two. There is the plea piteous with a lie, and the plea piteous with a truth. 'You shall have it again in two months as sure as the sun rises.' That is generally the plea piteous with a lie. Or it may be as follows: 'It is only fair to say that I don't quite know when I can pay it back.' This is the plea piteous with a truth, and upon the whole I think that this is generally the most successful mode of borrowing. And there is the assured demand, – which betokens a close intimacy. 'Old fellow, can you let me have thirty pounds? No? Just put your name, then, on the back of this, and I'll get it done in the City.' The worst of that manner is, that the bill so often does not get itself done in the City. Then there is the sudden attack, – that being the manner to which Crosbie had recourse in the present instance. That there are other modes of borrowing by means of which youth becomes indebted to age, and love to respect, and ignorance to experience, is a matter of course. It will be understood that I am here speaking only of borrowing and lending between the Butterwells and Crosbies of the world. 'I have come to you in great distress,' said Crosbie. 'I wonder whether you can help me. I want you to lend me five hundred pounds.' Mr Butterwell, when he heard the words, dropped the paper which he was reading from his hand, and stared at Crosbie over his spectacles.

'Five hundred pounds,' he said. 'Dear me, Crosbie; that's a large sum of money.'

'Yes, it is, – a very large sum. Half that is what I want at once; but I shall want the other half in a month.'

'I thought that you were always so much above the world in money matters. Gracious me; – nothing that I have heard for a long time has astonished me more. I don't know why, but I always thought that you had your things so very snug.'

Crosbie was aware that he had made one very great step towards success. The idea had been presented to Mr Butterwell's mind, and had not been instantly rejected as a scandalously iniquitous idea, as an idea to which no reception could be given for a moment. Crosbie had not been treated as was the needy knife-grinder,* and had ground to stand upon while he urged his request. 'I have been so pressed since my marriage,' he said, 'that it has been impossible for me to keep things straight.'

'But Lady Alexandrina—'

'Yes; of course; I know. I do not like to trouble you with my private affairs; – there is nothing, I think, so bad as washing one's dirty linen in public; – but the truth is, that I am only now free from the rapacity of the De Courcys. You would hardly believe me if I told you what I've had to pay. What do you think of two hundred and forty-five pounds for bringing her body over here, and burying it at De Courcy.

'I'd have left it where it was.'

'And so would I. You don't suppose I ordered it to be done. Poor dear thing. If it could do her any good, God knows I would not begrudge it. We had a bad time of it when we were together, but I would have spared nothing for her, alive or dead, that was reasonable. But to make me pay for bringing the body over here, when I never had a shilling with her! By George, it was too bad. And that oaf John De Courcy, – I had to pay his travelling bill too.'

'He didn't come to be buried; – did he?'

'It's too disgusting to talk of, Butterwell; it is indeed. And when I asked for her money that was settled upon me, – it was only two thousand pounds, – they made me go to law, and it seems there was no two thousand pounds to settle. If I like, I can have another lawsuit with the sisters, when the mother is dead. Oh, Butterwell, I have made such a fool of myself. I have come to such shipwreck! Oh, Butterwell, if you could but know it all.'

'Are you free from the De Courcys now?'

'I owe Gazebee, the man who married the other woman, over a thousand pounds. But I pay that off at two hundred a year, and he has a policy on my life.'

'What do you owe that for?'

'Don't ask me. Not that I mind telling you; furniture, and the lease of a house, and his bill for the marriage settlement. – d—him.'

'God bless me. They seem to have been very hard upon you.'

'A man doesn't marry an earl's daughter for nothing, Butterwell. And then to think what I lost! It can't be helped now, you know. As a man makes his bed he must lie on it. I am sometimes so mad with myself when I think over it all, – that I should like to blow my brains out.'

'You must not talk in that way, Crosbie. I hate to hear a man talk like that.'

'I don't mean that I shall. I'm too much of a coward, I fancy. A man who desires to soften another man's heart, should always abuse himself. In softening a woman's heart, he should abuse her. 'But life has been so bitter with me for the last three years! I haven't had an hour of comfort; – not an hour. I don't know why I should trouble you with all this, Butterwell. Oh, – about the money; yes; that's just how I stand. I owed Gazebee something over a thousand pounds, which is arranged as I have told you. Then there were debts, due by my wife, – at least some of them were, I suppose, – and that horrid, ghastly funeral, – and debts, I don't doubt, due by the cursed old countess. At any rate, to get myself clear I raised something over four hundred pounds, and now I owe five which must be paid, part to-morrow, and the remainder this day month.'

'And you've no security?'

'Not a rag, not a shred, not a line, not an acre. There's my salary, and after paying Gazebee what comes due to him, I can manage to let you have the money within twelve months, – that is, if you can lend it me. I can just do that and live; and if you will assist me with the money, I will do so. That's what I've brought myself to by my own folly.'

'Five hundred pounds is such a large sum of money.'

'Indeed it is.'

'And without any security!'

'I know, Butterwell, that I've no right to ask for it. I feel that. Of course I should pay you what interest you please.'

'Money's about seven now,' said Butterwell.

'I've not the slightest objection to seven per cent.,' said Crosbie.

'But that's on security,' said Butterwell.

'You can name your own terms,' said Crosbie.

Mr Butterwell got out of his chair, and walked about the room with his hands in his pockets. He was thinking at that moment what Mrs Butterwell would say to him. 'Will an answer do to-morrow morning?' he said. 'I would much rather have it to-day,' said Crosbie. Then Mr Butterwell took another turn about the room. 'I suppose I must let you have it,' he said.

'Butterwell,' said Crosbie, 'I'm eternally obliged to you. It's hardly too much to say that you've saved me from ruin.'

'Of course I was joking about the interest,' said Butterwell. 'Five per cent. is the proper thing. You'd better let me have a little acknowledgment. I'll give you the first half to-morrow.'

They were genuine tears which filled Crosbie's eyes, as he seized hold of the senior's hands. 'Butterwell,' he said, 'what am I to say to you?'

'Nothing at all, – nothing at all.'

'Your kindness makes me feel that I ought not to have come to you.'

'Oh, nonsense. By-the-by, would you mind telling Thompson to bring those papers to me which I gave him yesterday? I promised Optimist I would read them before three, and it's past two now.' So saying he sat himself down at his table, and Crosbie felt that he was bound to leave the room.

Mr Butterwell, when he was left alone, did not read the papers which Thompson brought him; but sat, instead, thinking of his five hundred pounds. 'Just put them down,' he said to Thompson. So the papers were put down, and there they lay all that day and all the next. Then Thompson took them away again, and it is to be hoped that somebody read them. Five hundred pounds! It was a large sum of money, and Crosbie was a man for whom Mr Butterwell in truth felt no very strong affection. 'Of course he must have it now,' he said to himself. 'But where should I be if anything happened to him?' And then he remembered that Mrs Butterwell especially disliked Mr Crosbie, – disliked him because she knew that he snubbed her husband. 'But it's hard to refuse, when one man has known another for more than ten years.' Then he comforted himself somewhat with the reflection, that Crosbie would no doubt make himself more pleasant for the future than he had done lately, and with a second reflection, that Crosbie's life was a good life, – and with a third, as to his own great goodness, in assisting a brother officer. Nevertheless, as he sat looking out of the omnibus-window, on his journey home to Putney, he was not altogether comfortable in his mind. Mrs Butterwell was a very prudent woman.

But Crosbie was very comfortable in his mind on that afternoon. He had hardly dared to hope for success, but he had been successful.

He had not even thought of Butterwell as a possible fountain of supply, till his mind had been brought back to the affairs of his office, by the voice of Sir Raffle Buffle at the corner of the street. The idea that his bill would be dishonoured, and that tidings of his insolvency would be conveyed to the Commissioners at his Board, had been dreadful to him. The way in which he had been treated by Musselboro and Dobbs Broughton had made him hate City men, and what he supposed to be City ways. Now there had come to him a relief which suddenly made everything feel light. He could almost think of Mr Mortimer Gazebee without disgust. Perhaps after all there might be some happiness yet in store for him. Might it not be possible that Lily would yet accept him in spite of the chilling letter, – the freezing letter which he had received from Lily's mother? Of one thing he was quite certain. If ever he had an opportunity of pleading his own cause with her, he certainly would tell her everything respecting his own money difficulties.

In that last resolve I think we may say that he was right. If Lily would ever listen to him again at all, she certainly would not be deterred from marrying him by his own story of his debts.

CHAPTER 45

Lily Dale goes to London

One morning towards the end of March the squire rapped at the window of the drawing-room of the Small House, in which Mrs Dale and her daughter were sitting. He had a letter in his hand, and both Lily and her mother knew that he had come down to speak about the contents of the letter. It was always a sign of good-humour on the squire's part, this rapping at the window. When it became necessary to him in his gloomy moods to see his sister-in-law, he would write a note to her, and she would go across to him at the Great House. At other times, if, as Lily would say, he was just then neither sweet not bitter, he would go round to the front door and knock, and be admitted after the manner of ordinary people; but when he was minded to make himself thoroughly pleasant he would come and rap at the drawing-room window, as he was doing now.

'I'll let you in, uncle; wait a moment,' said Lily, as she unbolted the window which opened out upon the lawn. 'It's dreadfully cold, so come in as fast as you can.'

'It's not cold at all,' said the squire. 'It's more like spring than any morning we've had yet. I've been sitting without a fire.'

'You won't catch us without one for the next two months; will he, mamma? You have got a letter uncle. Is it for us to see?'

'Well, – yes; I've brought it down to show you. Mary, what do you think is going to happen?'

A terrible idea occurred to Mrs Dale at that moment, but she was much too wise to give it expression. Could it be possible that the squire was going to make a fool of himself and get married? 'I am very bad at guessing,' said Mrs Dale. 'You had better tell us.'

'Bernard is going to be married,' said Lily.

'How did you know?' said the squire.

'I didn't know? I only guessed.'

'Then you've guessed right,' said the squire, a little annoyed at having the news taken out of his mouth.

'I am so glad,' said Mrs Dale; 'and I know from your manner that you like the match.'

'Well, — yes. I don't know the young lady, but I think that upon the whole I do like it. It's quite time, you know, that he got married.'

'He's not thirty yet,' said Mrs Dale.

'He will be, in a month or two.'

'And who is it, uncle?'

'Well; — as you're so good at guessing, I suppose you can guess that?'

'It's not that Miss Partridge he used to talk about?'

'No; it's not Miss Partridge, — I'm glad to say. I don't believe that the Partridges have a shilling among them.'

'Then I suppose it's an heiress?' said Mrs Dale.

'No; not an heiress; but she will have some money of her own. And she has connexions in Barsetshire, which makes it pleasant.'

'Connexions in Barsetshire!' Who can it be?' said Lily.

'Her name is Emily Dunstable,' said the squire, 'and she is the niece of Miss Dunstable who married Dr Thorne and who lives at Chaldicotes.'

'She was the woman who had millions upon millions,' said Lily, 'all got by selling ointment.'

'Never mind how it was got,' said the squire, angrily. 'Miss Dunstable married most respectably, and has always made a most excellent use of her money.'

'And will Bernard's wife have all her fortune?' asked Lily.

'She will have twenty thousand pounds the day she marries, and I suppose that will be all.'

'And quite enough, too,' said Mrs Dale.

'It seems that old Dr Dunstable, as he was called, who, as Lily says, sold the ointment, quarrelled with his son or with his son's widow, and left nothing either to her or her child. The mother is dead, and the aunt, Dr Thorne's wife, has always provided for the child. That's how it is, and Bernard is going to marry her. They are to be married at Chaldicotes in May.'

'I am delighted to hear it,' said Mrs Dale.

'I've known Dr Thorne for the last forty years;' and the squire now spoke in a low melancholy tone. 'I've written to him to say that the young people shall have the old place up there to themselves if they like it.'

'What! and turn you out?' said Mrs Dale.

'That would not matter,' said the squire.

'You'd have to come and live with us,' said Lily, taking him by the hand.

'It doesn't matter much now where I live,' said the squire.

'Bernard will never consent to that,' said Mrs Dale.

'I wonder whether she'll ask me to be a bridesmaid?' said Lily. 'They say that Chaldicotes is such a pretty place, and I should see all the Barsetshire people that I've been hearing about from Grace. Poor Grace! I know that the Grantlys and the Thornes are very intimate. Fancy Bernard having twenty thousand pounds from the making of ointment!'

'What does it matter to you where it comes from?' said the squire, half in anger.

'Not in the least; only it sounds so odd. I do hope she's a nice girl.'

Then the squire produced a photograph of Emily Dunstable which his nephew had sent to him, and they all pronounced her to be very pretty, to be very much like a lady, and to be very good-humoured. The squire was evidently pleased with the match, and therefore the ladies were pleased also. Bernard Dale was the heir to the estate, and his marriage was of course a matter of moment; and as on such properties as that of Allington money is always wanted, the squire may be forgiven for the great importance which he attached to the young lady's fortune. 'Bernard could hardly have married prudently without any money,' he said, – 'unless he had chosen to wait till I am gone.'

'And then he would have been too old to marry at all,' said Lily.

But the squire's budget of news had not yet been emptied. He told them soon afterwards that he himself had been summoned up to London. Bernard had written to him, begging him to come and see the young lady; and the family lawyer had written also, saying that his presence in town would be very desirable. 'It is very troublesome, of course; but I shall go,' said the squire. 'It will do you all the good in the world,' said Mrs Dale; 'and of course you ought to know her personally before the marriage.' And then the squire made a clean breast of it and declared his full purpose. 'I was thinking that, perhaps, Lily would not object to go up to London with me.'

'Oh, uncle Christopher, I should so like it,' said Lily.

'If your mamma does not object.'

'Mamma never objects to anything. I should like to see her objecting to that!' And Lily shook her head at her mother.

'Bernard says that Miss Dunstable particularly wants to see you.'

'Does she, indeed? And I particularly want to see Miss Dunstable. How nice! Mamma, I don't think I've ever been in London since I wore short frocks. Do you remember taking us to the pantomime? Only think how many years ago that is. I'm quite sure it's time that

Bernard should get married. Uncle, I hope you're prepared to take me to the play.'

'We must see about that!'

'And the opera, and Madame Tussaud, and the Horticultural Gardens, and the new conjuror who makes a woman lie upon nothing. The idea of my going to London! And then I suppose I shall be one of the bridesmaids. I declare a new vista of life is opening out to me! Mamma, you mustn't be dull while I'm away. It won't be very long, I suppose, uncle?'

'About a month, probably,' said the squire.

'Oh, mamma; what will you do?'

'Never mind me, Lily.'

'You must get Bell and the children to come. But I cannot imagine living away from home a month. I was never away from home a month in my life.'

And Lily did go up to town with her uncle, two days only having been allowed for her preparations. There was very much for her to think of in such a journey. It was not only that she would see Emily Dunstable who was to be her cousins's wife, and that she would go to the play and visit the new conjuror's entertainment, but that she would be in the same city both with Adolphus Crosbie and with John Eames. Not having personal experience of the wideness of London, and of the wilderness which it is; – of the distance which is set there between persons who are not purposely brought together – it seemed to her fancy as though for this month of her absence from home she would be brought into close contiguity with both her lovers. She had hitherto felt herself to be at any rate safe in her fortress at Allington. When Crosbie had written to her mother, making a renewed offer which had been rejected, Lily had felt that she certainly need not see him unless it pleased her to do so. He could hardly force himself upon her at Allington. And as to John Eames, though he would, of course, be welcome at Allington as often as he pleased to show himself, still there was a security in the place. She was so much at home there that she could always be mistress of the occasion. She knew that she could talk to him at Allington as though from ground higher than that on which he stood himself; but she felt that this would hardly be the case if she should chance to meet him in London. Crosbie probably would not come in her way. Crosbie she thought, – and she blushed for the man she loved, as the idea came across her mind, – would be afraid of meeting her uncle. But John Eames would certainly find her; and she was led by the experience of latter days to imagine that John would never cross her path without renewing his attempts.

But she said no word of all this, even to her mother. She was contented to confine her outspoken expectations to Emily Dunstable, and the play, and the conjuror. 'The chances are ten to one against my liking her, mamma,' she said.

'I don't see that, my dear.'

'I feel to be too old to think that I shall ever like any more new people. Three years ago I should have been quite sure that I should love a new cousin. It would have been like having a new dress. But I've come to think that an old dress is the most comfortable, and an old cousin certainly the best.'

The squire had taken for them a gloomy lodging in Sackville Street. Lodgings in London are always gloomy. Gloomy colours wear better than bright ones for curtains and carpets, and the keepers of lodgings in London seem to think that a certain dinginess of appearance is respectable. I never saw a London lodging in which any attempt at cheerfulness had been made, and I do not think that any such attempt, if made, would pay. The lodging-seeker would be frightened and dismayed, and would unconsciously be led to fancy that something was wrong. Ideas of burglars and improper persons would present themselves. This is so certainly the case that I doubt whether any well-conditioned lodging-house matron could be induced to show rooms that were prettily draped or pleasantly coloured. The big drawing-room and two large bedrooms which the squire took, were all that was proper, and were as brown, and as gloomy, and as ill-suited for the comforts of ordinary life as though they had been prepared for two prisoners. But Lily was not so ignorant as to expect cheerful lodgings in London, and was satisfied. 'And what are we to do now?' said Lily, as soon as they found themselves settled. It was still March, and whatever may have been the nature of the weather at Allington, it was very cold in London. They reached Sackville Street about five in the evening, and an hour was taken up in unpacking their trunks and making themselves as comfortable as their circumstances allowed. 'And now what are we to do?' said Lily.

'I told them to have dinner for us at half-past six.'

'And what after that? Won't Bernard come to us to-night? I expected him to be standing on the door-step waiting for us with his bride in his hand.'

'I don't suppose Bernard will be here to-night,' said the squire. 'He did not say that he would, and as for Miss Dunstable, I promised to take you to her aunt's house to-morrow.'

'But I wanted to see her to-night. Well; – of course bridesmaids must wait upon brides. And ladies with twenty thousand pounds can't be expected to run about like common people. As for Bernard, – but Bernard never was in a hurry.' Then they dined, and when the squire had very nearly fallen asleep over a bottle of port wine which had been sent in for him from some neighbouring public-house, Lily began to feel that it was very dull. And she looked round the room, and she thought that it was very ugly. And she calculated that thirty evenings so spent would seem to be very long. And she reflected that the hours were probably going much more quickly with Emily Dunstable, who, no doubt, at this moment had Bernard Dale by her side. And then she told herself that the hours were not tedious with her at home, while sitting with her mother, with all her daily occupations within her reach. But in so telling herself she took herself to task, inquiring of herself whether such an assurance was altogether true. Were not the hours sometimes tedious even at home? And in this way her mind wandered off to thoughts upon life in general, and she repeated to herself over and over again the two words which she had told John Eames that she would write in her journal. The reader will remember those two words; – Old Maid. And she had written them in her book, making each letter a capital, and round them she had drawn a scroll, ornamented after her own fashion, and she had added the date in quaintly formed figures, – for in such matters Lily had some little skill and a dash of fun to direct it; and she had inscribed below it an Italian motto, – 'Who goes softly, goes safely;'* and above her work of art she had put a heading – 'As arranged by Fate for L. D.' Now she thought of all this, and reflected whether Emily Dunstable was in truth very happy. Presently the tears came to her eyes, and she got up and went to the window, as though she were afraid that her uncle might wake and see them. And as she looked out on the blank street, she muttered a word or two – 'Dear mother! Dearest mother!' Then the door was opened, and her cousin Bernard announced himself. She had not heard his knock at the door as she had been thinking of the two words in her book.

'What; Bernard! – ah, yes, of course,' said the squire, rubbing his eyes as he strove to wake himself. 'I wasn't sure you would come, but I am delighted to see you. I wish you joy with all my heart, – with all my heart.'

'Of course, I should come,' said Bernard. Dear Lily, this is so good of you. Emily is so delighted.' Then Lily spoke her congratulations warmly, and there was no trace of a tear in her eye, and she was thoroughly happy as she sat by her cousin's side and listened to his raptures about Emily Dunstable. 'And you will be so fond of her aunt,' he said.

'But is she not awfully rich?' said Lily.

'Frightfully rich,' said Bernard; 'but really you would hardly find it out if nobody told you. Of course she lives in a big house, and has a heap of servants; but she can't help that.'

'I hate a heap of servants,' said Lily.

Then there came another knock at the door, and who should enter the room but John Eames. Lily for a moment was taken aback, but it was only for a moment. She had been thinking so much of him that his presence disturbed her for an instant. 'He probably will not know that I am here,' she had said to herself; but she had not yet been three hours in London, and he was already with her! At first he hardly spoke to her, addressing himself to the squire. 'Lady Julia told me you were to be here, and as I start for the Continent early to-morrow morning, I thought you would let me come and see you before I went.'

'I'm always glad to see you, John,' said the squire, – 'very glad. And so you're going abroad, are you?'

Then Johnny congratulated his old acquaintance, Bernard Dale, as to his coming marriage, and explained to them how Lady Julia in one of her letters had told him all about it, and had even given him the number in Sackville Street. 'I suppose she learned it from you Lily,' said the squire. 'Yes, uncle, she did.' And then there came questions as to John's projected journey to the Continent, and he explained that he was going on law-business, on behalf of Mr Crawley, to catch the dean and Mrs Arabin, if it might be possible. 'You see, sir, Mr Toogood, who is Mr Crawley's cousin, and also his lawyer, is my cousin, too; and that's why I'm going.' And still there had been hardly a word spoken between him and Lily.

'But you're not a lawyer, John; are you?' said the squire.

'No. I'm not a lawyer myself.'

'Nor a lawyer's clerk.'

'Certainly not a lawyer's clerk,' said Johnny, laughing.

'Then why should you go?' said Bernard Dale.

Then Johnny had to explain; and in doing so he became very eloquent as to the hardships of Mr Crawley's case. 'You see, sir, nobody can possibly believe that such a man as that stole twenty pounds.'

'I do not for one,' said Lily.

'God forbid that I should say he did said the squire.

'I'm quite sure he didn't,' said Johnny, warming to his subject. 'It couldn't be that such a man as that should become a thief all at once. It's not human nature, sir; is it?'

'It is very hard to know what is human nature,' said the squire.

'It's the general opinion down in Barsetshire that he did steal it,' said Bernard. 'Dr Thorne was one of the magistrates who committed him, and I know he thinks so.'

'I don't blame the magistrates in the least,' said Johnny.

'That's kind of you,' said the squire.

'Of course you'll laugh at me, sir; but you'll see that we shall come out right. There's some mystery in it of which we haven't got at the bottom as yet; and if there is anybody that can help us it's the dean.'

'If the dean knows anything, why has he not written and told what he knows?' said the squire.

'That's what I can't say. The dean has not had an opportunity of writing since he heard, — even if he has yet heard, — that Mr Crawley is to be tried. And then he and Mrs Arabin are not together. It's a long story, and I will not trouble you with it all; but at any rate I'm going off to-morrow. Lily, can I do anything for you in Florence?'

'In Florence?' said Lily; 'and are you really going to Florence? How I envy you.'

'And who pays your expenses?' said the squire.

'Well; — as to my expenses, they are to be paid by a person who won't raise any unpleasant questions about the amount.'

'I don't know what you mean,' said the squire.

'He means himself,' said Lily.

'Is he going to do it out of his own pocket?'

'He is,' said Lily, looking at her lover.

'I'm going to have a trip for my own fun,' said Johnny, 'and I shall pick up evidence on the road, as I'm going; that's all.'

Then Lily began to take an active part in the conversation, and a great deal was said about Mr Crawley, and about Grace and Lily declared that she would be very anxious to hear any news which John Eames might be able to send. 'You know, John, how fond we are of your cousin Grace, at Allington? Are we not, uncle?'

'Yes, indeed,' said the squire. 'I thought her a very nice girl.'

'If you should be able to learn anything that may be of use, John, how happy you will be.'

'Yes I shall,' said Johnny.

'And I think it so good of you to go, John. But it is just like you. You were always generous.' Soon after that he got up and went. It was very clear to him that he would have no moment in which to say a word alone to Lily; and if he could find such a moment, what good would such a word do him? It was as yet but a few weeks since she had positively refused him. And he too remembered very well those two words which she had told him that she would write in her book. As he had been coming to the house he had told himself that his coming would be, — could be of no use. And yet he was disappointed with the result of his visit, although she had spoken to him so sweetly.

'I suppose you'll be gone when I come back?' he said.

'We shall be here a month,' said the squire.

'I shall be back long before that, I hope,' said Johnny. 'Good-by, sir. Good-by, Dale. Good-by, Lily.' And he put out his hand to her.

'Good-by, John.' And then she added, almost in a whisper, 'I think you are very, very right to go.' How could he fail after that to hope as he walked home that she might still relent. And she also thought much of him, but her thoughts of him made her cling more firmly than ever to her two words. She could not bring herself to marry him; but, at least, she would not break his heart by becoming the wife of anyone else. Soon after this Bernard Dale went also. I am not sure that he had been well pleased at seeing John Eames become suddenly the hero of the hour. When a young man is going to perform so important an act as that of marriage, he is apt to think that he ought to be the hero of the hour himself – at any rate among his own family.

Early on the next morning Lily was taken by her uncle to call upon Mrs Thorne, and to see Emily Dunstable. Bernard was to meet them there, but it had been arranged that they should reach the house first. 'There is nothing so absurd as these introductions,' Bernard had said. 'You go and look at her, and when you've had time to look at her, then I'll come!' So the squire and Lily went off to look at Emily Dunstable.

'You don't mean to say that she lives in that house?' said Lily, when the cab was stopped before an enormous mansion in one of the most fashionable of the London squares.

'I believe she does,' said the squire.

'I never shall be able to speak to anybody living in such a house as that,' said Lily. 'A duke couldn't have anything grander.'

'Mrs Thorne is richer than half the dukes,' said the squire. Then the door was opened by a porter, and Lily found herself within the hall. Everything was very great, and very magnificent, and, as she thought, very uncomfortable. Presently she heard a loud jovial voice on the stairs. 'Mr Dale, I'm delighted to see you. And this is your niece Lily. Come up, my dear. There is a young woman upstairs, dying to embrace you. Never mind the umbrella. Put it down anywhere. I want to have a look at you, because Bernard swears that you're so pretty.' This was Mrs Thorne, once Miss Dunstable, the richest woman in England, and the aunt of Bernard's bride. The reader may perhaps remember the advice which she once gave to Major Grantly, and her enthusiasm on that occasion. 'There she is, Mr Dale; what do you think of her?' said Mrs Thorne, as she opened the door of a small sitting-room wedged in between two large saloons, in which Emily Dunstable was sitting.

'Aunt Martha, how can you be so ridiculous?' said the young lady.

'I suppose it is ridiculous to ask the question to which one really wants an answer,' said Mrs Thorne. 'But Mr Dale has, in truth, come to inspect you, and to form an opinion; and, in honest truth, I shall be very anxious to know what he thinks, – though, of course, he won't tell me.'

The old man took the girl in his arms, and kissed her on both cheeks. 'I have no doubt you'll find out what I think,' he said, 'though I should never tell you.'

'I generally do find out what people think,' she said. 'And so you're Lily Dale?'

'Yes, I'm Lily Dale.'

'I have so often heard of you, particularly of late; for you must know that a certain Major Grantly is a friend of mine. We must take care that that affair comes off all right, must we not?'

'I hope it will.' Then Lily turned to Emily Dunstable, and, taking her hand, went up and sat beside her, while Mrs Thorne and the squire talked of the coming marriage. 'How long have you been engaged?' said Lily.

'Really engaged, about three weeks. I think it is not more than three weeks ago.'

'How very discreet Bernard has been. He never told us a word about it while it was going on.'

'Men never do tell I suppose,' said Emily Dunstable.

'Of course you love him very dearly?' said Lily, not knowing what else to say.

'Of course I do.'

'So do we. You know he's almost a brother to us; that is, to me and my sister. We never had a brother of our own.' And so the morning was passed till Lily was told by her uncle to come away, and was told also by Mrs Thorne that she was to dine with them in the square on that day. 'You must not be surprised that my husband is not here,' she said. 'He is a very odd sort of man, and he never comes to London if he can help it.'

CHAPTER 46

The Bayswater romance

Eames had by no means done his work for that evening when he left Mr Dale and Lily at their lodgings. He had other business on hand to which he had promised to give attention, and another person to see who would welcome his coming quite as warmly, though by no means as pleasantly, as Lily Dale. It was then just nine o'clock, and as he had told Miss Demolines, – Madalina we may as well call her now, – that he would be in Porchester Terrace by nine at the latest, it was incumbent on him to make haste. He got into a cab, and bid the cabmen drive hard, and lighting a cigar, began to inquire of himself whether it was well for him to hurry away from the presence of Lily Dale to that of Madalina Demolines. He felt that he was half-ashamed of what he was doing. Though he declared to himself over and over again that he never had said a word, and never intended to say a word to Madalina, which all the world might not hear, yet he knew that he was doing amiss. He was doing amiss, and half repented it, and yet he was half proud of it. He was most anxious to be able to give himself credit for his constancy to Lily Dale; to be able to feel that he was steadfast in his passion; and yet he liked the idea of amusing himself with his Bayswater romance, as he would call it, and was not without something of conceit as he thought of the progress he had made in it. 'Love is one thing and amusement is another,' he said to himself as he puffed the cigar-smoke out of his mouth; and in his heart he was proud of his own capacity for enjoyment. He thought it a fine thing although at the same moment he knew it to be an evil thing – this hurrying away from the young lady whom he really loved to another as to whom he thought it very likely that he should be called upon to pretend to love her. And he sang a little song as he went, 'If she be not fair for me, what care I how fair she be.'* That was intended to apply to Lily, and was used as an excuse for his fickleness in going to Miss Demolines. And he was, perhaps,

too, a little conceited as to his mission to the Continent. Lily had
told him that she was very glad that he was going; that she thought
him very right to go. The words had been pleasant to his ears, and
Lily had never looked prettier in his eyes than when she had spoken
them. Johnny, therefore, was rather proud of himself as he sat in
the cab smoking his cigar. He had, moreover, beaten his old enemy
Sir Raffle Buffle in another contest, and he felt that the world was
smiling on him; – that the world was smiling on him in spite of his
cruel fate in the matter of his real lovesuit.

There was a mystery about the Bayswater romance which was
not without its allurement, and a portion of the mystery was
connected with Madalina's mother. Lady Demolines was very rarely
seen, and John Eames could not quite understand what was the
manner of life of that unfortunate lady. Her daughter usually spoke
of her with affectionate regret as being unable to appear on that
particular occasion on account of some passing malady. She was
suffering from a nervous headache, or was afflicted with bronchitis,
or had been touched with rheumatism, so that she was seldom on
the scene when Johnny was passing his time at Porchester Terrace.
And yet he heard of her dining out, and going to plays and operas;
and when he did chance to see her, he found that she was a sprightly
old woman enough. I will not venture to say that he much regretted
the absence of Lady Demolines, or that he was keenly alive to the
impropriety of being left alone with the gentle Madalina; but the
customary absence of the elder lady was an incident in the romance
which did not fail to strike him.

Madalina was alone when he was shown up into the drawing-
room on the evening of which we are speaking.

'Mr Eames,' she said,' will you kindly look at that watch which
is lying on the table.' She looked full at him with her great eyes
wide open, and the tone of her voice was intended to show him that
she was aggrieved.

'Yes, I see it,' said John, looking down on Miss Demolines' little
gold Geneva watch, with which he had already made sufficient
acquaintance to know that it was worth nothing. 'Shall I give it
you?'

'No, Mr Eames; let it remain there, that it may remind me, if it
does not remind you, by how long a time you have broken your
word.'

'Upon my word I couldn't help it; – upon my honour I couldn't.'

'Upon your honour, Mr Eames!'

'I was obliged to go and see a friend who has just come to town
from my part of the country.'

'That is the friend, I suppose, of whom I have heard from Maria.'

It is to be feared that Conway Dalrymple had not been so guarded as he should have been in some of his conversations with Mrs Dobbs Broughton, and that a word or two had escaped from him as to the love of John Eames for Lily Dale.

'I don't know what you may have heard,' said Johnny, 'but I was obliged to see these people before I left town. There is going to be a marriage and all that sort of thing.'

'Who is going to be married?'

'One Captain Dale is going to be married to one Miss Dunstable.'

'Oh! And as to one Miss Lily Dale, – is she to be married to anybody?'

'Not that I have heard of,' said Johnny.

'She is not going to become the wife of one Mr John Eames?'

He did not wish to talk to Miss Demolines about Lily Dale. He did not choose to disown the imputation, or to acknowledge its truth.

'Silence gives consent,' she said. 'If it be so, I congratulate you. I have no doubt she is a most charming young woman. It is about seven years, I believe, since that little affair with Mr Crosbie, and therefore that, I suppose, may be considered as forgotten.'

'It is only three years,' said Johnny, angrily. 'Besides, I don't know what that has to do with it.'

'You need not be ashamed,' said Madalina. 'I have heard how well you behaved on that occasion. You were quite the preux chevalier;* and if any gentleman ever deserved well of a lady you deserved well of her. I wonder how Mr Crosbie felt when he met you the other day at Maria's. I had not heard anything about it then, or I should have been much more interested in watching your meeting.'

'I really can't say how he felt.'

'I daresay not; but I saw him shake hands with you. And so Lily Dale has come to town?'

'Yes, – Miss Dale is here with her uncle.'

'And you are going away to-morrow?'

'Yes, – and I am going away to-morrow.'

After that there was a pause in the conversation. Eames was sick of it, and was very anxious to change the conversation. Miss Demolines was sitting in the shadow, away from the light, with her face half hidden by her hands. At last she jumped up, and came round and stood opposite to him. 'I charge you to tell me truly, John Eames,' she said, 'whether Miss Lilian Dale is engaged to you as your future wife?' He looked up into her face, but made no immediate answer. Then she repeated her demand. 'I ask you whether you are engaged to marry Miss Lilian Dale, and I expect a reply.'

'What makes you ask me such a question as that?'

'What makes me ask you? Do you deny my right to feel so much interest in you as to desire to know whether you are about to be married? Of course you decline to tell me if you choose.'

'And if I were to decline?'

'I should know then that it was true, and I should think that you were a coward.'

'I don't see any cowardice in the matter. One does not talk about that kind of thing to everybody.'

'Upon my word, Mr Eames, you are complimentary; – indeed you are. To everybody! I am everybody, – am I? That is your idea of – friendship! You may be sure that after that I shall ask no further questions.'

'I didn't mean it in the way you've taken it, Madalina.'

'In what way did you mean it, sir? Everybody! Mr Eames, you must excuse me if I say that I am not well enough this evening to bear the company of – everybody. I think you had better leave me. I think that you had better go.'

'Are you angry with me?'

'Yes, I am, – very angry. Because I have condescended to feel an interest in your welfare, and have asked you a question which I thought that our intimacy justified, you tell me that that is a kind of thing that you will not talk about to – everybody. I beg you to understand that I will not be your everybody. Mr Eames, there is the door.'

Things had now become very serious. Hitherto Johnny had been seated comfortably in the corner of a sofa, and had not found himself bound to move, though Miss Demolines was standing before him. But now it was absolutely necessary that he should do something. He must either go, or else he must make entreaty to be allowed to remain. Would it not be expedient that he should take the lady at her word and escape? She was still pointing to the door, and the way was open to him. If he were to walk out now of course he would never return, and there would be the end of the Bayswater romance. If he remained it might be that the romance would become troublesome. He got up from his seat, and had almost resolved that he would go. Had she not somewhat relaxed the majesty of her anger as he rose, had the fire of her eye not been somewhat quenched and the lines of her mouth softened, I think that he would have gone. The romance would have been over, and he would have felt that it had come to an inglorious end; but it would have been well for him that he should have gone. Though the fire was somewhat quenched and the lines were somewhat softened, she was still pointing to the door. 'Do you mean it?' he said.

'I do mean it, – certainly.'

'And this is to be the end of everything?'

'I do not know what you mean by everything. It is a very little everything to you, I should say. I do not quite understand your everything and your everybody.'

'I will go, if you wish me to go, of course.'

'I do wish it.'

'But before I go, you must permit me to excuse myself. I did not intend to offend you. I merely meant—'

'You merely meant! Give me an honest answer to a downright question. Are you engaged to Miss Lilian Dale?'

'No; – I am not.'

'Upon your honour?'

'Do you think that I would tell you a falsehood about it? What I meant was that it is a kind of thing one doesn't like talking about, merely because stories are bandied about. People are so fond of saying that this man is engaged to that woman, and of making up tales; and it seems to be so foolish to contradict such things.'

'But you know that you used to be very fond of her?'

He had taken up his hat when he had risen from the sofa, and was still standing with it ready in his hand. He was even now half-minded to escape; and the name of Lily Dale in Miss Demolines' mouth was so distasteful to him that he would have done so, – he would have gone in sheer disgust, had she not stood in his way, so that he could not escape without moving her, or going round behind the sofa. She did not stir to make way for him, and it may be that she understood that he was her prisoner, in spite of her late command to let him go. It may be, also, that she understood his vexation and the cause of it, and that she saw the expediency of leaving Lily Dale alone for the present. At any rate, she pressed him no more upon the matter. 'Are we to be friends again?' she said.

'I hope so,' replied Johnny.

'There is my hand, then.' So Johnny took her hand and pressed it, and held it a little while, – just long enough to seem to give a meaning to the action. 'You will get to understand me some day,' she said, 'and will learn that I do not like to be reckoned among the everybodies by those for whom I really – really – really have a regard. When I am angry, I am angry.'

'You were very angry just now, when you showed me the way to the door.'

'And I meant it too, – for the minute. Only think, – supposing you had gone! We should never have seen each other again; – never, never! What a change one word may make!'

'One word often does make a change.'

'Does it not? Just a little "yes," or "no." A "no" is said when a "yes" is meant, and then there comes no second chance, and what a change that may be from bright hopes to desolation! Or, worse again, a "yes" is said when a "no" should be said, – when the speaker knows that it should be "no." What a difference that "no" makes! When one thinks of it, one wonders that a woman should ever say anything but "no."'

'They never did say anything else to me,' said Johnny.

'I don't believe it. I daresay the truth is, you never asked anybody.'

'Did anybody ever ask you?'

'What would you give to know? But I will tell you frankly; – yes. And once, – once I thought that my answer would not have been a "no."'

'But you changed your mind?'

'When the moment came I could not bring myself to say the word that should rob me of my liberty for ever. I had said "no" to him often enough before, – poor fellow; and on this occasion he told me that he asked for the last time. "I shall not give myself another chance," he said, "for I shall be on board ship within a week." I merely bade him good-by. It was the only answer I gave him. He understood me, and since that day his foot has never pressed his native soil.'

'And was it all because you are so fond of your liberty?' said Johnny.

'Perhaps, – I did not – love him' said Miss Demolines, thoughtfully. She was now again seated in her chair, and John Eames had gone back to his corner of the sofa. 'If I had really loved him I suppose it would have been otherwise. He was a gallant fellow, and had two thousand a year of his own, in India stock and other securities.'

'Dear me! And he has not married yet?'

'He wrote me word to say that he would never marry till I was married, – but that on the day he should hear of my wedding, he would go to the first single woman near him and propose. It was a droll thing to say; was it not?'

'The single woman ought to feel herself flattered.'

'He would find plenty to accept him. Besides being so well off he was a very handsome fellow, and is connected with people of title. He had everything to recommend him.'

'And yet you refused him so often?'

'Yes. You think I was foolish; – do you not?'

'I don't think you were at all foolish if you didn't care for him.'

'It was my destiny, I suppose; I daresay I was wrong. Other girls marry without violent love, and do very well afterwards. Look at Maria Clutterbuck.'

The name of Maria Clutterbuck had become odious to John Eames. As long as Miss Demolines would continue to talk about herself he could listen with some amount of gratification. Conversation on that subject was the natural progress of the Bayswater romance. And if Madalina would only call her friend by her present name, he had no strong objection to an occasional mention of the lady; but the combined names of Maria Clutterbuck had come to be absolutely distasteful to him. He did not believe in the Maria Clutterbuck friendship, – either in its past or present existence, as described by Madalina. Indeed, he did not put strong faith in anything that Madalina said to him. In the handsome gentleman with two thousand a year, he did not believe at all. But the handsome gentleman had only been mentioned once in the course of his acquaintance with Miss Demolines, whereas Maria Clutterbuck had come up so often! 'Upon my word I must wish you goodby,' he said. 'It is going on for eleven o'clock, and I have to start tomorrow at seven.'

'What difference does that make?'

'A fellow wants to get a little sleep, you know.'

'Go then; – go and get your sleep. What a sleepy-headed generation it is.' Johnny longed to ask her whether the last generation was less sleepy-headed, and whether the gentleman with two thousand a year had sat up talking all night before he pressed his foot for the last time on his native soil; but he did not dare. As he said to himself afterwards, 'It would not do to bring the Bayswater romance too suddenly to its termination!' 'But before you go,' she continued, 'I must say the word to you about that picture. Did you speak to Mr Dalrymple?'

'I did not. I have been so busy with different things that I have not seen him.'

'And now you are going?'

'Well, – to tell the truth, I think I shall see him to-night, in spite of my being so sleepy-headed. I wrote him a line that I would look in and smoke a cigar with him if he chanced to be at home!'

'And that is why you want to go. A gentleman cannot live without his cigar now.'

'It is especially at your bidding that I am going to see him.'

'Go, then, – and make your friend understand that if he continues this picture of his, he will bring himself to great trouble, and will probably ruin the woman for whom he professes, I presume, to feel something like friendship. You may tell him that Mrs Van Siever has already heard of it.'

'Who told her?' demanded Johnny.

'Never mind. You need not look at me like that. It was not I. Do you suppose that secrets can be kept when so many people know them? Every servant in Maria's house knows all about it.'

'As for that, I don't suppose Mrs Broughton makes any great secret of it.'

'Do you think she has told Mr Broughton? I am sure she has not. I may say I know she has not. Maria Clutterbuck is infatuated. There is no other excuse to be made for her.'

'Good-by,' said Johnny, hurriedly.

'And you really are going?'

'Well, – yes. I suppose so.'

'Go then. I have nothing more to say to you.'

'I shall come and call directly I return,' said Johnny.

'You may do as you please about that, sir.'

'Do you mean that you won't be glad to see me again?'

'I am not going to flatter you, Mr Eames. Mamma will be well by that time, I hope, and I do not mind telling you that you are a favourite with her.' Johnny thought that this was particularly kind, as he had seen so very little of the old lady. 'If you choose to call upon her,' said Madalina, 'of course she will be glad to see you.'

'But I was speaking of yourself, you know?' and Johnny permitted himself for a moment to look tenderly at her.

'Then from myself pray understand that I will say nothing to flatter your self-love.'

'I thought you would be kinder just when I was going away.'

'I think I have been quite kind enough. As you observed yourself just now, it is nearly eleven o'clock, and I must ask you to go away. Bon voyage, and a happy return to you.'

'And you will be glad to see me when I am back? Tell me that you will be glad to see me.'

'I will tell you nothing of the kind. Mr Eames, if you do, I will be very angry with you.' And then he went.

On his way back to his own lodgings he did call on Conway Dalrymple, and in spite of his need for early rising, sat smoking with the artist for an hour. 'If you don't take care, young man,' said his friend, 'you will find yourself in a scrape with your Madalina.'

'What sort of a scrape?'

'As you walk away from Porchester Terrace some fine day, you will have to congratulate yourself on having made a successful overture towards matrimony.'

'You don't think I am such a fool as that comes to?'

'Other men as wise as you have done the same sort of thing. Miss Demolines is very clever, and I daresay you find it amusing.'

'It isn't so much that she's clever, and I can hardly say that it is amusing. One gets awfully tired of it, you know. But a fellow must have something to do, and that is as good as anything else.'

'I suppose you have not heard that one young man levanted last year to save himself from a breach of promise case?'

'I wonder whether he had any money in Indian securities?'

'What makes you ask that?'

'Nothing particular.'

'Whatever little he had he chose to save, and I think I heard that he went to Canada. His name was Shorter; and they say that, on the eve of his going, Madalina sent him word that she had no objection to the colonies, and that, under the pressing emergency of his expatriation, she was willing to become Mrs Shorter with more expedition than usually attends fashionable weddings. Shorter, however, escaped, and has never been seen back again.'

Eames declared that he did not believe a word of it. Nevertheless, as he walked home he came to the conclusion that Mr Shorter must have been the handsome gentleman with Indian securities, to whom 'no' had been said once too often.

While sitting with Conway Dalrymple, he had forgotten to say a word about Jael and Sisera.

CHAPTER 47

Dr Tempest at the palace

Intimation had been sent from the palace to Dr Tempest of Silverbridge of the bishop's intention that a commission should be held by him, as rural dean, with other neighbouring clergymen, as assessors with him, that inquiry might be made on the part of the church into the question of Mr Crawley's guilt. It must be understood that by this time the opinion had become very general that Mr Crawley had been guilty, – that he had found the cheque in his house, and that he had, after holding it for many months, succumbed to temptation, and applied it to his own purposes. But various excuses were made for him by those who so believed. In the first place it was felt by all who really knew anything of the man's character, that the very fact of his committing such a crime proved him to be hardly responsible for his actions. He must have known, had not all judgment in such matters been taken from him, that the cheque would certainly be traced back to his hands. No attempt had been made in the disposing of it to dispose of it in such a way that the trace should be obliterated. He had simply given it to a neighbour with a direction to have it cashed, and had written his own name on the back of it. And therefore, though there could be no doubt as to the theft in the mind of those who supposed that he had found the cheque in his own house, yet the guilt of the theft seemed to be almost annihilated by the folly of the thief. And then his poverty, and his struggles, and the sufferings of his wife, were remembered; and stories were told from mouth to mouth of his industry in his profession, of his great zeal among those brickmakers of Hoggle End, of acts of charity done by him which startled the people of the district into admiration; – how he had worked with his own hands for the sick poor to whom he could not give relief in money, turning a woman's mangle for a couple of hours, and carrying a boy's load along the lanes. Dr Tempest and others declared that he had derogated from the dignity of his position as an English parish clergyman by such acts; but, nevertheless, the stories of these deeds acted strongly on the minds of both men and women, creating an admiration for Mr Crawley which was much stronger than the condemnation of his guilt.

Even Mrs Walker and her daughter, and the Miss Prettymans, had so far given way that they had ceased to asseverate their belief in Mr Crawley's innocence. They contented themselves now with simply expressing a hope that he would be acquitted by a jury, and that when he should be so acquitted the thing might be allowed to rest. If he had sinned, no doubt he had repented. And then there were serious debates whether he might not have stolen the money without much sin, being mad or half-mad, – touched with madness when he took it; and whether he might not, in spite of such temporary touch of madness, be well fitted for his parish duties. Sorrow had afflicted him grievously; but that sorrow, though it had incapacitated him for the management of his own affairs, had not rendered him unfit for the ministrations of his parish. Such were the arguments now used in his favour by the women around him; and the men were not keen to contradict them. The wish that he should be acquitted and allowed to remain in his parsonage was very general.

When therefore it became known that the bishop had decided to put on foot another investigation, with the view of bringing Mr Crawley's conduct under ecclesiastical condemnation, almost everybody accused the bishop of persecution. The world of the diocese declared that Mrs Proudie was at work, and that the bishop himself was no better than a puppet. It was in vain that certain clear-headed men among the clergy, of whom Dr Tempest himself was one, pointed out that the bishop after all might perhaps be right; – that if Mr Crawley were guilty, and if he should be found to have been so by a jury, it might be absolutely necessary that an ecclesiastical court should take some cognizance of the crime beyond that taken by the civil law. 'The jury,' said Dr Tempest, discussing the case with Mr Roberts and other clerical neighbours, – 'the jury may probably find him guilty and recommend him to mercy. The judge will have heard his character, and will have been made acquainted with his manner of life and will deal as lightly with the case as the law will allow him. For aught I know he may be imprisoned for a month. I wish it might be for no more than a day, – or an hour. But when he comes out from his month's imprisonment, – how then? Surely it should be a case for ecclesiastical inquiry, whether a clergyman who has committed a theft should be allowed to go into his pulpit directly he comes out of prison?' But the answer to this was that Mr Crawley always had been a good clergyman, was a good clergyman at this moment, and would be a good clergyman when he did come out of prison.

But Dr Tempest, though he had argued in his way, was by no means eager for the commencement of the commission over which he was to be called upon to preside. In spite of such arguments as the above, which came from the man's head when his head was brought to bear upon the matter, there was a thorough desire within his heart to oppose the bishop. He had no strong sympathy with Mr Crawley, as had others. He would have had Mr Crawley silenced without regret, presuming Mr Crawley to have been guilty. But he had a much stronger feeling with regard to the bishop. Had there been any question of silencing the bishop, – could it have been possible to take any steps in that direction, – he would have been very active. It may therefore be understood that in spite of his defence of the bishop's present proceedings as to the commission, he was anxious that the bishop should fail, and anxious to put impediments in the bishop's way, should it appear to him that he could do so with justice. Dr Tempest was well known among his parishioners to be hard and unsympathetic, some said unfeeling also, and cruel; but it was admitted by those who disliked him the most that he was both practical and just, and that he cared for the welfare of many, though he was rarely touched by the misery of one. Such was the man who was rector of Silverbridge and rural dean in the district, and who was now called upon by the bishop to assist him in making further inquiry as to this wretched cheque for twenty pounds.

Once at this period Archdeacon Grantly and Dr Tempest met each other and discussed the question of Mr Crawley's guilt. Both these men were inimical to the present bishop of the diocese, and both had perhaps respected the old bishop beyond all other men. But they were different in this, that the archdeacon hated Dr Proudie as a partisan, – whereas Dr Tempest opposed the bishop on certain principles which he endeavoured to make clear, at any rate to himself. 'Wrong!' said the archdeacon, speaking of the bishop's intention of issuing a commission – 'of course he is wrong. How could anything right come from him or from her? I should be sorry to have to do his bidding.'

'I think you are a little hard upon Bishop Proudie,' said Dr Tempest.

'One cannot be hard upon him' said the archdeacon. 'He is so scandalously weak, and she is so radically vicious, that they cannot but be wrong together. The very fact that such a man should be a bishop among us is to me terribly strong evidence of evil days coming.'

'You are more impulsive than I am,' said Dr Tempest. 'In this case I am sorry for the poor man, who is, I am sure, honest in the main. But I believe that in such a case your father would have done just what the present bishop is doing; – that he could have done nothing else; and as I think that Dr Proudie is right I shall do all that I can to assist him in the commission.'

The bishop's secretary had written to Dr Tempest, telling him of the bishop's purpose; and now, in one of the last days of March, the bishop himself wrote to Dr Tempest, asking him to come over to the palace. The letter was worded most courteously, and expressed very feelingly the great regret which the writer felt at being obliged to take these proceedings against a clergyman in his diocese. Bishop Proudie knew how to write such a letter. By the writing of such letters, and by the making of speeches in the same strain, he had become Bishop of Barchester. Now, in this letter, he begged Dr Tempest to come over to him saying how delighted Mrs Proudie would be to see him at the palace. Then he went on to explain the great difficulty which he felt, and great sorrow also, in dealing with this matter of Mr Crawley. He looked, therefore, confidently for Dr Tempest's assistance. Thinking to do the best for Mr Crawley, and anxious to enable Mr Crawley to remain in quiet retirement till the trial should be over, he had sent a clergyman over to Hogglestock, who would have relieved Mr Crawley from the burden of the church-services; – but Mr Crawley would have none of this relief. Mr Crawley had been obstinate and overbearing, and had persisted in claiming his right to his own pulpit. Therefore was the bishop obliged to interfere legally, and therefore was he under the necessity of asking Dr Tempest to assist him. Would Dr Tempest come over on the Monday, and stay till the Wednesday?

The letter was a very good letter, and Dr Tempest was obliged to do as he was asked. He so far modified the bishop's proposition that he reduced the sojourn at the palace by one night. He wrote to say that he would have the pleasure of dining with the bishop and Mrs Proudie on the Monday, but would return home on the Tuesday, as soon as the business in hand would permit him. 'I shall get on very well with him,' he said to his wife before he started; 'but I am afraid of the woman. If she interferes, there will be a row.' 'Then, my dear,' said his wife, 'there will be a row, for I am told that she always interferes.' On reaching the palace about half-an-hour before dinner-time, Dr Tempest found that other guests were expected, and on descending to the great yellow drawing-room, which was used only on state occasions, he encountered Mrs Proudie and two of her daughters arrayed in a full panoply of female armour. She received him with her sweetest smiles, and if there had been any former enmity between Silverbridge and the palace, it was now all forgotten. She regretted greatly that Mrs Tempest had not accompanied the doctor; – for Mrs Tempest also had been invited. But Mrs Tempest was not quite as well as she might have been, the doctor had said, and very rarely slept away from home. And then the bishop came in and greeted his guest with his pleasantest good-humour. It was quite a sorrow to him that Silverbridge was so distant, and that he saw so little of Dr Tempest; but he hoped that that might be somewhat mended now, and that leisure might be found for social delights; – to all which Dr Tempest said but little, bowing to the bishop at each separate expression of his lordship's kindness.

There were guests there that evening who did not often sit at the bishop's table. The archdeacon and Mrs Grantly had been summoned from Plumstead, and had obeyed the summons. Great as was the enmity between the bishop and the archdeacon, it had never quite taken the form of open palpable hostility. Each, therefore, asked the other to dinner perhaps once every year; and each went to the other, perhaps, once in two years. And Dr Thorne from Chaldicotes was there, but without his wife, who in these days was up in London. Mrs Proudie always expressed a warm friendship for Mrs Thorne, and on this occasion loudly regretted her absence. 'You must tell her, Dr Thorne, how exceedingly much we miss her.' Dr Thorne, who was accustomed to hear his wife speak of her dear friend Mrs Proudie with almost unmeasured ridicule, promised that he would do so. 'We are so sorry the Luftons couldn't come to us,' said Mrs Proudie, – not alluding to the dowager, of whom it was well known that no earthly inducement would have sufficed to make her put her foot within Mrs Proudie's room; – 'but one of the children is ill, and she could not leave him.' But the Greshams were there from Boxall Hill, and the Thornes from Ullathorne, and, with the exception of a single chaplain, who pretended to carve, Dr Tempest and the archdeacon were the only clerical guests at the table. From all which Dr Tempest knew that the bishop was anxious to treat him with special consideration on the present occasion.

The dinner was rather long and ponderous, and occasionally almost dull. The archdeacon talked a good deal, but a bystander with an acute ear might have understood from the tone of his voice that he was not talking as he would have talked among friends. Mrs Proudie felt this, and understood it, and was angry. Her accurate ear would always appreciate the defiance of episcopal authority, as now existing in Barchester, which was concealed, or only half concealed, by all the archdeacon's words. But the bishop was not so keen, nor so easily roused to wrath; and though the presence of his enemy did to a certain degree cow him, he strove to fight against the feeling with renewed good-humour.

'You have improved so upon the old days,' said the archdeacon, speaking of some small matter with reference to the cathedral, 'that one hardly knows the old place.'

'I hope we have not fallen off,' said the bishop, with a smile.

'We have improved, Dr Grantly,' said Mrs Proudie, with great emphasis on her words. 'What you say is true. We have improved.'

'Not a doubt about that,' said the archdeacon. Then Mrs Grantly interposed, strove to change the subject, and threw oil upon the waters.

'Talking of improvements,' said Mrs Grantly, 'what an excellent row of houses they have built at the bottom of High Street. I wonder who is to live in them?'

'I remember when that was the very worst part of the town,' said Dr Thorne.

'And now they're asking seventy pounds apiece for houses which did not cost above six hundred each to build,' said Mr Thorne of Ullathorne, with that seeming dislike of modern success which is evinced by most of the elders of the world.

'And who is to live in them?' asked Mrs Grantly.

'Two of them have been already taken by clergymen,' said the bishop, in a tone of triumph.

'Yes,' said the archdeacon, 'and the houses in the Close which used to be the residences of the prebendaries have been leased out to tallow-chandlers and retired brewers. That comes of the working of the Ecclesiastical Commission.'

'And why not?' demanded Mrs Proudie.

'Why not, indeed, if you like to have tallow-chandlers next door to you?' said the archdeacon. 'In the old days, we would sooner have had our brethren near to us.'

'There is nothing, Dr Grantly, so objectionable in a cathedral town as a lot of idle clergymen,' said Mrs Proudie.

'It is beginning to be a question to me,' said the archdeacon, 'whether there is any use in clergymen at all for the present generation.'

'Dr Grantly, those cannot be your real sentiments,' said Mrs Proudie. Then Mrs Grantly, working hard in her vocation as a peacemaker, changed the conversation again, and began to talk of the American war. But even that was made matter of discord on church matters, – the archdeacon professing an opinion that the Southerners were Christian gentlemen, and the Northerners infidel snobs; whereas Mrs Proudie had an idea that the Gospel was preached with genuine zeal in the Northern States. And at each such outbreak the poor bishop would laugh uneasily, and say a word or two to which no one paid much attention. And so the dinner went on, not always in the most pleasant manner for those who preferred continued social good-humour to the occasional excitement of a half-suppressed battle.

Not a word was said about Mr Crawley. When Mrs Proudie and the ladies had left the dining-room, the bishop strove to get up a little lay conversation. He spoke to Mr Thorne about his game, and to Dr Thorne about his timber, and even to Mr Gresham about his hounds. 'It is not so very many years, Mr Gresham,' said he, 'since the Bishop of Barchester was expected to keep hounds himself,' and the bishop laughed at his own joke.

'Your lordship shall have them back at the palace next season,' said young Frank Gresham, 'if you will promise to do the county justice.'

'Ha, ha, ha!' laughed the bishop. 'What do you say, Mr Tozer?' Mr Tozer was the chaplain on duty.

'I have not the least objection in the world, my lord,' said Mr Tozer, 'to act as second whip.'

'I'm afraid you'll find them an expensive adjunct to the episcopate,' said the archeacon. And then the joke was over; for there had been a rumour, now for some years prevalent in Barchester, that Bishop Proudie was not liberal in his expenditure. As Mr Thorne said afterwards to his cousin the doctor, the archdeacon might have spared that sneer. 'The archdeacon will never spare the man who sits in his father's seat,' said the doctor. 'The pity of it is that men who are so thoroughly different in all their sympathies should ever be brought into contact.' 'Dear, dear,' said the archdeacon, as he stood afterwards on the rug before the drawing-room fire, 'how many rubbers of whist I have seen played in his room.' I sincerely hope that you will never see another played here,' said Mrs Proudie. 'I'm quite sure that I shall not,' said the archdeacon. For this last sally his wife scolded him bitterly on their way home. 'You know very well,' she said, 'that the times are changed, and that if you were Bishop of Barchester yourself you would not have whist played in the palace.' 'I only know,' said he, 'that when we had the whist we had some true religion along with it, and some good sense and good feeling also.' 'You cannot be right to sneer at others for doing what you would do yourself,' said his wife. Then the archdeacon threw himself sulkily into the corner of the carriage, and nothing more was said between him and his wife about the bishop's dinner-party.

Not a word was spoken that night at the palace about Mr Crawley; and when that obnoxious guest from Plumstead was gone, Mrs Proudie resumed her good-humour towards Dr Tempest. So intent was she on conciliating him that she refrained even from abusing the archdeacon, whom she knew to have been intimate for very many years with the rector of Silverbridge. In her accustomed moods she would have broken forth in loud anger, caring nothing for old friendships; but at present she was thoughtful of the morrow,* and desirous that Dr Tempest should, if possible, meet her in a friendly humour when the great discussion as to Hogglestock should be opened between them. But Dr Tempest understood her bearing, and as he pulled on his nightcap made certain resolutions of his own as to the morrow's proceedings. 'I don't suppose she will dare to interfere,' he had said to his wife; 'but if she does, I shall certainly tell the bishop that I cannot speak on the subject in her presence.'

At breakfast on the following morning there was no one present but the bishop, Mrs Proudie, and Dr Tempest. Very little was said at the meal. Mr Crawley's name was not mentioned, but there seemed to be a general feeling among them that there was a task hanging over them which prevented any general conversation. The eggs were eaten and the coffee was drunk, but the eggs and the coffee disappeared almost in silence. When these ceremonies had been altogether completed, and it was clearly necessary that something further should be done, the bishop spoke: 'Dr Tempest,' he said, 'perhaps you will join me in my study at eleven. We can then say a few words to each other about the unfortunate matter on which I shall have to trouble you.' Dr Tempest said he would be punctual to his appointment, and then the bishop withdrew, muttering something as to the necessity of looking at his letters. Dr Tempest took a newspaper in his hand, which had been brought in by a servant, but Mrs Proudie did not allow him to read it. 'Dr Tempest,' she said, 'this is a matter of most vital importance. I am quite sure that you feel that it is so.'

'What matter, madam?' said the doctor.

'This terrible affair of Mr Crawley's. If something be not done the whole diocese will be disgraced.' Then she waited for an answer, but receiving none she was obliged to continue. 'Of the poor man's guilt there can, I fear, be no doubt.' Then there was another pause, but still the doctor made no answer. 'And if he be guilty,' said Mrs Proudie, resolving that she would ask a question that must bring forth some reply, 'can any experienced clergyman think that he can be fit to preach from the pulpit of a parish church? I am sure that you must agree with me, Dr Tempest? Consider the souls of the people!'

'Mrs Proudie,' said he, 'I think that we had better not discuss the matter.'

'Not discuss it?'

'I think that we had better not do so. If I understand the bishop aright, he wishes that I should take some step in the matter.'

'Of course he does.'

'And therefore I must decline to make it a matter of common conversation.'

'Common conversation, Dr Tempest! I should be the last person in the world to make it a matter of common conversation. I regard this as by no means a common conversation. God forbid that it should be a common conversation. I am speaking now very seriously with reference to the interests of the Church, which I think will be endangered by having among her active servants a man who has been guilty of so base a crime as theft. Think of it, Dr Tempest. Theft! Stealing money! Appropriating to his own use a cheque for twenty pounds which did not belong to him! And then telling such terrible falsehoods about it! Can anything be worse, anything more scandalous, anything more dangerous? Indeed, Dr Tempest, I do not regard this as any common conversation.' The whole of this speech was not made at once, fluently, or without a break. From stop to stop Mrs Proudie paused, waiting for her companion's words; but as he would not speak she was obliged to continue. 'I am sure that you cannot but agree with me, Dr Tempest?' she said.

'I am quite sure that I shall not discuss it with you,' said the doctor, very brusquely.

'And why not? Are you not here to discuss it?'

'Not with you, Mrs Proudie. You must excuse me for saying so, but I am not here to discuss any such matter with you. Were I to do so, I should be guilty of a very great impropriety.'

'All these things are in common between me and the bishop,' said Mrs Proudie, with an air that was intended to be dignified, but which nevertheless displayed her rising anger.

'As to that I know nothing, but they cannot be in common between you and me. It grieves me much that I should have to speak to you in such a strain, but my duty allows me no alternative. I think if you will permit me, I will take a turn round the garden before I keep my appointment with his lordship.' And so saying he escaped from the lady without hearing her further remonstrance.

It still wanted nearly an hour to the time named by the bishop, and Dr Tempest used it in preparing for his withdrawal from the palace as soon as his interview with the bishop should be over. After what had passed he thought that he would be justified in taking his departure without bidding adieu formally to Mrs Proudie.

He would say a word or two, explaining his haste, to the bishop; and then, if he could get out of the house at once, it might be that he would never see Mrs Proudie again. He was rather proud of his success in their late battle, but he felt that, having been so completely victorious, it would be foolish in him to risk his laurels in the chance of another encounter. He would say not a word of what had happened to the bishop, and he thought it probable that neither would Mrs Proudie speak of it, – at any rate till after he was gone. Generals who are beaten out of the field are not quick to talk of their own repulses. He, indeed, had not beaten Mrs Proudie out of the field. He had, in fact, himself run away. But he had left his foe silenced; and with such a foe, and in such a contest, that was everything. He put up his portmanteau, therefore, and prepared for his final retreat. Then he rang his bell and desired the servant to show him to the bishop's study. The servant did so, and when he entered the room the first thing he saw was Mrs Proudie sitting in an arm-chair near the window. The bishop was also in the room, sitting with his arms upon the writing-table, and his head upon his hands. It was very evident that Mrs Proudie did not consider herself to have been beaten, and that she was prepared to fight another battle. 'Will you sit down, Dr Tempest?' she said, motioning him with her hand to a chair opposite to that occupied by the bishop. Dr Tempest sat down. He felt that at the moment he had nothing else to do, and that he must restrain any remonstrance that he might make till Mr Crawley's name should be mentioned. He was almost lost in admiration of the woman. He had left her, as he thought, utterly vanquished and prostrated by his determined but uncourteous usage of her; and here she was, present again upon the field of battle as though she had never been even wounded. He could see that there had been words between her and the bishop, and that she had carried a point on which the bishop had been very anxious to have his own way. He could perceive at once that the bishop had begged her to absent herself and was greatly chagrined that he should not have prevailed with her. There she was, – and as Dr Tempest was resolved that he would neither give advice nor receive instructions respecting Mr Crawley in her presence, he could only draw upon his courage and his strategy for the coming warfare. For a few moments no one said a word. The bishop felt that if Dr Tempest would only begin, the work on hand might be got through, even in his wife's presence. Mrs Proudie was aware that her husband should begin. If he would do so, and if Dr Tempest would listen and then reply, she might gradually make her way into the conversation; and if her words were once accepted then she could say all that she desired to say; then she could play her part and become somebody in the episcopal work. When once she should have been allowed liberty of speech, the enemy would be powerless to stop her. But all this Dr Tempest understood quite as well as she understood it, and had they waited till night he would not have been the first to mention Mr Crawley's name.

The bishop sighed aloud. The sigh might be taken as expressing grief over the sin of the erring brother whose conduct they were then to discuss, and was not amiss. But when the sigh with its attendant murmurs had passed away it was necessary that some initiative step should be taken. 'Dr Tempest,' said the bishop, 'what are we to do about this poor stiff-necked gentleman?' Still Dr Tempest did not speak. 'There is no clergyman in the diocese,' continued the bishop, 'in whose prudence and wisdom I have more confidence than in yours. And I know, too, that you are by no means disposed to severity where severe measures are not necessary. What ought we to do? If he has been guilty, he should not surely return to his pulpit after the expiration of such punishment as the law of his country may award to him.'

Dr Tempest looked at Mrs Proudie, thinking that she might perhaps say a word now; but Mrs Proudie knew her part better and was silent. Angry as she was, she contrived to hold her peace. Let the debate once begin and she would be able to creep into it, and then to lead it, – and so she would hold her own. But she had met a foe as wary as herself. 'My lord,' said the doctor, 'it will perhaps be well that you should communicate your wishes to me in writing. If it be possible for me to comply with them I will do so.'

'Yes; – exactly; no doubt; – but I thought that perhaps we might better understand each other if we had a few words of quiet conversation upon the subject. I believe you know the steps that I have—'

But here the bishop was interrupted. Dr Tempest rose from his chair, and advancing to the table put both his hands upon it. 'My lord,' he said, 'I feel myself compelled to say that which I would very much rather leave unsaid, were it possible. I feel the difficulty, and I may say delicacy, of my position; but I should be untrue to my conscience and to my feeling of what is right in such matters, if I were to take any part in a discussion on this matter in the presence, if I were to take any part in a discussion on this matter in the presence of – a lady.'

'Dr Tempest, what is your objection?' said Mrs Proudie, rising from her chair, and coming also to the table, so that from thence she might confront her opponent; and as she stood opposite to Dr Tempest she also put both her hands upon the table.

'My dear, perhaps you will leave us for a few moments,' said the bishop. Poor bishop! Poor weak bishop! As the words came from his mouth he knew that they would be spoken in vain, and that, if so, it would have been better for him to have left them unspoken.

'Why should I be dismissed from your room without a reason?' said Mrs Proudie. 'Cannot Dr Tempest understand that a wife may share her husband's counsels, – as she must share his troubles? If he cannot I pity him very much as to his own household.'

'Dr Tempest,' said the bishop, 'Mrs Proudie takes the greatest possible interest in everything concerning the diocese.'

'I am sure, my lord,' said the doctor, 'that you will see how unseemly it would be that I should interfere in any way between you and Mrs Proudie. I certainly will not do so. I can only say again that if you will communicate to me your wishes in writing, I will attend to them, – if it be possible.'

'You mean to be stubborn,' said Mrs Proudie, whose prudence was beginning to give way under the great provocation to which her temper was being subjected.

'Yes, madam; if it is to be called stubbornness, I must be stubborn. My lord, Mrs Proudie spoke to me on this subject in the breakfast-room after you had left it, and I then ventured to explain to her that in accordance with such light as I have on the matter, I could not discuss it in her presence. I greatly grieve that I failed to make myself understood by her, – as, otherwise this unpleasantness might have been spared.'

'I understood you very well, Dr Tempest, and I think you to be a most unreasonable man. Indeed, I might use a much harsher word.'

'You may use any word you please, Mrs Proudie,' said the doctor.

'My dear, I really think you had better leave us for a few minutes,' said the bishop.

'No, my lord, – no,' said Mrs Proudie, turning round upon her husband. 'Not so. It would be most unbecoming that I should be turned out of a room in this palace by an uncourteous word from a parish clergyman. It would be unseemly. If Dr Tempest forgets his duty, I will not forget mine. There are other clergymen in the diocese besides Dr Tempest who can undertake the very easy task of this commission. As for his having been appointed rural dean I don't know how many years ago, it is a matter of no consequence whatever. In such a preliminary inquiry any three clergymen will suffice. It need not be done by the rural dean at all.'

'My dear!'

'I will not be turned out of this room by Dr Tempest; – and that is enough.'

'My lord,' said the doctor, 'you had better write to me as I proposed to you just now.'

'His lordship will not write. His lordship will do nothing of the kind,' said Mrs Proudie.

'My dear!' said the bishop, driven in his perplexity beyond all carefulness of reticence. 'My dear, I do wish you wouldn't, – I do indeed. If you would only go away!'

'I will not go away, my lord,' said Mrs Proudie.

'But I will,' said Dr Tempest, feeling true compassion for the unfortunate man whom he saw writhing in agony before him. 'It will manifestly be for the best that I should retire. My lord, I wish you good morning. Mrs Proudie, good morning.' And so he left the room.

'A most stubborn and a most ungentlemanlike man,' said Mrs Proudie, as soon as the door was closed behind the retreating rural dean. 'I do not think that in the whole course of my life I ever met with any one so insubordinate and so ill-mannered. He is worse than the archdeacon.' As she uttered these words she paced about the room. The bishop said nothing; and when she herself had been silent for a few minutes she turned upon him. 'Bishop,' she said, 'I hope that you agree with me. I expect that you will agree with me in a matter that is of so much moment to my comfort, and I may say to my position generally in the diocese. Bishop, why do you not speak?'

'You have behaved in such a way that I do not know that I shall speak again,' said the bishop.

'What is this that you say?'

'I say that I do not know how I shall ever speak again. You have disgraced me.'

'Disgraced you! I disgrace you! It is you that disgrace yourself by saying such words.'

'Very well. Let it be so. Perhaps you will go away now and leave me to myself. I have got a bad headache, and I can't talk any more. Oh dear, oh dear, what will he think of it!'

'And you mean to tell me that I have been wrong!'

'Yes, you have been wrong, – very wrong. Why didn't you go away when I asked you? You are always being wrong. I wish I had never come to Barchester. In any other position I should not have felt it so much. As it is I do not know how I can ever show my face again.'

'Not have felt what so much, Mr Proudie?' said the wife, going back in the excitement of her anger to the nomenclature of old days. 'And this is to be my return for all my care in your behalf! Allow me to tell you, sir, that in any position in which you may be placed I know what is due to you, and that your dignity will never lose anything in my hands. I wish that you were as well able to take care of it yourself.' Then she stalked out of the room, and left the poor man alone.

Bishop Proudie sat alone in his study throughout the whole day. Once or twice in the course of the morning his chaplain came to him on some matter of business, and was answered with a smile, – the peculiar softness of which the chaplain did not fail to attribute to the right cause. For it was soon known throughout the household that there had been a quarrel. Could he quite have made up his mind to do so, – could he have resolved that it would be altogether better to quarrel with his wife, – the bishop would have appealed to the chaplain, and have asked at any rate for sympathy. But even yet he could not bring himself to confess his misery, and to own himself to another to be the wretch that he was. Then during the long hours of the day he sat thinking of it all. How happy could he be if it were only possible for him to go away, and become even a curate in a parish, without his wife! Would there ever come to him a time of freedom? Would she ever die? He was older than she, and of course he would die first. Would it not be a fine thing if he could die at once, and thus escape from his misery?

What could he do, even supposing himself strong enough to fight the battle? He could not lock her up. He could not even very well lock her out of his room. She was his wife, and must have the run of his house. He could not altogether debar her from the society of the diocesan clergymen. He had, on this very morning, taken strong measure with her. More than once or twice he had desired her to leave the room. What was there to be done with a woman who would not obey her husband, – who would not even leave him to the performance of his own work? What a blessed thing it would be if a bishop could go away from his home to his work every day like a clerk in a public office, – as a stone-mason does! But there was no such escape for him. He could not go away. And how was he to meet her again on this very day?

And then for hours he thought of Dr Tempest and Mr Crawley, considering what he had better do to repair the shipwreck of the morning. At last he resolved that he would write to the doctor; and before he had again seen his wife, he did write his letter, and he sent it off. In this letter he made no direct allusion to the occurrence of the morning, but wrote as though there had not been any fixed intention of a personal discussion between them. 'I think it will be better that there should be a commission,' he said, 'and I would suggest that you should have four other clergymen with you. Perhaps you will select two yourself out of your rural deanery; and, if you do not object, I will name as the other two Mr Thumble and Mr Quiverful, who are both resident in the city.' As he wrote these two names he felt ashamed of himself, knowing that he had chosen the two men as being special friends of his wife, and feeling that he should have been brave enough to throw aside all considerations of his wife's favour, – especially at this moment, in which he was putting on his armour to do battle against her. 'It is not probable,' he continued to say in his letter, 'that you will be able to make your report until after the trial of this unfortunate gentleman shall have taken place, and a verdict shall have been given. Should he be acquitted, that, I imagine, should end the matter. There can be no reason why we should attempt to go beyond the verdict of a jury. But should he be found guilty, I think we ought to be ready with such steps as it will be becoming for us to take at the expiration of any sentence which may be pronounced. It will be, at any rate, expedient that in such case the matter should be brought before an ecclesiastical court.' He knew well as he wrote this, that he was proposing something much milder than the course intended by his wife when she had instigated him to take proceedings in the matter; but he did not much regard that now. Though he had been weak enough to name certain clergymen as assessors with the rural dean, because he thought that by doing so he would to a certain degree conciliate his wife, – though he had been so far a coward, yet he was resolved that he would not sacrifice to her his own judgment and his own conscience in his manner of proceeding. He kept no copy of his letter, so that he might be unable to show her his very words when she should ask to see them. Of course he would tell her what he had done; but in telling her he would keep to himself what he had said as to the result of an acquittal in a civil court. She need not yet be told that he had promised to take such a verdict as sufficing also for an ecclesiastical acquittal. In this spirit his letter was written and sent off before he again saw his wife.

He did not meet her till they came together in the drawing-room before dinner. In explaining the whole truth as to circumstances as they existed at the palace at that moment, it must be acknowledged that Mrs Proudie herself, great as was her courage, and wide as were the resources which she possessed within herself, was somewhat appalled by the position of affairs. I fear that it may now be too late for me to excite much sympathy in the mind of any reader on behalf of Mrs Proudie. I shall never be able to make her virtues popular. But she had virtues, and their existence now made her unhappy. She did regard the dignity of her husband, and she felt at the present moment that she had almost compromised it. She did also regard the welfare of the clergymen around her, thinking of course in a general way that certain of them who agreed with her were the clergymen whose welfare should be studied, and that certain of them who disagreed with her were the clergymen whose welfare should be postponed. But now an idea made its way into her bosom that she was not perhaps doing the best for the welfare of the diocese generally. What if it should come to pass that all the clergymen of the diocese should refuse to open their mouths in her presence on ecclesiastical subjects, as Dr Tempest had done? This special day was not one on which she was well contented with herself, though by no means on that account was her anger mitigated against the offending rural dean.

During dinner she struggled to say a word or two to her husband, as though there had been no quarrel between them. With him the matter had gone so deep that he could not answer her in the same spirit. There were sundry members of the family present, – daughters, and a son-in-law, and a daughter's friend who was staying with them; but even in the hope of appearing to be serene before them he could not struggle through his deep despondence. He was very silent, and to his wife's words he answered hardly anything. He was courteous and gentle with them all, but he spoke as little as was possible, and during the evening he sat alone, with his head leaning on his hand, – not pretending even to read. He was aware that it was too late to make even an attempt to conceal his misery and his disgrace from his own family.

His wife came to him that night in his dressing room in a spirit of feminine softness that was very unusual with her. 'My dear,' said she, 'let us forget what occurred this morning. If there has been any anger we are bound as Christians to forget it.' She stood over him as she spoke, and put her hand upon his shoulder almost caressingly.

'When a man's heart is broken, he cannot forget it,' was his reply. She still stood by him, and still kept her hand upon him: but she could think of no other words of comfort to say. 'I will go to bed,' he said. 'It is the best place for me.' Then she left him, and he went to bed.

CHAPTER 48

The softness of Sir Raffle Buffle

We have seen that John Eames was prepared to start on his journey in search of the Arabins, and have seen him after he had taken farewell of his office and of his master there, previous to his departure; but that matter of his departure had not been arranged altogether with comfort as far as his official interests were concerned. He had been perhaps a little abrupt in his mode of informing Sir Raffle Buffle that there was a pressing cause for his official absence, and Sir Raffle had replied to him that no private pressure could be allowed to interfere with his public duties. 'I must go, Sir Raffle, at any rate,' Johnny had said; 'it is a matter affecting my family, and must not be neglected.' 'If you intend to go without leave,' said Sir Raffle, 'I presume you will first put your resignation into the hands of Mr Kissing.' Now, Mr Kissing was the secretary to the Board. This had been serious undoubtedly. John Eames was not specially anxious to keep his present position as private secretary to Sir Raffle, but he certainly had no desire to give up his profession altogether. He said nothing more to the great man on that occasion, but before he left the office he wrote a private note to the chairman expressing the extreme importance of his business, and begging that he might have leave of absence. On the next morning he received it back with a very few words written across it. 'It can't be done,' were the very few words which Sir Raffle Buffle had written across the note from his private secretary. Here was a difficulty which Johnny had not anticipated, and which seemed to be insuperable. Sir Raffle would not have answered him in that strain if he had not been very much in earnest.

'I should send him a medical certificate,' said Cradell, his friend of old.

'Nonsense,' said Eames.

'I don't see that it's nonsense at all. They can't get over a medical certificate from a respectable man; and everybody has got something the matter with him of some kind.'

'I should go and let him do his worst,' said Fisher, who was another clerk. 'It wouldn't be more than putting you down a place or two. As to losing your present berth you don't mind that, and they would never think of dismissing you.'

'But I do mind being put down a place or two,' said Johnny, who could not forget that were he so put down his friend Fisher would gain the step which he would lose.

'I should give him a barrel of oysters, and talk to him about the Chancellor of the Exchequer,' said FitzHoward, who had been private secretary to Sir Raffle before Eames, and might therefore be supposed to know the man.

'That might have done very well if I had not asked him and been refused first,' said John Eames. 'I'll tell you what I'll do, I'll write a long letter on a sheet of foolscap paper, with a regular margin, so that it must come before the board, and perhaps that will frighten him.'

When he mentioned his difficulty on that evening to Mr Toogood, the lawyer begged him to give up the journey. 'It will only be sending a clerk, and it won't cost so very much after all,' said Toogood. But Johnny's pride could not allow him to give way. 'I'm not going to be done about it,' said he. 'I'm not going to resign, but I will go even though they may dismiss me. I don't think it will come to that, but if it does it must.' His uncle begged of him not to think of such an alternative; but this discussion took place after dinner, and away from the office, and Eames would not submit to bow his neck to authority. 'If it comes to that,' said he, 'a fellow might as well be a slave at once. And what is the use of a fellow having a little money if it does not make him independent? You may be sure of one thing, I shall go; and that on the day fixed.'

On the next morning John Eames was very silent when he went into Sir Raffle's room at the office. There was now only this day and another before that fixed for his departure, and it was of course very necessary that matters should be arranged. But he said nothing to Sir Raffle during the morning. The great man himself was condescending and endeavoured to be kind. He knew that his stern refusal had greatly irritated his private secretary, and was anxious to show that, though in the cause of public duty he was obliged to be stern, he was quite willing to forget his sternness when the necessity for it had passed away. On this morning, therefore, he was very cheery. But to all his cheery good-humour John Eames would make no response. Late in the afternoon, when most of the men had left the office, Johnny appeared before the chairman for

the last time that day with a very long face. He was dressed in
black, and had changed his ordinary morning coat for a frock,
which gave him an appearance altogether unlike that which was
customary to him. And he spoke almost in a whisper, very slowly;
and when Sir Raffle joked, – and Sir Raffle often would joke, – he
not only did not laugh, but he absolutely sighed. 'Is there anything
the matter with you Eames?' asked Sir Raffle.

'I am in great trouble,' said Eames.

'And what is your trouble?'

'It is essential for the honour of one of my family that I should be
at Florence by this day week. I cannot make up my mind what I
ought to do. I do not wish to lose my position in the public service,
to which, as you know, I am warmly attached; but I cannot submit
to see the honour of my family sacrificed!'

'Eames,' said Sir Raffle, 'that must be nonsense; – that must be
nonsense. There can be no reason why you should always expect to
have your own way in everything.'

'Of course if I go without leave I shall be dismissed.'

'Of course you will. It is out of the question that a young man
should take the bit between his teeth in that way.'

'As for taking the bit between his teeth, Sir Raffle, I do not think
that any man was ever more obedient, perhaps I should say more
submissive, than I have been. But there must be a limit to
everything.'

'What do you mean by that, Mr Eames?' said Sir Raffle, turning
in anger upon his private secretary. But Johnny disregarded his
anger. Johnny, indeed, had made up his mind that Sir Raffle should
be very angry. 'What do you mean, Mr Eames, by saying that there
must be a limit? I know nothing about limits. One would suppose
that you intended to make an accusation against me.'

'So I do. I think, Sir Raffle, that you are treating me with great
cruelty. I have explained to you that family circumstances—'

'You hve explained nothing, Mr Eames.'

'Yes, I have, Sir Raffle. I have explained to you that matters
relating to my family, which materially affect the honour of a
certain one of its members, demand that I should go at once to
Florence. You tell me that if I go I shall be dismissed.'

'Of course you must not go without leave. I never heard of such
a thing in all my life.' And Sir Raffle lifted up his hands towards
heaven, almost in dismay.

'So I have drawn up a short statement of the circumstances,
which I hope may be read at the Board when the question of my
dismissal comes before it.'

'You mean to go, then?'

'Yes, Sir Raffle; I must go. The honour of a certain branch of my family demands that I should do so. As I have for some time been so especially under you, I thought it would be proper to show you what I have said before I send my letter in, and therefore I have brought it with me. Here it is.' And Johnny handed to Sir Raffle an official document of large dimensions.

Sir Raffle began to be uncomfortable. He had acquired a character for tyranny in the public service of which he was aware, though he thought that he knew well that he had never deserved it. Some official big-wig, – perhaps that Chancellor of the Exchequer of whom he was so fond, – had on one occasion hinted to him that a little softness of usage would be compatible with the prejudices of the age. Softness was impossible to Sir Raffle; but his temper was sufficiently under his control to enable him to encounter the rebuke, and to pull himself up from time to time when he found himself tempted to speak loud and to take things with a high hand. He knew that a clerk should not be dismissed for leaving his office, who could show that his absence had been caused by some matter really affecting the interest of his family; and that were he to drive Eames to go on this occasion without leave, Eames would be simply called in to state what was this matter of moment which had taken him away. Probably he had stated that matter of moment in this very document which Sir Raffle was holding in his hand. But Sir Raffle was not willing to be conquered by the document. If it was necessary that he should give way, he would much prefer to give way, – out of his own good-nature, let us say, – without looking at the document at all. 'I must, under the circumstances, decline to read this,' said he, 'unless it should come before me officially,' and he handed back the paper.

'I thought it best to let you see it if you pleased,' said John Eames. Then he turned round as though he were going to leave the room; but suddenly he turned back again. 'I don't like to leave you, Sir Raffle, without saying good-by. I do not suppose we shall meet again. Of course you must do your duty, and I do not wish you to think that I have any personal ill-will against you.' So saying, he put out his hand to Sir Raffle as though to take a final farewell. Sir Raffle looked at him in amazement. He was dressed, as has been said, in black, and did not look like the John Eames of every day to whom Sir Raffle was accustomed.

'I don't understand this at all,' said Sir Raffle.

'I was afraid that it was only too plain,' said John Eames.

'And you must go?'

'Oh, yes; – that's certain. I have pledged myself to go.'

'Of course I don't know anything of this matter that is so important to your family.'

'No; you do not,' said Johnny.

'Can't you explain it to me, then? so that I may have some reason, – if there is any reason.'

Then John told the story of Mr Crawley, – a considerable portion of the story; and in his telling of it, I think it probable that he put more weight upon the necessity of his mission to Italy than it could have fairly been made to bear. In the course of the narration Sir Raffle did once contrive to suggest that a lawyer by going to Florence might do the business at any rate as well as John Eames. But Johnny denied this. 'No, Sir Raffle, it is impossible; quite impossible,' he said. 'If you saw the lawyer who is acting in the matter, Mr Toogood, who is also my uncle, he would tell you the same.' Sir Raffle had already heard something of the story of Mr Crawley, and was now willing to accept the sad tragedy of that case as an excuse for his private secretary's somewhat insubordinate conduct. 'Under the circumstances, Eames, I suppose you must go; but I think you should have told me all about it before.'

'I did not like to trouble you, Sir Raffle, with private business.'

'It is always best to tell the whole of a story,' said Sir Raffle. Johnny being quite content with the upshot of the negotiations accepted this gentle rebuke in silence, and withdrew. On the next day he appeared again at the office in his ordinary costume, and an idea crossed Sir Raffle's brain that he had been partly 'done' by the affectation of a costume. 'I'll be even with him some day yet,' said Sir Raffle to himself.

'I've got my leave, boys,' said Eames when he went out into the room in which his three friends sat.

'No!' said Cradell.

'But I have,' said Johnny.

'You don't mean that old Huffle Scuffle has given it out of his own head?' said Fisher.

'Indeed he has,' said Johnny; 'and bade God bless me into the bargain.'

'And you didn't give him the oysters?' said FitzHoward.

'Not a shell,' said Johnny.

'I'm blessed if you don't beat cock-fighting,' said Cradell, lost in admiration at his friend's adroitness.

We know how John passed his evening after that. He went first to see Lily Dale at her uncle's lodgings in Sackville Street, from thence he was taken to the presence of the charming Madalina in Porchester Terrace, and then wound up the night with his friend Conway Dalrymple. When he got to his bed he felt himself to have been triumphant, but in spite of his triumph he was ashamed of himself. Why had he left Lily to go to Madalina? As he thought of this he quoted to himself against himself Hamlet's often-quoted appeal to the two portraits.* How could he not despise himself in that he could find any pleasure with Madalina, having a Lily Dale to fill his thoughts? 'But she is not fair for me,' he said to himself, – thinking thus to comfort himself. But he did not comfort himself.

On the next morning early his uncle, Mr Toogood, met him at the Dover Railway Station. 'Upon my word, Johnny, you're a clever fellow,' said he. 'I never thought that you'd make it all right with Sir Raffle.'

'As right as a trivet, uncle. There are some people, if you can only get to learn the length of their feet, you can always fit them with shoes afterwards.'

'You'll go on direct to Florence, Johnny?'

'Yes; I think so. From what we have heard, Mrs Arabin must be either there or at Venice, and I don't suppose I could learn from any one at Paris at which town she is staying at this moment.'

'Her address is Florence; – poste restante, Florence. You will be sure to find out at any of the hotels where she is staying, or where she has been staying.'

'But when I have found her, I don't suppose she can tell me anything,' said Johnny.

'Who can tell? She may or she may not. My belief is that the money was her present altogether, and not his. It seems that they don't mix their moneys. He has always had some scruple about it because of her son by a former marriage, and they always have different accounts at their bankers'. I found that out when I was at Barchester.'

'But Crawley was his friend.'

'Yes, Crawley was his friend; but I don't know that fifty-pound notes have always been so very plentiful with him. Deans' incomes ain't what they were, you know.'

'I don't know anything about that,' said Johnny.

'Well; they are not. And he has nothing of his own, as far as I can learn. It would be just the thing for her to do, – to give the money to his friend. At any rate she will tell you whether it was so or not.'

'And then I will go on to Jerusalem, after him.'

'Should you find it necessary. He will probably be on his way back, and she will know where you can hit him on the road. You must make him understand that it is essential that he should be here some little time before the trial. You can understand, Johnny,' – and as he spoke Mr Toogood lowered his voice to a whisper, though they were walking together on the platform of the railway station, and could not possibly have been overheard by any one. 'You can understand that it may be necessary to prove that he is not exactly compos mentis, and if so it will be essential that he should have some influential friend near him. Otherwise the bishop will trample him into dust.' If Mr Toogood could have seen the bishop at this time and have read the troubles of the poor man's heart, he would hardly have spoken of him as being so terrible a tyrant.

'I understand all that,' said Johnny.

'So that, in fact, I shall expect to see you both together,' said Toogood.

'I hope the dean is a good fellow.'

'They tell me he is a very good fellow.'

'I never did see much of bishops or deans as yet,' said Johnny, 'and I should feel rather awe-struck travelling with one.'

'I should fancy that a dean is very much like anybody else.'

'But the man's hat would cow me.'

'I daresay you'll find him walking about Jerusalem with a wide-awake* on, and a big stick in his hand, probably smoking a cigar. Deans contrive to get out of their armour sometimes, as the knights of old used to do. Bishops, I fancy, find it more difficult. Well; – good-by, old fellow. I'm very much obliged to you for going, – I am, indeed. I don't doubt but what we shall pull through, somehow.'

Then Mr Toogood went home to breakfast, and from his own house he proceeded to his office. When he had been there an hour or two, there came to him a messenger from the Income-tax Office, with an official note addressed to himself by Sir Raffle Buffle, – a note which looked to be very official. Sir Raffle Buffle presented his compliments to Mr Toogood, and could Mr Toogood favour Sir R. B. with the present address of Mr John Eames. 'Old fox' said Mr Toogood; – 'but then such a stupid old fox! As if it was likely that I should have peached on Johnny if anything was wrong.' So Mr Toogood sent his compliments to Sir Raffle Buffle, and begged to inform Sir R. B. that Mr John Eames was away on very particular family business, which would take him in the first instance to Florence; – but that from Florence he would probably have to go on to Jerusalem without the loss of an hour. 'Stupid old fool!' said Mr Toogood, as he sent off his reply by the messenger.

CHAPTER 49

Near the close

I wonder whether any one will read these pages who has never known anything of the bitterness of a family quarrel? If so, I shall have a reader very fortunate, or else very cold-blooded. It would be wrong to say that love produces quarrels; but love does produce those intimate relations of which quarrelling is too often one of the consequences, – one of the consequences which frequently seem to be so natural, and sometimes seem to be unavoidable. One brother rebukes the other, – and what brothers ever lived together between whom there was no such rebuking? – then some warm word is misunderstood and hotter words follow and there is a quarrel. The husband tyrannizes, knowing that it is his duty to direct, and the wife disobeys, or only partially obeys thinking that a little independence will become her, – and so there is a quarrel. The father, anxious only for his son's good, looks into that son's future with other eyes than those of his son himself, – and so there is a quarrel. They come very easily, these quarrels, but the quittance from them is sometimes terribly difficult. Much of thought is necessary before the angry man can remember that he too in part may have been wrong; and any attempt at such thinking is almost beyond the power of him who is carefully nursing his wrath, lest it cool! But the nursing of such quarrelling kills all happiness. The very man who is nursing his wrath, lest it cool, – his wrath against one whom he loves perhaps the best of all whom it has been given him to love, – is himself wretched as long as it lasts. His anger poisons every pleasure of his life. He is sullen at his meals, and cannot understand his book as he turns its pages. His work, let it be what it may, is ill done. He is full of his quarrel, – nursing it. He is telling himself how much he has loved that wicked one, how many have been his sacrifices for that wicked one, and that now that wicked one is repaying him simply with wickedness! And yet the wicked one is at that very moment dearer to him than ever. If that wicked one could only be forgiven how sweet would the world be again ! And yet he nurses his wrath.

So it was in these days with Archdeacon Grantly. He was very angry with his son. It is hardly too much to say that in every moment of his life, whether waking or sleeping, he was thinking of the injury that his son was doing him. He had almost come to forget the fact that his anger had first been roused by the feeling that his son was about to do himself an injury, – to cut his own throat. Various other considerations had now added themselves to that, and filled not only his mind but his daily conversation with his wife. How terrible would be the disgrace to Lord Hartletop, how incurable the injury to Griselda, the marchioness, should the brother-in-law of the one, and the brother of the other, marry the daughter of a convicted thief ! 'Of himself he would say nothing.' So he declared constantly, though of himself he did say a great deal. 'Of himself he would say nothing, though of course such a marriage would ruin him in the county.' 'My dear,' said his wife, 'that is nonsense. That really is nonsense. I feel sure there is not a single person in the county who would think of the marriage in such a light.' Then the archdeacon would have quarrelled with his wife too, had she not been too wise to admit such a quarrel. Mrs Grantly was very wise and knew that it took two persons to make a quarrel. He told her over and over again that she was in league with her son, – that she was encouraging her son to marry Grace Crawley. 'I believe that in your heart you wish it,' he once said to her. 'No, my dear, I do not wish it. I do not think it a becoming marriage. But if he does marry her, I should wish to receive his wife in my house, and certainly should not quarrel with him.' 'I will never receive her,' the archdeacon had replied; 'and as for him, I can only say that in such case I will make no provision for his family.'

It will be remembered that the archdeacon had on a former occasion instructed his wife to write to their son and tell him of his father's determination. Mrs Grantly had so manœuvred that a little time had been gained, and that those instructions had not been insisted upon in all their bitterness. Since that time Major Grantly had renewed his assurance that he would marry Grace Crawley if Grace Crawley would accept him, – writing on this occasion direct to his father, – and had asked his father whether, in such case, he was to look forward to be disinherited. 'It is essential that I should know,' the major had said, 'because in such case I must take immediate measures for leaving this place.' His father had sent him back his letter, writing a few words at the bottom of it. 'If you do as you propose above, you must expect nothing from me.' The words were written in large round handwriting, very hurriedly, and the son when he received them perfectly understood the mood of his father's mind when he wrote them.

Then there came tidings, addressed on this occasion to Mrs Grantly, that Cosby Lodge was to be given up. Lady-day had come, and the notice, necessarily to be given at that period, was so given. 'I know this will grieve you,' Major Grantly had said, 'but my father has driven me to it.' This, in itself, was a cause of great sorrow, both to the archdeacon and to Mrs Grantly, as there were circumstances connected with Cosby Lodge which made them think that it was a very desirable residence for their son. 'I shall sell everything about the place and go abroad at once,' he said in a subsequent letter. 'My present idea is that I shall settle myself at Pau, as my income will suffice for me to live there, and education for Edith will be cheap. At any rate I will not continue in England. I could never be happy here in circumstances so altered. Of course I should not have left my profession, unless I had understood from my father that the income arising from it would not be necessary to me. I do not, however, mean to complain, but simply tell you that I shall go.' There were many letters between the mother and son in those days. 'I shall stay till after the trial,' he said. 'If she will then go with me, well and good; but whether she will or not, I shall not remain here.' All this seemed to Mrs Grantly to be peculiarly unfortunate, for, had he not resolved to go, things might even yet have righted themselves. From what she could now understand of the character of Miss Crawley, whom she did not know personally, she thought it probable that Grace, in the event of her father being guilty by the jury, would absolutely and persistently refuse the offer made to her. She would be too good, as Mrs Grantly put it to herself, to bring misery and disgrace into another family. But should Mr Crawley be acquitted, and should the marriage then take place, the archdeacon himself might probably be got to forgive it. In either case there would be no necessity for breaking up the house at Cosby Lodge. But her dear son Henry, her best beloved, was obstinate and stiff-necked, and would take no advice. 'He is even worse than his father,' she said, in her short-lived anger, to her own father, to whom alone at this time she could unburden her griefs, seeking consolation and encouragement.

It was her habit to go over to the deanery at any rate twice a week at this time, and on the occasion of one of the visits so made, she expressed very strongly her distress at the family quarrel which had come among them. The old man took his grandson's part through and through. 'I do not at all see why he should not marry the young lady if he likes her. As for money, there ought to be enough without his having to look for a wife with a fortune.'

'It is not a question of money, papa.'

'And as to rank,' continued Mr Harding, 'Henry will not at any rate be going lower than his father did, when he married you; – not so low indeed, for at that time I was only a minor canon, and Mr Crawley is in possession of a benefice.'

'Papa, all that is nonsense. It is, indeed.'

Very likely, my dear.'

'It is not because Mr Crawley is only perpetual curate of Hogglestock, that the archdeacon objects to the marriage. It has nothing to do with that at all. At the present moment he is in disgrace.'

'Under a cloud, my dear. Let us pray that it may be only a passing cloud.'

'All the world thinks he was guilty. And then he is such a man: – so singular, so unlike anybody else! You know, papa, that I don't think very much of money, merely as money.'

'I hope not, my dear. Money is worth thinking of, but it is not worth very much thought.'

'But it does give advantages, and the absence of such advantages must be very much felt in the education of a girl. You would hardly wish Henry to marry a young woman who, from want of money, had not been brought up among ladies. It is not Miss Crawley's fault, but such has been her lot. We cannot ignore these deficiencies, papa.'

'Certainly not, my dear.'

'You would not, for instance, wish that Henry should marry a kitchen-maid.'

'But is Miss Crawley a kitchen-maid, Susan?'

'I don't quite say that.'

'I am told that she has been educated infinitely better than most of the young ladies in the neighbourhood,' said Mr Harding.

'I believe that her father has taught her Greek; and I suppose she has learned something of French at that school at Silverbridge.'

'Then the kitchen-maid theory is sufficiently disposed of,' said Mr Harding, with mild triumph.

'You know what I mean, papa. But the fact is, that it is impossible to deal with men. They will never be reasonable. A marriage such as this would be injurious to Henry; but it will not be ruinous; and as to disinheriting him for it, that would be downright wicked.'

'I think so,' said Mr Harding.

'But the archdeacon will look at it as though it would destroy Henry and Edith altogether, while you speak of it as though it were the best thing in the world.'

'If the young people love each other, I think it would be the best thing in the world,' said Mr Harding.

'But, papa, you cannot but think that his father's wish should go for something,' said Mrs Grantly, who desirous as she was on the one side to support her son, could not bear that her husband should, on the other side, be declared to be altogether in the wrong.

'I do not know, my dear,' said Mr Harding; 'but I do think, that if the two young people are fond of each other, and if there is anything for them to live upon, it cannot be right to keep them apart. You know, my dear, she is the daughter of a gentleman.' Mrs Grantly upon this left her father almost brusquely, without speaking another word on the subject; for, though she was opposed to the vehement anger of her husband, she could not endure the proposition now made by her father.

Mr Harding was at this time living all alone in the deanery. For some few years the deanery had been his home, and as his youngest daughter was the dean's wife, there could be no more comfortable resting-place for the evening of his life. During the last month or two the days had gone tediously with him; for he had had the large house all to himself, and he was a man who did not love solitude. It is hard to conceive that the old, whose thoughts have been all thought out, should ever love to live alone. Solitude is surely for the young, who have time before them for the execution of schemes, and who can, therefore, take delight in thinking. In these days the poor old man would wander about in the rooms, shambling from one chamber to another, and would feel ashamed when the servants met him ever on the move. He would make little apologies for his uneasiness, which they would accept graciously, understanding, after a fashion, why it was that he was uneasy. 'He ain't got nothing to do,' said the housemaid to the cook, 'and as for reading, they say that some of the young ones can read all day sometimes, and all night too; but, bless you, when you're nigh eighty, reading don't go for much.' The housemaid was right as to Mr Harding's reading. He was not one who had read so much in his earlier days as to enable him to make reading go far with him now that he was near eighty. So he wandered about the room, and sat here for a few minutes, and there for a few minutes, and though he did not sleep much, he made the hours of the night as many as was possible. Every morning he shambled across from the deanery to the cathedral, and attended the morning service, sitting in the stall which he had occupied for fifty years. The distance was very short, not exceeding, indeed, a hundred yards from a side-door in the deanery to another side-door into the cathedral; but short as it was there had come to be a question whether he should be allowed to

go alone. It had been feared that he might fall on his passage and
hurt himself; for there was a step here, and a step there, and the
light was not very good in the purlieus of the old cathedral. A word
or two had been said once, and the offer of an arm to help him had
been made; but he had rejected the proffered assistance, – softly,
in deed, but still firmly, – and every day he tottered off by himself,
hardly lifting his feet as he went, and aiding himself on his journey
by a hand upon the wall when he thought that nobody was looking
at him. But many did see him, and they who knew him, – ladies
generally of the city, – would offer him a hand. Nobody was milder
in his dislikings than Mr Harding; but there were ladies in
Barchester upon whose arm he would always decline to lean,
bowing courteously as he did so, and saying a word or two of
constrained civility. There were others whom he would allow to
accompany him home to the door of the deanery, with whom he
delighted to linger and chat if the morning was warm, and to whom
he would tell little stories of his own doings in the cathedral services
in the old days, when Bishop Grantly had ruled in the diocese.
Never a word did he say against Bishop Proudie, or against Bishop
Proudie's wife; but the many words which he did say in praise of
Bishop Grantly, – who, by his showing, was surely one of the best
of churchmen who ever walked through this vale of sorrow, – were
as eloquent in dispraise of the existing prelate as could have
been any more clearly-pointed phrases. This daily visit to the
cathedral, where he would say his prayers as he had said them for
so many years, and listen to the organ, of which he knew all the
power and every blemish as though he himself had made the stops
and fixed the pipes, was the chief occupation of his life. It was a
pity that it could not have been made to cover a larger portion of
the day.

It was sometimes sad enough to watch him as he sat alone. He
would have a book near him, and for a while would keep it in his
hands. It would generally be some volume of good old standard
theology with which he had been, or supposed himself to have
been, conversant from his youth. But the book would soon be laid
aside, and gradually he would move himself away from it, and he
would stand about in the room, looking now out of the window
from which he would fancy that he could not be seen, or gazing up
at some print which he had known for years; and then he would sit
down for a while in one chair, and for a while in another, while his
mind was wandering back into old days, thinking of old troubles
and remembering his old joys. And he had a habit, when he was
sure that he was not watched, of creeping up to a great black
wooden case, which always stood in one corner of the sitting-room

which he occupied in the deanery. Mr Harding, when he was younger, had been a performer on the violoncello, and in this case there was still the instrument from which he had been wont to extract the sounds which he had so dearly loved. Now in these latter days he never made any attempt to play. Soon after he had come to the deanery there had fallen upon him an illness, and after that he had never again asked for his bow. They who were around him, – his daughter chiefly and her husband, – had given the matter much thought, arguing with themselves whether or no it would be better to invite him to resume the task he had so loved; for of all the works of his life this playing on the violoncello had been the sweetest to him; but even before that illness his hand had greatly failed him, and the dean and Mrs Arabin had agreed that it would be better to let the matter pass without a word. He had never asked to be allowed to play. He had expressed no regrets. When he himself would propose that his daughter should 'give them a little music,' – and he would make such a proposition on every evening that was suitable, – he would never say a word of those former performances at which he himself had taken a part. But it had become known to Mrs Arabin, through the servants, that he had once dragged the instrument forth from its case when he had thought the house to be nearly deserted; and a wail of sounds had been heard, very low, very short-lived, recurring now and again at fitful intervals. He had at those times attempted to play, as though with a muffled bow, – so that none should know of his vanity and folly. Then there had been further consultations at the deanery, and it had been again agreed that it would be best to say nothing to him of his music.

In these latter days of which I am now speaking he would never draw the instrument out of its case. Indeed he was aware that it was too heavy for him to handle without assistance. But he would open the prison door, and gaze upon the thing that he loved, and he would pass his fingers among the broad strings, and ever and anon he would produce from one of them a low, melancholy, almost unearthly sound. And then he would pause, never daring to produce two such notes in succession, – one close upon the other. And these last sad moans of the old fiddle were now known through the household. They were the ghosts of the melody of days long past. He imagined that his visits to the box were unsuspected, – that none knew of the folly of his old fingers which could not keep themselves from touching the wires; but the voice of the violoncello had been recognized by the servants and by his daughter, and when that low wail was heard through the house, – like the last dying note of a dirge, – they would all know that Mr Harding was visiting his ancient friend.

When the dean and Mrs Arabin had first talked of going abroad for a long visit, it had been understood that Mr Harding should pass the period of their absence with his other daughter at Plumstead; but when the time came he begged of Mrs Arabin to be allowed to remain in his old rooms. 'Of course I shall go backwards and forwards,' he had said. 'There is nothing I like so much as a change now and then.' The result had been that he had gone once to Plumstead during the dean's absence. When he had thus remonstrated, begging to be allowed to remain in Barchester, Mrs Arabin had declared her intention of giving up her tour. In telling her father of this she had not said that her altered purpose had arisen from her disinclination to leave him alone; – but he had perceived that it was so, and had then consented to be taken over to Plumstead. There was nothing, he said, which he would like so much as going over to Plumstead for four or five months. It had ended in his having his own way altogether. The Arabins had gone upon their tour, and he was left in possession of the deanery. 'I should not like to die out of Barchester,' he said to himself in excuse to himself for his disinclination to sojourn long under the archdeacon's roof. But, in truth, the archdeacon, who loved him well and who, after a fashion, had always been good to him, – who had always spoken of the connexion which had bound the two families together as the great blessing of his life, – was too rough in his greetings for the old man. Mr Harding had even mixed something of fear with his warm affection for his elder son-in-law, and now in these closing hours of his life he could not avoid a certain amount of shrinking from that loud voice, – a certain inaptitude to be quite at ease in that commanding presence. The dean, his second son-in-law, had been a modern friend in comparison with the archdeacon; but the dean was more gentle with him; and then the dean's wife had ever been the dearest to him of human beings. It may be a doubt whether one of the dean's children was not now almost more dear, and whether in these days he did not have more free communication with that little girl than with any other human being. Her name was Susan, but he had always called her Posy, having himself invented for her that soubriquet. When it had been proposed to him to pass the winter and spring at Plumstead, the suggestion had been made alluring by a promise that Posy also should be taken to Mrs Grantly's house. But he, as we have seen, had remained at the deanery, and Posy had remained with him.

Posy was now five years old, and could talk well, and had her own ideas of things. Posy's eyes, – hers, and no others besides her own, – were allowed to see the inhabitant of the big black case; and now that the deanery was so nearly deserted, Posy's fingers had touched the strings, and had produced an infantine moan. 'Grandpa, let me do it again.' Twang! It was not, however, in truth, a twang, but a sound as of a prolonged dull, almost deadly, humm-m-m-m-m! On this occasion the moan was not entirely infantine, – Posy's fingers having been something too strong, – and the case was closed and locked, and grandpapa shook his head.

'But Mrs Baxter won't be angry,' said Posy. Mrs Baxter was the housekeeper in the deanery, and had Mr Harding under her especial charge.

'No, my darling; Mrs Baxter will not be angry, but we musn't disturb the house.'

'No,' said Posy, with much of important awe in her tone, 'we mustn't disturb the house; must we, grandpapa?' And so she gave in her adhesion to the closing of the case. But Posy could play cat's-cradle, and as cat's-cradle did not disturb the house at all, there was a good deal of cat's-cradle played in these days. Posy's fingers were so soft and pretty, so small and deft, that the dear old man delighted in taking the strings from them, and in having them taken from his own by those tender little digits.

'On the afternoon after the conversation respecting Grace Crawley which is recorded in the early part of this chapter, a messenger from Barchester went over to Plumstead, and a part of his mission consisted of a note from Mrs Baxter to Mrs Grantly, beginning, 'Honoured Madam,' and informing Mrs Grantly, among other things, that her 'respected papa,' as Mrs Baxter called him, was not quite so well as usual; not that Mrs Baxter thought there was much the matter. Mr Harding had been to the cathedral service, as was usual with him, but had come home leaning on a lady's arm, who had thought it well to stay with him at the door till it had been opened for him. After that 'Miss Posy' had found him asleep, and had been unable, – or if not unable, unwilling, to wake him. 'Miss Posy' had come down to Mrs Baxter somewhat in a fright, and hence this letter had been written. Mrs Baxter thought that there was nothing 'to fright' Mrs Grantly, and she wasn't sure that she should have written at all only that Dick was bound to go over to Plumstead with the wool; but as Dick was going, Mrs Baxter thought it proper to send her duty, and to say that to her humble way of thinking perhaps it might be best that Mr Harding shouldn't go alone to the cathedral every morning. 'If the dear reverence gentleman was to get a tumble, ma'am,' said the letter, 'it would be awkward.' Then Mrs Grantly remembered that she had left her father almost without a greeting on the previous day, and she resolved that she would go over very early on the following morning, – so early that she would be at the deanery before her father should have gone to the cathedral.

'He ought to have come over here, and not stayed there by himself,' said the archdeacon, when his wife told him of her intention.

'It is too late to think of that now, my dear; and one can understand, I think, that he should not like leaving the cathedral as long as he can attend it. The truth is he does not like being out of Barchester.'

'He would be much better here,' said the archdeacon. 'Of course you can have the carriage and go over. We can breakfast at eight; and if you can bring him back with you, do. I should tell him that he ought to come.' Mrs Grantly made no answer to this, knowing very well that she could not bring herself to go beyond the gentlest persuasion with her father, and on the next morning she was at the deanery by ten o'clock. Half-past ten was the hour at which the service began. Mrs Baxter contrived to meet her before she saw her father, and begged her not to let it be known that any special tidings of Mr Harding's failing strength had been sent from the deanery to Plumstead. 'And how is my father?' asked Mrs Grantly. 'Well, then, ma'am,' said Baxter, 'in one sense he's finely. He took a morsel of early lamb to his dinner yesterday, and relished it ever so well, – only he gave Miss Posy the best part of it. And then he sat with Miss Posy quite happy for an hour or so. And then he slept in his chair; and you know, ma'am, we never wakes him. And after that old Skulpit toddled up from the hospital,' – this was Hiram's Hospital, of which establishment, in the city of Barchester, Mr Harding had once been the warden and kind master, as has been told in former chronicles of the city,* – 'and your papa has said, ma'am, you know, that he is always to see any of the old men when they come up. And Skulpit is sly, and no better than he should be, and got money from your father, ma'am, I know. And then he had just a drop of tea, and after that I took him a glass of port wine with my own hands. And it touched me, ma'am, so it did, when he said, "Oh, Mrs Baxter, how good you are; you know well what it is I like." And then he went to bed. I listened hard, – not from idle cur'osity, ma'am, as you, who know me, will believe, but just because it's becoming to know what he's about, as there might be an accident, you know, ma'am.' 'You are very good, Mrs Baxter, very good.' 'Thank ye, ma'am, for saying so. And so I listened hard; but he didn't go to his music, poor gentleman; and I think he had a quiet night. He doesn't sleep much at nights, poor gentleman, but he's very quiet; leastwise he was last night.' This was the bulletin which Mrs Baxter gave to Mrs Grantly on that morning before Mrs Grantly saw her father.

She found him preparing himself for his visit to the cathedral. Some year or two, – but no more, – before the date of which we are speaking, he had still taken some small part in the service; and while he had done so he had of course worn his surplice. Living so close to the cathedral, – so close that he could almost walk out of the house into the transept, – he had kept his surplice in his own room, and had gone down in his vestment. It had been a bitter day to him when he had first found himself constrained to abandon the white garment which he loved. He had encountered some failure in the performance of the small task allotted to him, and the dean had tenderly advised him to desist. He did not utter one word of remonstrance. 'It will perhaps be better,' the dean had said. 'Yes, – it will be better,' Mr Harding had replied. 'Few have had accorded to them the high privilege of serving their Master in His house for so many years, – though few more humbly, or with lower gifts.' But on the following morning, and for nearly a week afterwards, he had been unable to face the minor canon and the vergers, and the old women who knew him so well, in his ordinary black garments. At last he went down with the dean, and occupied a stall close to the dean's seat, – far away from that in which he had sat for so many years, – and in this seat he had said his prayers ever since that day. And now his surplices were washed and ironed and folded and put away; but there were moments in which he would stealthily visit them, as he also stealthily visited his friend in the black wooden case. This was very melancholy, and the sadness of it was felt by all those who lived with him; but he never alluded himself to any of those bereavements which age brought upon him. Whatever might be his regrets, he kept them ever within his own breast.

Posy was with him when Mrs Grantly came into his room, holding for him his hat and stick while he was engaged in brushing a suspicion of dust from his black gaiters. 'Grandpapa, here is aunt Susan,' said Posy. The old man looked up with something, – with some slightest sign of that habitual fear which was always aroused within his bosom by visitations from Plumstead. Had Mrs Arabin thoroughly understood the difference in her father's feeling toward herself and toward her sister, I think she would hardly have gone forth upon any tour while he remained with her in the deanery. It is very hard sometimes to know how intensely we are loved, and of what value our presence is to those who love us! Mrs Grantly saw the look, – did not analyse it, did not quite understand it, – but felt, as she had so often felt before, that it was not altogether laden with welcome. But all this had nothing to do with the duty on which she had come; nor did it, in the slightest degree, militate against her own affection. 'Papa,' she said, kissing him, 'you are surprised to see me so early?'

'Well, my dear, yes; – but very glad all the same. I hope everybody is well at Plumstead?'

'Everybody, thank you, papa.'

'That is well, Posy and I are getting ready for church. Are we not, Posy?'

'Grandpapa is getting ready. Mrs Baxter won't let me go.'

'No, my dear, no; – not yet, Posy. When Posy is a great girl she can go to cathedral every day. Only then, perhaps, Posy won't want to go.'

'I thought that, perhaps, papa, you would sit with me a little while this morning, instead of going to morning prayers.'

'Certainly, my dear, – certainly. Only I do not like not going; – for who can say how often I may be able to go again? There is so little left, Susan, – so very little left.'

After that she had not the heart to ask him to stay, and therefore she went with him. As they passed down the stairs and out of the doors she was astonished to find how weak were his footsteps, – how powerless he was against the slightest misadventure. On this very day he would have tripped at the upward step at the cathedral door had she not been with him. 'Oh, papa,' she said, 'indeed, indeed, you should not come here alone.' Then he apologized for his little stumble with many words and much shame, assuring her that anybody might trip on any occasion. It was purely an accident; and though it was a comfort to him to have had her arm, he was sure that he should have recovered himself even had he been alone. He always, he said, kept quite close to the wall, so that there might be no mistake, – no possibility of an accident. All this he said volubly, but with confused words, in the covered stone passage leading into the transept. And as he thus spoke, Mrs Grantly made up her mind that her father should never again go to the cathedral alone. He never did go again to the cathedral, – alone.

When they returned to the deanery, Mr Harding was fluttered, weary, and unwell. When his daughter left him for a few minutes he told Mrs Baxter, in confidence, the story of his accident, and his great grief that his daughter should have seen it. 'Laws amercy, sir, it was a blessing she was with you,' said Mrs Baxter; 'it was, indeed, Mr Harding.' Then Mr Harding had been angry, and spoke almost crossly to Mrs Baxter; but, before she left the room, he found an opportunity of begging her pardon, – not in a set speech to that effect, but by a little word of gentle kindness, which she had understood perfectly. 'Papa,' said Mrs Grantly to him as soon as she had succeeded in getting both Posy and Mrs Baxter out of the room, – against the doing of which, Mr Harding had manœuvred with all his little impotent skill, – 'Papa, you must promise me that you will not go to the cathedral again alone, till Eleanor comes home.' When he heard the sentence he looked at her with blank misery in his eyes. He made no attempt at remonstrance. He begged for no respite. The word had gone forth, and he knew that it must be obeyed. Though he would have hidden the signs of his weakness had he been able, he would not condescend to plead that he was strong. 'If you think it wrong, my dear, I will not go alone,' he said. 'Papa, I do; indeed, I do. Dear papa, I would not hurt you by saying it if I did not know that I am right.' He was sitting with his hand upon the table, and, as she spoke to him, she put her hand upon his, caressing it. 'My dear,' he said, 'you are always right.'

She then left him again for awhile, having some business out in the city, and he was alone in his room for an hour. What was there left to him now in the world? Old as he was, and in some things almost childish, nevertheless, he thought of this keenly, and some half-realized remembrance of 'the lean and slippered pantaloon'* flitted across his mind, causing him a pang. What was there left to him now in the world? Posy and cat's-cradle! Then, in the midst of his regrets, as he sat with his back bent in his old easy-chair, with one arm over the shoulder of the chair, and the other hanging loose by his side, on a sudden there came across his face a smile as sweet as ever brightened the face of man or woman. He had been able to tell himself that he had no ground for complaint, – great ground rather for rejoicing and gratitude. Had not the world and all in it been good to him; had he not children who loved him, who had done him honour, who had been to him always a crown of glory, never a mark for reproach; had not his lines fallen to him in very pleasant places;* was it not his happy fate to go and leave it all amidst the good words and kind loving cares of devoted friends? Whose latter days had ever been more blessed than his? And for the future—? It was as he thought of this that that smile came across his face, – as though it were already the face of an angel. And then he muttered to himself a word or two. 'Lord now lettest Thou Thy servant depart in peace. Lord, now lettest Thou Thy servant depart in peace.'*

When Mrs Grantly returned she found him in jocund spirits. And yet she perceived that he was so weak that when he left his chair he could barely get across the room without assistance. Mrs Baxter, indeed, had not sent to her too soon, and it was well that the prohibition had come in time to prevent some terrible accident. 'Papa,' she said, 'I think you had better go with me to Plumstead.

The carriage is here, and I can take you home so comfortably.' But he would not allow himself to be taken on this occasion to Plumstead. He smiled and thanked her, and put his hand into hers, and repeated his promise that he would not leave the house on any occasion without assistance, and declared himself specially thankful to her for coming to him on that special morning; – but he would not be taken to Plumstead. 'When the summer comes,' he said, 'then, if you will have me for a few days!'

He meant no deceit, and yet he had told himself within the last hour that he should never see another summer. He could not tell even his daughter that after such a life as this, after more than fifty years spent in the ministrations of his darling cathedral, it specially behoved him to die, – as he had lived, – at Barchester. He could not say this to his eldest daughter; but had his Eleanor been at home, he could have said it to her. He thought he might yet live to see his Eleanor once again. If this could be given to him he would ask for nothing more.

On the afternoon of the next day, Mrs Baxter wrote another letter, in which she told Mrs Grantly that her father had declared, at his usual hour of rising that morning, that as he was not going to the cathedral he would, he thought, lie in bed a little longer. And then he had lain in bed the whole day. 'And, perhaps, honoured madam, looking at all things, it's best as he should,' said Mrs Baxter.

CHAPTER 50

Lady Lufton's proposition

It was now known throughout Barchester that a commission was to be held by the bishop's orders, at which inquiry would be made, – that is, ecclesiastical inquiry, – as to the guilt imputed to Mr Crawley in the matter of Mr Soames's cheque. Sundry rumours had gone abroad as to quarrels which had taken place on the subject among certain clergymen high in office; but these were simply rumours, and nothing was in truth known. There was no more discreet clergyman in all the diocese than Dr Tempest, and not a word had escaped from him as to the stormy nature of that meeting in the bishop's palace, at which he had attended with the bishop, – and at which Mrs Proudie had attended also. When it is said that the fact of this coming commission was known to all Barsetshire, allusion, is of course made to that portion of the inhab..ants of Barsetshire to which clerical matters were specially dear; – and as such matters were specially dear to the inhabitants of the parish of Framley, the commission was discussed very eagerly in that parish, and was specially discussed by the Dowager Lady Lufton.

And there was a double interest attached to the commission in the parish of Framley by the fact that Mr Robarts, the vicar, had been invited by Dr Tempest to be one of the clergymen who were to assist in making the inquiry. 'I also propose to ask Mr Oriel of Greshamsbury to join us,' said Dr Tempest. 'The bishop wishes to appoint the other two, and has already named Mr Thumble and Mr Quiverful, who are both residents in the city. Perhaps his lordship may be right in thinking it better that the matter should not be left altogether in the hands of clergymen who hold livings in the diocese. You are no doubt aware that neither Mr Thumble nor Mr Quiverful do hold any benefice.' Mr Robarts felt, – as everybody else did feel who knew anything of the matter, – that Bishop Proudie was singularly ignorant in his knowledge of men, and that he showed his ignorance on this sp_cial occasion. 'If he intended to

name two such men he should at any rate have named three,' said
Dr Thorne. 'Mr Thumble and Mr Quiverful will simply be outvoted
on the first day, and after that will give in their adhesion to the
majority.' 'Mr Thumble, indeed!' Lady Lufton had said, with much
scorn in her voice. To her thinking, it was absurd in the highest
degree that such men as Dr Tempest and her Mr Robarts should be
asked to meet Mr Thumble and Mr Quiverful on matters of
ecclesiastical business. Outvoted! Of course they would be outvoted. Of course they would be so paralyzed by fear at finding
themselves in the presence of real gentlemen, that they would hardly
be able to vote at all. Old Lady Lufton did not in fact utter words
so harsh as these; but thoughts as harsh passed through her mind.
The reader therefore will understand that much interest was felt on
the subject at Framley Court, where Lady Lufton lived with her son
and her daughter-in-law.

'They tell me,' said Lady Lufton, 'that both the archdeacon and
Dr Tempest think it right that a commission should be held. If so, I
have no doubt that it is right.'

'Mark says that the bishop could hardly do anything else,'
rejoined Mrs Robarts.

'I daresay not, my dear. I suppose the bishop has somebody near
him to tell him what he may do, and what he may not do. It would
be terrible to think of, if it were not so. But yet, when I hear that he
has named such men as Mr Thumble and Mr Quiverful, I cannot
but feel that the whole diocese is disgraced.'

'Oh, Lady Lufton, that is such a strong word,' said Mrs Robarts.

'It may be strong, but it is not the less true,' said Lady Lufton.

And from talking on the subject of the Crawleys, Lady Lufton
soon advanced, first to a desire for some action, and then to acting.
'I think, my dear, I will go over and see Mrs Crawley,' said Lady
Lufton the elder to Lady Lufton the younger. Lady Lufton the
younger had nothing to urge against this; but she did not offer to
accompany the elder lady. I attempted to explain in the early part
of this story that there still existed a certain understanding between
Mrs Crawley and Lord Lufton's wife, and that kindnesses occasionally passed from Framley Court to Hogglestock Parsonage; but on
this occasion young Lady Lufton, – the Lucy Robarts who had once
passed certain days of her life with the Crawleys at Hogglestock, –
did not choose to accompany her mother-in-law; and therefore
Mrs Robarts was invited to do so. 'I think it may comfort her to
know that she has our sympathy,' the elder woman said to the
younger as they made their journey together.

When the carriage stopped before the little wicket-gate, from
whence a path led through a ragged garden from the road to Mr

Crawley's house, Lady Lufton hardly knew how to proceed. The servant came to the door of the carriage, and asked for her orders. 'H – m – m, ha, yes; I think I'll send in my card; – and say that I hope Mrs Crawley will be able to see me. Won't that be best; eh, Fanny?' Fanny, otherwise Mrs Robarts, said that she thought that would be best; and the card and message were carried in.

It was happily the case that Mr Crawley was not at home. Mr Crawley was away at Hoggle End, reading to the brickmakers, or turning the mangles of their wives, or teaching them theology, or politics, or history, after his fashion. In these days he spent, perhaps, the happiest hours of his life down at Hoggle End. I say that his absence was a happy chance, because, had he been at home, he would certainly have said something, or done something, to offend Lady Lufton. He would either have refused to see her, or when seeing her he would have bade her hold her peace and not interfere with matters which did not concern her, or, – more probable still, – he would have sat still and sullen, and have spoken not at all. But he was away, and Mrs Crawley sent out word by the servant that she would be most proud to see her ladyship, if her ladyship would be pleased to alight. Her ladyship did alight, and walked into the parsonage, followed by Mrs Robarts.

Grace was with her mother. Indeed Jane had been there also when the message was brought in, but she fled into back regions, overcome by shame as to her frock. Grace, I think, would have fled too, had she not been bound in honour to support her mother. Lady Lufton, as she entered, was very gracious, struggling with all the power of her womanhood so to carry herself that there should be no outwardly visible sign of her rank or her wealth, – but not altogether succeeding. Mrs Robarts, on her first entrance, said only a word or two of greeting to Mrs Crawley, and kissed Grace, whom she had known intimately in early years. 'Lady Lufton,' said Mrs Crawley, 'I am afraid this is a very poor place for you to come to; but you have known that of old, and therefore I need hardly apologize.'

'Sometimes I like poor places best,' said Lady Lufton. Then there was a pause, after which Lady Lufton addressed herself to Grace, seeking some subject for immediate conversation. 'You have been down at Allington, my dear, have you not?' Grace, in a whisper, said that she had. 'Staying with the Dales, I believe? I know the Dales well by name, and I have always heard that they are charming people.'

'I like them very much,' said Grace. And then there was another pause.

'I hope your husband is pretty well, Mrs Crawley?' said Lady Lufton.

'He is pretty well, – not quite strong. I daresay you know, Lady Lufton, that he has things to vex him?' Mrs Crawley felt that it was the need of the moment that the only possible subject of conversation in that house should be introduced; and therefore she brought it in at once, not loving the subject, but being strongly conscious of the necessity. Lady Lufton meant to be good-natured, and therefore Mrs Crawley would do all in her power to make Lady Lufton's mission easy to her.

'Indeed yes,' said her ladyship; 'we do know that.'

'We feel so much for you and Mr Crawley,' said Mrs Robarts; 'and are so sure that your sufferings are unmerited.' This was not discreet on the part of Mrs Robarts, as she was the wife of one of the clergymen who had been selected to form the commission of inquiry; and so Lady Lufton told her on their way home.

'You are very kind,' said Mrs Crawley. 'We must only bear it with such fortitude as God will give us. We are told that He tempers the wind to the shorn lamb.'

'And so He does, my dear,' said the old lady, very solemnly. 'So He does. Surely you have felt that it is so?'

'I struggle not to complain,' said Mrs Crawley.

'I know that you struggle bravely. I hear of you, and I admire you for it, and I love you.' It was still the old lady who was speaking, and now she had at last been roused out of her difficulty as to words, and had risen from her chair, and was standing before Mrs Crawley. 'It is because you do not complain, because you are so great and so good, because your character is so high, and your spirit so firm, that I could not resist the temptation of coming to you. Mrs Crawley, if you will let me be your friend, I shall be proud of your friendship.'

'Your ladyship is too good,' said Mrs Crawley.

'Do not talk to me after that fashion,' said Lady Lufton. 'If you do I shall be disappointed, and feel myself thrown back. You know what I mean. ' She paused for an answer; but Mrs Crawley had no answer to make. She simply shook her head, not knowing why she did so. But we may know. We can understand that she had felt that the friendship offered to her by Lady Lufton was an impossibility. She had decided within her own breast that it was so, though she did not know that she had come to such decision. 'I wish you to take me at my word, Mrs Crawley,' continued Lady Lufton. 'What can we do for you? We know that you are distressed.'

'Yes, – we are distressed.'

'And we know how cruel circumstances have been to you. Will you not forgive me for being plain?'

'I have nothing to forgive,' said Mrs Crawley.

'Lady Lufton means,' said Mrs Robarts, 'that in asking you to talk openly to her of your affairs, she wishes you to remember that—I think you know what we mean,' said Mrs Robarts, knowing very well herself what she did mean, but not knowing at all how to express herself.

'Lady Lufton is very kind,' said Mrs Crawley, 'and so are you, Mrs Robarts. I know how good you both are, and for how much it behoves me to be grateful.' These words were very cold, and the voice in which they were spoken was very cold. They made Lady Lufton feel that it was beyond her power to proceed with the work of her mission in its intended spirit. It is ever so much easier to proffer kindness graciously than to receive it with grace. Lady Lufton had intended to say, 'Let us be women together; — women bound by humanity, and not separated by rank, and let us open our hearts freely. Let us see how we may be of comfort to each other.' And could she have succeeded in this, she would have spread out her little plans of succour with so loving a hand that she would have conquered the woman before her. But the suffering spirit cannot descend from its dignity of reticence. It has a nobility of its own, made sacred by many tears, by the flowing of streams of blood from unseen wounds, which cannot descend from its daïs to receive pity and kindness. A consciousness of undeserved woe produces a grandeur of its own, with which the high-souled sufferer will not easily part. Baskets full of eggs, pounds of eleemosynary butter, quarters of given pork, even second-hand clothing from the wardrobe of some richer sister, — even money, unsophisticated money, she could accept. She had learned to know that it was a portion of her allotted misery to take such things, — for the sake of her children and her husband, — and to be thankful for them. She did take them, and was thankful; and in the taking she submitted herself to the rod of cruel circumstances; but she could not even yet bring herself to accept spoken pity from a stranger, and to kiss the speaker.

'Can we not do something to help you?' said Mrs Robarts. She would not have spoken but that she perceived that Lady Lufton had completed her appeal, and that Mrs Crawley did not seem prepared to answer it.

'You have done much to help us,' said Mrs Crawley. 'The things you have sent to us have been very serviceable.'

'But we mean something more than that,' said Lady Lufton.

'I do not know what there is more,' said Mrs Crawley. 'A bit to eat and something to wear; – that seems to be all that we have to care for now.'

'But we were afraid that this coming trial must cause you so much anxiety.'

'Of course it causes anxiety; – but what can we do? It must be so. It cannot be put off, or avoided. We have made up our minds to it now, and almost wish that it would come quicker. If it were once over I think he would be better whatever the result might be.'

Then there was another lull in the conversation, and Lady Lufton began to be afraid that her visit would be a failure. She thought that perhaps she might get on better if Grace were not in the room, and she turned over in her mind various schemes for sending her away. And perhaps her task would be easier if Mrs Robarts also could be banished for a time. 'Fanny, my dear,' she said at last, boldly, 'I know you have a little plan to arrange with Miss Crawley. Perhaps you will be more likely to be successful if you can take a turn with her alone.' There was not much subtlety in her ladyship's scheme; but it answered the proposed purpose, and the two elder ladies were soon left face to face, so that Lady Lufton had a fair pretext for making another attempt. 'Dear Mrs Crawley,' she said, 'I do so long to say a word to you, but I fear that I may be thought to interfere.'

'Oh, no, Lady Lufton; I have no feeling of that kind.'

'I have asked your daughter and Mrs Robarts to go out because I can speak more easily to you alone. I wish I could teach you to trust me.'

'I do trust you.'

'As a friend, I mean; – as a real friend. If it should be the case, Mrs Crawley, that a jury should give a verdict against your husband, – what will you do then? Perhaps I ought not to suppose that it is possible.'

'Of course we know that is possible,' said Mrs Crawley. Her voice was stern, and there was in it a tone almost of offence. As she spoke she did not look at her visitor, but sat with her face averted and her arms akimbo on the table.

'Yes; – it is possible,' said Lady Lufton. 'I suppose there is not one in the county who does not truly wish that it may not be so. But it is right to be prepared for all alternatives. In such case have you thought what you will do?'

'I do not know what they would do to him,' said she.

'I suppose that for some time he would be—'

'Put in prison,' said Mrs Crawley, speaking very quickly, bringing out the words with a sharp eagerness that was quite unusual to her. 'They will send him to gaol. Is it not so, Lady Lufton?'

'I suppose it would be so; not for long I should hope; but I presume that such would be the sentence for some short period.'

'And I might not go with him?'

'No; that would be impossible.'

'And the house, and the living; would they let him have them again when he came out?'

'Ah; that I cannot say. That will depend much, probably, on what these clergymen will report. I hope he will not put himself in opposition to them.'

'I do not know. I cannot say. It is probable that he may do so. It is not easy for a man so injured as he has been, and one at the same time so great in intelligence, to submit himself gently to such inquiries. When ill is being done to himself or others he is very prone to oppose it.'

'But these gentlemen do not wish to do him ill, Mrs Crawley.'

'I cannot say. I do not know. When I think of it I see that there is nothing but ruin on every side. What is the use of talking of it? Do not be angry, Lady Lufton, if I say that it is of no use.'

'But I desire to be of use, – of real use. If it should be the case, Mrs Crawley, that your husband should be – detained at Barchester—'

'You mean imprisoned, Lady Lufton.'

'Yes, I mean imprisoned. If it should be so, then do you bring yourself and your children, – all of them, – over to Framley, and I will find a home for you while he is lost to you.'

'Oh, Lady Lufton; I could not do that.'

'Yes, you can. You have not heard me yet. It would not be a comfort to you in such a home as that to sit at table with people who are partly strangers to you. But there is a cottage nearly adjoining to the house, which you shall have all to yourself. The bailiff lived in it once, and others have lived in it who belong to the place; but it is empty now and it shall be made comfortable.' The tears were now running down Mrs Crawley's face, so that she could not answer a word. 'Of course it is my son's property, and not mine, but he has commissioned me to say that it is most heartily at your service. He begs that in such case you will occupy it. And I beg the same. And your old friend Lucy has desired me also to ask you in her name.'

'Lady Lufton, I could not do that,' said Mrs Crawley through her tears.

'You must think better of it, my dear. I do not scruple to advise you, because I am older than you, and have experience of the world.' This, I think, taken in the ordinary sense of the words, was a boast on the part of Lady Lufton, for which but little true pretence existed. Lady Lufton's experience of the world at large was not perhaps extensive. Nevertheless she knew what one woman might offer to another, and what one woman might receive from another. 'You would be better over with me, my dear, than you could be elsewhere. You will not misunderstand me if I say that, under such circumstances, it would do your husband good that you and your children should be under our protection during his period of temporary seclusion. We stand well in the county. Perhaps I ought not to say so, but I do not know how otherwise to explain myself; and when it is known, by the bishop and others, that you have come to us during that sad time, it will be understood that we think well of Mr Crawley, in spite of anything that a jury may say of him. Do you see that, my dear? And we do think well of him. I have known of your husband for many years, though I have not personally had the pleasure of much acquaintance with him. He was over at Framley once at my request, and I had great occasion then to respect him. I do respect him; and I shall feel grateful to him if he will allow you to put yourself and your children under my wing, as being an old woman, should this misfortune fall upon him. We hope that it will not fall upon him; but it is always well to be provided for the worst.'

In this way Lady Lufton at last made her speech and opened out the proposal with which she had come laden to Hogglestock. While she was speaking Mrs Crawley's shoulder was still turned to her; but the speaker could see that the quick tears were pouring themselves down the cheeks of the woman whom she addressed. There was a downright honesty of thorough-going well-wishing charity about the proposition which overcame Mrs Crawley altogether. She did not feel for a moment that it would be possible for her to go to Framley in such circumstances as those which had been suggested. As she thought of it all at the present moment, it seemed to her that her only appropriate home during the terrible period which was coming upon her, would be under the walls of the prison in which her husband would be incarcerated. But she fully appreciated the kindness which had suggested a measure, which, if carried into execution, would make the outside world feel that her husband was respected in the county, despite the degradation to which he was subjected. She felt all this, but her heart was too full to speak.

'Say that it shall be so, my dear,' continued Lady Lufton. 'Just give me one nod of assent, and the cottage shall be ready for you should it so chance that you should require it.'

But Mrs Crawley did not give the nod of assent. With her face still averted, while the tears were still running down her cheeks, she muttered but a word or two. 'I could not do that, Lady Lufton; I could not do that.'

'You know at any rate what my wishes are, and as you become calmer you will think of it. There is quite time enough, and I am speaking of an alternative which may never happen. My dear friend Mrs Robarts, who is now with your daughter, wishes Miss Crawley to go over to Framley Parsonage while this inquiry among the clergymen is going on. They all say is it the most ridiculous thing in all the world, – this inquiry. But the bishop you know is so silly! We all think that if Miss Crawley would go for a week or so to Framley Parsonage, that it will show how happy we all are to receive her. It should be while Mr Robarts is employed in his part of the work. What do you say, Mrs Crawley? We at Framley are all clearly of opinion that it will be best that it should be known that the people in the county uphold your husband. Miss Crawley would be back, you know, before the trial comes on. I hope you will let her come, Mrs Crawley?'

But even to this proposition Mrs Crawley could give no assent, though she expressed no direct dissent. As regarded her own feelings, she would much have preferred to have been left to live through her misery alone; but she could not but appreciate the kindness which endeavoured to throw over her and hers in their trouble the ægis of first-rate county respectability. She was saved from the necessity of giving a direct answer to this suggestion by the return of Mrs Robarts and Grace herself. The door was opened slowly, and they crept into the room as though they were aware that their presence would be hardly welcomed.

'Is the carriage there, Fanny?' said Lady Lufton. 'It is almost time for us to think of returning home.'

Mrs Robarts said that the carriage was standing within twenty yards of the door.

'Then I think we will make a start,' said Lady Lufton. 'Have you succeeded in persuading Miss Crawley to come over to Framley in April?'

Mrs Robarts made no answer to this, but looked at Grace; and Grace looked upon the ground.

'I have spoken to Mrs Crawley,' said Lady Lufton, 'and they will think of it.' Then the two ladies took their leave, and walked out to their carriage.

'What does she say about your plan?' Mrs Robarts asked.

'She is too broken-hearted to say anything,' Lady Lufton answered. 'Should it happen that he is convicted, we must come over and take her. She will have no power then to resist us in anything.

CHAPTER 51

Mrs Dobbs Broughton piles her fagots

The picture still progressed up in Mrs Dobbs Broughton's room, and the secret was still kept, or supposed to be kept. Miss Van Siever was, at any rate, certain that her mother had heard nothing of it, and Mrs Broughton reported from day to day that her husband had not yet interfered. Nevertheless, there was in these days a great gloom upon the Dobbs Broughton household, so much so that Conway Dalrymple had more than once suggested to Mrs Broughton that the work should be discontinued. But the mistress of the house would not consent to this. In answer to these offers, she was wont to declare in somewhat mysterious language, that any misery coming upon herself was matter of moment to nobody, – hardly even to herself, as she was quite prepared to encounter moral and social death without delay, if not an absolute physical demise; as to which latter alternative, she seemed to think that even that might not be so far distant as some people chose to believe. What was the cause of the gloom over the house neither Conway Dalrymple nor Miss Van Siever understood, and to speak the truth Mrs Broughton did not quite understand the cause herself. She knew well enough, no doubt, that her husband came home always sullen, and sometimes tipsy, and that things were not going well in the City. She had never understood much about the City, being satisfied with an assurance that had come to her in early days from her friends, that there was a mine of wealth in Hook Court, from whence would always come for her use, house and furniture, a carriage and horses, dresses and jewels, which latter, if not quite real, should be manufactured of the best sham substitute known. Soon after her brilliant marriage with Mr Dobbs Broughton, she had discovered that the carriage and horses, and the sham jewels, did not lift her so completely into a terrestrial paradise as she had taught herself to expect that they would do. Her brilliant drawing-room, with Dobbs Broughton for a companion, was not an elysium.

But though she had found out early in her married life that something was still wanting to her, she had by no means confessed to herself that the carriage and horses and sham jewels were bad, and it can hardly be said that she had repented. She had endeavoured to patch up matters with a little romance, and then had fallen upon Conway Dalrymple, – meaning no harm. Indeed, love with her, as it never could have meant much good, was not likely to mean much harm. That somebody should pretend to love her, to which pretence she might reply by a pretence of friendship, – this was the little excitement which she craved, and by which she had once flattered herself that something of an elysium might yet be created for her. Mr Dobbs Broughton had unreasonably expressed a dislike to this innocent amusement, – very unreasonably, knowing as he ought to have known, that he himself did so very little towards providing the necessary elysium by any qualities of his own. For a few weeks this interference from her husband had enhanced the amusement, giving an additional excitement to the game. She felt herself to be a woman misunderstood and ill-used; and to some women there is nothing so charming as a little mild ill-usage, which does not interfere with their creature comforts, with their clothes, or their carriage, or their sham jewels; but suffices to afford them the indulgence of a grievance. Of late, however, Mr Dobbs Broughton had become a little too rough in his language, and things had gone uncomfortably. She suspected that Conway Dalrymple was not the only cause of all this. She had an idea that Mr Musselboro and Mrs Van Siever had it in their power to make themselves unpleasant, and that they were exercising this power. Of his business in the City her husband never spoke to her, nor she to him. Her own fortune had been very small, some couple of thousand pounds or so, and she conceived that she had no pretext on which she could, unmasked, interrogate him about his money. She had no knowledge that marriage of itself had given her the right to such interference; and had such knowledge been hers she would have had no desire to interfere. She hoped that the carriage and sham jewels would be continued to her; but she did not know how to frame any question on the subject. Touching the other difficulty, – the Conway Dalrymple difficulty, – she had her ideas. The tenderness of her friendship had been trodden upon and outraged by the rough foot of an overbearing husband, and she was ill-used. She would obey. It was becoming to her as a wife that she should submit. She would give up Conway Dalrymple, and would induce him, – in spite of his violent attachment to herself, – to take a wife. She herself would choose a wife for him. She herself would, with suicidal hands, destroy the romance of her own life, since an overbearing, brutal husband demanded that it should be destroyed. She would sacrifice her own feelings, and do all in her power to bring Conway Dalrymple and Clara Van Siever together. If, after that, some poet did not immortalize her friendship in Byronic verse, she certainly would not get her due. Perhaps Conway Dalrymple would himself become a poet in order that this might be done properly. For it must be understood that, though she expected Conway Dalrymple to marry, she expected also that he should be Byronically wretched after his marriage on account of his love for herself.

But there was certainly something wrong over and beyond the Dalrymple difficulty. The servants were not as civil as they used to be, and her husband, when she suggested to him a little dinner-party, snubbed her most unmercifully. The giving of dinner-parties had been his glory, and she had made the suggestion simply with the view of pleasing him. 'If the world were going round the wrong way, a woman would still want a party,' he had said, sneering at her. 'It was of you I was thinking, Dobbs,' she replied; 'not of myself. I care little for such gatherings.' After that she retired to her own room with a romantic tear in each eye, and told herself that, had chance thrown Conway Dalrymple into her way before she had seen Dobbs Broughton, she would have been the happiest woman in the world. She sat for a while looking into vacancy, and thinking that it would be very nice to break her heart. How should she set about it? Should she take to her bed and grow thin? She would begin by eating no dinner for ever so many days together. At lunch her husband was never present, and therefore the broken heart could be displayed at dinner without much positive suffering. In the meantime she would implore Conway Dalrymple to get himself married with as little delay as possible, and she would lay upon him her positive order to restrain himself from any word of affection addressed to herself. She, at any rate, would be pure, high-minded, and self-sacrificing, – although romantic and poetic also, as was her nature.

The picture was progressing, and so also, as it had come about, was the love-affair between the artist and his model. Conway Dalrymple had begun to think that he might, after all, do worse than make Clara Van Siever his wife. Clara Van Siever was handsome, and undoubtedly clever, and Clara Van Siever's mother was certainly rich. And, in addition to this, the young lady herself began to like the man into whose society she was thrown. The affair seemed to flourish, and Mrs Dobbs Broughton should have been delighted. She told Clara, with a very serious air, that she was delighted, bidding Clara, at the same time, to be very cautious, as men were so fickle, and as Conway, though the best fellow in the world, was not, perhaps, altogether free from that common vice of men. Indeed, it might have been surmised, from a word or two which Mrs Broughton allowed to escape, that she considered poor Conway to be more than ordinarily afflicted in that way. Miss Van Siever at first only pouted, and said that there was nothing in it. 'There is something in it, my dear, certainly,' said Mrs Dobbs Broughton; 'and there can be no earthly reason why there should not be a great deal in it.' 'There is nothing in it,' said Miss Van Siever, impetuously; 'and if you will continue to speak of Mr Dalrymple in that way, I must give up the picture.' 'As for that,' said Mrs Broughton, 'I conceive that we are both of us bound to the young man now, seeing that he has given so much time to the work.' 'I am not bound to him at all,' said Miss Van Siever.'

Mrs Broughton also told Conway Dalrymple that she was delighted, – oh, so much delighted! He had obtained permission to come in one morning before the time of sitting, so that he might work at his canvas independently of his model. As was his custom, he made his own way upstairs and commenced his work alone, – having been expressly told by Mrs Broughton that she would not come to him till she brought Clara with her. But she did go up to the room in which the artist was painting, without waiting for Miss Van Siever. Indeed, she was at this time so anxious as to the future welfare of her two young friends that she could not restrain herself from speaking either to the one or to the other, whenever any opportunity for such speech came round. To have left Conway Dalrymple at work upstairs without going to him was impossible to her. So she went, and then took the opportunity of expressing to her friend her ideas as to his past and future conduct.

'Yes, it is very good; very good, indeed,' she said, standing before the easel, and looking at the half-completed work. 'I do not know that you ever did anything better.'

'I never can tell myself till a picture is finished whether it is going to be good or not,' said Dalrymple, thinking really of his picture and of nothing else.

'I am sure this will be good,' she said, 'and I suppose it is because you have thrown so much heart into it. It is not mere industry that will produce good work, nor yet skill, nor even genius: more than this is required. The heart of the artist must be thrust with all its gushing tides into the performance.' By this time he knew all the tones of her voice and their various meanings, and immediately became aware that at the present moment she was intent upon something beyond the picture. She was preparing for a little scene, and was going to give him some advice. He understood it all, but as he was really desirous of working at his canvas, and was rather averse to having a scene at that moment, he made a little attempt to disconcert her. 'It is the heart that gives success,' she said, while he was considering how he might best put an extinguisher upon her romance for the occasion.

'Not at all, Mrs Broughton; success depends on elbow-grease.'

'On what, Conway?'

'On elbow-grease, – hard work, that is, – and I must work hard now if I mean to take advantage of to-day's sitting. The truth is, I don't give enough hours of work to it.' And he leaned upon his stick, and daubed away briskly at the background, and then stood for a moment looking at his canvas with his head a little on one side, as though he could not withdraw his attention for a moment from the thing he was doing.

'You mean to say, Conway, that you would rather that I should not speak to you.'

'Oh, no, Mrs Broughton, I did not mean that at all.'

'I won't interrupt you at your work. What I have to say is perhaps of no great moment. Indeed, words between you and me never can have much importance now. Can they Conway?'

'I don't see that at all,' said he, still working away with his brush.

'Do you not? I do. They should never amount to more, – they can never amount to more than the common, ordinary courtesies of life; what I call the greetings and good-byings of conversation.' She said this in a low, melancholy tone of voice, not intending to be in any degree jocose. 'How seldom is it that conversation between ordinary friends goes beyond that.'

'Don't you think it does?' said Conway, stepping back and taking another look at his picture. 'I find myself talking to all manner of people about all manner of things.'

'You are different from me. I cannot talk to all manner of people.'

'Politics, you know, and art, and a little scandal, and the wars, with a dozen other things, make talking easy enough, I think. I grant you this, that it is very often a great bore. Hardly a day passes that I don't wish to cut out somebody's tongue.'

'Do you wish to cut out my tongue, Conway?'

He began to perceive that she was determined to talk about herself, and there was no remedy. He dreaded it, not because he did not like the woman, but from a conviction that she was going to make some comparison between herself and Clara Van Siever. In his ordinary humour he liked a little pretence at romance, and was rather good at that sort of love-making which in truth means anything but love. But just now he was really thinking of matrimony, and had on this very morning acknowledged to himself that he had become sufficiently attached to Clara Van Siever to justify him in asking her to be his wife. In his present mood he was not anxious for one of those tilts with blunted swords and half-severed lances in the lists of Cupid of which Mrs Dobbs Broughton was so fond. Nevertheless, if she insisted that he should now descend into the arena and go through the paraphernalia of a mock tournament, he must obey her. It is the hardship of men that when called upon by women for romance, they are bound to be romantic, whether the opportunity serves them or does not. A man must produce romance, or at least submit to it, when duly summoned, even though he should have a sore-throat or a headache. He is a brute if he decline such an encounter, – and feels that, should he so decline persistently, he will ever after be treated as a brute. There are many Potiphar's wives who never dream of any mischief, and Josephs* who are very anxious to escape, though they are asked to return only whisper for whisper. Mrs Dobbs Broughton had asked him whether he wished that her tongue should be cut out, and he had of course replied that her words had always been a joy to him, – never a trouble. It occurred to him as he made his little speech that it would only have served her right if he had answered her quite in another strain; but she was a woman, and was young and pretty, and was entitled to flattery. 'They have always been a joy to me,' he said, repeating his last words as he strove to continue his work.

'A deadly joy,' she replied, not quite knowing what she herself meant. 'A deadly joy, Conway. I wish with all my heart that we had never known each other.'

'I do not. I will never wish away the happiness of my life, even should it be followed by misery.'

'You are a man, and if trouble comes upon you, you can bear it on your own shoulders. A woman suffers more, just because another's shoulders may have to bear the burden.'

'When she has got a husband, you mean?'

'Yes, – when she has a husband.'

'It's the same with a man when he has a wife.' Hitherto the conversation had had so much of milk-and-water in its composition, that Dalrymple found himself able to keep it up and go on with his background at the same time. If she could only be kept in the same dim cloud of sentiment, if the hot rays of the sun of romance could be kept from breaking through the mist till Miss Van Siever should come, it might still be well. He had known her to wander about within the clouds for an hour together, without being able to find her way into the light. 'It's all the same with a man when he has got a wife,' he said. 'Of course one has to suffer for two, when one, so to say, is two.'

'And what happens when one has to suffer for three?' she asked.

'You mean when a woman has children?'

'I mean nothing of the kind, Conway; and you must know that I do not, unless your feelings are indeed blunted. But wordly success has, I suppose, blunted them.'

'I rather fancy not,' he said. 'I think they are pretty nearly as sharp as ever.'

'I know mine are. Oh, how I wish I could rid myself of them! But it cannot be done. Age will not blunt them, – I am sure of that,' said Mrs Broughton. 'I wish it would.'

He had determined not to talk about herself if the subject could be in any way avoided; but now he felt that he was driven up into a corner; – now he was forced to speak to her of her own personality. 'You have no experience yet as to that. How can you say what age will do?'

'Age does not go by years,' said Mrs Dobbs Broughton. 'We, all know that. "His hair was grey, but not with years."* Look here, Conway,' and she moved back her tresses from off her temples to show him that there were gray hairs behind. He did not see them; and had they been very visible she might not perhaps have been so ready to exhibit them. 'No one can say that length of years has blanched them. I have no secrets from you about my age. One should not be grey before one has reached thirty.'

'I did not see a changed hair.'

''Twas the fault of your eyes, then, for there are plenty of them. And what is it has made them grey?'

'They say that hot rooms will do it.'

'Hot rooms! No, Conway, it does not come from heated atmosphere. It comes from a cold heart, a chilled heart, a frozen heart, a heart that is all ice.' She was getting out of the cloud into the heat now, and he could only hope that Miss Van Siever would come soon. 'The world is beginning with you, Conway, and yet you are as old as I am. It is ending with me, and yet I am as young as you are. But I do not know why I talk of all this. It is simply folly, – utter folly. I had not meant to speak of myself; but I did wish to say a few words to you of your own future. I suppose I may still speak to you as a friend?'

'I hope you will always do that.'

'Nay, – I will make no such promise. That I will always have a friend's feeling for you, a friend's interest in your welfare, a friend's triumph in your success, – that I will promise. But friendly words, Conway, are sometimes misunderstood.'

'Never by me,' said he.

'No, not by you, – certainly not by you. I did not mean that. I did not expect that you should misinterpret them.' Then she laughed hysterically, – a little low, gurgling, hysterical laugh; and after that she wiped her eyes, and then she smiled, and then she put her hand very gently upon his shoulder. 'Thank God, Conway, we are quite safe there, – are we not?'

He had made a blunder, and it was necessary that he should correct it. His watch was lying in the trough of his easel, and he looked at it and wondered why Miss Van Siever was not there. He had tripped and he must make a little struggle and recover his step. 'As I said before, it shall never be misunderstood by me. I have never been vain enough to suppose for a moment that there was any other feeling, – not for a moment. You women can be so careful, while we men are always off our guard! A man loves because he cannot help it; but a woman has been careful, and answers him – with friendship. Perhaps I am wrong to say that I never thought of winning anything more; but I never think of winning more now.' Why the mischief didn't Miss Van Siever come! In another five minutes, despite himself, he would be on his knees, making a mock declaration, and she would be pouring forth the vial of her mock wrath, or giving him mock counsel as to the restraint of his passion. He had gone through it all before, and was tired of it; but for his life he did not know how to help himself.

'Conway,' said she, gravely, 'how dare you address me in such language.'

'Of course it is very wrong: I know that.'

'I'm not speaking of myself, now. I have learned to think so little of myself, as even to be indifferent to the feeling of the injury you are doing me. My life is a blank, and I almost think that nothing can hurt me further. I have not heart left enough to break; no, not enough to be broken. It is not of myself that I am thinking, when I ask you how you dare to address me in such language. Do you not know that it is an injury to another?'

'To what other?' asked Conway Dalrymple, whose mind was becoming rather confused, and who was not quite sure whether the other one was Mr Dobbs Broughton, or somebody else.

'To that poor girl who is coming here now, who is devoted to you, and to whom, I do not doubt, you have uttered words which ought to have made it impossible for you to speak to me as you spoke not a moment since.'

Things were becoming very grave and difficult. They would have been very grave, indeed, had not some god saved him by sending Miss Van Siever to his rescue at this moment. He was beginning to think what he would say in answer to the accusation now made, when his eager ear caught the sound of her step upon the stair; and before the pause in the conversation which the circumstances admitted had given place to the necessity for further speech, Miss Van Siever had knocked at the door and had entered the room. He was rejoiced, and I think that Mrs Broughton did not regret the interference. It is always well that these little dangerous scenes should be brought to sudden ends. The last details of such romances, if drawn out to their natural conclusions, are apt to be uncomfortable, if not dull. She did not want him to go down on his knees, knowing that the getting up again is always awkward.

'Clara, I began to think you were never coming,' said Mrs Broughton, with her sweetest smile.

'I began to think so myself also,' said Clara. 'And I believe this must be the last sitting, or, at any rate, the last but one.'

'Is anything the matter at home?' said Mrs Broughton, clasping her hands together.

'Nothing very much; mamma asked me a question or two this morning, and I said I was coming here. Had she asked me why, I should have told her.'

'But what did she ask? What did she say?

'She does not always make herself very intelligible. She complains without telling you what she complains of. But she muttered something about artists which was not complimentary, and I suppose therefore, that she has a suspicion. She stayed ever so late this morning, and we left the house together. She will ask some direct question to-night, or before long, and then there will be an end of it.'

'Let us make the best of our time then,'said Dalrymple; and the sitting was arranged; Miss Van Siever went down on her knees with her hammer in her hand, and the work began. Mrs Broughton had twisted a turban round Clara's head, as she always did on these occasions, and assisted to arrange the drapery. She used to tell herself as she did so, that she was like Isaac, piling the fagots for her own sacrifice.* Only Isaac had piled them in ignorance, and she piled them conscious of the sacrificial flames. And Isaac had been saved; whereas it was impossible that the catching of any ram in any thicket could save her. But, nevertheless, she arranged the drapery with all her skill, piling the fagots ever so high for her own pyre. In the meantime Conway Dalrymple painted away, thinking more of his picture than he did of one woman or of the other.

After a while, when Mrs Broughton had piled the fagots as high as she could pile them, she got up from her seat and prepared to leave the room. Much of the piling consisted, of course, in her own absence during a portion of these sittings. 'Conway,' she said, as she went, 'if this is to be the last sitting, or the last but one, you should make the most of it.' Then she threw upon him a very peculiar glance over the head of the kneeling Jael, and withdrew. Jael, who in those moments would be thinking more of the fatigue of her position than of anything else, did not at all take home to herself the peculiar meaning of her friend's words. Conway Dalrymple understood them thoroughly, and thought that he might as well take the advice given to him. He had made up his mind to propose to Miss Van Siever, and why should he not do so now? He went on with his brush for a couple of minutes without saying a word, working as well as he could work, and then resolved that he would at once begin the other task. 'Miss Van Siever,' he said, 'I'm afraid you are tired?'

'Not more than usually tired. It is fatiguing to be slaying Sisera by the hour together. I do get to hate this block.' The block was the dummy by which the form of Sisera was supposed to be typified.

'Another sitting will about finish it,' said he, 'so that you need not positively distress yourself now. Will you rest yourself for a minute or two?' He had already perceived that the attitude in which Clara was posed before him was not one in which an offer of marriage could be received and replied to with advantage.

'Thank you I am not tired yet,' said Clara, not changing the fixed glance of national wrath with which she regarded her wooden Sisera as she held her hammer on high.

'But I am. There; we will rest for a moment.' Dalrymple was aware that Mrs Dobbs Broughton, though she was very assiduous in piling her fagots, never piled them for long together. If he did not make haste she should be back upon them before he could get his word spoken. When he put down his brush, and got up from his chair, and stretched out his arm as a man does when he ceases for a moment from his work, Clara of course got up also, and seated herself. She was used to her turban and her drapery, and therefore thought not of it at all; but now that he intended to accomplish a special purpose, the turban and the drapery seemed to be in the way. 'I do so hope you will like the picture,' he said, as he was thinking of this.

'I don't think I shall. But you will understand that it is natural that a girl should not like herself in such a portraiture as that.'

'I don't know why. I can understand that you specially should not like the picture; but I think that most women in London in your place would at any rate say that they did.'

'Are you angry with me?'

'What; for telling the truth? No, indeed.' He was standing opposite to his easel, looking at the canvas shifting his head about so as to change the lights, and observing critically this blemish and that; and yet he was all the while thinking how he had best carry out his purpose. 'It will have been a prosperous picture to me,' he said at last, 'if it leads to the success of which I am ambitious.'

'I am told that all you do is successful now, – merely because you do it. That is the worst of success.'

'What is the worst of success?'

'That when won by merit it leads to further success, for the gaining of which no merit is necessary.'

'I hope it may be so in my case. If it is not I shall have a very poor chance. Clara, I think you must know that I am not talking about my pictures.'

'I thought you were.'

'Indeed I am not. As for success in my profession, far as I am from thinking I merit it, I feel tolerably certain that I shall obtain it.'

'You have obtained it.'

'I am in the way to do so. Perhaps one out of ten struggling artists is successful, and for him the profession is very charming. It is certainly a sad feeling that there is so much of chance in the distribution of the prizes. It is a lottery. But one cannot complain of that when one has drawn the prize.' Dalrymple was not a man without self-possession, nor was he readily abashed, but he found it easier to talk of his possession than to make his offer. The turban was his difficulty. He had told himself over and over again within the last five minutes, that he would have long since said what he had to say had it not been for the turban. He had been painting all his life from living models, – from women dressed up in this or that costume, to suit the necessities of his picture, – but he had never made love to any of them. They had been simply models to him, and now he found that there was a difficulty. 'Of that prize,' he said, 'I have made myself tolerably sure; but as to the other prize, I do not know. I wonder whether I am to have that.' Of course Miss Van Siever understood well what was the prize of which he was speaking; and as she was a young woman with a will and purpose of her own, no doubt she was already prepared with an answer. But it was necessary that the question should be put to her in properly distinct terms. Conway Dalrymple certainly had not put his question in properly distinct terms at present. She did not choose to make any answer to his last words; and therefore simply suggested that as time was pressing he had better go on with his work. 'I am quite ready now,' said she.

'Stop half a moment. How much more you are thinking of the picture than I am! I do not care twopence for the picture. I will slit the canvas from top to bottom without a groan, – without a single inner groan, – if you will let me.'

'For heaven's sake do nothing of the kind! Why should you?'

'Just to show you that it is not for the sake of the picture that I come here. Clara – ' Then the door was opened, and Isaac appeared, very weary, having been piling fagots with assiduity, till human nature could pile no more. Conway Dalrymple, who had made his way almost up to Clara's seat, turned round sharply towards his easel, in anger at having been disturbed. He should have been more grateful for all that his Isaac had done for him, and have recognized the fact that the fault had been with himself. Mrs Broughton had been twelve minutes out of the room. She had counted them to be fifteen, – having no doubt made a mistake as to three, – and had told herself that with such a one as Conway Dalrymple, with so much of the work ready done to his hand for him, fifteen minutes should have been amply sufficient. When we reflect what her own thoughts must have been during the interval, – what it is to have to pile up such fagots as those, how she was, as it were, giving away a fresh morsel of her own heart during each minute that she allowed Clara and Conway Dalrymple to remain together, it cannot surprise us that her eyes should have become dizzy, and that she should not have counted the minutes with accurate correctness. Dalrymple turned to his picture angrily, but Miss Van Siever kept her seat and did not show the slightest emotion.

'My friends,' said Mrs Broughton, 'this will not do. This is not working; this is not sitting.'

'Mr Dalrymple has been explaining to me the precarious nature of an artist's profession,' said Clara.

'It is not precarious with him' said Mrs Dobbs Broughton, sententiously.

'Not in a general way, perhaps; but to prove the truth of his words he was going to treat Jael worse than Jael treats Sisera.'

'I was going to slit the picture from the top to the bottom.'

'And why?' said Mrs Broughton, putting up her hands to heaven in tragic horror.

'Just to show Miss Van Siever how little I care about it.'

'And how little you care about her, too,' said Mrs Broughton.

'She might take that as she liked.' After this there was another genuine sitting and the real work went on as though there had been no episode. Jael fixed her face, and held her hammer as though her mind and heart was solely bent on seeming to be slaying Sisera. Dalrymple turned his eyes from the canvas to the model, and from the model to the canvas, working with his hand all the while, as though that last pathetic 'Clara' had never been uttered; and Mrs

Dobbs Broughton reclined on a sofa, looking at them and thinking of her own singularly romantic position, till her mind was filled with a poetic frenzy. In one moment she resolved that she would hate Clara as woman was never hated by woman; and then there were daggers, and poison-cups, and strangling cords in her eye. In the next she was as firmly determined that she would love Mrs Conway Dalrymple as woman never was loved by woman; and then she saw herself kneeling by a cradle, and tenderly nursing a baby, of which Conway was to be the father and Clara the mother. And so she went to sleep.

For some time Dalrymple did not observe this; but at last there was a little sound, – even the ill-nature of Miss Demolines could hardly have called it a snore, – and he became aware that for practical purposes he and Miss Van Siever were again alone together. 'Clara,' he said, in a whisper. Mrs Broughton instantly aroused herself from her slumbers, and rubbed her eyes. 'Dear, dear, dear,' she said, 'I declare it's past one. I'm afraid I must turn you both out. One more sitting, I suppose, will finish it, Conway ?'

'Yes, one more,' said he. It was always understood that he and Clara should not leave the house together, and therefore he remained painting when she left the room. 'And now, Conway,' said Mrs Broughton, 'I suppose that all is over ?'

'I don't know what you mean by all being over.'

'No, – of course not. You look at it in another light, no doubt. Everything is beginning for you. But you must pardon me, for my heart is distracted, – distracted, – distracted !' Then she sat down upon the floor, and burst into tears. What was he to do? He thought that the woman should either give him up altogether, or not give him up. All this fuss about it was irrational ! He would not have made love to Clara Van Siever in her room if she had not told him to do so !

'Maria,' he said, in a very grave voice, 'any sacrifice that is required on my part on your behalf I am ready to make.'

'No sir; the sacrifices shall all be made by me. It is the part of a woman to be ever sacrificial !' Poor Mrs Dobbs Broughton ! 'You shall give up nothing. The world is at your feet, and you shall have everything, – youth, beauty, wealth, station, love, – love; and friendship also, if you will accept it from one so poor, so broken, so secluded as I shall be.' At each of the last words there had been a desperate sob; and as she was still crouching in the middle of the room, looking up into Dalrymple's face while he stood over her, the scene was one which had much in it that transcended the doings of everyday life, much that would be ever memorable, and much, I have no doubt, that was thoroughly enjoyed by the principal actor.

As for Conway Dalrymple, he was so second-rate a personage in the whole thing, that it mattered little whether he enjoyed it or not. I don't think he did enjoy it. 'And now, Conway,' she said, 'I will give you some advice. And when in after-days you shall remember this interview, and reflect how that advice was given you, – with what solemnity,' – here she clasped both her hands together, – 'I think that you will follow it. Clara Van Siever will now become your wife.'

'I do not know that at all,' said Dalrymple.

'Clara Van Siever will now become your wife,' repeated Mrs Broughton in a louder voice, impatient of opposition. 'Love her. Cleave to her. Make her flesh of your flesh and bone of your bone.* But rule her! Yes, rule her! Let her be your second self, but not your first self. Rule her. Love her. Cleave to her. Do not leave her alone, to feed on her own thoughts as I have done, – as I have been forced to do. Now go. No, Conway, not a word; I will not hear a word. You must go, or I must.' Then she rose quickly from her lowly attitude, and prepared herself for a dart at the door. It was better by far that he should go, and so he went.

An American when he has spent a pleasant day will tell you that he has had 'a good time.' I think that Mrs Dobbs Broughton, if she had ever spoken the truth of that day's employment, would have acknowledged that she had had 'a good time.' I think that she enjoyed her morning's work. But as for Conway Dalrymple, I doubt whether he did enjoy his morning's work. 'A man may have too much of this sort of thing, and then he becomes very sick of his cake.' Such was the nature of his thoughts as he returned to his own abode.

CHAPTER 52

Why don't you have an 'it' for yourself?

Of course it came to pass that Lily Dale and Emily Dunstable were soon very intimate, and that they saw each other every day. Indeed, before long they would have been living together in the same house had it not been that the squire had felt reluctant to abandon the independence of his own lodgings. When Mrs Thorne had pressed her invitation for the second, and the for the third time, asking them both to come to her large house, he had begged his niece to go and leave him alone. 'You need not regard me,' he had said, speaking not with the whining voice of complaint, but with that thin tinge of melancholy which was usual to him. 'I am so much alone down at Allington, that you need not mind leaving me.' But Lily would not go on those terms, and therefore they still lived together in the lodgings. Nevertheless Lily was every day at Mrs Thorne's house, and thus a great intimacy grew up between the girls. Emily Dunstable had neither brother nor sister, and Lily's nearest male relative in her own degree was no *v* Miss Dunstable's betrothed husband. It was natural therefore that they should at any rate try to like each other. It afterwards came to pass that Lily did go to Mrs Thorne's house, and she stayed there for awhile; but when that occurred the squire had gone back to Allington.

Among other generous kindnesses Mrs Thorne insisted that Bernard should hire a horse for his cousin Lily. Emily Dunstable rode daily, and of course Captain Dale rode with her; – and now Lily joined the party. Almost before she knew what was being done she found herself provided with hat and habit and horse and whip. It was a way with Mrs Thorne that they who came within the influence of her immediate sphere should be made to feel that the comforts and luxuries arising from her wealth belonged to a common stock, and were the joint property of them all. Things were not offered and taken and talked about, but they made their appearance, and were used as a matter of course. If you go to stay at a gentleman's house you understand that, as a matter of course, you will be provided with meat and drink. Some hosts furnish you also with cigars. A small number give you stabling and forage for your horse; and a very select few mount you on hunting days, and send you out with a groom and a second horse. Mrs Thorne went beyond all others in this open-handed hospitality. She had enormous wealth at her command, and had but few of those all-absorbing drains upon wealth which in this country make so many rich men poor. She had no family property, – no place to keep up in which she did not live. She had no retainers to be maintained because they were retainers. She had neither sons nor daughters. Consequently she was able to be lavish in her generosity; and as her heart was very lavish, she would have given her friends gold to eat had gold been good for eating. Indeed there was no measure in her giving, – unless when the idea came upon her that the recipient of her favours was trading on them. Then she would hold her hand very stoutly.

Lily Dale had not liked the idea of being fitted out thus expensively. A box at the opera was all very well, as it was not procured especially for her. And tickets for other theatres did not seem to come unnaturally for a night or two. But her spirit had militated against the hat and the habit and the horse. The whip was a little present from Emily Dunstable, and that of course was accepted with a good grace. Then there came the horse, – as though from the heavens; there seemed to be ten horses, twenty horses, if anybody needed them. All these things seemed to flow naturally into Mrs Thorne's establishment, like the air through the windows. It was very pleasant, but Lily hesitated when she was told that a habit was to be given to her. 'My dear old aunt insists,' said Emily Dunstable. 'Nobody ever thinks of refusing anything from her. If you only knew what some people will take, and some people will even ask, who have nothing to do with her at all!' 'But I have nothing to do with her, – in that way I mean,' said Lily. 'Oh, yes, you have,' said Emily. 'You and Bernard are as good as brother and sister, and Bernard and I are as good as man and wife, and my aunt and I are as good as mother and daughter. So you see, in a sort of way you are a child of the house.' So Lily accepted the habit; but made a stand at the hat, and paid for that out of her own pocket. When the squire had seen Lily on horseback he asked her questions about it. 'It was a hired horse, I suppose?' he said. 'I think it came direct from heaven,' said Lily. 'What do you mean, Lily?' said the squire, angrily. 'I mean that when people are so rich and good-natured as Mrs Thorne it is not good inquiring where things come from. All that I know is that the horses come out of Potts' livery-stable. They talk of Potts as if he were a good-natured man who provides horses

for the world without troubling anybody.' Then, the squire spoke
to Bernard about it, saying that he should insist on defraying his
niece's expenses. But Bernard swore that he could give his uncle no
assistance. 'I would not speak to her about such a thing for all the
world,' said Bernard. 'Then I shall,' said the squire.

In those days Lily thought much of Johnny Eames, – gave to him
perhaps more of that thought which leads to love than she had ever
given him before. She still heard the Crawley question discussed
every day. Mrs Thorne, as we all know, was at this time a
Barsetshire personage, and was of course interested in Barsetshire
subjects; and she was specially anxious in the matter, having strong
hopes with reference to the marriage of Major Grantly and Grace,
and strong hopes also that Grace's father might escape the fangs of
justice. The Crawley case was constantly in Lily's ears, and as
constantly she heard high praise awarded to Johnny for his kindness
in going after the Arabins. 'He must be a fine young fellow,' said
Mrs Thorne, 'and we'll have him down at Chaldicotes some day.
Old Lord De Guest found him out and made a friend of him, and
old Lord De Guest was no fool.' Lily was not altogether free from
a suspicion that Mrs thorne knew the story of Johnny's love and
was trying to serve Johnny, – as other people had tried to do, very
ineffectually. When this suspicion came upon her she would shut
her heart against her lover's praises, and swear that she would stand
by those two letters which she had written in her book at home.
But the suspicion would not be always there, and there did come
upon her a conviction that her lover was more esteemed among
men and women than she had been accustomed to believe. Her
cousin, Bernard Dale, who certainly was regarded in the world as
somebody, spoke of him as his equal; whereas in former days
Bernard had always regarded Johnny Eames as standing low in the
world's regard. Then Lily, when alone, would remember a certain
comparison which she once made between Adolphus Crosbie and
John Eames, when neither of the men had as yet pleaded his cause
to her, and which had been very much in favour of the former. She
had then declared that Johnny was a 'mere clerk.' She had a higher
opinion of him now, – a much higher opinion, even though he
could never be more to her than a friend.

In these days Lily's new ally, Emily Dunstable, seemed to Lily to
be so happy! There was in Emily a complete realization of that idea
of ante-nuptial blessedness of which Lily had often thought so
much. Whatever Emily did she did for Bernard; and, to give
Captain Dale his due, he received all the sweets which were showered
upon him with becoming signs of gratitude. I suppose it is always
the case at such times that the girl has the best of it, and on this

occasion Emily Dunstable certainly made the most of her happiness. 'I do envy you,' Lily said one day. The acknowledgment seemed to have been extorted from her involuntarily. She did not laugh as she spoke, or follow up what she had said with other words intended to take away the joke of what she had uttered, – had it been a joke ; but she sat silent, looking at the girl who was re-arranging flowers which Bernard had brought to her.

'I can't give him up to you, you know,' said Emily.

'I don't envy you him but "it," ' said Lily.

'Then go and get an "it" for yourself. Why don't you have an "it" for yourself ? You can have an "it" to-morrow, if you like, – or two or three, if all that I hear is true.'

'No, I can't,' said Lily. 'Things have gone wrong with me. Don't ask me anything more about it. Pray don't. I shan't speak of it if you do.'

'Of course I will not if you tell me I must not.'

'I do tell you so. I have been a fool to say anything about it. However, I have got over my envy now, and am ready to go out with your aunt. Here she is.'

'Things have gone wrong with me.' She repeated the same words to herself over and over again. With all the efforts which she had made she could not quite reconcile herself to the two letters which she had written in the book. This coming up to London, and riding in the Park, and going to the theatres, seemed to unsettle her. At home she had schooled herself down into quiescence, and made herself think that she believed that she was satisfied with the prospects of her life. But now she was all astray again, doubting about herself, hankering after something over and beyond that which seemed to be allotted to her, – but, nevertheless, assuring herself that she never would accept of anything else.

I must not, if I can help it, let the reader suppose that she was softening her heart to John Eames because John Eames was spoken well of in the world. But with all of us, in the opinion which we form of those around us, we take unconsciously the opinion of others. A woman is handsome because the world says so. Music is charming to us because it charms others. We drink our wines with other men's palates, and look at our pictures with other men's eyes. When Lily heard John Eames praised by all around her, it could not be but that she should praise him too, – not out loud, as others did, but in the silence of her heart. And then his constancy to her had been so perfect ! If that other one had never come ! If it could be that she might begin again, and that she might be spared that episode in her life which had brought him and her together !

'When is Mr Eames going to be back ?' Mrs Thorne said at dinner one day. On this occasion the squire was dining at Mrs Thorne's house; and there were three or four others there, – among them a Mr Harold Smith, who was in Parliament, and his wife, and John Eames's especial friend, Sir Raffle Buffle. The question was addressed to the squire, but the squire was slow to answer, and it was taken up by Sir Raffle Buffle

'He'll be back on the 15th,' said the knight, 'unless he means to play truant. I hope he won't do that, as his absence has been a terrible inconvenience to me.' Then Sir Raffle explained that John Eames was his private secretary, and that Johnny's journey to the continent had been made with, and could not have been made without, his sanction. 'When I came to hear the story, of course I told him that he must go. "Eames," I said, "take the advice of a man who knows the world. Circumstanced as you are you are bound to go." And he went.'

'Upon my word that was very good-natured of you,' said Mrs Thorne.

'I never keep a fellow to his desk who has really got important business elsewhere,' said Sir Raffle. 'The country, I say, can afford to do as much as that for her servants. But then I like to know that the business is business. One doesn't choose to be humbugged.'

'I daresay you are humbugged, as you call it, very often,' said Harold Smith.

'Perhaps so; perhaps I am; perhaps that is the opinion which they have of me at the Treasury. But you were hardly long enough there, Smith, to have learned much about it, I should say.'

'I don't suppose I should have known much about it, as you call it, if I had stayed till Doomsday.'

'I daresay not; I daresay not. Men who begin as late as you did never know what official life really means. Now I've been at it all my life, and I think I do understand it.'

'It's not a profession I should like unless where it's joined with politics,' said Harold Smith.

But then it's apt to be so short,' said Sir Raffle Buffle. Now it had happened once in the life of Mr Harold Smith that he had been in a Ministry, but, unfortunately, that Ministry had gone out almost within a week of the time of Mr Smith's ahesion. Sir Raffle and Mr Smith had known each other for many years, and were accustomed to make civil little speeches to each other in society.

'I'd sooner be a horse in a mill than have to go to an office every day,' said Mrs Smith, coming to her husband's assistance. 'You, Sir Raffle, have kept yourself fresh and pleasant through it all; but who besides you ever did?'

I hope I am fresh,' said Sir Raffle, 'and as for pleasantness, I will leave that for you to determine.'

'There can be but one opinion,' said Mrs Thorne.

The conversation had strayed away from John Eames, and Lily was disappointed. It was a pleasure to her when people talked of him in her hearing, and as a question or two had been asked about him, making him the hero of the moment, it seemed to her that he was being robbed of his due when the little amenities between Mr and Mrs Harold Smith and Sir Raffle banished his name from the circle. Nothing more, however, was said of him at dinner, and I fear that he would have been altogether forgotten throughout the evening, had not Lily herself referred, – not to him, which she could not possibly have been induced to do, – but to the subject of his journey. 'I wonder whether poor Mr Crawley will be found guilty?' she said to Sir Raffle up in the drawing-room.

'I am afraid he will; I am afraid he will,' said Sir Raffle; 'and I fear, my dear Miss Dale, that I must go further than that. I fear I must express an opinion that he is guilty.'

'Nothing will ever make me think so,' said Lily.

'Ladies are always tender-hearted,' said Sir Raffle, 'and especially young ladies, – especially pretty young ladies. I do not wonder that such should be your opinion. But you see, Miss Dale, a man of business has to look at these things in a business light. What I want to know is, where did he get the cheque? He is bound to be explicit in answering that before anybody can acquit him.'

'That is just what Mr Eames has gone abroad to learn.'

'It is very well for Eames to go abroad, – though, upon my word, I don't know whether I should not have given him different advice if I had known how much I was to be tormented by his absence. The thing couldn't have happened at a more unfortunate time; – the Ministry going out, and everything. But, as I was saying, it is all very well for him to do what he can. He is related to them, and is bound to save the honour of his relations if it be possible. I like him for going. I always liked him. As I said to my friend De Guest, "That young man will make his way." And I rather fancy that the chance word which I spoke then to my valued old friend was not thrown away in Eames's favour. But, my dear Miss Dale, where did Mr Crawley get that cheque? That's what I want to know. If you can tell me that, then I can tell you whether or no he will be acquitted.'

Lily did not feel a strong prepossession in favour of Sir Raffle, in spite of his praise of John Eames. The harsh voice of the man annoyed her, and his egotism offended her. When, much later in the evening, his character came on for discussion between herself

and Mrs Thorne and Emily Dunstable, she had not a word to say
in his favour. But still she had been pleased to meet him, because he
was the man with whom Johnny's life was most specially concerned.
I think that a portion of her dislike to him arose from the fact that
in continuing the conversation he did not revert to his private
secretary, but preferred to regale her with stories of his own doings
in wonderful cases which had partaken of interest similar to that
which now attached itself to Mr Crawley's case. He had known a
man who had stolen a hundred pounds, and had never been found
out; and another man who had been arrested for stealing two-and-
sixpence which was found afterwards sticking to a bit of butter at
the bottom of a plate. Mrs Thorne had heard all this, and had
answered him, 'Dear me, Sir Raffle,' she had said, 'what a great
many thieves you have had among your acquaintance!' This had
rather disconcerted him, and then there had been no more talking
about Mr Crawley.

It had been arranged on this morning that Mr Dale should return
to Allington and leave Lily with Mrs Thorne. Some special need of
his presence at home, real or assumed, had arisen, and he had
declared that he must shorten his stay in London by about half the
intended period. The need would not have been so pressing,
probably, had he not felt that Lily would be more comfortable with
Mrs Thorne than in his lodgings in Sackville Street. Lily had at first
declared that she would return with him, but everybody had
protested against this. Emily Dunstable had protested against it very
stoutly; Mrs Dale herself had protested against it by letter; and
Mrs Thorne's protest had been quite imperious in its nature.
'Indeed, my dear, you'll do nothing of the kind. I'm sure your mother
wouldn't wish it. I look upon it as quite essential that you and
Emily should learn to know each other.' 'But we do know each
other; don't we, Emily?' said Lily. 'Not quite well yet,' said Emily.
Then Lily had laughed, and so the matter was settled. And now, on
this present occasion, Mr Dale was at Mrs Thorne's house for the
last time. His conscience had been perplexed about Lily's horse,
and if anything was to be said it must be said now. The subject was
very disagreeable to him, and he was angry with Bernard because
Bernard had declined to manage it for him after his own fashion.
But he had told himself so often that anything was better than a
pecuniary obligation, that he was determined to speak his mind to
Mrs Thorne, and to beg her to allow him to have his way. So he
waited till the Harold Smiths were gone, and Sir Raffle Buffle, and
then, when Lily was apart with Emily, – for Bernard Dale had left
them – he found himself at last alone with Mrs Thorne.

'I can't be too much obliged to you,' he said, 'for your kindness to my girl.'

'Oh, laws, that's nothing,' said Mrs Thorne. 'We look on her as one of us now.'

'I'm sure she is grateful, – very grateful; and so am I. She and Bernard have been brought up so much together that it is very desirable that she should be not unknown to Bernard's wife.'

'Exactly, – that's just what I mean. Blood's thicker than water; isn't it? Emily's child, if she has one, will be Lily's cousin.'

'Her first-cousin once removed,' said the squire, who was accurate in these matters. Then he drew himself up in his seat and compressed his lips together, and prepared himself for his task. It was very disagreeable. Nothing, he thought, could be more disagreeable. 'I have a little thing to speak about,' he said at last, 'which I hope will not offend you.'

'About Lily?'

'Yes; about Lily.'

'I'm not very easily offended, and I don't know how I could possibly be offended about her.'

'I'm an old-fashioned man, Mrs Thorne, and don't know much about the ways of the world. I have always been down in the county, and maybe I have prejudices. You won't refuse to humour one of them, I hope?'

'You're beginning to frighten me, Mr Dale; what is it?'

'About Lily's horse.'

'Lily's horse! What about her horse? I hope he's not vicious?'

'She is riding every day with your niece,' said the squire, thinking it best to stick to his own point.

'It will do her all the good in the world,' said Mrs Thorne.

'Very likely. I don't doubt it. I do not in the least disapprove of her riding. But—'

'But what, Mr Dale?'

'I should be so much obliged if I might be allowed to pay the livery-stable keeper's bill.'

'Oh, laws a' mercy.'

'I daresay it may sound odd, but as I have a fancy about it, I'm sure you'll gratify me.'

'Of course I will. I'll remember it. I'll make it all right with Bernard. Bernard and I have no end of accounts, – or shall have before long, – and we'll make an item of it. Then you can arrange with Bernard afterwards.'

Mr Dale as he got up to go away felt that he was beaten, but he did not know how to carry the battle any further on that occasion. He could not take out his purse and put down the cost of the horse on the table. 'I will then speak to my nephew about it,' he said, very gravely, as he went away. And he did speak to his nephew about it, and even wrote to him more than once. But it was all to no purpose. Mr Potts could not be induced to give a separate bill, and, – so said Bernard, – swore at last that he would furnish no account to anybody for horses that went to Mrs Thorne's door except to Mrs Thorne herself.

That night Lily took leave of her uncle and remained at Mrs Thorne's house. As things were now arranged she would, no doubt, be in London when John Eames returned. If he should find her in town – and she told herself that if she was in town he certainly would find her, – he would, doubtless, repeat to her the offer he had so often made before. She never ventured to tell herself that she doubted as to the answer to be made to him. The two letters were written in the book, and must remain there. But she felt that she would have had more courage for persistency down at Allington than she would be able to summon to her assistance up in London. She knew she would be weak, should she be found by him alone in Mrs Thorne's drawing-room. It would be better for her to make some excuse and go home. She was resolved that she would not become his wife. She could not extricate herself from the dominion of a feeling which she believed to be love for another man. She had given a solemn promise both to her mother and to John Eames that she would not marry that other man; but in doing so she had made a solemn promise to herself that she would not marry John Eames. She had sworn it and would keep her oath. And yet she regretted it! In writing home to her mother the next day, she told Mrs Dale that all the world was speaking well of John Eames, – that John had won for himself a reputation of his own, and was known far and wide to be a noble fellow. She could not keep herself from praising John Eames, though she knew that such praise might, and would, be used against her at some future time. 'Though I cannot love him I will give him his due,' she said to herself.

'I wish you would make up your mind to have an "it" for yourself,' Emily Dunstable said to her again that night; 'a nice "it," so that I could make a friend, perhaps a brother, of him.'

'I shall never have an "it," if I live to be a hundred,' said Lily Dale.

CHAPTER 53

Rotten Row

Lily had heard nothing as to the difficulty about her horse, and could therefore enjoy her exercise without the drawback of feeling that her uncle was subjected to an annoyance. She was in the habit of going out every day with Bernard and Emily Dunstable, and their party was generally joined by others who would meet them at Mrs Thorne's house. For Mrs Thorne was a very hospitable woman, and there were many who liked well enough to go to her house. Late in the afernoon there would be a great congregation of horses before the door, – sometimes as many as a dozen; and then the cavalcade would go off into the Park, and there it would become scattered. As neither Bernard nor Miss Dunstable were unconscionable lovers, Lily in these scatterings did not often find herself neglected or lost. Her cousin would generally remain with her, and as in those days she had no 'it' of her own she was well pleased that he should do so.

But it so happened that on a certain afternoon she found herself riding in Rotten Row alone with a certain stout gentleman whom she constantly met at Mrs Thorne's house. His name was Onesiphorus Dunn, and he was usually called Siph by his intimate friends. It had seemed to Lily that everybody was an intimate friend of Mr Dunn's, and she was in daily fear lest she should make a mistake and call him Siph herself. Had she done so it would not have mattered in the least. Mr Dunn, had he observed it at all, would neither have been flattered nor angry. A great many young ladies about London did call him Siph, and to him it was quite natural that they should do so. He was an Irishman, living on the best of everything in the world, with apparently no fortune of his own, and certainly never earning anything. Everybody liked him, and it was admitted on all sides that there was no safer friend in the world, either for young ladies or young men, than Mr Onesiphorus Dunn. He did not borrow money, and he did not encroach. He did like being asked out to dinner, and he did think that they to whom he gave the light of his countenance in town owed him the return of a week's run in the country. He neither shot, not hunted nor fished, nor read, and yet he was never in the way in any house. He did play billiards, and whist, and croquet – very badly. He was a good judge of wine, and would occasionally condescend to look after the bottling of it on behalf of some very intimate friend. He was a great friend of Mrs Thorne's, with whom he always spent ten days in the autumn at Chaldicotes.

Bernard and Emily were not insatiable lovers, but, nevertheless, Mrs Thorne had thought it proper to provide a fourth in the riding-parties, and had put Mr Dunn upon this duty. 'Don't bother yourself about it, Siph,' she had said; 'only if those lovers should go off philandering out of sight, our little country lassie might find herself to be nowhere in the Park.' Siph had promised to make himself useful, and had done so. There had generally been so large a number in their party that the work imposed on Mr Dunn had been very light. Lily had never found out that he had been especially consigned to her as her own cavalier, but had seen quite enough of him to be aware that he was a pleasant companion. To her, thinking, as she ever was thinking, about Johnny Eames, Siph was much more agreeable than might have been a younger man who would have endeavoured to make her think about himself.

Thus when she found herself riding alone in Rotten Row with Siph Dunn, she was neither disconcerted nor displeased. He had been talking to her about Lord De Guest, whom he had known, – for Siph knew everybody, – and Lily had begun to wonder whether he knew John Eames. She would have liked to hear the opinion of such a man about John Eames. She was making up her mind that she would say something about the Crawley matter, – not intending of course to mention John Eames's name, – when suddenly her tongue was paralyzed and she could not speak. At that moment they were standing near a corner, where a turning path made an angle in the iron rails, Mr Dunn having proposed that they should wait there for a few minutes before they returned home, as it was probable that Bernard and Miss Dunstable might come up. They had been there for some five or ten minutes, and Lily had asked her first question about the Crawleys, – inquiring of Mr Dunn whether he had heard of a terrible accusation which had been made against a clergyman in Barsetshire, – when on a sudden her tongue was paralyzed. As they were standing, Lily's horse was turned towards the diverging path, whereas Mr Dunn was looking the other way, towards Achilles and Apsley house.* Mr Dunn was nearer to the railings, but though they were thus looking different ways they were so placed that each could see the face of the other. Then, on a sudden, coming slowly towards her along the diverging path and leaning on the arm of another man, she saw, – Adolphus Crosbie.

She had never seen him since a day on which she had parted from him with many kisses, – with warm, pressing, eager kisses, – of which she had been nowhat ashamed. He had then been to her almost as her husband. She had trusted hin entirely, and had thrown herself into his arms with a full reliance. There is often much of reticence on the part of a woman towards a man to whom she is engaged, something also of shamefacedness occasionally. There exists a shadow of doubt, at least of that hesitation which shows that in spite of vows the woman knows that a change may come, and that provision for such possible steps backward should always be within her reach. But Lily had cast all such caution to the winds. She had given herself to the man entirely, and had determined that she would sink or swim, stand or fall, live or die, by him and by his truth. He had been as false as hell. She had been in his arms, clinging to him, kissing him, swearing that her only pleasure in the world was to be with him, – with him her treasure, her promised husband; and within a momth, a week, he had been false to her. There had come upon her crushing tidings, and she had for days wondered at herself that they had not killed her. But she had lived, and had forgiven him. She had still loved him, and had received new offers from him, which had been answered as the reader knows. But she had never seen him since the day on which she had parted from him at Allington, without a doubt as to his faith. Now he was before her, walking on the footpath, almost within reach of her whip.

He did not recognize her, but as he passed on he did recognize Mr Onesiphorous Dunn, and stopped to speak to him. Or it might have been that Crosbie's friend Fowler Pratt stopped with this special object, – for Siph Dunn was an intimate friend of Fowler Pratt's. Crosbie and Siph were also acquainted, but in those days Crosbie did not care much for stopping his friends in the Park or elsewhere. He had become moody and discontented, and was generally seen going about the world alone. On this special occasion he was having a little special conversation about money with his very old friend Fowler Pratt.

'What, Siph, is this you? You're always on horseback now,' said Fowler Pratt.

'Well, yes; I have gone in a good deal for cavalry work this last month. I've been lucky enough to have a young lady to ride with me.' This he said in a whisper, which the distance of Lily justified. 'How d'ye do, Crosbie? One doesn't often see you on horseback, or on foot either.'

'I've something to do besides going to look or to be looked at,'* said Crosbie. Then he raised his eyes and saw Lily's side-face, and recognized her. Had he seen her before he had been stopped on his way I think he would have passed on, endeavouring to escape observation. But as it was, his feet had been arrested before he knew of her close vicinity, and now it would seem that he was afraid of her, and was flying from her, were he at once to walk off, leaving his friend behind him. And he knew that she had seen him, and had recognized him, and was now suffering from his presence. He could not but perceive that it was so from the fixedness of her face, and from the constrained manner in which she gazed before her. His friend Fowler Pratt had never seen Miss Dale, though he knew very much of her history. Siph Dunn knew nothing of the history of Crosbie and his love, and was unaware that he and Lily had ever seen each other. There was thus no help near her to extricate her from her difficulty.

'When a man has any work to do in the world,' said Siph, 'he always boasts of it to his acquaintance, and curses his luck to himself. I have nothing to do and can go about to see and to be seen; – and I must own that I like it.'

'Especially the being seen, – eh, Siph?' said Fowler Pratt. 'I also have nothing on earth to do, and I come here every day because it is as easy to do that as to go anywhere else.'

Crosbie was still looking at Lily. He could not help himself. He could not take his eyes from off her. He could see that she was as pretty as ever, that she was but very little altered. She was, in truth, somewhat stouter than in the old days, but of that he took no special notice. Should he speak to her? Should he try to catch her eye, and then raise his hat? Should he go up to her horse's head boldly, and ask her to let bygones be bygones? He had an idea that of all courses which he could pursue that was the one which she would approve the best, – which would be most efficacious for him, if with her anything from him might have any efficacy. But he could not do it. He did not know what words he might best use. Would it become him humbly to sue to her for pardon? Or should he strive to express his unaltered love by some tone of his voice? Or should he simply ask her after her health? He made one step towards her, and he saw that the face became more rigid and more fixed than before, and then he desisted. He told himself that he was simply hateful to her. He thought that he could perceive that there was no tenderness mixed with her unabated anger.

At this moment Bernard Dale and Emily came close upon him, and Bernard saw him at once. It was through Bernard that Lily and Crosbie had come to know each other. He and Bernard Dale had been fast friends in old times, and had, of course, been bitter enemies since the day of Crosbie's treachery. They had never spoken since, though they had often seen each other, and Dale was not at all disposed to speak to him now. The moment that he recognized Crosbie he looked across to his cousin. For an instant, an idea had flashed across him that he was there by her permission, – with her assent; but it required no second glance to show him that this was not the case. 'Dunn,' he said, 'I think we will ride on,' and he put his horse into a trot. Siph, whose ear was very accurate, and who knew at once that something was wrong, trotted on with him, and Lily, of course, was not left behind. 'Is there anything the matter?' said Emily to her lover.

'Nothing specially the matter,' he replied; 'but you were standing in company with the greatest blackguard that ever lived, and I thought we had better change our ground.'

'Bernard!' said Lily, flashing on him with all the fire which her eyes could command. Then she remembered that she could not reprimand him for the offence of such abuse in such a company; so she reined in her horse and fell a-weeping.

Siph Dunn, with his wicked cleverness, knew the whole story at once, remembering that he had once heard something of Crosbie having behaved very ill to some one before he married Lady Alexandrina De Courcy. He stopped his horse also, falling a little behind Lily, so that he might not be supposed to have seen her tears, and began to hum a tune. Emily also, though not wickedly clever, understood something of it. 'If Bernard says anything to make you angry, I will scold him,' she said. Then the two girls rode on together in front, while Bernard fell back with Siph Dunn.

'Pratt,' said Crosbie, putting his hand on his friend's shoulder as soon as the party had ridden out of hearing, 'do you see that girl there in the dark blue habit?'

'What, the one nearest to the path?'

'Yes; the one nearest to the path. That is Lily Dale.'

'Lily Dale!' said Fowler Pratt.

'Yes; that is Lily Dale.'

'Did you speak to her?' Pratt asked.

'No; she gave me no chance. She was there but a moment. But it was herself. It seems so odd to me that I should have been thus so near her again.' If there was any man to whom Crosbie could have spoken freely about Lily Dale it was this man, Fowler Pratt. Pratt was the oldest friend he had in the world, and it had happened that when he first woke to the misery that he had prepared for himself in throwing over Lily and betrothing himself to his late wife, Pratt had been the first person to whom he had communicated his sorrow. Not that he had ever been really open in his communications. It is not given to such men as Crosbie to speak openly of themselves to their friends. Nor, indeed, was Fowler Pratt one who was fond of listening to such tales. He had no such tales to tell of himself, and he thought that men and women should go through the world quietly, not subjecting themselves or their acquaintances to anxieties and emotions from peculiar conduct. But he was conscientious, and courageous also as well as prudent, and he had dared to tell Crosbie that he was behaving very badly. He had spoken his mind plainly, and had then given all the assistance in his power.

He paused a moment before he replied, weighing, like a prudent man, the force of the words he was about to utter. 'It is much better as it is,' he said. 'It is much better that you should be as strangers for the future.'

'I do not see that at all,' said Crosbie. They were both leaning on the rails, and so they remained for the next twenty minutes. 'I do not see that at all.'

'I feel sure of it. What could come of any renewed intercourse, – even if she would allow it ?'

'I might make her my wife.'

'And do you think that you would be happy with her, or she with you, after what has passed ?'

'I do think so.'

'I do not. It might be possible that she should bring herself to marry you. Women delight to forgive injuries. They like the excitement of generosity. But she could never forget that you had had a former wife, or the circumstances under which you were married. And as for yourself, you would regret it after the first month. How could you ever speak to her of your love without speaking also of your shame ? If a man does marry he should at least be able to hold up his head before his wife.'

This was very severe, but Crosbie showed no anger. 'I think I should do so,' he said, – 'after a while.'

'And then, about money ? Of course you would have to tell her everything.'

'Everything – of course.'

'It is like enough that she might not regard that, – except that she would feel that if you could not afford to marry her when you were unembarrassed, you can hardly aford to do so when you are over head and ears in debt.'

'She has money now.'

'After all that has come and gone you would hardly seek Lily Dale because you want to marry a fortune.'

'You are to hard on me, Pratt. You know that my only reason for seeking her is that I love her.'

'I do not mean to be hard. But I have a very strong opinion that the quarrels of lovers, when they are of so very serious a nature, are a bad basis for the renewal of love.* Come, let us go and dress for dinner. I am going to dine with Mrs Thorne, the millionaire, who married a country doctor, and who used to be called Miss Dunstable.'

'I never dine out anywhere now,' said Crosbie. And then they walked out of the Park together. Neither of them, of course, knew that Lily Dale was staying at the house at which Fowler Pratt was going to dine.

Lily, as she rode home, did not speak a word. She would have given worlds to be able to talk, but she could not even make a beginning. She heard Bernard and Siph Dunn chatting behind her, and hoped that they would continue to do so till she was safe within the house. They all used her well, for no one tried to draw her into conversation. Once Emily said to her, 'Shall we trot a little, Lily ?' And then they had moved on quickly, and the misery was soon over. As soon as she was upstairs in the house, she got Emily by herself, and explained all the mystery in a word or two. 'I fear I have made a fool of myself. That was the man to whom I was once engaged.' 'What, Mr Crosbie ?' said Emily, who had heard the whole story from Bernard. 'Yes, Mr Crosbie; pray, do not say a word of it to anybody, – not even to your aunt. I am better now, but I was such a fool. No, dear; I won't go into the drawing-room. I'll go upstairs, and come down ready for dinner.'

When she was alone she sat down in her habit, and declared to herself that she certainly would never become the wife of Mr Crosbie. I do not know why she should make such a declaration. She had promised her mother and John Eames that she would not do so, and that promise would certainly have bound her without any further resolutions on her own part. But, to tell the truth, the vision of the man had disenchanted her. When last she had seen him he had been as it were a god to her; and though, since that day, his conduct to her had been as ungodlike as it well might be, still the memory of the outward signs of his divinity had remained with her. It is difficult to explain how it had come to pass that the glimpse which she had had of him should have altered so much within her mind; – why she should so suddenly have come to regard him in an altered light. It was not simply that he looked to be older, and because his face was careworn. It was not only that he had lost that look of an Apollo which Lily had once in her mirth attributed to him. I think it was chiefly that she herself was older, and could no longer see a god in such a man. She had never regarded John Eames as being gifted with divinity, and had therefore always been making comparisons to his discredit. Any such comparison now would tend quite the other way. Nevertheless she would adhere to the two letters in her book. Since she had seen Mr Crosbie she was altogether out of love with the prospect of matrimony.

She was in the room when Mr Pratt was announced, and she at once recognized him as the man who had been with Crosbie. And when, some minutes afterwards, Siph Dunn came into the room, she could see that in their greeting allusion was made to the scene in the Park. But still it was probable that this man would not recognize her, and, if he did so, what would it matter? There were twenty people to sit down to dinner, and the chances were that she would not be called upon to exchange a word with Mr Pratt. She had now recovered herself, and could speak freely to her friend Siph, and when Siph came and stood near her she thanked him graciously for his escort in the Park. 'If it wasn't for you, Mr Dunn, I really think I should not get any riding at all. Bernard and Miss Dunstable have only one thing to think about, and certainly I am not that one thing.' She thought it probable that if she could keep Siph close to her, Mrs Thorne, who always managed those things herself, might apportion her out to be led to dinner by her good-natured friend. But the fates were averse. The time had now come, and Lily was waiting her turn. 'Mr Fowler Pratt, let me introduce you to Miss Lily Dale,' said Mrs Thorne. Lily could perceive that Mr Pratt was startled. The sign he gave was the least possible sign in the world; but still it sufficed for Lily to perceive it. She put her hand upon his arm, and walked down with him to the dining-room without giving him the slightest cause to suppose that she knew who he was.

'I think I saw you in the Park riding?' he said.

'Yes, I was there; we go nearly every day.'

'I never ride; I was walking.'

'It seems to me that the people don't go there to walk, but to stand still,' said Lily. 'I cannot understand how so many people can bear to loiter about in that way – leaning on the rails and doing nothing.'

'It is about as good as the riding, and costs less money. That is all that can be said for it. Do you live chiefly in town?'

'O dear, no; I live altogether in the country. I'm only up here because a cousin is going to be married.'

'Captain Dale you mean – to Miss Dunstable?' said Fowler Pratt.

'When they have been joined together in holy matrimony, I shall go down to the country, and never, I suppose, come up to London again.'

'You do not like London?'

'Not as a residence, I think,' said Lily. 'But of course one's likings and dislikings on such a matter depend on circumstances. I live with my mother, and all my relatives live near us. Of course I like the country best, because they are there.'

'Young ladies so often have a different way of looking at this subject. I shouldn't wonder if Miss Dunstable's views about it were altogether of another sort. Young ladies generally expect to be taken away from their fathers and mothers, and uncles and aunts.'

'But you see I expect to be left with mine,' said Lily. After that she turned as much away from Mr Fowler Pratt as she could, having taken an aversion to him. What business had he to talk to her about being taken away from her uncles and aunts? She had seen him with Mr Crosbie, and it might be possible that they were intimate friends. It might be that Mr Pratt was asking questions in Mr Crosbie's interest. Let that be as it might, she would answer no more questions from him further than ordinary good breeding should require of her.

'She is a nice girl, certainly,' said Fowler Pratt to himself, as he walked home, 'and I have no doubt would make a good, ordinary, everyday wife. But she is not such a paragon that a man should condescend to grovel in the dirt for her.'

That night Lily told Emily Dunstable the whole of Mr Crosbie's history as far as she knew it, and also explained her new aversion to Mr Fowler Pratt. 'They are very great friends,' said Emily. 'Bernard has told me so; and you may be sure that Mr Pratt knew the whole history before he came here. I am so sorry that my aunt asked him.'

'It does not signify in the least,' said Lily. 'Even if I were to meet Mr Crosbie I don't think I should make such a fool of myself again. As it is, I can only hope he did not see it.'

'I am sure he did not.'

Then there was a pause, during which Lily sat with her face resting on both her hands. 'It is wonderful how much he is altered,' she said at last.

'Think how much he has suffered.'

'I suppose I am altered as much, only I do not see it in myself.'

'I don't know what you were, but I don't think you can have changed much. You no doubt have suffered too, but not as he has done.'

'Oh, as for that, I have done very well. I think I'll go to bed now. The riding makes me so sleepy.'

CHAPTER 54

The clerical commission

It was at last arranged that the five clergymen selected should meet at Dr Tempest's house in Silverbridge to make inquiry and report to the bishop whether the circumstances connected with the cheque for twenty pounds were of such a nature as to make it incumbent on him to institute proceedings against Mr Crawley in the Court of Arches. Dr Tempest had acted upon the letter which he had received from the bishop, exactly as though there had been no meeting at the palace, no quarrel to the death between him and Mrs Proudie. He was a prudent man, gifted with the great power of holding his tongue, and had not spoken a word, even to his wife, of what had occurred. After such a victory our old friend the archdeacon would have blown his own trumpet loudly among his friends. Plumstead would have heard of it instantly, and the pæan would have been sung out in the neighbouring parishes of Eiderdown, Stogpingum, and St Ewolds. The high-street of Barchester would have known of it, and the very bedesmen in Hiram's Hospital would have told among themselves the terrible discomfiture of the bishop and his lady. But Dr Tempest spoke no word of it to anybody. He wrote letters to the two clergymen named by the bishop, and himself selected two others out of his own rural deanery, and suggested to them all a day at which a preliminary meeting should be held at his own house. The two who were invited by him were Mr Oriel, the rector of Greshamsbury, and Mr Robarts, the vicar of Framley. They all assented to the proposition, and on the day named assembled themselves at Silverbridge.

It was now April, and the judges were to come into Barchester before the end of the month. What then could be the use of this ecclesiastical inquiry exactly at the same time? Men and women declared that it was a double prosecution, and that a double prosecution for the same offence was a course of action opposed to the feelings and traditions of the country. Miss Anne Prettyman went so far as to say that it was unconstitutional, and Mary Walker declared that no human being except Mrs Proudie would ever have been guilty of such cruelty. 'Don't tell me about the bishop, John,' she said; 'the bishop is a cypher.' You may be sure Dr Tempest would not have a hand in it if it were not right,' said John Walker. 'My dear Mr John,' said Miss Anne Prettyman, 'Dr Tempest is as hard as a bar of iron, and always was. But I am surprised that Mr Robarts should take a part in it.'

In the meantime, at the palace, Mrs Proudie had been reduced to learn what was going on from Mr Thumble. The bishop had never spoken a word to her respecting Mr Crawley since that terrible day on which Dr Tempest had witnessed his imbecility, – having absolutely declined to answer when his wife had mentioned the subject. 'You won't speak to me about it, my dear?' she had said to him, when he had thus declined, remonstrating more in sorrow than in anger. 'No; I won't,' the bishop had replied; 'there has been a great deal too much talking about it. It has broken my heart already, I know.' These were very bad days in the palace. Mrs Proudie affected to be satisfied with what was being done. She talked to Mr Thumble about Mr Crawley and the cheque, as though everything were arranged quite to her satisfaction, – as though everthing, indeed, had been arranged by herself. But everybody about the house could see that the manner of the woman was altogether altered. She was milder than usual with the servants and was almost too gentle in her usage of her husband. It seemed as though something had happened to frighten her and break her spirit, and it was whispered about through the palace that she was afraid that the bishop was dying. As for him, he hardly left his own sitting-room in these days, except when he joined the family at breakfast and at dinner. And in his study he did little or nothing. He would smile when his chaplain went to him, and give some trifling verbal directions; but for days he scarcely ever took a pen in his hands, and though he took up many books he read hardly a page. How often he told his wife in those days that he was broken-hearted, no one but his wife ever knew.

'What has happened that you should speak like that?' she said to him once. 'What has broken your heart?'

'You,' he replied. 'You; you have done it.'

'Oh, Tom,' she said, going back into the memory of very far distant days in her nomenclature, 'how can you speak to me so cruelly as that! That it should come to that between you and me, after all!'

'Why did you not go away and leave me that day when I told you?'

'Did you ever know a woman who liked to be turned out of a room in her own house?' said Mrs Proudie. When Mrs Proudie had condescended so far as this, it must be admitted that in those days there was great trouble in the palace.

Mr Thumble, on the day before he went to Silverbridge, asked for an audience with the bishop in order that he might receive instructions. He had been strictly desired to do this by Mrs Proudie, and had not dared to disobey her injunctions, – thinking, however, himself, that his doing so was inexpedient. 'I have got nothing to say to you about it; not a word,' said the bishop crossly. 'I thought that perhaps you might like to see me before I started,' pleaded Mr Thumble very humbly. 'I don't want to see you at all,' said the bishop; 'you are going there to exercise your own judgment, – if you have got any; and you ought not to come to me. After that Mr Thumble began to think that Mrs Proudie was right, and that the bishop was near his dissolution.

Mr Thumble and Mr Quiverful went over to Silverbridge together in a gig, hired from the Dragon of Wantly – as to the cost of which there arose among them a not unnatural apprehension which amounted at last almost to dismay. 'I don't mind it so much for once,' said Mr Quiverful, 'but if many such meetings are necessary, I for one can't afford it, and I won't do it. A man with my family can't allow himself to be money out of pocket in that way.' 'It is hard,' said Mr Thumble. 'She ought to pay it herself, out of her own pocket,' said Mr Quiverful. He had had concerns with the palace when Mrs Proudie was in the full swing of her dominion, and had not as yet begun to suspect that there might possibly be a change.

Mr Oriel and Mr Robarts were already sitting with Dr Tempest when the other two clergymen were shown into the room. When the first greetings were over luncheon was announced, and while they were eating not a word was said about Mr Crawley. The ladies of the family were not present, and the five clergymen sat round the table alone. It would have been difficult to have got together five gentlemen less likely to act with one mind and one spirit; – and perhaps it was all the better for Mr Crawley that it should be so. Dr Tempest himself was a man peculiarly capable of exercising the functions of a judge in such a matter, had he sat alone as a judge; but he was one who would be almost sure to differ from others who sat as equal assessors with him. Mr Oriel was a gentleman at all points; but he was very shy, very reticent, and altogether uninstructed in the ordinary daily intercourse of man with man. Any one knowing him might have predicted of him that he would be sure on such an occasion as this to be found floundering in a sea of doubts. Mr Quiverful was the father of a large family, whose whole life had been devoted to fighting a cruel world on behalf of his wife and children. That fight he had fought bravely; but it had left him no energy for any other business. Mr Thumble was a poor creature, – so poor a creature that, in spite of a small restless ambition to be doing something, he was almost cowed by the hard lines of Dr Tempest's brow. The Rev. Mark Robarts was a man of the world, and a clever fellow, and did not stand in awe of anybody, – unless it might be, in a very moderate degree, of his patrons the Luftons, whom he was bound to respect; but his cleverness was not the cleverness needed by a judge. He was essentially a partisan, and would be sure to vote against the bishop in such a matter as this now before him. There was a palace faction in the diocese, and an anti-palace faction. Mr Thumble and Mr Quiverful belonged to one, and Mr Oriel and Mr Robarts to the other. Mr Thumble was too weak to stick to his faction against the strength of such a man as Dr Tempest. Mr Quiverful would be too indifferent to do so, – unless his interest were concerned. Mr Oriel would be too conscientious to regard his own side on such an occasion as this. But Mark Robarts would be sure to support his friends and oppose his enemies, let the case be what it might. 'Now, gentlemen, if you please, we will go into the other room,' said Dr Tempest. They went into the other room, and there they found five chairs arranged for them round the table. Not a word had as yet been said about Mr Crawley, and no one of the four strangers knew whether Mr Crawley was to appear before them on that day or not.

'Gentlemen,' said Dr Temptest, seating himself at once in an armchair placed at the middle of the table, 'I think it will be well to explain to you at first what, as I regard the matter, is the extent of the work which we are called upon to perform. It is of its nature very disagreeable. It cannot but be so, let it be ever so limited. Here is a brother clergyman and a gentleman, living among us, and doing his duty, as we are told, in a most exemplary manner; and suddenly we hear that he is accused of a theft. The matter is brought before the magistrates, of whom I myself was one, and he was committed for trial. There is therefore primâ facie evidence of his guilt. But I do not think that we need go into the question of his guilt at all.' When he said this, the other four all looked up at him in astonishment. 'I thought that we had been summoned here for that purpose,' said Mr Robarts. 'Not at all, as I take it,' said the doctor. 'Were we to commence any such inquiry, the jury would have given their verdict before we could come to any conclusion; and it would be impossible for us to oppose that verdict, whether it declares this unfortunate gentleman to be innocent or to be guilty. If the jury shall say that he is innocent, there is an end of the matter altogether. He would go back to his parish amidst the sympathy and congratulations of his friends. That is what we should all wish.'

'Of course it is,' said Mr Robarts. They all declared that was their desire, as a matter of course; and Mr Thumble said it louder than any one else.

'But if he be found guilty, then will come that difficulty to the bishop, in which we are bound to give him any assistance within our power.'

'Of course we are,' said Mr Thumble, who, having heard his own voice once, and having liked the sound, thought that he might creep into a little importance by using it on any occasion that opened itself for him.

'If you will allow me, sir, I will venture to state my views as shortly as I can,' said Dr Tempest. 'That may perhaps be the most expeditious course for us all in the end.'

'Oh, certainly,' said Mr Thumble. 'I didn't mean to interrupt.'

'In the case of his being found guilty,' continued the doctor, 'there will arise the question whether the punishment awarded to him by the judge should suffice for ecclesiastical purposes. Suppose, for instance, that he should be imprisoned for two months, should he be allowed to return to his living at the expiration of that term?'

'I think he ought,' said Mr Robarts; – 'considering all things.'

'I don't see why he shouldn't,' said Mr Quiverful.

Mr Oriel sat listening patiently, and Mr Thumble looked up to the doctor, expecting to hear some opinion expressed by him with which he might coincide.

'There certainly are reasons why he should not,' said Dr Tempest; 'though I by no means say that those reasons are conclusive in the present case. In the first place, a man who has stolen money can hardly be a fitting person to teach others not to steal.'

'You must look to the circumstances,' said Robarts.

'Yes, that is true; but just bear with me a moment. It cannot, at any rate, be thought that a clergyman should come out of prison and go to his living without any notice from his bishop, simply because he has already been punished under the common law. If this were so, a clergyman might be fined ten days running for being drunk in the street, – five shillings each time, – and at the end of that time might set his bishop at defiance. When a clergyman has shown himself to be utterly unfit for clerical duties, he must not be held to be protected from ecclesiastical censure or from deprivation by the action of the common law.'

'But Mr Crawley has not shown himself to be unfit,' said Robarts.

'That is begging the question, Robarts,' said the doctor.

'Just so,' said Mr Thumble. Then Mr Robarts gave a look at Mr Thumble, and Mr Thumble retired into his shoes.

'That is the question as to which we are called upon to advise the bishop,' continued Dr Tempest. 'And I must say that I think the bishop is right. If he were to allow the matter to pass by without notice, – that is to say, in the event of Mr Crawley being pronounced to be guilty by a jury, – he would, I think, neglect his duty. Now, I have been informed that the bishop has recommended Mr Crawley to desist from his duties till the trial be over, and that Mr Crawley has declined to take the bishop's advice.

'That is true,' said Mr Thumble. 'He altogether disregarded the bishop.'

'I cannot say that I think he was wrong,' said Dr Tempest.

'I think he was quite right,' said Mr Robarts.

'A bishop in almost all cases is entitled to the obedience of his clergy,' said Mr Oriel.

'I must say that I agree with you, sir,' said Mr Thumble.

'The income is not large, and I suppose that it would have gone with the duties,' said Mr Quiverful. 'It is very hard for a man with a family to live when his income has been stopped.'

'Be that as it may,' continued the doctor, 'the bishop feels that it may be his duty to oppose the return of Mr Crawley to his pulpit, and that he can oppose it in no other way than by proceeding against Mr Crawley under the Clerical Offences Act. I propose, therefore, that we should invite Mr Crawley to attend here—'

'Mr Crawley is not coming here to-day, then ?' said Mr Robarts.

'I thought it useless to ask for his attendance until we had settled on our course of action,' said Dr Tempest. 'If we are all agreed, I will beg him to come here on this day week, when we will meet again. And we will then ask him whether he will submit himself to the bishop's decision, in the event of the jury finding him guilty. If he should decline to do so, we can only then form our opinion as to what will be the bishop's duty by reference to the facts as they are elicited at the trial. If Mr Crawley should choose to make to us any statement as to his own case, of course we shall be willing to receive it. That is my idea of what had better be done; and now, if any gentleman has any other proposition to make, of course we shall be pleased to hear him.' Dr Tempest, as he said this, looked round upon his companions, as though his pleasure, under the circumstances suggested by himself, would be very doubtful.

'I don't suppose we can do anything better,' said Mr Robarts. 'I think it a pity, however, that any steps should have been taken by the bishop before the trial.'

'The bishop has been placed in a very delicate position,' said Mr Thumble, pleading for his patron.

'I don't know the meaning of the word "delicate,"' said Robarts. 'I think his duty was very clear, to avoid interference whilst the matter is, so to say, before the judge.'

'Nobody has anything else to propose?' said Dr Tempest. 'Then I will write to Mr Crawley, and you, gentlemen, will perhaps do me the honour of meeting me here at one o'clock on this day week.' Then the meeting was over, and the four clergymen having shaken hands with Dr Tempest in the hall, all promised that they would return on that day week. So far, Dr Tempest had carried his point exactly as he might have done had the four gentlemen been represented by the chairs on which they had sat.

'I shan't come again, all the same, unless I know where I'm to get my expenses,' said Mr Quiverful, as he got into the gig.

'I shall come,' said Mr Thumble, 'because I think it a duty. Of course it is a hardship.' Mr Thumble liked the idea of being joined with such men as Dr Tempest, and Mr Oriel, and Mr Robarts, and would any day have paid the expense of a gig from Barchester to Silverbridge out of his own pocket, for the sake of sitting with such benchfellows on any clerical inquiry.

'One's first duty is to one's own wife and family,' said Mr Quiverful.

'Well, yes; in a way, of course, that is quite true, Mr Quiverful; and when we know how very inadequate are the incomes of the working clergy, we cannot but feel ourselves to be, if I may so say, put upon, when we have to defray the expenses incidental to special duties out of our own pockets. I think, you know, – I don't mind saying this to you, – that the palace should have provided us with a chaise and pair.' This was ungrateful on the part of Mr Thumble, who had been permitted to ride miles upon miles to various outlying clerical duties upon the bishop's worn-out cob. 'You see,' continued Mr Thumble, 'you and I go specially to represent the palace, and the palace ought to remember that. I think there ought to have been a chaise and pair; I do indeed.'

'I don't care much what the conveyance is,' said Mr Quiverful; 'but I certainly shall pay nothing more out of my own pocket; – certainly I shall not.'

'The result will be that the palace will be thrown over if they don't take care,' said Mr Thumble. 'Tempest, however, seems to be pretty steady. Tempest, I think, is steady. You see he is getting tired of parish work, and would like to go into the close. That's what he is looking out for. Did you ever see such a fellow as that Robarts, – just look at him; – quite indecent, wasn't he? He thinks he can have his own way in everything, just because his sister married a lord. I do hate to see all that meanness.'

Mark Robarts and Caleb Oriel left Silverbridge in another gig by the same road, and soon passed their brethren, as Mr Robarts was in the habit of driving a large, quick-stepping horse. The last remarks were being made as the dust from the vicar of Framley's wheels saluted the faces of the two slower clergymen. Mr Oriel had promised to dine and sleep at Framley, and therefore returned in Mr Robarts' gig.

'Quite unnecessary, all this fuss; don't you think so?' said Mr Robarts.

'I am not quite sure,' said Mr Oriel. 'I can understand that the bishop may have found a difficulty.'

'The bishop, indeed! The bishop doesn't care two straws about it. It's Mrs Proudie! She has put her finger on the poor man's neck because he has not put his neck beneath her feet; and now she thinks she can crush him, – as she would crush you or me, if it were in her power. That's about the long and the short of the bishop's solicitude.'

'You are very hard on him,' said Mr Oriel.

'I know him; – and am not at all hard on him. She is hard upon him if you like. Tempest is fair. He is very fair, and as long as no one meddles with him he won't do amiss. I can't hold my tongue always, but I often know that it is better that I should.'

Dr Tempest said not a word to any one on the subject, not even in his own defence. And yet he was sorely tempted. On the very day of the meeting he dined at Mr Walker's in Silverbridge, and there submitted to be talked at by all the ladies and most of the gentlemen present, without saying a word in his own defence. And yet a word or two would have been so easy and so conclusive.

'Oh, Dr Tempest,' said Mary Walker, 'I am so sorry that you have joined the bishop.'

'Are you, my dear?' said he. 'It is generally thought well that a parish clergyman should agree with his bishop.'

'But you know, Dr Tempest, that you don't agree with your bishop generally.'

'Then it is the more fortunate that I shall be able to agree with him on this occasion.'

Major Grantly was present at the dinner, and ventured to ask the doctor in the course of the evening what he thought would be done. 'I should not venture to ask such a question, Dr Tempest,' he said, 'unless I had the strongest possible reason to justify my anxiety.'

'I don't know that I can tell you anything, Major Grantly,' said the doctor. 'We did not even see Mr Crawley to-day. But the real truth is that he must stand or fall as the jury shall find him guilty or not guilty. It would be the same in any profession. Could a captain in the army hold up his head in his regiment after he had been tried and found guilty of stealing twenty pounds?'

'I don't think he could,' said the major.

'Neither can a clergyman,' said the doctor. 'The bishop can neither make him nor mar him. It is the jury that must do it.'

CHAPTER 55

Framley Parsonage

At this time Grace Crawley was at Framley Parsonage. Old Lady Lufton's strategy had been quite intelligible, but some people said that in point of etiquette and judgment and moral conduct, it was indefensible. Her vicar, Mr Robarts, had been selected to be one of the clergymen who was to sit in ecclesiastical judgment upon Mr Crawley, and while he was so sitting Mr Crawley's daughter was staying in Mr Robarts' house as a visitor with his wife! It might be that there was no harm in this. Lady Lufton, when the apparent impropriety was pointed out to her by no less a person than Archdeacon Grantly, ridiculed the idea. 'My dear archdeacon,' Lady Lufton had said, 'we all know the bishop to be such a fool and the bishop's wife to be such a knave, that we cannot allow ourselves to be governed in this matter by ordinary rules. Do you not think that it is expedient to show how utterly we disregard his judgment and her malice?' The archdeacon had hesitated much before he spoke to Lady Lufton, whether he should address himself to her or to Mr Robarts, – or indeed to Mrs Robarts. But he had become aware that the proposition as to the visit had originated with Lady Lufton, and he had therefore decided on speaking to her. He had not condescended to say a word as to his son, nor would he so condescend. Nor could he go from Lady Lufton to Mr Robarts, having once failed with her ladyship. Indeed, in giving him his due, we must acknowledge that his disapprobation of Lady Lufton's strategy arose rather from his true conviction as to its impropriety, than from any fear lest this attention paid to Miss Crawley should tend to bring about her marriage with his son. By this time he hated the very name of Crawley. He hated it the more because in hating it he had to put himself for the time on the same side with Mrs Proudie. But for all that he would not condescend to any unworthy mode of fighting. He thought it wrong that the young lady should be invited to Framley Parsonage at this moment, and he said so to the person who had, as he thought, in truth, given the invitation; but he would not allow his own personal motives to induce him to carry on the argument with Lady Lufton. 'The bishop is a fool,' he said, 'and the bishop's wife is a knave. Nevertheless I would not have had the young lady over to Framley at this moment. If, however, you think it right and Robarts thinks it right, there is an end of it.'

'Upon my word we do,' said Lady Lufton.

I am induced to think that Mr Robarts was not quite confident of the expediency of what he was doing by the way in which he mentioned to Mr Oriel the fact of Miss Crawley's presence at the parsonage as he drove that gentleman home in his gig. They had been talking about Mr Crawley when he suddenly turned himself round, so that he could look at his companion, and said, 'Miss Crawley is staying with us at the parsonage at the present moment.'

'What! Mr Crawley's daughter?' said Mr Oriel, showing plainly by his voice that the tidings had much surprised him.

'Yes; Mr Crawley's daughter.'

'Oh, indeed. I did not know that you were on those terms with the family.'

'We have known them for the last seven or eight years,' said Mark; 'and though I should be giving you a false notion if I were to say that I myself have known them intimately, – for Crawley is a man whom it is quite impossible to know intimately, – yet the womankind at Framley have known them. My sister stayed with them over at Hogglestock for some time.'

'What; Lady Lufton?'

'Yes; my sister Lucy. It was just before her marriage. There was a lot of trouble, and the Crawleys were all ill, and she went to nurse them. And then the old lady took them up, and altogether there came to be a sort of feeling that they were to be regarded as friends. They are always in trouble, and now in this special trouble the women between them have thought it best to have the girl over at Framley. Of course I had a kind of feeling about this commission; but as I knew that it would make no difference with me I did not think it necessary to put my veto upon the visit.' Mr Oriel said nothing further, but Mark Robarts was aware that Mr Oriel did not quite approve of the visit.

That morning old Lady Lufton herself had come across to the parsonage with the express view of bidding all the parsonage party to come across to the hall to dine. 'You can tell Mr Oriel, Fanny, with Lucy's compliments, how delighted she will be to see him.' Old Lady Lufton always spoke of her daughter-in-law as the mistress of the house. 'If you think he is particular, you know, we will send a note across.' Mrs Robarts said that she supposed Mr Oriel would not be particular, but, looking at Grace, made some faint excuse. 'You must come, my dear,' said Lady Lufton. 'Lucy wishes it particularly.' Mrs Robarts did not know how to say that she would not come; and so the matter stood, – when Mrs Robarts was called upon to leave the room for a moment, and Lady Lufton and Grace were left alone.

'Dear Lady Lufton,' said Grace, getting up suddenly from her chair; 'will you do me a favour, – a great favour?' She spoke with an energy which quite surprised the old lady, and caused her almost to start from her seat.

'I don't like making promises,' said Lady Lufton; 'but anything I can do with propriety I will.'

'You can do this. Pray let me stay here to-day. You don't understand how I feel about going out while papa is in this way. I know how kind and how good you all are; and when dear Mrs Robarts asked me here, and mamma said that I had better come, I could not refuse. But indeed, indeed, I had rather not go out to a dinner-party.'

'It is not a party, my dear girl,' said Lady Lufton, with the kindest voice which she knew how to assume. 'And you must remember that my daughter-in-law regards you as so very old a friend! You remember, of course, when she was staying over at Hogglestock?'

'Indeed I do. I remember it well.'

'And therefore you should not regard it as going out. There will be nobody there but ourselves and the people from this house.'

'But it will be going out, Lady Lufton; and I do hope you will let me stay here. You cannot think how I feel it. Of course I cannot go without something like dressing, and – and – and— In poor papa's state I feel that I ought not to do anything that looks like gaiety. I ought never to forget it; – not for a moment.'

There was a tear in Lady Lufton's eye as she said, – 'My dear, you shan't come. You and Fanny shall stop and dine here by yourselves. The gentlemen shall come.'

'Do let Mrs Robarts go, please,' said Grace.

'I won't do anything of the kind,' said Lady Lufton. Then, when Mrs Robarts returned to the room, her ladyship explained it all in two words. 'Whilst you have been away, my dear, Grace has begged off, and therefore we have decided that Mr Oriel and Mr Robarts shall come without you.'

'I am sorry, Mrs Robarts,' said Grace.

'Pooh, pooh,' said Lady Lufton. 'Fanny and I have known each other quite long enough not to stand on any compliments, – haven't we, my dear? I must get home now, as all the morning has gone by.

Fanny my dear, I want to speak to you.' Then she expressed her opinion of Grace Crawley as she walked across the parsonage garden with Mrs Robarts. 'She is a very nice girl, and a very good girl, I am sure; and she shows excellent feeling. Whatever happens we must take care of her. And, Fanny, have you observed how handsome she is?'

'We think her very pretty.'

'She is more than pretty when she has a little fire in her eyes. She is downright handsome, – or will be when she fills out a little. I tell you what, my dear; she'll make havoc with somebody yet; you see if she doesn't. By – by. Tell the two gentlemen to be up by seven punctually.' And then Lady Lufton went home.

Grace so contrived that Mr Oriel came and went without seeing her. There was a separate nursery breakfast at the parsonage, and by special permission Grace was allowed to have her tea and bread-and-butter on the next morning with the children. 'I thought you told me Miss Crawley was here,' said Mr Oriel, as the two clergymen stood waiting for the gig that was to take the visitor away to Barchester.

'So she is,' said Robarts; 'but she likes to hide herself, because of her father's trouble. You can't blame her.'

'No, indeed,' said Mr Oriel.

'Poor girl. If you knew her you would not only pity her, but like her.'

'Is she, – what you call— ?'

'You mean, is she a lady?'

'Of course she is by birth, and all that,' said Mr Oriel, apologizing for his inquiry.

'I don't think there is another girl in the county so well educated,' said Mr Robarts.

'Indeed! I had no idea of that.'

'And we think her a great beauty. As for manners, I never saw a girl with a prettier way of her own.'

'Dear me,' said Mr Oriel. 'I wish she had come down to breakfast.'

It will have been perceived that old Lady Lufton had heard nothing of Major Grantly's offence; that she had no knowledge that Grace had already made havoc, as she had called it, – had, in truth, made very sad havoc, at Plumstead. She did not, therefore, think much about it when her son told her upon her return home from the parsonage on that afternoon that Major Grantly had come over from Cosby Lodge, and that he was going to dine and sleep at Framley Court. Some slight idea of thankfulness came across her mind that she had not betrayed Grace Crawley into a meeting with a stranger. 'I asked him to come some day before we went up to town,' said his lordship; 'and I am glad he has come to-day, as two clergymen to one's self are, at any rate, one too many.' So Major Grantly dined and slept at the Court.

But Mrs Robarts was in a great flurry when she was told of this by her husband on his return from the dinner. Mrs Crawley had found an opportunity of telling the story of Major Grantly's love to Mrs Robarts before she had sent her daughter to Framley, knowing that the families were intimate, and thinking it right that there should be some precaution.

'I wonder whether he will come up here,' Mrs Robarts had said.

'Probably not,' said the vicar. 'He said he was going home early.'

'I hope he will not come — for Grace's sake,' said Mrs Robarts. She hesitated whether she should tell her husband. She always did tell him everything. But on this occasion she thought she had no right to do so, and she kept the secret. 'Don't do anything to bring him up, dear.'

'You needn't be afraid. He won't come,' said the vicar. On the following morning, as soon as Mr Oriel was gone, Mr Robarts went out, — about his parish he would probably have called it; but in half an hour he might have been seen strolling about the Court stable-yard with Lord Lufton. 'Where is Grantly?' asked the vicar. 'I don't know where he is,' said his lordship. 'He has sloped off somewhere.' The major had sloped off to the parsonage, well knowing in what nest his dove was lying hid; and he and the vicar had passed each other. The major had gone out at the front gate, and the vicar had gone in at the stable entrance.

The two clergymen had hardly taken their departure when Major Grantly knocked at the parsonage door. He had come so early that Mrs Robarts had taken no precautions, — even had there been any precautions which she would have thought it right to take. Grace was in the act of coming down the stairs, not having heard the knock at the door, and thus she found her lover in the hall. He had asked, of course, for Mrs Robarts, and thus they two entered the drawing-room together. They had not had time to speak when the servant opened the drawing-room door to announce the visitor. There had been no word spoken between Mrs Robarts and Grace about Major Grantly, but the mother had told the daughter of what she had said to Mrs Robarts.

'Grace,' said the major,' 'I am so glad to find you!' Then he turned to Mrs Robarts with his open hand. 'You won't take it uncivil of me if I say that my visit is not entirely to yourself? I think I may take upon myself to say that I and Miss Crawley are old friends. May I not?'

Grace could not answer a word. 'Mrs Crawley told me that you had known her at Silverbridge,' said Mrs Roberts, driven to say something, but feeling that she was blundering.

'I came over to Framley yesterday because I heard that she was here. Am I wrong to come up here to see her?'

'I think she must answer that for herself, Major Grantly.'

'Am I wrong, Grace?' Grace thought that he was the finest gentleman and the noblest lover that had ever shown his devotion to a woman, and was stirred by a mighty resolve that if it ever should be in her power to reward him after any fashion, she would pour out the reward with a very full hand indeed. But what was she to say on the present moment? 'Am I wrong, Grace?' he said, repeating his question with so much emphasis, that she was positively driven to answer it.

'I do not think you are wrong at all. How can I say you are wrong when you are so good? If I could be your servant I would serve you. But I can be nothing to you, because of papa's disgrace. Dear Mrs Roberts, I cannot stay. You must answer him for me.' And having thus made her speech she escaped from the room.

It may suffice to say further now that the major did not see Grace again during that visit at Framley.

CHAPTER 56

The archdeacon goes to Framley

By some of those unseen telegraphic wires which carry news about the country and make no charge for the conveyance, Archdeacon Grantly heard that his son the major was at Framley. Now in that itself there would have been nothing singular. There had been for years much intimacy between the Lufton family and the Grantly family, – so much that an alliance between the two houses had once been planned, the elders having considered it expedient that the young lord should marry that Griselda who had since mounted higher in the world even than the elders had then projected for her. There had come no such alliance; but the intimacy had not ceased, and there was nothing in itself surprising in the fact that Major Grantly should be staying at Framley Court. But the archdeacon, when he heard the news, bethought him at once of Grace Crawley. Could it be possible that his old friend Lady Lufton, – Lady Lufton whom he had known and trusted all his life, whom he had ever regarded as a pillar of the church in Barsetshire, – should now be untrue to him in a matter so closely affecting his interests? Men when they are worried by fears and teased by adverse circumstances become suspicious of those on whom suspicion should never rest. It was hardly possible, the archdeacon thought, that Lady Lufton should treat him so unworthily, – but the circumstances were strong against his friend. Lady Lufton had induced Miss Crawley to go Framley, much against his advice, at a time when such a visit seemed to him to be very improper; and it now appeared that his son was to be there at the same time, – a fact of which Lady Lufton had made no mention to him whatever. Why had not Lady Lufton told him that Henry Grantly was coming to Framley Court? The reader, whose interest in the matter will be less keen than was the archdeacon's, will know very well why Lady Lufton had said nothing about the major's visit. The reader will remember that Lady Lufton, when she saw the archdeacon, was as ignorant as to the intended visit as was the archdeacon himself. But the archdeacon was uneasy, troubled, and suspicious; – and he suspected his old friend unworthily.

He spoke to his wife about it within a very few hours of the arrival of the tidings by those invisible wires. He had already told her that Miss Crawley was to go to Framley parsonage, and that he thought that Mrs Robarts was wrong to receive her at such a time. 'It is only intended for good-nature,' Mrs Grantly had said. 'It is misplaced good-nature at the present moment,' the archdeacon had replied. Mrs Grantly had not thought it worth her while to undertake at the moment any strong defence of the Framley people. She knew well how odious was the name of Crawley in her husband's ears, and she felt that the less that was said at present about the Crawleys the better for the peace of the rectory at Plumstead. She had therefore allowed the expression of his disapproval to pass unchallenged. But now he came upon her with a more bitter grievance, and she was obliged to argue the matter with him.

'What do you think?' said he; 'Henry is at Framley.'

'He can hardly be staying there,' said Mrs Grantly, 'because I know that he is so very busy at home.' The business at home of which the major's mother was speaking was his projected moving from Cosby Lodge, a subject which was also very odious to the archdeacon. He did not wish his son to move from Cosby Lodge. He could not endure the idea that his son should be known throughout the county to be giving up a residence because he could not afford to keep it. The archdeacon could have afforded to keep up two Cosby Lodges for his son, and would have been well pleased to do so, if only his son would not misbehave against him so shamefully! He could not bear that his son should be punished, openly, before the eyes of all Barsetshire. Indeed he did not wish that his son should be punished at all. He simply desired that his son should recognize his father's power to inflict punishment. It would be henbane to Archdeacon Grantly to have a poor son, – a son living at Pau, – among Frenchmen! – because he could not afford to live in England. Why had the archdeacon been careful of his money, adding house to house and field to field? He himself was contented, – so he told himself, – to die as he had lived in a country parsonage, working with the collar round his neck up to the day of his death, if God would allow him so to do. He was ambitious of no grandeur for himself. So he would tell himself, – being partly oblivious of certain episodes in his own life. All his wealth had been got together for his children. He desired that his sons should be fitting brothers for their august sister. And now the son who was nearest to him, whom he was bent upon making a squire in his own county, wanted to marry the daughter of a man who had stolen twenty pounds, and when objection was made to so discreditable a connexion, replied by packing up all his things and saying that he would go and live – at Pau! The archdeacon therefore did not like to hear of his son being very busy at home.

'I don't know whether he's busy or not,' said the archdeacon, 'but I tell you he is staying at Framley.'

'From whom have you heard it?'

'What matter does that make if it is so? I heard it from Flurry.'

'Flurry may have been mistaken,' said Mrs Grantly.

'It is not at all likely. Those people always know about such things. He heard it from the Framley keeper. I don't doubt but it's true, and I think that it's a great shame.'

'A great shame that Henry should be at Framley! He has been there two or three times every year since he has lived in the county.'

'It is a great shame that he should be had over there just at the time when that girl is there also. It is impossible to believe that such a thing is an accident.'

'But, archdeacon, you do not mean to say that you think that Lady Lufton has arranged it?'

'I don't know who has arranged it. Somebody has arranged it. If it is Robarts, that is almost worse. One could forgive a woman in such a matter better than one could a man.'

'Psha!' Mrs Grantly's temper was never bitter, but at this moment it was not sweetened by her husband's very uncivil reference to her sex. 'The whole idea is nonsense, and you should get it out of your head.'

'Am I to get it out of my head that Henry wants to make this girl his wife, and that the two are at this moment at Framley together?' In this the archdeacon was wrong as to his facts. Major Grantly had left Framley on the previous day, having stayed there only one night. 'It is coming to that that one can trust no one – no one – literally no one.' Mrs Grantly perfectly understood that the archdeacon, in the agony of the moment, intended to exclude even herself from his confidence by that 'no one;' but to this she was indifferent, understanding accurately when his words should be accepted as expressing his thoughts, and when they should be supposed to express only his anger.

'The probability is that no one at Lufton knew anything about Henry's partiality for Miss Crawley,' said Mrs Grantly.

'I tell you I think they are both at Framley together.'

'And I tell you that if they are, which I doubt, they are there simply by an accident. Besides, what does it matter? If they choose to marry each other, you and I cannot prevent them. They don't want any assistance from Lady Lufton, or anybody else. They have simply got to make up their own minds, and then no one can hinder them.'

'And, therefore, you would like to see them brought together?'

'I say nothing about that, archdeacon; but I do say that we must take these things as they come. What can we do? Henry may go and stay with Lady Lufton if he pleases. You and I cannot prevent him.'

After this the archdeacon walked away, and would not argue the matter any further with his wife at that moment. He knew very well that he could not get the better of her, and was apt as such moments to think that she took an unfair advantage of him by keeping her temper. But he could not get out of his head the idea that perhaps on this very day things were being arranged between his son and Grace Crawley at Framley; and he resolved that he himself would go over and see what might be done. He would at any rate, tell all his trouble to Lady Lufton, and beg his old friend to assist him. He could not think that such a one as he had always known Lady Lufton to be would approve of a marriage between Henry Grantly and Grace Crawley. At any rate, he would learn the truth. He had once been told that Grace Crawley had herself refused to marry his son, feeling that she would do wrong to inflict so great an injury upon any gentleman. He had not believed in so great a virtue. He could not believe in it now, – now, when he heard that Miss Crawley and his son were staying together in the same parish. Somebody must be doing him an injury. It could hardly be chance. But his presence at Framley might even yet have a good effect, and he would at least learn the truth. So he had himself driven to Barchester, and from Barchester he took post-horses to Framley.

As he came near to the village, he grew to be somewhat ashamed of himself, or, at least, nervous as to the mode in which he would proceed. The driver, turning round to him, had suggested that he supposed he was to drive to 'My lady's.' This injustice to Lord Lufton, to whom the house belonged, and with whom his mother lived as a guest, was very common in the county; for old Lady Lufton had lived at Framley Court through her son's long minority, and had kept the house there till his marriage; and ever since his marriage she had been recognized as its presiding genius. It certainly was not the fault of old Lady Lufton, as she always spoke of everything as belonging either to her son or to her daughter-in-law. The archdeacon had been in doubt whether he would go to the Court or to the parsonage. Could he have done exactly as he wished, he would have left the chaise and walked to the parsonage, so as to reach it without the noise and fuss incidental to a postilion's arrival. But that was impossible. He could not drop into Framley as though he had come from the clouds, and, therefore, he told the man to do as he had suggested. 'To my lady's?' said the postilion. The archdeacon assented, and the man, with loud cracks of his whip, and with a spasmodic gallop along the short avenue, took the archdeacon up to the door of Lord Lufton's house. He asked for Lord Lufton first, putting on his pleasantest smile, so that the servant should not suspect the purpose, of which he was somewhat ashamed. Was Lord Lufton at home? Lord Lufton was not at home. Lord Lufton had gone up to London that morning, intending to return the day after to-morrow; but both my ladies were at home. So the archdeacon was shown into the room where both my ladies were sitting, – and with them he found Mrs Robarts. Any one who had become acquainted with the habits of the Framley ladies would have known that this might very probably be the case. The archdeacon himself was as well aware as any one of the modes of life at Framley. The lord's wife was the parson's sister, and the parson's wife had from her infancy been the petted friend of the old lady. Of course they all lived very much together. Of course Mrs Robarts was as much at home in the drawing-room of Framley Court as she was in her own drawing-room at the parsonage. Nevertheless, the archdeacon thought himself to be hardly used when he found that Mrs Robarts was at the house.

'My dear archdeacon, who ever expected to see you?' said old Lady Lufton. Then the two younger women greeted him. And they all smiled on him pleasantly, and seemed overjoyed to see him. He was, in truth, a great favourite at Framley, and each of the three was glad to welcome him. They believed in the archdeacon at Framley, and felt for him that sort of love which ladies in the country do feel for their elderly male friends. There was not one of the three who would not have taken much trouble to get anything for the archdeacon which they had thought the archdeacon would like. Even old Lady Lufton remembered what was his favourite soup, and always took care that he should have it when he dined at the Court. Young Lady Lufton would bring his tea to him as he sat in his chair. He was petted in the house, was allowed to poke the fire if he pleased, and called the servants by their names as though he were at home. He was compelled, therefore, to smile and to seem pleased; and it was not till after he had eaten his lunch, and had declared that he must return home to dinner, that the dowager gave him an opportunity of having the private conversation which he desired.

'Can I have a few minutes' talk with you?' he said to her,

whispering into her ear as they left the drawing-room together. So she led the way into her own sitting-room, telling him, as she asked him to be seated, that she had supposed that something special must have brought him over to Framley. 'I should have asked you to come up here, even if you had not spoken,' she said.

'Then perhaps you know what has brought me over?' said the archdeacon.

'Not in the least,' said Lady Lufton. 'I have not an idea. But I did not flatter myself that you would come so far on a morning call, merely to see us three ladies. I hope you did not want to see Ludovic, because he will not be back till to-morrow?'

'I wanted to see you, Lady Lufton.'

'That is lucky, as here I am. You may be pretty sure to find me here any day in the year.'

After this there was a little pause. The archdeacon hardly knew how to begin his story. In the first place he was in doubt whether Lady Lufton had ever heard of the preposterous match which his son had proposed to himself to make. In his anger at Plumstead he had felt sure that she knew all about it, and that she was assisting his son. But this belief had dwindled as his anger had dwindled; and as the chaise had entered the parish of Framley he had told himself that it was quite impossible that she should know anything about it. Her manner had certainly been altogether in her favour since he had been in her house. There had been nothing of the consciousness of guilt in her demeanour. But, nevertheless, there was the coincidence! How had it come to pass that Grace Crawley and his son should be at Framley together? It might, indeed, be just possible that Flurry might have been wrong, and that his son had not been there at all.

'I suppose Miss Crawley is at the parsonage?' he said at last.

'Oh, yes; she is still there, and will remain there I should think for the next ten days.'

'Oh; I did not know,' said the archdeacon very coldly.

It seemed to Lady Lufton, who was as innocent as an unborn babe in the matter of the projected marriage, that her old friend the archdeacon was in a mind to persecute the Crawleys. He had on a former occasion taken upon himself to advise that Grace Crawley should not be entertained at Framley, and now it seemed that he had come all the way from Plumstead to say something further in the same strain. Lady Lufton, if he had anything further to say of that kind, would listen to him as a matter of course. She would listen to him and reply to him without temper. But she did not approve of it. She told herself silently that she could not approve of persecution or of interference. She therefore drew herself up, and pursed her mouth, and put on something of that look of severity which she could assume very visibly, if it so pleased her.

'Yes; she is still there, and I think that her visit will do her a great deal of good,' said Lady Lufton.

'When we talk of doing good to people,' said the archdeacon, 'we often make terrible mistakes. It so often happens that we don't know when we are doing good and when we are doing harm.'

'That is true, of course, Dr Grantly, and must be so necessarily, as our wisdom here below is so very limited. But I should think, — as far as I can see, that is, — that the kindness which my friend Mrs Robarts is showing to this young lady must be beneficial. You know, archdeacon, I explained to you before that I could not quite agree with you in what you said as to leaving these people alone till after the trial. I thought that help was necessary to them at once.'

The archdeacon sighed deeply. He ought to have been somewhat renovated in spirit by the tone in which Lady Lufton spoke to him, as it conveyed to him almost an absolute conviction that his first suspicion was incorrect. But any comfort which might have come to him from this source was marred by the feeling that he must announce his own disgrace. At any rate he must do so, unless he were contented to go back to Plumstead without having learned anything by his journey. He changed the tone of his voice, however, and asked a question, — as it might be altogether on a different subject. 'I heard yesterday,' he said, 'that Henry was over here.'

'He was here yesterday. He came the evening before, and dined and slept here, and went home yesterday morning.'

'Was Miss Crawley with you that evening?'

'Miss Crawley? No; she would not come. She thinks it best not to go out while her father is in his present unfortunate position; and she is right.'

'She is quite right in that,' said the archdeacon; and then he paused again. He thought that it would be best for him to make a clean breast of it, and to trust to Lady Lufton's sympathy. 'Did Henry go up to the parsonage?' he asked.

But still Lady Lufton did not suspect the truth. 'I think he did,' she replied, with an air of surprise. 'I think I heard that he went up there to call on Mrs Robarts after breakfast.'

'No, Lady Lufton, he did not go up there to call on Mrs Robarts. He went up there because he is making a fool of himself about that Miss Crawley. That is the truth. Now you understand it all. I hope that Mrs Robarts does not know it. I do hope for her own sake that Mrs Robarts does not know it.'

The archdeacon certainly had no longer any doubt as to Lady Lufton's innocence when he looked at her face as she heard these tidings. She had predicted that Grace Crawley would 'make havoc,' and could not, therefore, be altogether surprised at the idea that some gentleman should have fallen in love with her; but she had never supposed that the havoc might be made so early in her days, or on so great a quarry. 'You don't mean to tell me that Henry Grantly is in love with Grace Crawley?' she replied.

'I mean to say that he says he is.'

'Dear, dear, dear! I'm sure, archdeacon, that you will believe me when I say that I knew nothing about it.'

'I am quite sure of that,' said the archdeacon dolefully.

'Or I certainly should not have been glad to see him here. But the house, you know, is not mine, Dr Grantly. I could have done nothing if I had known it. But only to think—; well, to be sure. She has not lost time, at any rate.'

Now this was not at all the light in which the archdeacon wished that the matter should be regarded. He had been desirous that Lady Lufton should be horror-stricken by the tidings, but it seemed to him that she regarded the iniquity almost as a good joke. What did it matter how young or how old the girl might be? She came of poor people, – of people who had no friends, – of disgraced people; and Lady Lufton ought to feel that such a marriage would be a terrible misfortune and a terrible crime. 'I need hardly tell you, Lady Lufton,' said the archdeacon, 'that I shall set my face against it as far as it is in my power to do so.'

'If they both be resolved I suppose you can hardly prevent it.'

'Of course I cannot prevent it. Of course I cannot prevent it. If he will break my heart and his mother's, – and his sister's, – of course I cannot prevent it. If he will ruin himself, he must have his own way.'

'Ruin himself, Dr Grantly!'

'They will have enough to live upon, – somewhere in Spain or France.' The scorn expressed in the archdeacon's voice as he spoke of Pau as being 'somewhere in Spain or France,' should have been heard to be understood. 'No doubt they will have enough to live upon.'

'Do you mean to say that it will make a difference as to your own property, Dr Grantly?'

'Certainly it will, Lady Lufton. I told Henry when I first heard of the thing, – before he had definitely made any offer to the girl, – that I should withdraw from him altogether the allowance that I now make him, if he married her. And I told him also, that if he persisted in his folly I should think it my duty to alter my will.'

'I am sorry for that, Dr Grantly.'

'Sorry! And am not I sorry? Sorrow is no sufficient word. I am broken-hearted. Lady Lufton, it is killing me. It is indeed. I love him; I love him; – I love him as you have loved your son. But what is the use? What can he be to me when he shall have married the daughter of such a man as that?'

Lady Lufton sat for a while silent, thinking of a certain episode in her own life. There had been a time when her son was desirous of making a marriage which she had thought would break her heart. She had for a time moved heaven and earth, – as far as she knew how to move them, – to prevent the marriage. But at last she had yielded, – not from lack of power, for the circumstances had been such that at the moment of yielding she had still the power in her hand of staying the marriage, – but she had yielded because she had perceived that her son was in earnest. She had yielded, and had kissed the dust; but from the moment in which her lips had so touched the ground, she had taken great joy in the new daughter whom her son had brought into the house. Since that she had learned to think that young people might perhaps be right, and that old people might perhaps be wrong. This trouble of her friend the archdeacon's was very like her own old trouble. 'And he is engaged to her now?' she said, when those thoughts had passed through her mind.

'Yes; – that is, no. I am not sure. I do not know how to make myself sure.'

'I am sure Major Grantly will tell you all the truth as it exists.'

'Yes; he'll tell me the truth, – as far as he knows it. I do not see that there is much anxiety to spare me in the matter. He is desirous rather of making me understand that I have no power of saving him from his own folly. Of course I have no power of saving him.'

'But is he engaged to her?'

'He says that she has refused him. But of course that means nothing.'

Again the archdeacon's position was very like Lady Lufton's position, as it had existed before her son's marriage. In that case also the young lady, who was now Lady Lufton's own daughter and dearest friend, had refused the lover who proposed to her, although the marriage was so much to her advantage, – loving him, too, the while, with her whole heart, as it was natural to suppose that Grace Crawley might so love her lover. The more she thought of the similarity of the stories, the stronger were her sympathies on the side of poor Grace. Nevertheless, she would comfort her old friend if she knew how; and of course she could not but admit to herself that the match was one which must be a cause of real sorrow to him. 'I don't know why her refusal should mean nothing,' said Lady Lufton.

'Of course a girl refuses at first, – a girl, I mean, in such circumstances as hers. She can't but feel that more is offered to her than she ought to take, and that she is bound to go through the ceremony of declining. But my anger is not with her, Lady Lufton.'

'I do not see how it can be.'

'No; it is not with her. If she becomes his wife I trust that I may never see her.'

'Oh, Dr Grantly !'

'I do; I do. How can it be otherwise with me? But I shall have no quarrel with her. With him I must quarrel.'

'I do not see why,' said Lady Lufton.

'You do not? Does he not set me at defiance?'

'At his age surely a son has a right to marry as he pleases.'

'If he took her out of the streets, then it would be the same?' said the archdeacon with bitter anger.

'No; – for such a one would herself be bad.'

'Or if she were the daughter of a huxter out of the city?'

'No again; – for in that case her want of education would probably unfit her for your society.'

'Her father's disgrace, then, should be a matter of indifference to me, Lady Lufton?'

'I did not say so. In the first place, her father is not disgraced, – not as yet; and we do not know whether he may ever be disgraced. You will hardly be disposed to say that persecution from the palace disgraces a clergyman in Barsetshire.'

'All the same, I believe that the man was guilty,' said the archdeacon.

'Wait and see, my friend, before you condemn him altogether. But, be that as it may, I acknowledge that the marriage is one which must naturally be distasteful to you.'

'Oh, Lady Lufton ! if you only knew ! If you only knew !'

'I do know; and I feel for you. But I think that your son has a right to expect that you should not show the same repugnance to such a marriage as this as you would have had a right to show had he suggested to himself such a wife as those at which you just now hinted. Of course you can advise him, and make him understand your feelings; but I cannot think you will be justified in quarrelling with him, or in changing your views towards him as regards money, seeing that Miss Crawley is an educated lady, who has done nothing to forfeit your respect.' A heavy cloud came upon the archdeacon's brow as he heard these words, but he did not make any immediate answer. 'Of course, my friend,' continued Lady Lufton, 'I should not have ventured to say so much to you, had you not come to me, as it were, for my opinion.'

'I came here because I thought Henry was here,' said the archdeacon.

'If I have said too much I beg your pardon.'

'No; you have not said too much. It is not that. You and I are such old friends that either may say almost anything to the other.'

'Yes; – just so. And therefore I have ventured to speak my mind,' said Lady Lufton.

'Of course; – and I am obliged to you. But, Lady Lufton, you do not understand yet how this hits me. Everything in life that I have done, I have done for my children. I am wealthy, but I have not used my wealth for myself, because I have desired that they should be able to hold their heads high in the world. All my ambition has been for them, and all the pleasure which I have anticipated for myself in my old age is that which I have hoped to receive from their credit. As for Henry, he might have had anything he wanted from me in the way of money. He expressed a wish, a few months since, to go into Parliament, and I promised to help him as far as ever I could go. I have kept up the game altogether for him. He, the younger son of a working parish parson, has had everything that could be given to the eldest son of a country gentleman, – more than is given to the eldest son of many a peer. I have hoped that he would marry again, but I have never cared that he should marry for money. I have been willing to do anything for him myself. But, Lady Lufton, a father does feel that he should have some return for all this. No one can imagine that Henry ever supposed that a bride from that wretched place at Hogglestock could be welcomed among us. He knew that he would break out hearts, and he did not care for it. That is what I feel. Of course he has the power to do as he likes; – and of course I have the power to do as I like also with what is my own.'

Lady Lufton was a very good woman, devoted to her duties, affectionate and just to those about her, truly religious, and charitable from her nature; but I doubt whether the thorough worldliness of the archdeacon's appeal struck her as it will strike the reader. People are so much more worldly in practice than they are in theory, so much keener after their own gratification in detail than they are in the abstract, that the narrative of many an adventure would shock us, though the same adventure would not shock us in the action. One girl tells another how she has changed her mind in love; and the friend sympathizes with the friend, and perhaps applauds. Had the story been told in print, the friend who had listened with equanimity would have read of such vacillation with indignation. She who vacillated herself would have hated her own performance when brought before her judgment as a matter in which she had no personal interest. Very fine things are written every day about honesty and truth, and men read them with a sort of external conviction that a man, if he be anything of a man at all, is of course honest and true. But when the internal convictions are brought out between two or three who are personally interested together, – between two or three who feel that their little gathering is, so to say, 'tiled,'* – those internal convictions differ very much from the external convictions. This man, in his confidences, asserts broadly that he does not mean to be thrown over, and that man has a project for throwing over somebody else; and the intention of each is that scruples are not to stand in the way of his success. The 'Ruat cœlum, fiat justitia,'* was said, no doubt, from an outside balcony to a crowd, and the speaker knew that he was talking buncombe. The 'Rem, si possis recte, si non, quocunque modo,'* was whispered into the ear in a club smoking-room, and the whisperer intended that his words should prevail.

Lady Lufton had often heard her friend the archdeacon preach, and she knew well the high tone which he could take as to the necessity of trusting to our hopes for the future for all our true happiness; and yet she sympathized with him when he told her that he was broken-hearted because his son would take a step which might possibly interfere with his worldly prosperity. Had the archdeacon been preaching about matrimony, he would have recommended young men, in taking wives to themselves, especially to look for young women who feared the Lord. But in talking about his own son's wife, no word as to her eligibility or non-eligibility in this respect escaped his lips. Had he talked on the subject till nightfall no such word would have been spoken. Had any friend of his own, man or woman, in discussing such a matter with him and asking his advice upon it, alluded to the fear of the Lord, the allusion would have been distasteful to him and would have smacked to his palate of hypocrisy. Lady Lufton, who understood as well as any woman what it was to be 'tiled' with a friend, took all this in good part. The archdeacon had spoken out of his heart what was in his heart. One of his children had married a marquis. Another might probably become a bishop, – perhaps an archbishop. The third might be a county squire, – high among county squires. But he could only so become by walking warily; – and now he was bent on marrying the penniless daughter of an impoverished half-mad country curate, who was about to be tried for stealing twenty pounds! Lady Lufton, in spite of all her arguments, could not refuse her sympathy to her old friend.

'After all, from what you say, I suppose they are not engaged.'

'I do not know,' said the archdeacon. 'I cannot tell!'

'And what do you wish me to do?'

'Oh, – nothing. I came over, as I said before, because I thought he was here. I think it right, before he has absolutely committed himself, to take every means in my power to make him understand that I shall withdraw from him all pecuniary assistance, – now and for the future.'

'My friend, that threat seems to me to be so terrible.'

'It is the only power I have left to me.'

'But you, who are so affectionate by nature, would never adhere to it.'

'I will try. I will do my best to be firm. I will at once put everything beyond my control after my death.' The archdeacon, as he uttered these terrible words, – words which were awful to Lady Lufton's ears, – resolved that he would endeavour to nurse his own wrath; but, at the same time, almost hated himself for his own pusillanimity, because he feared that his wrath would die away before he should have availed himself of its heat.

'I would do nothing rash of that kind,' said Lady Lufton. 'Your object is to prevent the marriage, – not to punish him for it when once he has made it.'

'He is not to have his own way in everything, Lady Lufton.'

'But you should first try to prevent it.'

'What can I do to prevent it?'

Lady Lufton paused for a couple of minutes before she replied. She had a scheme in her head, but it seemed to her to savour of cruelty. And yet at present it was her chief duty to assist her old friend, if any assistance could be given. There could hardly be a doubt that such a marriage as this, of which they were speaking, was in itself an evil. In her case, the case of her son, there had been no question of a trial, of money stolen, of aught that was in truth disgraceful. 'I think if I were you, Dr Grantly,' she said, 'that I would see the young lady while I was here.'

'See her myself?' said the archdeacon. The idea of seeing Grace Crawley himself had, up to this moment, never entered his head.

'I think I would do so.'

'I think I will,' said the archdeacon, after a pause. Then he got up from his chair. 'If I am to do it, I had better do it at once.'

'Be gentle with her, my friend.' The archdeacon paused again. He certainly had entertained the idea of encountering Miss Crawley with severity rather than gentleness. Lady Lufton rose from her seat, and coming up to him, took one of his hands between her own two. 'Be gentle to her,' she said. 'You have owned that she has done nothing wrong.' The archdeacon bowed his head in token of assent and left the room.

Poor Grace Crawley!

CHAPTER 57

A double pledge

The archdeacon, as he walked across from the court to the
parsonage, was very thoughtful and his steps were very slow. This
idea of seeing Miss Crawley herself had been suggested to him
suddenly, and he had to determine how he would bear himself
towards her, and what he would say to her. Lady Lufton had
beseeched him to be gentle with her. Was the mission one in which
gentleness would be possible? Must it not be his object to make
this young lady understand that she could not be right in desiring
to come into his family and share in all his good things when she
had got no good things of her own, – nothing but evil things to
bring with her? And how could this be properly explained to the
young lady in gentle terms? Must he not be round with her, and
give her to understand in plain words, – the plainest which he could
use, – that she would not get his good things, though she would
most certainly impose the burden of all her evil things on the man
whom she was proposing to herself as a husband. He remembered
very well as he went, that he had been told that Miss Crawley had
herself refused the offer, feeling herself to be unfit for the honour
tendered to her; but he suspected the sincerity of such a refusal.
Calculating in his own mind the unreasonably great advantages
which would be conferred on such a young lady as Miss Crawley
by a marriage with his son, he declared to himself that any girl must
be very wicked indeed who should expect, or even accept, so much
more than was her due; – but nevertheless he could not bring
himself to believe that any girl, when so tempted, would, in
sincerity, decline to commit this great wickedness. If he was to do
any good by seeing Miss Crawley, must it not consist in a proper
explanation to her of the selfishness, abomination, and altogether
damnable blackness of such wickedness as this on the part of a
young woman in her circumstances? 'Heaven and earth!' he must
say, 'here are you, without a penny in your pocket, with hardly

decent raiment on your back, with a thief for your father, and you think that you are to come and share in all the wealth that the Grantlys have amassed, that you are to have a husband with broad acres, a big house, and game preserves, and become one of a family whose name has never been touched by a single accusation, – no, not by a suspicion? No; – injustice such as that shall never be done betwixt you and me. You may wring my heart, and you may ruin my son; but the broad acres and the big house, and the game preserves, and the rest of it, shall never be your reward for doing so.' How was all that to be told effectively to a young woman in gentle words? And then how was a man in the archdeacon's position to be desirous of gentle words, – gentle words which would not be efficient, – when he knew well in his heart of hearts that he had nothing but his threats on which to depend. He had no more power of disinheriting his own son for such an offence as that contemplated than he had of blowing out his own brains, and he knew that it was so. He was a man incapable of such persistency of wrath against one whom he loved. He was neither cruel enough nor strong enough to do such a thing. He could only threaten to do it, and make what best use he might of threats, whilst threats might be of avail. In spite of all that he had said to his wife, to Lady Lufton, and to himself, he knew very well that if his son did sin in this way he, the father, would forgive the sin of the son.

In going across from the front gate of the Court to the parsonage there was a place where three roads met,* and on this spot there stood a finger-post. Round this finger-post there was now pasted a placard, which at once arrested the archdeacon's eye: – 'Cosby Lodge – Sale of furniture – Growing crops to be sold on the grounds. Three hunters. A brown gelding warranted for saddle of harness!' – The archdeacon himself had given the brown gelding to his son, as a great treasure. – 'Three Alderney cows, two cow-calves, a low phaeton, a gig, two ricks of hay.' In this fashion were proclaimed in odious details all those comfortable additions to a gentleman's house in the country, with which the archdeacon was so well acquainted. Only last November he had recommended his son to buy a certain new-invented clod-crusher, and the clod-crusher had of course been bought. The bright blue paint upon it had not as yet given way to the stains of the ordinary farmyard muck and mire; – and here was the clod-crusher* advertised for sale! The archdeacon did not want his son to leave Cosby Lodge. He knew well enough that his son need not leave Cosby Lodge. Why had the foolish fellow been in such a hurry with his hideous ill-conditioned advertisements? Gentle! How was he in such circumstances to be gentle? He raised his umbrella and poked angrily at the disgusting notice. The iron ferule caught the paper at a chink in the post, and tore it from the top to the bottom. But what was the use ? A horrid ugly bill lying torn in such a spot would attract only more attention than one fixed to a post. He could not condescend, however, to give to it further attention, but passed on up to the parsonage. Gentle, indeed !

Nevertheless Archdeacon Grantly was a gentleman, and never yet had dealt more harshly with any woman than we have sometimes seen him to with his wife, – when he would say to her an angry word or two with a good deal of marital authority. His wife, who knew well what his angry words were worth, never even suggested to herself that she had cause for complaint on that head. Had she known that the archdeacon was about to undertake such a mission as this which he had now in hand, she would not have warned him to be gentle. She, indeed, would have strongly advised him not to undertake the mission, cautioning him that the young lady would probably get the better of him.

'Grace my dear,' said Mrs Robarts, coming up into the nursery in which Miss Crawley was sitting with the children, 'come out here a moment, will you ?' Then Grace left the children and went out into the passage. 'My dear, there is a gentleman in the drawing-room who asks to see you.'

'A gentleman, Mrs Robarts ! What gentleman ?' But Grace, though she asked the question, conceived that the gentleman must be Henry Grantly. Her mind did not suggest to her the possibility of any other gentleman coming to see her.

'You must not be surprised, or allow yourself to be frightened.'

'Oh, Mrs Robarts, who is it ?'

'It is Major Grantly's father.'

'The archdeacon ?'

'Yes, dear ; Archdeacon Grantly. He is in the drawing-room.'

'Must I see him, Mrs Robarts ?'

'Well, Grace, – I think you must. I hardly know how you can refuse. He is an intimate friend of everybody here at Framley.'

'What will he say to me ?'

'Nay ; that I cannot tell. I suppose you know—'

'He has come, no doubt, to bid me have nothing to say to his son. He need not have troubled himself. But he may say what he likes. I am not a coward, and I will go to him.'

'Stop a moment, Grace. Come into my room for an instant. The children have pulled your hair about.' But, Grace, though she followed Mrs Robarts into the bedroom, would have nothing done to her hair. She was too proud for that, – and we may say, also, too little confident in any good which such resources might effect on her behalf. 'Never mind about that,' she said. 'What am I to say to him?' Mrs Robarts paused before she replied, feeling that the matter was one which required some deliberation. 'Tell me what I must say to him?' said Grace, repeating her question.

'I hardly know what your own feelings are, my dear.'

'Yes, you do. You do know. If I had all the world to give, I would give it all to Major Grantly.'

'Tell him that, then.'

'No, I will not tell him that. Never mind about my frock, Mrs Robarts. I do not care for that. I will tell him that I love his son and his granddaughter too well to injure them. I will tell him nothing else. I might as well go now.' Mrs Robarts, as she looked at Grace, was astonished at the serenity of her face. And yet when her hand was on the drawing-room door Grace hesitated, looked back, and trembled. Mrs Robarts blew a kiss to her from the stairs; and then the door was opened, and the girl found herself in the presence of the archdeacon. He was standing on the rug, with his back to the fire, and his heavy ecclesiastical hat was placed on the middle of the round table. The hat caught Grace's eye at the moment of her entrance, and she felt that all the thunders of the Church were contained within it. And then the archdeacon himself was so big and so clerical, and so imposing! Her father's aspect was severe, but the severity of her father's face was essentially different from that expressed by the archdeacon. Whatever impression came from her father came from the man himself. There was no outward adornment there; there was, so to say, no wig about Mr Crawley. Now the archdeacon was not exactly adorned; but he was so thoroughly imbued with high clerical belongings and sacerdotal fitnesses as to appear always as a walking, sitting, or standing impersonation of parsondom. To poor Grace, as she entered the room, he appeard to be an impersonation of parsondom in its severest aspect.

'Miss Crawley, I believe?' said he.

'Yes, sir,' said she, curtseying ever so slightly, as she stood before him at some considerable distance.

His first idea was that his son must be indeed a fool if he was going to give up Cosby Lodge and all Barsetshire, and retire to Pau, for so slight and unattractive a creature as he now saw before him. But this idea stayed with him only for a moment. As he continued to gaze at her during the interview he came to perceive that there was very much more than he had perceived at the first glance, and that his son, after all, had had eyes to see, though perhaps not a heart to understand.

'Will you not take a chair?' he said. Then Grace sat down, still at a distance from the archdeacon, and he kept his place upon the rug. He felt that there would be a difficulty in making her feel the full force of his eloquence all across the room; and yet he did not know how to bring himself nearer to her. She became suddenly very important in his eyes, and he was to some extent afraid of her. She was so slight, so meek, so young; and yet there was about her something so beautifully feminine, – and, withal, so like a lady, – that he felt instinctively that he could not attack her with harsh words. Had her lips been full, and her colour high, and had her eyes rolled, had she put forth against him any of that ordinary artillery with which youthful feminine batteries are charged, he would have been ready to rush to the combat. But this girl, about whom his son had gone mad, sat there as passively as though she were conscious of the possession of no artillery. There was not a single gun fired from beneath her eyelids. He knew not why, but he respected his son now more than he had respected him for the last two months; – more, perhaps, than he had ever respected him before. He was as eager as ever against the marriage; – but in thinking of his son in what he said and did after these few first moments of the interview, he ceased to think of him with contempt. The creature before him was a woman who grew in his opinion till he began to feel that she was in truth fit to be the wife of his son – if only she were not a pauper, and the daughter of a mad curate, and, alas! too probably, of a thief. Though his feeling towards the girl was changed, his duty to himself, his family, and his son, was the same as ever, and therefore he began his task.

'Perhaps you had not expected to see me?' he said.

'No, indeed, sir.'

'Nor had I intended when I came over here to call on my old friend, Lady Lufton, to come up to this house. But as I knew that you were here, Miss Crawley, I thought that upon the whole it would be better that I should see you.' Then he paused as though he expected that Grace would say something; but Grace had nothing to say. 'Of course you must understand, Miss Crawley, that I should not venture to speak to you on this subject unless I myself were very closely interested in it.' He had not yet said what was the subject, and it was not probable that Grace should give him any assistance by affecting to understand this without direct explanation from him. She sat quite motionless, and did not even aid him by showing by her altered colour that she understood his purpose. 'My son has told me,' said he, 'that he has professed an attachment for you, Miss Crawley.'

Then there was another pause, and Graced felt that she was compelled to say something. 'Major Grantly has been very good to me,' she said, and then she hated herself for having uttered words which were so tame and unwomanly in their spirit. Of course her lover's father would despise her for having so spoken. After all it did not much signify. If he would only despise her and go away, it would perhaps be for the best.

'I do not know about being good,' said the archdeacon. 'I think he is good. I think he means to be good.'

'I am sure he is good,' said Grace, warmly.

'You know he has a daughter, Miss Crawley?'

'Oh, yes; I know Edith well.'

'Of course his first duty is to her. Is it not? And he owes much to his family. Do you not feel that?'

'Of course I feel it, sir.' The poor girl had always heard Dr Grantly spoken of as the archdeacon, but she did not in the least know what she ought to call him.

'Now, Miss Crawley, pray listen to me; I will speak to you very openly. I must speak to you openly, because it is my duty on my son's behalf – but I will endeavour to speak to you kindly also. Of yourself I have heard nothing but what is favourable, and there is no reason as yet why I should not respect and esteem you.' Grace told herself that she would do nothing which ought to forfeit his respect and esteem, but that she did not care two straws whether his respect and esteem were bestowed on her or not. She was striving after something very different from that. 'If my son were to marry you, he would greatly injure himself, and would very greatly injure his child.' Again he paused. He had told her to listen, and she was resolved that she would listen, – unless he should say something which might make a word from her necessary at the moment. 'I do not know whether there does at present exist any engagement between you?'

'There is no engagement, sir.'

'I am glad of that, – very glad of it. I do not know whether you are aware that my son is dependent upon me for the greater part of his income. It is so, and as I am so circumstanced with my son, of course I feel the closest possible concern in his future prospects.' The archdeacon did not know how to explain clearly why the fact of his making a son an annual allowance should give him a warmer interest in his son's affairs than he might have had had the major been altogether independent of him; but he trusted that Grace would understand this by her own natural lights. 'Now, Miss Crawley, of course I cannot wish to say a word that shall hurt your feelings. But there are reasons—'

'I know,' said she, interrupting him. 'Papa is accused of stealing money. He did not steal it, but people think he did. And then we are so very poor.'

'You do understand me then, – and I feel grateful; I do indeed.'

'I don't think our being poor ought to signify a bit,' said Grace. 'Papa is a gentleman and a clergyman, and mamma is a lady.'

'But, my dear—'

'I know I ought not to be your son's wife as long as people think that papa stole the money. If he had stolen it, I ought never to be Major Grantly's wife, – or anybody's wife. I know that very well. And as for Edith, – I would sooner die than do anything that would be bad to her.'

The archdeacon had now left the rug, and advanced till he was almost close to the chair on which Grace was sitting. 'My dear,' he said, 'what you say does you very much honour, – very much honour indeed.' Now that he was close to her, he could look into her eyes, and he could see the exact form of her features, and could understand, – could not help understanding, – the character of her countenance. It was a noble face, having in it nothing that was poor, nothing that was mean, nothing that was shapeless. It was a face that promised infinite beauty, with a promise that was on the very verge of fulfilment. There was a play about her mouth as she spoke, and a curl in her nostril as the eager words came from her, which almost made the selfish father give way. Why had they not told him that she was such a one as this? Why had not Henry himself spoken of the speciality of her beauty? No man in England knew better than the archdeacon the difference between beauty of one kind and beauty of another kind in a woman's face, – the one beauty, which comes from health and youth and animal spirits, and which belongs to the miller's daughter, and the other beauty, which shows itself in fine lines and a noble spirit, – the beauty which comes from breeding. 'What you say does you very much honour indeed,' said the archdeacon.

'I should not mind at all about being poor,' said Grace.

'No; no; no,' said the archdeacon.

'Poor as we are, – and no clergyman, I think, ever was so poor, – I should have done as your son asked me at once, if it had been only that, – because I love him.'

'If you love him you will not wish to injure him.'

'I will not injure him. Sir, there is my promise.' And now as she spoke she rose from her chair, and standing close to the archdeacon, laid her hand very lightly on the sleeve of his coat. 'There is my promise. As long as people say that papa stole the money, I will never marry your son. There.'

The archdeacon was still looking down at her, and feeling the slight touch of her fingers, raised his arm a little as though to welcome the pressure. He looked into her eyes, which were turned eagerly towards his, and when doing so was quite sure that the promise would be kept. It would have been sacrilege, – he felt that it would have been sacrilege, – to doubt such a promise. He almost relented. His soft heart, which was never very well under his own control, gave way so far that he was nearly moved to tell her that, on his son's behalf, he acquitted her of the promise. What could any man's son do better than have such a woman for his wife? It would have been of no avail had he made her such offer. The pledge she had given had not been wrung from her by his influence, nor could his influence have availed ought with her towards the alteration of her purpose. It was not the archdeacon who had taught her that it would not be her duty to take disgrace into the house of the man she loved. As he looked down upon her face two tears formed themselves in his eyes, and gradually trickled down his old nose. 'My dear,' he said, 'if this cloud passes away from you, you shall come to us and be my daughter.' And thus he also pledged himself. There was a dash of generosity about the man, in spite of his selfishness, which always made him desirous of giving largely to those who gave largely to him. He would fain that his gifts should be the bigger, if it were possible. He longed at this moment to tell her that the dirty cheque should go for nothing. He would have done it, I think, but that it was impossible for him so to speak in her presence of that which moved her so greatly.

He had contrived that her hand should fall from his arm into his grasp, and now for a moment he held it. 'You are a good girl,' he said – 'a dear, dear, good girl. When this cloud had passed away, you shall come to us and be our daughter.'

'But it will never pass away,' said Grace.

'Let us hope that it may. Let us hope that it may.' Then he stooped over her and kissed her, and leaving the room, got out into the hall and thence into the garden, and so away, without saying a word of adieu to Mrs Robarts.

As he walked across to the Court, whither he was obliged to go, because of his chaise, he was lost in surprise at what had occurred. He had gone to the parsonage, hating the girl, and despising his son. Now, as he retraced his steps, his feelings were altogether changed. He admired the girl, – and as for his son, even his anger was for the moment altogether gone. He would write to his son at once and implore him to stop the sale. He would tell his son all that had occurred, or rather would make Mrs Grantly do so. In respect to his son he was quite safe. He thought at that moment that he was safe. There would be no use in hurling further threats at him.

If Crawley were found guilty of stealing the money, there was the girl's promise. If he were acquitted, there was his own pledge. He remembered perfectly well that the girl had said more than this, – that she had not confined her assurance to the verdict of a jury, that she had protested that she would not accept Major Grantly's hand as long as people thought that her father had stolen the cheque; but the archdeacon felt that it would be ignoble to hold her closely to her words. The event, according to his ideas of the compact, was to depend upon the verdict of the jury. If the jury should find Mr Crawley not guilty, all objection on his part to the marriage was to be withdrawn. And he would keep his word! In such case it should be withdrawn.

When he came to the rags of the auctioneer's bill, which he had before torn down with his umbrella, he stopped a moment to consider how he would act at once. In the first place he would tell his son that his threats were withdrawn, and would ask him to remain at Cosby Lodge. He would write the letter as he passed through Barchester, on his way home, so that his son might receive it on the following morning; and he would refer the major to his mother for a full explanation of the circumstances. Those odious bills must be removed from every barn-door and wall in the county. At the present moment his anger against his son was chiefly directed against his ill-judged haste in having put up those ill-omened posters. Then he paused to consider what must be his wish as to the verdict of the jury. He had pledged himself to abide by the verdict, and he could not but have a wish on the subject. Could he desire in his heart that Mr Crawley should be found guilty? He stood still for a moment thinking of this, and then he walked on, shaking his head. If it might be possible he would have no wish on the subject whatsoever.

'Well!' said Lady Lufton, stopping him in the passage, – 'have you seen her?'

'Yes; I have seen her.'

'Well?'

'She is a good girl, – a very good girl. I am in a great hurry, and hardly know how to tell you more now.'

'You say that she is a good girl?'

'I say that she is a very good girl. An angel could not have behaved better. I will tell you all some day, Lady Lufton, but I can hardly tell you now.'

When the archdeacon was gone old Lady Lufton confided to young Lady Lufton her very strong opinion that many months would not be gone by before Grace Crawley would be the mistress of Cosby Lodge. 'It will be great promotion,' said the old lady, with a little toss of her head.

When Grace was interrogated afterwards by Mrs Robarts as to what had passed between her and the archdeacon she had very little to say as to the interview. 'No, he did not scold me,' she replied to an inquiry from her friend. 'But he spoke about your engagement?' said Mrs Robarts. 'There is no engagement,' said Grace. 'But I suppose you acknowledged, my dear, that a future engagement is quite possible?' 'I told him, Mrs Robarts,' Grace answered, after hesitating for a moment, 'that I would never marry his son as long as papa was suspected by any one in the world of being a thief. And I will keep my word.' But she said nothing to Mrs Robarts of the pledge which the archdeacon had made to her.

CHAPTER 58

The cross-grainedness of men

By the time that the archdeacon reached Plumstead his enthusiasm in favour of Grace Crawley had somewhat cooled itself; and the language which from time to time he prepared for conveying his impressions to his wife, became less fervid as he approached his home. There was his pledge, and by that he would abide; – and so much he would make both his wife and his son understand. But any idea which he might have entertained for a moment of extending the promise he had given and relaxing that given to him was gone before he saw his own chimneys. Indeed, I fear he had by that time begun to feel that the only salvation now open to him must come from the jury's verdict. If the jury should declare Mr Crawley to be guilty, then—; he would not say even to himself that in such case all would be right, but he did feel that much as he might regret the fate of the poor Crawleys, and of the girl whom in his warmth he had declared to be almost an angel, nevertheless to him personally such a verdict would bring consolatory comfort.

'I have seen Miss Crawley,' he said to his wife, as soon as he had closed the door of his study, before he had been two minutes out of the chaise. He had determined that he would dash at the subject at once, and he thus carried his resolution into effect.

'You have seen Grace Crawley?'

'Yes; I went up to the parsonage and called upon her. Lady Lufton advised me to do so.'

'And Henry?'

'Oh, Henry has gone. He was only there one night. I suppose he saw her, but I am not sure.'

'Would not Miss Crawley tell you?'

'I forgot to ask her.' Mrs Grantly, at hearing this, expressed her surprise by opening wide her eyes. He had gone all the way over to Framley on purpose to look after his son, and learn what were his doings, and when there he had forgotten to ask the person who could have given him better information than any one else ! 'But it does not signify,' continued the archdeacon; 'she said enough to me to make that of no importance.'

'And what did she say?'

'She said that she would never consent to marry Henry as long as there was any suspicion abroad as to her father's guilt.'

'And you believe her promise?'

'Certainly I do; I do not doubt it in the least. I put implicit confidence in her. And I have promised her that if her father is acquitted, – I will withdraw my opposition.'

'No!'

'But I have. And you would have done the same had you been there.'

'I doubt that, my dear. I am not so impulsive as you are.'

'You could not have helped yourself. You would have felt yourself obliged to be equally generous with her. She came up to me and she put her hand upon me—' 'Psha!' said Mrs Grantly. 'But she did, my dear; and then she said, "I promise you that I will not become your son's wife while people think that papa stole this money." What else could I do?'

'And is she pretty?'

'Very pretty; very beautiful.'

'And like a lady?'

'Quite like a lady. There is no mistake about that.'

'And she behaved well?'

'Admirably,' said the archdeacon, who was in a measure compelled to justify the generosity into which he had been betrayed by his feelings.

'Then she is a paragon,' said Mrs Grantly.

'I don't know what you may call a paragon, my dear. I say that she is a lady, and that she is extremely good-looking, and that she behaved very well. I cannot say less in her favour. I am sure you would not say less yourself, if you had been present.'

'She must be a wonderful young woman.'

'I don't know anything about her being wonderful.'

'She must be wonderful when she has succeeded both with the son and with the father.'

'I wish you had been there instead of me,' said the archdeacon, angrily. Mrs Grantly very probably wished so also, feeling that in that case a more serene mode of business would have been adopted. How keenly susceptible the archdeacon still was to the influences of feminine charms, no one knew better than Mrs Grantly, and whenever she became aware that he had been in this way seduced from the wisdom of his cooler judgment she always felt something akin to indignation against the seducer. As for her husband, she probably told herself at such moments that he was an old goose. 'If you had been there, and Henry with you, you would have made a great deal worse job of it than I have done,' said the archdeacon.

'I don't say you have made a bad job of it, my dear,' said Mrs Grantly. 'But it's past eight, and you must be terribly in want of your dinner. Had you not better go up and dress?'

In the evening the plan of the future campaign was arranged between them. The archdeacon would not write to his son at all. In passing through Barchester he had abandoned his idea of despatching a note from the hotel, feeling that such a note as would be required was not easily written in a hurry. Mrs Grantly would now write to her son, telling him that circumstances had changed, that it would be altogether unnecessary for him to sell his furniture, and begging him to come over and see his father without a day's delay. She wrote her letter that night, and read to the archdeacon all that she had written, – with the exception of the postscript: – 'You may be quite sure that there will be no unpleasantness with your father.' That was the postscript which was not communicated to the archdeacon.

On the third day after that Henry Grantly did come over to Plumstead. His mother in her letter to him had not explained how it had come to pass that the sale of his furniture would be unnecessary. His father had given him to understand distinctly that his income would be withdrawn from him unless he would express his intention of giving up Miss Crawley; and it had been admitted among them all that Cosby Lodge must be abandoned if this were done. He certainly would not give up Grace Crawley. Sooner than that, he would give up every stick in his possession, and go and live in New Zealand if it were necessary. Not only had Grace's conduct to him made him thus firm, but the natural bent of his own disposition had tended that way also. His father had attempted to dictate to him, and sooner than submit to that he would sell the coat off his back. Had his father confined his opposition to advice, and had Miss Crawley been less firm in her view of her duty, the major might have been less firm also. But things had so gone that he was determined to be fixed as granite. If others would not be moved from their resolves, neither would he. Such being the state of his mind, he could not understand why he was thus summoned to Plumstead. He had already written over to Pau about his house, and it was well that he should, at any rate, see his mother before he started. He was willing, therefore, to go to Plumstead, but he took no steps as to the withdrawal of those auctioneer's bills to which the archdeacon so strongly objected. When he drove into the rectory yard, his father was standing there before him. 'Henry,' he said, 'I am very glad to see you. I am very much obliged to you for coming.' Then Henry got out of his cart and shook hands with his father, and the archdeacon began to talk about the weather. 'Your mother has gone into Barchester to see your grandfather,' said the archdeacon. 'If you are not tired, we might as well take a walk. I want to go up as far as Flurry's cottage.' The major of course declared that he was not at all tired, and that he should be delighted of all things to go up and see old Flurry, and thus they started. Young Grantly had not even been into the house before he left the yard with his father. Of course, he was thinking of the coming sale at Cosby Lodge, and of his future life at Pau, and of his injured position in the world. There would be no longer any occasion for him to be solicitous as to the Plumstead foxes. Of course these things were in his mind; but he could not begin to speak of them till his father did so. 'I'm afraid your grandfather is not very strong,' said the archdeacon, shaking his head. 'I fear he won't be with us very long.'

'Is it so bad as that, sir?'

'Well, you know, he is an old man, Henry; and he was always somewhat old for his age. He will be eighty, if he lives two years longer, I think. But he'll never reach eighty; – never. You must go and see him before you go back home; you must indeed.' The major, of course, promised that he would see his grandfather, and the archdeacon told his son how nearly the old man had fallen in the passage between the cathedral and the deanery. In this way they had nearly made their way up to the gamekeeper's cottage without a word of reference to any subject that touched upon the matter of which each of them was of course thinking. Whether the major intended to remain at home or to live at Pau, the subject of Mr Harding's health was a natural topic for conversation between him and his father; but when his father stopped suddenly, and began to tell him how a fox had been trapped on Darvell's farm, – 'and of course it was a Plumstead fox, – there can be no doubt that Flurry is right about that;' – when the archdeacon spoke of this iniquity with much warmth, and told his son how he had at once written off to Mr Thorne of Ullathorne, and how Mr Thorne had declared that he didn't believe a word of it, and how Flurry had produced the pad of the fox, with the marks of the trap on the skin, – then the son began to feel that the ground was becoming very warm, and that he could not go on much longer without rushing into details about Grace Crawley. 'I've no more doubt that it was one of our foxes than that I stand here,' said the archdeacon.

'It doesn't matter where the fox was bred. It shouldn't have been trapped,' said the major.

'Of course not,' said the archdeacon, indignantly. I wonder whether he would have been so keen had a Romanist priest come into his parish, and turned one of his Protestants into a Papist?'

Then Flurry came up, and produced the identical pad out of his pocket. 'I don't suppose it was intended,' said the major, looking at the interesting relic with scrutinizing eyes. 'I suppose it was caught in a rabbit-trap, – eh, Flurry?'

'I don't see what right a man has with traps at all, when gentlemen is particular about their foxes,' said Flurry. 'Of course they'd call it rabbits.'

'I never liked that man on Darvell's farm,' said the archdeacon.

'Nor I either,' said Flurry. 'No farmer ought to be on that land who don't have a horse of his own. And if I war Squire Thorne, I wouldn't have no farmer there who didn't keep no horse. When a farmer has a horse of his own, and follies the hounds, there ain't no rabbit-traps; – never. How does that come about, Mr Henry? Rabbits! I know very well what rabbits is!'

Mr Henry shook his head, and turned away, and the archdeacon followed him. There was an hypocrisy about this pretended care for the foxes which displeased the major. He could not, of course, tell his father that the foxes were no longer anything to him; but yet he must make it understood that such was his conviction. His mother had written to him, saying that the sale of furniture need not take place. It might be all very well for his mother to say that, or for his father; but, after what had taken place, he could consent to remain in England on no other understanding than that his income should be made permanent to him. Such permanence must not be any longer dependent on his father's caprice. In these days he had come to be somewhat in love with poverty and Pau, and had been feeding on the luxury of his grievance. There is, perhaps, nothing so pleasant as the preparation for self-sacrifice. To give up Cosby Lodge and the foxes, to marry a penniless wife, and go and live at Pau on six or seven hundred a year, seemed just now to Major Grantly to be a fine thing, and he did not intend to abandon this fine thing without receiving a very clear reason for doing so. 'I can't quite understand Thorne,' said the archdeacon. 'He used to be so particular about the foxes, and I don't suppose that a country gentleman will change his ideas because he has given up hunting himself.'

'Mr Thorne never thought much of Flurry,' said Henry Grantly, with his mind intent upon Pau and his grievance.

'He might take my word at any rate,' said the archdeacon.

It was a known fact that the archdeacon's solicitude about the Plumstead covers was wholly on behalf of his son the major. The major himself knew this thoroughly, and felt that his father's present special anxiety was intended as a corroboration of the tidings conveyed in his mother's letter. Every word so uttered was meant to have reference to his son's future residence in the country. 'Father,' he said, turning round shortly, and standing before the archdeacon in the pathway, 'I think you are quite right about the covers. I feel sure that every gentleman who preserves a fox does good to the country. I am sorry that I shall not have a closer interest in the matter myself.'

'Why shouldn't you have a closer interest in it?' said the archdeacon.

'Because I shall be living abroad.'

'You got your mother's letter?'

'Yes; I got my mother's letter.'

'Did she not tell you that you can stay where you are?'

'Yes, she said so. But, to tell you the truth, sir, I do not like the risk of living beyond my assured income.'

'But if I justify it?'

'I do not wish to complain, sir, but you have made me understand that you can, and that in certain circumstances you will, at a moment, withdraw what you give me. Since this was said to me, I have felt myself to be unsafe in such a house as Cosby Lodge.'

The archdeacon did not know how to explain. He had intended that the real explanation should be given by Mrs Grantly, and had been anxious to return to his old relations with his son without any exact terms on his own part. But his son was, as he thought, awkward, and would drive him to some speech that was unnecessary. 'You need not be unsafe there at all,' he said, half angrily.

'I must be unsafe if I am not sure of my income.'

'Your income is not in any danger. But you had better speak to your mother about it. For myself, I think I may say that I have never yet behaved to any of you with harshness. A son should, at any rate, not be offended because a father thinks that he is entitled to some consideration for what he does.'

'There are some points on which a son cannot give way even to his father, sir.'

'You had better speak to your mother, Henry. She will explain to you what has taken place. Look at that plantation. You don't remember it, but every tree there was planted since you were born. I bought that farm from old Mr Thorne, when he was purchasing St Ewold's Downs, and it was the first bit of land I ever had of my own.'

'That is not in Plumstead, I think?'

'No: this is Plumstead, where we stand, but that's in Eiderdown.

The parishes run in and out here. I never bought any other land as cheap as I bought that.'

'And did old Thorne make a good purchase at St Ewold's?'

'Yes, I fancy he did. It gave him the whole of the parish, which was a great thing. It is astonishing how land has risen in value since that, and yet rents are not so very much higher. They who buy land now can't have above two-and-a-half for their money.'

'I wonder people are so fond of land,' said the major.

'It is a comfortable feeling to know that you stand on your own ground. Land is about the only thing that can't fly away. And then, you see, land gives so much more than the rent. It gives position and influence and political power, to say nothing about the game. We'll go back now. I daresay your mother will be at home by this time.'

The archdeacon was striving to teach a great lesson to his son when he thus spoke of the pleasure which a man feels when he stands upon his own ground. He was bidding his son to understand how great was the position of an heir to a landed property, and how small the position of a man depending on what Dr Grantly himself would have called a scratch income, – an income made up of a few odds and ends, a share or two in this company and a share or two in that, a slight venture in foreign stocks, a small mortgage and such like convenient but uninfluential driblets. A man, no doubt, may live at Pau on driblets; may pay his way and drink his bottle of cheap wine, and enjoy life after a fashion while reading Galignani* and looking at the mountains. But, – as it seemed to the archdeacon, – when there was a choice between this kind of thing, and fox-covers at Plumstead, and a seat among the magistrates of Barsetshire, and an establishment full of horses, beeves, swine, carriages, and hayricks, a man brought up as his son had been brought up ought not to be very long in choosing. It never entered into the archdeacon's mind that he was tempting his son; but Henry Grantly felt that he was having the good things of the world shown to him, and that he was being told that they should be his – for a consideration.

The major, in his present mood, looked at the matter from his own point of view, and determined that the consideration was too high. He was pledged not to give up Grace Crawley, and he would not yield on that point, though he might be tempted by all the fox-covers in Barsetshire. At this moment he did not know how far his father was prepared to yield, or how far it was expected that he should yield himself. He was told that he had to speak to his mother. He would speak to his mother, but, in the meantime, he could not bring himself to make a comfortable answer to his father's eloquent praise of landed property. He could not allow himself to be enthusiastic on the matter till he knew what was expected of him if he chose to submit to be made a British squire. At present Galignani and the mountains had their charms for him. There was, therefore, but little conversation between the father and the son as they walked back to the rectory.

Late that night the major heard the whole story from his mother. Gradually, and as though unintentionally, Mrs Grantly told him all she knew of the archdeacon's visit to Framley. Mrs Grantly was quite as anxious as was her husband to keep her son at home, and therefore she omitted in her story those little sneers against Grace which she herself had been tempted to make by the archdeacon's fervour in the girl's favour. The major said as little as was possible while he was being told of his father's adventure, and expressed neither anger nor satisfaction till he had been made thoroughly to understand that Grace had pledged herself not to marry him as long as any suspicion should rest upon her father's name.

'Your father is quite satisfied with her,' said Mrs Grantly. 'He thinks that she is behaving very well.'

'My father had no right to exact such a pledge.'

'But she made it of her own accord. She was the first to speak about Mr Crawley's supposed guilt. Your father never mentioned it.'

'He must have led to it; and I think he had no right to do so. He had no right to go to her at all.'

'Now don't be foolish, Henry.'

'I don't see that I am foolish.'

'Yes, you are. A man is foolish if he won't take what he wants without asking exactly how he is to come by it. That your father should be anxious is the most natural thing in the world. You know how high he has always held his own head, and how much he thinks about the characters and position of clergymen. It is not surprising that he should dislike the idea of such a marriage.'

'Grace Crawley would disgrace no family,' said the lover.

'That's all very well for you to say, and I'll take your word that it is so; – that is as far as the young lady goes herself. And there's your father almost as much in love with her as you are. I don't know what you would have?'

'I would be left alone.'

'But what harm has been done you? From what you yourself have told me, I know that Miss Crawley has said the same thing to you that she has said to her father. You can't but admire her for the feeling.'

'I admire her for everything.'

'Very well. We don't say anything against that.'

'And I don't mean to give her up.'

'Very well again. Let us hope that Mr Crawley will be acquitted, and then all will be right. Your father never goes back from his promise. He is always better than his word. You'll find that if Mr Crawley is acquitted, or if he escapes in any way, your father will only be happy of an excuse to make much of the young lady. You should not be hard on him, Henry. Don't you see that it is his one great desire to keep you near to him? The sight of those odious bills nearly broke his heart.'

'Then why did he threaten me?'

'Henry, you are obstinate.'

'I am not obstinate, mother.'

'Yes, you are. You remember nothing, and you forget nothing. You expect everything to be made smooth for you, and will do nothing towards making things smooth for anybody else. You ought to promise to give up the sale. If the worst came to the worst, your father would not let you suffer in pocket for yielding to him in so much.

'If the worst comes to the worst, I wish to take nothing from my father.'

'You won't put off the sale, then?'

The son paused a moment before he answered his mother, thinking over all the circumstances of his position. 'I cannot do so as long as I am subject to my father's threat,' he said at last. 'What took place between my father and Miss Crawley can go for nothing with me. He has told me that his allowance to me is to be withdrawn. Let him tell me that he has reconsidered the matter.'

'But he has not withdrawn it. The last quarter was paid to your account only the other day. He does not mean to withdraw it.'

'Let him tell me so; let him tell me that my power of living at Cosby Lodge does not depend on my marriage, – that my income will be continued to me whether I marry or no, and I'll arrange matters with the auctioneer to-morrow. You can't suppose that I should prefer to live in France.'

'Henry, you are too hard on your father.'

'I think, mother, he has been too hard upon me.'

'It is you that are to blame now. I tell you plainly that that is my opinion. If evil comes of it, it will be your own fault.'

'If evil come of it I must bear it.'

'A son ought to give up something to his father; – especially to a father so indulgent as yours.'

But it was of no use. And Mrs Grantly when she went to her bed could only lament in her own mind over what, in discussing the matter afterwards with her sister, she called the cross-grainedness of men. 'They are as like each other as two peas,' she said, 'and though each of them wished to be generous, neither of them would condescend to be just.' Early on the following morning there was, no doubt, much said on the subject between the archdeacon and his wife before they met their son at breakfast; but neither at breakfast nor afterwards was there a word said between the father and son that had the slightest reference to the subject in dispute between them. The archdeacon made no more speeches in favour of land, nor did he revert to the foxes. He was very civil to his son; — too civil by half, as Mrs Grantly continued to say to herself. And then the major drove himself away in his cart, going through Barchester, so that he might see his grandfather. When he wished his father good-by, the archdeacon shook hands with him, and said something about the chance of rain. Had he not better take the big umbrella? The major thanked him courteously, and said that he did not think it would rain. Then he was gone. 'Upon his own head be it,' said the archdeacon when his son's step was heard in the passage leading to the back-yard. Then Mrs Grantly got up quietly and followed her son. She found him settling himself in his dog-cart, while the servant who was to accompany him was still at the horse's head. She went up close to him, and, standing by the wheel of the gig, whispered a word or two into his ear. 'If you love me, Henry, you will postpone the sale. Do it for my sake.' There came across his face a look of great pain, but he answered her not a word.

The archdeacon was walking about the room striking one hand open with the other closed, clearly in a tumult of anger, when his wife returned to him. 'I have done all that I can,' he said, — 'all that I can; more, indeed, than was becoming for me. Upon his own head be it. Upon his own head be it!'

'What is it that you fear?' she asked.

'I fear nothing. But if he chooses to sell his things at Cosby Lodge he must abide the consequences. They shall not be replaced with my money.'

'What will it matter if he does sell them?'

'Matter! Do you think there is a single person in the county who will not know that his doing so is a sign that he has quarrelled with me?'

'But he has not quarrelled with you.'

'I can tell you then, that in that case I shall have quarrelled with him! I have not been a hard father, but there are some things which a man cannot bear. Of course you will take his part.'

'I am taking no part. I only want to see peace between you.'

'Peace! – yes; peace indeed. I am to yield in everything. I am to be nobody. Look here; – as sure as ever an auctioneer's hammer is raised at Cosby Lodge, I will alter the settlement of the property. Every acre shall belong to Charles. There is my word for it.' The poor woman had nothing more to say; – nothing more to say at that moment. She thought that at the present conjuncture her husband was less in the wrong than her son, but she could not tell him so lest she should strengthen him in his wrath.

Henry Grantly found his grandfather in bed, with Posy seated on the bed beside him. 'My father told me that you were not quite well, and I thought that I would look in,' said the major.

'Thank you, my dear; – it is very good of you. There is not much the matter with me, but I am not quite so strong as I was once.' And the old man smiled as he held his grandson's hand.

'And how is cousin Posy?' said the major.

'Posy is quite well; – isn't she, my darling?' said the old man.

'Grandpa doesn't go to the cathedral now,' said Posy; 'so I come in to talk to him. Don't I, grandpa?'

'And to play cat's-cradle; – only we have not had any cat's-cradle this morning, – have we, Posy?'

'Mrs Baxter told me not to play this morning, because it's cold for grandpa to sit up in bed,' said Posy.

When the major had been there about twenty minutes he was preparing to take his leave, – but Mr Harding, bidding Posy to go out of the room, told his grandson that he had a word to say to him. 'I don't like to interfere, Henry,' he said, 'but I am afraid that things are not quite smooth at Plumstead.'

'There is nothing wrong between me and my mother,' said the major.

'God forbid that there should be; but, my dear boy, don't let there be anything wrong between you and your father. He is a good man, and the time will come when you will be proud of his memory.'

'I am proud of him now.'

'Then be gentle with him, – and submit yourself. I am an old man now, – very fast going away from all those I love here. But I am happy in leaving my children because they have ever been gentle to me and kind. If I am permitted to remember them whither I am going, my thoughts of them will all be pleasant. Should it not be much to them that they have made my death-bed happy?'

The major could not but tell himself that Mr Harding had been a man easy to please, easy to satisfy, and, in that respect, very different from his father. But of course he said nothing of this. 'I will do my best,' he replied.

'Do, my boy. Honour thy father, – that thy days may be long in the land.'*

It seemed to the major as he drove away from Barchester that everybody was against him; and yet he was sure that he himself was right. He could not give up Grace Crawley; and unless he were to do so he could not live at Cosby Lodge.

CHAPTER 59

A lady presents her compliments to Miss L. D.

One morning, while Lily Dale was staying with Mrs Thorne in London, there was brought up to her room, as she was dressing for dinner, a letter which the postman had just left for her. The address was written with a feminine hand, and Lily was at once aware that she did not know the writing. The angles were very acute, and the lines were very straight, and the vowels looked to be cruel and false, with their sharp points and their open eyes. Lily at once knew that it was the performance of a woman who had been taught to write at school, and not at home, and she became prejudiced against the writer before she opened the letter. When she had opened the letter and read it, her feelings towards the writer were not of a kindly nature. It was as follows : —

'A lady presents her compliments to Miss L. D., and earnestly implores Miss L. D. to give her an answer to the following question. Is Miss L. D. engaged to marry Mr J. E. ? The lady in question pledges herself not to interfere with Miss L. D. in any way, should the answer be in the affirmative. The lady earnestly requests that a reply to this question may be sent to M. D., Post-office, 455 Edgeware Road. In order that L. D. may not doubt that M. D. has an interest in J. E., M. D. encloses the last note she received from him before he started for the Continent.' Then there was a scrap, which Lily well knew to be in the handwriting of John Eames, and the scrap was as follows : — 'Dearest M. — Punctually at 8.30. Ever and always your unalterable J. E.' Lily, as she read this, did not comprehend that John's note to M. D. had been in itself a joke.

Lily Dale had heard of anonymous letters before, but had never received one, or even seen one. Now that she had one in her hand, it seemed to her that there could be nothing more abominable than the writing of such a letter. She let it drop from her, as though the receiving, and opening, and reading it had been a stain to her. As it lay on the ground at her feet, she trod upon it. Of what sort could a woman be who would write such a letter as that? Answer it! Of course she would not answer it. It never occurred to her for a moment that it could become her to answer it. Had she been at home or with her mother, she would have called her mother to her, and Mrs Dale would have taken it from the ground, and have read it, and then destroyed it. As it was, she must pick it up herself. She did so, and declared to herself that there should be an end to it. It might be right that somebody should see it, and therefore she would show it to Emily Dunstable. After that it should be destroyed.

Of course the letter could have no effect upon her. So she told herself. But it did have a very strong effect, and probably the exact effect which the writer had intended that it should have. J. E. was, of course, John Eames. There was no doubt about that. What a fool the writer must have been to talk of L. D. in the letter, when the outside cover was plainly addressed to Miss Lilian Dale! But there are some people for whom the pretended mystery of initial letters has a charm, and who love the darkness of anonymous letters. As Lily thought of this, she stamped on the letter again. Who was the M. D. to whom she was required to send an answer – with whom John Eames corresponded in the most affectionate terms? She had resolved that she would not even ask herself a question about M. D., and yet she could not divert her mind from the inquiry. It was, at any rate, a fact that there must be some woman designated by the letters, – some woman who had, at any rate, chosen to call herself M. D. And John Eames had called her M. There must, at any rate, be such a woman. This female, be she who she might, had thought it worth her while to make this inquiry about John Eames, and had manifestly learned something of Lily's own history. And the woman had pledged herself not to interfere with John Eames, if L. D. would only condescend to say that she was engaged to him! As Lily thought of the proposition, she trod upon the letter for the third time. Then she picked it up, and having no place of custody under lock and key ready to her hand, she put it in her pocket.

At night, before she went to bed, she showed the letter to Emily Dunstable. 'Is it not surprising that any woman could bring herself to write such a letter?' said Lily.

But Miss Dunstable hardly saw it in the same light. 'If anybody were to write me such a letter about Bernard,' said she, 'I should show it to him as a good joke.'

'That would be very different. You and Bernard, of course, understand each other.'

'And so will you and Mr Eames – some day, I hope.'

'Never more than we do now, dear. The thing that annoys me is that such a woman as that should have even heard my name at all.'

'As long as people have got ears and tongues, people will hear other people's names.'

Lily paused a moment, and then spoke again, asking another question. 'I suppose this woman does know him? She must know him, because he has written to her.'

'She knows something about him, no doubt, and has some reason for wishing that you should quarrel with him. If I were you, I should take care not to gratify her. As for Mr Eames's note, it is a joke.'

'It is nothing to me,' said Lily.

'I suppose,' continued Emily, 'that most gentlemen become acquainted with some people that they would not wish all their friends to know that they knew. They go about so much more than we do, and meet people of all sorts.'

'No gentleman should become intimately acquainted with a woman who could write such a letter as that,' said Lily. And as she spoke she remembered a certain episode to John Eames's early life, which had reached her from a source which she had not doubted, and which had given her pain and offended her. She had believed that John Eames had in that case behaved cruelly to a young woman, and had thought that her offence had come simply from that feeling. 'But of course it is nothing to me,' she said. 'Mr Eames can choose his friends as he likes. I only wish that my name might not be mentioned to them.'

'It is not from him that she has heard it.'

'Perhaps not. As I said before, of course it does not signify; only there is something very disagreeable in the whole thing. The idea is so hateful! Of course this woman means me to understand that she considers herself to have a claim upon Mr Eames, and that I stand in her way.'

'And why should you not stand in her way?'

'I will stand in nobody's way. Mr Eames has a right to give his hand to any one that he pleases. I, at any rate, can have no cause of offence against him. The only thing is that I do wish that my name could be left alone.' Lily, when she was in her own room again, did destroy the letter; but before she did so she read it again, and it became so indelibly impressed on her memory that she could not forget even the words of it. The lady who wrote had pledged herself, under certain conditions, 'not to interfere with Miss L. D.' 'Interfere with me!' Lily said to herself; 'nobody can interfere with me; nobody has power to do so.' As she turned it over in her mind, her heart became hard against John Eames. No woman would have troubled herself to write such a letter without some cause for the writing. That the writer was vulgar, false, and unfeminine, Lily thought that she could perceive from the letter itself; but no doubt the woman knew John Eames had some interest in the question of his marriage, and was entitled to some answer to her question; — only was not entitled to such answer from Lily Dale.

For some weeks past now, up to the hour at which this anonymous letter had reached her hands, Lily's heart had been growing soft and still softer towards John Eames; and now again it had become hardened. I think that the appearance of Adolphus Crosbie in the park, that momentary vision of the real man by which the divinity of the imaginary Apollo had been dashed to the ground, had done a service to the cause of the other lover; of the lover who had never been a god, but who of late years had at any rate grown into the full dimensions of a man. Unfortunately for the latter, he had commenced his love-making when he was but little more than a boy. Lily, as she had thought of the two together, in the days of her solitude, after she had been deserted by Crosbie, had ever pictured to herself the lover whom she had preferred as having something godlike in his favour, as being far the superior in wit, in manner, in acquirement, and in personal advantage. There had been good nature and true hearty love on the side of the other man; but circumstances had seemed to show that his good-nature was equal to all, and that he was able to share even his hearty love among two or three. A man of such a character, known by a girl from his boyhood as John Eames had been known by Lily Dale, was likely to find more favour as a friend than as a lover. So it had been between John Eames and Lily. While the untrue memory of what Crosbie was, or ever had been, was present to her, she could hardly bring herself to accept in her mind the idea of a lover who was less noble in his manhood than the false picture which that untrue memory was ever painting for her. Then had come before her eyes the actual man; and though he had been seen but for a moment, the false image had been broken into shivers. Lily had discovered that she had been deceived, and that her forgiveness had been asked, not by a god, but by an ordinary human being. As regarded the ungodlike man himself, this could make no difference. Having thought upon the matter deeply, she had resolved that she would not marry Mr Crosbie, and had pledged herself to that effect to friends who never could have brought themselves to feel affection for him, even had she married him. But the shattering of the false image might have done John Eames a good turn. Lily knew that she had at any rate full permission from all her friends to throw in her lot with his, — if she could persuade herself to do so. Mother, uncle, sister, brother-in-law, cousin, — and now this new cousin's bride that was to be, — together with Lady Julia and a whole crowd of

Allington and Guestwick friends, were in favour of such a marriage. There had been nothing against it but the fact that the other man had been dearer to her; and that other fact that poor Johnny lacked something, – something of earnestness, something of manliness, something of that Phoebus divinity with which Crosbie had contrived to invest his own image. But, as I have said above, John had gradually grown, if not into divinity, at least into manliness; and the shattering of the false image had done him yeoman's service. Now had come this accursed letter, and Lily, despite herself, despite her better judgment, could not sweep it away from her mind and make the letter as nothing to her. M. D. had promised not to interfere with her! There was no room for such interference, no possibility that such interference should take place. She hoped earnestly, – so she told herself, – that her old friend John Eames might have nothing to do with a woman so impudent and vulgar as must be this M. D.; but except as regarded old friendship, M. D. and John Eames, apart or together, could be as nothing to her. Therefore, I say that the letter had had the effect which the writer of it had desired.

All London was new to Lily Dale, and Mrs Thorne was very anxious to show her everything that could be seen. She was to return to Allington before the flowers of May would have come, and the crowd and the glare and the fashion and the art of the Academy's great exhibition must therefore remain unknown to her; but she was taken to see many pictures, and among others she was taken to see the pictures belonging to a certain nobleman who, with that munificence which is so amply enjoyed and so little recognized in England, keeps open house for the world to see the treasures which the wealth of his family has collected. The necessary order was procured, and on a certain brilliant April afternoon Mrs Thorne and her party found themselves in this nobleman's drawing-room. Lily was with her, of course, and Emily Dunstable was there, and Bernard Dale, and Mrs Thorne's dear friend Mrs Harold Smith, and Mrs Thorne's constant and useful attendant, Siph Dunn. They had nearly completed their delightful but wearying task of gazing at pictures, and Mrs Harold Smith had declared that she would not look at another painting till the exhibition was open; three of the ladies were seated in the drawing-room, and Siph Dunn was standing before them, lecturing about art as though he had been brought up on the ancient masters; Emily and Bernard were lingering behind, and the others were simply delaying their departure till the truant lovers should have caught them. At this moment two gentlemen entered the room from the gallery, and the two gentlemen were Fowler Pratt and Adolphus Crosbie.

All the party except Mrs Thorne knew Crosbie personally, and all of them except Mrs Harold Smith knew something of the story of what had occurred between Crosbie and Lily. Siph Dunn had learned it all since the meeting in the Park, having nearly learned it all from what he had seen there with his eyes. But Mrs Thorne, who knew Lily's story, did not know Crosbie's appearance. But there was his friend Fowler Pratt, who, as will be remembered, had dined with her but the other day; and she, with that outspoken and somewhat loud impulse which was natural to her, addressed him at once across the room, calling him by name. Had she not done so, the two men might probably have escaped through the room, in which case they would have met Bernard Dale and Emily Dunstable in the doorway. Fowler Pratt would have endeavoured so to escape, and to carry Crosbie with him, as he was quite alive to the expedience of saving Lily from such a meeting. But, as things turned out, escape from Mrs Thorne was impossible.

'There's Fowler Pratt,' she had said when they first entered, quite loud enough for Fowler Pratt to hear her. 'Mr Pratt, come here. How d'ye do? You dined with me last Tuesday, and you've never been to call.'

'I never recognize that obligation till after the middle of May,'* said Mr Pratt, shaking hands with Mrs Thorne and Mrs Smith, and bowing to Miss Dale.

'I don't see the justice of that at all,' said Mrs Thorne. 'It seems to me that a good dinner is as much entitled to a morsel of pasteboard in April as at any other time. You won't have another till you have called, – unless you're specially wanted.'

Crosbie would have gone on, but that in his attempt to do so he passed close by the chair on which Mrs Harold Smith was sitting, and that he was accosted by her. 'Mr Crosbie,' she said, 'I haven't seen you for an age. Has it come to pass that you have buried yourself entirely?' He did not know how to extricate himself so as to move on at once. He paused, and hesitated, and then stopped, and made an attempt to talk to Mrs Smith as though he were at his ease. The attempt was anything but successful; but having once stopped, he did not know how to put himself in motion again, so that he might escape. At this moment Bernard Dale and Emily Dunstable came up and joined the group; but neither of them had discovered who Crosbie was till they were close upon him.

Lily was seated between Mrs Thorne and Mrs Smith, and Siph Dunn had been standing immediately opposite to them. Fowler Pratt, who had been drawn into the circle against his will, was now standing close to Dunn, almost between him and Lily, – and Crosbie was standing within two yards of Lily, on the other side of

Dunn. Emily and Bernard had gone behind Pratt and Crosbie to Mrs Thorne's side before they had recognized the two men; – and in this way Lily was completely surrounded. Mrs Thorne, who, in spite of her eager, impetuous ways, was as thoughtful of others as any woman could be, as soon as she heard Crosbie's name understood it all, and knew that it would be well that she should withdraw Lily from her plight. Crosbie, in his attempt to talk to Mrs Smith, had smiled and simpered, – and had then felt that to smile and simper before Lily Dale, with a pretended indifference to her presence, was false on his part, and would seem to be mean. He would have avoided Lily for both their sakes, had it been possible; but it was no longer possible, and he could not keep his eyes from her face. Hardly knowing what he did, he bowed to her, lifted his hat, and uttered some word of greeting.

Lily, from the moment that she had perceived his presence, had looked straight before her, with something almost of fierceness in her eyes. Both Pratt and Siph Dunn had observed her narrowly. It had seemed as though Crosbie had been altogether outside the ken of her eyes, or the notice of her ears, and yet she had seen every motion of his body, and had heard every word which had fallen from his lips. Now, when he saluted her, she turned her face full upon him, and bowed to him. Then she rose from her seat, and made her way, between Siph Dunn and Pratt, out of the circle. The blood had mounted to her face and suffused it all, and her whole manner was such that it could escape the observation of none who stood there. Even Mrs Harold Smith had seen it, and had read the story. As soon as she was on her feet, Bernard had dropped Emily's hand, and offered his arm to his cousin. 'Lily,' he had said out loud, 'you had better let me take you away. It is a misfortune that you have been subjected to the insult of such a greeting.' Bernard and Crosbie had been early friends, and Bernard had been the unfortunate means of bringing Crosbie and Lily together. Up to this day, Bernard had never had his revenge for the ill-treatment which his cousin had received. Some morsel of that revenge came to him now. Lily almost hated her cousin for what he said; but she took his arm, and walked with him from the room. It must be acknowledged in excuse for Bernard Dale, and as an apology for the apparent indiscretion of his words, that all the circumstances of the meeting had become apparent to every one there. The misfortune of the encounter had become too plain to admit of its being hidden under any of the ordinary veils of society. Crosbie's salutation had been made before the eyes of them all, and in the midst of absolute silence, and Lily had risen with so queen-like a demeanour, and had moved with so stately a step, that it was impossible that any one concerned should pretend to ignore the facts of the scene that had occurred. Crosbie was still standing close to Mrs Harold Smith, Mrs Thorne had risen from her seat, and the words which Bernard Dale had uttered were still sounding in the ears of them all. 'Shall I see after the carriage?' said Siph Dunn. 'Do,' said Mrs Thorne; 'or, stay a moment; the carriage will of course be there, and we will go together. Good-morning, Mr Pratt. I expect that, at any rate, you will send me your card by post.' Then they all passed on, and Crosbie and Fowler Pratt were left among the pictures.

'I think you will agree with me now that you had better give her up,' said Fowler Pratt.

'I will never give her up,' said Crosbie, 'till I shall hear that she has married some one else.'

'You may take my word for it, that she will never marry you after what has just now occurred.'

'Very likely not; but still the attempt, even the idea of the attempt, will be a comfort to me. I shall be endeavouring to do that which I ought to have done.'

'What you have got to think of, I should suppose, is her comfort, – not your own.'

Crosbie stood for a while silent, looking at a portrait which was hung just within the doorway of a smaller room into which they had passed, as though his attention were entirely riveted by the picture. But he was thinking of the picture not at all, and did not even know what kind of painting was on the canvas before him.

'Pratt,' he said at last, 'you are always hard to me.'

'I will say nothing more to you on the subject, if you wish me to be silent.'

'I do wish you to be silent about that.'

'That shall be enough,' said Pratt.

'You do not quite understand me. You do not know how thoroughly I have repented of the evil that I have done, or how far I would go to make retribution, if retribution were possible!'

Fowler Pratt, having been told to hold his tongue as regarded that subject, made no reply to this, and began to talk about the pictures.

Lily, leaning on her cousin's arm, was out in the courtyard in front of the house before Mrs Thorne or Siph Dunn. It was but for a minute, but still there was a minute in which Bernard felt that he ought to say a word to her.

'I hope you are not angry with me, Lily, for having spoken.'

'I wish, of course, that you had not spoken; but I am not angry. I have no right to be angry. I made the misfortune for myself. Do not say anything more about it, dear Bernard; – that is all.'

They had walked to the picture-gallery; but, by agreement, two carriages had come to take them away, – Mrs Thorne's and Mrs Harold Smith's. Mrs Thorne easily managed to send Emily Dunstable and Bernard away with her friend, and to tell Siph Dunn that he must manage for himself. In this way it was contrived that no one but Mrs Thorne should be with Lily Dale.

'My dear,' said Mrs Thorne, 'it seemed to me that you were a little put out, and so I thought it best to send them all away.'

'It was very kind.'

'He ought to have passed on and not to have stood an instant when he saw you,' said Mrs Thorne, with indignation. 'There are moments when it is a man's duty simply to vanish, to melt into the air, or to sink into the ground, – in which he is bound to overcome the difficulties of such sudden self-removal, or must ever after be accounted poor and mean.'

'I did not want him to vanish; – if only he had not spoken to me.'

'He should have vanished. A man is sometimes bound in honour to do so, even when he himself has done nothing wrong; – when the sin has been all with the woman. Her femininity has still a right to expect that so much shall be done in its behalf. But when the sin has been all his own, as it was in this case, – and such damning sin too,—'

'Pray do not go on, Mrs Thorne.'

'He ought to go out and hang himself simply for having allowed himself to be seen. I thought Bernard behaved very well, and I shall tell him so.'

'I wish you could manage to forget it all, and say no word more about it.'

'I won't trouble you with it, my dear; I will promise you that. But, Lily, I can hardly understand you. This man who must have been and must ever be a brute,—'

'Mrs Thorne, you promised me this instant that you would not talk of him.'

'After this I will not; but you must let me have my way now for one moment. I have so often longed to speak to you, but have not done so from fear of offending you. Now the matter has come up by chance, and it was impossible that what has occurred should pass by without a word. I cannot conceive why the memory of that bad man should be allowed to destroy your whole life.'

'My life is not destroyed. My life is anything but destroyed. It is a very happy life.'

'But, my dear, if all that I hear is true, there is a most estimable young man, whom everybody likes, and particularly all your own family, and whom you like very much yourself; and you will have nothing to say to him, though his constancy is like the constancy of an old Paladin, – and all because of this wretch who just now came in your way.'

'Mrs Thorne, it is impossible to explain it all.'

'I do not want you to explain it all. Of course I would not ask any young woman to marry a man whom she did not love. Such marriages are abominable to me. But I think that a young woman ought to get married if the thing fairly comes in her way, and if her friends approve, and if she is fond of the man who is fond of her. It may be that some memory of what has gone before is allowed to stand in your way, and that it should not be so allowed. It sometimes happens that a morbid sentiment will destroy a life. Excuse me, then, Lily, if I say too much to you in my hope that you may not suffer after this fashion.'

'I know how kind you are, Mrs Thorne.'

'Here we are at home, and perhaps you would like to go in. I have some calls which I must make.' Then the conversation was ended, and Lily was alone.

As if she had not thought of it all before! As if there was anything new in this counsel which Mrs Thorne had given her! She had received the same advice from her mother, from her sister, from her uncle, and from Lady Julia, till she was sick of it. How had it come to pass that matters which with others are so private, should with her have become the public property of so large a circle? Any other girl would receive advice on such a subject from her mother alone, and there the secret would rest. But her secret had been published, as it were, by the town-crier in the High Street! Everybody knew that she had been jilted by Adolphus Crosbie, and that it was intended that she should be consoled by John Eames. And people seemed to think that they had a right to rebuke her if she expressed an unwillingness to carry out this intention which the public had so kindly arranged for her.

Morbid sentiment! Why should she be accused of morbid senti-ment because she was unable to transfer her affections to the man who had been fixed on as her future husband by the large circle of acquaintance who had interested themselves in her affairs? There was nothing morbid in either her desires or her regrets. So she assured herself, with something very like anger at the accusation made against her. She had been contented, and was contented, to live at home as her mother lived, asking for no excitement beyond that given by the daily routine of her duties. There could be nothing morbid in that. She would go back to Allington as soon as might be, and have done with this London life, which only made her wretched. This seeing of Crosbie had been terrible to her. She did not tell herself that his image had been shattered. Her idea was that all her misery had come from the untowardness of the meeting. But there was the fact that she had seen the man and heard his voice, and that the seeing him and hearing him had made her miserable. She certainly desired that it might never be her lot either to see him or to hear him again.

And as for John Eames, – in those bitter moments of her reflection she almost wished the same in regard to him. If he would only cease to be her lover, he might be very well; but he was not very well to her as long as his pretensions were dinned into her ear by everybody who knew her. And then she told herself that John would have had a better chance if he had been content to plead for himself. In this, I think, she was hard upon her lover. He had pleaded for himself as well as he knew how, and as often as the occasion had been given to him. It had hardly been his fault that his case had been taken in hand by other advocates. He had given no commission to Mrs Thorne to plead for him.

Poor Johnny. He had stood in much better favour before the lady had presented her compliments to Miss L. D. It was that odious letter, and the thoughts which it had forced upon Lily's mind, which were now most inimical to his interests. Whether Lily loved him or not, she did not love him well enough not to be jealous of him. Had any such letter reached her respecting Crosbie in the happy days of her young love, she would simply have laughed at it. It would have been nothing to her. But now she was sore and unhappy, and any trifle was powerful enough to irritate her. 'Is Miss L. D. engaged to marry Mr J. E ?' 'No,' said Lily, out loud. 'Lily Dale is not engaged to marry John Eames, and never will be so engaged.' She was almost tempted to sit down and write the required answer to Miss M. D. Though the letter had been destroyed, she well remembered the number of the post-office in the Edgeware Road. Poor John Eames !

That evening she told Emily Dunstable that she thought she would like to return to Allington before the day that had been appointed for her. 'But why,' said Emily, 'should you be worse than your word ?'

'I daresay it will seem silly, but the fact is I am homesick. I'm not accustomed to be away from mamma for so long.'

'I hope it is not what occurred to-day at the picture-gallery.'

'I won't deny that it is that in part.'

'That was a strange accident, you know, that might never occur again.'

'It has occurred twice already, Emily.'

'I don't call the affair in the Park anything. Anybody may see anybody else in the Park, of course. He was not brought so near you that he could annoy you there. You ought certainly to wait till Mr Eames has come back from Italy.'

Then Lily declared that she must and would go back to Allington on the next Monday, and she actually did write a letter to her mother that night to say that such was her intention. But on the morrow her heart was less sore, and the letter was not sent.

CHAPTER 60

The end of Jael and Sisera

There was to be one more sitting for the picture, as the reader will remember, and the day for that sitting had arrived. Conway Dalrymple had in the meantime called at Mrs Van Siever's house, hoping that he might be able to see Clara, and make his offer to her there. But he had failed in his attempt to reach her. He had found it impossible to say all that he had to say in the painting-room, during the very short intervals which Mrs Broughton left to him. A man should be allowed to be alone more than fifteen minutes with a young lady on the occasion in which he offers to her his hand and his heart; but hitherto he had never had more than fifteen minutes at his command; and then there had been the turban! He had also in the meantime called on Mrs Broughton, with the intention of explaining to her that if she really intended to favour his views in respect to Miss Van Siever, she ought to give him a little more liberty for expressing himself. On this occasion he had seen his friend, but had not been able to go as minutely as he had wished into the matter that was so important to himself. Mrs Broughton had found it necessary during this meeting to talk almost exclusively about herself and her own affairs. 'Conway,' she had said, directly she saw him, 'I am so glad you have come. I think I should have gone mad if I had not seen some one who cares for me.' This was early in the morning, not much after eleven, and Mrs Broughton, hearing first his knock at the door, and then his voice, had met him in the hall and taken him into the dining-room.

'Is anything the matter?' he asked.

'Oh, Conway!'

'What is it? Has anything gone wrong with Dobbs?'

'Everything has gone wrong with him. He is ruined.'

'Heaven and earth! What do you mean?'

'Simply what I say. But you must not speak a word of it. I do not know it from himself.'

'How do you know it?'

'Wait a moment. Sit down there, will you? – and I will sit by you. No, Conway; do not take my hand. It is not right. There; – so. Yesterday Mrs Van Siever was here. I need not tell you all that she said to me, even if I could. She was very harsh and cruel, saying all manner of things about Dobbs. How can I help it, if he drinks? I have not encouraged him. And as for expensive living, I have been as ignorant as a child. I have never asked for anything. When we were married somebody told me how much we should have to spend. It was either two thousand, or three thousand, or four thousand, or something like that. You know, Conway, how ignorant I am about money; – that I am like a child. Is it not true?' She waited for an answer and Dalrymple was obliged to acknowledge that it was true. And yet he had known the times in which his dear friend had been very sharp in her memory with reference to a few pounds. 'And now she says that Dobbs owes her money which he cannot pay her, and that everything must be sold. She says that Musselboro must have the business, and that Dobbs must shift for himself elsewhere.'

'Do you believe that she has the power to decide that things shall go this way or that, – as she pleases?'

'How am I to know? She says so, and she says it is because he drinks. He does drink. That at least is true; but how can I help it? Oh, Conway, what am I to do? Dobbs did not come home at all last night, but sent for his things, – saying that he must stay in the City. What am I to do if they come and take the house, and sell the furniture, and turn me out into the street?' Then the poor creature began to cry in earnest, and Dalrymple had to console her as best he might. 'How I wish I had known you first,' she said. To this Dalrymple was able to make no direct answer. He was wise enough to know that a direct answer might possibly lead him into terrible trouble. He was by no means anxious to find himself 'protecting' Mrs Dobbs Broughton from the ruin which her husband had brought upon her.

Before he left her she had told him a long story, partly of matters of which he had known something before, and partly made up of that which she had heard from the old woman. It was settled, Mrs Broughton said, that Mr Musselboro was to marry Clara Van Siever. But it appeared, as far as Dalrymple could learn, that this was a settlement made simply between Mrs Van Siever and Musselboro. Clara, as he thought, was not a girl likely to fall into such a settlement without having an opinion of her own. Musselboro was to have the business, and Dobbs Broughton was to be 'sold up,' and then look for employment in the City. From her husband the wife had not heard a word on this matter, and the above story was simply what had been told to Mrs Broughton by Mrs Van Siever. 'For myself it seems that there can be but one fate,' said Mrs Broughton. Dalrymple, in his tenderest voice, asked what that one fate must be. 'Never mind,' said Mrs Broughton. 'There are some things which one cannot tell even to such a friend as you.' He was sitting near her and had all but got his arm behind her waist. He was, however, able to be prudent. 'Maria,' he said, getting up on his feet, 'if it should really come about that you should want anything, you will send to me. You will promise me that, at any rate?' She rubbed a tear from her eye and said that she did not know. 'There are moments in which a man must speak plainly,' said Conway Dalrymple; – 'in which it would be unmanly not to do so, however prosaic it may seem. I need hardly tell you that my purse shall be yours if you want it.' But just at that moment she did not want his purse, nor must it be supposed that she wanted to run away with him and to leave her husband to fight the battle alone with Mrs Van Siever. The truth was that she did not know what she wanted, over and beyond an assurance from Conway Dalrymple that she was the most ill-used, the most interesting, and the most beautiful woman ever heard of, either in history or romance. Had he proposed to her to pack up a bundle and go off with him in a cab to the London, Chatham, and Dover railway station, en route for Boulogne, I do not for a moment think that she would have packed up her bundle. She would have received intense gratification from the offer, – so much so that she would have been almost consoled for her husband's ruin; but she would have scolded her lover, and would have explained to him the great iniquity of which he was guilty.

It was clear to him that at this present time he could not make any special terms with her as to Clara Van Siever. At such a moment as this he could hardly ask her to keep out of the way, in order that he might have his opportunity. But when he suggested that probably it might be better, in the present emergency, to give up the idea of any further sitting in her room, and proposed to send for his canvas, colour-box, and easel, she told him that, as far as she was concerned, he was welcome to have that one other sitting for which they had all bargained. 'You had better come to-morrow, as we had agreed,' she said; 'and unless I shall have been turned out into the street by the creditors, you may have the room as you did before. And you must remember, Conway, that though Mrs Van says that Musselboro is to have Clara, it doesn't follow that Clara should give way.' When we consider everything, we must acknowledge that this was, at any rate, good-natured. Then there was a tender parting, with many tears, and Conway Dalrymple escaped from the house.

He did not for a moment doubt the truth of the story which Mrs Broughton had told, as far, at least, as it referred to the ruin of Dobbs Broughton. He had heard something of this before, and for some weeks had expected that a crash was coming. Broughton's rise had been very sudden, and Dalrymple had never regarded his friend as firmly placed in the commercial world. Dobbs was one of those men who seem born to surprise the world by a spurt of prosperity, and might, perhaps, have had a second spurt, or even a third, could he have kept himself from drinking in the morning. But Dalrymple, though he was hardly astonished by the story, as it regarded Broughton, was put out by that part of it which had reference to Musselboro. He had known that Musselboro had been introduced to Broughton by Mrs Van Siever, but, neverthelss, he had regarded the man as being no more than Broughton's clerk. And now he was told that Musselboro was to marry Clara Van Siever, and have all Mrs Van Siever's money. He resolved, at last, that he would run his risk about the money, and take Clara either with or without it, if she would have him. And as for that difficulty in asking her, if Mrs Broughton would give him no opportunity of putting the question behind her back, he would put it before her face. He had not much leisure for consideration on these points, as the next day was the day for the last sitting.

On the following morning he found Miss Van Siever already seated in Mrs Broughton's room when he reached it. And at the moment Mrs Broughton was not there. As he took Clara's hand, he could not prevent himself from asking her whether she had heard anything? 'Heard what?' said Clara. 'Then you have not,' said he. 'Never mind now, as Mrs Broughton is here.' Then Mrs Broughton had entered the room. She seemed to be quite cheerful, but Dalrymple perfectly understood, from a special glance which she gave to him, that he was to perceive that her cheerfulness was assumed for Clara's benefit. Mrs Broughton was showing how great a heroine she could be on behalf of her friends. 'Now, my dear,' she said, 'do remember that this is the last day. It may be all very well, Conway, and, of course, you know best; but as far as I can see, you have not made half as much progress as you ought to have done.' 'We shall do excellently well,' said Dalrymple. 'So much the better,' said Mrs Broughton; 'and now, Clara, I'll place you.' And so Clara was placed on her knees, with the turban on her head.

Dalrymple began his work assiduously, knowing that Mrs Broughton would not leave the room for some minutes. It was certain that she would remain for a quarter of an hour, and it might be as well that he should really use that time on his picture. The peculiar position in which he was placed probably made his work difficult to him. There was something perplexing in the necessity which bound him to look upon the young lady before him both as Jael and as the future Mrs Conway Dalrymple, knowing as he did that she was at present simply Clara Van Siever. A double personification was not difficult to him. He had encountered it with every model that had sat to him, and with every young lady he had attempted to win, – if he had ever made such an attempt with one before. But the triple character, joined to the necessity of the double work, was distressing to him. 'The hand a little further back, if you don't mind,' he said, 'and the wrist more turned towards me. That is just it. Lean a little more over him. There – that will do exactly.' If Mrs Broughton did not go very quickly, he must begin to address his model on a totally different subject, even while she was in the act of slaying Sisera.

'Have you made up your mind who is to be Sisera?' asked Mrs Broughton.

'I think I shall put in my own face,' said Dalrymple; 'if Miss Van Siever does not object.'

'Not in the least,' said Clara, speaking without moving her face – almost without moving her lips.

'That will be excellent,' said Mrs Broughton. She was still quite cheerful, and really laughed as she spoke. 'Shall you like the idea, Clara, of striking the nail right through his head?'

'Oh, yes; as well his head as another's. I shall seem to be having my revenge for all the trouble he has given me.'

There was a slight pause, and then Dalrymple spoke. 'You have had that already, in striking me right through the heart.'

'What a very pretty speech! Was it not, my dear?' said Mrs Broughton. And then Mrs Broughton laughed. There was something slightly hysterical in her laugh which grated on Dalrymple's ears, – something which seemed to tell him that at the present moment his dear friend was not going to assist him honestly in his effort.

'Only that I should put him out, I would get up and make a curtsey,' said Clara. No young lady could ever talk of making a curtsey for such a speech if she supposed it to have been made in earnestness. And Clara, no doubt, understood that a man might make a hundred such speeches in the presence of a third person without any danger that they would be taken as meaning anything. All this Dalrymple knew, and began to think that he had better put down his palette and brush, and do the work which he had before him in the most prosaic language that he could use. He could, at any rate, succeed in making Clara acknowledge his intention in this way. He waited still for a minute or two, and it seemed to him that Mrs Broughton had no intention of piling her fagots on the present occasion. It might be that the remembrance of her husband's ruin prevented her from sacrificing herself in the other direction also.

'I am not very good at pretty speeches, but I am good at telling the truth,' said Dalrymple.

'Ha, ha, ha!' laughed Mrs Broughton, still with a touch of hysterical action in her throat. 'Upon my word, Conway, you know how to praise yourself.'

'He dispraises himself most unnecessarily in denying the prettiness of his language,' said Clara. As she spoke she hardly moved her lips, and Dalrymple went on painting from the model. It was clear that Miss Van Siever understood that the painting, and not the pretty speeches, was the important business on hand.

Mrs Broughton had now tucked her feet up on the sofa, and was gazing at the artist as he stood at his work. Dalrymple, remembering how he had offered her his purse, – an offer which, in the existing crisis of her affairs, might mean a great deal, – felt that she was ill-natured. Had she intended to do him a good turn, she would have gone now; but there she lay, with her feet tucked up, clearly purposing to be present through the whole of that morning's sitting. His anger against her added something to his spirit, and made him determine that he would carry out his purpose. Suddenly, therefore, he prepared himself for action.

He was in the habit of working with a Turkish cap on his head, and with a short apron tied round him. There was something picturesque about the cap, which might not have been incongruous with love-making. It is easy to suppose that Juan wore a Turkish cap when he sat with Haidee in Lambro's island.* But we may be quite sure that he did not wear an apron. Now Dalrymple had thought of all this, and had made up his mind to work to-day without his apron; but when arranging his easel and his brushes, he had put it on from force of habit, and was now disgusted with himself as he remembered it. He put down his brush, divested his thumb of his palette, then took off his cap, and after that untied the apron.

'Conway, what are you going to do?' said Mrs Broughton.

'I am going to ask Clara Van Siever to be my wife,' said Dalrymple. At that moment the door was opened, and Mrs Van Siever entered the room.

Clara had not risen from her kneeling posture when Dalrymple began to put off his trappings. She had not seen what he was doing as plainly as Mrs Broughton had done, having her attention naturally drawn towards her Sisera; and, besides this, she understood that she was to remain as she was placed till orders to move were given to her. Dalrymple would occasionally step aside from his easel to look at her in some altered light, and on such occasions she would simply hold her hammer somewhat more tightly than before. When, therefore, Mrs Van Siever entered the room Clara was still slaying Sisera, in spite of the artist's speech. The speech, indeed, and her mother both seemed to come to her at the same time. The old woman stood for a moment holding the open door in her hand. 'You fool!' she said, 'what are you doing there, dressed up in that way like a guy?' Then Clara got up from her feet and stood before her mother in Jael's dress and Jael's turban. Dalrymple thought that the dress and turban did not become her badly. Mrs Van Siever apparently thought otherwise. 'Will you have the goodness to tell me, miss, why you are dressed up after that Mad Bess of Bedlam fashion?'

The reader will no doubt bear in mind that Clara had other words of which to think besides those which were addressed to her by her mother. Dalrymple had asked her to be his wife in the plainest possible language, and she thought that the very plainness of the language became him well. The very taking off of his apron, almost as he said the words, though to himself the action had been so distressing as almost to overcome his purpose, had in it something to her of direct simple determination which pleased her. When he had spoken of having had a nail driven by her right through his heart, she had not been in the least gratified; but the taking off of the apron, and the putting down of the palette, and the downright way in which he had called her Clara Van Siever, – attempting to be neither sentimental with Clara, nor polite with Miss Van Siever, – did please her. She had often said to herself that she would never give a plain answer to a man who did not ask her a plain question; – to a man who, in asking this question, did not say plainly to her, 'Clara Van Siever, will you become Mrs Jones?' – or Mrs Smith, or Mrs Tomkins, as the case might be. Now Conway Dalrymple had asked her to become Mrs Dalrymple very much after this fashion. In spite of the apparition of her mother, all this had passed through her mind. Not the less, however, was she obliged to answer her mother, before she could give any reply to the other questioner. In the meantime Mrs Dobbs Broughton had untucked her feet.

'Mamma,' said Clara, 'who ever expected to see you here?'

'I daresay nobody did,' said Mrs Van Siever; 'but here I am, nevertheless.'

'Madam,' said Mrs Dobbs Broughton, 'you might at any rate have gone through the ceremony of having yourself announced by the servant.'

'Madam,' said the old woman, attempting to mimic the tone of the other, 'I thought that on such a very particular occasion as this I might be allowed to announce myself. You tomfool, you, why don't you take that turban off ?' Then Clara, with slow and graceful motion, unwound the turban. If Dalrymple really meant what he had said, and would stick to it, she need not mind being called a tomfool by her mother.

'Conway, I am afraid that our last sitting is disturbed,' said Mrs Broughton, with her little laugh.

'Conway's last sitting certainly is disturbed,' said Mrs Van Siever, and then she mimicked the laugh. 'And you'll all be disturbed, – I can tell you that. What an ass you must be to go on with this kind of thing, after what I said to you yesterday ! Do you know that he got beastly drunk in the City last night, and that he is drunk now, while you are going on with your tomfooleries ?' Upon hearing this, Mrs Dobbs Broughton fainted into Dalrymple's arms.

Hitherto the artist had not said a word, and had hardly known what part it would best become him now to play. If he intended to marry Clara, – and he certainly did intend to marry her if she would have him, – it might be as well not to quarrel with Mrs Van Siever. At any rate there was nothing in Mrs Van Siever's intrusion, disagreeable as it was, which need make him take up his sword to do battle with her. But now, as he held Mrs Broughton in his arms, and as the horrid words which the old woman had spoken rung in his ears, he could not refrain himself from uttering reproach. 'You ought not to have told her in this way, before other people, even if it be true,' said Conway.

'Leave me to be my own judge of what I ought to do, if you please, sir. If she had any feeling at all, what I told her yesterday would have kept her from all this. But some people have no feeling, and will go on being tomfools though the house is on fire.' As these words were spoken, Mrs Broughton fainted more persistently than ever, – so that Dalrymple was convinced that whether she felt or not, at any rate she heard. He had now dragged her across the room, and laid her upon the sofa, and Clara had come to her assistance. 'I daresay you think me very hard because I speak plainly, but there are things much harder than plain speaking. How much do you expect to be paid, sir, for this picture of my girl ?'

'I do not expect to be paid for it at all,' said Dalrymple.

'And who is it to belong to ?'

'It belongs to me at present.'

'Then, sir, it mustn't belong to you any longer. It won't do for you to have a picture of my girl to hang up in your painting-room for all your friends to come and make their jokes about, nor yet to make a show of it in any of your exhibitions. My daughter has been a fool, and I can't help it. If you'll tell me what's the cost, I'll pay you; then I'll have the picture home, and I'll treat it as it deserves.'

Dalrymple thought for a moment about his picture and about Mrs Van Siever. What had he better do? He wanted to behave well, and he felt that the old woman had something of justice on her side. 'Madam,' he said, 'I will not sell this picture; but it shall be destroyed, if you wish it.'

'I certainly do wish it, but I won't trust to you. If it's not sent to my house at once you'll hear from me through my lawyers.'

Then Dalrymple deliberately opened his penknife and slit the canvas across, through the middle of the picture each way. Clara, as she saw him do it, felt that in truth she loved him. 'There, Mrs Van Siever,' he said; 'now you can take the bits home with you in your basket if you wish it.' At this moment, as the rent canvas fell and fluttered upon the stretcher, there came a loud voice of lamentation from the sofa, a groan of despair and a shriek of wrath. 'Very fine indeed,' said Mrs Van Siever. 'When ladies faint they always ought to have their eyes about them. I see that Mrs Broughton understands that.'

'Take her away, Conway – for God's sake take her away,' said Mrs Broughton.

'I shall take myself away very shortly,' said Mrs Van Siever, 'so you needn't trouble Mr Conway about that. Not but what I thought the gentleman's name was Mr Something else.'

'My name is Conway Dalrymple,' said the artist.

'Then I suppose you must be her brother, or her cousin, or something of that sort?' said Mrs Van Siever.

'Take her away,' screamed Mrs Dobbs Broughton.

'Wait a moment, madam. As you've chopped up your handiwork there, Mr Conway Dalrymple, and as I suppose my daughter has been more to blame than anybody else—'

'She has not been to blame at all,' said Dalrymple.

'That's my affair, and not yours,' said Mrs Van Siever, very sharply. 'But as you've been at all this trouble, and have now chopped it up, I don't mind paying you for your time and paints; only I shall be glad to know how much it will come to?'

'There will be nothing to pay, Mrs Van Siever.'

'How long has he been at it, Clara?'

'Mamma, indeed you had better not say anything about paying him.'

'I shall say whatever I please, miss. Will ten pounds do it, sir?'

'If you choose to buy the picture, the price will be seven hundred and fifty,' said Dalrymple, with a smile, pointing to the fragments.

'Seven hundred and fifty pounds ?' said the old woman.

'But I strongly advise you not to make the purchase,' said Dalrymple.

'Seven hundred and fifty pounds ! I certainly shall not give you seven hundred and fifty pounds, sir.'

'I certainly think you could invest your money better, Mrs Van Siever. But if the thing is to be so at all, that is my price. I've thought that there was some justice in your demand that it should be destroyed, – and therefore I have destroyed it.'

Mrs Van Siever had been standing on the same spot ever since she had entered the room, and now she turned round to leave the room.

'If you have any demand to make, I beg that you will send in your account for work done to Mr Musselboro. He is my man of business. Clara, are you ready to come home ? The cab is waiting at the door, – at sixpence the quarter of an hour, if you will be pleased to remember.'

'Mrs Broughton,' said Clara, thoughtful of her raiment, and remembering that it might not be well that she should return home, even in a cab, dressed as Jael; 'if you will allow me, I will go into your room for a minute or two.'

'Certainly, Clara,' said Mrs Broughton, preparing to accompany her.

'But before you go, Mrs Broughton,' said Mrs Van Siever, 'it may be as well that I should tell you that my daughter is going to become the wife of Mr Musselboro. It may simplify matters that you should know this.' And Mrs Van Seiver, as she spoke, looked hard at Conway Dalrymple.

'Mamma !' exclaimed Clara.

'My dear,' said Mrs Van Siever, 'you had better change your dress and come away with me.'

'Not till I have protested against what you have said, mamma.'

'You had better leave your protesting alone, I can tell you.'

'Mrs Broughton,' continued Clara, 'I must beg you to understand that mamma has not the slightest right in the world to tell you what she just now said about me. Nothing on earth would induce me to become the wife of Mr Broughton's partner.'

There was something which made Clara unwilling even to name the man whom her mother had publicly proposed as her future husband.

'He isn't Mr Broughton's partner,' said Mrs Van Siever. 'Mr Broughton has not got a partner. Mr Musselboro is the head of the firm. And as to your marrying him, of course, I can't make you.'

'No, mamma ; you cannot.'

'Mrs Broughton understands that, no doubt; – and so, probably, does Mr Dalrymple. I only tell them what are my ideas. If you choose to marry the sweep at the crossing, I can't help it. Only I don't see what good you would do the sweep, when he would have to sweep for himself and you too. At any rate, I suppose you mean to go home with me now ?' Then Mrs Broughton and Clara left the room, and Mrs Van Siever was left with Conway Dalrymple. 'Mr Dalrymple,' said Mrs Van Siever, 'do not deceive yourself. What I told you just now will certainly come to pass.'

'It seems to me that that must depend on the young lady,' said Dalrymple.

'I'll tell you what certainly will not depend on the young lady,' said Mrs Van Siever, 'and that is whether the man who marries her will have more with her than the clothes she stands up in. You will understand that argument, I suppose ?'

'I'm not quite sure that I do,' said Dalrymple.

'Then you'd better try to understand it. Good-morning, sir. I'm sorry you've had to slit your picture.' Then she curtseyed low, and walked out on to the landing-place. 'Clara,' she cried, 'I'm waiting for you – sixpence a quarter of an hour, – remember that.' In a minute or two Clara came out to her, and then Mrs Van Siever and Miss Van Siever took their departure.

'Oh, Conway, what am I to do ? what am I to do ?' said Mrs Dobbs Broughton. Dalrymple stood perplexed for a few minutes, and could not tell her what she was to do. She was in such a position that it was very hard to tell her what to do. 'Do you believe, Conway, that he is really ruined ?'

'What am I to say ? How am I to know ?'

'I see that you believe it,' said the wretched woman.

'I cannot but believe that there is something of truth in what this woman says. Why else should she come here with such a story ?' Then there was a pause, during which Mrs Broughton was burying her face on the arm of the sofa. 'I'll tell you what I'll do,' continued he. 'I'll go into the City, and make inquiry. It can hardly be but what I shall learn the truth there.'

Then there was another pause, at the end of which Mrs Broughton got up from the sofa.

'Tell me,' said she; – 'what do you mean to do about that girl ?'

'You heard me ask her to be my wife ?'

'I did. I did !'

'Is it not what you intended ?'

'Do not ask me. My mind is bewildered. My brain is on fire ! Oh, Conway !'

'Shall I go into the City as I proposed ?' said Dalrymple, who felt that he might at any rate improve the position of circumstances by leaving the house.

'Yes; – yes; go into the City! Go anywhere. Go. But stay! Oh, Conway!' There was a sudden change in her voice as she spoke. 'Hark, – there he is, as sure as life.' Then Conway listened, and heard a footstep on the stairs, as to which he had then but little doubt that it was the footstep of Dobbs Broughton. 'O heavens! he is tipsy!' exclaimed Mrs Broughton; 'and what shall we do?' Then Dalrymple took her hand and pressed it, and left the room, so that he might meet the husband on the stairs. In the one moment that he had for reflection he thought it was better that there should be no concealment.

CHAPTER 61

It's dogged as does it.

In accordance with the resolution to which the clerical commission had come on the first day of their sitting, Dr Tempest wrote the following letter to Mr Crawley:

> *Rectory, Silverbridge, April 9, 186–.*

Dear Sir, –

I have been given to understand that you have been informed that the Bishop of Barchester has appointed a commission of clergymen of the diocese to make inquiry respecting certain accusations which, to the great regret of us all, have been made against you, in respect to a cheque for twenty pounds which was passed by you to a tradesman in this town. The clergymen appointed to form this commission are Mr Oriel, the rector of Greshamsbury, Mr Robarts, the vicar of Framley, Mr Quiverful, the warden of Hiram's Hospital at Barchester, Mr Thumble, a clergyman established in that city, and myself. We held our first meeting on last Monday, and I now write to you in compliance with a resolution to which we then came. Before taking any other steps we thought it best to ask you to attend us here on next Monday, at two o'clock, and I beg that you will accept this letter as an invitation to that effect.

We are, of course, aware that you are about to stand your trial at the next assizes for the offence in question. I beg you to understand that I do not express any opinion as to your guilt. But I think it right to point out to you that in the event of a jury finding an adverse verdict, the bishop might be placed in great difficulty unless he were fortified with the opinion of a commission formed from your fellow clerical labourers in the diocese. Should such adverse verdict unfortunately be given, the bishop would hardly be justified in allowing a clergyman placed as you then would be placed, to return to his cure after the expiration of such punishment as the judge might award, without a further decision from an ecclesiastical court. This decision he could only obtain by proceeding against you under the Act in reference to clerical offences, which empowers him as bishop of the diocese to bring you before the Court of Arches, – unless you would think well to submit yourself entirely to his judgment. You will, I think, understand what I mean. The judge at assizes might find it his duty to imprison a clergyman for a month, – regarding that clergyman simply as he would regard any other person found guilty by a jury and thus made subject to his judgment, – and might do this for an offence which the ecclesiastical judge would find himself obliged to visit with the severer sentence of prolonged suspension, or even with deprivation.

We are, however, clearly of opinion that should the jury find themselves able to acquit you, no further action whatsoever should be taken. In such case we think that the bishop may regard your innocence to be fully established, and in such case we shall recommend his lordship to look upon the matter as altogether at an end. I can assure you that in such case I shall so regard it myself.

You will perceive that, as a consequence of this resolution, to which we have already come, we are not minded to make any inquiries ourselves into the circumstances of your alleged guilt, till the verdict of the jury shall be given. If you are acquitted, our course will be clear. But should you be convicted, we must in that case advise the bishop to take the proceedings to which I have alluded, or to abstain from taking them. We wish to ask you whether, now that our opinion has been conveyed to you, you will be willing to submit to the bishop's decision, in the event of an adverse verdict being given by the jury; and we think that it will be better for us all that you should meet us here at the hour I have named on Monday next, the 15th instant. It is not our intention to make any report to the bishop until the trial shall be over.

> I have the honour to be,
> My dear sir,
> Your very obedient servant,
> Mortimer Tempest.

The Rev. Josiah Crawley,
    Hogglestock.

In the same envelope Dr Tempest sent a short private note, in which he said that he should be very happy to see Mr Crawley at half-past one on the Monday named, that luncheon would be ready at that hour, and that, as Mr Crawley's attendance was required on public grounds, he would take care that a carriage was provided for the day.

Mr Crawley received this letter in his wife's presence, and read it in silence. Mrs Crawley saw that he paid close attention to it, and was sure, – she felt that she was sure, – that it referred in some way to the terrible subject of the cheque for twenty pounds. Indeed, everything that came into the house, almost every word spoken there, and every thought that came into the breasts of any of the family, had more or less reference to the coming trial. How could it be otherwise? There was ruin coming on them all, – ruin and complete disgrace coming on father, mother, and children! To have been accused itself was very bad; but now it seemed to be the opinion of every one that the verdict must be against the man. Mrs Crawley herself, who was perfectly sure of her husband's innocence before God, believed that the jury would find him guilty, – and believed also that he had become possessed of the money in some manner that would have been dishonest, had he not been so different from other people as to be entitled to be considered innocent where another man would have been plainly guilty. She was full of the cheque for twenty pounds, and of its results. When, therefore, he had read the letter through a second time, and even then had spoken no word about it, of course she could not refrain from questioning him. 'My love,' she said, 'what is the letter?'

'It is on business,' he answered.

She was silent for a moment before she spoke again. 'May I not know the business?'

'No,' said he; 'not at present.'

'Is it from the bishop?'

'Have I not answered you? Have I not given you to understand that, for a while at least, I would prefer to keep the contents of this epistle to myself?' Then he looked at her very sternly, and afterwards turned his eyes upon the fireplace and gazed at the fire, as though he were striving to read there something of his future fate. She did not much regard the severity of his speech. That, too, like the taking of the cheque itself, was to be forgiven him, because he was different from other men. His black mood had come upon him, and everything was to be forgiven him now. He was as a child when cutting his teeth. Let the poor wayward sufferer be ever so petulant, the mother simply pities and loves him, and is never angry. 'I beg your pardon, Josiah,' she said, 'but I thought it would comfort you to speak to me about it.'

'It will not comfort me,' he said. 'Nothing comforts me. Nothing can comfort me. Jane, give me my hat and my stick.' His daughter brought to him his hat and stick, and without another word he went out and left them.

As a matter of course he turned his steps towards Hoggle End. When he desired to be long absent from the house, he always went among the brickmakers. His wife, as she stood at the window and watched the direction in which he went, knew that he might be away for hours. The only friends out of his own family with whom he ever spoke freely were some of these rough parishioners. But he was not thinking of the brickmakers when he started. He was simply desirous of again reading Dr Tempest's letter, and of considering it, in some spot where no eye could see him. He walked away with long steps, regarding nothing, – neither the ruts in the dirty lane, nor the young primroses which were fast showing themselves on the banks, nor the gathering clouds which might have told him of the coming rain. He went on for a couple of miles, till he had nearly reached the outskirts of the colony of Hoggle End, and then he sat himself down upon a gate. He had not been there a minute before a few slow large drops began to fall, but he was altogether too much wrapped up in his thoughts to regard the rain. What answer should he make to this letter from the man at Silverbridge?

The position of his own mind in reference to his own guilt or his own innocence was very singular. It was simply the truth that he did not know how the cheque had come to him. He did know that he had blundered about it most egregiously, especially when he had averred that this cheque for twenty pounds had been identical with a cheque for another sum which had been given to him by Mr Soames. He had blundered since, in saying that the dean had given it to him. There could be no doubt as to this, for the dean had denied that he had done so. And he had come to think it very possible that he had indeed picked the cheque up, and had afterwards used it, having deposited it by some strange accident, – not knowing then what he was doing, or what was the nature of the bit of paper in his hand, – with the notes which he had accepted from the dean with so much reluctance, with such an agony of spirit. In all these thoughts of his own about his own doings, and his own position, he almost admitted to himself his own insanity, his inability to manage his own affairs with that degree of rational sequence which is taken for granted as belonging to a man when he is made subject to criminal laws. As he puzzled his brain in his efforts to create a memory as to the cheque, and succeeded in bringing to his mind a recollection that he had once known something about the cheque, – that the cheque had at one time been the subject of a thought and of a resolution, – he admitted to himself that in accordance with all law and all reason he must be regarded as a thief. He had taken and used and spent that which he ought to have known was not his own; – which he would have known not to be his own but for some terrible incapacity with which God had afflicted him. What then must be the result? His mind was clear enough about this. If the jury could see everything and know everything, – as he would wish that they should do; and if this bishop's commission, and the bishop himself, and the Court of Arches with its judge, could see and know everything; and if so seeing and so knowing they could act with clear honesty and perfect wisdom, – what would they do? They would declare of him that he was not a thief, only because he was so muddy-minded, so addle-pated as not to know the difference between meum and tuum! There could be no other end to it, let all the lawyers and all the clergymen in England put their wits to it. Though he knew himself to be muddy-minded and addle-pated, he could see that. And could any one say of such a man that he was fit to be the acting clergyman of a parish, – to have a freehold possession in a parish as curer of men's souls! The bishop was in the right of it, let him be ten times as mean a fellow as he was.

And yet as he sat there on the gate, while the rain came down heavily upon him, even when admitting the justice of the bishop, and the truth of the verdict which the jury would no doubt give, and the propriety of the action which that cold, reasonable, prosperous man at Silverbridge would take, he pitied himself with a tenderness of commiseration which knew no bounds. As for those belonging to him, his wife and children, his pity for them was of a different kind. He would have suffered any increase of suffering, could he by such agony have released them. Dearly as he loved them, he would have severed himself from them, had it been possible. Terrible thoughts as to their fate had come into his mind in the worst moments of his moodiness, – thoughts which he had had sufficient strength and manliness to put away from him with a strong hand, lest they should drive him to crime indeed; and these had come from the great pity which he had felt for them. But the commiseration which he had felt for himself had been different from this, and had mostly visited him at times when that other pity was for the moment in abeyance. What though he had taken the cheque, and spent the money though it was not his? He might be guilty before the law, but he was not guilty before God. There had never been a thought of theft in his mind, or a desire to steal in his heart. He knew that well enough. No jury could make him guilty of theft before God. And what though this mixture of guilt and innocence had come from madness, – from madness which these courts must recognize if they chose to find him innocent of the crime? In spite of his aberrations of intellect, if there were any such, his ministrations in his parish were good. Had he not preached fervently and well, – preaching the true gospel? Had he not been very diligent among his people, striving with all his might to lessen the ignorance of the ignorant, and to gild with godliness the learning of the instructed? Had he not been patient, enduring, instant, and in all things amenable to the laws and regulations laid down by the Church for his guidance in his duties as a parish clergyman? Who could point out in what he had been astray, or where he had gone amiss? But for the work which he had done with so much zeal the Church which he served had paid him so miserable a pittance that, though life and soul had been kept together, the reason, or a fragment of the reason, had at moments escaped from his keeping in the scramble. Hence it was that this terrible calamity had fallen upon him! Who had been tried as he had been tried, and had gone through such fire with less loss of intellectual power than he had done? He was still a scholar, though no brother scholar ever came near him, and would make Greek iambics as he walked along the lanes. His memory was stored with poetry, though no book ever came to his hands, except those shorn and tattered volumes which lay upon his table. Old problems in trigonometry were the pleasing relaxations of his mind, and complications of figures were a delight to him. There was not one of those prosperous clergymen around him, and who scorned him, whom he could not have instructed in Hebrew. It was always a gratification to him to remember that his old friend the dean was weak in his Hebrew. He, with these acquirements, with these fitnesses, had been thrust down to the ground, – to the very granite, – and because in that harsh heartless thrusting his intellect had for moments wavered as to common things, cleaving still to all its grander, nobler possessions, he was now to be rent in pieces and scattered to the winds, as being altogether vile, worthless, and worse than worthless. It was thus that he thought of himself, pitying himself, as he sat upon the gate, while the rain fell ruthlessly on his shoulders.

He pitied himself with a commiseration that was sickly in spite of its truth. It was the fault of the man that he was imbued too strongly with self-consciousness. He could do a great thing or two. He could keep up his courage in positions which would wash all courage out of most men. He could tell the truth though truth should ruin him. He could sacrifice all that he had to duty. He could do justice though the heaven should fall.* But he could not forget to pay a tribute to himself for the greatness of his own actions; nor, when accepting with an effort of meekness the small payment made by the world to him, in return for his great works, could he forget the great payments made to others for small work. It was not sufficient for him to remember that he knew Hebrew, but he must remember also that the dean did not.

Nevertheless, as he sat there under the rain, he made up his mind with a clearness that certainly had in it nothing of that muddiness of mind of which he had often accused himself. Indeed, the intellect of this man was essentially clear. It was simply his memory that would play him tricks, – his memory as to things which at the moment were not important to him. The fact that the dean had given him money was very important, and he remembered it well. But the amount of the money, and its form, at a moment in which he had flattered himself that he might have strength to leave it unused, had not been important to him. Now, he resolved that he would go to Dr Tempest, and that he would tell Dr Tempest that there was no occasion for any further inquiry. He would submit to the bishop, let the bishop's decision be what it might. Things were different since the day on which he had refused Mr Thumble admission to his pulpit. At that time people believed him to be innocent, and he so believed of himself. Now, people believed him to be guilty, and it could not be right that a man held in such slight esteem should exercise the functions of a parish priest, let his own opinion of himself be what it might. He would submit himself, and go anywhere, – to the galleys or the workhouse, if they wished it. As for his wife and children, they would, he said to himself, be better without him than with him. The world would never be so hard to a woman or to children as it had been to him.

He was sitting saturated with rain, – saturated also with thinking, – and quite unobservant of anything around him, when he was accosted by an old man from Hoggle End, with whom he was well acquainted. 'Thee be wat, Master Crawley,' said the old man.

'Wet!' said Crawley, recalled suddenly back to the realities of life. 'Well, – yes. I am wet. That's because it's raining.'

'Thee be teeming o' wat. Hadn't thee better go whome ?'

'And are not you wet also ?' said Mr Crawley, looking at the old man, who had been at work in the brickfield, and who was soaked with mire, and from whom there seemed to come a steam of muddy mist.

'Is it me, yer reverence ? I'm wat in course. The loikes of us is always wat, – that is barring the insides of us. It comes to us natural to have the rheumatics. How is one of us to help hisself against having on 'em ? But there ain't no call for the loikes of you to have the rheumatics.'

'My friend,' said Crawley, who was now standing on the road, –

and as he spoke he put out his arm and took the brickmaker by the hand, 'there is a worse complaint than rheumatism, – there is, indeed.'

'There's what they calls the collerer,' said Giles Hoggett, looking up into Mr Crawley's face. 'That ain't a got a hold of yer?'

'Ay, and worse than the cholera. A man is killed all over when he is struck in his pride; – and yet he lives.'

'Maybe that's bad enough too,' said Giles, with his hand still held by the other.

'It is bad enough,' said Mr Crawley, striking his breast with his left hand. 'It is bad enough.'

'Tell'ee what, Master Crawley; – and yer reverence mustn't think as I means to be preaching; there ain't nowt a man can't bear if he'll only be dogged. You go whome, Master Crawley, and think o' that, and maybe it'll do ye a good yet. It's dogged as does it. It ain't thinking about it.' Then Giles Hoggett withdrew his hand from the clergyman's, and walked away towards his home at Hoggle End. Mr Crawley also turned homewards, and as he made his way through the lanes, he repeated to himself Giles Hoggett's words. 'It's dogged as does it. It's not thinking about it.'

He did not say a word to his wife on that afternoon about Dr Tempest; and she was so much taken up with his outward condition when he returned, as almost to have forgotten the letter. He allowed himself, but barely allowed himself, to be made dry, and then for the remainder of the day applied himself to learn the lesson which Hoggett had endeavoured to teach him. But the learning of it was not easy, and hardly became more easy when he had worked the problem out in his own mind, and discovered that the brickmaker's doggedness simply meant self-abnegation; – that a man should force himself to endure anything that might be sent upon him, not only without outward grumbling, but also without grumbling inwardly.

Early on the next morning, he told his wife that he was going into Silverbridge. 'It is that letter, – the letter which I got yesterday that calls me,' he said. And then he handed her the letter as to which he had refused to speak to her on the preceding day.

'But this speaks of your going next Monday, Josiah,' said Mrs Crawley.

'I find it to be more suitable that I should go to-day,' said he. 'Some duty I do owe in this matter, both to the bishop, and to Dr Tempest, who, after a fashion, is, as regards my present business, the bishop's representative. But I do not perceive that I owe it as a duty to either to obey implicitly their injunctions, and I will not submit myself to the cross-questionings of the man Thumble. As I am purposed at present I shall express my willingness to give up the parish.'

'Give up the parish altogether?'

'Yes, altogether.' As he spoke he clasped both his hands together, and having held them for a moment on high, allowed them to fall thus clasped before him. 'I cannot give it up in part; I cannot abandon the duties and reserve the honorarium. Nor would I if I could.'

'I did not mean that, Josiah. But pray think of it before you speak.'

'I have thought of it, and I will think of it. Farewell, my dear.' Then he came up to her and kissed her, and started on his journey on foot to Silverbridge.

It was about noon when he reached Silverbridge, and he was told that Doctor Tempest was at home. The servant asked him for a card. 'I have no card,' said Mr Crawley, 'but I will write my name for your behoof if your master's hospitality will allow me paper and pencil.' The name was written, and as Crawley waited in the drawing-room he spent his time in hating Dr Tempest because the door had been opened by a man-servant dressed in black. Had the man been in livery he would have hated Dr Tempest all the same. And he would have hated him a little had the door been opened even by a smart maid.

'You letter came to hand yesterday morning, Dr Tempest,' said Mr Crawley, still standing, though the doctor had pointed to a chair for him after shaking hands with him; 'and having given yesterday to the consideration of it, with what judgment I have been able to exercise, I have felt it to be incumbent upon me to wait upon you without further delay, as by doing so I may perhaps assist your views and save labour to those gentlemen who are joined with you in this commission of which you have spoken. To some of them it may possibly be troublesome that they should be brought together here on next Monday.'

Dr Tempest had been looking at him during this speech, and could see by his shoes and trousers that he had walked from Hogglestock to Silverbridge. 'Mr Crawley, will you not sit down?' said he, and then he rang his bell. Mr Crawley sat down, not on the chair indicated, but on one further removed and at the other side of the table. When the servant came, – the objectionable butler in black clothes that were so much smarter than Mr Crawley's own, – his master's orders were communicated without any audible word, and the man returned with a decanter and wine-glasses.

'After your walk, Mr Crawley,' said Dr Tempest, getting up from his seat to pour out the wine.

'None, I thank you.'

'Pray let me persuade you. I know the length of the miles so well.'

'I will take none, if you please, sir,' said Mr Crawley.

'Now, Mr Crawley,' said Dr Tempest, 'do let me speak to you as a friend. You have walked eight miles, and are going to talk to me on a subject which is of vital importance to yourself. I won't discuss it unless you'll take a glass of wine and a biscuit.'

'Dr Tempest!'

'I'm quite in earnest. I won't. If you do as I ask you, you shall talk to me till dinner-time, if you like it. There. Now you may begin.'

Mr Crawley did eat the biscuit and did drink the wine, and as he did so, he acknowledged to himself that Dr Tempest was right. He felt that the wine made him stronger to speak. 'I hardly know why you have preferred to-day to next Monday,' said Dr Tempest; 'but if anything can be done by your presence here to-day, your time shall not be thrown away.'

'I have preferred to-day to Monday,' said Crawley, 'partly because I would sooner talk to one man than to five.'

'There is something in that, certainly,' said Dr Tempest.

'And as I have made up my mind as to the course of action which it is my duty to take in the matter to which your letter of the 9th of this month refers, there can be no reason why I should postpone the declaration of my purpose. Dr Tempest, I have determined to resign my preferment at Hogglestock, and shall write to-day to the Dean of Barchester, who is the patron, acquainting him of my purpose.'

'You mean in the event – in the event—'

'I mean, sir, to do this without reference to any event that is future. The bishop, Dr Tempest, when I shall have been proved to be a thief, shall have no trouble either in causing my suspension or my deprivation. The name and fame of a parish clergyman should be unstained. Mine have become foul with infamy. I will not wait to be deprived by any court, by any bishop, or by any commission. I will bow my head to that public opinion which has reached me, and I will deprive myself.'

He had got up from his chair, and was standing as he pronounced the final sentence against himself. Dr Tempest still remained seated in his chair, looking at him, and for a few moments there was silence. 'You must not do that, Mr Crawley,' Dr Tempest said at last.

'But I shall do it.'

'Then the dean must not take your resignation. Speaking to you frankly, I tell you that there is no prevailing opinion as to the verdict which the jury may give.'

'My decision has nothing to do with the jury's verdict. My decision—'

'Stop a moment, Mr Crawley. It is possible that you might say that which should not be said.'

'There is nothing to be said, – nothing which I could say, which I would not say at the town cross if it were possible. As to this money, I do not know whether I stole it or whether I did not.'

'That is just what I have thought.'

'It is so.'

'Then you did not steal it. There can be no doubt about that.'

'Thank you, Dr Tempest. I thank you heartily for saying so much. But, sir, you are not the jury. Nor, if you were, could you whitewash me from the infamy which has been cast on me. Against the opinion expressed at the beginning of these proceedings by the bishop of the diocese, – or rather against that expressed by his wife, – I did venture to make a stand. Neither the opinion which came from the palace, nor the vehicle by which it was expressed, commanded my respect. Since that, others have spoken to whom I feel myself bound to yield; – yourself not the least among them, Dr Tempest; – and to them I shall yield. You may tell the Bishop of Barchester that I shall at once resign the perpetual curacy of Hogglestock into the hands of the Dean of Barchester, by whom I was appointed.'

'No, Mr Crawley; I shall not do that. I cannot control you, but thinking you to be wrong, I shall not make that communication to the bishop.'

'Then I shall do so myself.'

'And your wife, Mr Crawley, and your children ?'

At that moment Mr Crawley called to mind the advice of his friend Giles Hoggett. 'It's dogged as does it.' He certainly wanted something very strong to sustain him in his difficulty. He found that this reference to his wife and children required him to be dogged in a very marked manner. 'I can only trust that the wind may be tempered to them,' he said. 'They will, indeed, be shorn lambs.'

Dr Tempest got up from his chair, and took a couple of turns about the room before he spoke again. 'Man,' he said, addressing Mr Crawley with all his energy, 'if you do this thing, you will then at least be very wicked. If the jury find a verdict in your favour you are safe, and the chances are that the verdict will be in your favour.'

'I care nothing now for the verdict,' said Mr Crawley.

'And you will turn your wife into the poorhouse for an idea !'

'It's dogged as does it,' said Mr Crawley to himself. 'I have thought of that,' he said aloud. 'That my wife is dear to me, and that my children are dear, I will not deny. She was softly nurtured, Dr Tempest, and came from a house in which want was never known. Since she has shared my board she has had some experience of that nature. That I should have brought her to all this is very terrible to me, – so terrible, that I often wonder how it is that I live. But, sir, you will agree with me, that my duty as a clergyman is above everything. I do not dare, even for their sake, to remain in the parish. Good morning, Dr Tempest.' Dr Tempest, finding that he could not prevail with him, bade him adieu, feeling that any service to the Crawleys within his power might be best done by intercession with the bishop and with the dean.

Then Mr Crawley walked back to Hogglestock, repeating to himself Giles Hoggett's words, 'It's dogged as does it.'

CHAPTER 62

Mr Crawley's letter to the dean

Mr Crawley, when he got home after his walk to Silverbridge, denied that he was at all tired. 'The man at Silverbridge, whom I went to see administered refreshment to me ; – nay, he administered it with salutary violence,' he said, affecting even to laugh. 'And I am bound to speak well of him on behalf of mercies over and beyond that exhibited by the persistent tender of some wine. That I should find him judicious I had expected. What little I have known of him taught me so to think of him. But I found with him also a softness of heart for which I had not looked.'

'And you will not give up the living, Josiah ?'

'Most certainly I will. A duty, when it is clear before a man, should never be made less so by any tenderness in others.' He was still thinking of Giles Hoggett. 'It's dogged as does it.' The poor woman could not answer him. She knew well that it was vain to argue with him. She could only hope that in the event of his being acquitted at the trial, the dean, whose friendship she did not doubt, might re-endow him with the small benefice which was their only source of bread.

On the following morning there came by post a short note from Dr Tempest. 'My dear Mr Crawley,' the note ran, 'I implore you, if there be yet time, to do nothing rashly. And even although you should have written to the bishop or to the dean, your letters need have no effect, if you will allow me to make them inoperative. Permit me to say that I am a man much older than you, and one who has mixed much both with clergymen and with the world at large. I tell you with absolute confidence, that it is not your duty in your present position to give up your living. Should your conduct ever be called in question on this matter you will be at perfect liberty to say that you were guided by my advice. You should take no step till after the trial. Then, if the verdict be against you, you should submit to the bishop's judgment. If the verdict be in your favour, the bishop's interference will be over.

'And you must remember that if it is not your duty as a clergyman to give up your living, you can have no right, seeing that you have a wife and family, to throw it away as an indulgence to your pride. Consult any other friend you please; – Mr Robarts, or the dean himself. I am quite sure that any friend who knows as many of the circumstances as I know will advise you to hold the living, at any rate till after the trial. You can refer any such friend to me.

> Believe me to be, yours very truly,
> Mortimer Tempest.

Mr Crawley walked about again with this letter in his pocket, but on this occasion he did not go in the direction of Hoggle End. From Hoggle End he could hardly hope to pick up further lessons of wisdom. What could any Giles Hoggett say to him beyond what he had said to him already? If he were to read the doctor's letter to Hoggett, and to succeed in making Hoggett understand it all, Hoggett could only caution him to be dogged. But it seemed to him that Hoggett and his new friend at Silverbridge did not agree in their doctrines, and it might be well that he should endeavour to find out which of them had most of justice on his side. He was quite sure that Hoggett would advise him to adhere to his project of giving up the living, – if only Hoggett could be made to understand the circumstances.

He had written, but had not as yet sent away his letter to the dean.

His letter to the bishop would be but a note, and he had postponed the writing of that till the other should be copied and made complete.

He had sat up into the night composing and altering his letter to his old friend, and now that the composition was finished he was loth to throw it away. Early in this morning, before the postman had brought to him Dr Tempest's urgent remonstrance, he had shown to his wife the draught of his letter to the dean. 'I cannot say that it is not true,' she had said.

'It is certainly true.'

'But I wish, dear, you would not send it. Why should you take any step till the trial be over?'

'I shall assuredly send it,' he had replied. 'If you will peruse it again, you will see that the epistle would be futile were it kept till I shall have been proved to be a thief.'

'Oh, Josiah, such words kill me.'

'They are not pleasant, but it will be well that you should become used to them. As for the letter, I have taken some trouble to express myself with perspicuity, and I trust that I may have succeeded.' At that time Hoggett was altogether in the ascendant; but now, as he started on his walk, his mind was somewhat perturbed by the contrary advice of one, who after all, might be as wise as Hoggett. There would be nothing dogged in the conduct recommended to him by Dr Tempest. Were he to follow the doctor's advice, he would be trimming his sails, so as to catch any slant of a breeze that might be favourable to him. There could be no doggedness in a character that would submit to such trimming.

The postman came to Hogglestock but once in a day, so that he could not despatch his letter till the next morning, – unless, indeed, he chose to send it a distance of four miles to the nearest post-office. As there was nothing to justify this, there was another night for the copying of his letter, – should he at last determine to send it. He had declared to Dr Tempest that he would send it. He had sworn to his wife that it should go. He had taken much trouble with it. He believed in Hoggett. But, nevertheless, this incumbency of Hogglestock was his all in the world. It might be that he could still hold it, and have bread at least for his wife to eat. Dr Tempest had told him that he would be probably acquitted. Dr Tempest knew as much of all the circumstances as did he himself, and had told him that he was not guilty. After all Dr Tempest knew more about it than Hoggett knew.

If he resigned the living, what would become of him, – of him, – of him and his wife? Whither would they first go when they turned their back upon the door inside which there had at any rate been shelter for them for many years? He calculated everything that he had, and found that at the end of April, even when he should have received his rentcharge,* there would not be five pounds in hand among them. As for his furniture, he still owed enough to make it impossible that he should get anything out of that. And these thoughts all had reference to his position if he should be acquitted. What would become of his wife if he should be convicted? And as for himself, 'whither should he go when he came out of prison?'

He had completely realized the idea that Hoggett's counsel was opposed to that given to him by Dr Tempest; but then it might certainly be the case that Hoggett had not known all the facts. A man should, no doubt, be dogged when the evils of life are insuperable; but need he be so when the evils can be overcome? Would not Hoggett himself undergo any treatment which he believed to be specific for rheumatism? Yes; Hoggett would undergo any treatment that was not in itself opposed to his duty. The best treatment for rheumatism might be to stay away from the brick-field on a rainy day; but if so, there would be no money to keep the pot boiling, and Hoggett would certainly go the the brickfield, rheumatism and all, as long as his limbs would carry him there. Yes; he would send his letter. It was his duty, and he would do it. Men looked askance at him, and pointed at him as a thief. He would send the letter, in spite of Dr Tempest. Let justice be done, though the heaven may fall.

He had heard of Lady Lufton's offer to his wife. The offers of the Lady Luftons of the world had been sorely distressing to his spirit, since it had first come to pass that such offers had reached him in consequence of his poverty. But now there was something almost of relief to him in the thought that the Lady Luftons would, after some fashion, save his wife and children from starvation; – would save his wife from the poorhouse, and enable his children to have a start in the world. For one of his children a brilliant marriage might be provided, – if only he himself were out of the way. How could he take himself out of the way? It had been whispered to him that he might be imprisoned for two months, – or for two years. Would it not be a grand thing if the judge would condemn him to be imprisoned for life? Was there ever a man whose existence was so purposeless, so useless, so deleterious, as his own? And yet he knew Hebrew well, whereas the dean knew but very little Hebrew. He could make Greek iambics, and doubted whether the bishop knew the difference between an iambus and a trochee. He could disport himself with trigonometry, feeling confident that Dr Tempest had forgotten his way over the asses' bridge. he knew 'Lycidas' by heart; and as for Thumble, he felt quite sure that Thumble was imcompetent of understanding a single allusion in that divine poem. Nevertheless, though all this wealth of acquirement was his, it would be better for himself, better for those who belonged to him, better for the world at large, that he should be put an end to. A sentence of penal servitude for life, without any trial, would be of all things the most desirable. Then there would be ample room for the practice of that virtue which Hoggett had taught him.

When he returned home the Hoggethan doctrine prevailed, and he prepared to copy his letter. But before he commenced his task, he sat down with his youngest daughter, and read, – or made her read to him, – a passage out of a Greek poem, in which are described the troubles and agonies of a blind giant.* No giant would have been more powerful, – only that he was blind, and could not see to avenge himself on those who had injured him. 'The same story is always coming up,' he said, stopping the girl in her reading. 'We have it in various versions, because it is so true to life.

> Ask for this great deliverer now, and find him
> Eyeless in Gaza, at the mill with the slaves.*

It is the same story. Great power reduced to impotence, great glory to misery, by the hand of Fate, – Necessity, as the Greeks called her; the goddess that will not be shunned! At the mill with slaves! People, when they read it, do not appreciate the horror of the picture. Go on, my dear. It may be a question whether Polyphemus had mind enough to suffer; but, from the description of his power, I should think that he had. 'At the mill with slaves!' Can any picture be more dreadful than that? Go on, my dear. Of course you remember Milton's Samson Agonistes. Agonistes indeed!' His wife was sitting stiching at the other side of the room; but she heard his words, – heard and understood them; and before Jane could again get herself into the swing of the Greek verse, she was over at her husband's side, with her arms round his neck. 'My love!' she said. 'My love!

He turned to her, and smiled as he spoke to her. 'These are old thoughts with me. Polyphemus and Belisarius,* and Samson and Milton, have always been pets of mine. The mind of the strong blind creature must be so sensible of the injury that has been done to him! The impotency, combined with his strength and former aspirations, is so essentially tragic!'

She looked into his eyes as he spoke, and there was something of the flash of old days, when the world was young to them, and when he would tell her of his hopes, and repeat to her long passages of poetry, and would criticize for her advantage the works of old writers. 'Thank God,' she said, 'that you are not blind. It may yet be all right with you.'

'Yes, – it may be,' he said.

'And you shall not be at the mill with slaves.'

'Or, at any rate, not eyeless in Gaza, if the Lord is good to me. Come, Jane, we will go on.' Then he took up the passage himself, and read it on with clear, sonorous voice, every now and then explaining some passage or expressing his own ideas upon it, as though he were really happy with his poetry.

It was late in the evening before he got out his small stock of best letter-paper, and sat down to work at his letter. He first addressed himself to the bishop; and what he wrote to the bishop was as follows:

Hogglestock Parsonage, April 11th, 186–.

My Lord Bishop,

I have been in communication with Dr Tempest, of Silverbridge, from whom I have learned that your lordship has been pleased to appoint a commission of inquiry, – of which commission he is the chairman, – with reference to the proceedings which it may be necessary that you should take, as bishop of this diocese, after my forthcoming trial at the approaching Barchester assizes. My lord, I think it right to inform you, partly with a view to the comfort of the gentlemen named on that commission, and partly with the purport of giving you that information which I think that a bishop should possess in regard to the clerical affairs of his own diocese, that I have by this post resigned my preferment at Hogglestock into the hands of the Dean of Barchester, by whom it was given to me. In these circumstances, it will, I suppose, be unnecessary for you to continue the commission which you have set in force; but as to that, your lordship will, of course, be the only judge.

I have the honour to be, my Lord Bishop,
Your most obedient and very humble servant,
Josiah Crawley,
Perpetual Curate of Hoogglestock

The Right Reverend
  The Bishop of Barchester,
    &c.   &c.   &c.
    The Palace, Barchester.

But the letter which was of real importance, – which was intended to say something, – was that to the dean, and that also shall be given to the reader. Mr Crawley had been for a while in doubt how he should address his old friend in commencing this letter, understanding that its tone throughout must, in a great degree, be made conformable with its first words. He would fain, in his pride, have begun 'Sir.' The question was between that and 'My dear Arabin.' It had once between them always been 'Dear Frank' and 'Dear Joe;' but the occasions for 'Dear Frank' and 'Dear Joe' between them had long been past. Crawley would have been very angry had he now been called Joe by the dean, and would have bitten his tongue out before he would have called the dean Frank. His better nature, however, now prevailed, and he began his letter, and completed it as follows: –

My dear Arabin,

Circumstances, of which you have probably heard something, compel me to write to you, as I fear, at some length. I am sorry that the trouble of such a letter should be forced upon you during your holidays; – Mr Crawley, as he wrote this, did not forget to remind himself that he never had any holidays; – but I think you will admit, if you will bear with me to the end, that I have no alternative.

I have been accused of stealing a cheque for twenty pounds, which cheque was drawn by my Lord Lufton on his London bankers, and was lost out of his pocket by Mr Soames, his lordship's agent, and was so lost, as Mr Soames states, – not with an absolute assertion, – during a visit which he made to my parsonage here at Hogglestock. Of the fact that I paid the cheque to a tradesman in Silverbridge there is no doubt. When questioned about it, I first gave an answer which was so manifestly incorrect that it has seemed odd to me that I should not have had credit for a mistake from those who must have seen that detection was so evident. The blunder was undoubtedly stupid, and it now bears heavy on me. I then, as I have learned, made another error, – of which I am aware that you been i formed. I said that the cheque had come to me from you, and in saying so, I thought that it had formed portion of that alms which your open-handed benevolence bestowed upon me when I attended on you, not long before your departure, in your library. I have striven to remember the facts. It may be, – nay, it probably is the case, – that such struggles to catch some accurate glimpse of bygone things do not trouble you. Your mind is, no doubt, clearer and stronger than mine, having been kept to its proper tune by greater and fitter work. With me, memory is all but gone, and the power of thinking is on the wane ! I struggled to remember, and I thought that the cheque had been in the envelope which you handed to me, – and I said so. I have since learned, from tidings received, as I am told, direct from yourself, that I was as wrong in the second statement as I had been in the first. The double blunder has, of course, been very heavy on me.

I was taken before the magistrates at Silverbridge, and was by them committed to stand my trial at the assizes to be holden in Barchester on the 28th of this month. Without doubt, the magistrates had no alternative but to commit me, and I am indebted to them that they have allowed me my present liberty upon bail. That my sufferings in all this should have been grievous, you will understand. But on that head I should not touch, were it not that I am bound to explain to you that my troubles in reference to this parish of Hogglestock, to which I was appointed by you, have not been the slightest of those sufferings. I felt at first, believing then that the world around me would think it unlikely that such a one as I had wilfully stolen a sum of money, that it was my duty to maintain myself in my church. I did so maintain myself against an attack made upon me by the bishop, who sent over to Hogglestock one Mr Thumble, a gentleman doubtless in holy orders, though I know nothing and can learn nothing of the place of his cure, to dispossess me of my pulpit and to remove me from my ministrations among my people. To Mr Thumble I turned a deaf ear, and would not let him so much as open his mouth inside the porch of my church. Up to this time I myself have read the services, and have preached to the people, and have continued, as best I could, my visits to the poor and my labours in the school, though I know, – no one knows as well, – how unfitted I am for such work by the grief which has fallen upon me.

Then the bishop sent for me, and I thought it becoming on my part to go to him. I presented myself to his lordship at his palace, and was minded to be much governed in my conduct by what he might say to me, remembering that I am bound to respect the office, even though I may not approve the man; and I humbled myself before his lordship, waiting patiently for any directions which he in his discretion might think it proper to bestow on me. But there arose up between us that very pestilent woman, his wife, – to his dismay, seemingly, as much as to mine, – and she would let there be place for no speech but her own. If there be aught clear to me in ecclesiastical matters, it is this, – that no authority can be delegated to a female. The special laws of this and of some other countries do allow that women shall sit upon the temporal thrones of the earth, but on the lowest step of the throne of the Church no woman has been allowed to sit as bearing authority, the romantic tale of the woman Pope* notwithstanding. Thereupon, I left the palace in wrath, feeling myself aggrieved that a woman should have attempted to dictate to me, and finding it hopeless to get a clear instruction from his lordship, – the woman taking up the word whenever I put a question to my lord the bishop. Nothing, therefore, came of that interview but fruitless labour to myself, and anger, of which I have since been ashamed.

Since that time I have continued in my parish, – working, not without zeal, though in truth, almost without hope, – and learning even from day to day that the opinions of men around me have declared me to be guilty of the crime imputed to me. And now the bishop has issued a commission as preparatory to proceeding against me under the Act for the punishment of clerical offences. In doing this, I cannot say that the bishop has been ill-advised, even though the advice may have come from that evil-tongued lady, his wife. And I hold that a woman may be called on for advice, with most salutary effect, in affairs as to which any show of female authority would be equally false and pernicious. With me it has ever been so, and I have had a counsellor by me as wise as she has been devoted.' It must be noticed that in the draught copy of his letter which Mr Crawley gave to his wife to read this last sentence was not inserted. Intending that she should read his letter, he omitted it till he made the fair copy. 'Over this commission his lordship has appointed Dr Tempest of Silverbridge to preside, and with him I have been in communication. I trust that the labours of the gentlemen of whom it is composed may be brought to a speedy close; and, having regard to their trouble, which in such a matter is, I fear, left without remuneration, I have informed Dr Tempest that I should write this letter to you with the intent and assured purpose of resigning the perpetual curacy of Hogglestock into your hands.

You will be good enough, therefore, to understand that I do so resign the living, and that I shall continue to administer the services of the church only till some clergyman, certified to me as coming from you or from the bishop, may present himself in the parish, and shall declare himself prepared to undertake the cure. Should it be so that Mr Thumble be sent hither again, I will sit under him, endeavouring to catch improvement from his teaching, and striving to overcome the contempt which I felt for him when he before visited this parish. I annex beneath my signature a copy of the letter which I have written to the bishop on this subject.

And now it behoves me, as the guardianship of the souls of those around me was placed in my hands by you, to explain to you as shortly as may be possible the reasons which have induced me to abandon my work. One or two whose judgment I do not discredit, – and I am allowed to name Dr Tempest of Silverbridge as one, – have suggested to me that I should take no step myself till after my trial. They think that I should have regard to the chance of the verdict, so that the preferment may still be mine should I be acquitted; and they say, that should I be acquitted, the bishop's action against me must of necessity cease. That they are right in these facts I do not doubt; but in giving such advice they look only to facts, having no regard to the conscience. I do not blame them. I should give such advice myself, knowing that a friend may give counsel as to outer things, but that a man must satisfy his inner conscience by his own perceptions of what is right and what is wrong.

I find myself to be ill-spoken of, to be regarded with hard eyes by those around me, my people thinking that I have stolen this money. Two farmers in this parish have, as I am aware, expressed opinions that no jury could acquit me honestly, and neither of these men have appeared in my church since the expression of that opinion. I doubt whether they have gone to other churches; and if not they have been deterred from all public worship by my presence. If this be so, how can I with a clear conscience remain among these men? Shall I take from their hands wages for those administrations, which their deliberately formed opinions will not allow them to accept from my hands?' And yet, though he thus pleaded against himself, he knew that the two men of whom he was speaking were thick-headed dolts who were always tipsy on Saturday nights, and who came to church perhaps once in three weeks.

Your kind heart will doubtless prompt you to tell me that no clergyman could be safe in his parish if he were to allow the opinion of chance parishioners to prevail against him; and you would probably lay down for my guidance that grand old doctrine, "Nil conscire sibi, nulla pallescere culpa."* Presuming that you may do so, I will acknowledge such guidance to be good. If my mind were clear in this matter, I would not budge an inch for any farmer, – no, nor for any bishop, further than he might by law compel me! But my mind is not clear. I do grow pale, and my hair stands on end with horror, as I confess to myself that I do not know whether I stole this money or no! Such is the fact. In all sincerity I tell you that I know not whether I be guilty or innocent. It may be that I picked up the cheque from the floor of my room, and afterwards took it out and used it, not knowing whence it had come to me. If it be so, I stole it, and am guilty before the laws of my country. If it be so, I am not fit to administer the Lord's sacraments to these people. When the cup was last in my hand and I was blessing them, I felt that I was not fit, and I almost dropped the chalice. That God will know me weakness and pardon me the perplexity of my mind, – that is between Him and His creature.

As I read my letter over to myself I feel how weak are my words, and how inefficient to explain to you the exact position in which I stand; but they will suffice to convince you that I am assuredly purposed to resign this parish of Hogglestock, and that it is therefore incumbent on you, as patron of the living, to nominate my successor to the benefice. I have only further to ask your pardon for this long letter, and to thank you again for the many and great marks of friendship which you have conferred on me. Alas, could you have foreseen in those old days how barren of all good would have been the life of him you then esteemed, you might perhaps have escaped the disgrace of being called the friend of one whom no one now regards with esteem.

> Nevertheless, I may still say that I am,
> With all affection, yours truly,
> Josiah Crawley.

The last paragraph of the letter was also added since his wife had read it. When he had first composed his letter, he had been somewhat proud of his words thinking that he had clearly told his story. But when, sitting alone at his desk, he read it again, filling his mind as he went on with ideas which he would fain have expressed to his old friend, were it not that he feared to indulge himself with too many words, he began to tell himself that his story was anything but well told. There was no expression there of the Hoggethan doctrine. In answer to such a letter as that the dean might well say, 'Think again of it. Try yet to save yourself. Never mind the two farmers, or Mr Thumble, or the bishop. Stick to the ship while there is a plank above the water.' Whereas it had been his desire to use words that should make the dean clearly understand that the thing was decided. He had failed, – as he had failed in everything throughout his life; but nevertheless the letter must go. Were he to begin again he would not do it better. So he added to what he had written a copy of his note to the bishop, and the letter was fastened and sent.

Mrs Crawley might probably have been more instant in her efforts to stop the letter, had she not felt that it would not decide everything. In the first place it was not improbable that the letter might not reach the dean till after his return home, – and Mrs Crawley had long since made up her mind that she would see the dean as soon as possible after his return. She had heard from Lady Lufton that it was not doubted in Barchester that he would be back at any rate before the judges came into the city. And then, in the next place, was it probable that the dean would act upon such a letter by filling up the vacancy, even if he did get it? She trusted in the dean, and knew that he would help them, if any help were possible. Should the verdict go against her husband, then indeed it might be that no hope would be possible. In such case she thought that the bishop with his commission might prevail. But she still believed that the verdict would be favourable, – if not with an assured belief, still with a hope that was sufficient to stand in lieu of a belief. No single man, let alone no twelve men, could think that her husband had intended to appropriate that money dishonestly. That he had taken it improperly, – without real possession, – she herself believed; but he had not taken it as a thief, and could not merit a thief's punishment.

After two days he got a reply from the bishop's chaplain, in which the chaplain expressed the bishop's commendation of Mr Crawley's present conduct. 'Mr Thumble shall proceed from hence to Hogglestock on next Sunday,' said the chaplain, 'and shall relieve you for the present from the burden of your duties. As to the future status of the parish, it will perhaps be best that nothing shall be done till the dean returns, – or perhaps till the assizes shall be over. This is the bishop's opinion.' It need hardly be explained that the promised visit of Mr Thumble to Hogglestock was gall and wormwood* to Mr Crawley. He had told the dean that should Mr Thumble come, he would endeavour to learn something even from him. But it may be doubted whether Mr Crawley in his present mood could learn anything useful from Mr Thumble. Giles Hoggett was a much more effective teacher.

'I will endure even that,' he said to his wife, as she handed to him back the letter from the bishop's chaplain.

CHAPTER 63

Two visitors to Hogglestock

The cross-grainedness of men is so great that things will often be forced to go wrong, even when they have the strongest possible natural tendency of their own to go right. It was so now in these affairs between the archdeacon and his son. The original difficulty was solved by the good feeling of the young lady, – by that and by the real kindness of the archdeacon's nature. They had come to terms which were satisfactory to both of them, and those terms admitted of perfect reconciliation between the father and his son. Whether the major did marry the lady or whether he did not, his allowance was to be continued to him, the archdeacon being perfectly willing to trust himself in the matter to the pledge which he had received from Miss Crawley. All that he required from his son was simply this, – that he should pull down the bills advertising the sale of his effects. Was any desire ever more rational? The sale had been advertised for a day just one week in advance of the assizes, and the time must have been selected, – so thought the archeacon, – with a malicious intention. Why, at any rate, should the things be sold at all, when the archdeacon had tacitly withdrawn his threats, – when he had given his son to understand that the allowance would still be paid quarterly with the customary archidiaconal regularity, and that no alteration was intended in those settlements under which the Plumstead foxes would, in the ripeness of time, become the property of the major himself. It was thus that the archdeacon looked at it, and as he did so, he thought that his son was the most cross-grained of men.

But the major had his own way of looking at the matter. He had, he flattered himself, dealt very fairly with his father. When he had first made up his mind to make Miss Crawley his wife, he had told his father of his intention. The archdeacon had declared that, if he did so, such and such results would follow, – results which, as was apparent to every one, would make it indispensable that the major should leave Cosby Lodge. The major had never complained. So he told himself. He had simply said to his father, – 'I shall do as I have said. You can do as you have said. Therefore, I shall prepare to leave Cosby Lodge.' He had so prepared; and as a part of that preparation, the auctioneer's bills had been stuck up on the posts and walls. Then the archdeacon had gone to work surreptitiously with the lady, – the reader will understand that we are still following the workings of the major's mind, – and having succeeded in obtaining a pledge which he had been wrong to demand, came forward very graciously to withdraw his threats. He withdrew his threats because he had succeeded in his object by other means. The major knew nothing of the kiss that had been given, of the two tears that had trickled down his father's nose, of the generous epithets which the archdeacon had applied to Grace. He did not guess how nearly his father had yielded altogether beneath the pressure of Grace's charms, – how willing he was to yield altogether at the first decent opportunity. His father had obtained a pledge from Grace that she would not marry in certain circumstances, – as to which circumstances the major was strongly resolved that they should form no bar to his marriage, – and then came forward with his eager demand that the sale should be stopped! The major could not submit to so much indignity. He had resolved that his father should have nothing to do with his marriage one way or the other. He would not accept anything from his father on the understanding that his father had any such right. His father had asserted such right with threats, and he, the major, taking such threats as meaning something, had seen that he must leave Cosby Lodge. Let his father come forward, and say that they meant nothing, that he abandoned all right to any interference as to his son's marriage, and then the son – would dutifully consent to accept his father's bounty! They were both cross-grained, as Mrs Grantly declared; but I think that the major was the most cross-grained of the two.

Something of the truth made its way into Henry Grantly's mind as he drove himself home from Barchester after seeing his grand-father. It was not that he began to think that his father was right, but that he almost perceived that it might be becoming in him to forgive some fault in his father. He had been implored to honour his father, and he was willing to do so, understanding that such honour must, to a certain degree, imply obedience, – if it could be done at no more than a moderate expense to his feelings. The threatened auctioneer was the cause of offence to his father, and he might see whether it would not be possible to have the sale postponed. There would, of course, be a pecuniary loss, and that in his diminished circumstances, – he would still talk to himself of his diminished circumstances, – might be inconvenient. But so much he thought himself bound to endure on his father's behalf. At any rate, he would consult the auctioneer at Silverbridge.

But he would not make any pause in the measure which he had proposed to himself, as likely to be conducive to his marriage. As for Grace's pledge, such pledges from young ladies never went for anything. It was out of the question that she should be sacrificed, even though her father had taken the money. And, moreover, the very gist of the major's generosity was to consist in his marrying her whether the father were guilty or innocent. He understood that perfectly, and understood also that it was his duty to make his purpose in this resepct known to Grace's family. He determined, therefore, that he would go over to Hogglestock, and see Mr Crawley before he saw the auctioneer.

Hitherto Major Grantly had never even spoken to Mr Crawley. It may be remembered that the major was at the present moment one of the bailsmen for the due appearance of Mr Crawley before the judge, and that he had been present when the magistrates sat at the inn in Silverbridge. He therefore knew the man's presence, but except on that occasion he had never even seen his intended future father-in-law. From the moment when he had first allowed himself to think of Grace, he had desired, yet almost feared, to make acquaintance with the father; but had been debarred from doing so by the peculiar position in which Mr Crawley was placed. He had felt that it would be impossible to speak to the father of his affection for the daughter without any allusion to the coming trial; and he did not know how such allusion could be made. Thinking of this, he had at different times almost resolved not to call at Hogglestock till the trial should be over. Then he would go there, let the result of the trial have been what it might. But it had now become necessary for him to go on at once. His father had precipitated matters by his appeal to Grace. He would appeal to Grace's father, and reach Grace through his influence.

He drove over to Hogglestock, feeling himself to be anything but comfortable as he came near to the house. And when he did reach the spot he was somewhat disconcerted to find that another visitor was in the house before him. He presumed this to be the case, because there stood a little pony horse, – an animal which did not strongly recommend itself to his instructed eye, – attached by its rein to the palings. It was a poor humble-looking beast, whose knees had very lately become acquainted with the hard and sharp stones of a newly-mended highway. The blood was even now red upon the wounds.

'He'll never be much good again,' said the major to his servant.

'That he won't sir,' said the man. 'But I don't think he's been very much good for some time back.'

'I shouldn't like to have to ride him into Silverbridge,' said the major, descending from the gig, and instructing his servant to move the horse and gig about as long as he might remain within the house. Then he walked across the little garden and knocked at the door. The door was immediately opened, and in the passage he found Mr Crawley, and another clergyman whom the reader will recognize as Mr Thumble. Mr Thumble had come over to make arrangements as to the Sunday services and the parochial work, and had been very urgent in impressing on Mr Crawley that the duties were to be left entirely to himself. Hence had come some bitter words, in which Mr Crawley, though no doubt he said the sharper things of the two, had not been able to vanquish his enemy so completely as he had done on former occasions.

'There must be no interference, my dear sir, – none whatever, if you please,' Mr Thumble had said.

'There shall be none of which the bishop shall have reason to complain,' Mr Crawley had replied.

'There must be none at all, Mr Crawley, if you please. It is only on that understanding that I have consented to take the parish temporarily into my hands. Mrs Crawley, I hope that there may be no mistake about the schools. It must be exactly as though I were residing on the spot.'

'Sir,' said Mr Crawley, very irate at this appeal to his wife, and speaking in a loud voice, 'do you misdoubt my word; or do you think that if I were minded to be false to you, that I should be corrected in my falsehood by the firmer faith of my wife?'

'I meant nothing about falsehood, Mr Crawley.'

'Having resigned this benefice for certain reasons of my own, with which I shall not trouble you, and acknowledging as I do, – and have done in writing under my hand to the bishop, – the propriety of his lordship's interference in providing for the services of the parish till my successor shall have been instituted, I shall, with what feelings of regret I need not say, leave you to the performance of your temporary duties.'

'That is all that I require, Mr Crawley.'

'But it is wholly unnecessary that you should instruct me in mine.'

'The bishop especially desires' – began Mr Thumble. But Mr Crawley interrupted him instantly.—

'If the bishop has directed you to give me such instruction, the bishop has been much in error. I will submit to receive none from him through you, sir. If you please, sir, let there be an end of it;'

and Mr Crawley waved his hand. I hope that the reader will conceive the tone of Mr Crawley's voice, and will appreciate the aspect of his face, and will see the motion of his hand, as he spoke these latter words. Mr Thumble felt the power of the man so sensibly that he was unable to carry on the contest. Though Mr Crawley was now but a broken reed, and was beneath his feet, yet Mr Thumble acknowledged to himself that he could not hold his own in debate with this broken reed. But the words had been spoken, and the tone of the voice had died away, and the fire in the eyes had burned itself out before the moment of the major's arrival. Mr Thumble was now returning to his horse, and having enjoyed, – if he did enjoy, – his little triumph about the parish, was becoming unhappy at the future dangers that awaited him. Perhaps he was the more unhappy because it had been proposed to him by authorities at the palace that he should repeatedly ride on the same animal from Barchester to Hogglestock and back. Mr Crawley was in the act of replying to lamentations on this subject, with his hand on the latch, when the major arrived – 'I regret to say, sir, that I cannot assist you by supplying any other steed.' Then the major had knocked, and Mr Crawley had at once opened the door.

'You probably do not remember me, Mr Crawley?' said the major. 'I am Major Grantly.' Mrs Crawley, who heard these words inside the room, sprang up from her chair, and could hardly resist the temptation to rush into the passage. She too had barely seen Major Grantly; and now the only bright gleam which appeared on her horizon depended on his constancy under circumstances which would have justified his inconstancy. But had he meant to be inconstant, surely he would never have come to Hogglestock!

'I remember you well, sir,' said Mr Crawley. 'I am under no common obligation to you. You are at present one of my bailsmen.'

'There's nothing in that,' said the major.

Mr Thumble, who had caught the name of Grantly, took off his hat, which he had put on his head. He had not been particular in keeping off his hat before Mr Crawley. But he knew very well that Archdeacon Grantly was a big man in the diocese; and though the Grantlys and the Proudies were opposed to each other, still it might be well to take off his hat before any one who had to do with the big ones of the diocese. 'I hope your respected father is well, sir?' said Mr Thumble.

'Pretty well, I thank you.' The major stood close up against the wall of the passage, so as to allow room for Mr Thumble to pass out. His business was one on which he could hardly begin to speak until the other visitor should have gone. Mr Crawley was standing with the door wide open in his hand. He also was anxious to be rid of Mr Thumble, – and was perhaps not so solicitous as a brother clergyman should have been touching the future fate of Mr Thumble in the matter of the bishop's old cob.

'Really I don't know what to do as to getting upon him again,' said Mr Thumble.

'If you will allow him to progress slowly,' said Mr Crawley, 'he will probably travel with the greater safety.'

'I don't know what you call slow, Mr Crawley. I was ever so much over two hours coming here from Barchester. He stumbled almost at every step.'

'Did he fall while you were on him?' asked the major.

'Indeed he did, sir. You never saw such a thing, Major Grantly. Look here.' Then Mr Thumble, turning round, showed that the rear portion of his clothes had not escaped without injury.

'It was well he was not going fast, or you would have come on to your head,' said Grantly.

'It was a mercy,' aid Thumble. 'But, sir, as it was, I came to the ground with much violence. It was on Spigglewick Hill, where the road is covered with loose stones. I see, sir, you have a gig and horse here, with a servant. Perhaps, as the circumstances are so very peculiar,—' Then Mr Thumble stopped, and looked up into the major's face with imploring eyes. But the major had no tenderness for such sufferings. 'I'm sorry to say that I am going quite the other way,' he said. 'I am returning to Silverbridge.'

Mr Thumble hesitated, and then made a renewed request. 'If you would not mind taking me to Silverbridge, I could get home from thence by railway; and perhaps you would allow your servant to take the horse to Barchester.'

Major Grantly was for a moment dumfounded. 'The request is most unreasonable, sir,' said Mr Crawley.

'That is as Major Grantly pleases to look at it,' said Mr Thumble.

'I am sorry to say that it is quite out of my power,' said the major.

'You can surely walk, leading the beast, if you fear to mount him,' said Mr Crawley.

'I shall do as I please about that,' said Mr Thumble. 'And, Mr Crawley, if you will have the kindness to leave things in the parish just as they are, – just as they are, I will be obliged to you. It is the bishop's wish that you should touch nothing.' Mr Thumble was by this time on the step, and Mr Crawley instantly slammed the door. 'The gentleman is a clergyman from Barchester,' said Mr Crawley, modestly folding his hands upon his breast, 'whom the bishop has sent over here to take upon himself temporarily the services of the church, and, as it appears, the duties also of the parish. I refrain from animadverting upon his lordship's choice.'

'And are you leaving Hogglestock?'

'When I have found a shelter for my wife and children I shall do so; nay, peradventure, I must do so before any such shelter can be found. I shall proceed in that matter as I am bid. I am one who can regard myself as no longer possessing the privilege of free action in anything. But while I have a room at your service, permit me to ask you to enter it.' Then Mr Crawley motioned him in with his hand, and Major Grantly found himself in the presence of Mrs Crawley and her younger daughter.

He looked at them both for a moment, and could trace much of the lines of that face which he loved so well. But the troubles of life had almost robbed the elder lady of her beauty; and with the younger, the awkward thinness of the last years of feminine childhood had not yet given place to the fulfilment of feminine grace. But the likeness in each was quite enough to make him feel that he ought to be at home in that room. He thought that he could love the woman as his mother, and the girl as his sister. He found it very difficult to begin any conversation in their presence, and yet it seemed to be his duty to begin. Mr Crawley had marshalled him into the room, and having done so, stood aside near the door. Mrs Crawley had received him very graciously, and having done so, seemed to be ashamed of her own hospitality. Poor Jane had shrunk back into a distant corner, near the open standing desk at which she was accustomed to read Greek to her father, and, of course, could not be expected to speak. If Major Grantly could have found himself alone with any one of the three, – nay, if he could have been there with any two, he could have opened his budget at once; but, before all the family, he felt the difficulty of his situation. 'Mrs Crawley,' said he, 'I have been most anxious to make your acquaintance, and I trust you will excuse the liberty I have taken in calling.'

'I feel grateful to you, as I am sure does also my husband.' So much she said, and then felt angry with herself for saying so much. Was she not expressing her strong hope that he might stand fast by her child, whereby the whole Crawley family would gain so much, – and the Grantly family lose much, in the same proportion?

'Sir,' said Mr Crawley, 'I owe you thanks, still unexpressed, in that you came forward, together with Mr Robarts of Framley, to satisfy the not unnatural requisition of the magistrates before whom I was called upon to appear in the early winter. I know not why any one should have ventured into such jeopardy on my account.'

'There was no jeopardy, Mr Crawley. Any one in the county would have done it.'

'I know not that; nor can I see that there was no jeopardy. I trust that I may assure you that there is no danger; – none, I mean, to you. The danger to myself and those belonging to me is, alas, very urgent. The facts of my position are pressing close upon me. Methinks I suffer more from the visit of the gentleman who has just departed from me than from anything that has yet happened to me. And yet he is in his right; – he is altogether in his right.'

'No, papa; he is not,' said Jane, from her standing ground near the upright desk.

'My dear,' said her father, 'you should be silent on such a subject. It is a matter hard to be undertstood in all its bearings, – even by those who are most conversant with them. But as to this we need not trouble Major Grantly.'

After that there was silence among them, and for a while it seemed as though there could be no approach to the subject on which Grantly had come thither to express himself. Mrs Crawley, in her despair, said something about the weather; and the major, trying to draw near the special subject, became bold enough to remark 'that he had had the pleasure of seeing Miss Crawley at Framley.' 'Mrs Robarts has been very kind,' said Mrs Crawley, 'very kind indeed. You can understand Major Grantly, that this must be a very sad house for any young person.' 'I don't think it is at all sad,' said Jane, still standing in the corner by the upright desk.

Then Major Grantly rose from his seat and walked across to the girl and took her hand. 'You are so like your sister,' said he. 'Your sister is a great friend of mine. She has often spoken to me of you. I hope we shall be friends some day.' But Jane could make no answer to this, though she had been able to vindicate the general character of the house while she was left in her corner by herself. 'I wonder whether you would be angry with me,' continued the major, 'if I told you that I wanted to speak a word to your father and mother alone?' To this Jane made no reply, but was out of the room almost before the words had reached the ears of her father and mother. Though she was only sixteen, and had as yet read nothing but Latin and Greek, – unless we are to count the twelve books of Euclid and Wood's Algebra, and sundry smaller exercises of the same description, – she understood, as well as any one then present, the reason why her absence was required.

As she closed the door the major paused for a moment, expecting, or perhaps hoping, that the father or the mother would say a word. But neither of them had a word to say. They sat silent, and as though conscience-stricken. Here was a rich man come, of whom they had heard that he might probably wish to wed their daughter. It was manifest enough to both of them that no man could marry into their family without subjecting himself to a heavy portion of that reproach and disgrace which was attached to them. But how was it possible that they should not care more for their daughter, – for their own flesh and blood, than for the incidental welfare of this rich man? As regarded the man himself they had heard everything that was good. Such a marriage was like the opening of paradise to their child. 'Nil conscire sibi,' said the father to himself, as he buckled on his armour for the fight.

When he had waited for a moment or two the major began. 'Mrs Crawley,' he said, addressing himself to the mother, 'I do not quite know how far you may be aware that I, – that I have for some time been, – been acquainted with your eldest daughter.'

'I have heard from her that she is acquainted with you,' said Mrs Crawley, almost panting with anxiety.

'I may as well make a clean breast of it at once,' said the major, smiling, 'and say outright that I have come here to request your permission and her father's to ask her to be my wife.' Then he was silent, and for a few moments neither Mr nor Mrs Crawley replied to him. She looked at her husband, and he gazed at the fire, and the smile died away from the major's face, as he watched the solemnity of them both. There was something almost forbidding in the peculiar gravity of Mr Crawley's countenance when, as at present, something operated within him to cause him to express dissent from any proposition that was made to him. 'I do not know how far this may be altogether new to you, Mrs Crawley,' said the major, waiting for a reply.

'It is not new to us,' said Mrs Crawley.

'May I hope, then, that you will not disapprove?'

'Sir,' said Mr Crawley, 'I am so placed by the untoward circumstances of my life that I can hardly claim to exercise over my own daughter that authority which should belong to a parent.'

'My dear, do not say that,' exclaimed Mrs Crawley.

'But I do say it. Within three weeks of this time I may be a prisoner, subject to the criminal laws of my country. At this moment I am without the power of earning bread for myself, or for my wife, or for my children. Major Grantly, you have even now seen the departure of the gentleman who has been sent here to take my place in this parish. I am, as it were, an outlaw here, and entitled neither to obedience nor respect from those who under other circumstances would be bound to give me both.'

'Major Grantly,' said the poor woman, 'no husband or father in the county is more closely obeyed or more thoroughly respected and loved.'

'I am sure of it,' said the major.

'All this, however, matters nothing,' continued Mr Crawley, 'and all speech on such homely matters would amount to an impertinence before you, sir, were it not that you have hinted at a purpose of connecting yourself at some future time with this unfortunate family.'

'I meant to be plain-spoken, Mr Crawley.'

'I did not mean to insinuate, sir, that there was aught of reticence in your words, so contrived that you might fall back upon the vagueness of your expression for protection, should you hereafter see fit to change your purpose. I should have wronged you much by such a suggestion. I rather was minded to make known to you that I, – or I should rather say, we,' and Mr Crawley pointed to his wife, – 'shall not accept your plainness of speech as betokening aught beyond a conceived idea in furtherance of which you have thought it expedient to make certain inquiries.'

'I don't quite follow you,' said the major. 'But what I want you to do is give me your consent to visit your daughter; and I want Mrs Crawley to write to Grace and tell her that it's all right.' Mrs Crawley was quite sure that it was all right, and was ready to sit down and write the letter that moment, if her husband would permit her to do so.

'I am sorry that I have not been explicit,' said Mr Crawley, 'but I will endeavour to make myself more plainly intelligible. My daughter, sir, is so circumstanced in reference to her father, that I, as her father and as a gentleman, cannot encourage any man to make a tender to her of his hand.'

'But I have made up my mind about all that.'

'And I, sir, have made up mine. I dare not tell my girl that I think she will do well to place her hand in yours. A lady, when she does that, should feel at least that her hand is clean.'

'It is the cleanest and the sweetest and the fairest hand in Barsetshire,' said the major. Mrs Crawley could not restrain herself, but running up to him, took his hand in hers and kissed it.

'There is unfortunately a stain, which is vicarial,' began Mr Crawley, sustaining up to that point his voice with Roman fortitude, – with a fortitude which would have been Roman had it not at that moment broken down under human feeling. He could keep it up no longer, but continued his speech with broken sobs, and with a voice altogether changed in its tone, – rapid now, whereas it had before been slow, – natural, whereas it had hitherto been affected, – human, whereas it had hitherto been Roman. 'Major Grantly,' he said, 'I am sore beset; but what can I say to you? My darling is as pure as the light of day, – only that she is soiled with my impurity. She is fit to grace the house of the best gentleman in England, had I not made her unfit.'

'She shall grace mine,' said the major. 'By God, she shall! – tomorrow, if she'll have me.' Mrs Crawley, who was standing beside him, again raised his hand and kissed it.

'It may not be so. As I began by saying, – or rather strove to say, for I have been overtaken by weakness, and cannot speak my mind, – I cannot claim authority over my child as would another man. How can I exercise authority from between a prison's bars?'

'She would obey your slightest wish,' said Mrs Crawley.

'I could express no wish,' said he. ' But I know my girl, and I am sure that she will not consent to take infamy with her into the house of the man who loves her.'

'There will be no infamy,' said the major. 'Infamy! I tell you that I shall be proud of the connexion.'

'You, sir, are generous in your prosperity. We will strive to be at least just in our adversity. My wife and children are to be pitied, – because of the husband and the father.'

'No!' said Mrs Crawley. 'I will not hear that said without denying it.'

'But they must take their lot as it has been given to them,' continued he. 'Such a position in life as that which you have proposed to bestow upon my child would be to her, as regards human affairs, great elevation. And from what I have heard, – I may be permitted to add also from what I now learn by personal experience, – such a marriage would be laden with fair promise of future happiness. But if you ask my mind, I think that my child is not free to make it. You, sir, have many relatives, who are not in love, as you are, all of whom would be affected by the stain of my disgrace. You have a daughter, to whom all your solicitude is due. No one should go to your house as your second wife who cannot feel that she will serve your child. My daughter would feel that she was bringing an injury upon the babe. I cannot bid her do this, – and I will not. Nor do I believe that she would do so if I bade her.' Then he turned his chair round, and sat with his face to the wall, wiping away the tears with a tattered handkerchief.

Mrs Crawley led the major away to the further window, and there stood looking up into his face. It need hardly be said that they also were crying. Whose eyes could have been dry after such a scene, – upon hearing such words? 'You had better go,' said Mrs Crawley. 'I know him so well. You had better go.'

'Mrs Crawley,' he said, whispering to her, 'if I ever desert her, may all that I love desert me! But you will help me?'

'You would want no help, were it not for this trouble.'

'But you will help me?'

Then she paused a moment. 'I can do nothing,' she said, 'but what he bids me.'

'You will trust me, at any rate?' said the major.

'I do trust you,' she replied. Then he went without saying a word further to Mr Crawley. As soon as he was gone, the wife went over to her husband, and put her arm gently round his neck as he was sitting. For a while the husband took no notice of his wife's caress, but sat motionless, with his face still turned to the wall. Then she spoke to him a word or two, telling him that their visitor was gone.

'My child!' he said. 'My poor child! my darling! She has found grace in this man's sight; but even of that has her father robbed her! The Lord has visited upon the children the sins of the father, and will do so to the third and fourth generation.'*

CHAPTER 64

The tragedy in Hook Court

Conway Dalrymple had hurried out of the room in Mrs Broughton's house in which he had been painting Jael and Sisera, thinking that it would be better to meet an angry and perhaps tipsy husband on the stairs, than it would be either to wait for him till he should make his way into his wife's room, or to hide away from him with the view of escaping altogether from so disagreeable an encounter. He had no fear of the man. He did not think that there would be any violence, – nor, as regarded himself, did he much care if there was to be violence. But he felt that he was bound, as far as it might be possible, to screen the poor woman from the ill effects of her husband's temper and condition. He was, therefore, prepared to stop Broughton on the stairs, and to use some force in arresting him on his way, should he find the man to be really intoxicated. But he had not descended above a stair or two before he was aware that the man below him, whose step had been heard in the hall, was not intoxicated, and that he was not Dobbs Broughton. It was Mr Musselboro.

'It is you, is it?' said Conway. 'I thought it was Broughton.' Then he looked into the man's face and saw that he was ashy pale. All that appearance of low-bred jauntiness which used to belong to him seemed to have been washed out of him. His hair had forgotten to curl, his gloves had been thrown aside, and even his trinkets were out of sight. 'What has happened?' said Conway. 'What is the matter? Something is wrong.' Then it occurred to him that Musselboro had been sent to the house to tell the wife of the husband's ruin.

'The servant told me that I should find you upstairs,' said Musselboro.

'Yes; I have been painting here. For some time past I have been doing a picture of Miss Van Siever. Mrs Van Siever has been here to-day.' Conway thought that this information would produce some strong effect on Clara's proposed husband; but he did not seem to regard the matter of the picture nor the mention of Miss Van Siever's name.

'She knows nothing of it?' said he. 'She doesn't know yet?'

Know what?' asked Conway. 'She knows that her husband has lost money.'

'Dobbs has — destroyed himself.'

'What!'

'Blew his brains out this morning just inside the entrance at Hook Court. The horror of drink was on him, and he stood just in the pathway and shot himself. Bangles was standing at the top of their vaults and saw him do it. I don't think Bangles will ever be a man again. O Lord! I shall never get over it myself. The body was there when I went in.' Then Musselboro sank back against the wall of the staircase, and stared at Dalrymple as though he still saw before him the terrible sight of which he had just spoken.

Dalrymple seated himself on the stairs and strove to bring his mind to bear on the tale which he had just heard. What was he to do, and how was that poor woman upstairs to be informed? 'You came here intending to tell her,' he said, in a whisper. He feared every moment that Mrs Broughton would appear on the stairs, and learn from a word or two what had happened without any hint to prepare her for the catastrophe.

'I thought you would be here. I knew you were doing the picture. He knew it. He'd had a letter to say so, — one of those anonymous ones.'

'But that didn't influence him?'

'I don't think it was that,' said Musselboro. 'He meant to have had it out with her; but it wasn't that as brought this about. Perhaps you didn't know that he was clean ruined?'

'She had told me.'

'Then she knew it?'

'Oh, yes; she knew that. Mrs Van Siever had told her. Poor creature! How are we to break this to her?'

'You and she are very thick,' said Mussleboro. 'I suppose you'll do it best.' By this time they were in the drawing-room, and the door was closed, Dalrymple had put his hand on the other man's arm, and had led him downstairs, out of reach of hearing from the room above. 'You'll tell her, — won't you?' said Musselboro. then Dalrymple tried to think what loving female friend there was who could break the news to the unfortunate woman. He knew of the Van Sievers, and he knew of the Demolines, and he almost knew that there was no other woman within reach whom he was entitled to regard as closely connected with Mrs Broughton. He was well aware that the anonymous letter of which Musselboro had just spoken had come from Miss Demolines, and he could not go there for sympathy and assistance. Nor could he apply to Mrs Van Siever after what had passed this morning. To Clara Van Siever he would have applied, but that it was impossible he should reach Clara except through her mother. 'I suppose I had better go to her,' he said, after a while. And then he went, leaving Musselboro in the drawing-room. 'I'm so bad with it,' said Musselboro, 'that I really don't know how I shall ever go up that court again.'

Conway Dalrymple made his way up the stairs with very slow steps, and as he did so he could not but think seriously of the nature of his friendship with this woman, and could not but condemn himself heartily for the folly and iniquity of his own conduct. Scores of times he had professed his love to her with half-expressed words, intended to mean nothing, as he said to himself when he tried to excuse himself, but enough to turn her head, even if they did not reach her heart. Now, this woman was a widow, and it came to be his duty to tell her that she was so. What if she should claim from him now the love which he had so often proffered to her! It was not that he feared that she would claim anything from him at this moment, – neither now, nor to-morrow, not the next day, – but the agony of the present meeting would produce others in which there would be some tenderness mixed with the agony; and so from one meeting to another the thing would progress. Dalrymple knew well enough how such things might progress. But in this danger before him, it was not of himself that he was thinking, but of her. How could he assist her at such a time without doing her more injury than benefit? And, if he did not assist her, who would do so? He knew her to be heartless; but even heartless people have hearts which can be touched and almost broken by certain sorrows. Her heart would not be broken by her husband's death, but it would become very sore if she were utterly neglected. He was now at the door, with his hand on the lock, and was wondering why she should remain so long within without making herself heard. Then he opened it, and found her seated in a lounging-chair, with her back to the door, and he could see that she had a volume of a novel in her hand. He understood it all. She was pretending to be indifferent to her husband's return. He walked up to her, thinking that she would recognize his step; but she made no sign of turning towards him. He saw the motion of her hair over the back of the chair as she affected to make herself luxuriously comfortable. She was striving to let her husband see that she cared nothing for him, or for his condition, or for his jealousy, if he were jealous, – or even for his ruin. 'Mrs Broughton,' he said, when he was close to her.

Then she jumped up quickly, and turned round, facing him. 'Where is Dobbs?' she said. 'Where is Broughton?'

'He is not here.'

'He is in the house, for I heard him. Why have you come back?'

Dalrymple's eye fell on the tattered canvas, and he thought of the doings of the past month. He thought of the picture of three Graces, which was hanging in the room below, and he thoroughly wished that he had never been introduced to the Broughton establishment. How was he to get through his present difficulty? 'No,' said he, 'Broughton did not come. It was Mr Musselboro whose steps you heard below.'

'What is he here for? What is he doing here? Where is Dobbs? Conway, there is something the matter. He has gone off!'

'Yes; – he has gone off.'

'The coward!'

'No; he was not a coward; – not in that way.'

The use of the past tense, unintentional as it had been, told the story to the woman at once. 'He is dead,' she said. Then he took both her hands in his and looked into her face without speaking a word. And she gazed at him with fixed eyes, and rigid mouth, while the quick coming breath just moved the curl of her nostrils. It occurred to him at the moment that he had never before seen her so wholly unaffected, and had never before observed that she was so totally deficient in all the elements of real beauty. She was the first to speak again. 'Conway,' she said, 'Tell it me all. Why do you not speak to me?'

'There is nothing further to tell,' said he.

Then she dropped his hands and walked away from him to the window, – and stood there looking out upon the stuccoed turret of a huge house that stood opposite. As she did so she was employing herself in counting the windows. Her mind was paralysed by the blow, and she knew not how to make any exertion with it for any purpose. Everything was changed with her, – and was changed in such a way that she could make no guess as to her future mode of life. She was suddenly a widow, a pauper, and utterly desolate, – while the only person in the whole world that she really liked was standing close to her. But in the midst of it all she counted the windows of the house opposite. Had it been possible for her she would have put her mind altogether to sleep.

He let her stand for a few minutes and then joined her at the window. 'My friend,' he said, 'what shall I do for you?'

'Do?' she said. 'What do you mean by – doing?'

'Come and sit down and let me talk to you,' he replied. Then he led her to the sofa, and as she seated herself I doubt whether she had not almost forgotten that her husband was dead.

'What a pity it was to cut it up,' she said, pointing to the rags of Jael and Sisera.

'Never mind the picture now. Dreadful as it is, you must allow yourself to think of him for a few minutes.'

'Think of what! O God! yes. Conway, you must tell me what to do. Was everything gone? It isn't about myself. I don't mind about myself. I wish it was me instead of him. I do. I do.'

'No wishing is of any avail.'

'But, Conway, how did it happen? Do you think it is true? That man would say anything to gain his object. Is he here now?'

'I believe he is here still.'

'I won't see him. Remember that. Nothing on earth shall make me see him.'

'It may be necessary, but I do not think it will be; – at any rate not yet.'

'I will never see him. I believe that he has murdered my husband. I do. I feel sure of it. Now I think of it I am quite sure of it. And he will murder you too; – about that girl. He will. I tell you I know the man.' Dalrymple simply shook his head, smiling sadly. 'Very well! you will see. But, Conway, how do you know that it is true? Do you believe it yourself?'

'I do believe it.'

'And how did it happen?'

'He could not bear the ruin that he had brought upon himself and you.'

'Then; – then—' She went no further in her speech; but Dalrymple assented by a slight motion of his head, and she had been informed sufficiently that her husband had perished by his own hand. 'What am I do do?' she said. 'Oh, Conway; – you must tell me. Was there ever so miserable a woman! Was it—poison?'

He got up and walked quickly across the room and back again to the place where she was sitting. 'Never mind about that now. You shall know all that in time. Do not ask any questions about that. If I were you I think I would go to bed. You will be better there than up, and this shock will make you sleep.'

'No,' she said. 'I will not go to bed. How should I know that that man would not come to me and kill me? I believe he murdered Dobbs; – I do. You are not going to leave me, Conway?'

'I think I had better, for a while. There are things which should be done. Shall I send one of the women to you?'

'There is not one of them that cares for me in the least. Oh, Conway, do not go; not yet. I will not be left alone in the house with him. You will be very cruel if you go and leave me now, — when you have so often said that you, — that you, — that you were my friend.' And now, at last, she began to weep.

'I think it will be best,' he said, 'that I should go to Mrs Van Siever. If I can manage it I will get Clara to come to you.'

'I do not want her,' said Mrs Broughton. 'She is a heartless cold creature, and I do not want to have her near me. My poor husband was ruined among them; — yes, ruined among them. It has all been done that she may marry that horrid man and live here in this house. I have known ever so long that he has not been safe among them.'

'You need fear nothing from Clara,' said Dalrymple, with some touch of anger in his voice.

'Of course you will say so. I can understand that very well. And it is natural that you should wish to be with her. Pray go.'

Then he sat beside her, and took her hand, and endeavoured to speak to her so seriously, that she herself might become serious, and if it might be possible, in some degree comtemplative. He told her how necessary it was that she should have some woman near her in her trouble, and explained to her that as far as he knew her female friends, there would be no one who would be so considerate with her as Clara Van Siever. She at one time mentioned the name of Miss Demolines; but Dalrymple altogether opposed the notion of sending for that lady, — expressing his opinion that the amiable Madalina had done all in her power to create quarrels both between Mrs Broughton and her husband and between Dobbs Broughton and Mrs Van Siever. And he spoke his opinion very fully about Miss Demolines. 'And yet you liked her once,' said Mrs Broughton. 'I never liked her,' said Dalrymple with energy. 'But all that matters nothing now. Of course you can send for her if you please; but I do not think her trustworthy, and I will not willingly come in contact with her.' Then Mrs Broughton gave him to understand that of course she must give way, but that in giving way she felt herself to be submitting to that ill-usage which is the ordinary lot of women, and to which she, among women, had been specially subjected. She did not exactly say as much, fearing that if she did he would leave her altogether, but that was the gist of her plaints and wails, and final acquiescence.

'And you are going?' she said, catching hold of his arm.

'I will employ myself altogether and only about your affairs, till I see you again.'

'But I want you to stay.'

'It would be madness. Look here; — lie down till Clara comes or till I return. Do not go beyond this room and your own. If she cannot come this evening I will return. Good-by now. I will see the servants as I go out, and tell them what ought to be told.'

'Oh, Conway,' she said, clutching hold of him again, 'I know that you despise me.'

'I do not despise you, and I will be as good a friend to you as I can. God bless you.' Then he went, and as he descended the stairs he could not refrain from telling himself that he did in truth despise her.

His first object was to find Musselboro, and to dismiss that gentleman from the house. For though he himself did not attribute to Mrs Van Siever's favourite any of those terrible crimes and potentialities for crime, with which Mrs Dobbs Broughton had invested him, still he thought it reasonable that the poor woman upstairs should not be subjected to the necessity of either seeing him or hearing him. But Musselboro had gone, and Dalrymple could not learn from the head woman-servant whom he saw, whether before going he had told to any one in the house the tale of the catastrophe which had happened in the City. Servants are wonderful actors, looking often as though they knew nothing when they know everything, – as though they understood nothing, when they understand all. Dalrymple made known all that was necessary, and the discreet upper servant listened to the tale with a proper amount of awe and horror and commiseration. 'Shot hisself in the City; – laws! You'll excuse me, sir, but we all know'd as master was coming to no good.' But she promised to do her best with her mistress, – and kept her promise. It is seldom that servants are not good in such straits as that.

From Mrs Broughton's house Dalrymple went directly to Mrs Van Siever's, and learned that Musselboro had been there about half an hour before, and had then gone off in a cab with Mrs Van Siever. It was now nearly four o'clock in the afternoon, and no one in the house knew when Mrs Van Siever would be back. Miss Van Siever was out, and had been out when Mr Musselboro had called, but was expeced in every minute. Conway therefore said that he would call again, and on returning found Clara alone. She had not then heard a word of the fate of Dobbs Broughton. Of course she would go at once to Mrs Broughton, and if necessary stay with her during the night. She wrote a line at once to her mother, saying where she was, and went across to Mrs Broughton leaning on Dalrymple's arm. 'Be good to her,' said Conway, as he left her at the door. 'I will,' said Clara. 'I will be as kind as my nature will allow me.' 'And remember,' said Conway, whispering into her ear as he pressed her hand at leaving her, 'that you are all the world to me.' It was perhaps not a proper time for an expression of love, but Clara Van Siever forgave the impropriety.

CHAPTER 65

Miss Van Siever makes her choice

Clara Van Siever did stay all that night with Mrs Broughton. In the course of the evening she received a note from her mother, in which she was told to come home to breakfast. 'You can go back to her afterwards,' said Mrs Van Siever; 'and I will see her myself in the course of the day, if she will let me.' The note was written on a scrap of paper, and had neither beginning nor end; but this was after the manner of Mrs Van Siever, and Clara was not in the least hurt or surprised. 'My mother will come to see you after breakfast,' said Clara, as she was taking her leave.

'Oh, goodness! And what shall I say to her?'

'You will have to say very little. She will speak to you.'

'I suppose everything belongs to her now,' said Mrs Broughton.

'I know nothing about that. I never do know anything of mamma's money matters.'

'Of course she'll turn me out. I do not mind a bit about that, – only I hope she'll let me have some mourning.' Then she made Clara promise that she would return as soon as possible, having in Clara's presence overcome all that feeling of dislike which she had expressed to Conway Dalrymple. Mrs Broughton was generally affectionate to those who were near to her. Had Musselboro forced himself into her presence, she would have become quite confidential with him before he left her.

'Mr Musselboro will be here directly,' said Mrs Van Siever, as she was starting for Mrs Broughton's house. 'You had better tell him to come to me there; or, stop, – perhaps you had better keep him here till I come back. Tell him to be sure and wait for me.'

'Very well, mamma. I suppose he can wait below?'

'Why should he wait below?' said Mrs Van Siever, very angrily.

Clara had made the uncourteous proposition to her mother with the express intention of making it understood that she would have nothing to say to him. 'He can come upstairs if he likes it,' said Clara; 'and I will go up to my room.'

'If you fight shy of him, miss, you may remember this, – that you will fight shy of me at the same time.'

'I am sorry for that, mamma, for I shall certainly fight shy of Mr Musselboro.'

'You can do as you please. I can't force you, and I shan't try. But I can make your life a burden to you, – and I will. What's the matter with the man that he isn't good enough for you? He's as good as any of your own people ever was. I hate your new-fangled airs, – with pictures painted on the sly, and all the rest of it. I hate such ways. See what they have brought that wretched man to, and the poor fool his wife. If you go and marry that painter, some of these days you'll be very much like what she is. Only I doubt whether he has got courage enough to blow his brains out.' With these comfortable words, the old woman took herself off, leaving Clara to entertain her lover as best she might choose.

Mr Musselboro was not long in coming, and, in accordance with Mrs Van Siever's implied directions to her daughter, was shown up into the drawing-room. Clara gave him her mother's message in a very few words. 'I was expressly told, sir, to ask you to stop, if it is not inconvenient, as she very much wants to see you.' Mr Musselboro declared that of course he would stop. He was only too happy to have an opportunity of remaining in such delightful society. As Clara answered nothing to this, he went on to say that he hoped that the melancholy occasion of Mrs Van Siever's visit to Mrs Broughton might make a long absence necessary, – he did not, indeed, care how long it might be. He had recovered now from that paleness, and that want of gloves and jewellery which had befallen him on the previous day immediately after the sight he had seen in the City. Clara made no answer to the last speech, but, putting some things together in her work-basket, prepared to leave the room. 'I hope you are not going to leave me?' he said, in a voice that was intended to convey much of love, and something of melancholy.

'I am so shocked by what has happened, Mr Musselboro, that I am altogether unfit for conversation. I was with poor Mrs Broughton last night, and I shall return to her when mamma comes home.'

'It is sad, certainly; but what was there to be expected? If you'd only seen how he used to go on.' To this Clara made no answer. 'Don't go yet,' said he; 'there is something that I want to say to you. There is, indeed.'

Clara Van Siever was a young woman whose presence of mind rarely deserted her. It occurred to her now that she must undergo on some occasion the nuisance of a direct offer from this man, and that she could have not better opportunity of answering him after her own fashion than the present. Her mother was absent, and the field was her own. And, moreover, it was a point in her favour that the tragedy which had so lately occurred, and to which she had just now alluded, would give her a fair excuse for additional severity. At such a moment no man could, she told herself, be justified in making an offer of his love, and therefore she might rebuke him with the less remorse. I wonder whether the last words which Conway Dalrymple had spoken to her stung her conscience as she thought of this! She had now reached the door, and was standing close to it. As Mr Musselboro did not at once begin, she encouraged him. 'If you have anything special to tell me, of course I will hear you,' she said.

'Miss Clara,' he began, rising from his chair, and coming into the middle of the room, 'I think you know what my wishes are.' Then he put his hand upon his heart. 'And your respected mother is the same way of thinking. It's that that emboldens me to be so sudden. Not but what my heart has been yours and yours only all along, before the old lady so much as mentioned it.' Clara would give him no assistance, not even the aid of a negative, but stood there quite passive, with her hand on the door. 'Since I first had the pleasure of seeing you I have always said to myself, "Augustus Musselboro, that is the woman for you, if you can only win her." But then there was so much against me, – wasn't there?' She would not even take advantage of this by assuring him that there certainly always had been much against him, but allowed him to go on till he should run out all the length of his tether. 'I mean, of course, in the way of money,' he continued. 'I hadn't much that I could call my own when your respected mamma first allowed me to become acquainted with you. But it's different now; and I think I may say that I'm all right in that respect. Poor Broughton's going in this way will make it a deal smoother to me; and I may say that I and your mamma will be all in all to each other now about money.' Then he stopped.

'I don't quite understand what you mean by all this,' said Clara.

'I mean that there isn't a more devoted fellow in all London than what I am to you.' Then he was about to go down on one knee, but it occurred to him that it would not be convenient to kneel to a lady who would stand quite close to the door. 'One and one, if they're put together well, willl often make more than two, and so they shall with us,' said Musselboro, who began to feel that it might be expedient to throw a little spirit into his words.

'If you have done,' said Clara, 'you may as well hear me for a minute. And I hope you will have sense to understand that I really mean what I say.'

'I hope you will remember what are your mamma's wishes.'

'Mamma's wishes have no influence whatsoever with me in such matters as this. Mamma's arrangements with you are for her own convenience, and I am not a party to them. I do not know anything about mamma's money, and I do not want to know. But under no possible circumstances will I consent to become your wife. Nothing that mamma could say or do would induce me even to think of it. I hope you will be man enough to take this for an answer, and say nothing more about it.'

'But, Miss Clara—'

'It's no good your Miss Claraing me, sir. What I have said you may be sure I mean. Good-morning, sir.' Then she opened the door, and left him.

'By Jove, she is a Tartar,' said Musselboro to himself, when he was alone. 'They're both Tartars, but the younger is the worse.' Then he began to speculate whether Fortune was not doing the best for him in so arranging that he might have the use of the Tartar-mother's money without binding himself to endure for life the Tartar qualities of the daughter.

It had been understood that Clara was to wait at home till her mother should return before she again went across to Mrs Broughton. At about eleven Mrs Van Siever came in, and her daughter intercepted her at the dining-room door before she had made her way upstairs to Mr Musselboro. 'How is she, mamma?' said Clara with something of hypocrisy in her assumed interest for Mrs Broughton.

'She is an idiot,' said Mrs Van Siever.

'She has had a terrible misfortune!'

'That is no reason why she should be an idiot; and she is heartless too. She never cared a bit for him; — not a bit.'

'He was a man whom it was impossible to care for much. I will go to her now, mamma.'

'Where is Musselboro?'

'He is upstairs.'

'Well?'

'Mamma, that is quite out of the question. Quite. I would not marry him to save myself from starving.'

'You do not know what starving is yet, my dear. Tell me the truth at once. Are you engaged to that painter?' Clara paused a moment before she answered, not hesitating as to the expediency of telling her mother any truth on the matter in question, but doubting what the truth might really be. Could she say that she was engaged to Mr Dalrymple, or could she say that she was not? 'If you tell me a lie, miss, I'll have you put out of the house.'

'I certainly shall not tell you a lie. Mr Dalrymple has asked me to be his wife, and I have made him no answer. If he asks me again I shall accept him.'

'Then I order you not to leave this house,' said Mrs Van Siever.

'Surely I may go to Mrs Broughton?'

'I order you not to leave this house,' said Mrs Van Siever again, – and thereupon she stalked out of the dining-room and went upstairs. Clara had been standing with her bonnet on, ready dressed to go out, and the mother made no attempt to send the daughter up to her room. That she did not expect to be obeyed in her order may be inferred from the first words which she spoke to Mr Musselboro. 'She has gone off to that man now. You are no good, Musselboro, at this kind of work.'

'You see, Mrs Van, he had the start of me so much. And then being at the West End, and all that, gives a man such a standing with a girl!'

'Bother!' said Mrs Van Siever, as her quick ear caught the sound of the closing hall-door. Clara had stood a minute or two to consider, and then had resolved that she would disobey her mother. She tried to excuse her own conduct to her own satisfaction as she went. 'There are some things,' she said, 'which even a daughter cannot hear from her mother. If she chooses to close the door against me, she must do so.'

She found Mrs Broughton still in bed, and could not but agree with her mother that the woman was both silly and heartless.

'Your mother says that everything must be sold up,' said Mrs Broughton.

'At any rate you would hardly choose to remain here,' said Clara.

'But I hope she'll let me have my own things. A great many of them are altogether my own. I know there's a law that a woman may have her own things, even though her husband has, – done what poor Dobbs did. And I think she was hard upon me about the mourning. They never do mind giving credit for such things as that, and though there is a bill due to Mrs Morell now, she has had a deal of Dobbs's money.' Clara promised her that she should have mourning to her heart's content. 'I will see to that myself,' she said.

Presently there was a knock at the door, and the discreet head-servant beckoned Clara out of the room. 'You are not going away,' said Mrs Proughton. Clara promised her that she would not go without coming back again. 'He will be here soon, I suppose, and perhaps you had better see him; though, for the matter of that, perhaps you had better not, because he is so much cut up about poor Dobbs.' The servant had come up to tell Clara that the 'he' in question was at the present moment waiting for her below stairs.

The first words which passed between Dalrymple and Clara had reference to the widow. He told her what he had learned in the City, — that Broughton's property had never been great, and that his personal liabilities at the time of his death were supposed to be small. But he had fallen lately altogether into the hands of Musselboro, who, though penniless himself in the way of capital, was backed by the money of Mrs Van Siever. There was no doubt that Broughton had destroyed himself in the manner told by Musselboro, but the opinion in the City was that he had done so rather through the effects of drink than because of his losses. As to the widow, Dalrymple thought that Mrs Van Siever, or nominally, perhaps, Musselboro, might be induced to settle an annuity on her, if she would give up everything quietly.

'I doubt whether your mother is not responsible for everything Broughton owed when he died, — for everything, that is, in the way of business; and if so, Mrs Broughton will certainly have a claim upon the estate.' It occurred to Dalrymple once or twice that he was talking to Clara about Mrs Van Siever as though he and Clara were more closely bound together than were Clara and her mother; but Clara seemed to take this in good part, and was as solicitous as was he himself in the matter of Mrs Broughton's interest.

Then the discreet head-servant knocked and told them that Mrs Broughton was very anxious to see Mr Dalrymple, but that Miss Van Siever was on no account to go away. She was up, and in her dressing-gown, and had gone into the sitting-room. 'I will come directly,' said Dalrymple, and the discreet head-servant retired.

'Clara,' said Conway, 'I do not know when I may have another chance of asking for an answer to my question. You heard my question?'

'Yes, I heard it.'

'And will you answer it?'

'If you wish it, I will.'

'Of course I wish it. You understood what I said upon the doorstep yesterday.'

'I don't think much of that; men say those things so often. What you said before was serious, I suppose?'

'Serious! Heavens! do you think that I am joking?'

'Mamma wants me to marry Mr Musselboro.'

'He is a vulgar brute. It would be impossible.'

'It is impossible; but mamma is very obstinate. I have no fortune of my own, — not a shilling. She told me to-day that she would turn me into the street. She forbade me to come here, thinking I should meet you, but I came, because I had promised Mrs Broughton. I am sure that she will never give me one shilling.'

Dalrymple paused for a moment. It was certainly true that he had regarded Clara Van Siever as an heiress, and had at first been attracted to her because he thought it expedient to marry an heiress. But there had since come something beyond that, and there was perhaps less of regret than most men would have felt as he gave up his golden hopes. He took her into his arms and kissed her, and called her his own. 'Now we understand each other,' he said.

'If you wish it to be so.'

'I do wish it.'

'And I shall tell my mother to-day that I am engaged to you, — unless she refuses to see me. Go to Mrs Broughton now. I feel that we are almost cruel to be thinking of ourselves in this house at such a time.' Upon this Dalrymple went, and Clara Van Siever was left to her reflections. She had never before had a lover. She had never had even a friend whom she loved and trusted. Her life had been passed at school till she was nearly twenty, and since then she had been vainly endeavouring to accommodate herself and her feelings to her mother. Now she was about to throw herself into the absolute power of a man who was nearly a stranger to her! But she did love him, as she had never loved any one else; — and then, on the other side, there was Mr Musselboro!

Dalrymple was upstairs for an hour, and Clara did not see him again before he left the house. It was clear to her, from Mrs Broughton's first words, that Conway had told her what had passed. 'Of course I shall never see anything more of either of you now?' said Mrs Broughton.

'I should say that probably you will see a great deal of us both.'

'There are some people,' said Mrs Broughton, 'who can do well for their friends, but can never do well for themselves. I am one of them. I saw at once how great a thing it would be for both of you to bring you two together, — especially for you, Clara; and therefore I did it. I may say that I never had it out of my mind for months past. Poor Dobbs misunderstood what I was doing. God knows how far that may have brought about what has happened.'

'Oh, Mrs Broughton!'

'Of course he could not be blind to one thing; — nor was I. I mention it now because it is right, but I shall never, never allude to it again. Of course he saw, and I saw, that Conway—was attached to me. Poor Conway meant no harm. I was aware of that. But there was the terrible fact. I knew at once that the only coure for him was a marriage with some girl that he could respect. Admiring you as I do, I immediately resolved on bringing you two together. My dear,

I have been successful, and I heartily trust that you may be happier than Maria Broughton.'

Miss Van Siever knew the woman, understood all the facts, and pitying the condition of the wretched creature, bore all this without a word of rebuke. She scorned to put out her strength against one who was in truth so weak.

CHAPTER 67

Requiescat in pace

Things were very gloomy at the palace. It has been already said that for many days after Dr Tempest's visit to Barchester the intercourse between the bishop and Mrs Proudie had not been of a pleasant nature. He had become so silent, so sullen, and so solitary in his ways, that even her courage had been almost cowed, and for a while she had condescended to use gentler measures, with the hope that she might thus bring her lord round to his usual state of active submission; or perhaps, if we strive to do her full justice, we may say of her that her effort was made conscientiously, with the idea of inducing him to do his duty with proper activity. For she was a woman not without a conscience, and by no means indifferent to the real service which her husband, as bishop of the diocese, was bound to render to the affairs of the Church around her. Of her own struggles after personal dominion she was herself unconscious; and no doubt they gave her, when recognized and acknowledged by herself, many stabs to her inner self, of which no single being in the world knew anything. And now, as after a while she failed in producing any amelioration in the bishop's mood, her temper also gave way, and things were becoming very gloomy and very unpleasant.

The bishop and his wife were at present alone in the palace. Their married daughter and her husband had left them, and their unmarried daughter was also away. How far the bishop's mood may have produced this solitude in the vast house I will not say. Probably Mrs Proudie's state of mind may have prevented her from having other guests in the place of those who were gone. She felt herself to be almost disgraced in the eyes of all those around her by her husband's long absence from the common rooms of the house and by his dogged silence at meals. It was better, she thought, that they two should be alone in the palace.

Her own efforts to bring him back to something like life, to some activity of mind if not of body, were made constantly; and when she failed, as she did fail day after day, she would go slowly to her own room, and lock her door, and look back in her solitude at all the days of her life. She had agonies in these minutes of which no one near her knew anything. She would seize with her arm the part of the bed near which she would stand, and hold by it, rasping it, as though she were afraid to fall; and then, when it was at the worst with her, she would go to her closet, – a closet that no eyes ever saw unlocked but her own, – and fill for herself and swallow some draught; and then she would sit down with the Bible before her, and read it sedulously. She spent hours every day with her Bible before her, repeating to herself whole chapters, which she almost knew by heart.

It cannot be said that she was a bad woman, though she had in her time done an indescribable amount of evil. She had endeavoured to do good, failing partly by ignorance and partly from the effects of an unbridled, ambitious temper. And now, even amidst her keenest sufferings, her ambition was by no means dead. She still longed to rule the diocese by means of her husband, – but was made to pause and hesitate by the unwonted mood that had fallen upon him. Before this, on more than one occasion, and on one very memorable occasion, he had endeavoured to combat her. He had fought with her, striving to put her down. He had failed, and given up the hope of any escape for himself in that direcion. On those occasions her courage had never quailed for a moment. While he openly struggled to be master, she could openly struggle to be mistress, – and could enjoy the struggle. But nothing like this moodiness had ever come upon him before.

She had yielded to it for many days, striving to coax him by little softnesses of which she herself had been ashamed as she practised them. They had served her nothing, and at last she determined that something else must be done. If only for his sake, to keep some life in him, something else must be done. Were he to continue as he was now, he must give up his diocese, or, at any rate, declare himself too ill to keep the working of it in his own hands. How she hated Mr Crawley for all the sorrow that he had brought upon her and her house!

And it was still the affair of Mr Crawley which urged her on to further action. When the bishop received Mr Crawley's letter he said nothing of it to her; but he handed it over to his chaplain. The chaplain, fearing to act upon it himself, handed it to Mr Thumble, whom he knew to be one of the bishop's commission, and Mr Thumble, equally fearing responsibility in the present state of affairs at the palace, found himself obliged to consult Mrs Proudie. Mrs

Proudie had no doubt as to what should be done. The man had abdicated his living, and of course some provision must be made for the services. She would again make an attempt upon her husband, and therefore she went into his room holding Mr Crawley's letter in her hand.

'My dear,' she said, 'here is Mr Crawley's letter. I suppose you have read it?'

'Yes,' said the bishop; 'I have read it.'

'And what will you do about it? Something must be done.'

'I don't know,' said he. He did not even look at her as he spoke. He had not turned his eyes upon her since she had entered the room.

'But, bishop, it is a letter that requires to be acted upon at once. We cannot doubt that the man is doing right at last. He is submitting himself where his submission is due; but his submission will be of no avail unless you take some action upon his letter. Do you not think that Mr Thumble had better go over?'

'No, I don't. I think Mr Thumble had better stay where he is,' said the irritated bishop.

'What, then, would you wish to have done?'

'Never mind,' said he.

'But, bishop, that is nonsense,' said Mrs Proudie, adding something of severity to the tone of her voice.

'No, it isn't nonsense,' said he. Still he did not look at her, nor had he done so for a moment since she had entered the room. Mrs Proudie could not bear this, and as her anger became strong within her breast, she told herself that she would be wrong to bear it. She had tried what gentleness would do, and she had failed. It was now imperatively necessary that she should resort to sterner measures. She must make him understand that he must give her authority to send Mr Thumble to Hogglestock.

'Why do you not turn round and speak to me properly?' she said.

'I do not want to speak to you at all,' the bishop answered.

This was very bad; – almost anything would be better than this. He was sitting now over the fire, with his elbows on his knees, and his face buried in his hands. She had gone round the room so as to face his countenance. 'This will not do at all,' she said. 'My dear, do you know that you are forgetting yourself altogether?'

'I wish I could forget myself.'

'That might be all very well if you were in a position in which you owed no service to any one; or, rather, it would not be well then, but the evil would not be so manifest. You cannot do your duty in the diocese if you continue to sit there doing nothing, with your head upon your hands. Why do you not rally, and get to your work like a man?'

'I wish you would go away and leave me,' he said.

'No, bishop, I will not go away and leave you. You have brought yourself to such a condition that it is my duty as your wife to stay by you; and if you neglect your duty, I will not neglect mine.'

'It was you that brought me to it.'

'No, sir, that is not true. I did not bring you to it.'

'It is the truth.' And now he got up and looked at her. For a moment he stood upon his legs, and then again he sat down with his face turned towards her. 'It is the truth. You have brought on me such disgrace that I cannot hold up my head. You have ruined me. I wish I were dead; and it is all through you that I am driven to wish it.'

Of all that she had suffered in her life this was the worst. She clasped both her hands to her side as she listened to him, and for a minute or two she made no reply. When he ceased from speaking he again put his elbows on his knees and again buried his face in his hands. What had she better do, or how was it expedient that she should treat him? At this crisis the whole thing was so important to her that she would have postponed her own ambition and would have curbed her temper had she thought that by doing so she might in any degree have benefited him. But it seemed to her that she could not rouse him by conciliation. Neither could she leave him as he was. Something must be done. 'Bishop,' she said, 'the words that you speak are sinful, very sinful.'

'You have made them sinful,' he replied.

'I will not hear that from you. I will not indeed. I have endeavoured to do my duty by you, and I do not deserve it. I am endeavouring to do my duty now, and you must know that it would ill become me to remain quiescent while you are in such a state. The world around you is observing you, and knows that you are not doing your work. All I want of you is that you should arouse yourself, and go to your work.'

'I could do my work very well,' he said, 'if you were not here.'

'I suppose, then you wish that I were dead?' said Mrs Proudie. To this he made no reply, nor did he stir himself. How could flesh and blood bear this, – female flesh and blood, – Mrs Proudie's flesh and blood? Now, at last, her temper once more got the better of her judgment, probably much to her immediate satisfaction, and she spoke out. 'I'll tell you what it is, my lord; if you are imbecile, I must be active. It is very sad that should have to assume your authority—'

'I will not allow you to assume my authority.'

'I must do so, or must else obtain a medical certificate as to your incapacity, and beg that some neighbouring bishop may administer the diocese. Things shall not go on as they are now. I, at any rate, will do my duty. I shall tell Mr Thumble that he must go over to Hogglestock, and arrange for the duties of the parish.'

'I desire that you will do no such thing,' said the bishop, now again looking up at her.

'You may be sure that I shall,' said Mrs Proudie, and then she left the room.

He did not even yet suppose that she would go about this work at once. The condition of his mind was in truth bad, and was becoming worse, probably, from day to day; but still he did make his calculations about things, and now reflected that it would be sufficient if he spoke to his chaplain to-morrow about Mr Crawley's letter. Since the terrible scene that Dr Tempest had witnessed, he had never been able to make up his mind as to what great step he would take, but he had made up his mind that some great step was necessary. There were moments in which he thought that he would resign his bishopric. For such resignation, without acknowledged incompetence on the score of infirmity, the precedents were very few; but even if there were no precedents, it would be better to do that than to remain where he was. Of course there would be disgrace. But then it would be disgrace from which he could hide himself. Now there was equal disgrace; and he could not hide himself. And then such a measure as that would bring punishment where punishment was due. It would bring his wife to the ground, – her who had brought him to the ground. The suffering should not be all his own. When she found that her income, and her palace, and her position were all gone, then perhaps she might repent the evil that she had done him. Now, when he was left alone, his mind went back to this, and he did not think of taking immediate measures, – measures on that very day, – to prevent the action of Mr Thumble.

But Mrs Proudie did take immediate steps. Mr Thumble was at this moment in the palace waiting for instructions. It was he who had brought Mr Crawley's letter to Mrs Proudie, and she now returned to him with that letter in her hand. The reader will know what was the result. Mr Thumble was sent off to Hogglestock at once on the bishop's old cob, and, – as will be remembered, – fell into trouble on the road. Late in the afternoon he entered the palace yard, having led the cob by the bridle the whole way home from Hogglestock.

Some hour or two before Mr Thumble's return Mrs Proudie returned to her husband, thinking it better to let him know what she had done. She resolved to be very firm with him, but at the same time she determined not to use harsh language if it could be avoided. 'My dear,' she said, 'I have arranged with Mr Thumble.' She found him on this occasion sitting at his desk with papers before him, with a pen in his hand; and she could see at a glance that nothing had been written on the paper. What would she have thought had she known that when he placed the sheet before him he was proposing to consult the archbishop as to the propriety of his resignation! He had not, however, progressed so far as to write even the date of his letter.

'You have done what?' said he, throwing down the pen.

'I have arranged with Mr Thumble as to going out to Hogglestock,' said she firmly. 'Indeed he has gone already.' Then the bishop jumped up from his seat and rang the bell with violence. 'What are you going to do?' said Mrs Proudie.

'I am going to depart from here,' said he. 'I will not stay here to be the mark of scorn for all men's fingers. I will resign the diocese.'

'You cannot do that,' said his wife.

'I can try, at any rate,' said he. Then the servant entered. 'John,' said he, addressing the man, 'let Mr Thumble know the moment he returns to the palace that I wish to see him here. Perhaps he may not come to the palace. In that case let word be sent to his house.'

Mrs Proudie allowed the man to go before she addressed her husband again. 'What do you mean to say to Mr Thumble when you see him?'

'That is nothing to you.'

She came up to him and put her hand upon his shoulder, and spoke to him very gently. 'Tom,' she said, 'is that the way in which you speak to your wife?'

'Yes, it is. You have driven me to it. Why have you taken upon yourself to send that man to Hogglestock?'

'Because it was right to do so. I came to you for instruction, and you would give none.'

'I should have given what instruction I pleased in proper time. Thumble shall not go to Hogglestock next Sunday.'

'Who shall go, then?'

'Never mind. Nobody. It does not matter to you. If you will leave me now I shall be obliged to you. There will be an end of all this very soon, – very soon.'

Mrs Proudie after this stood for a while thinking what she would say; but she left the room without uttering another word. As she looked at him a hundred different thoughts came into her mind. She had loved him dearly, and she loved him still; but she knew now, – at this moment felt absolutely sure, – that by him she was hated! In spite of all her roughness and temper, Mrs Proudie was in this like other women, – that she would fain have been loved had it been possible. She had always meant to serve him. She was conscious of that; conscious also in a way that, although she had been industrious, although she had been faithful, although she was clever, yet she had failed. At the bottom of her heart she knew that she had been a bad wife. And yet she had meant to be a pattern wife! She had meant to be a good Christian; but she had so exercised her Christianity that not a soul in the world loved her, or would endure her presence if it could be avoided! She had sufficient insight to the minds and feelings of those around her to be aware of this. And now her husband had told her that her tyranny to him was so overbearing that he must throw up his great position, and retire to an obscurity that would be exceptionally disgraceful to them both, because he could no longer endure the public disgrace which her conduct brought upon him in his high place before the world! Her heart was too full for speech; and she left him, very quietly closing the door behind her.

She was preparing to go up to her chamber, with her hand on the bannisters and with her foot on the stairs, when she saw the servant who had answered the bishop's bell. 'John,' she said, 'when Mr Thumble comes to the palace, let me see him before he goes to my lord.'

'Yes, ma'am,' said John, who well understood the nature of these quarrels between his master and his mistress. But the commands of the mistress were still paramount among the servants, and John proceeded on his mission with the view of accomplishing Mrs Proudie's behests. Then Mrs Proudie went upstairs to her chamber, and locked her door.

Mr Thumble returned to Barchester that day, leading the broken-down cob; and a dreadful walk he had. He was not good at walking, and before he came near Barchester he had come to entertain a violent hatred for the beast he was leading. The leading of a horse that is tired, or in pain, or lame, or even stiff in his limbs, is not pleasant work. The brute will not accommodate his paces to the man, and will contrive to make his head very heavy on the bridle. And he will not walk on the part of the road which the man intends for him, but will lean against the man, and will make himself altogether very disagreeable. It may be understood, therefore, that Mr Thumble was not in a good humour when he entered the palace yard. Nor was he altogether quiet in his mind as to the injury which he had done to the animal. 'It was the brute's fault,' said Mr Thumble. 'It comes generally of not knowing how to ride 'em,' said the groom. For Mr Thumble, though he often had a horse out of the episcopal stables, was not ready with his shillings to the man who waited upon him with the steed.

He had not, however, come to any satisfactory understanding respecting the broken knees when the footman from the palace told him he was wanted. It was in vain that Mr Thumble pleaded that he was nearly dead with fatigue, that he had walked all the way from Hogglestock and must go home to change his clothes. John was peremptory with him, insisting that he must wait first upon Mrs Proudie and then upon the bishop. Mr Thumble might perhaps have turned a deaf ear to the latter command, but the former was one which he felt himself bound to obey. So he entered the palace, rather cross, very much soiled as to his outer man; and in this condition went up a certain small staircase which was familiar to him, to a small parlour which adjoined Mrs Proudie's room, and there awaited the arrival of the lady. That he should be required to wait some quarter of an hour was not surprising to him; but when half an hour was gone, and he remembered himself of his own wife at home, and of the dinner which he had not yet eaten, he ventured to ring the bell. Mrs Proudie's own maid, Mrs Draper by name, came to him and said that she had knocked twice at Mrs Proudie's door and would knock again. Two minutes after that she returned, running into the room with her arms extended, and exclaiming, 'Oh, heavens, sir; mistress is dead!' Mr Thumble, hardly knowing what he was about, followed the woman into the bedroom and there he found himself standing awestruck before the corpse of her who had so lately been the presiding spirit of the palace.

The body was still resting on its legs, leaning against the end of the side of the bed, while one of the arms was close clasped round the bed-post. The mouth was rigidly close, but the eyes were open as though staring at him. Nevertheless there could be no doubt from the first glance that the woman was dead. He went up close to it, but did not dare to touch it. There was no one as yet there but he and Mrs Draper; – no one else knew what had happened.

'It's her heart,' said Mrs Draper.

'Did she suffer from heart complaint ?' he asked.

'We suspected it, sir, though nobody knew it. She was very shy of talking about herself.'

'We must send for the doctor at once,' said Mr Thumble. 'We had better touch nothing till he is here.' Then they retreated and the door was locked.

In ten minutes everybody in the house knew it except the bishop; and in twenty minutes the nearest apothecary with his assistant were in the room, and the body had been properly laid upon the bed. Even then the husband had not been told, – did not know either his relief or his loss. It was now past seven, which was the usual hour for dinner at the palace, and it was probable that he would come out of his room among the servants, if he were not summoned. When it was proposed to Mr Thumble that he should go in to him and tell him, he positively declined, saying that the sight which he had just seen and the exertions of the day together, had so unnerved him, that he had not physical strength for the task. The apothecary, who had been summoned in a hurry, had escaped, probably being equally unwilling to be the bearer of such a communication. The duty therefore fell to Mrs Draper, and under the pressing instance of the other servants she descended to her master's room. Had it not been that the hour of dinner had come, so that the bishop could not have been left much longer to himself, the evil time would have been still postponed.

She went very slowly along the passage, and was just going to pause ere she reached the room, when the door was opened and the bishop stood close before her. It was easy to be seen that he was cross. His hands and face were unwashed and his face was haggard. In these days he would not even go through the ceremony of dressing himself before dinner. 'Mrs Draper,' he said, 'why don't they tell me that dinner is ready? Are they going to give me any dinner?' She stood a moment without answering him, while the tears streamed down her face. 'What is the matter?' said he. 'Has your mistress sent you here?'

'Oh, laws!' said Mrs Draper, – and she put out her hands to support him if such support should be necessary.

'What is the matter?' he demanded angrily.

'Oh, my lord; – bear it like a Christian. Mistress isn't no more.' He leaned back against the door-post, and she took hold of him by the arm. 'It was the heart, my lord. Dr Filgrave hisself has not been yet; but that's what it was.' The bishop did not say a word, but walked back to his chair before the fire.

CHAPTER 67

In memoriam

The bishop when he had heard the tidings of his wife's death walked back to his seat over the fire, and Mrs Draper, the housekeeper, came and stood over him without speaking. Thus she stood for ten minutes looking down at him and listening. But there was no sound; not a word, nor a moan, nor a sob. It was as though he also were dead, but that a slight irregular movement of his fingers on the top of his bald head, told her that his mind and body were still active. 'My lord,' she said at last, 'would you wish to see the doctor when he comes?' She spoke very low and he did not answer her. Then, after another minute of silence, she asked the same question again.

'What doctor?' he said.

'Dr Filgrave. We sent for him. Perhaps he is here now. Shall I go and see, my lord?' Mrs Draper found that her position there was weary and she wished to escape. Anything on his behalf requiring trouble or work she would have done willingly; but she could not stand there for ever watching the motion of his fingers.

'I suppose I must see him,' said the bishop. Mrs Draper took this as an order for her departure and crept silently out of the room, closing the door behind her with the long protracted elaborate click which is always produced by an attempt at silence on such occasions. He did not care for noise or for silence. Had she slammed the door he would not have regarded it. A wonderful silence had come upon him which for the time almost crushed him. He would never hear that well-known voice again!

He was free now. Even in his misery, – for he was very miserable, – he could not refrain from telling himself that. No one could now press uncalled-for into his study, contradict him in the presence of those before whom he was bound to be authoritative, and rob him of all his dignity. There was no one else of whom he was afraid. She had at least kept him out of the hands of other tyrants. He was now his own master, and there was a feeling, – I may not call it of relief, for as yet there was more of pain in it than of satisfaction, – a feeling as though he had escaped from an old trouble at a terrible cost of which he could not as yet calculate the amount. He knew that he might now give up all idea of writing to the archbishop.

She had in some ways, and at certain periods of his life, been very good to him. She had kept his money for him and made things go straight, when they had been poor. His interests had always been her interests. Without her he would never have been a bishop. So, at least, he told himself now, and so told himself probably with truth. She had been very careful of his children. She had never been idle. She had never been fond of pleasure. She had neglected no acknowledged duty. He did not doubt that she was now on her way to heaven. He took his hands down from his head, and clasping them together, said a little prayer. It may be doubted whether he quite knew for what he was praying. The idea of praying for her soul, now that she was dead, would have scandalized him.* He certainly was not praying for his own soul. I think he was praying that God might save him from being glad that his wife was dead.

But she was dead; – and, as it were, in a moment! He had not stirred out of that room since she had been there with him. Then there had been angry words between them, – perhaps more determined enmity on his part than ever had before existed; and they had parted for the last time with bitter animosity. But he told himself that he had certainly been right in what he had done then. He thought he had been right then. And so his mind went back to the Crawley and Thumble question, and he tried to alleviate the misery which that last interview with his wife now created by assuring himself that he at least had been justified in what he had done.

But yet his thoughts were very tender to her. Nothing reopens the springs of love so fully as absence, and no absence so thoroughly as that which must needs be endless. We want that which we have not; and especially that which we can never have. She had told him in the very last moments of her presence with him that he was wishing that she were dead, and he had made her no reply. At the moment he had felt, with savage anger, that such was his wish. Her words had now come to pass, and he was a widower, – and he assured himself that he would give all that he possessed in the world to bring her back again.

Yes, he was a widower, and he might do as he pleased. The tyrant was gone, and he was free. The tyrant was gone, and the tyranny had doubtless been very oppressive. Who had suffered as he had done? But in thus being left without his tyrant he was

wretchedly desolate. Might it not be that the tyranny had been
good for him? – that the Lord had known best what wife was fit
for him? Then he thought of a story which he had read, – and had
well marked as he was reading, – of some man who had been
terribly afflicted by his wife, whose wife had starved him and beaten
him and reviled him; and yet this man had been able to thank his
God for having thus mortified him in the flesh. Might it not be that
the mortification which he himself had doubtless suffered in his
flesh had been intended for his welfare, and had been very good for
him? But if this were so, it might be that the mortification was now
removed because the Lord knew that his servant had been sufficiently mortified. He had not been starved or beaten, but the
mortification had been certainly severe. Then there came words –
into his mind, not into his mouth – 'The Lord sent the thorn, and
the Lord has taken it away. Blessed be the name of the Lord.'*
After that he was very angry with himself, and tried to pray that he
might be forgiven. While he was so striving there came a low knock
at the door, and Mrs Draper again entered the room.

'Dr Filgrave, my lord, was not at home,' said Mrs Draper; 'but
he will be sent the very moment he arrives.'

'Very well, Mrs Draper.'

'But, my lord, will you not come to your dinner? A little soup, or
a morsel of something to eat, and a glass of wine, will enable your
lordship to bear it better.' He allowed Mrs Draper to persuade him,
and followed her into the dining-room. 'Do not go, Mrs Draper,'
he said; 'I would rather that you should stay with me.' So Mrs
Draper stayed with him, and administered to his wants. He was
desirous of being seen by as few eyes as possible in these the first
moments of his freedom.

He saw Dr Filgrave twice, both before and after the doctor had
been upstairs. There was no doubt, Dr Filgrave said, that it was as
Mrs Draper had surmised. The poor lady was suffering, and had
for years been suffering, from heart-complaint. To her husband she
had never said a word on the subject. To Mrs Draper a word had
been said now and again, – a word when some moment of fear
would come, when some sharp stroke of agony would tell of
danger. But Mrs Draper had kept the secret of her mistress, and
none of the family had known that there was aught to be feared.
Dr Filgrave, indeed, did tell the bishop that he had dreaded all
along exactly that which had happened. He had said the same to
Mr Rerechild, the surgeon, when they two had had a consultation
together at the palace on the occasion of a somewhat alarming birth
of a grandchild. But he mixed up this information with so much
medical Latin, and was so pompous over it, and the bishop was so

anxious to be rid of him, that his words did not have much effect. What did it all matter? The thorn was gone, and the wife was dead, and the widower must balance his gain and loss as best he might.

He slept well, but when he woke in the morning the dreariness of his loneliness was very strong on him. He must send of course for his chaplain, and tell his chaplain to open all letters and to answer them for a week. Then he remembered how many of his letters in days of yore had been opened and been answered by the helpmate who had just gone from him. Since Dr Tempest's visit he had insisted that the palace letterbag should always be brought in the first instance to him; – and this had been done, greatly to the annoyance of his wife. In order that it might be done the bishop had been up every morning an hour before his usual time; and everybody in the household had known why it was so. He thought of this now as the bag was brought to him on the first morning of his freedom. He could have it where he pleased now; – either in his bedroom or left for him untouched on the breakfast-table till he should go to it. 'Blessed be the name of the Lord,' he said as he thought of all this; but he did not stop to analyse what he was saying. On this morning he would not enjoy his liberty, but desired that the letter-bag might be taken to Mr Snapper, the chaplain.

The news of Mrs Proudie's death had spread all over Barchester on the evening of its occurrence, and had been received with that feeling of distant awe which is always accompanied by some degree of pleasurable sensation. There was no one in Barchester to lament a mother, or a sister, or a friend who was really loved. There were those, doubtless, who regretted the woman's death, – and even some who regretted it without any feeling of personal damage done to themselves. There had come to be around Mrs Proudie a party who thought as she thought on church matters, and such people had lost their head, and thereby their strength. And she had been staunch to her own party, preferring bad tea from a low-church grocer, to good tea from a grocer who went to the ritualistic church or to no church at all. And it is due to her to say that she did not forget those who were true to her, – looking after them mindfully where looking after might be profitable, and fighting their battles where fighting might be more serviceable. I do not think that the appetite for breakfast of any man or woman in Barchester was disturbed by the news of Mrs Proudie's death, but there were some who felt that a trouble had fallen on them.

Tidings of the catastrophe reached Hiram's Hospital on the evening of its occurrentce, – Hiram's Hospital, where dwelt Mr and Mrs Quiverful with all their children. Now Mrs Quiverful owed a debt of gratitude to Mrs Proudie, having been placed in her present comfortable home by that lady's patronage. Mrs Quiverful perhaps understood the character of the deceased woman, and expressed her opinion respecting it, as graphically as did any one in Barchester. There was the natural surprise felt at the Warden's lodge in the Hospital when the tidings were first received ther, and the Quiverful family was at first too full of dismay, regrets and surmises, to be able to give themselves impartially to criticism. But on the following morning, conversation at the breakfast-table naturally referring to the great loss which the bishop had sustained, Mrs Quiverful thus pronounced her opinion of her friend's character: 'You'll find that he'll feel it, Q,' she said to her husband, in answer to some sarcastic remark made by him as to the removal of the thorn. 'He'll feel it, though she was almost too many for him while she was alive.'

'I daresay he'll feel it at first,' said Quiverful; 'but I think he'll be more comfortable than he has been.'

'Of course he'll feel it, and go on feeling it till he dies, if he's the man I take him to be. You're not to think that there has been no love because there used to be some words, that he'll find himself the happier because he can do things more as he pleases. She was a great help to him, and he must have known that she was, in spite of the sharpness of her tongue. No doubt she was sharp. No doubt she was upsetting. And she could make herself a fool too in her struggles to have everything her own way. But, Q, there were worse women than Mrs Proudie. She was never one of your idle ones, and I'm quite sure that no man or woman ever heard her say a word against her husband behind his back.'

'All the same, she gave him a terribly bad life of it, if all is true that we hear.'

'There are men who must have what you call a terribly bad life of it, whatever way it goes with them. The bishop is weak, and he wants somebody near to him to be strong. She was strong, – perhps too strong; but he had his advantage out of it. After all I don't know that his life has been so terribly bad. I daresay he's had everything very comfortable about him. And a man ought to be grateful for that, though very few men ever are.'

Mr Quiverful's predecessor at the Hospital, old Mr Harding, whose halcyon days in Barchester had been passed before the coming of the Proudies, was in bed playing cat's-cradle with Posy seated on the counterpane, when the tidings of Mrs Proudie's death were brought to him by Mrs Baxter. 'Oh, sir,' said Mrs Baxter, seating herself on a chair by the bed-side. Mr Harding liked Mrs Baxter to sit down, because he was almost sure on such occasions to have the advantage of a prolonged coversation.

'What is it, Mrs Baxter?'

'Oh, sir!'

'Is anything the matter?' And the old man attempted to raise himself in his bed.

'You mustn't frighten grandpa,' said Posy.

'No, my dear; and there isn't nothing to frighten him. There isn't indeed, Mr Harding. They're all well at Plumstead, and when I heard from the missus at Venice, everything was going on well.'

'But what is it, Mrs Baxter?'

'God forgive her all her sins – Mrs Proudie ain't no more.' Now there had been terrible feud between the palace and the deanery for years, in carrying on which the persons of the opposed households were wont to express themselves with eager animosity. Mrs Baxter and Mrs Draper never spoke to each other. The two coachmen each longed for an opportunity to take the other before a magistrate for some breach of the law of the road in driving. The footmen abused each other, and the grooms occasionally fought. The masters and mistresses contented themselves with simple hatred. Therefore it was not surprising that Mrs Baxter, in speaking of the death of Mrs Proudie, should remember first her sins.

'Mrs Proudie dead!' said the old man.

'Indeed she is, Mr Harding, ' said Mrs Baxter, putting both her hands together piously. 'We're just grass, ain't we, sir! and dust and clay and flowers of the field?' Whether Mrs Proudie had most partaken of the clayey nature or of the flowery nature, Mrs Baxter did not stop to consider.

'Mrs Proudie dead!' said Posy, with a solemnity that was all her own. 'Then she won't scold the poor bishop any more.'

'No, my dear; she won't scold anybody any more; and it will be a blessing for some, I must say. Everybody is always so considerate in this house, Miss Posy, that we none of us know nothing about what that is.'

'Dead!' said Mr Harding again. 'I think, if you please, Mrs Baxter, you shall leave me for a little time, and take Miss Posy with you.' He had been in the city of Barchester some fifty years, and here was one who might have been his daughter, who had come there scarcely ten years since, and who now had gone before him! He had never loved Mrs Proudie. Perhaps he had gone as near to disliking Mrs Proudie as he had ever gone to disliking any person. Mrs Proudie had wounded him in every part that was most sensitive. It would be long to tell, nor need it be told now, how she had despised him, always manifesting her contempt plainly. He had been even driven to rebuke her, and it had perhaps been the only personal rebuke which he had ever uttered in Barchester. But now she was gone; and he thought of her simply as an active pious woman, who had been taken away from her work before her time. And for the bishop, no idea ever entered Mr Harding's mind as to the removal of a thorn. The man had lost his life's companion at that time of life when such a companion is most needed; and Mr Harding grieved for him with sincerity.

The news went out to Plumstead Episcopi by the postman, and happened to reach the archdeacon as he was talking to his rector at the little gate leading into the churchyard. 'Mrs Proudie dead!' he almost shouted, as the postman notified the fact to him. 'Impossible!'

'It be so for zartain, yer reverence,' said the postman, who was proud of his news.

'Heavens!' ejaculated the archdeacon, and then hurried in to his wife. 'My dear,' he said – and as he spoke he could hardly deliver himself of his words, so eager was he to speak them – 'who do you think is dead? Gracious heavens! Mrs Proudie is dead!' Mrs Grantly dropped from her hand the teaspoonful of tea that was just going into the pot, and repeated her husband's words. 'Mrs Proudie dead?' There was a pause, during which they looked into each other's faces. 'My dear, I don't believe it,' said Mrs Grantly.

But she did believe it very shortly. There were no prayers at Plumstead rectory that morning. The archdeacon immediately went out into the village, and soon obtained sufficient evidence of the truth of that which the postman had told him. Then he rushed back to his wife. 'It's true,' he said. 'It's quite true. She's dead. There's no doubt about that. She's dead. It was last night about seven. That was when they found her, at least, and she may have died about an hour before. Filgrave says not more than an hour.'

'And how did she die?'

'Heart-complaint. She was standing up, taking hold of the bedstead, and so they found her.' Then there was a pause, during which the archdeacon sat down to his breakfast. 'I wonder how he felt when he heard it?'

'Of course he was terribly shocked.'

'I've no doubt he was shocked. Any man would be shocked. But when you come to think of it, what a relief!'

'How can you speak of it in that way?' said Mrs Grantly.

'How am I to speak of it in any other way?' said the archdeacon. 'Of course I shouldn't go and say it out in the street.'

'I don't think you ought to say it anywhere,' said Mrs Grantly. 'The poor man no doubt feels about his wife in the same way that anybody else would.'

'And if any other poor man has got such a wife as she was, you may be quite sure that he would be glad to be rid of her. I don't say that

he wished her to die, or that he would have done anything to
contrive her death—'

'Gracious, archdeacon; do, pray, hold your tongue.'

'But it stands to reason that her going will be a great relief to
him. What has she done for him? She has made him contemptible
to everybody in the diocese by her interference, and his life has been
a burden to him through her violence.'

'Is that the way you carry out your proverb of De mortuis?'*
said Mrs Grantly.

'The proverb of De mortuis is founded on humbug. Humbug out
of doors is necessary. It would not do for you and me to go into the
High Street just now and say what we think about Mrs Proudie;
but I don't suppose that kind of thing need be kept up in here,
between you and me. She was an uncomfortable woman, – so
uncomfortable that I cannot believe that any one will regret her.
Dear me! Only to think that she has gone! You may as well give
me my tea.'

I do not think that Mrs Grantly's opinion differed much from
that expressed by her husband, or that she was, in truth, the least
offended by the archdeacon's plain speech. But it must be remembered that there was probably no house in the diocese in which Mrs
Proudie had been so thoroughly hated as she had been at the
Plumstead rectory. There had been hatred at the deanery; but the
hatred at the deanery had been mild in comparison with the hatred
at Plumstead. The archeacon was a sound friend; but he was also a
sound enemy. From the very first arrival of the Proudies at
Barchester, Mrs Proudie had thrown down her gauntlet to him, and
he had not been slow in picking it up. The war had been internecine,
and each had given the other terrible wounds. It had been understood that there should be no quarter, and there had been none.
His enemy was now dead, and the archdeacon could not bring
himself to adopt before his wife the namby-pamby every-day
decency of speaking well of one of whom he had ever thought ill,
or of expressing regret when no regret could be felt. 'May all her
sins be forgiven her,' said Mrs Grantly. 'Amen,' said the archdeacon. There was something in the tone of his Amen which thoroughly
implied that it was uttered only on the understanding that her
departure from the existing world was to be regarded as an
unmitigated good, and that she should, at any rate, never come
back again to Barchester.

When Lady Lufton heard the tidings, she was not so bold in
speaking of it as was her friend the archdeacon. 'Mrs Proudie
dead!' she said to her daughter-in-law. This was some hours after
the news had reached the house, and when the fact of the poor

lady's death had been fully recognized. 'What will he do without her?'

'The same as other men do,' said young Lady Lufton.

'But, my dear, he is not the same as other men. He is not at all like other men. He is so weak that he cannot walk without a stick to lean upon. No doubt she was a virago, a woman who could not control her temper for a moment! No doubt she had led him a terrible life! I have often pitied him with all my heart. But, nevertheless, she was useful to him. I suppose she was useful to him. I can hardly believe that Mrs Proudie is dead. Had he gone, it would have seemed so much more natural. Poor woman. I daresay she had her good points.' The reader will be pleased to remember that the Luftons had ever been strong partisans on the side of the Grantlys.

The news made its way even to Hogglestock on the same day. Mrs Crawley, when she heard it, went out after her husband, who was in the school. 'Dead!' said he, in answer to her whisper. 'Do you tell me that the woman is dead?' Then Mrs Crawley explained that the tidings were credible. 'May God forgive her all her sins,' said Mr Crawley. 'She was a violent woman, certainly, and I think that she misunderstood her duties; but I do not say that she was a bad woman. I am inclined to think that she was earnest in her endeavours to do good.' It never occurred to Mr Crawley that he and his affair had, in truth, been the cause of her death.

It was thus that she was spoken of for a few days; and then men and women ceased to speak much of her, and began to talk of the bishop instead. A month had not passed before it was surmised that a man so long accustomed to the comforts of married life would marry again; and even then one lady connected with low-church clergymen in and around the city was named as a probable successor to the great lady who was gone. For myself, I am inclined to think that the bishop will for the future be content to lean upon his chaplain.

The monument that was put up to our old friend's memory in one of the side aisles of the choir of the cathedral was supposed to be designed and executed in good taste. There was a broken column, and on the column simply the words, 'My beloved wife!' Then there was a slab by the column, bearing Mrs Proudie's name, with the date of her life and death. Beneath this was the common inscription, —

Requiescat in pace.*

CHAPTER 68

The obstinacy of Mr Crawley

Dr Tempest, when he heard the news, sent immediately to Mr Robarts, begging him to come over to Silverbridge. But this message was not occasioned solely by the death of Mrs Proudie. Dr Tempest had also heard that Mr Crawley had submitted himself to the bishop, that instant advantage, – and as Dr Tempest thought, unfair advantage, – had been taken of Mr Crawley's submission, and that the pernicious Thumble had been at once sent over to Hogglestock. Had these palace doings with reference to Mr Crawley been unaccompanied by the catastrophe which had happened, the doctor, much as he might have regretted them, would probably have felt that there was nothing to be done. He could not in such case have prevented Thumble's journey to Hogglestock on the next Sunday, and certainly he could not have softened the heart of the presiding genius at the palace. But things were very different now. The presiding genius was gone. Everybody at the palace would for a while be weak and vacillating. Thumble would be then thoroughly cowed; and it might at any rate be possible to make some movement in Mr Crawley's favour. Dr Tempest, therefore, sent for Mr Robarts.

'I'm giving you a great deal of trouble, Robarts,' said the doctor; 'but then you are so much younger than I am, and I've an idea that you would do more for this poor man than any one else in the diocese.' Mr Robarts of course declared that he did not begrudge his trouble, and that he would do anything in his power for the poor man. 'I think that you should see him again, and that you should then see Thumble also. I don't know whether you can condescend to be civil to Thumble. I could not.'

'I am not quite sure that incivility would not be more efficacious,' said Mr Robarts.

'Very likely. There are men who are deaf as adders to courtesy,* but who are compelled to obedience at once by ill-usage. Very likely

Thumble is one of them; but of that you will be the best judge yourself. I would see Crawley first, and get his consent.'

'That's the difficulty.'

'Then I should go on without his consent, and I would see Thumble and the bishop's chaplain, Snapper. I think you might manage just at this moment, when they will all be a little abashed and perplexed by this woman's death, to arrange that simply nothing shall be done. The great thing will be that Crawley should go on with the duty till the assizes. If it should then happen that he goes into Barchester, is acquitted, and comes back again, the whole thing will be over, and there will be no further interference in the parish. If I were you, I think I would try it.' Mr Robarts said that he would try it. 'I daresay Mr Crawley will be a little stiff-necked with you.'

'He will be very stiff-necked with me,' said Mr Robarts.

'But I can hardly think that he will throw away the only means he has of supporting his wife and children, when he finds that there can be no occasion for his doing so. I do not suppose that any person wishes him to throw up his work now that the poor woman has gone.'

Mr Crawley had been almost in good spirits since the last visit which Mr Thumble had made to him. It seemed as though the loss of everything in the world was in some way satisfactory to him. He had now given up his living by his own doing, and had after a fashion acknowledged his guilt by this act. He had proclaimed to all around him that he did not think himself to be any longer fit to perform the sacred functions of his office. He spoke of his trial as though a verdict against him must be the result. He knew that in going into prison he would leave his wife and children dependent on the charity of their friends, – on charity which they must condescend to accept, though he could not condescend to ask it. And yet he was able to carry himself now with a greater show of fortitude than had been within his power when the extent of his calamity was more doubtful. I must not ask the reader to suppose that he was cheerful. To have been cheerful under such circumstances would have been inhuman. But he carried his head on high, and walked firmly, and gave his orders at home with a clear voice. His wife, who was necessarily more despondent than ever, wondered at him, – but wondered in silence. It certainly seemed as though the very extremity of ill-fortune was good for him. And he was very diligent with his school, passing the greater part of the morning with the children. Mr Thumble had told him that he would come on Sunday, and that he would then take charge of the parish. Up to the coming of Mr Thumble he would do everything in the parish that could be done by a clergyman with a clear spirit and a free heart. Mr Thumble should not find that spiritual weeds had grown rank in the parish because of his misfortunes.

Mrs Proudie had died on the Tuesday, – that having been the day of Mr Thumble's visit to Hogglestock, – and Mr Robarts had gone over to Silverbridge, in answer to Dr Tempest's invitation, on the Thursday. He had not, therefore, the command of much time, it being his express object to prevent the appearance of Mr Thumble at Hogglestock on the next Sunday. He had gone to Silverbridge by railway, and had, therefore, been obliged to postpone his visit to Mr Crawley till the next day; but early on the Friday morning he rode over to Hogglestock. That he did not arrive there with a broken-knee'd horse, the reader may be quite sure. In all matters of that sort, Mr Robarts was ever above reproach. He rode a good horse, and drove a neat gig, and was always well dressed. On this account Mr Crawley, though he really liked Mr Robarts, and was thankful to him for many kindnesses, could never bear his presence with perfect equanimity. Robarts was no scholar, was not a great preacher, had obtained no celebrity as a churchman, – had, in fact, done nothing to merit great reward; and yet everything had been given to him with an abundant hand. Within the last twelvemonth his wife had inherited Mr Crawley did not care to know how many thousand pounds. And yet Mr Robarts had won all that he possessed by being a clergyman. Was it possible that Mr Crawley should regard such a man with equanimity? Robarts rode over with a groom behind him, – really taking the groom because he knew that Mr Crawley would have no one to hold his horse for him; – and the groom was the source of great offence. He came upon Mr Crawley standing at the school door, and stopping at once, jumped off his nag. There was something in the way in which he sprang out of the saddle and threw the reins to the man, which was not clerical in Mr Crawley's eyes. No man could be so quick in the matter of a horse who spent as many hours with the poor and with the children as should be spent by a parish clergyman. It might be probable that Mr Robarts had never stolen twenty pounds, – might never be accused of so disgraceful a crime, – but, nevertheless, Mr Crawley had his own ideas, and made his own comparisons.

'Crawley,' said Robarts, 'I am so glad to find you at home.'

'I am generally to be found in the parish,' said the perpetual curate of Hogglestock.

'I know you are,' said Robarts, who knew the man well, and cared nothing for his friend's peculiarities when he felt his own withers to be unwrung.* 'But you might have been down at Hoggle

End with the brickmakers, and then I should have had to go after you.'

'I should have grieved—,' began Crawley; but Robarts interrupted him at once.

'Let us go for a walk, and I'll leave the man with the horses. I've something special to say to you, and I can say it better out here than in the house. Grace is quite well, and sends her love. She is growing to look so beautiful!'

'I hope she may grow in grace with God,' said Mr Crawley.

'She's a good a girl as I ever knew. By-the-by, you had Henry Grantly over here the other day?'

'Major Grantly, whom I cannot name without expressing my esteem for him, did do us the honour of calling upon us not very long since. If it be with reference to him that you have taken this trouble—'

'No, no; not at all. I'll allow him and the ladies to fight out that battle. I've not the least doubt in the world how that will go. When I'm told that she made a complete conquest of the archdeacon, there cannot be a doubt about that.'

'A conqest of the archdeacon!'

But Mr Robarts did not wish to have to explain anything further about the archdeacon. 'Were you not terribly shocked, Crawley,' he asked, 'when you heard of the death of Mrs Proudie?'

'It was sudden and very awful,' said Mr Crawley. 'Such deaths are always shocking. Not more so, perhaps, as regards the wife of a bishop, than with any other woman.'

'Only we happened to know her.'

'No doubt the finite and meagre nature of our feelings does prevent us from extending our sympathies to those whom we have not seen in the flesh. It should not be so, and would not with one who had nurtured his heart with proper care. And we are prone to permit an evil worse than that to canker our regards and to foster and to mar our solicitudes. Those who are high in station strike us more by their joys and sorrows than do the poor and lowly. Were some young duke's wife, wedded but the other day, to die, all England would put on some show of mourning, – nay would feel some true gleam of pity; but nobody cares for the widowed brickmaker seated with his starving infant on his cold hearth.'

'Of course we hear more of the big people,' said Robarts.

'Ay; and think more of them. But do not suppose, sir, that I complain of this man or that woman because his sympathies, or hers, runs out of that course which my reason tells me they should hold. The man with whom it would not be so would simply be a god among men. It is in his perfection as a man that we recognize the divinity of Christ. It is in the imperfection of men that we recognize our necessity for a Christ. Yes, sir, the death of the poor lady at Barchester was very sudden. I hope that my lord the bishop bears with becoming fortitude the heavy misfortune. They say that he was a man much beholden to his wife, – prone to lean upon her in his goings out and comings in. For such a man such a loss is more dreadful perhaps than for another.'

'They say she led him a terrible life, you know.'

'I am not prone, sir, to believe much of what I hear about the domesticities of other men, knowing how little any other man can know of my own. And I have, methinks, observed a proneness in the world to riducule that dependence on a woman which every married man should acknowledge in regard to the wife of his bosom, if he can trust her as well as love her. When I hear jocose proverbs spoken as to men, such as that in this house the gray mare is the better horse, or that in that house the wife wears that garment which is supposed to denote virile command, knowing that the joke is easy, and that meekness in a man is more truly noble than a habit of stern authority, I do not allow them to go far with me in influencing my judgment.'

So spoke Mr Crawley, who never permitted the slightest interference with his own word in his own family, and who had himself been a witness of one of those scenes between the bishop and his wife in which the poor bishop had been so cruelly misused. But to Mr Crawley the thing which he himself had seen under such circumstances was as sacred as though it had come to him under the seal of confession. In speaking of the bishop and Mrs Proudie, – nay, as far as was possible in thinking of them, – he was bound to speak and to think as though he had not witnessed that scene in the palace study.

'I don't suppose that there is much doubt about her real character,' said Robarts. 'But you and I need not discuss that.'

'By no means. Such discussion would be both useless and unseemly.'

'And just at present there is something else that I specially want to say to you. Indeed, I went to Silverbridge on the same subject yesterday, and have come here expressly to have a little conversation with you.'

'If it be about affairs of mine, Mr Robarts, I am indeed troubled in spirit that so great labour should have fallen upon you.'

'Never mind my labour. Indeed your saying that is a nuisance to me, because I hoped that by this time you would have understood that I regard you as a friend, and that I think nothing any trouble that I do for a friend. Your position just now is so peculiar that it requires a great deal of care.'

'No care can be of any avail to me.'

'There I disagree with you. You must excuse me, but I do; and so does Dr Tempest. We think that you have been a little too much in a hurry since he communicated to you the result of our first meeting.'

'As how, sir?'

'It is, perhaps, hardly worth while for us to go into the whole question; but that man, Thumble, must not come here on next Sunday.'

'I cannot say, Mr Robarts, that the Reverend Mr Thumble has recommended himself to me strongly either by his outward symbols of manhood or by such manifestation of his inward mental gifts as I have succeeded in obtaining. But my knowledge of him has been so slight, and has been acquired in a manner so likely to bias me prejudicially against him, that I am inclined to think my opinion should go for nothing. It is, however, the fact that the bishop has nominated him to this duty; and that, as I have myself simply notified my desire to be relieved from the care of the parish, on account of certain unfitness of my own, I am the last man who should interfere with the bishop in the choice of my temporary successor.'

'It was her choice, not his.'

'Excuse me, Mr Robarts, but I cannot allow that assertion to pass unquestioned. I must say that I have adequate cause for believing that he came here by his lordship's authority.'

'No doubt he did. Will you just listen to me for a moment? Ever since this unfortunate affair of the cheque became known, Mrs Proudie has been anxious to get you out of this parish. She was a violent woman, and chose to take this matter up violently. Pray hear me out before you interrupt me. There would have been no commission at all but for her.'

'The commission is right and proper and just,' said Mr Crawley, who could not keep himself silent.

'Very well. Let it be so. But Mr Thumble's coming over here is not proper or right; and you may be sure the bishop does not wish it.'

'Let him send any other clergyman whom he may think more fitting,' said Mr Crawley.

'But we do not want him to send anybody.'

'Somebody must be sent, Mr Robarts.'

'No, not so. Let me go over and see Thumble and Snapper, – Snapper, you know, is the domestic chaplain; and all that you need do is to go on with your services on Sunday. If necessary, I will see the bishop. I think you may be sure that I can manage it. If not, I will come back to you.' Mr Robarts paused for an answer, but it seemed for awhile that all Mr Crawley's impatient desire to speak was over. He walked on silently along the lane by his visitor's side, and when, after some five or six minutes, Robarts stood still in the road, Mr Crawley even then said nothing. 'It cannot be but that you should be anxious to keep the income of the parish for your wife and children,' said Mark Robarts.

'Of course, I am anxious for my wife and children,' Crawley answered.

'Then let me do as I say. Why should you throw away a chance, even if it be a bad one? But here the chance is all in your favour. Let me manage it for you at Barchester.'

'Of course I am anxious for my wife and children,' said Crawley, repeating his words; 'how anxious, I fancy no man can conceive who has not been near enough to absolute want to know how terrible is its approach when it threatens those who are weak and who are very dear! But, Mr Robarts, you spoke just now of the chance of the thing, – the chance of your arranging on my behalf that I should for a while longer be left in the enjoyment of the freehold of my parish. It seemeth to me that there should be no chance on such a subject; that in the adjustment of so momentous a matter there should be a consideration of right and wrong, and no consideration of aught beside. I have been growing to feel, for some weeks past, that circumstances, – whether through my own fault or not is an outside question as to which I will not further delay you by offering even an opinion, – that unfortunate circumstances have made me unfit to remain here as guardian of the souls of the people of this parish. Then there came to me the letter from Dr Tempest, – for which I am greatly beholden to him, – strengthening me altogether in this view. What could I do then, Mr Robarts? Could I allow myself to think of my wife and my children when such a question as that was before me for self-discussion?'

'I would, – certainly,' said Robarts.

'No, sir! Excuse the bluntness of my contradiction, but I feel assured that in such emergency you would look solely to duty, – as by God's help, I will endeavour to do. Mr Robarts, there are many of us who in many things, are much worse than we believe ourselves to be. But in other matters, and perhaps of larger moment, we can rise to ideas of duty as the need for such ideas comes upon us. I say not this at all as praising myself. I speak of men as I believe that they will be found to be; – of yourself, of myself, and of others who strive to live with clean hands and a clear conscience. I do not for a moment think that you would retain your benefice at Framley if there had come upon you, after much thought, an assured conviction that you could not retain it without grievous injury to the souls of others and grievous sin to your own. Wife and children, dear as they are to you and to me, – as dear to me as to you, – fade from the sight when the time comes for judgment on such a matter as that!' They were standing quite still now, facing each other, and Crawley, as he spoke with a low voice, looked straight into his friend's eyes, and kept his hand firmly fixed on his friend's arm.

'I cannot interfere further,' said Robarts.

'No, – you cannot interfere further.' Robarts, when he told the story of the interview to his wife that evening, declared that he had never heard a voice so plaintively touching as was the voice of Mr Crawley when he uttered those last words.

They returned back to the servant and the house almost without a word, and Robarts mounted without offering to see Mrs Crawley. Nor did Mr Crawley ask him to do so. It was better now that Robarts should go. 'May God send you through all your troubles,' said Mr Robarts.

'Mr Robarts, I thank you warmly, for your friendship,' said Mr Crawley. And then they parted. In about half an hour Mr Crawley returned to the house. 'Now for Pindar, Jane,' he said, seating himself at his old desk.

CHAPTER 69

Mr Crawley's last appearance in his own pulpit

No word or message from Mr Crawley reached Barchester throughout the week, and on the Sunday morning Mr Thumble was under a positive engagement to go out to Hogglestock, and perform the services of the church. Dr Tempest had been quite right in saying that Mr Thumble would be awed by the death of his patroness. Such was altogether the case, and he was very anxious to escape from the task he had undertaken at her instance, if it were possible. In the first place, he had never been a favourite with the bishop himself, and had now, therefore, nothing to expect in the diocese. The crusts from bits of loaves and the morsels of broken fishes which had come in his way had all come from the bounty of Mrs Proudie. And then, as regarded this special Hogglestock job, how was he to get paid for it? Whence, indeed, was he to seek repayment for the actual money which he would be out of pocket in finding his way to Hogglestock and back again? But he could not get to speak to the bishop, nor could he induce any one who had access to his lordship to touch upon the subject. Mr Snapper expressed his opinion that Mr Thumble was bound to go out to Hogglestock; and, when Mr Thumble declared petulantly that he would not stir a step out of Barchester, Mr Snapper protested that Mr Thumble would have to answer for it in this world and in the next if there were not services at Hogglestock on that Sunday. On the Saturday evening Mr Thumble made a desperate attempt to see the bishop, but was told by Mrs Draper that the bishop had positively declined to see him. The bishop himself probably felt unwilling to interfere with his wife's doings so soon after her death! So Mr Thumble, with a heavy heart, went across to 'The Dragon of Wantly,' and ordered a gig, resolving that the bill should be sent in to the palace. He was not going to trust himself again upon the bishop's cob!

Up to Saturday evening Mr Crawley did the work of his parish, and on the Saturday evening he made an address to his parishioners from his pulpit. He had given notice among the brickmakers and labourers that he wished to say a few words to them in the school-room; but the farmers also heard of this and came with their wives and daughters, and all the brickmakers came, and most of the labourers were there, so that there was no room for them in the school-house. The congregation was much larger than was customary even in the church. 'They will come,' he said to his wife, 'to hear a ruined man declare his own ruin, but they will not come to hear the word of God.' When it was found that the persons assembled were too many for the school-room, the meeting was adjourned to the church, and Mr Crawley was forced to get into his pulpit. He said a short prayer, and then he began his story.

His story as he told it then shall not be repeated now, as the same story has been told too often already in these pages. Surely it was a singular story for a parish clergyman to tell of himself in so solemn a manner. That he had applied the cheque to his own purposes, and was unable to account for the possession of it, was certain. He did not know when or how he had got it. Speaking to them then in God's house he told them that. He was to be tried by a jury, and all he could do was to tell the jury the same. He would not expect the jury to believe him. The jury would, of course, believe only that which was proved to them. But he did expect his old friends at Hogglestock, who had known him so long, to take his word as true. That there was no sufficient excuse for his conduct, even in his own sight, this, his voluntary resignation of his parish, was, he said, sufficient evidence. Then he explained to them, as clearly as he was able, what the bishop had done, what the commission had done, and what he had done himself. That he spoke no word of Mrs Proudie to that audience need hardly be mentioned here. 'And now, dearest friends, I leave you,' he said, with that weighty solemnity which was so peculiar to the man, and which he was able to make singularly impressive even on such a congregation as that of Hogglestock, 'and I trust that the heavy but pleasing burden of the charge which I have had over you may fall into hands better fitted than mine have been for such work. I have always known my own unfitness, by reason of the worldly cares with which I have been laden. Poverty makes the spirit poor, and the hands weak, and the heart sore, – and too often makes the conscience dull. May the latter never be the case with any of you.' Then he uttered another short prayer, and, stepping down from the pulpit, walked out of the church, with his weeping wife hanging on his arm, and his daughter following them, almost dissolved in tears. He never again entered that church as the pastor of the congregation.

There was an old lame man from Hoggle End leaning on his stick

near the door as Mr Crawley went out, and with him was his old
lame wife. 'He'll pull through yet,' said the old man to his wife;
'you'll see else. He'll pull through because he's so dogged. It's
dogged as does it.'

On that night the position of the members of Mr Crawley's
household seemed to have been changed. There was something
almost of elation in his mode of speaking, and he said soft loving
words, striving to comfort his wife. She, on the other hand, could
say nothing to comfort him. She had been averse to the step he was
taking, but had been unable to press her objection in opposition to
his great argument as to duty. Since he had spoken to her in that
strain which he had used with Robarts, she also had felt that she
must be silent. But she could not even feign to feel the pride which
comes from the performance of a duty. 'What will he do when he
comes out?' she said to her daughter. The coming out spoken of by
her was the coming out of prison. It was natural enough that she
should feel no elation.

The breakfast on Sunday morning was to her, perhaps, the
saddest scene of her life. They sat down, the three together, at the
usual hour, – nine o'clock, – but the morning had not been passed
as was customary on Sundays. It had been Mr Crawley's practice
to go into the school from eight to nine; but on this Sunday he felt,
as he told his wife, that his presence would be an intrusion there.
But he requested Jane to go and perform her usual task. 'If Mr
Thumble should come,' he said to her, 'be submissive to him in all
things.' Then he stood at his door, watching to see at what hour
Mr Thumble would reach the school. But Mr Thumble did not
attend the school on that morning. 'And yet he was very express to
me in his desire that I would not myself meddle with the duties,'
said Mr Crawley to his wife as he stood at the door, – 'Unnecessarily
urgent, as I must say I thought at the time.' If Mrs Crawley could
have spoken out her thoughts about Mr Thumble at that moment,
her words would, I think, have surprised her husband.

At breakfast there was hardly a word spoken. Mr Crawley took
his crust and eat it mournfully, – almost ostentatiously. Jane tried
and failed, and tried to hide her failure, failing in that also. Mrs
Crawley made no attempt. She sat behind her old teapot, with her
hands clasped and her eyes fixed. It was as though some last day
had come upon her, – this, the first Sunday of her husband's
degradation. 'Mary,' he said to her, 'why do you not eat?'

'I cannot,' she replied, speaking not in a whisper, but in words
which would hardly get themselves articulated. 'I cannot. Do not
ask me.'

'For the honour of the Lord you will want the strength which bread alone can give you,' he said, intimating to her that he wished her to attend the service.

'Do not ask me to be there, Josiah. I cannot. It is too much for me.'

'Nay; I will not press it,' he said. 'I can go alone.' He uttered no word expressive of a wish that his daughter should attend the church; but when the moment came, Jane accompanied him. 'What shall I do, mamma,' she said, 'If I find I cannot bear it?'

'Try to bear it,' the mother said. 'Try, for his sake. You are stronger now than I am.'

The tinkle of the church bell was heard at the usual time, and Mr Crawley, hat in hand, stood ready to go forth. He had heard nothing of Mr Thumble, but had made up his mind that Mr Thumble would not trouble him. He had taken the precaution to request his church-warden to be early at the church, so that Mr Thumble might encounter no difficulty. The church was very near to the house, and any vehicle arriving might have been seen had Mr Crawley watched closely. But no one had cared to watch Mr Thumble's arrival at the church. He did not doubt that Mr Thumble would be at the church. With reference to the school, he had had some doubt.

But just as he was about to start he heard the clatter of a gig. Up came Mr Thumble to the door of the parsonage, and having come down from his gig was about to enter the house as though it were his own. Mr Crawley greeted him in the pathway, raising his hat from his head, and expressing a wish that Mr Thumble might not feel himself fatigued with his drive. 'I will not ask you into my poor house,' he said, standing in the middle of the pathway; 'for that my wife is ill.'

'Nothing catching, I hope?' said Mr Thumble.

'Her malady is of the spirit rather than of the flesh,' said Mr Crawley. 'Shall we go on to the church?'

'Certainly, – by all means. How about the surplice?'

'You will find, I trust, that the churchwarden has everything in readiness. I have notified to him expressly your coming, with the purport that it may be so.'

'You'll take a part in the service, I suppose?' said Mr Thumble.

'No part, – no part whatever,' said Mr Crawley, standing still for a moment as he spoke, and showing plainly by the tone of his voice how dismayed he was, how indignant he had been made, by so indecent a proposition. Was he giving up his pulpit to a stranger for any reason less cogent than one which made it absolutely imperative on him to be silent in that church which had so long been his own?

'Just as you please,' said Mr Thumble. 'Only it's rather hard lines to have to do it all myself after coming all the way from Barchester this morning.' To this Mr Crawley condescended to make no reply whatever.

In the porch of the church, which was the only entrance, Mr Crawley introduced Mr Thumble to the churchwarden, simply by a wave of the hand, and then passed on with his daughter to a seat which opened upon the aisle. Jane was going on to that which she had hitherto always occupied with her mother in the little chancel; but Mr Crawley would not allow this. Neither to him nor to any of his family was there attached any longer the privilege of using the chancel of the church of Hogglestock.

Mr Thumble scrambled into the reading-desk some ten minutes after the proper time, and went through the morning service under, what must be admitted to be, serious difficulties. There were the eyes of Mr Crawley fixed upon him throughout the work, and a feeling pervaded him that everybody there regarded him as an intruder. At first this was so strong upon him that Mr Crawley pitied him, and would have encouraged him had it been possible. But as the work progressed, and as custom and the sound of his own voice emboldened him, there came to the man some touches of the arrogance which so generally accompanies cowardice, and Mr Crawley's acute ear detected the moment when it was so. An observer might have seen that the motion of his hands was altered as they were lifted in prayer. Though he was praying, even in prayer he could not forget the man who was occupying his desk.

Then came the sermon, preached very often before, lasting exactly half-an-hour, and then Mr Thumble's work was done. Itinerant clergymen, who preach now here and now there, as it had been the lot of Mr Thumble to do, have at any rate this relief, – that they can preach their sermons often. From the communion-table Mr Thumble had stated that, in the present peculiar circumstances of the parish, there would be no second service at Hogglestock for the present; and this was all he said or did peculiar to the occasion. The moment the service was over he got into his gig, and was driven back to Barchester.

'Mamma,' said Jane, as they sat at their dinner, 'such a sermon I am sure was never heard in Hogglestock before. Indeed, you can hardly call it a sermon. It was downright nonsense.'

'My dear,' said Mr Crawley, energetically, 'keep your criticisms for matters that are profane; then, though they be childish and silly, they may at least be innocent. Be critical on Euripides, if you must be critical.' But when Jane kissed her father after dinner, she, knowing his humour well, felt assured that her remarks had not been taken altogether in ill part.

Mr Thumble was neither seen nor heard of again in the parish during the entire week.

CHAPTER 70

Mrs Arabin is caught

One morning about the middle of April Mr Toogood received a telegram from Venice which caused him instantly to leave his business in Bedford Row and take the first train for Silverbridge. 'It seems to me that this job will be a deal of time and very little money,' said his partner to him, when Toogood on the spur of the moment was making arrangements for his sudden departure and uncertain period of absence. 'That's about it,' said Toogood. 'A deal of time, some expense, and no returns. It's not the kind of business a man can live upon; is it?' The partner growled, and Toogood went. But as we must go with Mr Toogood down to Silverbridge, and as we cannot make the journey in this chapter, we will just indicate his departure and then go back to John Eames, who, as will be remembered, was just starting for Florence when we last saw him.

Our dear old friend Johnny had been rather proud of himself as he started form London. He had gotten an absolute victory over Sir Raffle Buffle, and that alone was gratifying to his feelings. He liked the excitement of a journey, and especially of a journey to Italy; and the importance of the cause of his journey was satisfactory to him. But above all things he was delighted at having found that Lily Dale was pleased at his going. He had seen clearly that she was much pleased, and that she made something of a hero of him because of his alacrity in the cause of his cousin. He had partially understood, – had understood in a dim sort of way, – that his want of favour in Lily's eyes had come from some deficiency of his own in this respect. She had not found him to be a hero. She had known him first as a boy, with boyish belongings around him, and she had seen him from time to time as he became a man, almost with too much intimacy for the creation of that love with which he wished to fill her heart. His rival had come before her eyes for the first time with all the glories of Pall Mall heroism about him, and Lily in her weakness had been conquered by them. Since that she had learned how weak she had been, – how silly, how childish, she would say to herself when she allowed her memory to go back to the details of her own story; but not the less on that account did she feel the want of something heroic in a man before she could teach herself to look upon him as more worthy of her regard than other men. She had still unconsciously hoped in regard to Crosbie, but now that hope had been dispelled as unconsciously, simply by his appearance. There had been moments in which John Eames had almost risen to the necessary point, – had almost made good his footing on the top of some moderate, but still sufficient mountain. But there had still been a succession of little tumbles, – unfortunate slips for which he himself should not always have been held responsible; and he had never quite stood upright on his pinnacle, visible to Lily's eyes as being really excelsior.* Of all this John Eames himself had an inkling which had often made him very uncomfortable. What the mischief was it she wanted of him; and what was he to do? The days for plucking glory from the nettle danger* were clean gone by. He was well dressed. He knew a good many of the right sort of people. He was not in debt. He had saved an old nobleman's life once upon a time, and had been a good deal talked about on that score. He had even thrashed the man who had ill-treated her. His constancy had been as the constancy of a Jacob! What was it that she wanted of him? But in a certain way he did know what was wanted; and now, as he started for Florence, intending to stop nowhere till he reached that city, he hoped that by this chivalrous journey he might even yet achieve the thing necessary.

But on reaching Paris he heard tidings of Mrs Arabin which induced him to change his plans and make for Venice instead of for Florence. A banker at Paris, to whom he brought a letter, told him that Mrs Arabin would now be found at Venice. This did not perplex him at all. It would have been delightful to see Florence, – but was more delightful still to see Venice. His journey was the same as far as Turin; but from Turin he proceeded through Milan to Venice, instead of going by Bologna to Florence. He had fortunately come armed with an Austrian passport, – as was necessary in those bygone days of Venetia's thraldom.* He was almost proud of himself, as though he had done something great, when he tumbled in to his inn at Venice, without having been in a bed since he left London.

But he was barely allowed to swim in a gondola,* for on reaching Venice he found that Mrs Arabin had gone back to Florence. He had been directed to the hotel which Mrs Arabin had used, and was there told that she had started the day before. She had received some letter, from her husband as the landlord thought, and had done so. That was all the landlord knew. John now was vexed, but became a little prouder than before as he felt it to be his duty to go on to Florence before he went to bed. There would be another night in a railway carriage, but he would live through it. There was just time to have a tub and a breakfast, to swim in a gondola, to look at the outside of the Doge's palace, and to walk up and down the piazza before he started again. It was hard work, but I think he would have been pleased had he heard that Mrs Arabin had retreated from Florence to Rome. Had such been the case, he would have folded his cloak around him, and have gone on, – regardless of brigands, – thinking of Lily, and wondering whether anybody else had ever done so much before without going to bed. As it was, he found that Mrs Arabin was at the hotel in Florence, – still in bed, as he had arrived early in the morning. So he had another tub, another breakfast, and sent up his card. 'Mr John Eames,' – and across the top of it he wrote, 'has come from England about Mr Toogood.' Then he threw himself on to a sofa in the hotel reading-room, and went fast to sleep.

John had found an opportunity of talking to a young lady in the breakfast-room, and had told her of his deeds. 'I only left London on Tuesday night, and I have come here taking Venice on the road.'

'Then you have travelled fast,' said the young lady.

'I haven't seen a bed, of course,' said John.

The young lady immediately afterwards told her father. 'I suppose he must be one of those Foreign Office messengers,' said the young lady.

'Anything but that,' said the gentleman. 'People never talk about their own trades. He's probably a clerk with a fortnight's leave of absence, seeing how many towns he can do in the time. It's the usual way of travelling now-a-days. When I was young and there were no railways, I remember going from Paris to Vienna without sleeping.' Luckily for his present happiness, John did not hear this.

He was still fast asleep when a servant came to him from Mrs Arabin to say that she would see him at once. 'Yes, yes; I'm quite ready to go on,' said Johnny, jumping up, and thinking of the journey to Rome. But there was no journey to Rome before him. Mrs Arabin was almost in the next room, and there he found her.

The reader will understand that they had never met before, and hitherto knew nothing of each other. Mrs Arabin had never heard the name of John Eames till John's card was put into her hands, and would not have known his business with her had he not written those few words upon it. 'You have come about Mr Crawley ?' she said to him, eagerly. 'I have heard from my father that somebody was coming.'

'Yes, Mrs Arabin; as hard as I could travel. I had expected to find you at Venice.'

'Have you been at Venice?'

'I have just arrived from Venice. They told me at Paris I should find you there. However, that does not matter, as I have found you here. I wonder whether you can help us?'

'Do you know Mr Crawley? Are you a friend of his?'

'I never saw him in my life; but he married my cousin.'

'I gave him the cheque, you know,' said Mrs Arabin.

'What!' exclaimed Eames, literally almost knocked backwards by the easiness of the words which contained a solution for so terrible a difficulty. The Crawley case had assumed such magnitude, and the troubles of the Crawley family had been so terrible, that it seemed to him to be almost sacrilegious that words so simply uttered should suffice to cure everything. He had hardly hoped, – had at least barely hoped, – that Mrs Arabin might be able to suggest something which would put them all on a track towards discovery of the truth. But he found that she had the clue in her hand and that the clue was one which required no further delicacy of investigation. There would be nothing more to unravel; no journey to Jerusalem would be necessary!

'Yes,' said Mrs Arabin, 'I gave it to him. They have been writing to my husband about it, and never wrote to me; and till I received a letter about it from my father, and another from my sister, at Venice the day before yesterday I knew nothing of the particulars of Mr Crawley's trouble.'

'Had you not heard that he had been taken before the magistrates?'

'No; not so much even as that. I had seen in "Galignani" something about a clergyman, but I did not know what clergyman; and I heard that there was something wrong about Mr Crawley's money, but there has always been something wrong about money with poor Mr Crawley; and as I knew that my husband had been written to also, I did not interfere, further than to ask the particulars. My letters have followed me about, and I only learned at Venice, just before I came here, what was the nature of the case.'

'And did you do anything?'

'I telegraphed at once to Mr Toogood, who I understand is acting as Mr Crawley's solicitor. My sister sent me his address.'

'He is my uncle.'

'I telegraphed to him, telling him that I had given Mr Crawley the cheque, and then I wrote to Archdeacon Grantly giving him the whole history. I was obliged to come here before I could return home, but I intended to start this evening.'

'And what is the whole history?' asked John Eames.

The history of the gift of the cheque was very simple. It has been told how Mr Crawley in his dire distress had called upon his old friend at the deanery asking for pecuniary assistance. This he had done with so much reluctance that his spirit had given way while he was waiting in the dean's library, and he had wished to depart without accepting what the dean was quite willing to bestow upon him. From this cause it had come to pass there had been no time for explanatory words, even between the dean and his wife, – from whose private funds had in truth come the money which had been given to Mr Crawley. For the private wealth of the family belonged to Mrs Arabin, and not to the dean; and was left entirely in Mrs Arabin's hands, to be disposed of as she might please. Previously to Mr Crawley's arrival at the deanery this matter had been discussed between the dean and his wife, and it had been agreed between them that a sum of fifty pounds should be given. It should be given by Mrs Arabin, but it was thought that the gift would come with more comfort to the recipient from the hands of his old friend than from those of his wife. There had been much discussion between them as to the mode in which this might be done with least offence to the man's feelings, – for they knew Mr Crawley and his peculiarities well. At last it was agreed that the notes should be put into an envelope, which envelope the dean should have ready with him. But when the moment came the dean did not have the envelope ready, and was obliged to leave the room to seek his wife. And Mrs Arabin explained to John Eames that even she had not had it ready, and had been forced to go to her own desk to fetch it. Then, at the last moment, with the desire of increasing the good to be done to people who were so terribly in want, she put the cheque for twenty pounds, which was in her possession as money of her own, along with the notes, and in this way the cheque had been given by the dean to Mr Crawley. 'I shall never forgive myself for not telling the dean,' she said. 'Had I done that all this trouble would have been saved!'

'But where did you get the cheque?' Eames asked with natural curiosity.

'Exactly,' said Mrs Arabin. 'I have got to show now that I did not steal it, – have I not? Mr Soames will indict me now. And, indeed, I have had some trouble to refresh my memory as to all the particulars, for you see it is more than a year past.' But Mrs Arabin's mind was clearer on such matters than Mr Crawley's, and she was able to explain that she had taken the cheque as part of the rent due to her from the landlord of 'The Dragon of Wantly,' which inn was her property, having been the property of her first husband. For some years past there had been a difficulty about the rent, things not having gone at 'The Dragon of Wantly' as smoothly as they had used to go. At one time the money had been paid half-yearly by the landlord's cheque on the bank at Barchester. For the last year-and-a-half this had not been done, and the money had come into Mrs Arabin's hands at irregular periods and in irregular sums. There was at this moment rent due for twelve months, and Mrs Arabin expressed her doubt whether she would get it on her return to Barchester. On the occasion to which she was now alluding, the money had been paid into her own hands, in the deanery breakfast-parlour, by a man she knew very well, – not the landlord himself, but one bearing the landlord's name, whom she believed to be the landlord's brother, or at least his cousin. The man in question was named Daniel Stringer, and he had been employed in 'The Dragon of Wantly,' as a sort of clerk or managing man, as long as she had known it. The rent had been paid to her by Daniel Stringer quite as often as by Daniel's brother or cousin, John Stringer, who was, in truth, the landlord of the hotel. When questioned by John respecting the persons employed at the inn, she said that she did believe that there had been rumours of something wrong. The house had been in the hands of the Stringers for many years, – before the property had been purchased by her husband's father – and therefore there had been an unwillingness to move them; but gradually, so she said, there had come upon her and her husband a feeling that the house must be put into other hands. 'But did you say nothing about the cheque ?' John asked. 'Yes, I said a good deal about it. I asked why a cheque of Mr Soames's was brought to me, instead of being taken to the bank for money ; and Stringer explained to me that they were not very fond of going to the bank, as they owed money there, but that I could pay it into my account. Only I kept my account at the other bank.'

'You might have paid it in there ?' said Johnny.

'I suppose I might, but I didn't. I gave it to poor Mr Crawley instead, – like a fool, as I know now that I was. And so I have brought all this trouble on him and on her; and now I must rush home, without waiting for the dean, as fast as the trains will carry me.'

Eames offered to accompany, and this offer was accepted. 'It is hard upon you, though,' she said ; 'you will see nothing of Florence. Three hours in Venice, and six in Florence, and no hours at all anywhere else, will be a hard fate to you on your first trip to Italy.' But Johnny said 'Excelsior' to himself once more, and thought of

Lily Dale, who was still in London, hoping that she might hear of his exertions; and he felt, perhaps, also, that it would be pleasant to return with a dean's wife, and never hesitated. Nor would it do, he thought, for him to be absent in the excitement caused by the news of Mr Crawley's innocence and injuries. 'I don't care a bit about that,' he said. 'Of course, I should like to see Florence, and, of course, I should like to go to bed; but I will live in hopes that I may do both some day.' And so there grew to be a friendship between him and Mrs Arabin even before they had started.

He was driven once through Florence, he saw the Venus de'Medici, and he saw the Seggiola; he looked up from the side of the Duomo to the top of the Campanile, and he walked round the back of the cathedral itself; he tried to inspect the doors of the Baptistery, and declared that the 'David' was very fine. Then he went back to the hotel, dined with Mrs Arabin, and started for England.

The dean was to have joined his wife at Venice, and then they were to have returned together, coming round by Florence. Mrs Arabin had not, therefore, taken her things away from Florence when she left it, and had been obliged to return to pick them up on her journey homewards. He, – the dean, – had been delayed in his Eastern travels. Neither Syria not Constantinople had got themselves done as quickly as he had expected, and he had, consequently, twice written to his wife, begging her to pardon the transgression of his absence for even yet a few days longer. 'Everything, therefore,' as Mrs Arabin said, 'has conspired to perpetuate this mystery, which a word from me would have solved. I owe more to Mr Crawley than I can ever pay him.'

'He will be very well paid, I think,' said John, 'when he hears the truth. If you could see inside his mind at this moment, I'm sure you'd find that he thinks he stole the cheque.'

'He cannot think that, Mr Eames. Besides, at this moment I hope he has heard the truth.'

'That may be, but he did think so. I do believe that he had not the slightest notion where he got it; and, which is more, not a single person in the whole county had a notion. People thought that he had picked it up, and used it in his despair. And the bishop has been so hard upon him.'

'Oh, Mr Eames, that is the worst of all.'

'So I am told. The bishop has a wife, I believe.'

'Yes, he has a wife, certainly,' said Mrs Arabin.

'And people say that she is not very good-natured.'

'There are some of us at Bartchester who do not love her very dearly. I cannot say that she is one of my own especial friends.'

'I believe she has been hard to Mr Crawley,' said John Eames.

'I should not be in the least surprised,' said Mrs Arabin.

Then they reached Turin, and there, taking up 'Galignani's Messenger' in the reading-room of Trompetta's Hotel, John Eames saw that Mrs Proudie was dead. 'Look at that,' said he, taking the paragraph to Mrs Arabin; 'Mrs Proudie is dead!' 'Mrs Proudie dead!' she exclaimed. 'Poor woman! Then there will be peace at Barchester!' 'I never knew her very intimately,' she afterwards said to her companion, 'and I do not know that I have a right to say that she ever did me an injury. But I remember well her first coming into Barchester. My sister's father-in-law, the late bishop, was just dead. He was a mild, kind, dear old man, whom my father loved beyond all the world, except his own children. You may suppose we were all a little sad. I was not specially connected with the cathedral then, except through my father,' – and Mrs Arabin, as she told all this, remembered that in the days of which she was speaking she was a young mourning widow, – 'but I think I can never forget the sort of harsh-toned pæan of low-church trumpets with which that poor woman made her entry into the city. She might have been more lenient, as we had never sinned by being very high. She might, at any rate, have been more gentle with us at first. I think we had never attempted much beyond decency, good-will and comfort. Our comfort she utterly destroyed. Good-will was not to her taste. And as for decency, when I remember some things, I must say that when the comfort and good-will went, the decency went along with them. And now she is dead! I wonder how the bishop will get on without her.'

'Like a house on fire, I should think,' said Johnny.

'Fie, Mr Eames; you shouldn't speak in such a way on such a subject.'

Mrs Arabin and Johnny became fast friends as they journeyed home. There was a sweetness in his character which endeared him readily to women; though, as we have seen, there was a want of something to make one woman cling to him. He could be soft and pleasant-mannered. He was fond of making himself useful, and was a perfect master of all those little caressing modes of behaviour in which the caress is quite impalpable, and of which most women know the value and appreciate the comfort. By the time that they had reached Paris John had told Mrs Arabin the whole story of Lily Dale and Crosbie, and Mrs Arabin had promised to assist him, if any assistance might be in her power.

'Of course I have heard of Miss Dale,' she said, 'because we know the De Courcys.' Then she turned away her face, almost blushing, as she remembered the first time that she had seen that

Lady Alexandrina De Courcy whom Mr Crosbie had married. It had been at Mr Thorne's house at Ullathorne, and on that day she had done a thing which she had never since remembered without blushing. But it was an old story now, and a story of which her companion knew nothing, – of which he never could know anything. That day at Ullathorne Mrs Arabin, the wife of the Dean of Barchester, than whom there was no more discreet clerical matron in the diocese, had—boxed a clergyman's ears!*

'Yes,' said John, speaking of Crosbie, 'he was a wise fellow; he knew what he was about; he married an earl's daughter.'

'And now I remember hearing that somebody gave him a terrible beating. Perhaps it was you?'

'It wasn't terrible at all,' said Johnny.

'Then it was you?'

'Oh, yes; it was I.'

'Then it was you who saved poor old Lord De Guest from the bull?'

'Go on, Mrs Arabin. There is no end of the grand things I've done.'

'You're quite a hero of romance.'

He bit his lip as he told himself that he was not enough of a hero. 'I don't know about that,' said Johnny. 'I think what a man ought to do in these days is to seem not to care what he eats and drinks, and to have his linen very well got up. Then he'll be a hero.' But that was hard upon Lily.

'Is that what Miss Dale requires?' said Mrs Arabin.

'I was not thinking about her particularly,' said Johnny, lying.

They slept a night in Paris, as they had done also at Turin, – Mrs Arabin not finding herself able to accomplish such marvels in the way of travelling as her companion had achieved – and then arrived in London in the evening. She was taken to a certain quiet clerical hotel at the top of Suffolk Street, much patronized by bishops and deans of the better sort, expecting to find a message there from her husband. And there was the message – just arrived. The dean had reached Florence three days after her departure; and as he would do the journey home in twenty-four hours less than she had taken, he would be there, at the hotel, on the day after to-morrow. 'I suppose I may wait for him, Mr Eames?' said Mrs Arabin.

'I will see Mr Toogood to-night, and I will call here to-morrow, whether I see him or not. At what hour will you be in?'

'Don't trouble yourself to do that. You must take care of Sir Raffle Buffle, you know.'

'I shan't go near Sir Raffle Buffle to-morrow, nor yet the next day. You mustn't suppose that I am afraid of Sir Raffle Buffle.'

'You are only afraid of Lily Dale.' From all which it may be seen that Mrs Arabin and John Eames had become very intimate on their way home.

It was then arranged that he should call on Mr Toogood that same night or early the next morning, and that he should come to the hotel at twelve o'clock on the next day. Going along one of the passages he passed two gentlemen in shovel-hats, with very black new coats, and knee-breeches; and Johnny could not but hear a few words which one clerical gentleman said to the other. 'She was a woman of great energy, of wonderful spirit, but a firebrand, my lord, – a complete firebrand!' Then Johnny knew that the Dean of A. was talking to the Bishop of B. about the late Mrs Proudie.

CHAPTER 71

Mr Toogood at Silverbridge

We will now go back to Mr Toogood as he started for Silverbridge, on the receipt of Mrs Arabin's telegram from Venice. 'I gave cheque to Mr Crawley. It was part of a sum of money. Will write to Archdeacon Grantly to-day, and return home at once.' That was the telegram which Mr Toogood received at his office, and on receiving which he resolved that he must start to Barchester immediately. 'It isn't certainly what you may call a paying business,' he said to his partner, who continued to grumble; 'but it must be done all the same. If it don't get into the ledger in one way it will in another.' So Mr Toogood started for Silverbridge, having sent to his house in Tavistock Square for a small bag, a clean shirt, and a toothbrush. And as he went down in the railway-carriage, before he went to sleep, he turned it all over in his mind. 'Poor devil! I wonder whether any man ever suffered so much before. And as for that woman, – it's ten thousand pities that she should have died before she heard it. Talk of heart-complaint; she'd have had a touch of heart-complaint if she had known this!' Then, as he was speculating how Mrs Arabin could have become possessed of the cheque, he went to sleep.

He made up his mind that the first person to be seen was Mr Walker, and after that he would, if possible, go to Archdeacon Grantly. He was at first minded to go at once out to Hogglestock; but when he remembered how very strange Mr Crawley was in all his ways, and told himself professionally that telegrams were but bad sources of evidence on which to depend for details, he thought that it would be safer if he were first to see Mr Walker. There would be very little delay. In a day or two the archdeacon would receive his letter, and in a day or two after that Mrs Arabin would probably be at home.

It was late in the evening before Mr Toogood reached the house of the Silverbridge solicitor, having the telegram carefully folded in his pocket; and he was shown into the dining-room while the servant took his name up to Mr Walker. The clerks were gone, and the office was closed; and persons coming on business at such times, – as they often did come to that house, – were always shown into the parlour.

'I don't know whether master can see you to-night,' said the girl; 'but if he can, he'll come down.'

When the card was brought up to Mr Walker he was sitting alone with his wife. 'It's Toogood,' said he; 'poor Crawley's cousin.'

'I wonder whether he has found anything out,' said Mrs Walker. 'May he not come up here?' Then Mr Toogood was summoned into the drawing-room, to the maid's astonishment; for Mr Toogood had made no toilet sacrifices to the goddess or grace who presides over evening society in provincial towns, – and presented himself with the telegram in his hand. 'We have found out all about poor Crawley's cheque,' he said, before the maid-servant had closed the door. 'Look at that,' and he handed the telegram to Mr Walker. The poor girl was obliged to go, though she would have given one of her ears to know the exact contents of that bit of paper.

'Walker, what is it?' said his wife, before Walker had had time to make the contents of the document his own.

'He got it from Mrs Arabin,' said Toogood.

'No!' said Mrs Walker. 'I thought that was it all along.'

'It's a pity you didn't say so before,' said Mr Walker.

'So I did; but a lawyer thinks that nobody can ever see anything but himself; – begging your pardon, Mr Toogood, but I forgot you were one of us. But, Walker, do read it.' Then the telegram was read. 'I gave cheque to Mr Crawley. It was part of a sum of money,' – with the rest of it. 'I knew it would come out,' said Mrs Walker. 'I was quite sure of it.'

'But why the mischief didn't he say so?' said Walker.

'He did say that he got it from the dean,' said Toogood.

'But he didn't get it from the dean; and the dean clearly knew nothing about it.'

'I'll tell you what it is,' said Mrs Walker; 'it has been some private transaction between Mr Crawley and Mrs Arabin, which the dean was to know nothing about; and so he wouldn't tell. I must say I honour him.'

'I don't think it has been that,' said Walker. 'Had he known all through that it had come from Mrs Arabin, he would never have said that Mr Soames gave it to him, and then that the dean gave it him.'

'The truth has been that he has known nothing about it,' said Toogood; 'and we shall have to tell him.'

At that moment Mary Walker came into the room, and Mrs Walker could not constrain herself. 'Mary, Mr Crawley is all right. He didn't steal the cheque. Mrs Arabin gave it to him.'

'Who says so? How do you know? Oh, dear; I am so happy, if it's true.' Then she saw Mr Toogood and curtseyed.

'It is quite true, my dear,' said Mr Walker. 'Mr Toogood has had a message by the wires from Mrs Arabin at Venice. She is coming home at once, and no doubt everything will be put right. In the meantime, it may be a question whether we should not hold our tongues. Mr Crawley himself, I suppose, knows nothing of it yet?'

'Not a word,' said Toogood.

'Papa, I must tell Miss Prettyman,' said Mary.

'I should think that probably all Silverbridge knows it by this time,' said Mrs Walker, 'because Jane was in the room when the announcement was made. You may be sure that every servant in the house has been told.' Mary Walker, not waiting for any further command from her father, hurried out of the room to convey the secret to her special circle of friends.

It was known throughout Silverbridge that night, and indeed it made so much commotion that it kept many people for an hour out of their beds. Ladies who were not in the habit of going out late at night without the fly from the 'George and Vulture,' tied their heads up in their handkerchiefs, and hurried up and down the street to tell each other that the great secret had been discovered, and that in truth Mr Crawley had not stolen the cheque. The solution of the mystery was not known to all, – was known on that night only to the very select portion of the aristocracy of Silverbridge to whom it was communicated by Mary Walker or Miss Anne Prettyman. For Mary Walker, when earnestly entreated by Jane, the parlour-maid, to tell her something more of the great news, had so far respected her father's caution as to say not a word about Mrs Arabin. 'Is it true, Miss Mary, that he didn't steal it?' Jane asked imploringly. 'It is true. He did not steal it.' 'And who did, Miss Mary? Indeed I won't tell anybody.'

'Nobody. But don't ask any more questions, for I won't answer them. Get me my hat at once, for I want to go up to Miss Prettyman's.' Then Jane got Miss Walker's hat, and immediately afterwards scampered into the kitchen with the news. 'Oh, law, cook, it's all come out! Mr Crawley's as innocent as the unborn babe. The gentleman upstairs what's just come, and was here once before, – for I know'd him immediate, – I heard him say so. And master said so too.'

'Did master say so his own self?' asked the cook.

'Indeed he did; and Miss Mary told me the same this moment.'

'If master said so, then there ain't a doubt as they'll find him innocent. And who took'd it, Jane?'

'Miss Mary says as nobody didn't steal it.'

'That's nonsense, Jane. It stands to reason as somebody had it as hadn't ought to have had it. But I'm as glad as anything as how that poor reverent gent'll come off; – I am. They tells me it's weeks sometimes before a bit of butcher's meat finds its way into his house.' Then the groom and the housemaid and the cook, one after another, took occasion to slip out of the back-door, and poor Jane, who had really been the owner of the news, was left alone to answer the bell.

Miss Walker found the two Miss Prettymans sitting together over their accounts in the elder Miss Prettyman's private room. And she could see at once by signs which were not unfamiliar to her that Miss Anne Prettyman was being scolded. It often happened that Miss Anne Prettyman was scolded, especially when the accounts were brought out upon the table. 'Sister, they are illegible,' Mary Walker heard, as the servant opened the door for her.

'I don't think it's quite so bad as that,' said Miss Anne, unable to restrain her defence. Then, as Mary entered the room, Miss Prettyman the elder laid her hands down on certain books and papers as though to hide them from profane eyes.

'I am glad to see you, Mary,' said Miss Prettyman, gravely.

'I've brought such a piece of news,' said Mary. 'I knew you'd be glad to hear it, so I ventured to disturb you.'

'Is it good news?' said Anne Prettyman.

'Very good news. Mr Crawley is innocent.

Both the ladies sprung on to their legs. Even Miss Prettyman herself jumped up on to her legs. 'No!' said Anne. 'Your father has discovered it?' said Miss Prettyman.

'Not exactly that. Mr Toogood has come down from London to tell him. Mr Toogood, you know, is Mr Crawley's cousin; and he is a lawyer, like papa.' It may be observed that ladies belonging to the families of solicitors always talk about lawyers, and never about attorneys or barristers.

'And does Mr Toogood say that Mr Crawley is innocent?' asked Miss Prettyman.

'He has heard it by a message from Mrs Arabin. But you mustn't mention this. You won't, please, because papa has asked me not. I told him that I should tell you.' Then, for the first time, the frown passed away entirely from Miss Prettyman's face, and the papers and account-books were pushed aside, as being of no moment. The news had been momentous enough to satisfy her. Mary continued her story almost in a whisper. 'It was Mrs Arabin who sent the cheque to Mr Crawley. She says so herself. So that makes Mr Crawley quite innocent. I am so glad.'

'But isn't it odd he didn't say so?' said Miss Prettyman.

'Nevertheless, it's true,' said Mary.

'Perhaps he forgot,' said Anne Prettyman.

'Men don't forget such things as that,' said the elder sister.

'I really do think Mr Crawley could forget anything,' said the younger sister.

'You may be sure it's true,' said Mary Walker, 'because papa said so.'

'If he said so, it must be true,' said Miss Prettyman; 'and I am rejoiced. I really am rejoiced. Poor man! Poor ill-used man! And nobody has ever believed that he has really been guilty, even though they may have thought that he spent the money without any proper right to it. And now he will get off. But dear me, Mary, Mr Smithe told me yesterday that he had already given up his living, and that Mr Spooner, the minor canon, was trying to get it from the dean. But that was because Mr Spooner and Mrs Proudie had quarrelled; and as Mrs Proudie is gone, Mr Spooner very likely won't want to move now.'

'They'll never go and put anybody into Hogglestock, Annabella, over Mr Crawley's head,' said Anne.

'I didn't say they would. Surely I may be allowed to repeat what I hear, like another person, without being snapped up.'

'I didn't mean to snap you up, Annabella.'

'You're always snapping me up. But if this is true, I cannot say how glad I am. My poor Grace! Now, I suppose there will be no difficulty, and Grace will become a great lady.' Then they discussed very minutely the chances of Grace Crawley's promotion.

John Walker, Mr Winthrop, and several others of the chosen spirits of Silverbridge, were playing whist at a provincial club, which had established itself in the town, when the news was brought to them. Though Mr Winthrop was the partner of the great Walker, and though John Walker was the great man's son, I fear that the news reached their ears in but an underhand sort of way. As for the great man himself, he never went near the club, preferring his slippers and tea at home. The Walkerian groom, rushing up the street to the 'George and Vulture,' paused a moment to tell his tidings to the club porter; from the club porter it was whispered respectfully to the Silverbridge apothecary, who, by special grace, was a member of the club; – and was by him repeated with much cautious solemnity over the card-table. 'Who told you that, Balsam?' said John Walker, throwing down his cards.

'I've just heard it,' said Balsam.

'I don't believe it,' said John.

'I shouldn't wonder if it's true,' said Winthrop. 'I always said that something would turn up.'

'Will you bet three to one he is not found guilty?' said John Walker.

'Done,' said Winthrop; 'in pounds.' That morning the odds in the club against the event had been only two to one. But as the matter was discussed, the men in the club began to believe the tidings, and before he went home John Walker would hvave been glad to hedge his bet on any terms. After he had spoken to his father, he gave his money up for lost.

But Mr Walker, – the great Walker, – had more to do that night before his son came home from the club. He and Mr Toogood agreed that it would be right that they should see Dr Tempest at once, and they went over together, to the rectory. It was past ten at this time, and they found the doctor almost in the act of putting out the candles for the night. 'I could not but come to you, doctor,' said Mr Walker, 'with the news my friend has brought. Mrs Arabin gave the cheque to Crawley. Here is a telegram from her saying so.' And the telegram was handed to the doctor.

He stood perfectly silent for a few minutes, reading it over and over again. 'I see it all,' he said, when he spoke at last. 'I see it all now; and I must own I was never before so much puzzled in my life.'

'I own I can't see why she should have given him Mr Soames's cheque,' said Mr Walker.

'I can't say where she got it, and I own I don't much care,' said Dr Tempest. 'But I don't doubt but what she gave it him without telling the dean, and that Crawley though it came from the dean. I'm very glad. I am, indeed, very glad. I do not know that I ever pitied a man so much in my life as I have pitied Mr Crawley.'

'It must have been a hard case when it has moved him,' said Mr Walker to Mr Toogood as they left the clergyman's house; and then the Silverbridge attorney saw the attorney from London home to his inn.

It was the general opinion at Silverbridge that the news from Venice ought to be communicated to the Crawleys by Major Grantly. Mary Walker had expressed this opinion very strongly, and her mother had agreed with her. Miss Prettyman also felt that poetical justice, or, at least, the romance of justice, demanded this; and, as she told her sister Anne after Mary Walker left her, she was of opinion that such an arrangement might tend to make things safe. 'I do think he is an honest man and a fine fellow,' said Miss Prettyman; 'but, my dear, you know what the proverb says,

"There's many a slip 'twixt the cup and the lip".' Miss Prettyman thought that anything which might be done to prevent a slip ought to be done. The idea that the pleasant task of taking the news out to Hogglestock ought to be confided to Major Grantly was very general; but then Mr Walker was of opinion that the news ought not to be taken to Hogglestock at all till something more certain than the telegram had reached them. Early on the following morning the two lawyers again met, and it was arranged between them that the London lawyer should go over at once to Barchester, and that the Silverbridge lawyer should see Major Grantly. Mr Toogood was still of opinion that with due diligence something might yet be learned as to the cheque, by inquiry among the denizens of 'The Dragon of Wantly.' And his opinion to this effect was stronger than ever when he learned from Mr Walker that 'The Dragon of Wantly' belonged to Mrs Arabin.

Mr Walker, after breakfast, had himself driven up in his open carriage to Cosby Lodge, and, as he entered the gates, observed that the auctioneer's bills as to the sale had been pulled down. The Mr Walkers of the world know everything, and our Mr Walker had quite understood that the major was leaving Cosby Lodge because of some misunderstanding with his father. The exact nature of the misunderstanding he did not know, even though he was Mr Walker, but had little doubt that it referred in some way to Grace Crawley. If the archdeacon's objection to Grace arose from the imputation against the father, that objection would now be removed, but the abolition of the posters could not as yet have been owing to any such cause as that. Mr Walker found the major at the gate of the farmyard attached to Cosby Lodge, and perceived that at that very moment he was engaged in superintending the abolition of sundry other auctioneer's bills fom sundry other posts. 'What is all this about?' said Mr Walker, greeting the major. 'Is there to be no sale after all?'

'It has been postponed,' said the major.

'Postponed for good, I hope? Bill to be read again this day six months!' said Mr Walker.

'I rather think not. But circumstances have induced me to have it put off.'

Mr Walker had got out of the carriage and had taken Major Grantly aside. 'Just come a little further,' he said; 'I've something special to tell you. News reached me last night which will clear Mr Crawley altogether . We know now where he got the cheque.'

'You don't tell me so!'

'Yes, I do. And though the news has reached us in such a way that we cannot act upon it till it's confirmed, I do not in the least doubt it.'

'And how did he get it ?'

'You cannot guess ?'

'Not in the least,' said the major; 'unless, after all, Soames gave it to him.'

'Soames did not give it to him, but Mrs Arabin did.'

'Mrs Arabin ?'

'Yes, Mrs Arabin.'

'Not the dean ?'

'No, not the dean. What we know is this, that your aunt has telegraphed to Crawley's cousin, Toogood, to say that she gave Crawley that cheque, and that she has written to your father about it at length. We do not like to tell Crawley till that letter has been received. It is so easy, you know, to misunderstand a telegram, and the wrong copying of a word may make such a mistake !'

'When was it received ?'

'Toogood received it in London only yesterday morning. Your father will not get his letter, as I calculate, till the day after to-morrow. But, perhaps, you had better go over and see him, and prepare him for it. Toogood has gone to Barchester this morning.' To this propositon Grantly made no immediate answer. He could not but remember the terms on which he had left his father; and though he had, most unwillingly, pulled down the auctioneer's bills, in compliance with his mother's last prayer to him, – and, indeed, had angrily told the auctioneer to send him in his bill when the auctioneer had demurred to these proceedings, – nevertheless he was hardly prepared to discuss the matter of Mr Crawley with his father in pleasant words, – in words which should be full of rejoicing. It was a great thing for him, Henry Grantly, that Mr Crawley should be innocent, and he did rejoice; but he had intended his father to understand that he meant to persevere, whether Mr Crawley were innocent or guilty, and thus he would now lose an opportunity for exhibiting his obstinacy, – an opportunity which had not been without a charm for him. He must console himself as best he might with the returning prospect of assured prosperity, and with his renewed hopes as to the Plumstead foxes ! 'We think, major, that when the time comes you ought to be the bearer of the news to Hogglestock,' said Mr Walker. Then the major did undertake to convey the news to Hogglestock, but he made no promise as to going over to Plumstead.

CHAPTER 72

Mr Toogood at 'The Dragon of Wantly'

In accordance with his arrangement with Mr Walker, Mr Toogood went over to Barchester early in the morning and put himself up at 'The Dragon of Wantly.' He now knew the following facts; that Mr Soames, when he lost his cheque, had had with him one of the servants from that inn, – that the man who had been with Mr Soames had gone to New Zealand, – that the cheque had found its way into the hands of Mrs Arabin, and that Mrs Arabin was the owner of the inn in question. So much he believed to be within his knowledge, and if his knowledge should prove to be correct, his work would be done as far as Mr Crawley was concerned. If Mr Crawley had not stolen the cheque, and if that could be proved, it would be a question of no great moment to Mr Toogood who had stolen it. But he was a sportsman in his own line who liked to account for his own fox. As he was down at Barchester, he thought that he might as well learn how the cheque had got into Mrs Arabin's hands. No doubt that for her own personal possession of it she would be able to account on her return. Probably such account would be given in her first letter home. But it might be well that he should be prepared with any small circumstantial details which he might be able to pick up at the inn.

He reached Barchester before breakfast, and in ordering his tea and toast, reminded the old waiter with the dirty towel of his former acquaintance with him. 'I remember you, sir,' said the old waiter. 'I remember you very well. You were asking questions about the cheque which Mr Soames lost afore Christmas.' Mr Toogood certainly had asked one question on the subject. He had inquired whether a certain man who had gone to New Zealand had been the post-boy who accompanied Mr Soames when the cheque was lost; and the waiter had professed to know nothing about Mr Soames or the cheque. He now pervceived at once that the gist of the question had remained on the old man's mind, and that he was recognized as being in some way connected with the lost money.

'Did I? Ah, yes; I think I did. And I think you told me that he was the man?'

'No, sir; I never told you that.'

'Then you told me that he wasn't.'

'Nor I didn't tell you that neither,' said the waiter angrily.

'Then what the devil did you tell me?' To this further question the waiter sulkily declined to give any answer, and soon afterwards left the room. Toogood, as soon as he had done his breakfast, rang the bell, and the same man appeared. 'Will you tell Mr Stringer that I should be glad to see him if he's disengaged,' said Mr Toogood. 'I know he's bad with the gout, and therefore if he'll allow me, I'll go to him instead of his coming to me.' Mr Stringer was the landlord of the inn. The waiter hesitated a moment, and then declared that to the best of his belief his master was not down. He would go and see. Toogood, however, would not wait for that; but rising quickly and passing the waiter, crossed the hall from the coffee-room, and entered what was called the bar. The bar was a small room connected with the hall by a large open window, at which orders for rooms were given and cash was paid, and glasses of beer were consumed, — and a good deal of miscellaneous conversation was carried on. The barmaid was here at the window, and there was also, in a corner of the room, a man at a desk with a red nose. Toogood knew that the man at the desk with the red nose was Mr Stringer's clerk. So much he had learned in his former rummaging about the inn. And he also remembered at this moment that he had observed the man with the red nose standing under a narrow archway in the close as he was coming out of the deanery, on the occasion of his visit to Mr Harding. It had not occurred to him then that the man with the red nose was watching him, but it did occur to him now that the man with the red nose had been there, under the arch, with the express purpose of watching him on that occasion. Mr Toogood passed quickly through the bar into an inner parlour, in which was sitting Mr Stringer, the landlord, propped among his cushions. Toogood, as he had entered the hotel, had seen Mr Stringer so placed, through the two doors, which at that moment had both happened to be open. He knew therefore that his old friend the waiter had not been quite true to him in suggesting that his master was not as yet down. As Toogood cast a glance of his eye on the man with the red nose, he told himself the old story of the apparition under the archway.

'Mr Stringer,' said Mr Toogood to the landlord, 'I hope I'm not intruding.'

'O dear, no, sir,' said the forlorn man. 'Nobody ever intrudes coming in here. I'm always happy to see gentlemen, – only mostly, I'm so bad with the gout.'

'Have you got a sharp touch of it just now, Mr Stringer?'

'Not just to-day, sir. I've been a little easier since Saturday. The worst of this burst is over. But Lord bless you, sir, it don't leave me, – not for a fortnight at a time, now; it don't. And it ain't what I drink, nor it ain't what I eat.'

'Constitution, I suppose?' said Toogood.

'Look here, sir;' and Mr Stringer shewed his visitor the chalk stones in all his knuckles. 'They say I'm a mass of chalk. I sometimes think they'll break me up to mark the scores behind my own door with.' And Mr Stringer laughed at his own wit.

Mr Toogood laughed too. He laughed loud and cheerily. And then he asked a sudden question, keeping his eye as he did so upon a little square open window, which communicated between the landlord's private room and the bar. Through this small aperture he could see as he stood a portion of the hat worn by the man with the red nose. Since he had been in the room with the landlord, the man with the red nose had moved his head twice, on each occasion drawing himself closer into his corner; but Mr Toogood, by moving also, had still contrived to keep a morsel of the hat in sight. He laughed cheerily at the landlord's joke, and then he asked a sudden question, – looking well at the morsel of the hat as he did so. 'Mr Stringer,' said he, 'how do you pay your rent, and to whom do you pay it?' There was immediately a jerk in the hat, and then it disappeared. Toogood, stepping to the open door, saw that the red-nosed clerk had taken his hat off and was very busy at his accounts.

'How do I pay my rent?' said Mr Stringer, the landlord. 'Well, sir, since this cursed gout has been so bad, it's hard enough to pay it at all sometimes. You ain't sent here to look for it, sir, are you?'

'Not I,' said Toogood. 'It was only a chance question.' He felt that he had nothing more to do with Mr Stringer, the landlord. Mr Stringer, the landlord, knew nothing about Mr Soames's cheque. 'What's the name of your clerk?' said he.

'The name of my clerk?' said Mr Stringer. 'Why do you want to know the name of my clerk?'

'Does he ever pay your rent for you?'

'Well, yes; he does, at times. He pays it into the bank for the lady as owns the house. Is there any reason for your asking these questions, sir? It isn't usual, you know, for a stranger, sir.'

Toogood during the whole of this time was standing with his eye upon the red-nosed man, and he red-nosed man could not move. The red-nosed man heard all the questions and the landlord's answers, and could not even pretend that he did not hear them. 'I am my cousin's clerk,' said he, putting on his hat, and coming up to Mr Toogood with a swagger. 'My name is Dan Stringer, and I'm Mr John Stringer's cousin. I've lived with Mr John Stringer for twelve year and more, and I'm a'most as well known in Barchester as himself. Have you anything to say to me, sir?'

'Well, yes; I have,' said Toogood.

'I believe you're one of them attorneys from London?' said Mr Dan Stringer.

'That's true. I am an attorney from London.'

'I hope there's nothing wrong?' said the gouty man, trying to get off his chair, but not succeeding. 'If there is anything wronger than usual, Dan, do tell me. Is there anything–wrong, sir?' and the landlord appealed piteously to Mr Toogood.

'Never you mind, John,' said Dan. 'You keep yourself quiet, and don't answer none of his questions. He's one of them low sort, he is. I know him. I knowed him for what he is directly I saw him. Ferreting about, – that's his game; to see if there's anything to be got.'

'But what is he ferreting here for?' said Mr John Stringer.

'I'm ferreting for Mr Soames's cheque for twenty pounds,' said Mr Toogood.

'That's the cheque that the parson stole,' said Dan Stringer. 'He's to be tried for it at the 'sizes.'

'You've heard about Mr Soames and his cheque, and about Mr Crawley, I daresay?' said Toogood.

'I've heard a deal about them,' said the landlord.

'And so, I daresay, have you?' said Toogood, turning to Dan Stringer. But Dan Stringer did not seem inclined to carry on the conversation any further. When he was hardly pressed, he declared that he just had heard that there was some parson in trouble about a sum of money; but that he knew no more about it than that. He didn't know whether it was a cheque or a note that the parson had taken, and had never been sufficiently interested in the matter to make any inquiry.

'But you've just said that Mr Soames's cheque was the cheque the parson stole,' said the astonished landlord, turning with open eyes upon his cousin.

'You be blowed,' said Dan Stringer, the clerk, to Mr John Stringer, the landlord; and then walked out of the room back to the bar.

'I understand nothing about it, – nothing at all,' said the gout man.

'I understand pretty nearly all about it,' said Mr Toogood,

following the red-nosed clerk. There was no necessity that he should trouble the landlord any further. He left the room, and went through the bar, and as he passed out along the hall, he found Dan Stringer with his hat on talking to the waiter. The waiter immediately pulled himself up, and adjusted his dirty napkin under his arm, after the fashion of waiters, and showed that he intended to be civil to the customers of the house. But he of the red nose cocked his hat, and looked with insolence at Mr Toogood, and defied him. 'There's nothing I do hate so much as them low-bred Old Bailey attorneys,' said Mr Dan Striinger to the waiter, in a voice intended to reach Mr Toogood's ears. Then Mr Toogood told himself that Dan Stringer was not the thief himself, and that it might be very difficult to prove that Dan had even been the receiver of stolen goods. He had, however, no doubt in his own mind but that such was the case.

He first went to the police office, and there explained his business. Nobody at the police office pretended to forget Mr Soames's cheque, or Mr Crawley's position. The constable went so far as to swear that there wasn't a man, woman, or child in all Barchester who was not talking of Mr Crawley at that very moment. Then Mr Toogood went with the constable to the private house of the mayor, and had a little conversation with the mayor. 'Not guilty!' said the mayor, with incredulity, when he first heard the news about Crawley. But when he heard Mr Toogood's story, or as much of it as it was necessary that he should hear, he yielded reluctantly. 'Dear, dear!' he said. 'I'd have bet anything 'twas he who stole it.' And after that the mayor was quite sad. Only let us think what a comfortable excitement it would create throughout England if it was surmised that an archbishop had forged a deed; and how much England would lose when it was discovered that the archbishop was innocent! As the archbishop and his forgery would be to England, so was Mr Crawley and the cheque for twenty pounds to Barchester and its mayor. Nevertheless, the mayor promised his assistance to Mr Toogood.

'Mr Toogood, still neglecting his red-nosed friend, went next to the deanery, hoping that he might again see Mr Harding. Mr Harding was, he was told, too ill to be seen. Mr Harding, Mrs Baxter said, could never be seen now by strangers, nor yet by friends, unless they were very old friends. 'There's been a deal of change since you were here last, sir. I remember your coming, sir. You were talking to Mr Harding about the poor clergyman as is to be tried.' He did not stop to tell Mrs Baxter the whole story of Mr Crawley's innocence; but having learned that a message had been received to say that Mrs Arabin would be home on the next

Tuesday, – this being Friday, – he took his leave of Mrs Baxter. His next visit was to Mr Soames, who lived three miles out in the country.

He found it very difficult to convince Mr Soames. Mr Soames was more staunch in his belief of Mr Crawley's guilt than any one whom Toogood had yet encountered. 'I never took the cheque out of his house,' said Mr Soames. 'But you have not stated that on oath,' said Mr Toogood. 'No,' rejoined the other; 'and I never will. I can't swear to it; but yet I'm sure of it.' He acknowledged that he had been driven by a man named Scuttle, and that Scuttle might have picked up the cheque, if it had been dropped in the gig. But the cheque had not been dropped in the gig. The cheque had been dropped in Mr Crawley's house. 'Why did he say then that I paid it to him?' said Mr Soames, when Mr Toogood spoke confidently of Crawley's innocence. 'Ah, why indeed?' answered Toogood. 'If he had not been fool enough to do that, we should have been saved all this trouble. All the same, he did not steal your money, Mr Soames; and Jem Scuttle did steal it. Unfortunately, Jem Scuttle is in New Zealand by this time.' 'Of course, it is possible,' said Mr Soames, as he bowed Mr Toogood out. Mr Soames did not like Mr Toogood.

That evening a gentleman with a red nose asked at the Barchester station for a second-class ticket for London by the up night-mail train. He was well known at the station, and the station-master made some little inquiry. 'All the way to London to-night, Mr Stringer?' he said.

'Yes, – all the way,' said the red-nosed man, sulkily.

'I don't think you'd better go to London to-night, Mr Stringer,' said a tall man, stepping out of the door of the booking-office. 'I think you'd better come back with me to Barchester. I do indeed.' There was some little argument on the occasion; but the stranger, who was a detective policeman, carried his point, and Mr Dan Stringer did return to Barchester.

CHAPTER 73

There is comfort at Plumstead

Henry Grantly had written the following short letter to Mrs Grantly when he made up his mind to pull down the auctioneer's bills. 'Dear Mother, – I have postponed that sale, not liking to refuse you anything. As far as I can see, I shall still be forced to leave Cosby Lodge, as I certainly shall do all I can to make Grace Crawley my wife. I say this that there may be no misunderstanding with my father. The auctioneer has promised to have the bills removed.

Your affectionate son,
Henry Grantly.'

This had been written by the major on the Friday before Mr Walker had brought up to him the tidings of Mr Toogood and Mrs Arabin's solution of the Crawley difficulty; but it did not reach Plumstead till the following morning. Mrs Grantly immediately took the good news about the sale to her husband, – not of course showing him the letter, being far too wise for that, and giving him credit for being too wise to ask for it. 'Henry has arranged with the auctioneer,' she said joyfully; 'and the bills have been all pulled down.'

'How do you know?'

'I've just heard from him. He had told me so. Come, my dear, let me have the pleasure of hearing you say that things shall be pleasant again between you and him. He has yielded.'

'I don't see much yielding in it.'

'He has done what you wanted. What more can he do?'

'I want him to come over here, and take an interest in things, and not treat me as though I were nobody.' Within an hour of this the major had arrived at Plumstead, laden with the story of Mrs Arabin and the cheque, and of Mr Crawley's innocence, – laden not only with such tidings as he had receivd from Mr Walker, but also with further details, which he had received from Mr Toogood. For he had come through Barchester, and had seen Mr Toogood on his way. This was on the Saturday morning, and he had breakfasted with Mr Toogood at 'The Dragon of Wantly.' Mr Toogood had told him of his suspicions, – how the red-nosed man had been stopped, and had been summoned as a witness for Mr Crawley's trial, – and how he was now under the surveillance of the police. Grantly had not cared very much about the red-nosed man, confining his present solicitude to the question whether Grace Crawley's father would certainly be shown to have been innocent of the theft. 'There's not a doubt about it, major,' said Mr Toogood; 'not a doubt on earth. But we'd better be a little quiet till your aunt comes home, – just a little quiet. She'll be here in a day or two, and I won't budge till she comes.' In spite of his desire for quiescence Mr Toogood consented to a revelation being at once made to the archdeacon and Mrs Grantly. 'And I'll tell you what, major; as soon as ever Mrs Arabin is here, and has given us her own word to act on, you and I will go over to Hogglestock and astonish them. I should like to go myself, because, you see, Mrs Crawley is my cousin, and we have taken a little trouble about this matter.' To this the major assented; but he altogether declined to assist in Mr Toogood's speculations respecting the unfortunate Dan Stringer. It was agreed between them that for the present no visit should be made to the palace, as it was thought that Mr Thumble had better be allowed to do the Hogglestock duties on the next Sunday. As matters went, however, Mr Thumble did not do so. He had paid his last visit to Hogglestock.

It may be as well to explain here that the unfortunate Mr Snapper was constrained to go out to Hogglestock on the next Sunday which was now approaching; – which fell out as follows. It might be all very well for Mr Toogood to arrange that he would not tell this person or that person of the news which he had brought down from London; but as he had told various people in Silverbridge, as he had told Mr Soames, and as he had told the police at Barchester, of course the tale found its way to the palace. Mr Thumble heard it, and having come by this time thoroughly to hate Hogglestock and all that belonged to it, he pleaded to Mr Snapper that this report afforded ample reason why he need not again visit that detestable parish. Mr Snapper did not see it in the same light. 'You may be sure Mr Crawley will not get into the pulpit after his resignation, Mr Thumble,' said he.

'His resignation means nothing,' said Thumble.

'It means a great deal,' said Snapper; 'and the duties must be provided for.'

'I won't provide for them,' said Thumble; 'and so you may tell the bishop.' In these days Mr Thumble was very angry with the bishop, for the bishop had not yet seen him since the death of Mrs Proudie.

Mr Snapper had no alternative but to go to the bishop. The bishop in these days was very mild to those whom he saw, given but to few words, and a little astray, – as though he had had one of his limbs cut off, – as Mr Snapper expressed it to to Mrs Snapper. 'I shouldn't wonder if he felt as though all his limbs were cut off,' said Mrs Snapper; 'you must give him time, ane he'll come round by-and-by.' I am inclined to think that Mrs Snapper's opinion of the bishop's feelings and condition was correct. In his diffficulty respecting Hogglestock and Mr Thumble Mr Snapper went to the bishop, and spoke perhaps a little harshly of Mr Thumble.

'I think, upon the whole, Snapper, that you had better go yourself,' said the bishop.

'Do you think so, my lord?' said Snapper. 'It will be inconvenient.'

'Everything is inconvenient; but you'd better go. And look here, Snapper, if I were you, I wouldn't say anything out at Hogglestock about the cheque. We don't know what it may come to yet.' Mr Snapper, with a heavy heart, left his patron, not at all liking the task that was before him. But his wife encouraged him to be obedient. He was the owner of a one-horse carriage, and the work was not, therefore, so hard to him as it would have been and had been to poor Mr Thumble. And, moreover, his wife promised to go with him. Mr Snapper and Mrs Snapper did go over to Hogglestock, and the duty was done. Mrs Snapper spoke a word or two to Mrs Crawley, and Mr Snapper spoke a word or two to Mr Crawley; but not a word was said about the new news as to Mr Soames's cheque, which were now almost current in Barchester. Indeed, no whisper about it had as yet reached Hogglestock.

'One word with you, reverend sir,' said Mr Crawley to the chaplain, as the latter was coming out of the church, 'as to the parish work, sir, during the week; – I should be glad if you would favour me with your opinion.'

'About what, Mr Crawley?'

'Whether you think that I may be allowed, without scandal, to visit the sick, – and to give instruction in the school.'

'Surely; – surely, Mr Crawley. Why not?'

'Mr Thumble gave me to understand that the bishop was very urgent that I should interfere in no way in the ministrations of the parish. Twice did he enjoin on me that I should not interfere, – unnecessarily, as it seeemed to me.'

'Quite unnecessary,' said Mr Snapper. 'And the bishop will be obliged to you, Mr Crawley, if you'll just see that the things go on all straight.'

'I wish it were possible to know with accuracy what his idea of straightness is,' said Mr Crawley to his wife. 'It may be that things are straight to him when they are buried as it were out of sight, and put away without trouble. I hope it be not so with the bishop.' When he went into his school and remembered, – as he did remember through every minute of his teaching – that he was to receive no portion of the poor stipend which was allotted for the clerical duties of the parish, he told himself that there was gross injustice in the way in which things were being made straight at Hogglestock.

But we must go back to the major and the archdeacon at Plumstead, – in which comfortable parish things were generally made straight more easily than at Hogglestock. Henry Grantly went over from Barchester to Plumstead in a gig from the 'Dragon,' and made his way at once into his father's study. The archdeacon was seated there with sundry manuscripts before him, and with one half-finished manuscript, – as was his wont on every Saturday morning. 'Halloo, Harry,' he said. 'I didn't expect you in the least.' It was barely an hour since he had told Mrs Grantly that his complaint against his son was that he wouldn't come and make himself comfortable at the rectory.

'Father,' said he, giving he archdeacon his hand, 'you have heard nothing yet about Mr Crawley?'

'No,' said the archdeacon jumping up; 'nothing new; – what is it?' Many ideas about Mr Crawley at that moment flitted across the archdeacon's mind. Could it be that the unfortunate man had committed suicide, overcome by his troubles?

'It has all come out. He got the cheque from my aunt.'

'From your aunt Eleanor?'

'Yes; from my aunt Eleanor. She has telegraphed over from Venice to say that she gave the identical cheque to Crawley. That is all we know at present, – except that she has written an account of the matter to you, and that she will be here herself as quick as she can come.'

'Who got the message, Henry?'

'Crawley's lawyer, – a fellow named Toogood, a cousin of his wife's; – a very decent fellow,' added the major, remembering how necessary it was that he should reconcile his father to all the Crawley belongings. 'He's to be over here on Monday, and then will arrange what is to be done.'

'Done in what way, Henry?'

'There's a great deal to be done yet. Crawley does not know

himself at this moment how the cheque got into his hands. He must be told, and something must be settled about the living. They've taken the living away from him among them. And then the indictment must be quashed, or something of that kind done. Toogood has got hold of the scoundrel at Barchester who really stole the cheque from Soames; – or thinks that he has. It's that Dan Stringer.'

'He's got hold of a regular scamp then. I never knew any good of Dan Stringer,' said the archdeacon.

Then Mrs Grantly was told, and the whole story was repeated again, with many expressions of commiseration in reference to all the Crawleys. The archdeacon did not join in these at first, being rather shy on that head. It was very hard to him to have to speak to his son about the Crawleys as though they were people in all respects estimable and well-conducted, and satisfactory. Mrs Grantly understood this so well, that every now and then she said some half-laughing word respecting Mr Crawley's peculiarities, feeling that in this way she might ease her husband's difficulties. 'He must be the oddest man that ever lived,' said Mrs Grantly, 'not to have known where he got the cheque.' The archdeacon shook his head, and rubbed his hands as he walked about the room. 'I suppose too much learning has upset him,' said the archdeacon. 'They say he's not very good at talking English, but put him on in Greek and he never stops.'

The archdeacon was perfectly aware that he had to admit Mr Crawley to his goodwill, and that as for Grace Crawley, – it was essentially necessary that she should be admitted to his heart of hearts. He had promised as much. It must be acknowledged that Archdeacon Grantly always kept his promises, and especially such promises as these. And indeed it was the nature of the man that when he had been very angry with those he loved, he should be unhappy until he had found some escape from his anger. He could not endure to have to own himself to have been in the wrong, but he could be content with a very incomplete recognition of his having been in the right. The posters had been pulled down and Mr Crawley, as he was now told, had not stolen the cheque. That was sufficient. If his son could only drink a glass or two of wine with him comfortably, and talk dutifully about the Plumstead foxes, all should be held to be right, and Grace Crawley should be received with lavish paternal embraces. The archdeacon had kissed Grace once, and felt that he could do so again without an unpleasant strain upon his feelings.

'Say something to your father about the property after dinner,' said Mrs Grantly to her son when they were alone together.

'About what property?'

'About this property, or any property; you know what I mean; — something to show that you are interested about his affairs. He is doing the best he can to make things right.' After dinner, over the claret, Mr Thorne's terrible sin in reference to the trapping of foxes was accordingly again brought up, and the archdeacon became beautifully irate, and expressed his animosity, — which he did not in the least feel, — against an old friend with an energy which would have delighted his wife, if she could have heard him. 'I shall tell Thorne my mind, certainly. He and I are very old friends; we have known each other all our lives; but I cannot put up with this kind of thing, — and I will not. It's all because he's afraid of his own gamekeeper.' And yet the archdeacon had never ridden after a fox in his life, and never meant to do so. Nor had he in truth been always so very anxious that foxes should be found in his covers. That fox which had been so fortunately trapped just outside the Plumstead property afforded almost pleasant escape for the steam of his anger. When he bagan to talk to his wife that evening about Mr Thorne's wicked gamekeeper, she was so sure that all was right, that she said a word of her extreme desire to see Grace Crawley.

'If he is to marry her, we might as well have her over here,' said the archdeacon.

That's just what I was thinking,' said Mrs Grantly. And thus things at the rectory got themselves arranged.

On the Sunday morning the expected letter from Venice came to hand, and was read on that morning very anxiously, not only by Mrs Grantly and the major, but by the archedeacon also, in spite of the sanctity of the day. Indeed the archdeacon had been very stoutly anti-sabbatarial when the question of stopping the Sunday post to Plumstead had been mooted in the village, giving those who on that occasion were the special friends of the postman to understand that he considered them to be numskulls, and little better than idiots. The postman, finding the parson to be against him, had seen that there was no chance for him, and had allowed the matter to drop. Mrs Arabin's letter was long and eager, and full of repetitions, but it did explain clearly to them the exact manner in which the cheque had found its way into Mr Crawley's hand. 'Francis came up to me,' she said in her letter, — Francis being her husband, the dean, — 'and asked me for the money, which I had promised to make up in a packet. The packet was not ready, and he would not wait, declaring that Mr Crawley was in such a flurry that he did not like to leave him. I was therefore to bring it down to the door. I went to my desk, and thinking that I could spare the twenty pounds as well as the fifty, I put the cheque into the envelope, together with the notes, and handed the packet to Francis at the door. I think I told Francis afterwards that I put seventy pounds into the envelope, instead of fifty, but of this I will not be sure. *At any rate, Mr Crawley got Mr Soames's cheque from me.*' These last words she underscored, and then went on to explain how the cheque had been paid to her a short time before by Dan Stringer.

'Then Toogood has been right about the fellow,' said the archdeacon.

'I hope they'll hang him,' said Mrs Grantly. 'He must have known all the time what dreadful misery he was bringing upon this unfortunate family.'

'I don't suppose Dan Stringer cared much about that,' said the major.

'Not a straw,' said the archdeacon, and then all hurried off to church; and the archdeacon preached the sermon in the fabrication of which he had been interrupted by his son, and which therefore barely enabled him to turn the quarter of an hour from the giving out of his text. It was his constant practice to preach for full twenty minutes.

As Barchester lay on the direct road from Plumstead to Hogglestock, it was thought well that word should be sent to Mr Toogood, desiring him not to come out to Plumstead on the Monday morning. Major Grantly proposed to call for him at 'The Dragon,' and to take him on from thence to Hogglestock. 'You had better take your mother's horses all through,' said the archdeacon. The distance was very nearly twenty miles, and it was felt both by the mother and the son, that the archdeacon must be in a good humour when he made such a proposition as that. It was not often that the rectory carriage-horses were allowed to make long journeys. A run into Barchester and back, which altogether was under ten miles, was generally the extent of their work. 'I meant to have posted from Barchester,' said the major. 'You may as well take the horses through,' said the archdeacon. 'Your mother will not want them. And I suppose you might as well bring your friend Toogood back to dinner. We'll give him a bed.'

'He must be a good sort of man,' said Mrs Grantly; 'for I suppose he has done all this for love?'

'Yes; and spent a lot of money out of his own pocket too!' said the major enthusiastically. 'And the joke of it is, that he has been defending Crawley in Crawley's teeth. Mr Crawley had refused to employ counsel; but Toogood had made up his mind to have a barrister, on purpose that there might be a fuss about it in court. He thought that it would tell with the jury in Crawley's favour.'

'Bring him here, and we'll hear all about that from himself,' said the archdeacon. The major, before he started, told his mother that he should call at Framley Parsonage on his way back but he said nothing on this subject to his father.

'I'll write to her in a day or two,' said Mr Grantly, 'and we'll have things settled pleasantly.'

CHAPTER 74

The Crawleys are informed

Major Grantly made an early start, knowing that he had a long day's work before him. He had written over-night to Mr Toogood, naming the hour at which he would reach 'The Dragon,' and was there punctual to the moment. When the attorney came out and got into the open carriage, while the groom held the steps for him, it was plain to be seen that the respect in which he was held at 'The Dragon' was greatly increased. It was already known that he was going to Plumstead that night, and it was partly understood that he was engaged with the Grantly and Arabin faction in defending Mr Crawley the clergyman against the Proudie faction. Dan Stringer, who was still at the inn, as he saw his enemy get into the Plumstead carriage, felt himself to be one of the palace party, and felt that if Mrs Proudie had only lived till after the assizes all this heavy trouble would not have befallen him. The waiter with the dirty napkin stood at the door and bowed, thinking perhaps that as the Proudie party was going down in Barchester, it might be as well to be civil to Mr Toogood. The days of the Stringers were probably drawing to a close at 'The Dragon of Wantly,' and there was no knowing who might be the new landlord.

Henry Grantly and the lawyer found very little to say to each other on their long way out to Hogglestock. They were thinking, probably, much of the coming interview, and hardly knew how to express their thoughts to each other. 'I will not take the carriage up to the house,' said the major, as they were entering the parish of Hogglestock; 'particularly as the man must feed the horses.' So they got out at a farmhouse about half a mile from the church, where the offence of the carriage and livery-servant would be well out of Mr Crawley's sight, and from thence walked towards the parsonage. The church, and the school close to it, lay on their way, and as they passed by the school door they heard voices within. 'I'll bet twopence he's there,' said Toogood. 'They tell me he's always either in one shop or the other. I'll slip in and bring him out.' Mr Toogood had assumed a comfortable air, as though the day's work was to be good pastime, and even made occasional attempts at drollery. He had had his jokes about Dan Stringer, and had attempted to describe the absurdities of Mr Crawley's visit to Bedford Row. All this would have angered the major, had he not seen that it was assumed to cover something below of which Mr Toogood was a little ashamed, but of which, as the major thought, Mr Toogood had no cause to be ashamed. When, therefore, Toogood proposed to go into the school and bring Mr Crawley out, as though the telling of their story would be the easiest in the world, the major did not stop him. Indeed he had no plan of his own ready. His mind was too intent on the tragedy which had occurred, and which was now to be brought to a close, to enable him to form any plan as to the best way of getting up the last scene. So Mr Toogood, with quick and easy steps, entered the school, leaving the major still standing in the road. Mr Crawley was in the school; – as was also Jane Crawley. 'So here you are,' said Toogood. 'That's fortunate. I hope I find you pretty well?'

'If I am not mistaken in the identity, my wife's relative, Mr Toogood?' said Mr Crawley, stepping down from his humble desk.

'Just so, my friend,' said Toogood, with his hand extended, 'just so; and there's another gentleman outside who wants to have a word with you also. Perhaps you won't mind stepping out. These are the young Hogglestockians; are they?'

The young Hogglestockians stared at him, and so did Jane. Jane, who had before heard of him did not like him at first sight, seeing that her father was clearly displeased by the tone of the visitor's address. Mr Crawley was displeased. There was a familiarity about Mr Toogood which made him sore, as having been exhibited before his pupils. 'If you will be pleased to step out, sir, I will follow you,' he said, waving his hand towards the door. 'Jane, my dear, if you will remain with the children, I will return to you presently. Bobby Studge has failed in saying his Belief. You had better set him on again from the beginning. Now, Mr Toogood.' And again he waved with his hand towards the door.

'So that's my young cousin, is it?' said Toogood, stretching over and just managing to touch Jane's fingers, – of which act of touching Jane was very chary. Then he went forth, and Mr Crawley followed him. There was the major standing in the road, and Toogood was anxious to be the first to communicate the good news. It was the only reward he had proposed to himself for the money he had expended and the time he had lost and the trouble he had taken. 'It's all right, old fellow,' he said, clapping his hand

on Crawley's shoulder. 'We've got the right sow by the ear at last.*
We know all about it.' Mr Crawley could hardly remember the
time when he had been called an old fellow last, and now he did
not like it; nor, in the confusion of his mind, could he understand
the allusion to the right sow. He supposed that Mr Toogood had
come to him about his trial, but it did not occur to him that the
lawyer might be bringing him news which might make the trial
altogether unnecessary. 'If my eyes are not mistaken, there is my
friend, Major Grantly,' said Mr Crawley.

'There he is, as large as life,' said Toogood. 'But stop a moment
before you go to him, and give me your hand. I must have the first
shake of it.' Hereupon Crawley extended his hand. 'That's right.
And now let me tell you we know all about the cheque, – Soames's
cheque. We know where you got it. We know who stole it. We
know how it came to the person who gave it to you. It's all very
well talking, but when you're in trouble always go to a lawyer.'

By this time Mr Crawley was looking full into Mr Toogood's
face, and seeing that his cousin's eyes were streaming with tears,
began to get some insight into the man's character, and also some
very dim insight into the facts which the man intended to communicate to himself.

'I do not as yet fully understand you, sir,' said he, 'being perhaps
in such matters somewhat dull of intellect, but it seemeth to me that
you are a messenger of glad tidings, whose feet are beautiful upon
the mountains.'*

'Beautiful!' said Toogood. 'By George, I should think they are
beautiful! Don't you hear me tell you that we have found out all
about the cheque, and that you're as right as a trivet?' They were
still on the little causeway leading from the school up to the road,
and Henry Grantly was waiting for them at the small wicket-gate.
'Mr Crawley,' said the major, 'I congratulate you with all my heart.
I could not but accompany my friend, Mr Toogood, when he
brought you this good news.'

'I do not even yet altogether comprehend what has been told to
me,' said Crawly, now standing out on the road between the other
two men. 'I am doubtless dull, – very dull. May I beg some clearer
word of explanation before I ask you to go with me to my wife?'

'The cheque was given to you by my aunt Eleanor.'

'Your aunt Eleanor!' said Crawley, now altogether in the clouds.
Who was the major's aunt Eleanor? Though he had, no doubt, at
different times heard all the circumstances of the connection, he
had never realized the fact that his daughter's lover was the nephew
of his old friend, Arabin.

'Yes; by my aunt, Mrs Arabin.'

'She put it into the envelope what the notes,' said Toogood; — 'slipped it in without saying a word to any one. I never heard of a woman doing such a mad thing in my life before. If she had died, or if we hadn't caught her where should we all have been? Not but what I think I should have run Dan Srtinger to ground too, and worked it out of him.'

'Then, after all, it was given to me by the dean?' said Crawley, drawing himself up.

'It was in the envelope, but the dean did not know it,' said the major.

'Gentlemen,' said Mr Crawley, 'I was sure of it. I knew it. Weak as my mind may be, — and at times it is very weak, — I was certain that I could not have erred in such a matter. The more I struggled with my memory, the more fixed with me became the fact, — which I had forgotten but for a moment, — that the document had formed a part of that small packet handed to be me by the dean. But look you, sirs, — bear with me yet for a moment. I said that it was so, and the dean denied it.'

'The dean did not know it, man,' said Toogood, almost in a passion.

'Bear with me yet awhile. So far have I been from misdoubting the dean, — whom I have long known to be in all things a true and honest gentleman, — that I postponed the elaborated result of my own memory to his word. And I felt myself the more constrained to do this, because, in a moment of forgetfulness, in the wantonness of inconsiderate haste, with wicked thoughtlessness, I had allowed myself to make a false statement, — unwittingly false, indeed, nathless very false, unpardonably false. I had declared, without thinking, that the money had come to me from the hands of Mr Soames, thereby seeming to cast a reflection upon that gentleman. When I had been guilty of so great a blunder, of so gross a violation of that ordinary care which should govern all words between man and man, especially when any question of money may be in doubt, — how could I expect that any one should accept my statement when contravened by that made by the dean? How, in such an embarrassment, could I believe my own memory? Gentlemen, I did not believe my own memory. Though all the little circumstances of that envelope, with its rich but perilous freightage, came back upon me from time to time with an exactness that has appeared to me to be almost marvellous, yet I have told myself that it was not so! Gentlemen, if you please, we will go into the house; my wife is there, and should no longer be left in suspense.' They passed on in silence for a few steps, till Crawley spoke again. 'Perhaps you will allow me the privilege to be alone with her for one minute, — but for a minute. Her thanks shall not be delayed, where thanks are so richly due.'

'Of course,' said Toogood, wiping his eyes with a large red bandana handkerchief. 'By all means. We'll take a little walk. Come along, major.' The major had turned his face away, and he also was weeping. 'By George! I never heard such a thing in all my life,' said Toogood. 'I wouldn't have believed it if I hadn't seen it. I wouldn't indeed. If I were to tell that up in London, nobody would believe me.'

'I call that man a hero,' said Grantly.

'I don't know about being a hero. I never quite knew what makes a hero, if it isn't having three or four girls dying in love for you at once. But to find a man who was going to let everything in the world go against him, because he believed another fellow better than himself! There's many a chap thinks another man is wool-gathering; but this man has thought he was wool-gathering himself! It's not natural; and the world wouldn't go on if there were many like that. He's beckoning, and we had better go in.'

Mr Toogood went first, and the major followed him. When they entered the front door they saw the skirt of a woman's dress flitting away through the door at the end of the passage, and on entering the room to the left they found Mr Crawley alone. 'She has fled, as though from an enemy,' he said, with a little attempt at a laugh; 'but I will pursue her, and bring her back.'

'No, Crawley, no,' said the lawyer. 'She's a little upset, and all that kind of thing. We know what women are. Let her alone.'

'Nay, Mr Toogood; but then she would be angered with herself afterwards, and would lack the comfort of having spoken a word of gratitude. Pardon me, Major Grantly; but I would not have you leave us till she has seen you. It is as her cousin says. She is somewhat over-excited. But still it will be best that she should see you. Gentlemen, you will excuse me.'

Then he went out to fetch his wife, and while he was away not a word was spoken. The major looked out of one window and Mr Toogood out of the other, and they waited patiently till they heard the coming steps of the husband and wife. When the door was opened, Mr Crawley appeared, leading his wife by the hand. 'My dear,' he said, 'you know Major Grantly. This is your cousin, Mr Toogood. It is well that you know him too, and remember his great kindness to us.' Bu Mrs Crawley could not speak. She could only sink on the sofa, and hide her face, while she strove in vain to repress her sobs. She had been very strong through all her husband's troubles, – very strong in bearing for him what he could not bear for himself, and in fighting on his behalf battles in which he was altogether unable to couch a lance; but the endurance of so many troubles, and the great overwhelming sorrow at last, had so nearly overpowered her, that she could not sustain the shock of this turn in their fortunes. 'She was never like this, sirs, when ill news came to us,' said Mr Crawley, standing somewhat apart from her.

The major sat himself by her side, and put his hand upon hers, and whispered some word to her about her daughter. Upon this she threw her arms around him, and kissed his face, and then his hands, and then looked up into his face through her tears. She murmured some few words, or attempted to do so. I doubt whether the major understood their meaning, but he knew very well what was in her heart.

'And now I think we might as well be moving,' said Mr Toogood. 'I'll see about having the indictment quashed. I'll arrange all that with Walker. It may be necessary that you should go into Barchester the first day the judges sit, and if so, I'll come and fetch you. You may be sure I won't leave the place till it's all square.'

As they were going, Grantly, – speaking now altogether with indifference as to Toogood's presence, – asked Mr Crawley's leave to be the bearer of these tidings to his daughter.

'She can hear it in no tones that can be more grateful to her,' said Mr Crawley.

'I shall ask her for nothing for myself now,' said Grantly. 'It would be ungenerous. But hereafter, – in a few days, – when she shall be more at ease, may I then use your permission— ?'

'Major Grantly,' said Mr Crawley, solemnly, 'I respect you so highly, and esteem you so thoroughly, that I give willingly that which you ask. If my daughter can bring herself to regard you, as a woman should regard her husband, with the love that can worship and cling and be constant, she will, I think, have a fair promise of worldly happiness. And for you, sir, in giving to you my girl, – if so it be that she is given you, – I shall bestow upon you a great treasure.' Had Grace been a king's daughter, with a queen's dowry, the permission to address her could not have been imparted to her lover with a more thorough appreciation of the value of the privilege conferred.

'He is a rum 'un,' said Mr Toogood, as they got into the carriage together; 'but they say he's a very good 'un to go.'

After their departure Jane was sent for, that she might hear the family news; and when she expressed some feeling not altogether in favour of Mr Toogood, Mr Crawley thus strove to correct her views. 'He is a man, my dear, who conceals a warm heart, and an active spirit, and healthy sympathies, under an affected jocularity of manner, and almost with a touch of assumed vulgarity. But when the jewel itself is good, any fault in the casket may be forgiven.'

'Then, papa, the next time I see him I'll like him, – if I can,' said Jane.

The village of Framley lies slightly off the road from Hogglestock to Barchester, – so much so as to add perhaps a mile on the journey if the traveller goes by the parsonage gate. On their route to Hogglestock our two travellers had passed Framley without visiting the village, but on the return journey the major asked Mr Toogood's permission to make the deviation. 'I'm not in a hurry,' said Toogood. 'I never was more comfortable in my life. I'll just light a cigar while you go in and see your friends.' Toogood lit his cigar, and the major, getting down from the carriage, entered the parsonage. It was his fortune to find Grace alone. Robarts was in Barchester, and Mrs Robart was across the road, at Lufton Court. 'Miss Crawley was certainly in,' the servant told him and he soon found himself in Miss Crawley's presence.

'I have only called to tell you the news about your father,' said he.

'What news?'

'We have just come from Hogglestock, – your cousin, Mr Toogood, that is, and myself. They have found out all about the cheque. My aunt, Mrs Arabin, the dean's wife, you know, – she gave it to your father.'

'Oh, Major Grantly!'

'It seems so easily settled, does it not?'

'And is it settled?'

'Yes; everthing. Everything about that.' Now he had hold of her hand as if he were going. 'Good-by. I told your father that I would just call and tell you.'

'It seems almost more than I can believe.'

'You may believe it; indeed you may.' He still held her hand. 'You will write to your mother I daresay to-night. Tell her I was here. Good-by now.'

'Good-by,' she said. Her hand was still in his, and she looked up into his face.

'Dear, dear, dearest Grace! My darling Grace!' Then he took her into his arms and kissed her, and went his way without another word, feeling that he had kept his word to her father like a gentleman. Grace, when she was left alone, though that she was the happiest girl in Christendom. If she could only get to her mother, and tell everything, and be told everything! She had no idea of any promise that her lover might have made to her father, nor did she make inquiry of her own thoughts as to his reasons for staying with her so short a time; but looking back at it all she thought his conduct had been perfect.

In the meantime the major, with Mr Toogood, was driven home to dinner at Barchester.

CHAPTER 75

Madalina's heart is bleeding

John Eames, as soon as he had left Mrs Arabin at the hotel and had taken his travelling-bag to his own lodgings, started off for his uncle Toogood's house. There he found Mrs Toogood, not in the most serene state of mind as to her husband's absence. Mr Toogood had now been at Barchester for the best part of a week, – spending a good deal of money at the inn. Mrs Toogood was quite sure that he must be doing that. Indeed, how could he help himself? Johnny remarked that he did not see how in such circumstances his uncle was to help himself. And then Mr Toogood had only written one short scrap of a letter, – just three words, and they were written in triumph. 'Crawley is all right, and I think I've got the real Simon Pure by the heels.' 'It's all very well, John,' Mrs Toogood said; 'and of course it would be a terrible thing to the family if anybody connected with it were made out to be a thief.' 'It would be quite dreadful,' said Johnny. 'Not that I ever looked upon the Crawleys as connections of ours. But, however, let that pass. I'm sure I'm very glad that your uncle should have been able to be of service to them. But there's a reason in the roasting of eggs, and I can tell you that money is not so plenty in this house, that your uncle can afford to throw it into the Barchester gutters. Think what twelve children are, John. It might be all very well if Toogood were a bachelor, and if some lord had left him a fortune.' John Eames did not stay very long in Tavistock Square. His cousins Polly and Lucy were gone to the play with Mr Summerkin, and his aunt was not in one of her best humours. He took his uncle's part as well as he could, and then left Mrs Toogood. The little allusion to Lord De Guest's generosity had not been pleasant to him. It seemed to rob him of all his own merit. He had been rather proud of his journey to Italy, having contrived to spend nearly forty pounds in ten days. He had done everything in the most expensive way, feeling that every napoleon wasted had been laid out on behalf of Mr Crawley. But, as Mrs Toogood had just told him, all this was nothing to what Toogood was doing. Toogood with twelve children was living at his own charges at Barchester, and was neglecting his business besides. 'There's Mr Crump,' said Mrs Toogood. 'Of course he doesn't like it, and what can I say to him when he comes to me?' This was not quite fair on the part of Mrs Toogood, as Mr Crump had not troubled her even once as yet since her husband's departure.

What was Johnny to do, when he left Tavistock Square? His club was open to him. Should he go to his club, play a game of billiards, and have some supper? When he asked himself the question he knew that he would not go to his club, and yet he pretended to doubt about it, as he made his way to a cabstand in Tottenham Court Road. It would be slow, he told himself, to go to his club. He would have gone to see Lily Dale, only that his intimacy with Mrs Thorne was not sufficient to justify his calling at her house between nine and ten o'clock at night. But, as he must go somewhere, – and as his intimacy with Lady Demolines was, he thought, sufficient to justify almost anything, – he would go to Bayswater. I regret to say that he had written a mysterious note from Paris to Madalina Demolines, saying that he should be in London on this very night, and that it was just on the cards that he might make his way up to Porchester Terrace before he went to bed. The note was mysterious, because it had neither beginning nor ending. It did not contain even initials. It was written like a telegraph message, and was about as long. It was the kind of thing Miss Demolines liked, Johnny thought; and there could be no reason why he should not gratify her. It was her favourite game. Some people like whist, some like croquet, and some like intrigue. Madalina would probably have called it romance, – because by nature she was romantic. John, who was made of sterner stuff, laughed at this. He knew that there was no romance in it. He knew that he was only amusing himself, and gratifying her at the same time, by a little innocent pretence. He told himself that it was his nature to prefer the society of women to that of men. He would have liked the society of Lily Dale, no doubt, much better than that of Miss Demolines; but as the society of Lily Dale was not to be had at that moment, the society of Miss Demolines was the best substitute within his reach. So he got into a cab and had himself driven to Porchester Terrace. 'Is Lady Demolines at home?' he said to the servant. He always asked for Lady Demolines. But the page who was accustomed to open the door for him was less false, being young, and would now tell him, without any further fiction, that Miss Madalina was in the drawing-room. Such was the answer he got from the page on this evening. What Madalina did with her mother on these occasions he had never yet discovered. There used to be some little excuses given about Lady Demolines' state of health, but latterly Madalina had discontinued her references to her mother's headaches. She was standing in the centre of the drawing-room when he entered it, with both her hands raised, and an almost terrible expression of mystery in her face. Her hair, however, had been very carefully arranged so as to fall with copious carelessness down her shoulders, and altogether she was looking her best. 'Oh, John,' she said. She called him John by accident in the tumult of the moment. 'Have you heard what has happened? But of course you have heard it.'

'Heard what? I have heard nothing,' said Johnny, arrested almost in the doorway by the nature of the question, – and partly also, no doubt, by the tumult of the moment. He had no idea how terrible a tragedy was in truth in store for him; but he perceived that the moment was to be tumultuous, and that he must carry himself accordingly.

'Come in, and close the door,' she said. He came in and closed the door. 'Do you mean to say that you haven't heard what has happened in Hook Court?'

'No; – what has happened in Hook Court?' Miss Demolines threw herself back into an arm-chair, closed her eyes, and clasped both her hands upon her forehead. 'What has happened in Hook Court?' said Johnny, walking up to her.

'I do not think I can bring myself to tell you,' she answered.

Then he took one of her hands down from her forehead and held it in his, – which she allowed passively. She was thinking, no doubt, of something far different from that.

'I never saw you looking better in my life,' said Johnny.

'Don't,' said she. 'How can you talk in that way, when my heart is bleeding, – bleeding.' Then she pulled away her hands, and again clasped it with the other upon her forehead.

'But why is your heart bleeding? What has happened in Hook Court?' Still she answered nothing, but she sobbed violently and the heaving of her bosom showed how tumultuous was the tumult within it. 'You don't mean to say that Dobbs Broughton has come to grief; – that he's to be sold out?'

'Man,' said Madalina, jumping from her chair, standing at her full height, and stretching out both her arms, 'he has destroyed himself!' The revelation was at last made with so much tragic propriety, in so excellent a tone, and with such an absence of all the customary redundances of commonplace relation, that I think that she must have rehearsed the scene, – either with her mother or with the page. Then there was a minute's silence, during which she did not move even an eyelid. She held her outstretched hands without dropping a finger half an inch. Her face was thrust forward, her chin projecting, with tragic horror; but there was no vacillation even in her chin. She did not wink an eye, or alter to the breadth of a hair the aperture of her lips. Surely she was a great genius if she did it all without previous rehearsal. Then, before he had thought of words in which to answer her, she let her hands fall by her side, she closed her eyes, and shook her head, and fell back again into her chair. 'It is too horrible to be spoken of, – to be thought about,' she said. 'I could not have brought myself to tell the tale to a living being, – except to you.'

This would naturally have been flattering to Johnny had it not been that he was in truth absorbed by the story which he had heard.

'Do you mean to tell me,' he said, 'that Broughton has— committed suicide?' She could not speak of it again, but nodded her head at him thrice, while her eyes were still closed. 'And how was the manner of it?' said he, asking the question in a low voice. He could not even as yet quite bring himself to believe it. Madalina was so fond of a little playful intrigue, that even this story might have something in it of the nature of fiction. He was not quite sure of the facts, and yet he was shocked by what he had heard.

'Would you have me repeat to you all the bloody details of that terrible scene?' she said. 'It is impossible. Go to your friend Dalrymple. He will tell you. He knows it all. He has been with Maria all through. I wish, – I wish it had not been so.' But nevertheless she did bring herself to narrate all the details with something more of circumstance than Eames desired. She soon succeeded in making him understand that the tragedy of Hook Court was a reality, and that poor Dobbs Broughton had brought his career to an untimely end. She had heard everything, – having indeed gone to Musselboro in the City, and having penetrated even to the sanctum of Mr Bangles. To Mr Bangles she had explained that she was bosom-friend of the widow of the unfortunate man, and that it was her miserable duty to make herself the mistress of all the circumstances. Mr Bangles, – the reader may remember him, Burton and Bangles, who kept the stores for Himalaya wines at 22s. 6d. the dozen, in Hook Court, – was a bachelor, and rather liked the visit, and told Miss Demolines very freely all he had seen. And when she suggested that it might be expedient for the sake of the family that she should come back to Mr Bangles for further information at a subsequent period, he very politely assured her that she would 'do him proud,' whenever she might please to call in Hook Court. And then he saw her into Lombard Street, and put her into an omnibus. She was therefore well qualified to tell Johnny all the particulars of the tragedy, – and she did so far overcome her horror as to tell them all. She told her tale somewhat after the manner of Æneas, not forgetting the 'quorum pars magna fui.'* 'I feel that it almost makes an old woman of me,' said she, when she had finished.

'No,' said Johnny, remonstrating; – 'not that.'

'But it does. To have been concerned in so terrible a tragedy takes more of life out of one than years of tranquil existence.' As she had told him nothing of her intercourse with Bangles, – with Bangles who had literally picked the poor wretch up, – he did not see how she herself had been concerned in the matter; but he said nothing about that, knowing the character of his Madalina. 'I shall see – that – body, floating before my eyes while I live,' she said, 'and the gory wound, and – and—' 'Don't,' said Johnny, recoiling in truth from the picture, by which he was revolted. 'Never again,' she said; 'never again! But you forced it from me, and now I shall not close my eyes for a week.'

She then became very comfortably confidential, and discussed the affairs of poor Mrs Dobbs Broughton with a great deal of satisfaction. 'I went to see her, of course, but she sent me down word to say that the shock would be too much for her. I do not wonder that she should not see me. Poor Maria! She came to me for advice, you know, when Dobbs Broughton first proposed to her; and I was obliged to tell her what I really thought. I knew her character so well! 'Dear Maria,' I said, 'if you think that you can love him, take him!' 'I think I can,' she replied. 'But,' said I, 'make yourself quite sure about the business.' And how has it turned out? She never loved him. What heart she has she has given to that wretched Dalrymple.'

'I don't see that he is particularly wretched,' said Johnny, pleading for his friend.

'He is wretched, and so you'll find. She gave him her heart after giving her hand to poor Dobbs; and as for the business, there isn't as much left as will pay for her mourning. I don't wonder that she could not bring herself to see me.'

'And what has become of the business?'

'It belongs to Mrs Van Siever, – to her and Musselboro. Poor Broughton had some little money, and it has gone among them. Musselboro, who never had a penny, will be a rich man. Of course you know that he is going to marry Clara?'

'Nonsense!'

'I always told you that it would be so. And now you may perhaps acknowledge that Conway Dalrymple's prospects are not very brilliant. I hope he likes being cut out by Mr Musselboro! Of course he will have to marry Maria. I do not see how he can escape.

Indeed, she is too good for him; — only after such a marriage as
that, there would be an end to all his prospects as an artist. The
best thing for them would be to go to New Zealand.'

John Eames certainly liked these evenings with Miss Demolines.
He sat at his ease in a comfortable chair, and amused himself by
watching her different little plots. And then she had bright eyes,
and she flattered him, and allowed him to scold her occasionally.
And now and again there might be some more potent attraction,
when she would admit him to take her hand, — or the like. It was
better than to sit smoking with men at the club. But he could not
sit all night even with Madalina Demolines, and at eleven he got up
to take his leave. 'When shall you see Miss Dale?' she asked him
suddenly.

'I do not know,' he answered, frowning at her. He always
frowned at her when she spoke to him of Miss Dale.

'I do not in the least care for your frowns,' she said playfully,
putting up her hands to smooth his brows. 'I think I know you
intimately enough to name your goddess to you.'

'She isn't my goddess.'

'A very cold goddess, I should think, from what I hear. I wish to
ask you for a promise respecting her.'

'What promise?'

'Will you grant it me?'

'How can I tell till I hear?'

'You must promise me not to speak of me to her when you see
her.'

'But why must I promise that?'

'Promise me.'

'Not unless you tell me why.' Johnny had already assured himself
that nothing could be more improbable than that he should mention
the name of Miss Demolines to Lily Dale.

'Very well, sir. Then you may go. And I must say that unless you
can comply with so slight a request as that, I shall not care to see
you here again. Mr Eames, why should you want to speak evil of
me to Miss Dale?'

'I do not want to speak evil of you.'

'I know that you could not speak of me to her without at least
ridicule. Come, promise me. You shall come here on Thursday
evening, and I will tell you why I have asked you.'

'Tell me now.'

She hesitated a moment, and then shook her head. 'No, I cannot
tell you now. My heart is still bleeding with the memory of that
poor man's fate. I will not tell you now. And yet it is now that you
must give me the promise. Will you not trust me so far as that?'

'I will not speak of you to Miss Dale.'

'There is my own friend! And now, John, mind you are here at half-past eight on Thursday. Punctually at half-past eight. There is a thing I have to tell you, which I will tell you then if you will come. I had thought to have told you to-day.'

'And why not now?'

'I cannot. My feelings are too many for me. I should never go through with it after all that has passed between us about poor Broughton. I should break down; indeed I should. Go now, for I am tired.' Then, having probably taken a momentary advantage of that more potent attraction to which we have before alluded, he left the room very suddenly.

He left the room very suddenly because Madalina's movements had been so sudden, and her words so full of impulse. He had become aware that in this little game which he was playing in Porchester Terrace everything ought to be done after some unaccustomed and special fashion. So, – having clasped Madalina for one moment in his arms, – he made a rush at the room door, and was out on the landing in a second. He was a little too quick for old Lady Demolines, the skirt of whose night-dress, – as it seemed to Johnny, – he saw whisking away, in at another door. It was nothing, however, to him if old Lady Demolines, who was always too ill to be seen, chose to roam about her own house in her night-dress.

When he found himself alone in the street, his mind reverted to Dobbs Broughton and the fate of the wretched man, and he sauntered slowly down Palace Gardens, that he might look at the house in which he had dined with a man who had destroyed himself by his own hands. He stood for a moment looking up at the windows, in which there was now no light, thinking of the poor woman whom he had seen in the midst of luxury, and who was now left a widow in such miserable circumstances! As for the suggestion that his friend Conway would marry her, he did not believe it for a moment. He knew too well what the suggestions of his Madalina were worth, and the motives from which they sprung. But he thought it might be true that Mrs Van Siever had absorbed all there was of property, and possibly, also, that Musselboro was to marry her daughter. At any rate, he would go to Dalrymple's rooms, and if he could find him, would learn the truth. He knew enough of Dalrymple's ways of life, and of the ways of his friend's chambers and studio, to care nothing for the lateness of the hour, and in a very few minutes he was sitting in Dalrymple's armchair. He found Siph Dunn there, smoking in unperturbed tranquillity, and as long as that lasted he could ask no questions about Mrs

Broughton. He told them, therefore, of his adventures abroad, and of Crawley's escape. But at last, having finished his third pipe, Siph Dunn took his leave.

'Tell me,' said John, as soon as Dunn had closed the door, 'what is this I hear about Dobbs Broughton ?'

'He has blown his brains out. That is all.'

'How terribly shocking !'

'Yes ; it shocked us all at first. We are used to it now.'

'And the business ?'

'That had gone to the dogs. They say at least that his share of it had done so.'

'And he was ruined ?'

'They say so. That is, Musselboro says so, and Mrs Van Siever.'

'And what do you say, Conway ?'

'The less I say the better. I have my hopes, — only you're such a talkative fellow, one can't trust you.'

'I never told any secret of yours, old fellow.'

'Well; — the fact is, I have an idea that something may be saved for the poor woman. I think that they are wronging her. Of course all I can do is to put the matter into a lawyer's hands, and pay the lawyer's bill. So I went to your cousin, and he has taken the case up. I hope he won't ruin me.'

'Then I suppose you are quarrelling with Mrs Van ?'

'That doesn't matter. She has quarrelled with me.'

'And what about Jael, Conway ? They tell me that Jael is going to become Mrs Musselboro.'

'Who has told you that ?'

'A bird.'

'Yes ; I know who the bird is. I don't think that Jael will become Mrs Musselboro. I don't think that Jael would become Mrs Musselboro, if Jael were the only woman, and Musselboro the only man in London. To tell you a little bit of secret, Johnny, I think that Jael will become the wife of one Conway Dalrymple. That is my opinion ; and as far as I can judge, it is the opinion of Jael also.'

'But not the opinion of Mrs Van. The bird told me another thing, Conway.'

'What was the other thing ?'

'The bird hinted that all this would end in your marrying the widow of that poor wretch who destroyed himself.'

'Johnny, my boy,' said the artist, after a moment's silence, 'if I give you a bit of advice, will you profit by it ?'

'I'll try, if it's not disagreeable.'

'Whether you profit by it, or whether you do not, keep it to yourself. I know the bird better than you do, and I strongly caution you to beware of the bird. The bird is a bird of prey, and altogether an unclean bird. The bird wants a mate and doesn't much care how she finds one. And the bird wants money, and doesn't much care how she gets it. The bird is a decidedly bad bird, and not at all fit to take the place of domestic hen in a decent farmyard. In plain English, Johnny, you'll find some day, if you go over too often to Porchester Terrace, either that you are employing your cousin Toogood for your defence in an action for breach of promise, brought against you by that venerable old bird, the bird's mamma.'

'If it's to be either, it will be the latter,' said Johnny as he took up his hat to go away.

CHAPTER 76

I think he is light of heart

Mrs Arabin remained one day in town. Mr Toogood, in spite of his asseveration that he would not budge from Barchester till he had seen Mr Crawley through all his troubles, did run up to London as soon as the news reached him that John Eames had returned. He came up and took Mrs Arabin's deposition, which he sent down to Mr Walker. It might still be necessary, Mrs Arabin was told, that she should go into court, and there state on oath that she had given the cheque to Mr Crawley; but Mr Walker was of opinion that the circumstances would enable the judge to call upon the grand jury not to find a true bill against Mr Crawley, and that the whole affair, as far as Mr Crawley was concerned, would thus be brought to an end. Toogood was still very anxious to place Dan Stringer in the dock, but Mr Walker declared that they would fail if they made the attempt. Dan had been examined before the magistrates at Barchester, and had persisted in his statement that he had heard nothing about Mr Crawley and the cheque. This he said in the teeth of the words which had fallen from him unawares in the presence of Mr Toogood. But they could not punish him for a lie, – not even for such a lie as that! He was not upon oath, and they could not make him responsible to the law because he had held his tongue upon a matter as to which it was manifest to them all that he had known the whole history during the entire period of Mr Crawley's persecution. They could only call upon him to account for his possession of the cheque, and this he did by saying it had been paid to him by Jem Scuttle, who received all moneys appertaining to the hotel stables, and accounted for them once a week. Jem Scuttle had simply told him that he had taken the cheque from Mr Soames, and Jem had since gone to New Zealand. It was quite true that Jem's departure had followed suspiciously close upon the payment of the rent to Mrs Arabin, and that Jem had been in close amity with Dan Stringer up to the moment of his departure. That Dan Stringer had not become honestly possessed of the cheque, everybody knew; but, nevertheless, the magistrates were of opinion, Mr Walker coinciding with them, that there was no evidence against him sufficient to secure a conviction. The story, however, of Mr Crawley's injuries was so well known in Barchester, and the feeling against the man who had permitted him to be thus injured was so strong, that Dan Stringer did not altogether escape without punishment. Some rough spirits in Barchester called one night at 'The Dragon of Wantly,' and begged that Mr Dan Stringer would be kind enough to come out and take a walk with them that evening; and when it was intimated to them that Dan Stringer had not just then any desire for such exercise, they requested to be allowed to go into the back parlour and make an evening with Dan Stringer in that recess. There was a terrible row at 'The Dragon of Wantly' that night, and Dan with difficulty was rescued by the police. On the following morning he was smuggled out of Barchester by an early train, and has never more been seen in that city. Rumours of him, however, were soon heard, from which it appeared that he had made himself acquainted with the casual ward of more than one workhouse in London. His cousin John left the inn almost immediately, – as, indeed, he must have done had there been no question of Mr Soames's cheque, – and then there was nothing more heard of the Stringers in Barchester.

Mrs Arabin remained in town one day, and would have remained longer, waiting for her husband, had not a letter from his sister impressed upon her that it might be as well that she should be with their father as soon as possible. 'I don't mean to make you think that there is any immediate danger,' Mrs Grantly said, 'and, indeed, we cannot say that he is ill; but it seems that the extremity of old age has come upon him almost suddenly, and that he is as weak as a child. His only delight is with the children, especially with Posy, whose gravity in her management of him is wonderful. He has not left his room now for more than a week, and he eats very little. It may be that he will live yet for years; but I should be deceiving you if I did not let you know that both the archdeacon and I think that the time of his departure from us is near at hand.' After reading this letter, Mrs Arabin could not wait in town for her husband, even though he was expected in two days, and though she had been told that her presence at Barchester was not immediately required on behalf of Mr Crawley.

But during that one day she kept her promise to John Eames by going to Lily Dale. Mrs Arabin had become very fond of Johnny, and felt that he deserved the prize which he had been so long trying to win. The reader, perhaps, may not agree with Mrs Arabin. The

reader, who may have caught a closer insight into Johnny's character than Mrs Arabin had obtained, may, perhaps, think that a
young man who could amuse himself with Miss Demolines was
unworthy of Lily Dale. If so, I may declare for myself that I and the
reader are not in accord about John Eames. It is hard to measure
worth and worthlessness in such matters, as there is no standard
for such measurement. My old friend John was certainly no hero, –
was very unheroic in many phases of his life; but then, if all the
girls are to wait for heroes, I fear that the difficulties in the way of
matrimonial arrangements, great as they are at present, will be very
seriously enhanced. Johnny was not ecstatic, nor heroic, nor transcendental, nor very beautiful in his manliness; he was not a man
to break his heart for love, or to have his story written in an epic;
but he was an affectionate, kindly, honest young man; and I think
most girls might have done worse than take him. Whether he was
wise to ask assistance in his love-making so often as he had done,
that may be another question.

Mrs Arabin was intimately acquainted with Mrs Thorne, and
therefore there was nothing odd in her going to Mrs Thorne's
house. Mrs Thorne was very glad to see her, and told her all the
Barsetshire news, – much more than Mrs Arabin would have
learned in a week at the deanery; for Mrs Thorne had a marvellous
gift of picking up news. She had already heard the whole story of
Mr Soames's cheque, and expressed her conviction that the least
that could be done in amends to Mr Crawley was to make him a
bishop. 'And you see the palace is vacant,' said Mrs Thorne.

'The palace vacant!' said Mrs Arabin.

'It is just as good. Now that Mrs Proudie has gone I don't
suppose the poor bishop will count for much. I can assure you, Mrs
Arabin, I felt that poor woman's death so much! She used to regard
me as one of the staunchest of the Proudieites! She once whispered
to me such a delightfully wicked story about the dean and the
archdeacon. When I told her that they were my particular friends,
she put on a look of horror. But I don't think she believed me.'
Then Emily Dunstable entered the room, and with her came Lily
Dale. Mrs Arabin had never before seen Lily, and of course they
were introduced. 'I am sorry to say Miss Dale is going home to
Allington to-morrow,' said Emily. 'But she is coming to Chaldicotes
in May,' said Mrs Thorne. 'Of course, Mrs Arabin, you know what
gala doings we are going to have in May?' Then there were various
civil little speeches made on each side, and Mrs Arabin expressed a
wish that she might meet Miss Dale again in Barsetshire. But all this
did not bring her at all nearer to her object.

'I particularly wish to say a word to Miss Dale, – here to-day, if she will allow me,' said Mrs Arabin.

'I'm sure she will, – twenty words; won't you, Lily?' said Mrs Thorne, preparing to leave the room. Then Mrs Arabin apologized, and Mrs Thorne, bustling up, said that it did not signify, and Lily, remaining quite still on the sofa, wondered what it was all about, – and in two minutes Lily and Mrs Arabin were alone together. Lily had just time to surmise that Mrs Arabin's visit must have some reference to Mr Crosbie, – remembering that Crosbie had married his wife out of Barsetshire, and forgetting altogether that Mrs Arabin had been just brought home from Italy by John Eames.

'I am afraid, Miss Dale, you will think me very impertinent,' said Mrs Arabin.

'I am sure I shall not think that,' said Lily.

'I believe you knew, before Mr Eames started, that he was going to Italy to find me and my husband?' said Mrs Arabin. Then Lily put Mr Crosbie altogether out of her head, and became aware that he was not to be the subject of the coming conversation. She was almost sorry that it was so. There was no doubt in her mind as to what she would have said to any one who might have taken up Crosbie's cause. On that matter she could now have given a very decisive answer in a few words. But on that other matter she was much more in doubt. She remembered, however, every word of the note she had received from M. D. She remembered also the words of John's note to that young woman. And her heart was still hard against him. 'Yes,' she said; 'Mr Eames came here one night and told us why he was going. I was very glad that he was going, because I thought it was right.'

'You know, of course, how successful he has been? It was I who gave the cheque to Mr Crawley.'

'So Mrs Thorne has heard. Dr Thorne has written to tell her the whole story.'

'And now I've come to look for Mr Eames's reward.'

'His reward, Mrs Arabin?'

'Yes; or rather to plead for him. You will not, I hope, be angry with him because he has told me much of his history while we were travelling home alone together.'

'Oh, no,' said Lily, smiling. 'How could he have chosen a better friend in whom to trust?'

'He could certainly have chosen none who would take his part more sincerely. He is so good and so amiable! He is so pleasant in his ways, and so fitted to make a woman happy! And then, Miss Dale, he is also so devoted!'

'He is an old friend of ours, Mrs Arabin.'

'So he has told me.'

'And we all of us love him dearly. Mamma is very much attached to him.'

'Unless he flatters himself, there is no one belonging to you who would not wish that he should be nearer and dearer still.'

'It may be so. I do not say that it is not so. Mamma and my uncle are both fond of him.'

'And does not that go a long way?' said Mrs Arabin.

'It ought not to do so,' said Lily. 'It ought not to go any way at all.'

'Ought it not? It seems to me that I could never have brought myself to marry any one whom my old friends had not liked.'

'Ah! that is another thing.'

'But is it not a recommendation to a man that he has been so successful with your friends as to make them all feel that you might trust yourself to him with perfect safety?' To this Lily made no answer, and Mrs Arabin went on to plead her friend's cause with all the eloquence she could use, insisting on all his virtues, his good temper, his kindness, his constancy, – and not forgetting the fact that the world was inclined to use him very well. Still Lily made no answer. She had promised Mrs Arabin that she would not regard her interference as impertinent, and therefore she refrained from any word that might seem to show offence. Nor did she feel offence. It was something gained by John Eames in Lily's estimation that he should have such a friend as Mrs Arabin to take an interest in his welfare. But there was a self-dependence, perhaps one may call it an obstinacy about Lily Dale, which made her determined that she would not be driven hither or thither by any pressure from without. Why had John Eames, at the very moment when he should have been doing his best to drive from her breast the memory of past follies, – when he would have striven to do so had he really been earnest in his suit, – why at such a moment had he allowed himself to correspond in terms of affection with such a woman as this M. D.? While Mrs Arabin was pleading for John Eames, Lily was repeating to herself certain words which John had written to the woman – 'Ever and always yours unalterably.' Such were not the exact words, but such was the form in which Lily, dishonestly, chose to repeat them to herself. And why was it so with her? In the old days she would have forgiven Crosbie any offence at a word or a look, – any possible letter to any M. D., let her have been ever so abominable! Nay, – had she not even forgiven him the offence of deserting herself altogether on behalf of a woman as detestable as could be any M. D. of Johnny's choosing; – a woman whose only recommendation had been her title? And yet she would not forgive

John Eames, though the evidence against him was of so flimsy a nature, – but rather strove to turn the flimsiness of that evidence into strength ! Why was it so ? Unheroic as he might be, John Eames was surely a better man and a bigger man than Adolphus Crosbie. It was simply this; – she had fallen in love with the one, and had never fallen in love with the other ! She had fallen in love with the one man, though in her simple way she had made a struggle against such feeling; and she had not come to love the other man, though she had told herself that it would be well that she should do so if it were possible. Again and again she had half declared to herself that she would take him as her husband and leave the love to come afterwards; but when the moment came for doing so, she could not do it.

'May I not say a word of comfort to him ?' said Mrs Arabin.

'He will be very comfortable without any such word,' said Lily, laughing.

'But he is not comfortable; of that you may be very sure.' 'Yours ever and unalterably, J. E.,' said Lily to herself. 'You do not doubt his affection ?' continued Mrs Arabin.

'I neither doubt it nor credit it.'

'Then I think you wrong him. And the reason why I have ventured to come to you is that you may know the impression which he has made upon one who was but the other day a stranger to him. I am sure that he loves you.'

'I think he is light of heart.'

'Oh, no, Miss Dale.'

'And how am I to become his wife unless I love him well enough myself ? Mrs Arabin, I have made up my mind about it. I shall never become any man's wife. Mamma and I are all in all together, and we shall remain together.' As soon as these words were out of her mouth, she hated herself for having spoken them. There was a maudlin, missish, namby-mamby sentimentality about them which disgusted her. She specially desired to be straightforward, resolute of purpose, honest-spoken, and free from all touch of affectation. And yet she had excused herself from marrying John Eames after the fashion of a sick schoolgirl. 'It is no good talking about it any more,' she said, getting up from her chair meekly.

'You are not angry with me; – or at any rate you will forgive me ?'

'I'm quite sure you have meant to be very good, and I am not a bit angry.'

'And you will see him before you go ?'

'Oh, yes; that is if he likes to come to-day, or early to-morrow. I go home to-morrow. I cannot refuse him, because he is such an old

friend, – almost like a brother. But it is of no use, Mrs Arabin.'
Then Mrs Arabin kissed her and left her, telling her that Mr Eames
would come to her that afternoon at half-past five. Lily promised
that she would be at home to receive him.

'Won't you ride with us for the last time?' said Emily Dunstable
when Lily gave notice that she would not want the horse on that
afternoon.

'No; not to-day.'

'You'll never have another opportunity of riding with Emily
Dunstable,' said the bride elect; – 'at least I hope not.'

'Even under those circumstances I must refuse, though I would
give a guinea to be with you. John Eames is coming here to say
good-by.'

'Oh; then indeed you must not come with us. Lily, what will you
say to him?'

'Nothing.'

'Oh, Lily, think of it.'

'I have thought of it. I have thought of nothing else. I am tired of
thinking of it. It is not good to think of anything so much. What
does it matter?'

'It is very good to have some one to love one better than all the
world besides.'

'I have some one,' said Lily, thinking of her mother, but not
caring to descend again to the mawkish weakness of talking about
her.

'Yes; but some one to be always with you, to do everything for
you, to be your very own.'

'It is all very well for you,' said Lily, 'and I think that Bernard is
the luckiest fellow in the world; but it will not do for me. I know
in what college I'll take my degree, and I wish they'd let me write
the letters after my name as the men do.'

'What letters, Lily?'

'O. M., for Old Maid. I don't see why it shouldn't be as good as
B. A. for Bachelor of Arts. It would mean a great deal more.'

CHAPTER 77

The shattered tree

When Mrs Arabin saw Johnny in the middle of that day, she could hardly give him much encouragement. And yet she felt by no means sure that he might not succeed even yet. Lily had been very positive in her answers, and yet there had been something, either in her words or in the tone of her voice, which had made Mrs Arabin feel that even Lily was not quite sure of herself. There was still room for relenting. Nothing, however, had been said which could justify her in bidding John Eames simply 'to go in and win.' 'I think he is light of heart,' Lily had said. Those were the words which, of all that had been spoken, most impressed themselves on Mrs Arabin's memory. She would not repeat them to her friend, but she would graft upon them such advice as she had to give him.

And this she did, telling him that she thought that perhaps Lily doubted his actual earnestness. 'I would marry her this moment,' said Johnny. But that was not enough, as Mrs Arabin knew, to prove his earnestness. Many men, fickle as weathercocks, are ready to marry at the moment, – are ready to marry at the moment, because they are fickle, and think so little about it. 'But she hears, perhaps, of your liking other people,' said Mrs Arabin. 'I don't care a straw for any other person,' said Johnny. 'I wonder whether if I was to shut myself up in a cage for six months, it would do any good?' 'If she had the keeping of the cage, perhaps it might,' said Mrs Arabin. She had nothing more to say to him on that subject, but to tell him that Miss Dale would expect him that afternoon at half-past five. 'I told her that you would come to wish her good-by, and she promised to see you.'

'I wish she'd say she wouldn't see me. Then there would be some chance,' said Johnny.

Between him and Mrs Arabin the parting was very affectionate. She told him how thankful she was for his kindness in coming to her, and how grateful she would ever be, – and the dean also, – for his attention to her. 'Remember, Mr Eames, that you will always be most welcome at the deanery of Barchester. And I do hope that before long you may be there with your wife.' And so they parted.

He left her at about two, and went to Mr Toogood's office in Bedford Row. He found his uncle, and the two went out to lunch together in Holborn. Between them there was no word said about Lily Dale, and John was glad to have some other subject in his mind for half an hour. Toogood was full of his triumph about Mr Crawley and of his successes in Barsetshire. He gave John a long account of his visit to Plumstead, and expressed his opinion that if all clergymen were like the archdeacon there would not be so much room for Dissenters. 'I've seen a good many parsons in my time,' said Toogood; 'but I don't think I ever saw such a one as him. You know he is a clergyman somehow, and he never lets you forget it; but that's about all. Most of 'em are never contented without choking you with their white cravats all the time you're with 'em. As for Crawley himself,' Mr Toogood continued, 'he's not like anybody else that never was born saint or sinner, parson or layman. I never heard of such a man in all my experience. Though he knew where he got the cheque as well as I know it now, he wouldn't say so, because the dean had said it wasn't so. Somebody ought to write a book about it, – indeed they ought.' Then he told the whole story of Dan Stringer, and how he had found Dan out, looking at the top of Dan's hat through the little aperture in the wall of the inn parlour. 'When I saw the twitch in his hat, John, I knew he had handled the cheque himself. I don't mean to say that I'm sharper than another man, and I don't think so; but I do mean to say that when you are in any difficulty of that sort, you ought to go to a lawyer. It's his business, and a man does what is his business with patience and perseverance. It's a pity, though, that that scoundrel should get off.' Then Eames gave his uncle an account of his Italian trip, to and fro, and was congratulated also upon his success. John's great triumph lay in the fact that he had been only two nights in bed, and that he would not have so far condescended on those occasions but for the feminine weakness of his fellow-traveller. 'We shan't forget it all in a hurry – shall we, John?' said Mr Toogood, in a pleasant voice, as they parted at the door of the luncheon-house in Holborn. Toogood was returning to his office, and John Eames was to prepare himself for his last attempt.

He went home to his lodgings, intending at first to change his dress, – to make himself smart for the work before him, – but after standing for a moment or two leaning on the chest of drawers in his bed-room, he gave up this idea. 'After all that's come and gone,' he said to himself, 'if I cannot win her as I am now, I cannot win her at all.' And then he swore to himself a solemn oath, resolving that he would repeat the purport of it to Lily herself, – that this should be the last attempt. 'What's the use of it? Everybody ridicules me. And I am ridiculous. I am an ass. It's all very well wanting to be prime minister; but if you can't be prime minister, you must do without being prime minister.' Then he attempted to sing the old song – 'Shall I, sighing in despair, die because a woman's fair? If she be not fair for me, what care I how fair she be?'* But he did care, and he told himself that the song did him no good. As it was not time for him as yet to go to Lily, he threw himself on the sofa, and strove to read a book. Then all the weary nights of his journey prevailed over him, and he fell asleep.

When he awoke it wanted a quarter to six. He sprang up, and rushing out, jumped into a cab. 'Berkeley Square, – as hard as you can go,' he said. 'Number – ' He thought of Rosalind, and her counsels to lovers as to the keeping of time,* and reflected that in such an emergency as his, he might really have ruined himself by that unfortunate slumber. When he got to Mrs Thorne's door he knocked hurriedly, and bustled up to the drawing-room as though everything depended on his saving a minute. 'I'm afraid I'm ever so much behind my time,' he said.

'It does not matter in the least,' said Lily. 'As Mrs Arabin said that perhaps you might call, I would not be out of the way. I supposed that Sir Raffle was keeping you and that you wouldn't come.'

'Sir Raffle was not keeping me. I fell asleep. That is the truth of it.'

'I am sorry that you should have been disturbed!'

'Do not laugh at me, Lily, – to-day. I had been travelling a good deal, and I suppose I was tired.'

'I won't laugh at you,' she said, and of a sudden her eyes became full of tears, – she did not know why. But there they were, and she was ashamed to put up her handkerchief, and she could not bring herself to turn away her face, and she had no resource but that he should see them.

'Lily!' he said.

'What a paladin you have been, John, rushing all about Europe on your friend's behalf!'

'Don't talk about that.'

'And such a successful paladin too! Why am I not to talk about it? I am going home tomorrow, and I mean to talk about nothing else for a week. I am so very, very glad that you have saved your cousin.' Then she did put up her handkerchief, making believe that her tears had been due to Mr Crawley. But John Eames knew better than that.

'Lily,' he said, 'I've come for the last time. It sounds as though I meant to threaten you; but you won't take it in that way. I think you will know what I mean. I have come for the last time – to ask you to be my wife.' She had got up to greet him when he entered, and they were both still standing. She did not answer him at once, but turning away from him walked towards the window. 'You knew why I was coming to-day, Lily?'

'Mrs Arabin told me. I could not be away when you were coming, but perhaps it would have been better.'

'Is it so? Must it be so? Must you say that to me, Lily? Think of it for a moment, dear.'

'I have thought of it.'

'One word from you, yes or no, spoken now is to be everything to me for always. Lily, cannot you say yes?' She did not answer him, but walked further away from him to another window. 'Try to say yes. Look round at me with one look that may only half mean it; – that may tell me that it shall not positively be no for ever.' I think that she almost tried to turn her face to him; but be that as it may, she kept her eyes steadily fixed upon the window-pane. 'Lily,' he said, 'it is not that you are hard-hearted, – perhaps not altogether that you do not like me. I think that you believe things against me that are not true.' As she heard this she moved her foot angrily upon the carpet. She had almost forgotten M. D., but now he had reminded her of the note. She assured herself that she had never believed anything against him except on evidence that was incontrovertible. But she was not going to speak to him on such a matter as that! It would not become her to accuse him. 'Mrs Arabin tells me that you doubt whether I am in earnest,' he said.

Upon hearing this she flashed round upon him almost angrily. 'I never said that.'

'If you will ask me for any token of earnestness, I will give it you.'

'I want no token.'

'The best sign of earnestness a man can give generally in such a matter, is to show how ready he is to be married.'

'I never said anything about earnestness.'

'At the risk of making you angry I will go on, Lily. Of course when you tell me that you will have nothing to say to me, I try to amuse myself' – 'Yes; by writing love-letters to M.D.,' said Lily to herself. – 'What is a poor fellow to do? I tell you fairly that when I leave you I swear to myself that I will make love to the first girl I can see who will listen to me – to twenty, if twenty will let me. I feel I have failed, and it is so I punish myself for my failure.' There was something in this which softened her brow, though she did not intend that it should be so; and she turned away again, that he might not see that her brow was softened. 'But, Lily, the hope ever comes back again, and then neither the one nor the twenty are of avail, – even to punish me. When I look forward and see what it might be if you were with me, how green it all looks and how lovely, in spite of all the vows I have made, I cannot help coming back again.' She was now again near the window, and he had not followed her. As she neither turned towards him nor answered him, he moved from the table near which he was standing on to the rug before the fire, and leaned with both his elbows on the mantelpiece. He could still watch her in the mirror over the fireplace, and could see that she was still seeming to gaze out upon the street. And had he not moved her? I think he had so far moved her now, that she had ceased to think of the woman who had written to her, – that she had ceased to reject him in her heart on the score of such levities as that! If there were M. D.'s, like sunken rocks, in his course, whose fault was it? He was ready enough to steer his bark into the tranquil blue waters, if only she would aid him. I think that all his sins on that score were at this moment forgiven him. He had told her now what to him would be green and beautiful, and she did not find herself able to disbelieve him. She had banished M. D. out of her mind, but in doing so she admitted other reminiscences into it. And then, – was she in a moment to be talked out of the resolution of years; and was she to give up herself, not because she loved, but because the man who talked to her talked so well that he deserved a reward? Was she now to be as light, as foolish, as easy, as in those former days from which she had learned her wisdom? A picture of green lovely things could be delicious to her eyes as to his; but even for such a picture as that the price might be too dear! Of all living men, – of all men living in their present lives, – she loved best this man who was now waiting for some word of answer to his words, and she did love him dearly; she would have tended him if sick, have supplied him if in want, have mourned for him if dead, with the bitter grief of true affection; – but she could not say to herself that he should be her lord and master, the head of her house, the owner of herself, the ruler of her life. The shipwreck to which she had once come, and the fierce regrets which had thence arisen, had forced her to think too much of these things. 'Lily,' he said, still facing towards the mirror, 'will you not come to me and speak to me?' She turned round, and stood a moment looking at him, and then, having again resolved that it could not be as he wished, she drew near to him. 'Certainly I will speak to you, John. Here I am.' And she came close to him.

He took both her hands, and looked into her eyes. 'Lily, will you be mine?'

'No, dear; it cannot be so.'

'Why not, Lily?'

'Because of that other man.'

'And is that to be a bar for ever?'

'Yes; for ever.'

'Do you still love him?'

'No; no, no!'

'Then why should this be so?'

'I cannot tell, dear. It is so. If you take a young tree and split it, it still lives, perhaps. But it isn't a tree. It is only a fragment.'

'Then be my fragment.'

'So I will, if it can serve you to give standing ground to such a fragment in some corner of your garden. But I will not have myself planted out in the middle, for people to look at. What there is left would die soon.' He still held her hands, and she did not attempt to draw them away. 'John,' she said, 'next to mamma, I love you better than all the world. Indeed I do. I can't be your wife, but you need never be afraid that I shall be more to another than I am to you.'

'That will not serve me,' he said, grasping both her hands till he almost hurt them, but not knowing that he did so. 'That is no good.'

'It is all the good that I can do you. Indeed I can do you, – can do no one any good. The trees that the storms have splintered are never of use.'

'And is this to be the end of all, Lily?'

'Not of our loving friendship.'

'Friendship! I hate the word. I hear some one's step, and I had better leave you. Good-by.'

'Good-by, John. Be kinder than that to me as you are going.' He turned back for a moment, took her hand, and held it tight against his heart, and then he left her. In the hall he met Mrs Thorne, but, as she said afterwards, he had been too much knocked about to be able to throw a word to a dog.

To Mrs Thorne Lily said hardly a word about John Eames, and when her cousin Bernard questioned her about him she was dumb. And in these days she could assume a manner, and express herself with her eyes as well as with her voice, after a fashion, which was apt to silence unwelcome questioners, even though they were as intimate with her as was her cousin Bernard. She had described her feelings more plainly to her lover than she had ever done to any one, – even to her mother; and having done so she meant to be silent on that subject for evermore. But of her settled purpose she did say some word to Emily Dunstable that night. 'I do feel,' she said, 'that I have got the thing settled at last.'

'And you have settled it, as you call it, in opposition to the wishes of all your friends?'

'That is true; and yet I have settled it rightly, and I would not for worlds have it unsettled again. There are matters on which friends should not have wishes, or at any rate should not express them.'

'Is that meant to be severe to me?'

'No; not to you. I was thinking about mamma, and Bell, and my uncle, and Bernard, who all seem to think that I am to be looked upon as a regular castaway because I am not likely to have a husband of my own. Of course you, in your position, must think a girl a castaway who isn't going to be married?'

'I think that a girl who is going to be married has the best of it.'

'And I think a girl who isn't going to be married has the best of it; – that's all. But I feel that the thing is done now, and I am contented. For the last six or eight months there has come up, I know not how, a state of doubt which has made me so wretched that I have done literally nothing. I haven't been able to finish old Mrs Heard's tippet, literally because people would talk to me about that dearest of all dear fellows, John Eames. And yet all along I have known how it would be, – as well as I do now.'

'I cannot understand you, Lily; I can't indeed.'

'I can understand myself. I love him so well, – with that intimate, close, familiar affection, – that I could wash his clothes for him to-morrow, out of pure personal regard, and think it no shame. He could not ask me to do a single thing for him, – except the one thing, – that I would refuse. And I'll go further. I would sooner marry him than any man in the world I ever saw, or, as I believe, that I ever shall see. And yet I am very glad that it is settled.'

On the next day Lily Dale went down to the Small House of Allington, and so she passes out of our sight. I can only ask the reader to believe that she was in earnest, and express my own opinion, in this last word, that I shall ever write respecting her, that she will live and die as Lily Dale.

CHAPTER 78

The Arabins return to Barchester

In these days Mr Harding was keeping his bed at the deanery, and most of those who saw him declared that he would never again leave it. The archdeacon had been slow to believe so, because he had still found his father-in-law able to talk to him; – not indeed with energy, but then Mr Harding had never been energetic on ordinary matters, – but with the same soft cordial interest in things which had ever been customary with him. He had latterly been much interested about Mr Crawley, and would make both the archdeacon and Mrs Grantly tell him all that they heard, and what they thought of the case. This of course had been before the all-important news had been received from Mrs Arabin. Mr Harding was very anxious, 'Firstly,' as he said, 'for the welfare of the poor man, of whom I cannot bring myself to think ill; and then for the honour of the cloth in Barchester.' 'We are as liable to have black sheep here as elsewhere,' the archdeacon replied. 'But, my dear, I do not think that the sheep is black; and we never have had black sheep in Barchester.' 'Haven't we though?' said the archdeacon, thinking, however, of sheep who were black with a different kind of blackness from this which was now attributed to poor Mr Crawley, – of a blackness which was not absolute blackness to Mr Harding's milder eyes. The archdeacon, when he heard his father-in-law talk after this fashion, expressed his opinion that he might live yet for years. He was just the man to linger on, living in bed, – as indeed he had lingered all his life out of bed. But the doctor who attended him thought otherwise, as did also Mrs Grantly, and as did Mrs Baxter, and as also did Posy. 'Grandpa won't get up any more, will he?' Posy said to Mrs Baxter. 'I hope he will, my dear; and that very soon.' 'I don't think he will,' said Posy, 'because he said he would never see the big fiddle again.' 'That comes of his being a little melancholy like, my dear,' said Mrs Baxter.

Mrs Grantly at this time went into Barchester almost every day, and the archdeacon, who was very often in the city, never went there without passing half-an-hour with the old man. These two clergymen, essentially different in their characters and in every detail of conduct, had been so much thrown together by circumstances that the life of each had almost become a part of the life of the other. Although the fact of Mr Harding's residence of the deanery had of late years thrown him oftener into the society of the dean than that of his other son-in-law, yet his intimacy with the archdeacon had been so much earlier, and his memories of the archdeacon were so much clearer, that he depended almost more upon the rector of Plumstead, who was absent, than he did upon the dean, whom he customarily saw every day. It was not so with his daughters. His Nelly, as he had used to call her, had ever been his favourite, and the circumstances of their joint lives had been such, that they had never been further separated than from one street of Barchester to another, – and that only for the very short period of the married life of Mrs Arabin's first husband. For all that was soft and tender therefore, – which with Mr Harding was all in the world that was charming to him, – he looked to his youngest daughter; but for authority and guidance and wisdom, and for information as to what was going on in the world, he had still turned to his son-in-law the archdeacon, – as he had done for nearly forty years. For so long had the archdeacon been potent as a clergyman in the diocese, and throughout the whole duration of such potency his word had been law to Mr Harding in most of the affairs of life, – a law generally to be obeyed, and if sometimes to be broken, still a law. And now, when all was so nearly over, he would become unhappy if the archdeacon's visits were far between. Dr Grantly, when he found that this was so, would not allow that they should be far between.

'He puts me so much in mind of my father,' the archdeacon said to his wife one day.

'He is not so old as your father was when he died, by many years,' said Mrs Grantly, 'and I think one sees that difference.'

'Yes; – and therefore I say that he may still live for years. My father, when he took to his bed at last, was manifestly near his death. The wonder with him was that he continued to live so long. Do you not remember how the London doctor was put out because his prophecies were not fulfilled?'

'I remember it well; – as if it were yesterday.'

'And in that way there is a great difference. My father, who was physically a much stronger man, did not succumb so easily. But the likeness is in their characters. There is the same mild sweetness, becoming milder and sweeter as they increased in age; – a sweetness that never could believe much evil, but that could believe less, and still less, as the weakness of age came on them. No amount of evidence would induce your father to think that Mr Crawley stole that money.' This was said of course before the telegram had come from Venice.

'As far as that goes I agree with him,' said Mrs Grantly, who had her own reasons for choosing to believe Mr Crawley to be innocent. If your son, my dear, is to marry a man's daughter, it will be as well that you should at least be able to say that you do not believe that man to be a thief.

'That is neither here nor there,' said the archdeacon. 'A jury must decide it.'

'No jury in Barchester shall decide it for me,' said Mrs Grantly.

'I'm sick of Mr Crawley, and I'm sorry I spoke of him,' said the archdeacon. 'But look at Mrs Proudie. You'll agree that she was not the most charming woman in the world.'

'She certainly was not,' said Mrs Grantly, who was anxious to encourage her husband, if she could do so without admitting anything which might injure herself afterwards.

'And she was at one time violently insolent to your father. And even the bishop thought to trample upon him. Do you remember the bishop's preaching against your father's chaunting? If I ever forget it!' And the archdeacon slapped his closed fist against his open hand.

'Don't, dear; don't. What is the good of being violent now?'

'Paltry little fool! It will be long enough before such a chaunt as that is heard in any English cathedral again.' Then Mrs Grantly got up and kissed her husband, but he, somewhat negligent of the kiss, went on with his speech. 'But your father remembers nothing of it, and if there was a single human being who shed a tear in Barchester for that woman, I believe it was your father. And it was the same with mine. It came to that at last, that I could not bear to speak to him of any shortcoming as to one of his own clergymen. I might as well have pricked him with a penknife. And yet they say men become heartless and unfeeling as they grow old!'

'Some do, I suppose.'

'Yes; the heartless and unfeeling do. As the bodily strength fails and the power of control becomes lessened, the natural aptitude of the man pronounces itself more clearly. I take it that that is it. Had Mrs Proudie lived to be a hundred and fifty, she would have spoken spiteful lies on her deathbed.' Then Mrs Grantly told herself that her husband, should he live to be a hundred and fifty, would still be expressing his horror of Mrs Proudie, – even on his deathbed.

As soon as the letter from Mrs Arabin had reached Plumstead, the archdeacon and his wife arranged that they would both go together to the deanery. There were the double tidings to be told, – those of Mr Crawley's assured innocence, and those also of Mrs Arabin's instant return. And as they went together various ideas were passing through their minds in reference to the marriage of their son with Grace Crawley. They were both now reconciled to it. Mrs Grantly had long ceased to feel any opposition to it, even though she had not seen Grace; and the archdeacon was prepared to give way. Had he not promised that in a certain case he would give way, and had not that case now come to pass? He had no wish to go back from his word. But he had a difficulty in this, – that he liked to make all the affairs of his life matter for enjoyment, almost for triumph; but how was he to be triumphant over this marriage, or how even was he to enjoy it, seeing that he had opposed it so bitterly? Those posters, though they were now pulled down, had been up on all barn ends and walls, patent – alas, too patent – to all the world of Barsetshire! 'What will Mr Crawley do now, do you suppose?' said Mr Crawley.

'What will he do?'

'Yes; must he go on at Hogglestock?'

'What else?' said the archdeacon.

'It is a pity something could not be done for him after all he has undergone. How on earth can he be expected to live there with a wife and family, and no private means?' To this the archdeacon made no answer. Mrs Grantly had spoken almost immediately upon their quitting Plumstead, and the silence was continued till the carriage had entered the suburbs of the city. Then Mrs Grantly spoke again, asking a question, with some internal trepidation, which, however, she managed to hide from her husband. 'When poor papa does go, what shall you do about St Ewold's?' Now, St Ewold's was a rural parish lying about two miles out of Barchester, the living of which was in the gift of the archdeacon, and to which the archdeacon had presented his father-in-law, under certain circumstances, which need not be repeated in this last chronicle of Barchester. Have they not been written in other chronicles?* 'When poor papa does go, what will you do about St Ewold's?' said Mrs Grantly, trembling inwardly. A word too much might, as she well knew, settle the question against Mr Crawley for ever. But were she to postpone the word till too late, the question would be settled as fatally.

'I haven't thought about it,' he said sharply. 'I don't like thinking of such things while the incumbent is still living.' Oh, archdeacon, archdeacon! unless that other chronicle be a false chronicle, how hast thou forgotten thyself and thy past life!* 'Particularly not, when that incumbent is your father,' said the archdeacon. Mrs Grantly said nothing more about St Ewold's. She would have said as much as she had intended to say if she had succeeded in making the archdeacon understand that St Ewold's would be a very nice refuge for Mr Crawley after all the miseries which he had endured at Hogglestock.

They learned as they entered the deanery that Mrs Baxter had already heard of Mrs Arabin's return. 'O yes, ma'am. Mr Harding got a letter hisself, and I got another, – separate; both from Venice, ma'am. But when master is to come, nobody seems to know.' Mrs Baxter knew that the dean had gone to Jerusalem, and was inclined to think that from such distant bournes there was no return for any traveller.* The east is always further than the west in the estimation of the Mrs Baxters of the world. Had the dean gone to Canada, she would have thought that he might come back to-morrow. But still there was the news to be told of Mr Crawley, and there was also joy to be expressed at the sudden coming back of the much-wished-for mistress.

'It's so good of you to come both together,' said Mr Harding.

'We thought we should be too many for you,' said the archdeacon.

'Too many! O dear, no. I like to have people by me; and as for voices, and noise, and all that, the more the better. But I am weak. I'm weak in my legs. I don't think I shall ever stand again.'

'Yes, you will,' said the archdeacon.

'We have brought you good news,' said Mrs Grantly.

'Is it not good news that Nelly will be home this week? You can't understand what a joy it is to me. I used to think sometimes, at night, that I should never see her again. That she would come back in time was all I have had to wish for.' He was lying on his back, and as he spoke he pressed his withered hands together above the bed-clothes. They could not begin immediately to tell him of Mr Crawley, but as soon as his mind had turned itself away from the thoughts of his absent daughter, Mrs Grantly again reverted to her news.

'We have come to tell you about Mr Crawley, papa.'

'What about him?'

'He is quite innocent.'

'I knew it, my dear. I always said so. Did I not always say so, archdeacon?'

'Indeed you did. I'll give you that credit.'

'And is it all found out?' asked Mr Harding.

'As far as he is concerned, everything is found out,' said Mrs Grantly. 'Eleanor gave him the cheque herself.'

'Nelly gave it to him?'

'Yes, papa. The dean meant her to give him fifty pounds. But it seems she got to be soft of heart and made it seventy. She had the cheque by her, and put it into the envelope with the notes.'

'Some of Stringer's people seem to have stolen the cheque from Mr Soames,' said the archdeacon.

'O dear; I hope not.'

'Somebody must have stolen it, papa.'

'I had hoped not, Susan,' said Mr Harding. Both the archdeacon and Mrs Grantly knew that it was useless to argue with him on such a point, and so they let that go.

Then they came to discuss Mr Crawley's present position, and Mr Harding ventured to ask a question or two as to Grace's chance of marriage. He did not often interfere in the family arrangements of his son-in-law, – and never did so when those family arrangements were concerned with high matters. He had hardly opened his mouth in reference to the marriage of that august lady who was now the Marchioness of Hartletop. And of the Lady Anne, the wife of the Rev. Charles Grantly, who was always prodigiously civil to him, speaking to him very loud, as though he were deaf because he was old, and bringing him cheap presents from London of which he did not take much heed, – of her he rarely said a word, or of her children, to either of his daughters. But now his grandson, Henry Grantly, was going to marry a girl of whom he felt that he might speak without impropriety. 'I suppose it will be a match; won't it, my dears?'

'Not a doubt about it,' said Mrs Grantly. Mr Harding looked at his son-in-law, but his son-in-law said nothing. The archdeacon did not even frown, – but only moved himself a little uneasily in his chair.

'Dear, dear! What a comfort that must be,' said the old man.

'I have not seen her yet,' said Mrs Grantly; 'but the archdeacon declared that she is all the graces rolled into one.'

'I never said anything half so absurd,' replied the archdeacon.

'But he really is quite in love with her, papa,' said Mrs Grantly. 'He confessed to me that he gave her a kiss, and he only saw her once for five minutes.'

'I should like to give her a kiss,' said Mr Harding.

'So you shall, papa, and I'll bring her here on purpose. As soon as ever the thing is settled, we mean to ask her to Plumstead.'

'Do you though? How nice! How happy Henry will be!'

'And if she comes – and of course she will – I'll lose no time in bringing her over to you. Nelly must see her of course.'

As they were leaving the room Mr Harding called the archdeacon back, and taking him by the hand, spoke one word to him in a whisper. 'I don't like to interfere,' he said; 'but might not Mr Crawley have St Ewold's?' The archdeacon took up the old man's hand and kissed it. Then he followed his wife out of the room, without making any answer to Mr Harding's question.

Three days after this Mrs Arabin reached the deanery, and the joy at her return was very great. 'My dear, I have been sick for you,' said Mr Harding.

'Oh, papa, I ought not to have gone.'

'Nay, my dear; do not say that. Would it make me happy that you should be a prisoner here for ever? It was only when I seemed to get so weak that I thought about it. I felt that it must be near when they bade me not to go to the cathedral any more.'

'If I had been here, I could have gone with you, papa.'

'It is better as it is. I know now that I was not fit for it. When your sister came to me, I never thought of remonstrating. I knew then that I had seen it for the last time.'

'We need not say that yet, papa.'

'I did think that when you came home we might crawl there together some warm morning. I did think of that for a time. But it will never be so, dear. I shall never see anything now that I do not see from here, – and not that for long. Do not cry, Nelly. I have nothing to regret, nothing to make me unhappy. I know how poor and weak has been my life; but I know how rich and strong is that other life. Do not cry, Nelly, – not till I am gone; and then not beyond measure. Why should any one weep for those who go away full of years, – and full of hope?'

On the day but one following the dean also reached his home. The final arrangements of his tour, as well as those of his wife, had been made to depend on Mr Crawley's trial; for he also had been hurried back by John Eames's visit to Florence. 'I should have come at once,' he said to his wife, 'when they wrote to ask me whether Crawley had taken the cheque from me, had anybody then told me that he was in actual trouble; but I had no idea then that they were charging him with theft.'

'As far as I can learn, they never really suspected him until after your answer had come. They had been quite sure that your answer would be in the affirmative.'

'What he must have endured it is impossible to conceive. I shall go out to him to-morrow.'

'Would he not come to us?' said Mrs Arabin.

'I doubt it. I will ask him, of course. I will ask them all here. This about Henry and the girl may make a difference. He has resigned the living, and some of the palace people are doing the duty.'

'But he can have it again?'

'Oh, yes; he can have it again. For the matter of that, I need simply give him back his letter. Only he is so odd, – so unlike other people! And he has tried to live there, and has failed; and is now in debt. I wonder whether Grantly would give him St Ewold's?'

'I wish he would. But you must ask him. I should not dare.'

As to the matter of the cheque, the dean acknowledged to his wife at last that he had some recollection of her having told him that she had made the sum of money up to seventy pounds. 'I don't feel certain of it now; but I think you may have done so.' 'I am quite sure I could not have done it without telling you,' she replied. 'At any rate you said nothing of the cheque,' pleaded the dean. 'I don't suppose I did,' said Mrs Arabin. 'I thought that cheques were like any other money; but I shall know better for the future.'

On the following morning the dean rode over to Hogglestock, and as he drew near to the house of his old friend, his spirits flagged, – for to tell the truth, he dreaded the meeting. Since the day on which he had brought Mr Crawley from a curacy in Cornwall into the diocese of Barchester, his friend had been a trouble to him rather than a joy. The trouble had been a trouble of spirit altogether, – not at all of pocket. He would willingly have picked the Crawleys out from the pecuniary mud into which they were ever falling, time after time, had it been possible. For, though the dean was hardly to be called a rich man, his lines had fallen to him not only in pleasant places,* but in easy circumstances; – and Mr Crawley's embarrassments, though overwhelming to him, were not so great as to have been heavy to the dean. But in striving to do this he had always failed, had always suffered, and had generally been rebuked. Crawley would attempt to argue with him as to the improper allotment of Church endowments, – declaring that he did not do so with any reference to his own circumstances, but simply because the subject was one naturally interesting to clergymen. And this he would do, as he was waving off with his hand offers of immediate assistance which were indispensable. Then there had been scenes between the dean and Mrs Crawley, – terribly painful, – and which had taken place in direct disobedience to the husband's positive injunctions. 'Sir,' he had once said to the dean, 'I request that nothing may pass from your hands to the hands of my wife.' 'Tush, tush,' the dean had answered. 'I will have no tushing or pshawing on such a matter. A man's wife is his very own, the breath of his nostril, the blood of his heart, the rib from his body. It is for me to rule my wife, and I tell you that I will not have it.' After that the gifts had come from the hands of Mrs Arabin; – and then again, after that, in the direst hour of his need, Crawley had himself come and taken money from the dean's hands! The interview had been so painful that Arabin would hardly have been able to count the money or to know of what it had consisted, had he taken the notes and cheque out of the envelope in which his wife had put them. Since that day the two had not met each other, and since that day these new troubles had come. Arabin as yet knew but little of the manner in which they had been borne, except that Crawley had felt himself compelled to resign the living of Hogglestock. He knew nothing of Mrs Proudie's persecution, except what he gathered from the fact of the clerical commission of which he had been informed; but he could imagine that Mrs Proudie would not lie easy on her bed while a clergyman was doing duty almost under her nose, who was guilty of the double offence of being accused of a theft, and of having been put into his living by the dean. The dean, therefore, as he rode on, pictured to himself his old friend in a terrible condition. And it might be that even now that condition would hardly have been improved. He was no longer suspected of being a thief; but he could have no money in his pocket; and it might well be that his sufferings would have made him almost mad.

The dean also got down and left his horse at a farm-yard, – as Grantly had done with his carriage; and walked on first to the school. He heard voices inside, but could not distinguish from them whether Mr Crawley was there or not. Slowly he opened the door, and looking round saw that Jane Crawley was in the ascendant. Jane did not know him at once, but told him when he had introduced himself that her father had gone down to Hoggle End. He had started two hours ago, but it was impossible to say when he might be back. 'He sometimes stays all day long with the brickmakers,' said Jane. Her mother was at home, and she would take the dean into the house. As she said this she told him that her father was sometimes better and sometimes worse. 'But he has never been so very, very bad, since Henry Grantly and mamma's cousin came and told us about the cheque.' That word Henry Grantly made the dean understand that there might yet be a ray of sunshine among the Crawleys.

'There is papa,' said Jane, as they got to the gate. Then they waited for a few minutes till Mr Crawley came up, very hot, wiping the sweat from his forehead.

'Crawley,' said the dean. 'I cannot tell you how glad I am to see you, and how rejoiced I am that this accusation has fallen off from you.'

'Verily the news came in time, Arabin,' said the other; 'but it was a narrow pinch – a narrow pinch. Will you not enter, and see my wife?'

CHAPTER 79

Mr Crawley speaks of his coat

At this time Grace had returned home from Framley. As long as the terrible tragedy of the forthcoming trial was dragging itself on she had been content to stay away, at her mother's bidding. It has not been possible in these pages to tell of all the advice that had been given to the ladies of the Crawley family in their great difficulty, and of all the assistance that had been offered. The elder Lady Lufton and the younger, and Mrs Robarts had continually been in consultation on the subject; Mrs Grantly's opinion had been asked and given; and even the Miss Prettymans and Mrs Walker had found means of expressing themselves. The communications to Mrs Crawley had been very frequent, – though they had not of course been allowed to reach the ears of Mr Crawley. What was to be done when the living should be gone and Mr Crawley should be in prison? Some said that he might be there for six weeks, and some for two years. Old Lady Lufton made anxious inquiries about Judge Medlicote, before whom it was said that the trial would be taken. Judge Medlicote was a Dissenter, and old Lady Lufton was in despair. When she was assured by some liberally-disposed friend that this would certainly make no difference, she shook her head woefully. 'I don't know why we are to have Dissenters at all,' she said, 'to try people who belong to the Established Church.' When she heard that Judge Medlicote would certainly be the judge, she made up her mind that two years would be the least of it. She would not have minded it, she said, if he had been a Roman Catholic. And whether the punishment might be for six weeks or for two years, what should be done with the family? Where should they be housed? how should they be fed? What should be done with the poor man when he came out of prison? It was a case in which the generous, soft-hearted old Lady Lufton was almost beside herself. 'As for Grace,' said young Lady Lufton, 'it will be great deal better that we should keep her amongst us. Of course she will become Mrs Grantly, and it will be nicer for her that it should be so.' In those days the posters had been seen, and the flitting to Pau had been talked of, and the Framley opinion was that Grace had better remain at Framley till she should be carried off to Pau. There were schemes, too, about Jane. But what was to be done for the wife? And what was to be done for Mr Crawley? Then came the news from Mrs Arabin, and all interest in Judge Medlicote was at an end.

But even now, after this great escape, what was to be done? As to Grace, she had felt the absolute necessity of being obedient to her friends, – with the consent of course of her mother, – during the great tribulation of her family. Things were so bad that she had not the heart to make them worse by giving any unnecessary trouble as to herself. Having resolved, – and having made her mother so understand, – that on one point she would guide herself by her own feelings, she was contented to go hither and thither as she was told, and to do as she was bid. Her hope was that Miss Prettyman would allow her to go back to her teaching, but it had come to be understood among them all that nothing was to be said on that subject till the trial should be over. Till that time she would be passive. But then, as I have said, had come the news from Mrs Arabin, and Grace, with all the others, understood that there would be no trial. When this was known and acknowledged, she declared her purpose of going back to Hogglestock. She would go back at once. When asked both by Lady Lufton and by Mrs Robarts why she was in so great a haste, she merely said that it must be so. She was, as it were, absolved from her passive obedience to Framley authorities by the diminution of the family misfortunes.

Mrs Robarts understood the feeling by which Grace was hurried away. 'Do you know why she is so obstinate?' Lady Lufton asked.

'I think I do,' said Mrs Robarts.

'And what is it?'

'Should Major Grantly renew his offer to her she is under a pledge to accept him now.'

'Of course he will renew it, and of course she will accept him.'

'Just so. But she prefers that he should come for her to her own house, – because of its poverty. If he chooses to seek her there, I don't think she will make much difficulty.' Lady Lufton demurred to this, not however with anger, and expressed a certain amount of mild displeasure. She did not quite see why Major Grantly should not be allowed to come and do his love-making comfortably, where there was a decent dinner for him to eat, and chairs and tables and sofas and carpets. She said that she thought that something was due to Major Grantly. She was in truth a little disappointed that she was not allowed to have her own way, and to arrange the marriage at Framley under her own eye. But, through it all, she appreciated Grace; and they who knew her well and heard what she said upon the occasion, understood that her favour was not to be withdrawn. All young women were divided by old Lady Lufton into sheep and goats, – very white sheep and very black goats; – and Grace was to be a sheep. Thus it came to pass that Grace Crawley was at home when the dean visited Hogglestock. 'Mamma,' she said, looking out of the window, 'there is the dean with papa at the gate.'

'It was a narrow squeak – a very narrow squeak,' Mr Crawley had said when his friend congratulated him on his escape. The dean felt at the moment that not for many years had he heard the incumbent of Hogglestock speak either of himself or of anything else with so manifest an attempt at jocularity. Arabin had expected to find the man broken down by the weight of his sorrows, and lo! at the first moment of their first interview he himself began to ridicule them! Crawley having thus alluded to the narrow squeak had asked his visitor to enter the house and see his wife.

'Of course I will,' said Arabin, 'but I will speak just a word to you first.' Jane, who had accompanied the dean from the school, now left them, and went into the house to her mother. 'My wife cannot forgive herself about the cheque,' continued he.

'There is nothing to be forgiven,' said Mr Crawley; 'nothing.'

'She feels that what she did was awkward and foolish. She ought never to have paid a cheque away in such a manner. She knows that now.'

'It was given, – not paid,' said Crawley; and as he spoke something of the black cloud came back upon his face. 'And I am well aware how hard Mrs Arabin strove to take away from the alms she bestowed the bitterness of the sting of eleemosynary aid. If you please, Arabin, we will not talk any more of that. I can never forget that I have been a beggar, but I need not make my beggary the matter of conversation. I hope the Holy Land has fulfilled your expectation?'

'It has more than done so,' said the dean, bewildered by the sudden change.

'For myself, it is, of course, impossible that I should ever visit any scenes except those to which my immediate work may call me, – never in this world. The new Jerusalem is still within my reach, – if it be not forfeited by pride and obstinacy; but the old Jerusalem I can never behold. Methinks, because it is so, I would sooner stand with my foot on Mount Olivet, or drink a cup of water in the village of Bethany, than visit any other spot within the traveller's compass. The sources of the Nile, of which men now talk so much,*

– I see it in the papers and reviews which the ladies at Framley are so good as to send to my wife, – do not interest me much. I have no ambition to climb Mont Blanc or the Matterhorn; Rome makes my mouth water but little, nor even Athens much. I can realize without seeing all that Athens could show me, and can fancy that the existing truth would destroy more than it would build up. But to have stood on Calvary!'

'We don't know where Calvary was,' said the dean.

'I fancy that I should know, – should know enough,' said the illogical and unreasonable Mr Crawley. 'Is it true that you can look over from the spot on which He came across the brow of the hill, and see the huge stones of the Temple placed there by Solomon's men, – as He saw them; – right across the brook Cedron, is it not?'

'It is all there, Crawley, – just as your knowledge of it tells you.'

'In the privilege of seeing those places I can almost envy a man his – money.' The last word he uttered after a pause. He had been about to say that under such temptation he could almost envy a man his promotion; but he bethought himself that on such an occasion as this it would be better that he should spare the dean. 'And now, if you wish it, we will go in. I fancy that I see my wife at the window, as though she were waiting for us.' So saying, he strode on along the little path, and the dean was fain to follow him, though he had said so little of all that he had intended to say.

As soon as he was with Mrs Crawley he repeated his apology about the cheque, and found himself better able to explain himself than he could do when alone with her husband. 'Of course, it has been our fault,' he said.

'Oh, no,' said Mrs Crawley, 'how can you have been in fault when your only object was to do us good?' But, nevertheless, the dean took the blame upon his own shoulders, or, rather upon those of his wife, and declared himself to be responsible for all the trouble about the cheque.

'Let it go,' said Crawley, after sitting for awhile in silence; 'let it pass.'

'You cannot wonder, Crawley,' said the dean, 'that I should have felt myself obliged to speak of it.'

'For the future it will be well that it should be forgotten,' said Crawley; 'or, if not forgotten, treated as though forgotten. And now, dean, what must I do about the living?'

'Just resume it, as though nothing had happened.'

'But that may hardly be done without the bishop's authority. I speak, of course, with deference to your higher and better information on such subjects. My experience in the taking up and laying down of livings has not been extended. But it seemeth to me that though it may certainly be in your power to nominate me again to the perpetual curacy of this parish, – presuming your patronage to be unlimited and not to reach you in rotation only, – yet the bishop may demand to institute again, and must so demand, unless he pleases to permit that my letter to him shall be revoked and cancelled.'

'Of course he will do anything of that kind. He must know the circumstances as well as you and I do.'

'At present they tell me that he is much afflicted by the death of his wife, and, therefore, can hardly be expected to take immediate action. There came here on the last Sunday one Mr Snapper, his lordship's chaplain.'

'We all know Snapper,' said the dean. 'Snapper is not a bad little fellow.'

'I say nothing of his being bad, my friend, but merely mention the fact that on Sunday morning last he performed the service in our church. On the Sunday previous, one Mr Thumble was here.'

'We all know Thumble, too,' said the dean; 'or, at least, know something about him.'

'He has been a thorn in our sides,' said Mrs Crawley, unable to restrain the expression of her dislike when Mr Thumble's name was mentioned.

'Nay, my dear, nay; – do not allow yourself the use of language so strong against a brother. Our flesh at that time was somewhat prone to fester, and little thorns made us very sore.'

'He is a horrible man,' said Jane, almost in a whisper; but the words were distinctly audible by the dean.

'They need not come any more,' said Arabin.

'That is where I fear we differ. I think they must come, – or some others in their place, – till the bishop shall have expressed his pleasure to the contrary. I have submitted myself to his lordship, and, having done so, feel that I cannot again go up into my pulpit till he shall have authorized me to do so. For a time, Arabin, I combated the bishop, believing, – then and now, – that he put forth his hand against me after a fashion which the law had not sanctioned. And I made bold to stand in his presence and to tell him that I would not obey him, except in things legal. But afterwards, when he proceeded formally, through the action of a commission, I submitted myself. And I regard myself still as being under submission.'

It was impossible to shake him. Arabin remained there for more than an hour, trying to pass on to another subject, but being constantly brought back by Mr Crawley himself to the fact of his own dependent position. Nor would he condescend to supplicate the bishop. It was, he surmised, the duty of Dr Tempest, together with the other four clergymen, to report to the bishop on the question of the alleged theft; and then doubtless the bishop, when he had duly considered the report, and, – as Mr Crawley seemed to think was essentially necessary, – had sufficiently recovered from the grief at his wife's death, would, at his leisure, communicate his decision to Mr Crawley. Nothing could be more complete than Mr Crawley's humility in reference to the bishop; and he never seemed to be tired of declaring that he had submitted himself!

And then the dean, finding it to be vain to expect to be left alone with Mr Crawley for a moment, – in vain also to wait for a proper opening for that which he had to say, – rushed violently at his other subject. 'And now, Mrs Crawley,' he said, 'Mrs Arabin wishes you all to come over to the deanery for a while and stay with us.'

'Mrs Arabin is too kind,' said Mrs Crawley, looking across at her husband.

'We should like it of all things,' said the dean, with perhaps more of good nature than of truth. 'Of course you must have been knocked about a good deal.'

'Indeed we have,' said Mrs Crawley.

'And till you are somewhat settled again, I think that the change of scene would be good for all of you. Come, Crawley, I'll talk to you every evening about Jerusalem for as long as you please; – and then there will perhaps come back to us something of the pleasantness of old days.' As she heard this Mrs Crawley's eyes became full of tears, and she could not altogether hide them. What she had endured during the last four months had almost broken her spirit. The burden had at last been too heavy for her strength. 'You cannot fancy, Crawley, how often I have thought of the old days and wished that they might return. I have found it very hard to get an opportunity of saying so much to you; but I will say it now.'

'It may hardly be as you say,' said Crawley, grimly.

'You mean that the old days can never be brought back?'

'Assuredly they cannot. But it was not that that I meant. It may not be that I and mine should transfer ourselves to your roof and sojourn there.'

'Why should you not?'

'The reasons are many, and on the face of things. The reason, perhaps, the most on the face is to be found in my wife's gown, and in my coat.' This Mr Crawley said very gravely, looking neither to the right nor to the left, nor at the face of any of them, nor at his own garment, nor at hers, but straight before him; and when he had so spoken he said not a word further, – not going on to dilate on his poverty as the dean expected that he would do.

'At such a time such reasons should stand for nothing,' said the dean.

'And why not now as they always do, and always must till the power of tailors shall have waned, and the daughters of Eve shall toil and spin no more? Like to like is true, and should be held to be true of all societies and of all compacts for co-operation and mutual living. Here, where, if I may venture to say so, you and I are like to like; – for the new gloss of your coat,' – the dean, as it happened, had on at the moment a very old coat, his oldest coat, selected perhaps with some view to this special visit, – 'does not obtrude itself in my household, as would the threadbare texture of mine in yours; – I can open my mouth to you and converse with you at my ease; you are now to me that Frank Arabin who has so often comforted me and so often confuted me; whom I may perhaps on an occasion have confuted – and perhaps have comforted. But were I sitting with you in your library in Barchester, my threadbare coat would be too much for me. I should be silent, if not sullen. I should feel the weight of all my poverty, and the greater weight of all your wealth. For my children, let them go. I have come to know that they will be better away from me.'

'Papa!' said Jane.

'Papa does not mean it,' said Grace, coming up to him and standing close to him.

There was silence amongst them for a few moments, and then the master of the house shook himself, – literally shook himself, till he had shaken off the cloud. He had taken Grace by the hand, and thrusting out the other arm had got it round Jane's waist. 'When a man has girls, Arabin,' he said, 'as you have, but not big girls yet like Grace here, of course he knows that they will fly away.'

'I shall not fly away,' said Jane.

'I don't know what papa means,' said Grace.

Upon the whole the dean thought it the pleasantest visit he had ever made to Hogglestock, and when he got home he told his wife that he believed that the accusation made against Mr Crawley had done him good. 'I could not say a word in private to her,' he said, 'but I did promise that you would go and see her.' On the very next day Mrs Arabin went over, and I think that the visit was a comfort to Mrs Crawley.

CHAPTER 80

Miss Demolines desires to become a finger-post

John Eames had passed Mrs Thorne in the hall of her own house almost without noticing her as he took his departure from Lily Dale. She had told him as plainly as words could speak that she could not bring herself to be his wife, – and he had believed her. He had sworn to himself that if he did not succeed now he would never ask her again. 'It would be foolish and unmanly to do so,' he said to himself as he rushed along the street towards his club. No! That romance was over. At last there had come an end to it! 'It has taken a good bit out of me,' he said, arresting his steps suddenly that he might stand still and think of it all. 'By George, yes! A man doesn't go through that kind of thing without losing some of the calorie.* I couldn't do it again if an angel came my way.' He went to his club, and tried to be jolly. He ordered a good dinner, and got some man to come and dine with him. For an hour or so he held himself up, and did appear to be jolly. But as he walked home at night, and gave himself time to think over what had taken place with deliberation, he stopped in the gloom of a deserted street and leaning against the rails burst into tears. He had really loved her and she was never to be his. He had wanted her, – and it is so painful a thing to miss what you want when you have done your very best to obtain it! To struggle in vain always hurts the pride; but the wound made by the vain struggle for a woman is sorer than any other wound so made. He gnashed his teeth, and struck the iron railings with his stick; – and then he hurried home, swearing that he would never give another thought to Lily Dale. In the dead of the night, thinking of it still, he asked himself whether it would not be a fine thing to wait another ten years, and then go to her again. In such a way would he not make himself immortal as a lover beyond any Jacob or any Leander?

The next day he went to his office and was very grave. When Sir Raffle complimented him on being back before his time, he simply said that when he had accomplished that for which he had gone, he had, of course, come back. Sir Raffle could not get a word out from him about Mr Crawley. He was very grave, and intent upon his work. Indeed he was so serious that he quite afflicted Sir Raffle, – whose mock activity felt itself to be confounded by the official zeal of his private secretary. During the whole of that day Johnny was resolving that there could be no cure for his malady but hard work. He would not only work hard at the office if he remained there, but he would take to heavy reading. He rather thought that he would go deep into Greek and do a translation, or take up the exact sciences and make a name for himself that way. But as he had enough for the life of a secluded literary man without his salary, he rather thought that he would give up his office altogether. He had a mutton chop at home that evening, and spent his time in endeavouring to read out loud to himself certain passages from the Iliad; – for he had bought a Homer as he returned from his office. At nine o'clock he went, half-price, to the Strand Theatre.* How he met there his old friend Boulger and went afterwards to 'The Cock' and had a supper need not here be told with more accurate detail.

On the evening of the next day he was bound by his appointment to go to Porchester Terrace. In the moments of his enthusiasm about Homer he had declared to himself that he would never go near Miss Demolines again. Why should he ? All that kind of thing was nothing to him now. He would simply send her his compliments and say that he was prevented by business from keeping his engagement. She, of course, would go on writing to him for a time, but he would simply leave her letters unanswered, and the thing, of course, would come to an end at last. He afterwards said something to Boulger about Miss Demolines, – but that was during the jollity of their supper, – and he then declared that he would follow out that little game. 'I don't see why a fellow isn't to amuse himself, eh, Boulger, old boy ?' Boulger winked and grinned, and said that some amusements were dangerous. 'I don't think that there is any danger there,' said Johnny. 'I don't believe she is thinking of that kind of thing herself; – not with me at least. What she likes is the pretence of a mystery ; and as it is amusing I don't see why a fellow shouldn't indulge her.' But that determination was pronounced after two mutton chops at 'The Cock,' between one and two o'clock in the morning. On the next day he was cooler and wiser. Greek he thought might be tedious as he discovered that he would have to begin again from the very alphabet. He would therefore abandon that idea. Greek was not the thing for him, but he would take up the sanitary condition of the poor in London. A fellow could be of some use in that way. In the meantime he would keep his appointment with Miss Demolines, simply because it was an appointment. A gentleman should always keep his word to a lady !

He did keep his appointment with Miss Demolines, and was with her almost precisely at the hour she had named. She received him with a mysterious tranquillity which almost perplexed him. He remembered, however, that the way to enjoy the society of Miss Demolines was to take her in all her moods with perfect seriousness, and was therefore very tranquil himself. On the present occasion she did not rise as he entered the room, and hardly spoke as she tendered to him the tips of her fingers to be touched. As she said almost nothing, he said nothing at all, but sank into a chair and stretched his legs out comfortably before him. It had been always understood between them that she was to bear the burden of the conversation.

'You'll have a cup of tea ?' she said.

'Yes; – if you do.' Then the page brought the tea, and John Eames amused himself with swallowing three slices of very thin bread and butter.

'None for me, – thanks,' said Madalina. 'I rarely eat after dinner, and not often much then. I fancy that I should best like a world in which there was no eating.'

'A good dinner is a very good thing,' said John. And then there was again silence. He was aware that some great secret was to be told to him during this evening, but he was much too discreet to show any curiosity upon that subject. He sipped his tea to the end, and then, having got up to put his cup down, stood on the rug with his back to the fire. 'Have you been out to-day ?' he asked.

'Indeed I have.'

'And are you tired ?'

'Very tired !'

'Then perhaps I had better not keep you up.'

'Your remaining will make no difference in that respect. I don't suppose that I shall be in bed for the next four hours. But do as you like about going.'

'I am in no hurry,' said Johnny. Then he sat down again, stretched out his legs and made himself comfortable.

'I have been to see that woman,' said Madalina after a pause.

'What woman ?'

'Maria Clutterbuck, – as I must always call her; for I cannot bring myself to pronounce the name of that poor wretch who was done to death.'

'He blew his brains out in delirium tremens,' said Johnny.

'And what made him drink ?' said Madalina with emphasis. 'Never mind. I decline altogether to speak of it. Such a scene as I have had! I was driven at last to tell her what I thought of her. Anything so callous, so heartless, so selfish, so stone-cold, and so childish, I never saw before! That Maria was childish and selfish I always knew; – but I thought there was some heart, – a vestige of heart. I found to-day that there was none, – none. If you please we won't speak of her any more.'

'Certainly not,' said Johnny.

'You need not wonder that I am tired and feverish.'

'That sort of thing is fatiguing, I dare say. I don't know whether we do not lose more than we gain by those strong emotions.'

'I would rather die and go beneath the sod at once, than live without them,' said Madalina.

'It's a matter of taste,' said Johnny.

'It is there that that poor wretch is so deficient. She is thinking now, this moment, of nothing but her creature comforts. That tragedy has not even stirred her pulses.'

'If her pulses were stirred over so, that would not make her happy.'

'Happy! Who is happy? Are you happy?'

Johnny thought of Lily Dale and paused before he answered. No; certainly he was not happy. But he was not going to talk about his unhappiness to Miss Demolines! 'Of course I am; – as jolly as a sandboy,' he said.

'Mr Eames,' said Madalina raising herself on her sofa, 'if you can not express yourself in language more suitable to the occasion and to the scene than that, I think that you had better—'

'Hold my tongue.'

'Just so; – though I should not have chosen myself to use words so abruptly discourteous.'

'What did I say, – jolly as a sandboy? There is nothing wrong in that. What I meant was, that I think that this world is a very good sort of world, and that a man can get along in it very well, if he minds his *p*s and *q*s.'

'But suppose it's a woman?'

'Easier still.'

'And suppose she does not mind her *p*s and *q*s?'

'Women always do.'

'Do they? Your knowledge of women goes as far as that, does it? Tell me fairly; – do you think you know anything about women?' Madalina as she asked the question, looked full into his face, and shook her locks and smiled. When she shook her locks and smiled, there was a certain attraction about her of which John Eames was fully sensible. She could throw a special brightness into her eyes, which, though it probably betokened nothing truly beyond ill-natured mischief, seemed to convey a promise of wit and intellect.

'I don't mean to make any boast about it,' said Johnny.

'I doubt whether you know anything. The pretty simplicity of your excellent Lily Dale has suffered for you.'

'Never mind about her,' said Johnny impatiently.

'I do not mind about her in the least. But an insight into that sort of simplicity will not teach you the character of a real woman. You cannot learn the flavour of wines by sipping sherry and water. For myself I do not think that I am simple. I own it fairly. If you must have simplicity, I cannot be to your taste.'

'Nobody likes partridge always,' said Johnny laughing.

'I understand you, sir. And though what you say is not complimentary, I am willing to forgive the fault for its truth. I don't consider myself to be always partridge, I can assure you. I am as changeable as the moon.'

'And as fickle?'

'I say nothing about that, sir. I leave you to find that out. It is a man's business to discover that for himself. If you really do know aught of women—'

'I did not say that I did.'

'But if you do, you will perhaps have discovered that a woman may be as changeable as the moon, and yet as true as the sun; — that she may flit from flower to flower, quite unheeding while no passion exists, but that a passion fixes her at once. Do you believe me?' Now she looked into his eyes again, but did not smile and did not shake her locks.

'Oh yes; — that's true enough. And when they have a lot of children, then they become steady as milestones.'

'Children!' said Madalina, getting up and walking about the room.

'They do have them you know,' said Johnny.

'Do you mean to say, sir, that I should be a milestone?'

'A finger-post,' said Johnny, 'to show a fellow the way he ought to go.'

She walked twice across the room without speaking. Then she came and stood opposite to him, still without speaking, — and then she walked about again. 'What could a woman better be, than a finger-post, as you call it, with such a purpose?'

'Nothing better of course; — though a milestone to tell a fellow his distances, is very good.'

'Psha!'

'You don't like the idea of being a milestone?'

'No!'

'Then you can make up your mind to be a finger-post.'

'John, shall I be a finger-post for you?' She stood and looked at him for a moment or two, with her eyes full of love, as though she were going to throw herself into his arms. And she would have done so, no doubt, instantly, had he risen to his legs. As it was, after having gazed at him for the moment with her love-laden eyes, she flung herself on the sofa, and hid her face among the cushions.

He had felt that it was coming for the last quarter of an hour and he had felt, also, that he was quite unable to help himself. He did not believe that he should ever be reduced to marrying Miss Demolines, but he did see plainly enough that he was getting into trouble; and yet, for his life, he could not help himself. The moth who flutters round the light knows that he is being burned, and yet he cannot fly away from it. When Madalina had begun to talk to him about women in general, and then about herself, and had told him that such a woman as herself, – even one so liable to the disturbance of violent emotions, – might yet be as true and honest as the sun, he knew that he ought to get up and make his escape. He did not excactly know how the catastrophe would come, but he was quite sure that if he remained there he would be called upon in some way for a declaration of his sentiments, – and that the call would be one which all his wit would not enable him to answer with any comfort. It was very well jesting about milestones, but every jest brought him nearer to the precipice. He perceived that however ludicrous might be the image which his words produced, she was clever enough in some way to turn that image to her own purpose. He had called a woman a finger-post, and forthwith she had offered to come to him and be finger-post to him for life! What was he to say to her? It was clear that he must say something. As at this moment she was sobbing violently, he could not pass the offer by as a joke. Women will say that his answer should have been very simple, and his escape very easy. But men will understand that it is not easy to reject even a Miss Demolines when she offers herself for matrimony. And moreoever, – as Johnny bethought himself at this crisis of his fate, – Lady Demolines was no doubt at the other side of the drawing-room door, ready to stop him, should he attempt to run away. In the meantime the sobs on the sofa became violent, and still more violent. He had not even yet made up his mind what to do, when Madalina, springing to her feet, stood before him, with her curls wilding waving and her arms extended. 'Let it be as though it were unsaid,' she exclaimed. John Eames had not the slightest objection; but, nevertheless, there was a difficulty even in this. Were he simply to assent to this latter proposition, it could not be but that the feminine nature of Miss

Demolines would be outraged by so uncomplimentary an acquiescence. He felt that he ought at least to hesitate a little, – to make some pretence at closing upon the rich offer that had been made to him; only that were he to show any such pretence the rich offer would, no doubt, be repeated. His Madalina had twitted him in the earlier part of their interview with knowing nothing of the nature of women. He did not enough to feel assured that any false step on his part now would lead him into very serious difficulties. 'Let it be as though it were unsaid! Why, oh, why, have I betrayed myself?' exclaimed Madalina.

John now had risen from his chair, and coming up to her took her by the arm and spoke a word. 'Compose yourself,' he said. He spoke in his most affectionate voice, and he stood very close to her.

'How easy it is to bid me do that,' said Madalina. 'Tell the sea to compose itself when it rages!'

'Madalina!' said he.

'Well, – what of Madalina? Madalina has lost her own respect, – for ever.'

'Do not say that.'

'Oh, John, – why did you ever come here? Why? Why did we meet at that fatal woman's house? Or, meeting so, why did we not part as strangers? Sir, why have you come here to my mother's house day after day, evening after evening, if— Oh, heavens, what am I saying? I wonder whether you will scorn me always?'

'I will never scorn you.'

'And you will pardon me?'

'Madalina, there is nothing to pardon.'

'And – you will love me?' Then, without waiting for any more encouraging reply, – unable, probably, to wait a moment longer, she sunk upon his bosom. He caught her, of course, – and at that moment the drawing-room door was opened, and Lady Demolines entered the chamber. John Eames detected at a glance the skirt of the old white dressing gown which he had seen whisking away on the occasion of his last visit at Porchester Terrace. But on the present occasion Lady Demolines wore over it a short red opera cloak, and the cap on her head was ornamented with coloured ribbons. 'What is this,' she said, 'and why am I thus disturbed?' Madalina lay motionless in Johnny's arms, while the old woman glowered at him from under the coloured ribbons. 'Mr Eames, what is that I behold?' she said.

'Your daughter, madam, seems to be a little unwell,' said Johnny. Madalina kept her feet firm upon the ground, but did not for a moment lose her purchase against Johnny's waistcoat. Her respirations came very strong, but they came a good deal stronger when he mentioned the fact that she was not so well as she might be.

'Unwell! said Lady Demolines. And John was stricken at the moment with a conviction that her ladyship must have passed the early years of her life upon the stage. 'You would trifle with me, sir. Beware that you do not trifle with her, – with Madalina !'

'My mother,' said Madalina; but still she did not give up her purchase, and the voice seemed to come half from her and half from Johnny. 'Come to me, my mother.' Then Lady Demolines hastened to her daughter, and Madalina between them was gradually laid at her length upon the sofa. The work of laying her out, however, was left almost entirely to the stronger arm of Mr John Eames. 'Thanks, mother,' said Madalina; but she had not as yet opened her eyes, even for an instant. 'Perhaps I had better go now,' said Johnny. The old woman looked at him with eyes which asked him whether 'he didn't wish he might get it' as plainly as though the words had been pronounced. 'Of course I'll wait if I can be of any service,' said Johnny.

'I must know more of this, sir, before you leave the house,' said Lady Demolines. He saw that between them both there might probably be a very bad quarter of an hour in store for him; but he swore to himself that no union of dragon and tigress should extract from him a word that could be taken as a promise of marriage.

The old woman was now kneeling by the head of the sofa, and Johnny was standing close by her side. Suddenly Madalina opened her eyes, – opened them very wide and gazed around her. Then slowly she raised herself on the sofa, and turned her face first upon her mother and then upon Johnny. 'You here, mamma!' she said.

'Dearest one, I am near you. Be not afraid,' said her ladyship.

'Afraid! Why should I be afraid? John! My own John! Mamma, he is my own.' And she put out her arms to him, as though calling to him to come to her. Things were now very bad with John Eames, – so bad that he would have given a considerable lump out of Lord de Guest's legacy to be able to escape at once into the street. The power of a woman, when she chooses to use it recklessly, is, for the moment, almost unbounded.

'I hope you find yourself a little better,' said John, struggling to speak, as though he were not utterly crushed by the occasion.

Lady Demolines slowly raised herself from her knees, helping herself with her hands against the shoulder of the sofa, – for though still very clever, she was old and stiff, – and then offered both her hands to Johnny. Johnny cautiously took one of them, finding himself unable to decline them both. 'My son!' she exclaimed; and before he knew where he was the old woman had succeeded in kissing his nose and his whiskers. 'My son !' she said again.

Now the time had come for facing the dragon and the tigress in their wrath. If they were to be faced at all, time for facing them had certainly arrived. I fear that John's heart sank low in his bosom at that moment. 'I don't quite understand,' he said, almost in a whisper. Madalina put out one arm towards him, and the fingers trembled. Her lips were opened, and the white row of interior ivory might be seen plainly ; but at the present conjuncture of affairs she spoke not a word ; but her arm remained stretched out towards him, and her fingers did not cease to tremble.

'You do not understand !' said Lady Demolines, drawing herself back, and looking, in her short open cloak, like a knight who has donned his cuirass, but has forgotten to put on his leg-gear. And she shook the bright ribbons of her cap, as a knight in his wrath shakes the crest of his helmet. 'You do not understand, Mr Eames ! What is it, sir, that you do not understand ?'

'There is some misconception, I mean,' said Johnny.

'Mother !' said Madalina, turning her eyes from her recreant lover to her tender parent ; trembling all over, but still keeping her head extended. 'Mother !'

'My darling ! But leave him to me, dearest. Compose yourself.'

''Twas the word that he said – this moment ; before he pressed me to his heart.'

'I thought you were fainting,' said Johnny.

'Sir !' And Lady Demolines, as she spoke, shook her crest, and glared at him, and almost flew at him in her armour.

'It may be that nature has given way with me, and that I have been in a dream,' said Madalina.

'That which mine eyes saw was no dream,' said Lady Demolines. 'Mr Eames, I have given to you the sweetest name that can fall from an old woman's lips. I have called you my son.'

'Yes, you did, I know. But, as I said before, there is some mistake. I know how proud I ought to be, and how happy, and all that kind of thing. But—' Then there came a screech from Madalina, which would have awakened the dead, had there been any dead in that house. The page and the cook, however, took no notice of it, whether they were awakened or not. And having screeched, Madalina stood erect upon the floor, and she also glared upon her recreant lover. The dragon and the tiger were there before him now, and he knew that it behoved him to look to himself. As he had a battle to fight, might it not be best to put a bold face upon it ? 'The truth is,' said he, 'that I don't understand this kind of thing at all.'

'Not understand it, sir ?' said the dragon.

'Leave him to me, mother,' said the tigress, shaking her head again, but with a kind of shake differing from that which she had used before. 'This is my business, and I'll have it out for myself. If he thinks I'm going to put up with his nonsense he's mistaken. I've been straightforward and above board with you, Mr Eames, and I expect to be treated in the same way in return. Do you mean to tell my mother that you deny that we are engaged?'

'Well; yes; I do. I'm very sorry, you know, if I seem to be uncivil—'

'It's because I've no brother,' said the tigress. 'He thinks that I have no man near me to protect me. But he shall find that I can protect myself. John Eames, why are you treating me like this?'

'I shall consult my cousin the serjeant to-morrow,' said the dragon. 'In the meantime he must remain in this house. I shall not allow the front door to be unlocked for him.'

This, I think, was the bitterest moment of all to Johnny. To be confined all night in Lady Demolines' drawing-room would, of itself, be an intolerable nuisance. And then the absurdity of the thing, and the story that would go abroad! And what should he say to the dragon's cousin the serjeant, if the serjeant should be brought upon the field before he was able to escape from it. He did not know what a serjeant might not do to him in such circumstances. There was one thing no serjeant should do, and no dragon! Between them all they should never force him to marry the tigress. At this moment Johnny heard a t amp along the pavement, and he rushed to the window. Before the dragon or even the tigress could arrest him, he had thrown up the sash, and had appealed in his difficulty to the guardian of the night. 'I say, old fellow,' said Johnny, 'don't you stir from that till I tell you.' The policeman turned his bull's-eye* upon the window, and stood perfectly motionless. 'Now, if you please, I'll say good-night,' said Johnny. But, as he spoke, he still held the open window in his hand.

'What means this violence in my house?' said the dragon.

'Mamma, you had better let him go,' said the tigress. 'We shall know where to find him.'

'You will certainly be able to find me,' said Johnny.

'Go,' said the dragon, shaking her crest, – shaking all her armour at him, 'dastard, go!'

'Policeman,' shouted Johnny, while he still held the open window in his hand, 'mind you don't stir till I come out.' The bull's-eye was shifted a little, but the policeman spoke never a word.

'I wish you good-night, Lady Demolines,' said Johnny. 'Good-night, Miss Demolines.' Then he left the window and made a run for the door. But the dragon was there before him.

'Let him go, mamma,' said the tigress as she closed the window, 'We shall only have a rumpus.'

'That will be all,' said Johnny. 'There isn't the slightest use in your trying to keep me here.'

'And are we never to see you again?' said the tigress, almost languishing again with one eye.

'Well; no. What would be the use? No man likes to be shut in, you know.'

'Go then,' said the tigress; 'but if you think that this is to be the end of it, you'll find yourself wonderfully mistaken. You poor false, drivelling creature! Lily Dale won't touch you with a pair of tongs. It's no use your going to her.'

'Go away, sir, at this moment, and don't contaminate my room an instant longer by your presence,' said the dragon, who had observed through the window that the bull's-eye was still in full force before the house. Then John Eames withdrew, and descending into the hall made his way in the dark to the front door. For aught he knew there might still be treachery in regard to the lock; but his heart was comforted as he heard the footfall of the policeman on the door-step. With much fumbling he succeeded at last in turning the key and drawing the bolt, and then he found himself at liberty in the street. Before he even spoke a word to the policeman he went out into the road and looked up at the window. He could just see the figure of the dragon's helmet as she was closing the shutters. It was the last he ever saw of Lady Demolines or of her daughter.

'What was it all about?' said the policeman.

'I don't know that I can just tell you,' said Johnny, searching in his pocket-book for half a sovereign which he tendered to the man. 'There was a little difficulty, and I'm obliged to you for waiting.'

'There ain't nothing wrong?' said the man suspiciously, hesitating for a moment before he accepted the coin.

'Nothing on earth. I'll wait with you, while you have the house opened and inquire, if you wish it. The truth is somebody inside refused to have the door opened, and I didn't want to stay there all night.'

'They're a rummy couple, if what I hear is true.'

'They are a rummy couple,' said Johnny.

'I suppose it's all right,' said the policeman, taking the money. And then John walked off home by himself, turning in his mind all the circumstances of his connection with Miss Demolines. Taking his own conduct as a whole, he was rather proud of it; but he acknowledged to himself that it would be well that he should keep himself free from the society of Madalina for the future.

CHAPTER 81

Barchester cloisters

On the morning of the Sunday after the dean's return Mr Harding was lying on his bed, and Posy was sitting on the bed beside him. It was manifest to all now that he became feebler and feebler from day to day and that he would never leave his bed again. Even the archdeacon had shaken his head, and had acknowledged to his wife that the last day for her father was near at hand. It would very soon be necessary that he should select another vicar for St Ewolds.

'Grandpa won't play cat's-cradle,' said Posy, as Mrs Arabin entered the room.

'No darling, – not this morning,' said the old man. He himself knew well enough that he would never play cat's-cradle again. Even that was over for him now.

'She teases you, papa,' said Mrs Arabin.

'No, indeed,' said he. 'Posy never teases me;' and he slowly moved his withered hand down outside the bed, so as to hold the child by her frock. 'Let her stay with me, my dear.'

'Dr Filgrave is downstairs, papa. You will see him, if he comes up?' Now Dr Filgrave was the leading physician of Barchester, and nobody of note in the city, – or for the matter of that in the eastern division of the county, – was allowed to start upon the last great journey without some assistance from him as the hour of going drew nigh. I do not know that he had much reputation for prolonging life, but he was supposed to add a grace to the hour of departure. Mr Harding had expressed no wish to see the doctor, – had rather declared his conviction that Dr Filgrave could be of no possible service to him. But he was not a man to persevere in his objection in opposition to the wishes of the friends around him; and as soon as the archdeacon had spoken a word on the subject he assented.

'Of course, my dear, I will see him.'

'And Posy shall come back when he has gone,' said Mrs Arabin.

'Posy will do me more good than Dr Filgrave I am quite sure; – but Posy shall go now.' So Posy scrambled off the bed, and the doctor was ushered into the room.

'A day or two will see the end of it, Mr Archdeacon; – I should say a day or two,' said the doctor, as he met Dr Grantly in the hall. 'I should say that a day or two would see the end to it. Indeed I will not undertake that twenty-four hours may not see the close of his earthly troubles. He has no suffering, no pain, no disturbing cause. Nature simply retires to rest.' Dr Filgrave, as he said this, made a slow falling motion with his hands, which alone on various occasions had been thought to be worth all the money paid for his attendance. 'Perhaps you would wish that I should step in in the evening, Mr Dean ? As it happens, I shall be at liberty.' The dean of course said that he would take it as an additional favour. Neither the dean nor the archdeacon had the slightest belief in Dr Filgrave, and yet they would hardly have been contented that their father-in-law should have departed without him.

'Look at that man, now,' said the archdeacon, when the doctor had gone, 'who talks so glibly about nature going to rest. I've known him all my life. He's an older man by some months than our dear old friend upstairs. And he looks as if he were going to attend death-beds in Barchester for ever.'

'I suppose he is right in what he tells us now ?' said the dean.

'No doubt he is ; but my belief doesn't come from his saying it.' Then there was a pause as the two church dignitaries sat together, doing nothing, feeling that the solemnity of the moment was such that it would be hardly becoming that they should even attempt to read. 'His going will make an old man of me,' said the archdeacon. 'It will be different with you.'

'It will make an old woman of Eleanor, I fear.'

'I seem to have know him all my life,' said the archdeacon. 'I have known him ever since I left college ; and I have known him as one man seldom knows another. There is nothing that he has done, – as I believe, nothing that he has thought, – with which I have not been cognizant. I feel sure that he never had an impure fancy in his mind, or a faulty wish in his heart. His tenderness has surpassed the tenderness of woman;* and yet, when an occasion came for showing it, he had all the spirit of a hero. I shall never forget his resignation of the hospital, and all that I did and said to make him keep it.'

'But he was right ?'

'As Septimus Harding he was, I think, right ; but it would have been wrong in any other man. And he was right, too, about the deanery.' For promotion had once come in Mr Harding's way, and he, too, might have been Dean of Barchester. 'The fact is, he never was wrong. He couldn't go wrong. He lacked guile, and he feared God, – and a man who does both will never go far astray. I don't think he ever coveted aught in his life, – except a new case for his violoncello and somebody to listen to him when he played it.' Then the archdeacon got up, and walked about the room in his enthusiasm; and, perhaps, as he walked some thoughts as to the sterner ambition of his own life passed through his mind. What things had he coveted? Had he lacked guile? He told himself that he had feared God, – but he was not sure that he was telling himself true in that.

During the whole of the morning Mrs Arabin and Mrs Grantly were with their father, and during the greater part of the day there was absolute silence in the room. He seemed to sleep; and they, though they knew that in truth he was not sleeping, feared to disturb him by a word. About two Mrs Baxter brought him his dinner, and he did rouse himself, and swallowed a spoonful or two of soup and half a glass of wine. At this time Posy came to him, and stood at the bedside, looking at him with her great wide eyes. She seemed to be aware that life had now gone so far with her dear old friend that she must not be allowed to sit upon his bed again. But he put his hand out to her, and she held it, standing quite still and silent. When Mrs Baxter came to take away the tray, Posy's mother got up, and whispered a word to the child. Then Posy went away, and her eyes never beheld the old man again. That was a day which Posy will never forget, – not though she should live to be much older than her grandfather was when she thus left him.

'It is so sweet to have you both here,' he said, when he had been lying silent for nearly an hour after the child had gone. Then they got up, and came and stood close to him. 'There is nothing left for me to wish, my dears; – nothing.' Not long after that he expressed a desire that the two husbands, – his two sons-in-law, – should come to him; and Mrs Arabin went to them, and brought them to the room. As he took their hands he merely repeated the same words again. 'There is nothing left for me to wish, my dears; – nothing.' He never spoke again above his breath; but ever and anon his daughters, who watched him, could see that he was praying. The two men did not stay with him long, but returned to the gloom of the library. The gloom had almost become the darkness of night, and they were still sitting there without any light, when Mrs Baxter entered the room. 'The dear gentleman is no more,' said Mrs Baxter; and it seemed to the archdeacon that the very moment of his father's death had repeated itself. When Dr Filgrave called he was told that his services could be of no further use. 'Dear, dear !' said the doctor. 'We are all dust, Mrs Baxter ; are we not ?' There were people in Barchester who pretended to know how often the doctor had repeated this little formula during the last thirty years.

There was no violence of sorrow in the house that night ; but there were aching hearts, and one heart so sore that it seemed that no cure for its anguish could ever reach it. 'He has always been with me,' Mrs Arabin said to her husband, as he strove to console her. 'It was not that I loved him better than Susan, but I have felt so much more of his loving tenderness. The sweetness of his voice has been in my ears almost daily since I was born.'

They buried him in the cathedral which he had loved so well, and in which nearly all the work of his life had been done ; and all Barchester was there to see him laid in his grave within the cloisters. There was no procession of coaches, no hearse, nor was there any attempt at funeral pomp. From the dean's side door, across the vaulted passage, and into the transept, – over the little step upon which he had so nearly fallen when last he made his way out of the building, – the coffin was carried on men's shoulders. It was but a short journey from his bedroom to his grave. But the bell had been tolling sadly all the morning, and the nave and the aisles and the transepts, close up to the door leading from the transept into the cloister, were crowded with those who had known the name and the figure and the voice of Mr Harding as long as they had known anything. Up to this day no one would have said specially that Mr Harding was a favourite in the town. He had never been forward enough in anything to become the acknowledged possessor of popularity. But, now that he was gone, men and women told each other how good he had been. They remembered the sweetness of his smile, and talked of loving little words which he had spoken to them, – either years ago or the other day, for his words had always been loving. The dean and the archdeacon came first, shoulder to shoulder, and after them came their wives. I do not know that it was the proper order for mourning, but it was a touching sight to be seen, and was long remembered in Barchester. Painful as it was for them, the two women would be there, and the two sisters would walk together ; – nor would they go before their husbands. Then there were the archdeacon's two sons, – for the Rev. Charles Grantley had come to Plumstead on the occasion. And in the vaulted passage which runs between the deanery and the end of the transept all the chapter, with the choir, the prebendaries, with the fat old chancellor, the precentor, and the minor canons down to the little choristers, – they all were there, and followed in at the transept door, two by two. And in the transept they were joined by another clergyman whom no one had expected to see that day. The bishop was there, looking old and worn, – almost as though he were unconscious of what he was doing. Since his wife's death no one had seen him out of the palace or of the palace grounds till that day. But there he was, – and they made way for him into the procession behind the two ladies, – and the archdeacon, when he saw it, resolved that there should be peace in his heart, if peace might be possible.

They made their way into the cloisters where the grave had been dug, – as many as might be allowed to follow. The place indeed was open to all who chose to come; but they who had only slightly known the man, refrained from pressing upon those who had a right to stand around his coffin. But there was one other there whom the faithful chronicler of Barchester should mention. Before any other one had reached the spot, the sexton and the verger between them had led in between them, among the graves beneath the cloisters, a blind man, very old, with a wondrous stoop, but who must have owned a grand stature before extreme old age had bent him, and they placed him sitting on a stone in the corner of the archway. But as soon as the shuffling of steps reached his ears, he raised himself with the aid of his stick, and stood during the service leaning against the pillar. The blind man was so old that he might almost have been Mr Harding's father. This was John Bunce, a bedesman from Hiram's Hospital, – and none perhaps there had known Mr Harding better than he had known him. When the earth had been thrown on to the coffin, and the service was over, and they were about to disperse, Mrs Arabin went up to the old man, and taking his hand between hers whispered a word into his ear. 'Oh, Miss Eleanor,' he said. 'Oh, Miss Eleanor!' Within a fortnight he also was lying within the cathedral precincts.

And so they buried Mr Septimus Harding, formerly Warden of Hiram's Hospital in the city of Barchester, of whom the chronicler may say that that city never knew a sweeter gentleman or a better Christian.

CHAPTER 82

The last scene at Hogglestock

The fortnight following Mr Harding's death was passed quietly at
Hogglestock, for during that time no visitor made an appearance in
the parish except Mr Snapper on the Sundays. Mr Snapper, when
he had completed the service on the first of these Sundays, intimated
to Mr Crawley his opinion that probably that gentleman might
himself wish to resume the duties on the following Sabbath. Mr
Crawley, however, courteously declined to do anything of the kind.
He said that it was quite out of the question that he should do so
without a direct communication made to him from the bishop, or
by the bishop's order. The assizes had, of course, gone by, and all
question of the trial was over. Nevertheless, – as Mr Snapper said,
– the bishop had not, as yet, given any order. Mr Snapper was of
opinion that the bishop in these days was not quite himself. He had
spoken to the bishop about it and the bishop had told him peevishly,
– 'I must say quite peevishly,' Mr Snapper had said, – that nothing
was to be done at present. Mr Snapper was not the less clearly of
opinion that Mr Crawley might resume his duties. To this, however,
Mr Crawley would not assent.

But even during the fortnight Mr Crawley had not remained
altogether neglected. Two days after Mr Harding's death he had
received a note from the dean in which he was advised not to
resume the duties at Hogglestock for the present. 'Of course you
can understand that we have a sad house here at present,' the dean
had said. 'But as soon as ever we are able to move in the matter we
will arrange things for you as comfortably as we can. I will see the
bishop myself.' Mr Crawley had no ambitious idea of any comfort
which might accrue to him beyond that of an honourable return to
his humble preferment at Hogglestock; but, nevertheless, he was in
this case minded to do as the dean counselled him. He had
submitted himself to the bishop, and he would wait till the bishop
absolved him from his submission.

On the day after the funeral, the bishop had sent his compliments to the dean with the expression of a wish that the dean would call upon him on any early day that might be convenient with reference to the position of Mr Crawley of Hogglestock. The note was in the bishop's own handwriting and was as mild and civil as a bishop's note could be. Of course the dean named an early day for the interview; but it was with the archdeacon. If St Ewolds might be given to Mr Crawley, the Hogglestock difficulties would all be brought to an end. The archdeacon, after the funeral, had returned to Plumstead, and thither the dean went to him before he saw the bishop. He did succeed, – he and Mrs Grantly between them, – but with very great difficulty, in obtaining a conditional promise. They had both thought that when the archdeacon became fully aware that Grace was to be his daughter-in-law, he would at once have been delighted to have an opportunity of extricating from his poverty a clergyman with whom it was his fate to be so closely connected. But he fought the matter on twenty different points. He declared at first that as it was his primary duty to give to the people of St Ewolds the best clergyman he could select for them he could not give the preferment to Mr Crawley, because Mr Crawley, in spite of all his zeal and piety, was a man so quaint in his manners and so eccentric in his mode of speech as not to be the best clergyman whom he could select. 'What is my old friend Thorne to do with a man in his parish who won't drink a glass of wine with him?' For Ullathorne, the seat of that Mr Wilfred Thorne who had been so guilty in the matter of the foxes, was situated in the parish of St Ewolds. When Mrs Grantly proposed that Mr Thorne's consent should be asked, the archdeacon became very angry. He had never heard so unecclesiastical a proposition in his life. It was his special duty to do the best he could for Mr Thorne, but it was specially his duty to do so without consulting Mr Thorne about it. As the archdeacon's objection had been argued simply on the point of the glass of wine, both the dean and Mrs Grantly thought that he was unreasonable. But they had their point to gain, and therefore they only flattered him. They were sure that Mr Thorne would like to have a clergyman in the parish who would himself be closely connected with the archdeacon. Then Dr Grantly alleged that he might find himself in a trap. What if he conferred the living of St Ewolds on Mr Crawley and after all there should be no marriage between his son and Grace? 'Of course they'll be married,' said Mrs Grantly. 'It's all very well for you to say that, my dear; but the whole family are so queer that there is no knowing what the girl may do. She may take up some other fad now, and refuse him point blank.' 'She has never taken up any fad,' said Mrs Grantly, who now mounted almost to wrath in defence of her future daughter-in-law, 'and you are wrong to say that she has. She has behaved beautifully; – as nobody knows better than you do.' Then the archdeacon gave way so far as to promise that St Ewolds should be offered to Mr Crawley as soon as Grace Crawley was in truth engaged to Harry Grantly.

After that, the dean went to the palace. There had never been any quarrelling between the bishop and the dean, either direct or indirect; – nor, indeed, had the dean ever quarrelled even with Mrs Proudie. But he had belonged to the anti-Proudie faction. He had been brought into the diocese by the Grantly interest; and therefore, during Mrs Proudie's life-time, he had always been accounted among the enemies. There had never been any real intimacy between the houses. Each house had been always asked to dine with the other house once a year; but it had been understood that such dinings were ecclesiastico-official, and not friendly. There had been the same outside diocesan civility between even the palace and Plumstead. But now, when the great chieftain of the palace was no more, and the strength of the palace faction was gone, peace, or perhaps something more than peace, – amity, perhaps, might be more easily arranged with the dean than the archdeacon. In preparation for such arrangements the bishop had gone to Mr Harding's funeral.

And now the dean went to the palace at the bishop's behest. He found his lordship alone, and was received with almost reverential courtesy. He thought that the bishop was looking wonderfully aged since he last saw him, but did not perhaps take into account the absence of clerical sleekness which was incidental to the bishop's private life in his private room, and perhaps in a certain measure to his recent great affliction. The dean had been in the habit of regarding Dr Proudie as a man almost young for his age, – having been in the habit of seeing him at his best, clothed in authority, redolent of the throne, conspicuous as regarded his apron and outward signs of episcopality. Much of all this was now absent. The bishop, as he rose to greet the dean, shuffled with his old slippers, and his hair was not brushed so becomingly as used to be the case when Mrs Proudie was always near him.

It was necessary that a word should be said by each as to the loss which the other had suffered. 'Mr Dean,' said his lordship, 'allow me to offer you my condolements in regard to the death of that very excellent clergyman and most worthy gentleman, your father-in-law.'

'Thank you, my lord. He was excellent and worthy. I do not suppose that I shall live to see any man who was more so. You also have a great, – a terrible loss.'

'O, Mr Dean, yes; yes, indeed, Mr Dean. That was a loss.'

'And hardly past the prime of life!'

'Ah, yes; – just fifty-six, – and so strong! Was she not? At least everybody thought so. And yet she was gone in a minute; – gone in a minute. I haven't held up my head since, Mr Dean.'

'It was a great loss, my lord; but you must struggle to bear it.'

'I do struggle. I am struggling. But it makes one feel so lonely in this great house. Ah, me! I often wish, Mr Dean, that it had pleased Providence to have left me in some humble parsonage, where duty would have been easier than it is here. But I will not trouble you with all that. What are we to do, Mr Dean, about this poor Mr Crawley?'

'Mr Crawley is a very old friend of mine, and a very dear friend.'

'Is he? Ah! A very worthy man, I am sure, and one who has been much tried by undeserved adversities.'

'Most severely tried, my lord.'

'Sitting among the potsherds, like Job;* has he not, Mr Dean? Well; let us hope that all that is over. When this accusation about the robbery was brought against him, I found myself bound to interfere.'

'He has no complaint to make on that score.'

'I hope not. I have not wished to be harsh, but what could I do, Mr Dean? They told me that the civil authorities found the evidence so strong against him that it could not be withstood.'

'It was very strong.'

'And we thought that he should at least be relieved, and we sent for Dr Tempest, who is his rural dean.' Then the bishop, remembering all the circumstances of that interview with Dr Tempest, – as to which he had ever felt assured that one of the results of it was the death of his wife, whereby there was no longer any 'we' left in the palace of Barchester, – sighed piteously, looking up at the dean with hopeless face.

'Nobody doubts, my lord, that you acted for the best.'

'I hope we did. I think we did. And now what shall we do? He has resigned his living, both to you and to me, as I hear, – you being the patron. It will simply be necessary, I think, that he should ask to have the letters cancelled. Then, as I take it, there need be no reinstitution. You cannot think, Mr Dean, how much I have thought about it all.'

Then the dean unfolded his budget, and explained to the bishop how he hoped that the living of St Ewolds, which was, after some ecclesiastical fashion, attached to the rectory of Plumstead, and which was now vacant by the demise of Mr Harding, might be conferred by the archdeacon upon Mr Crawley. It was necessary to explain also that this could not be done quite immediately, and in doing this the dean encountered some little difficulty. The archdeacon, he said, wished to be allowed another week to think about it; and therefore perhaps provision for the duties at Hogglestock might yet be made for a few Sundays. The bishop, the dean said, might easily understand that, after what had occurred, Mr Crawley would hardly wish to go again into that pulpit, unless he did so as resuming duties which would necessarily be permanent with him. To all this the bishop assented, but he was apparently struck with much wonder at the choice made by the archdeacon. 'I should have thought, Mr Dean,' he said, 'that Mr Crawley was the last man to have suited the archdeacon's choice.'

'The archdeacon and I married sisters, my lord.'

'Oh, ah! yes. And he puts the nomination of St Ewolds at your disposition. I am sure I shall be delighted to institute so worthy a gentleman as Mr Crawley.' Then the dean took his leave of the bishop, – as will we also. Poor dear bishop! I am inclined to think that he was right in his regrets as to the little parsonage. Not that his failure at Barchester, and his present consciousness of lonely incompetence, were mainly due to any positive inefficiency on his own part. He might have been a sufficiently good bishop, had it not been that Mrs Proudie was so much more than a sufficiently good bishop's wife. We will now say farewell to him, with a hope that the lopped tree may yet become green again, and to some extent fruitful, although all its beautiful head and richness of waving foliage have been taken from it.

About a week after this Henry Grantly rode over from Cosby Lodge to Hogglestock. It has been just said that though the assizes had passed by and though all question of Mr Crawley's guilt was now set aside, no visitor had of late made his way over to Hogglestock. I fancy that Grace Crawley forgot, in the fulness of her memory as to other things, that Mr Harding, of whose death she heard, had been her lover's grandfather, – and that therefore there might possibly be some delay. Had there been much said between the mother and the daughter about the lover, no doubt all this would have been explained; but Grace was very reticent, and there were other matters in the Hogglestock household which in those days occupied Mrs Crawley's mind. How were they again to begin life? for, in very truth, life as it had existed with them before, had been brought to an end. But Grace remembered well the sort of compact which existed between her and her lover; – the compact which had been made in very words between herself and her lover's father. Complete in her estimation as had been the heaven opened to her by Henry Grantly's offer, she had refused it all, – lest she should bring disgrace upon him. But the disgrace was not certain; and if her father should be made free from it, then, – then, – then Henry Grantly ought to come to her and be at her feet with all the expedition possible to him. That was her reading of the compact. She had once declared, when speaking of the possible disgrace which might attach itself to her family, and to her name, that her poverty did not 'signify a bit.' She was not ashamed of her father, – only of the accusation against her father. Therefore she had hurried home when that accusation was withdrawn, desirous that her lover should tell her of his love, – if he chose to repeat such telling, – amidst all the poor things of Hogglestock, and not among the chairs and tables and good dinners of luxurious Framley. Mrs Robarts had given a true interpretation to Lady Lufton of the haste which Grace had displayed. But she need not have been in so great a hurry. She had been at home already above a fortnight, and as yet he had made no sign. At last she said a word to her mother. 'Might I not ask to go back to Miss Prettyman's now, mamma?' 'I think, dear, you had better wait till things are a little settled. Papa is to hear again from the dean very soon. You see they are all in a great sorrow at Barchester about poor Mr Harding's death.' 'Grace!' said Jane, rushing into the house almost speechless, at that moment, 'here he is! – on horseback.' I do not know why Jane should have talked about Major Grantly as simply 'he.' There had been no conversation among the sisters to justify her in such a mode of speech. Grace had not a moment to put two and two together, so that she might realize the meaning of what her mother had said; but nevertheless, she felt at the moment that the man, coming as he had done now, had come with all commendable speed. How foolish had she been with her wretched impatience!

There he was certainly, tying his horse up to the railing. 'Mamma, what am I to say to him?'

'Nay, dear; he is your own friend, – of your own making. You must say what you think fit.'

'You are not going.'

'I think we had better, dear.' Then she went, and Jane with her, and Jane opened the door for Major Grantly. Mr Crawley himself was away, at Hoggle End, and did not return till after Major Grantly had left the parsonage. Jane, as she greeted the grand gentleman, whom she had seen and no more than seen, hardly knew what to say to him. When, after a minute's hesitation, she told him that Grace was in there, – pointing to the sitting-room door, she felt that she had been very awkward. Henry Grantly, however, did not, I think, feel her awkwardness, being conscious of some small difficulties of his own. When, however, he found that Grace was alone, the task before him at once lost half its difficulties. 'Grace,' he said, 'am I right to come to you now?'

'I do not know,' she said. 'I cannot tell.'

'Dearest Grace, there is no reason on earth now why you should not be my wife.'

'Is there not?'

'I know of none, – if you can love me. You saw my father?'

'Yes, I saw him.'

'And you heard what he said?'

'I hardly remember what he said; – but he kissed me, and I thought he was very kind.'

What little attempt Henry Grantly then made, thinking that he could not do better than follow closely the example of so excellent a father, need not be explained with minuteness. But I think that his first effort was not successful. Grace was embarrassed and retreated, and it was not till she had been compelled to give a direct answer to a direct question that she submitted to allow his arm round her waist. But when she had answered that question she was almost more humble than becomes a maiden who has just been wooed and won. A maiden who has been wooed and won, generally thinks that it is she who has conquered, and chooses to be triumphant accordingly. But Grace was even mean enough to thank her lover. 'I do not know why you should be so good to me,' she said.

'Because I love you,' said he, 'better than all the world.'

'But why should you be so good to me as that? Why should you love me? I am such a poor thing for a man like you to love.'

'I have had the wit to see that you are not a poor thing, Grace; and it is thus that I have earned my treasure. Some girls are poor things, and some are rich treasures.'

'If love can make me a treasure, I will be your treasure. And if love can make me rich, I will be rich for you.' After that I think he had no difficulty in following in his father's footsteps.

After a while Mrs Crawley came in, and there was much plesant talking among them, while Henry Grantly sat happily with his love, as though waiting for Mr Crawley's return. But though he was there nearly all the morning Mr Crawley did not return. 'I think he likes the brickmakers better than anybody in all the world, except ourselves,' said Grace. 'I don't know how he will manage to get on without his friends.' Before Grace had said this, Major Grantly had told all his story, and had produced a letter from his father, addressed to Mr Crawley, of which the reader shall have a copy, although at this time the letter had not been opened. The letter was as follows: –

Plumstead Rectory, – May, 186–.

My dear Sir,

You will no doubt have heard that Mr Harding, the vicar of St Ewolds, who was the father of my wife and of Mrs Arabin, has been taken from us. The loss to us of so excellent and so dear a man has been very great. I have conferred with my friend the Dean of Barchester as to a new nomination, and I venture to request your acceptance of the preferment, if it should suit you to move from Hogglestock to St Ewolds. It may be as well that I should state plainly my reasons for making this offer to a gentleman with whom I am not personally acquainted. Mr Harding, on his deathbed, himself suggested it, moved thereto by what he had heard of the cruel and undeserved persecution to which you have lately been subjected; as also, – on which point he was very urgent in what he said, – by the character which you bear in the diocese for zeal and piety. I may also add, that the close connection which, as I understand, is likely to take place between your family and mine has been an additional reason for my taking this step, and the long friendship which has existed between you and my wife's brother-in-law, the Dean of Barchester, is a third.

'St Ewolds is worth 350*l.* per annum, besides the house, which is sufficiently commodious for a moderate family. The population is about twelve hundred, of which more than a half consists of persons dwelling in an outskirt of the city, – for the parish runs almost into Barchester.

'I shall be glad to have your reply with as little delay as may suit your convenience, and in the event of your accepting the offer, – which I sincerely trust you may be enabled to do, – I shall hope to have an early opportunity of seeing you, with reference to your institution to the parish.

'Allow me also to say to you and to Mrs Crawley that, if we have been correctly informed as to that other event to which I have alluded, we both hope that we may have an early opportunity of making ourselves personally acquainted with the parents of a young lady who is to be so dear to us. As I have met your daughter, I may perhaps be allowed to send her my kindest love. If, as my daughter-in-law, she comes up to the impression which she gave me at our first meeting, I, at any rate, shall be satisfied.

> I have the honour to be, my dear sir,
> Your most faithful servant,
> Theophilus Grantly.

This letter the archdeacon had shown to his wife, by whom it had not been very warmly approved. Nothing, Mrs Grantly had said, could be prettier than what the archdeacon had said about Grace. Mrs Crawley, no doubt, would be satisfied with that. But Mr Crawley was such a strange man! 'He will be stranger than I take him to be if he does not accept St Ewolds,' said the archdeacon. 'But in offering it,' said Mrs Grantly 'you have not said a word of your own high opinion of his merits.' 'I have not a very high opinion of them,' said the archdeacon. 'Your father had, and I have said so. And as I have the most profound respect for your father's opinion in such a matter, I have permitted that to overcome my own hesitation.' This was pretty from the husband to the wife as it regarded her father, who had now gone from them; and, therefore, Mrs Grantly accepted it without further argument. The reader may probably feel assured that the archdeacon had never, during their joint lives, acted in any church matter upon the advice given to him by Mr Harding; and it was probably the case also that the living would have been offered to Mr Crawley, if nothing had been said by Mr Harding on the subject; but it did not become Mrs Grantly even to think of all this. The archdeacon, having made his gracious speech about her father, was not again asked to alter his letter. 'I suppose he will accept it,' said Mrs Grantly. 'I should think that he probably may,' said the archdeacon.

So Grace, knowing what was the purport of the letter, sat with it between her fingers, while her lover sat beside her, full of various plans for the future. This was his first lover's present to her; – and what a present it was! Comfort, and happiness, and a pleasant home for all her family. 'St Ewolds isn't the best house in the world,' said the major, 'because it is old, and what I call piecemeal; but it is very pretty, and certainly nice.' 'That is just the sort of parsonage that I dream about,' said Jane. 'And the garden is plesant with old trees,' said the major. 'I always dream about old trees,' said Jane, 'only I'm afraid I'm too old myself to be let to climb up them now.' Mrs Crawley said very little, but sat by with her eyes full of tears. Was it possible that, at last, before the world had closed upon her, she was to enjoy something again of the comforts which she had known in her early years, and to be again surrounded by those decencies of life which of late had been almost banished from her home by poverty!

Their various plans for the future, – for the immediate future, – were very startling. Grace was to go over at once to Plumstead, whither Edith had been already transferred from Cosby Lodge. That was all very well; there was nothing very startling or impracticable in that. The Framley ladies, having none of those doubts as to what was coming which had for a while perplexed Grace herself, had taken little liberties with her wardrobe, which enabled such a visit to be made without overwhelming difficulties. But the major was equally eager, – or at any rate equally imperious, – in his requisition for a visit from Mr and Mrs Crawley themselves to Plumstead rectory. Mrs Crawley did not dare to put forward the plain unadorned reasons against it, as Mr Crawley had done when discussing the subject of a visit to the deanery. Nor could she quite venture to explain that she feared that the archdeacon and her husband would hardly mix well together in society. With whom, indeed, was it possible that her husband should mix well, after his long and hardly-tried seclusion? She could only plead that both her husband and herself were so little used to going out that she feared, – she feared, – she feared she knew not what. 'We'll get over all that,' said the major almost contemptuously. 'It is only the first plunge that is disagreeable.' Perhaps the major did not know how very disagreeable a first plunge may be!

At two o'clock Henry Grantly got up to go. 'I should very much like to have seen him, but I fear I cannot wait longer. As it is, the patience of my horse has been surprising.' Then Grace walked out with him to the gate, and put her hand upon his bridle as he mounted, and thought how wonderful was the power of Fortune, that the goddess should have sent so gallant a gentleman to be her lord and her lover. 'I declare I don't quite believe it even yet,' she said, in the letter which she wrote to Lily Dale that night.

It was four before Mr Crawley returned to his house, and then he was very weary. There were many sick in these days at Hoggle End, and he had gone from cottage to cottage through the day. Giles Hoggett was almost unable to work from rheumatism, but still was of opinion that doggedness might carry him on. 'It's been a deal o' service to you, Muster Crawley,' he said. 'We hears about it all. If you hadn't a been dogged, where'd you been now?' With Giles Hoggett and others he had remained all the day, and now he came home weary and beaten. 'You'll tell him first,' Grace had said, 'and then I'll give him the letter.' The wife was the first to tell him of the good fortune that was coming.

He flung himself into the old chair as soon as he entered, and asked for some bread and tea. 'Jane has already gone for it, dear,' said his wife. 'We have had a visitor here, Josiah.'

'A visitor, – what visitor?'

'Grace's own friend, – Henry Grantly.'

'Grace, come here, that I may kiss you and bless you,' he said, very solemnly. 'It would seem that the world is going to be very good to you.'

'Papa, you must read this letter first.'

'Before I kiss my own darling?' Then she knelt at his feet. 'I see,' he said, taking the letter; 'it is from your lover's father. Peradventure he signifies his consent, which would be surely needful before such a marriage would be seemly.'

'It isn't about me, papa, at all.'

'Not about you? If so, that would be most unpromising. But, in any case, you are my best darling.' Then he kissed her and blessed her, and slowly opened the letter. His wife had now come close to him, and was standing over him, touching him, so that she also could read the archdeacon's letter. Grace, who was still in front of him, could see the working of his face as he read it; but even she could not tell whether he was gratified, or offended, or dismayed. When he had got as far as the first offer of the presentation, he ceased reading for a while, and looked round about the room as though lost in thought. 'Let me see what further he writes to me,' he then said; and after that he continued the letter slowly to the end. 'Nay, my child, you were in error in saying that he wrote not about you. 'Tis in writing of you he has put some real heart into his words. He writes as though his home would be welcome to you.'

'And does he not make St Ewolds welcome to you, papa?'

'He makes me welcome to accept it, – if I may use the word after the ordinary and somewhat faulty parlance of mankind.'

'And you will accept it, – of course?'

'I know not that, my dear. The acceptance of a cure of souls is a thing not to be decided on in a moment, – as is the colour of a garment or the shape of a toy. Nor would I condescend to take this thing from the archdeacon's hands, if I thought that he bestowed it simply that the father of his daughter-in-law might no longer be accounted poor.'

'Does he say that, papa?'

'He gives it as a collateral reason, basing his offer first on the kindly expressed judgment of one who is now no more. Then he refers to the friendship of the dean. If he believed that the judgment of his late father-in-law in so weighty a matter were the best to be relied upon of all that were at his command, then he would have done well to trust to it. But in such case he should have bolstered up a good ground for action with no collateral supports which are weak, – and worse than weak. However, it shall have my best consideration, whereunto I hope that wisdom will be given me where only such wisdom can be had.'

'Josiah,' said his wife to him, when they were alone, 'you will not refuse it?'

'Not willingly, – not if it may be accepted. Alas! you need not urge me, when the temptation is so strong!'

CHAPTER 83

Mr Crawley is conquered

It was more than a week before the archdeacon received a reply
from Mr Crawley, during which time the dean had been over at
Hogglestock more than once, as had also Mrs Arabin and Lady
Lufton the younger, – and there had been letters written without
end, and the archdeacon had been nearly beside himself. 'A man
who pretends to conscientious scruples of that kind is not fit to
have a parish,' he had said to his wife. His wife understood what
he meant, and I trust that the reader may also understand it. In the
ordinary cutting of blocks a very fine razor is not an appropriate
instrument. The archdeacon, moreover, loved the temporalities of
the Church as temporalities. The Church was beautiful to him
because one man by interest might have a thousand a year, while
another man equally good, but without interest, could only have a
hundred. And he liked the men who had the interest a great deal
better than the men who had it not. He had been willing to admit
this poor perpetual curate, who had so long been kept out in the
cold, within the pleasant circle which was warm with ecclesiastical
good things, and the man hesitated, – because of scruples, as the
dean told him! 'I always button up my pocket when I hear of
scruples,' the archdeacon said.

But at last Mr Crawley condescended to accept St Ewolds.
'Reverend and dear Sir,' he said in his letter. 'For the personal
benevolence of the offer made to me in your letter of the – instant,
I beg to tender you my most grateful thanks; as also for your
generous kindness to me, in telling me of the high praise bestowed
upon me by a gentleman who is now no more, – whose character I
have esteemed and whose good opinion I value. There is, methinks,
something inexpressibly dear to me in the recorded praise of the
dead. For the further instance of the friendship of the Dean of
Barchester, I am also thankful.

'Since the receipt of your letter I have doubted much as to my fitness for the work you have proposed to entrust to me, – not from any feeling that the parish of St Ewolds may be beyond my intellectual power, but because the latter circumstances of my life have been of a nature so strange and perplexing, that they left me somewhat in doubt as to my own aptitude for going about among men without giving offence and becoming a stumbling block.

'Nevertheless, reverend and dear sir, if after this confession on my part of a certain faulty demeanour with which I know well that I am afflicted, you are still willing to put the parish into my hands, I will accept the charge, – instigated to do so by the advice of all whom I have consulted on the subject; and in thus accepting it, I hereby pledge myself to vacate it at a month's warning, should I be called upon by you to do so at any period within the next two years. Should I be so far successful during those twenty-four months as to have satisfied both yourself and myself, I may then perhaps venture to regard the preferment as my own in perpetuity for life.

> I have the honour to be, reverend and dear sir,
> Your most humble and faithful servant,
> Josiah Crawley.'

'Psha!' said the archdeacon, who professed that he did not at all like the letter. 'I wonder what he would say if I sent him a month's notice at next Michaelmas?'

'I'm sure he would go,' said Mrs Grantly.

'The more fool he,' said the archdeacon.

At this time Grace was at the parsonage in a seventh heaven of happiness. The archdeacon was never rough to her, nor did he make any of his harsh remarks about her father in her presence. Before her St Ewolds was spoken of as the home that was to belong to the Crawleys for the next twenty years. Mrs Grantly was very loving with her, lavishing upon her pretty presents, and words that were prettier than the presents. Grace's life had hitherto been so destitute of those prettinesses and softnesses, which can hardly be had without money though money alone will not purchase them, that it seemed to her now that the heavens rained graciousness upon her. It was not that the archdeacon's watch, or her lover's chain, or Mrs Grantly's locket, or the little toy from Italy which Mrs Arabin brought to her from the treasures of the deanery, filled her heart with undue exultation. It was not that she revelled in her new delights of silver and gold and shining gems: but that the silver and gold and shining gems were constant indications to her that things had changed, not only for her, but for her father and mother, and brother and sister. She felt now more sure than ever that she could not have enjoyed her love had she accepted her lover while the disgrace of the accusation against her father remained. But now, – having waited till that had passed away, everything was a new happiness to her.

At last it was settled that Mr and Mrs Crawley were to come to Plumstead, – and they came. It would be too long to tell now how gradually had come about that changed state of things which made such a visit possible. Mr Crawley had at first declared that such a thing was quite out of the question. If St Ewolds was to depend upon it, St Ewolds must be given up. And I think that it would have been impossible for him to go direct from Hogglestock to Plumstead. But it fell out after this wise.

Mr Harding's curate at St Ewolds was nominated to Hogglestock, and the dean urged upon his friend Crawley the expediency of giving up the house as quickly as he could do so. Gradually at this time Mr Crawley had been forced into a certain amount of intimacy with the haunts of men. He had been twice or thrice at Barchester, and had lunched with the dean. He had been at Framley for an hour or two, and had been forced into some communication with old Mr Thorne, the squire of his new parish. The end of this had been that he had at last consented to transfer himself and wife and daughter to the deanery for a fortnight. He had preached one farewell sermon at Hogglestock, – not, as he told his audience, as their pastor, which he had ceased to be now for some two or three months, – but as their old and loving friend, to whom the use of his former pulpit had been lent, that he might express himself thus among them for the last time. His sermon was very short, and was preached without book or notes, – but he never once paused for a word or halted in the string or rhythm of his discourse. The dean was there and declared to him afterwards that he had not given him credit for such powers of utterance. 'Any man can utter out of a full heart,' Crawley had answered. 'In this trumpery affair about myself, my heart is full! If we could only have our hearts full in other matters, our utterances thereanent would receive more attention.' To all of which the dean made no reply.

On the day after this the Crawleys took their final departure from Hogglestock, all the brickmakers from Hoggle End having assembled on the occasion, with a purse containing seventeen pounds seven shillings and sixpence, which they insisted on presenting to Mr Crawley, and as to which there was a little difficulty. And at the deanery they remained for a fortnight. How Mrs Crawley, under the guidance of Mrs Arabin, had there so far trenched upon the revenues of St Ewolds as to provide for her husband and herself raiment fitting for the worldly splendour of Plumstead, need not here be told in detail. Suffice to say, the raiment was forthcoming, and Mr Crawley found himself to be the perplexed possessor of a black dress coat, in addition to the long frock, coming nearly to his feet, which was provided for his daily wear. Touching this garment, there had been some discussion between the dean and the new vicar. The dean had desired that it should be curtailed in length. The vicar had remonstrated, – but still with something of the weakness of compliance in his eye. Then the dean had persisted. 'Surely the price of the cloth wanted to perfect the comeliness of the garment cannot be much,' said the vicar, almost woefully. After that, the dean relented, and the comeliness of the coat was made perfect. The new black long frock, I think Mr Crawley liked; but the dress coat, with the suit complete, perplexed him sorely.

With his new coats, and something, also, of new manners, he and his wife went over to Plumstead, leaving Jane at the deanery with Mrs Arabin. The dean also went to Plumstead. They arrived there not much before dinner, and as Grace was there before them the first moments were not so bad. Before Mr Crawley had had time to feel himself lost in the drawing-room, he was summoned away to prepare himself for dinner, – for dinner, and for the coat, which at the deanery he had been allowed to leave unworn. 'I would with all my heart that I might retire to rest,' he said to his wife, when the ceremony had been perfected.

'Do not say so. Go down and take your place with them, and speak your mind with them, – as you so well know how. Who among them can do it so well?'

'I have been told,' said Mr Crawley, 'that you shall take a cock which is lord of the farmyard, – the cock of all that walk, – and when you have daubed his feathers with mud, he shall be thrashed by every dunghill coward. I say not that I was ever the cock of the walk, but I know that they have daubed my feathers.' Then he went down among the other poultry into the farmyard.

At dinner he was very silent, answering, however, with a sort of graceful stateliness any word that Mrs Grantly addressed to him. Mr Thorne, from Ullathorne, was there also to meet his new vicar, as was also Mr Thorne's very old sister, Miss Monica Thorne. And Lady Anne Grantly was there, – she having come with the expressed intention that the wives of the two brothers should know each other, – but with a warmer desire, I think, of seeing Mr Crawley, of whom the clerical world had been talking much since some notice of the accusation against him had become general. There were, therefore, ten or twelve at the dinner-table, and Mr Crawley had not made one at such a board certainly since his marriage. All went fairly smooth with him till the ladies left the room; for though Lady Anne, who sat at his left hand, had perplexed him somewhat with clerical questions, he had found that he was not called upon for much more than monosyllabic responses. But in his heart he feared the archdeacon, and he felt that when the ladies were gone the archdeacon would not leave him alone in his silence.

As soon as the door was closed, the first subject mooted was that of the Plumstead fox, which had been so basely murdered on Mr Thorne's ground. Mr Thorne had confessed the iniquity, had dismissed the murderous keeper, and all was serene. But the greater on that account was the feasibility of discussing the question, and the archdeacon had a good deal to say about it. Then Mr Thorne turned to the new vicar, and asked him whether foxes abounded in Hogglestock. Had he been asked as to the rats or the moles, he would have known more about it.

'Indeed, sir, I know not whether or no there be any foxes in the parish of Hogglestock. I do not remember me that I ever saw one. It is an animal whose habits I have not watched.'

'There is an earth at Hoggle Bushes,' said the major; 'and I never knew it without a litter.'

'I think I know the domestic whereabouts of every fox in Plumstead,' said the archdeacon, with an ill-natured intention of astonishing Mr Crawley.

'Of foxes with two legs our friend is speaking, without doubt,' said the vicar of St Ewolds, with an attempt at grim pleasantry.

'Of them we have none at Plumstead. No, – I was speaking of the dear old fellow with the brush. Pass the bottle, Mr Crawley. Won't you fill your glass?' Mr Crawley passed the bottle, but would not fill his glass. Then the dean, looking up slily, saw the vexation written in the archdeacon's face. The parson whom the archdeacon feared most of all parsons was the parson who wouldn't fill his glass.

Then the subject was changed. 'I'm told that the bishop has at last made his reappearance on his throne,' said the archdeacon.

'He was in the cathedral last Sunday,' said the dean.

'Does he ever mean to preach again?'

'He never did preach very often,' said the dean.

'A great deal too often, from all that people say,' said the archdeacon. 'I never heard him myself, and never shall, I dare say. You have heard him, Mr Crawley?'

'I have never had that good fortune, Mr Archdeacon. But living as I shall now do, so near to the city, I may perhaps be enabled to attend the cathedral service on some holyday of the Church, which may not require prayers in my own rural parish. I think that the clergy of the diocese should be acquainted with the opinions, and with the voice, and with the very manner and words of their bishop. As things are now done, this is not possible. I could wish that there were occasions on which a bishop might assemble his clergy, and preach to them sermons adapted to their use.'

'What do you call a bishop's charge, then?'

'It is usually in the printed form that I have received it,' said Mr Crawley.

'I think we have quite enough of that kind of thing,' said the archdeacon.

'He is a man whose conversation is not pleasing to me,' Mr Crawley said to his wife that night.

'Do not judge of him too quickly, Josiah,' his wife said. 'There is so much of good in him! He is kind, and generous, and I think affectionate.'

'But he is of the earth, earthy.* When you and the other ladies had retired, the conversation at first fell on the habits and value of, – foxes. I have been informed that in these parts the fox is greatly prized, as without a fox to run before the dogs, that scampering over the country which is called hunting, and which delights by the quickness and perhaps by the peril of the exercise, is not relished by the riders. Of the wisdom or taste herein displayed by the hunters of the day I say nothing. But it seemed to me that in talking of foxes Dr Grantly was master of his subject. Thence the topic glided to the duties of a bishop and to questions of preaching, as to which Dr Grantly was not slow in offering his opinion. But I thought that I would rather have heard him talk about the foxes for a week together.' She said nothing more to him, knowing well how useless it was to attempt to turn him by any argument. To her thinking the kindness of the archdeacon to them personally demanded some indulgence in the expression, and even in the formation, of an opinion, respecting his clerical peculiarities.

On the next day, however, Mr Crawley, having been summoned by the archdeacon into the library for a little private conversation, found that he got on better with him. How the archdeacon conquered him may perhaps be best described by a further narration of what Mr Crawley said to his wife. 'I told him that in regard to money matters, as he called them, I had nothing to say. I only trusted that his son was aware that my daughter had no money, and never would have any. 'My dear Crawley,' the archdeacon said, – for of late there seems to have grown up in the world a habit of greater familiarity than that which I think did prevail when last I moved much among men; – my dear Crawley, I have enough for both.' 'I would we stood on more equal grounds,' I said. Then as he answered me, he rose from his chair. 'We stand,' said he, 'on the only perfect level on which such men can meet each other. We are both gentlemen.' 'Sir,' I said, rising also, 'from the bottom of my heart I agree with you. I could not have spoken such words; but coming from you who are rich to me who am poor, they are honourable to the one and comfortable to the other.'

'And after that?'

'He took down from the shelves a volume of sermons which his father published many years ago, and presented it to me. I have it now under my arm. It hath the old bishop's manuscript notes, which I will study carefully.' And thus the archdeacon had hit his bird on both wings.

CHAPTER 84

Conclusion

It now only remains for me to gather together a few loose strings, and tie them together in a knot, so that my work may not become untwisted. Early in July, Henry Grantly and Grace Crawley were married in the parish church of Plumstead, – a great impropriety, as to which neither Archdeacon Grantly nor Mr Crawley could be got to assent for a long time, but which was at last carried, not simply by a union of Mrs Grantly and Mrs Crawley, nor even by the assistance of Mrs Arabin, but by the strong intervention of old Lady Lufton herself. 'Of course Miss Crawley ought to be married from St Ewolds vicarage; but when the furniture has only half been got in, how is it possible?' When Lady Lufton thus spoke, the archdeacon gave way, and Mr Crawley hadn't a leg to stand upon. Henry Grantly had not an opinion upon the matter. He told his father that he expected that they would marry him among them, and that that would be enough for him. As for Grace, nobody even thought of asking her; and I doubt whether she would have heard anything about the contest, had not some tidings of it reached her from her lover. Married they were at Plumstead, – and the breakfast was given with all that luxuriance of plenty which was so dear to the archdeacon's mind. Mr Crawley was the officiating priest. With his hands dropping before him, folded humbly, he told the archdeacon, – when that Plumstead question had been finally settled in opposition to his wishes, – that he would fain himself perform the ceremony by which his dearest daughter would be bound to her marriage duties. 'And who else should?' said the archdeacon. Mr Crawley muttered that he had not known how far his reverend brother might have been willing to waive his rights. But the archdeacon, who was in high good humour, – having just bestowed a little pony carriage on his new daughter-in-law, – only laughed at him; and, if the rumour which was handed about the families be true, the archdeacon before the interview was over, had poked

Mr Crawley in the ribs. Mr Crawley married them; but the archdeacon assisted, – and the dean gave away the bride. The Rev. Charles Grantly was there also; and as there was, as a matter of course, a cloud of curates floating in the distance, Henry Grantly was perhaps to be excused for declaring to his wife, when the pair had escaped, that surely no couple had ever been so tightly buckled since marriage had first become a Church ceremony.

Soon after that, Mr and Mrs Crawley became quiet at St Ewolds, and, as I think, contented. Her happiness began very quickly. Though she had been greatly broken by her troubles, the first sight she had of her husband in his new long frock-coat went far to restore her, and while he was declaring himself to be a cock so daubed with mud as to be incapable of crowing, she was congratulating herself on seeing her husband once more clothed as became his position. And they were lucky, too, as regarded the squire's house; for Mr Thorne was old, and quiet, and old-fashioned; and Miss Thorne was older, and though she was not exactly quiet, she was very old-fashioned indeed. So that there grew to be a pleasant friendship between Miss Thorne and Mrs Crawley.

Johnny Eames, when last I heard of him, was still a bachelor, and, as I think, likely to remain so. At last he had utterly thrown over Sir Raffle Buffle, declaring to his friends that the special duties of private secretaryship were not exactly to his taste. 'You get so sick at the thirteenth private note,' he said, 'that you find yourself unable to carry on the humbug any farther.' But he did not leave his office. 'I'm the head of a room, you know,' he told Lady Julia De Guest; 'and there's nothing to trouble me, – and a fellow, you know, ought to have something to do.' Lady Julia told him, with a great deal of energy, that she would never forgive him if he gave up his office. After that eventful night when he escaped ignominiously from the house of Lady Demolines under the protection of the policeman's lantern, he did hear more than once from Porchester Terrace, and from allies employed by the enemy who was there resident. 'My cousin, the serjeant,' proved to be a myth. Johnny found out all about that Serjeant Runter, who was distantly connected, indeed, with the late husband of Lady Demolines, but had always persistently declined to have any intercourse whatever with her ladyship. For the serjeant was a rising man, and Lady Demolines was not exactly progressing in the world. Johnny heard nothing from the serjeant; but from Madalina he got letter after letter. In the first she asked him not to think too much of the little joke that had occurred. In her second she described the vehemence of her love. In her third the bitterness of her wrath. Her fourth she simply invited him to come and dine in Porchester Terrace. Her fifth was the outpouring of injured innocence. And then came letters from an attorney. Johnny answered not a word to any of them, and gradually the letters were discontinued. Within six months of the receipt of the last, he was delighted by reading among the marriages in the newspapers a notice that Peter Bangles, Esq., of the firm of Burton and Bangles, wine merchants, of Hook Court, had been united to Madalina, daughter of the late Sir Confucius Demolines, at the church of Peter the Martyr. 'Most appropriate,' said Johnny, as he read the notice to Conway Dalrymple, who was then back from his wedding tour; 'for most assuredly there will be now another Peter the Martyr.'

'I'm not so sure of that,' said Conway, who had heard something of Mr Peter Bangles. 'There are men who have strong wills of their own, and strong hands of their own.'

'Poor Madalina!' said Johnny. 'If he does beat her, I hope he will do it tenderly. It may be that a little of it will suit her fevered temperament.'

Before the summer was over Conway Dalrymple had been married to Clara Van Siever, and by a singular arrangement of circumstances had married her with the full approval of old Mrs Van. Mr Musselboro, – whose name I hope has not been altogether forgotten, though the part played by him has been subordinate, – had opposed Dalrymple in the efforts made by the artist to get something out of Broughton's estate for the benefit of the widow. From circumstances of which Dalrymple learned the particulars with the aid of an attorney, it seemed to him that certain facts were wilfully kept in the dark by Musselboro, and he went with his complaint to Mrs Van Siever, declaring that he would bring the whole affair into court, unless all the workings of the firm were made clear to him. Mrs Van was very insolent to him, – and even turned him out of the house. But, nevertheless, she did not allow Mr Musselboro to escape. Whoever was to be left in the dark she did not wish to be there herself; – and it began to dawn upon her that her dear Musselboro was deceiving her. Then she sent for Dalrymple, and without a word of apology for her former conduct, put him upon the right track. As he was pushing his inquiries, and working heaven and earth for the unfortunate widow, – as to whom he swore daily that when this matter was settled he would never see her again, so terrible was she to him with her mock affection and pretended hysterics, and false moralities, – he was told one day that she had gone off with Mr Musselboro! Mr Musselboro, finding that this was the surest plan of obtaining for himself the little business in Hook Court, married the widow of his late partner, and is at this moment probably carrying on a law-suit with Mrs Van. For the law-suit Conway Dalrymple cared nothing. When the quarrel had become hot between Mrs Van and her late myrmidon, Clara fell into Conway's hands without opposition; and, let the law-suit go as it may, there will be enough left of Mrs Van's money to make the house of Mr and Mrs Conway Dalrymple very comfortable. The picture of Jael and Sisera was stitched up without any difficulty, and I daresay most of my readers will remember it hanging on the walls of the exhibition.

Before I take my leave of the diocese of Barchester for ever, which I purpose to do in the succeeding paragraph, I desire to be allowed to say one word of apology for myself, in answer to those who have accused me, — always without bitterness, and generally with tenderness, — of having forgotten, in writing of clergymen, the first and most prominent characteristic of the ordinary English clergyman's life. I have described many clergymen, they say, but have spoken of them all as though their professional duties, their high calling, their daily workings for the good of those around them, were matters of no moment, either to me, or, in my opinion, to themselves. I would plead, in answer to this, that my object has been to paint the social and not the professional lives of clergymen; and that I have been led to do so, firstly, by a feeling that as no men affect more strongly, by their own character, the society of those around than do country clergymen, so, therefore, their social habits have been worth the labour necessary for painting them; and secondly, by a feeling that though I, as a novelist, may feel myself entitled to write of clergymen out of their pulpits, as I may also write of lawyers and doctors, I have no such liberty to write of them in their pulpits. When I have done so, if I have done so, I have so far transgressed. There are those who have told me that I have made all my clergymen bad, and none good. I must venture to hint to such judges that they have taught their eyes to love a colouring higher than nature justifies. We are, most of us, apt to love Raphael's madonnas better than Rembrandt's matrons. But, though we do so, we know that Rembrandt's matrons existed; but we have a strong belief that no such woman as Raphael painted ever did exist. In that he painted, as he may be surmised to have done, for pious purposes, — at least for Church purposes, — Raphael was justified; but had he painted so for family portraiture he would have been false. Had I written an epic about clergymen, I would have taken St Paul for my model; but describing, as I have endeavoured to do, such clergymen as I see around me, I could not venture to be transcendental. For myself I can only say that I shall always be happy to sit, when allowed to do so, at the table of Archdeacon Grantly, to walk through the High Street of Barchester arm in arm with Mr Robarts of Framley, and to stand alone and shed a tear beneath the modest black stone in the north transept of the cathedral on which is inscribed the name of Septimus Harding.

And now, if the reader will allow me to seize him affectionately by the arm, we will together take our last farewell of Barset and of the towers of Barchester. I may not venture to say to him that, in this country, he and I together have wandered often through the country lanes, and have ridden together over the too-well wooded fields, or have stood together in the cathedral nave listening to the peals of the organ, or have together sat at good men's tables, or have confronted together the angry pride of men who were not good. I may not boast that any beside myself have so realized the place, and the people, and the facts, as to make such reminiscences possible as those which I should attempt to evoke by an appeal to perfect fellowship. But to me Barset has been a real county, and its city a real city, and the spires and towers have been before my eyes, and the voices of the peoples are known to my ears, and the pavement of the city ways are familiar to my footsteps. To them all I now say farewell. That I have been induced to wander among them too long by my love of old friendships, and by the sweetness of old faces, is a fault for which I may perhaps be more readily forgiven, when I repeat, with some solemnity of assurance, the promise made in my title, that this shall be the last chronicle of Barset.

THE END

EXPLANATORY NOTES

p.7   *It is declared that a good wife is a crown to her husband*: Proverbs 12.4: 'A virtuous woman is a crown to her husband.'

p.9   *rentcharge*: a charge upon lands, granted to one who is not owner of those lands.

p.9   *large tithes*: originally the 'great tithes' (or one tenth of the main crops of the parish) would have gone to the rector, and the 'small tithes' (or one tenth of the lesser produce of the parish) to the vicar. In Hogglestock the great tithes probably originally belonged to a monastic foundation and passed to the secular landowners to whom the monastic lands were granted on the dissolution of the monasteries in the sixteenth century. Under the Commutation Act of 1836, Lord Lufton's tithes now come in money as commuted tithes, and no longer in kind.

p.12   *the waters were meeting over his head*: compare Lamentations 3.54: 'Waters flowed over mine head; then I said, I am cut off.'

p.18   *unaccoutred as he was*: see *Julius Caesar* I.ii.105 – 'Accoutred as I was'.

p.21   *honour and glory*: Revelations 5.13: 'And every creature which is in heaven, and on earth, and under the earth, and such as are in the sea, and all that are in them, heard I saying, Blessing, and honour, and glory, and power, be unto him that sitteth upon the throne, and unto the Lamb for ever and ever.'

p.22   *does her duty in her sphere of life*: 'to do my duty in that state of life, unto which it shall please God to call me' – from the Catechism in the *Book of Common Prayer*.

p.33   *the very noble ballad of Lord Bateman*: *The Loving Ballad of Lord Bateman* was a facetious little publication in which Dickens, Thackeray and Cruickshank collaborated in 1839, being the adaptation of a ballad which Thackeray had heard outside 'The Black Bear' in Piccadilly, Dickens supplying mock-learned footnotes to the text, and Cruickshank the illustrations.

p.38   *a certain interview between himself and Mr Crawley*: this interview occurs in Chapter 15 of *Framley Parsonage*, when Crawley rebukes Robarts for his worldliness.

p.47 *a stool of repentance*: a stool on which offenders were placed in Scottish churches to make public repentance, particularly for unchastity.

p.57 *state of life to . . . call her*: see note to p.22.

p.63 *Was St Paul not bound in prison*: in Acts chapters 21, 24 and 28.

p.64 *that my lines should be cast in such terrible places*: contrast Psalm 16.6, 'The lines are fallen unto me in pleasant places'.

p.74 *petty sessions*: a court held by justices of the peace or stipendiary magistrates.

p.74 *lictor . . . fasces*: the lictor was the officer who preceded Roman magistrates and carried the fasces, or bundle of rods with an axe at the centre, which were symbols of the authority of law and of punishment.

p.79 *bare bodkin*: instrument of suicide in *Hamlet* III.i.76.

p.80 *the labour I delight in shall physic my pain*: see *Macbeth* II.iii.48: 'The labour we delight in physics pain.'

p.91 *Mrs Proudie was ready for the battle, and was even now sniffing the blood afar-off*: compare Job 39.25: 'He saith among the trumpets, Ha, ha; and he smelleth the battle afar off.'

p.91 *roaring lion*: see Ezekiel 22.25: 'like a roaring lion ravening the prey; they have devoured souls . . .'

p.92 *the eighth commandment*: 'Thou shalt not steal.'

p.97 *auricular confession*: some of the Tractarian High Church party approved of the Roman Catholic practice of auricular confession to a priest (though not of the granting of absolution after penance), but such things were anathema to Mrs Proudie's Low Church party.

p.100 *bare bodkin*: see note to p.79.

p.100 *hemlock*: a poison associated with the death of Socrates, who was condemned to death by poisoning, and rather than avail himself of a chance of escape, drank the hemlock.

p.108 *eat the hay of idleness*: compare Proverbs 31.27: 'eateth not the bread of idleness'.

p.109 *all those rich revenues which they had stolen from the bishops*: Since Bishop Proudie was appointed in the Whig interest, Mrs Proudie is politically inconsistent in resenting the operation of the Ecclesiastical Commission, established by the Whigs, and which since the Established Church Act (1836) and the Ecclesiastical Duties Act (1840) had been reducing disparities between the incomes of different bishops.

p.116 *the bishop's thumb*: Mr Thumble's name is carefully chosen, since 'to thumble' means to touch with the thumb or handle clumsily, and 'thumb' suggests the exercise of power (as in 'to be under someone's thumb'), sometimes by means of a low instrument or agent, as in the case of Pollex, whose name means thumb in Latin, and who was Cicero's slave.

p.116 *one of the angels of the church*: 'angel' derives from the Greek word for 'messenger'.

p.116 *the Seven against Thebes*: the tragedy of Aeschylus (467 BC), now best known in film, reworked as *The Seven Samurai* and *The Magnificent Seven*.

p.127 *his stockings ungartered ... signs of unrequited affection*: see for example *As You Like It* III.ii.528 or *Hamlet* II.i.79–80.

p.133 *to have out-Jacobed Jacob*: by analogy with 'out-Herod Herod' (*Hamlet*), to have waited longer to marry his loved one than Jacob, who 'served seven years for Rachel' (Genesis 29.20).

p.136 *is utilitarian*: prefers usefulness to beauty.

p.145 *off the reel*: without stopping.

p.145 *a Pope Joan board*: the board for holding the stakes in the card game called Pope Joan, which is played by three or more players with a pack of cards from which the eight of diamonds has been removed.

p.153 *the story of Oedipus*: the description better suits the *Oedipus Tyrannus* of Sophocles (c. 428 BC) than his *Oedipus at Colonnus* (401 BC).

p.167 *'Vengeance is mine. I will repay,' saith the Lord*: Romans 12.19.

p.173 *mens sana*: a sound mind (Latin).

p.175 *six-and-eightpenny considerations*: the minimum standard fee for a legal consultation was six shillings and eightpence, or one–third of a pound.

p.187 *the camel and the needle's eye*: 'It is easier for a camel to go through the eye of a needle, than for a rich man to enter the kingdom of God', Matthew 19.24.

p.189 *Galignani*: *Galignani's Messenger*, a newspaper published in Paris for English-speaking readers on the Continent.

p.202 *Out of the full heart the mouth speaketh*: compare Matthew 12.34: 'out of the abundance of the heart the mouth speaketh'.

p.204 *to gather grapes from thistles*: see Matthew 7.16: 'Do men gather figs of thorns, or grapes of thistles?'

p.210 *the Dean of Arches*: the judge of the ecclesiastical court of appeal, or Court of Arches, so called because it was formerly held in the church of St Mary-le-Bow, known as 'St Mary of the Arches'.

p.215 *Judith with the disseevered head, or as Jael using her hammer over the temple of Sisera*: Judith and Jael were Israelite heroines who killed enemy commanders, and whose stories are told in the Book of Judith in the Apocrypha and in Judges 4, respectively. Having 'decked herself bravely, to allure the eyes of all men that should see her', Judith went to the Assyrian general, Holofernes, to plead for her native town of Bethulia, and after feasting with him, cut off his head.

Jael drove a tent-peg through the temple of Sisera, the captain of the Canaanite army, as he lay hidden in her tent.

p.215 Madame Rachel: from her shop in New Bond Street, Mrs Levison or Levinson, otherwise 'Madame Rachel', marketed products which she claimed would make women 'Beautiful for Ever!' Her 'Teeth Enamel' and 'Pearly Tooth Powder' each sold at a guinea a bottle. In 1868, shortly after *The Last Chronicle* was published, she was condemned to five years' penal servitude for fraud.

p.220 *with my stockings cross-gartered*: like Malvolio when, in *Twelfth Night* II.v and III.ii, he aspires to the hand of Olivia.

p.232 *the Lucretias, and the Charlotte Cordays*: Lucretia Borgia (1480–1519), the Renaissance beauty, art-patron and poisoner, and Charlotte Corday (1768–93), who was guillotined for stabbing Jean-Paul Marat to death in his bath to avenge the Girondins, who had been executed for refusing to vote for the death of Louis XVI.

p.233 *Still climbing trees in the Hesperides*: *Love's Labours Lost* IV.iii.337: 'For valour, is not Love a Hercules/Still climbing trees in the Hesperides?' One of the labours of Hercules was to get possession of the Golden Apples of the Hesperides.

p.234 *comb my hair*: Conrad Dalyrmple is thinking of himself and Clara Van Siever in the roles of Samson and Delilah.

p.239 *the ... Saturday and the ... Spectator*: the *Saturday Review* and the *Spectator* were the two leading political and literary weekly papers of the day, founded in 1828 and 1855 respectively.

p.239 *the Pall Mall Gazette*: this afternoon daily paper, to which Trollope was a contributor, was named after a fictional journal in Thackeray's *Pendennis*, and launched in 1865 by George Smith, the publisher of *The Last Chronicle of Barset*.

p.241 *Berlin wool*: fine, dyed wool used for tapestry, knitting, etc.

p.254 *chevalier sans peur et sans reproche*: the chevalier Bayard (1473–1524), the French model of knightly perfection, 'the knight without fear and without reproach'.

p.256 *his ox, nor his ass*: the Tenth Commandment says, 'Thou shalt not covet thy neighbour's house ... thy neighbour's wife, nor his servant, nor his maid, nor his ox, nor his ass, nor any thing that is his.'

p.261 *In the Bible it is said of some season that it is not a time for marrying, or for giving in marriage*: see Matthew 22.30: 'For in the resurrection they neither marry, nor are given in marriage.'

p.271 *In forma pauperis*: in the character of a poor man (Latin).

p.275 *the Quirk, Gammon and Snaps of the profession, or the Dodson and Foggs*: unscrupulous firms of lawyers in Samuel Warren's *Ten Thousand a Year* (1839–41) and Dickens's *Pickwick Papers* (1836–7) respectively.

p.276 *the text about the quiver*: Psalm 127.3–5 – 'Lo, children are an heritage of the Lord . . . Happy is the man that hath his quiver full of them . . .'

p.276 *'The lovely Thais . . . provide you'*: Dryden, *Alexander's Feast*, ll. 106–7. Though these lines were much quoted in the period, not all who used them realized that Thais was an Athenian concubine who accompanied Alexander the Great on his Asian campaigns.

p.277 *Byron and Tom Moore*: enthusiasm for these Romantic poets contrasts with the seriousness of Grace's reading of the Classics.

p.281 *I know myself as no one else can know me, in spite of the wise man's motto*: perhaps the words written up in the temple at Delphi: 'Know thyself'.

p.283 *You can't get into the box*: Until the passing of the Criminal Evidence Act of 1898, the accused was not a competent witness in a criminal trial.

p.287 *Grizel*: the model of a patient and submissive wife in medieval literature, in particular Boccaccio's *Decameron* and Chaucer's *Clerkes Tale*.

p.288 *the sun shall go down upon your wrath*: Ephesians 4.26: 'let not the sun go down upon your wrath'.

p.294 *the Court of Arches*: see note to p.210.

p.295 *vicar chorals*: the assistants to the canons or prebendaries of a cathedral, particularly in relation to the choir or the chancel. The plural 'vicar chorals' is said by the *Oxford English Dictionary* to be rare.

p.296 *the Church Discipline Act'*: this act, for better regulating 'the Correction of Clerks in Holy Orders', was passed in 1840.

p.296 *the Consistorial Court*: a bishop's court for trying ecclesiastical offences dealt with under ecclesiastical law.

p.310 *with all my heart and all my strength and all my soul*: see Luke 10.27: 'Thou shalt love the Lord thy God with all thy heart, and with all thy soul, and with all thy strength, and with all thy mind' (See also Mark 12.30).

p.314 *stricken deer*: Hamlet III.ii 265.

p.326 *the court*: Capel Court, i.e. the Stock Exchange.

p.337 *Honi soit qui mal y pense*: 'Shame be to him who evil thinks of this' – the motto of the Knights of the Garter.

p.338 *That way madness lies*: *King Lear* III.iv.21.

p.340 *Imogen*: the virtuous wife in Shakespeare's *Cymbeline*, who is proof against temptation.

p.345 *Sir Charles Grandison*: the protagonist and paragon of Samuel Richardson's novel of that name, 1753–4.

p.350 *à la Russe*: a dinner *à la russe* (or in the Russian style) involved considerable formality, including one servant to each diner.

p.352 *Who thundering comes on blackest steed, With slackened bit and hoof of speed*: Byron, *The Giaour* (1813), ll. 180–81.

p.352 *a hideous monster behind a veil*: Hakim ben Allah, the Veiled Prophet of Khorassan, in Thomas Moore's *Lalla Rookh* (1817).

p.353 *'Light toil . . . promised best'*: Byron, *The Corsair* (1814) canto xiv, ll.422–3.

p.353 *arrow in her quiver*: see note to p.276, *the text about the quiver*.

p.356 *Gladstone claret*: low-grade French wine which had been made cheaper when Gladstone reduced Customs duty in 1860.

p.360 *year on top of a pillar*: St Simeon Stylites (*c.* 390–459) was the first and most famous of numerous saints to mortify the flesh by living for many years (in his case thirty) on top of a pillar.

p.372 *No one of a sudden becomes most base*: 'Nemo repente fuit turpissimus', Juvenal, *Satires* II, l. 83.

p.394 *the needy knife-grinder*: in 'The Friend of Humanity and the Knife Grinder', an anti-revolutionary poem which was widely known in the nineteenth century, the revolutionary 'Friend of Humanity' responds to the knife-grinder's request for alms thus:

> Wretch! whom no sense of wrongs can rouse to vengeance-
> Sordid, unfeeling, reprobate, degraded,
> Spiritless outcast!

[Kicks the knife-grinder, overturns his wheel, and exit in a transport of Republican enthusiasm and universal philanthropy.] – *Poetry of the Anti-Jacobin* ed. George Canning and John Hookham Frere, 1799, p.10.

p.403 *an Italian motto, – 'Who goes softly, goes safely'*: 'chi va piano va sano.'

p.408 *'If she be not fair for me, what care I how fair she be'*: a popular misquotation of lines by George Wither (1588–1667):

> For, if she be not for me,
> What care I how fair she be?

p.410 *preux chevalier*: valiant knight (French).

p.424 *thoughtful of the morrow*: Matthew 6.34: 'Take therefore no thought for the morrow: for the morrow shall take thought for the things of itself.'

p.438 *Hamlet's often-quoted appeal to the two portraits*: *Hamlet* III.iv.53: 'Look here upon this picture and on this . . .'

p.439 *a wide-awake*: a soft felt hat with a broad brim and low crown.

p.449 *old Skulpit . . . Hiram's Hospital . . . told in former chronicles of the city*: Skulpit is one of the inmates of Hiram's Hospital, the story of the wardenship of which is told in *The Warden* (1855) and *Barchester Towers* (1857).

p.452 *the lean and slippered pantaloon*: the sixth age in Jaques's speech on the seven ages of man, *As You Like It* III.vii.158.

p.452 *had not his lines fallen to him in very pleasant places*: see note to p.64.

p.452 *Lord, now lettest Thou Thy servant depart in peace*: the Nunc Dimittis, from the Order for Evening Prayer in the *Book of Common Prayer*, and which is taken from Luke 2.29.

p.468 *many Potiphar's wives ... and Josephs*: when Joseph was a slave to Pharaoh's captain, Potiphar, his master's wife 'caught him by his garment, saying, Lie with me: and he left his garment in her hand, and fled' – Genesis 39.12.

p.469 *His hair was grey, but not with years*: Byron, *The Prisoner of Chillon*, line 1: 'My hair is grey ...'

p.471 *like Isaac, piling the fagots for her own sacrifice*: see Genesis 22.

p.476 *Cleave to her ... bone of your bone*: echoes of the marriage service from the *Book of Common Prayer*.

p.487 *Achilles and Apsley house*: a large male nude, representing Achilles and put up in honour of the Duke of Wellington by a subscription among ladies, stands near Hyde Park Corner, close to the Duke's town house, Apsley House.

p.489 *to look at or to be looked at*: a glance at a Latin tag often quoted in the period to mean that women have no serious business to conduct when they appear in public: 'Spectatum veniunt; veniunt specentur ut ipsae' – Ovid, *De arte amandi*, I.99, 'The ladies come to see and to be seen.'

p.492 *the quarrels of lovers ... are a bad basis for the renewal of love*: compare Terence, *Andria* 1. 555: 'Amantium irae amoris integratio': 'lovers' quarrels are love's renewal.'

p.521 *tiled*: kept strictly private, as though protected by a Freemason's door-keeper, or 'tiler'.

p.521 *Ruat coelum, fiat justitia*: 'Though the heavens fall, let justice be done' (Latin) – attributed to the Emperor Ferdinand 1.

p.521 *Rem, si possis recte, si non quocunque modo*: 'Make (money), honestly if you can; if not, by any means possible' – Horace, *Epistles* I.i.65–6.

p.524 *a place where three roads met*: an echo of the description of the place at which Oedipus killed his father.

p.524 *clod-crusher*: a machine for crushing the clods left by a plough.

p.539 Galignani: see note to p.189.

p.544 *Honour thy father, – that thy days may be long in the land*: the fifth commandment.

p.550 *till after the middle of May*: i.e. until the start of the London 'season', when such politeness with 'pasteboard' visiting cards would be expected.

p.562 *Juan ... sat with Haidee in Lambro's island*: in Byron's *Don Juan*, canto ii.

p.574   *do justice though the heaven should fall*: see note to p.521, *Ruat coelum, fiat justitia*.

p.583   rentcharge: see note to p.9.

p.584   *the troubles and agonies of a blind giant*: the Cyclops, Polyphemus, who is blinded by Ulysses and his sailors in Book Nine of the *Odyssey*.

p.584   *Eyeless in Gaza, at the mill with the slaves*: Milton, *Samson Agonistes*, 1.41.

p.585   *Belisarius*: medieval tradition had it that this famous sixth-century Illyrian general was blinded for his part in a conspiracy against the Emperor Justinian in 563.

p.588   *the romantic tale of the woman Pope*: legend recounts the story of Pope Joan, a woman who is said to have disguised herself as a monk, and risen so far that she was elected Pope, some said in 855, others around 1100. She is supposed to have died after giving birth to a child.

p.590   *Nil conscire sibi, nulla pallescere culpa*: Horace, *Epistles* I.i.61: 'to be conscious of no guilt, to turn pale at no charge'.

p.592   *gall and wormwood*: Lamentations 3.19.

p.604   *to the third and fourth generation*: see the second commandment.

p.630   *praying for her soul, now that she was dead ... would have scandalized him*: such prayers would have smacked of Roman Catholicism or Tractarianism.

p.631   *The Lord sent ... Blessed be the name of the Lord*: compare Job 1.21, used in the service of the Burial of the Dead: 'The Lord gave, and the Lord hath taken away; blessed be the Name of the Lord.'

p.636   *Du mortuis*: 'De mortuis nil nisi bonum' (Latin): 'Speak nothing but good of the dead.'

p.637   Requiescat in pace: May she rest in peace (Latin).

p.638   *deaf as adders to courtesy*: See Psalm 58.4−5:

>   'Their poison is like the poison of a serpent: they are like the deaf adder that stoppeth her ear;
>   'Which will not harken to the voice of charmers, charming never so wisely.'

p.640   *felt his own withers to be unwrung*: *Hamlet* III.ii.235−7: 'Let the galled jade wince, our withers are unwrung.'

p.652   excelsior : higher (Latin); the motto of the USA, usually rendered in English as 'Aim higher!', was best known in Britain from Longfellow's poem of this title, set by M. W. Balfe as an enormously popular drawing-room song, in which a young man battles upwards through snow and ice, and ends frozen to death on the mountain.

p.652   *plucking glory from the nettle danger*: compare *I Henry IV* II.iii.12−14: 'out of the nettle, danger, we pluck this flower, safety'.

p.652 *an Austrian passport – as was necessary in those bygone days of Venetia's thraldom*: that is, until 1866 (the year in which publication of *The Last Chronicle of Barset* commenced), when Venetia was incorporated into the new Kindom of Italy, having been ruled by Austria since 1815.

p.652 *to swim in a gondola*: see *As You Like It* IV.1.34–5: 'I will scarce think you have swam in a gondola.'

p.659 *boxed a clergyman's ears*: this and other events from Mrs Arabin's earlier life are recorded in *Barchester Towers* (1857).

p.685 *the right sow by the ear*: Henry VIII said of Cranmer, 'this man hath the right sow by the ear.'

p.685 *a messenger of glad tidings, whose feet are beautiful upon the mountains*: 'How beautiful upon the mountains are the feet of him that bringeth good tidings' – Isaiah 52.7.

p.695 *quorum pars magna fui*: 'of which I was a large part': Virgil, *Aeneid* II.5–6: 'Quaeque ipse miserrima vidi/Et quorum pars magna fui' – 'I myself have seen these sad events, in which I played a large part.'

p.709 *what care I how fair she be?*: see note to p.408.

p.709 *Rosalind, and her counsels to lovers as to the keeping of time*: see *As You Like It* IV.1.36–45.

p.717 *other chronicles*: the archdeacon's presentation of the living of St Ewold's to Mr Harding is not in fact related in the previous novels.

p.717 *thy past life*: in Chapter 1 of *Barchester Towers*, while the archdeacon's father, the then Bishop of Barchester, lay dying, the son knew that his own chance of being appointed to the bishopric by the outgoing Prime Minister would be lost if his father survived another night, and he 'at last dared to ask himself whether he really longed for his father's death . . . The proud, wishful, worldly man, sank on his knees by the bedside, and . . . prayed eagerly that his sins might be forgiven him.'

p.718 *from such distant bournes there was no return for any traveller*: see *Hamlet* III.i.78–80: 'death/The undiscover'd country, from whose bourn/No traveller returns'.

p.721 *his lines had fallen to him not only in pleasant places*: see note to p.64.

p.725 *The sources of the Nile, of which men now talk so much*: In January 1866, David Livingstone had set out on his third and greatest African journey, to explore the central Africa watershed, and locate the ultimate source of the Nile.

p.730 *the caloric*: the name given by Lavoisier to a fluid, which he supposed diffused all things and was responsible for the phenomena of heat.

p.731 *At nine o'clock he went, half-price, to the Strand Theatre*: in a theatre having a programme of more than one play, admission was half-price after the first piece.

p.739　*bull's eye*: a lantern with which London policemen were equipped, and which threw a beam.

p.742　*His tenderness has surpassed the tenderness of woman*: see 2 Samuel, I.26: 'my brother Jonathan . . . thy love to me was wonderful, passing the love of women'.

p.749　*Sitting among potsherds, like Job*: see Job 2.8: 'And he took a potsherd to scrape himself withal; and he sat down among the ashes.'

p.762　*of the earth, earthy*: 1 Corinthians 15.47.

TEXT SUMMARY

1. How did he get it?
... ask the Walker family, alluding to Mr Crawley's alleged theft of a cheque for twenty pounds.

2. By Heavens, he had better not!
Rumours of Major Grantly's love for Grace Crawley reach his father, the archdeacon, who swears such a marriage shall not take place.

3. The archdeacon's threat
... to halt the major's income, should he marry Grace, does not intimidate his son.

4. The clergyman's house at Hogglestock
The narrative describes Crawley's 'darker moments', and his wife's faith in his innocence.

5. What the world thought about it
Opinion is divided throughout Barset over the issue of Crawley's guilt.

6. Grace Crawley
... determines to leave the Prettymans' school, over the possible scandal arising from the accusations against her father.

7. Miss Prettyman's private room
The Major is advised by Miss Prettyman not to propose to Grace; 'these hours of her father's sorrow are not hours in which love should be either proffered or accepted'.

8. Mr Crawley is taken to Silverbridge
The Silverbridge magistrates commit Crawley to trial at the Barchester assizes.

9. Grace Crawley goes to Allington
... at the invitation of Lily Dale and her mother, to reside there until the resolution of her father's troubles.

10. Dinner at Framley Court
Deciding on Crawley's innocence, the Framley set make Mr Robarts responsible for persuading the curate that he must obtain proper legal representation.

11. The bishop sends his inhibition
At his wife's insistence, Dr Proudie writes to Crawley, instructing him to cease the 'performance of any of his sacred duties'.

12. Mr Crawley seeks for sympathy
... among the brickmakers of Hoggle End. It appears that even they think that he is guilty.

13. The bishop's angel
Mr Thumble delivers the bishop's letter to Hogglestock. Crawley immediately replies, stating his avowed intention to ignore the 'inhibition'.

14. Major Grantly consults a friend
... about his love for Grace. The 'friend' in question, Mrs Thorne, advises him to marry her, in spite of the archdeacon's objections.

15. Up in London
John Eames broods over his long-unrequited love for Lily. He decides to propose to her for one last time.

16. Down at Allington
Lady Julia De Guest drops broad hints to Lily about Eames's continuing love for her. Lily resents such interference.

17. Mr Crawley is summoned to Barchester
... to appear before Dr Proudie, because of his refusal to let Thumble carry out the services at Hogglestock.

18. The Bishop of Barchester is crushed
Crawley arrives at the palace. He is resolute in his defiance of both Dr and Mrs Proudie.

19. Where did it come from?
... asks Mrs Crawley of the missing cheque. Her husband is still unable to give a clear answer.

20. What Mr Walker thought about it
As talk of Crawley dominates the county, Walker suggests to Robarts that the curate put in a plea of temporary insanity.

21. Mr Robarts on his embassy
Crawley refuses the idea of employing an attorney, declaring that he wants 'no-one there paid ... to obstruct the course of justice or to hoodwink a jury' on his behalf.

22. *Major Grantly at home*
An oblique threat by the archdeacon to disinherit his son should he wed Grace serves only to make the latter more determined so to do.

23. *Miss Lily Dale's resolution*
The widowed Mr Crosbie writes to Mrs Dale, asking permission to renew his courtship of Lily. Despite still loving him, Lily declines.

24. *Mrs Dobbs Broughton's dinner-party*
. . . forms the introduction of the London subplot, as the artist Dalrymple conceives a wish to make a portrait of the wealthy Clara Van Siever.

25. *Miss Madalina Demolines*
Eames begins a flirtation with Madalina, who seems determined to prevent the portrait of Clara from going ahead.

26. *The picture*
Clara is persuaded to sit for the portrait by Dalrymple and Mrs Broughton, who are carrying on a flirtation of their own.

27. *A hero at home*
Eames and the major encounter each other as they both travel down to Guestwick.

28. *Showing how Major Grantly took a walk*
The major introduces himself to Mrs Dale. On a subsequent walk around Allington, he chances upon Squire Dale, Lily and Grace.

29. *Miss Lily Dale's logic*
Grace tells Lily that, for the major's own sake, she will not consent to marry him.

30. *Showing what Major Grantly did after his walk*
The major refuses to accept his rejection by Grace: 'I declare that we are engaged.'

31. *Showing how Major Grantly returned to Guestwick*
The major and Eames discuss the Crawley affair. Meanwhile, Grace tells the Dales she intends to be firm in her decision.

32. *Mr Toogood*
. . . is visited, in London by a reluctant Crawley. The attorney undertakes to offer his cousin assistance.

33. *The Plumstead foxes*
Learning of the major's proposal to Grace, the archdeacon reiterates his intention to disinherit his son.

34. *Mrs Proudie sends for her lawyer*
. . . to set in motion the organizing of a clerical commission to investigate the Crawley affair.

35. *Lily Dale writes two words in her book*
. . . as she once more rejects Eames, the two words being 'Old Maid'.

36. *Grace Crawley returns home*
. . . after receiving a letter from her mother informing her that her father is ill.

37. *Hook Court*
Mrs Van Siever demands of Dobbs Broughton and Musselboro money owed to her by their investment company.

38. *Jael*
As Clara's sittings for the portrait get under way, Dalrymple continues his flirtation with Mrs Broughton.

39. *A new flirtation*
Eames begins flirting with Madalina in earnest; 'because he was too weak to keep out of it'.

40. *Mr Toogood's ideas about society*
Toogood, Walker and Eames decide that the latter should head abroad to track down Dean Arabin.

41. *Grace Crawley at home*
Grace tends to her father, and confesses to her mother the story of her proposal.

42. *Mr Toogood travels professionally*
. . . to Barset, and begins 'rummaging' in the Crawley affair.

43. *Mr Crosbie goes into the City*
. . . in a bid to raise money, his late marriage having brought him to financial ruin.

44. *I suppose I must let you have it*
. . . says a reluctant Mr Butterwell, after Crosbie pleads for money.

45. *Lily Dale goes to London*
. . . to take lodgings for a month with her uncle. Eames bids her farewell, as he prepares for his journey to Jerusalem.

46. *The Bayswater romance*
Dalrymple warns Eames against Madalina's likely matrimonial ambitions.

47. *Dr Tempest at the palace*
A confrontation between Dr Tempest and Mrs Proudie leaves the bishop feeling thoroughly disgraced.

48. *The softness of Sir Raffle Buffle*
Eames manages to obtain official leave to take his journey abroad.

49. *Near the close*
Mr Harding quietly comes to terms with old age and his approaching death.

50. *Lady Lufton's proposition*
. . . is that Mrs Crawley and family should come and live at Framley in the event of her husband's imprisonment.

51. *Mrs Dobbs Broughton piles her fagots*
Dalrymple misses his first opportunity to propose to Clara.

52. *Why don't you have an 'it' for yourself?'*
Lily learns of the high esteem in which Eames is now held, but is still determined to refuse him.

53. *Rotten Row*
Lily and Crosbie encounter each other for the first time since his jilting her.

54. *The clerical commission*
. . . has a preliminary meeting. It decides it will interview Crawley before any further steps are taken.

55. *Framley Parsonage*
The major is again rejected by Grace: 'I can be nothing to you, because of papa's disgrace.'

56. *The archdeacon goes to Framley*
. . . and tries to persuade Lady Lufton to take his side against the major's.

57. *A double pledge*
As Grace promises she will never accept the major while her father stands accused, so the archdeacon vows that the establishment of Crawley's innocence will remove all obstacles between herself and the major.

58. *The cross-grainedness of men*
The archdeacon and his son are still at loggerheads, this time over the latter's proposed sale of Cosby Lodge.

59. *A lady presents her compliments to Miss L. D.*
Lily is disturbed, by both an anonymous letter from 'M. D.', and another accidental meeting with Crosbie.

60. *The end of Jael and Sisera*
Mrs Van Siever brings financial ruin upon Dobbs Broughton, and supervises the destruction of Dalrymple's painting.

61. *It's dogged as does it*
Against Tempest's advice, Crawley decides to resign his curacy.

62. *Mr Crawley's letter to the dean*
. . . together with his letter to the bishop, inform both parties of his decision to resign.

63. *Two visitors to Hogglestock*
The major seeks approval from the Crawleys of his love for Grace.

64. *The tragedy in Hook Court*
Musselboro informs Dalrymple of Dobbs Broughton's suicide. The artist conveys the news to Mrs Broughton.

65. *Miss Van Siever makes her choice*
Clara defies her mother, by refusing Musselboro in favour of Dalrymple.

66. *Requiescat in pace*
The bishop finally tells his wife what he thinks of her. She is later found dead in her chambers.

67. *In memoriam*
News of Mrs Proudie's death reaches all parts of the county.

68. *The obstinacy of Mr Crawley*
Robarts offers to intercede with the bishop on Crawley's behalf. Crawley rejects him.

69. *Mr Crawley's last appearance in his own pulpit*
Crawley delivers a farewell address to his parishioners.

70. *Mrs Arabin is caught.*
. . . and the Crawley affair is at once resolved: 'I gave him the cheque, you know.'

71. *Mr Toogood at Silverbridge*
The news of Crawley's innocence soon spreads over Silverbridge.

72. *Mr Toogood at 'The Dragon of Wantly'*
Toogood's investigations yield proof that the cheque had been stolen by one Jem Scuttle.

73. *There is comfort at Plumstead*
. . . as all the Grantlys' problems are resolved by the news of Crawley's innocence.

74. *The Crawleys are informed*
. . . by Toogood and the major. The latter calls at Framley and is finally accepted by Grace.

75. *Madalina's heart is bleeding*
Eames catches up on the news of his London acquaintances.

76. *I think he is light of heart*
Mrs Arabin tries to plead Eames's cause to Lily.

77. *The shattered tree*
Eames goes to Lily for the very last time. They both resign themselves to remaining forever unmarried.

78. *The Arabins return to Barchester*
Harding's life draws nearer to its close. There is talk amongst the Grantly faction of bestowing the living of St Ewold's upon Crawley.

79. *Mr Crawley speaks of his coat*
Arabin visits Crawley, who turns down an offer to come and stay at the deanery.

80. *Miss Demolines desires to become a finger-post*
Eames narrowly escapes being manoeuvred into an engagement to Madalina.

81. *Barchester cloisters.*
Harding dies. He is buried among the cloisters of the cathedral.

82. *The last scene at Hogglestock*
The encumbency of St Ewold's is offered to Crawley.

83. *Mr Crawley is conquered*
Crawley accepts the living. He meets the archdeacon for the first time. Eventually both admit a mutual respect.

84. *Conclusion*
The narrator bids farewell to his imaginary county.

SUGGESTED FURTHER READING

Such is the status of *The Last Chronicle of Barset* in Trollope's œuvre that most books on his fiction, and many on Victorian fiction in general contain a treatment of it. Examples of general works on Trollope are Bradford A. Booth, *Anthony Trollope: Aspects of His Life and Art* (London, 1958), A.O.J. Cockshut, *Anthony Trollope* (London, 1955), P.D. Edwards, *Anthony Trollope: His Art and Scope* (St Lucia, Queensland, 1977), John Halperin, *Trollope and Politics: A Study of the Pallisers and Others* (London, 1977), Geoffrey Harvey, *The Art of Anthony Trollope* (London, 1980), James R. Kincaid, *The Novels of Anthony Trollope* (Oxford, 1977), Coral Lansbury, *The Reasonable Man: Trollope's Legal Fiction* (Princeton, 1981), Robert M. Polhemus, *The Changing World of Anthony Trollope* (Berkeley and Los Angeles, 1968), Arthur Pollard, *Anthony Trollope* (London, 1978), Michael Sadleir, *Trollope: A Commentary* (London, 1927), L.P. and R.P. Stebbins, *The Trollopes: The Chronicle of a Writing Family* (London, 1946), R.C. Terry, *Anthony Trollope: The Artist in Hiding* (London, 1977), Robert Tracy, *Trollope's Later Novels* (Berkeley, CA, 1978), and Stephen Wall, *Trollope and Character* (London, 1988).

Despite a number of serious bibliographical errors, Donald Smalley (ed.), *Anthony Trollope: The Critical Heritage* (London, 1969), contains a useful collection of Victorian criticism of Trollope's fiction. Trollope's contemporary reception is analysed in David Skilton, *Anthony Trollope and His Contemporaries: A Study in the Theory and Conventions of Mid-Victorian Fiction* (London, 1972). An annotated bibliography of later criticism is found in J.C. Olmsted and J.E. Welch, *The Reputation of Trollope: An Annotated Bibliography 1925–1975* (New York, 1978), and a fuller listing of Trollope editions as well as selected secondary works is found in *Anthony Trollope: A Collector's Catalogue 1847–1990* (London: the Trollope Society, 1992). The standard descriptive bibliography of Trollope's works in their original editions is Michael Sadleir, *Trollope: A Bibliography* (London, 1928).

The most scholarly biographies are N. John Hall, *Trollope: A*

Biography (Oxford, 1991), and R.H. Super, *The Chronicler of Barsetshire: A Life of Anthony Trollope* (Ann Arbor, 1988), while Richard Mullen, *Anthony Trollope: A Victorian in His World* (London, 1990), gives a more opinionated account. Victoria Glendinning's *Anthony Trollope* (London, 1992) is fascinating and exceptionally readable, and contains very plausible speculations about unknown aspects of the author's life, including his marriage. Trollope's letters are admirably collected in N. John Hall (ed.), *The Letters of Anthony Trollope* (Stanford, CA, 1983). Also useful in the study of Trollope as a public and private figure is R.C. Terry (ed.), *Trollope: Interviews and Recollections* (London, 1987).